Fair Housing Act Design Manual

A Manual to Assist Designers and Builders in Meeting the Accessibility Requirements of the Fair Housing Act

U. S. Department
of Housing and Urban Development
Office of Fair Housing and Equal Opportunity
Office of Housing

Preface

The Department is pleased to present the Fair Housing Act Design Manual. The manual was first published in August, 1996, and was updated in 1998. This republication of the 1998 manual is intended to provide clear and helpful guidance about ways to design and construct housing that complies with the Fair Housing Act.

The manual provides comprehensive information about accessibility requirements which must be incorporated into the design and construction of multifamily housing covered by the Act. It carries out two statutory responsibilities:

- first, it provides a clear statement of HUD's interpretation of the accessibility requirements of the Act, so that readers may know what actions on their part will provide them with a "safe harbor," and

- second, it provides guidance in the form of recommendations which meet the Department's obligation to provide technical assistance on alternative accessibility approaches.

Readers following the revised manual can rely on it. They will be in compliance with the Act's accessibility provisions if they carry them out. However, it should be noted that when the manual uses the terms: recommended, preferred, should, could, or uses italics or text labeled as "recommended," the material involved is provided as a suggestion for accessibility and not a requirement under the Act. In addition, HUD currently recognizes six other safe harbors for compliance with the Fair Housing Act's design and construction requirements. The other safe harbors are:

1. HUD's March 6, 1991 Fair Housing Accessibility Guidelines (the Guidelines), and the June 28, 1994 Supplemental Notice to Fair Housing Accessibility Guidelines: Questions and Answers about the Guidelines;
2. ANSI A117.1-1986, used in conjunction with the Act and HUD's regulations, and the Guidelines;
3. CABO/ANSI A117.1-1992, used in conjunction with the Act, HUD's regulations, and the Guidelines;
4. ICC/ANSI A117.1-1998, used in conjunction with the Act, HUD's regulations, and the Guidelines;
5. *Code Requirements for Housing Accessibility 2000* (CRHA), approved and published by the International Code Council (ICC), October 2000;
6. *International Building Code 2000* (IBC) as amended by the IBC *2001 Supplement to the International Codes.*

It is important to note that the ANSI A117.1 standard contains only technical criteria, whereas the Fair Housing Act, the regulations and the Guidelines contain both scoping and technical criteria. Therefore, in using any of the ANSI standards it is necessary to also consult the Act, HUD's regulations, and the Guidelines for the scoping requirements.

Providing an environment where persons with disabilities can have the same access to, and ability to use, housing that persons without disabilities enjoy is both a worthwhile goal and the law. The Department is committed to helping those who develop housing to meet the requirements of the law, so that we can reach the goal of providing meaningful access for people with disabilities.

FAIR HOUSING ACT DESIGN MANUAL

A MANUAL TO ASSIST DESIGNERS AND BUILDERS IN MEETING THE ACCESSIBILITY REQUIREMENTS OF THE FAIR HOUSING ACT

designed and developed by

Barrier Free Environments, Inc.
Raleigh, North Carolina

for

The U.S. Department of Housing and Urban Development
Office of Fair Housing and Equal Opportunity
and the Office of Housing
Contract # 15903

August 1996
Revised April 1998

Credits

Project Director **Ronald L. Mace, FAIA**

Project Manager **Leslie C. Young**

Technical Assistance **Cheryl Kent, FHEO, HUD**

Authorship **Leslie C. Young**
Ronald L. Mace
Geoff Sifrin

Architectural Design and Conceptual Illustration **Ronald L. Mace**
Leslie C. Young
Rex J. Pace
Geoff Sifrin

Graphic Design **Christopher A. B. McLachlan**

Illustration **Rex J. Pace**
Mark Pace

Photography **Kelly Houk**
Leslie C. Young

Acknowledgements Creation of this design manual involved the close cooperation of many people. Among them are the reviewers and technical staff at the Department of Housing and Urban Development, including Cheryl Kent, Judy Keeler, Merle Morrow, Alan Rothman, Nelson Carbonell, and Gail Williamson.

Special appreciation to the Barrier Free Environments, Inc. staff who contributed to this publication, including Leslie Young, Rex Pace, and Ron Mace. Special thanks also to Geoff Sifrin in South Africa and Lucy Harber.

Every attempt was made with this project to provide a concise and easy-to-follow guide on the construction requirements of the Fair Housing Act. Our hope is that the construction and disability communities to whom this manual is directed will be able to use and benefit from our efforts.

Contents

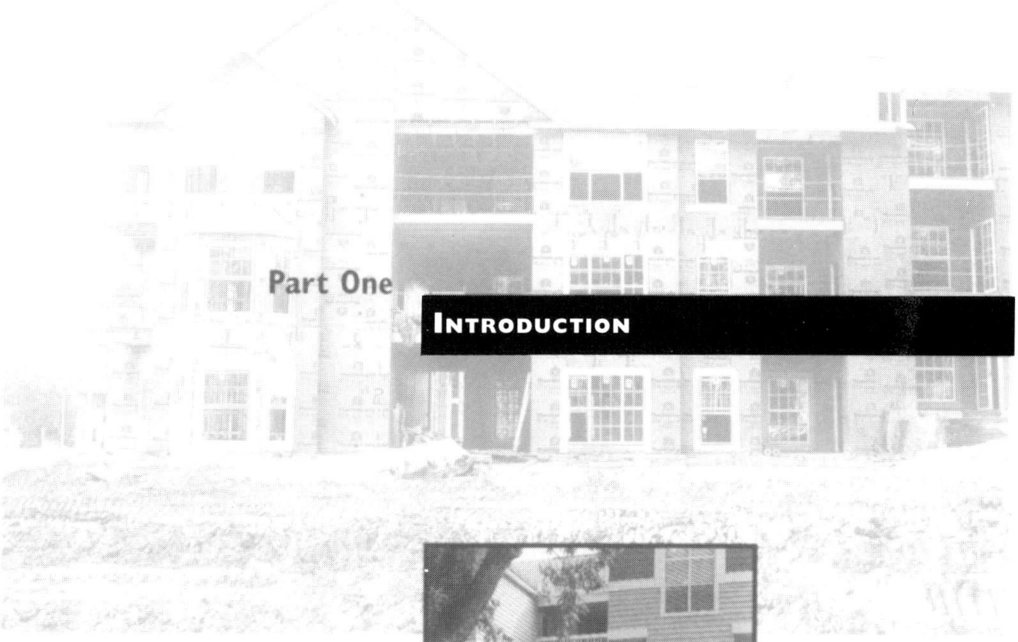

Part One
Introduction

INTRODUCTION

THE FAIR HOUSING ACT

Title VIII of the Civil Rights Act of 1968, commonly known as the Fair Housing Act, prohibits discrimination in the sale, rental, and financing of dwellings based on race, color, religion, sex, and national origin. In 1988, Congress passed the Fair Housing Amendments Act. The Amendments expand coverage of Title VIII to prohibit discriminatory housing practices based on disability[1] and familial status. Now it is unlawful to deny the rental or sale of a dwelling unit to a person because that person has a disability.

As a protected class, people with disabilities are unique in at least one respect because they are the only minority that can be discriminated against solely by the design of the built environment. The Fair Housing Act remedies that in part by establishing design and construction requirements for multifamily housing built for first occupancy after March 13, 1991. The law provides that a failure to design and construct certain multifamily dwellings to include certain features of accessible design will be regarded as unlawful discrimination.

The design and construction requirements of the Fair Housing Act apply to all new multifamily housing consisting of four or more dwelling units. Such buildings must meet specific design requirements so public and common use spaces and facilities are accessible to people with disabilities. In addition, the interior of dwelling units covered by the Fair Housing Act must be designed so they too meet certain accessibility requirements.

The Fair Housing Act is intended to place "**modest** accessibility requirements on covered multifamily dwellings .... These **modest** requirements will be incorporated into the design of new buildings, resulting in features which do not look unusual and will not add significant additional costs" (House Report 711[2] at 25 and 18). Fair Housing units are not fully accessible, nor are they purported to be; however, new multifamily housing built to comply with the Guidelines will be a dramatic improvement over units built in the past.

The Fair Housing Act gives people with disabilities greater freedom to choose where they will live and greater freedom to visit friends and relatives. But the Fair Housing Act has other broad implications. It proactively addresses the needs of an evolving population, looking ahead at future needs. With the aging of the population and the increase in incidence of disability that accompanies aging, significant numbers of people will be able to remain in and safely use their dwellings longer. For example, housing designed in accordance with the Fair Housing Act will have accessible entrances, wider doors, and provisions to allow for easy installation of grab bars around toilets and bathtubs, i.e., features that make housing safer and more responsive to all users.

---

[1]The Fair Housing Act statute uses the term "handicap"; however, this manual uses the terms "disability" or "persons with disabilities" to the greatest extent possible to be consistent with current preferred terminology as reflected in the Americans with Disabilities Act of 1990.

[2]House Report No. 711, 100th Congress, 2nd Session

The Role of HUD

The U.S. Department of Housing and Urban Development (HUD) is the Federal agency responsible for enforcement of compliance with the Fair Housing Act. On January 23, 1989, HUD published its final rule implementing the Fair Housing Act. In the preamble to this rule, HUD indicated that it would provide further guidance on meeting the new construction requirements of the Act by developing accessibility guidelines. The preamble stated that until these guidelines are published, designers and builders may be guided by the requirements of the ANSI A117.1-1986 *American National Standard for Buildings and Facilities – Providing Accessibility and Usability for Physically Handicapped People.* More information on the ANSI standard appears on page 13.

The final Fair Housing Accessibility Guidelines (the Guidelines) were published on March 6, 1991 (56 Federal Register 9472-9515, 24 CFR[3] Chapter I, Subchapter A, Appendix II and III). The Guidelines provide technical guidance on designing dwelling units as required by the Fair Housing Act. The Guidelines are not mandatory, but are intended to provide a safe harbor for compliance with the accessibility requirements of the Fair Housing Act. The Guidelines are included in this manual as Appendix B.

The Guidelines published on March 6, 1991, remain unchanged. However, on June 28, 1994, HUD published a supplemental notice to the Guidelines, "Supplement to Notice of Fair Housing Accessibility Guidelines: Questions and Answers About the Guidelines." This supplemental notice reproduces questions that have been most frequently asked by members of the public, and HUD's answers to those questions. The Supplement also is included in this manual as Appendix C.

Under the Fair Housing Act, HUD is not required to review builders' plans or issue a certification of compliance with the Fair Housing Act. HUD prepared the Guidelines and will answer technical questions. HUD also provides this publication as additional guidance.

The burden of compliance rests with the person or persons who design and construct covered multifamily dwellings. HUD or an individual who thinks he or she may have been discriminated against may file a complaint against the building owner, the architect, the contractor, and any other persons involved in the design and construction of the building. See page 22 for additional information on enforcement.

The Purpose of the Manual

This design manual has been produced by HUD to assist designers, builders, and developers in understanding and conforming with the design requirements of the Fair Housing Act. It contains explanations and uses detailed illustrations to explain the application of the Guidelines to all aspects of multifamily housing projects.

The manual consists of three parts:

Part One: The Introduction contains an overview of the Fair Housing Act, outlines other national laws and standards that regulate accessible design, presents the types of buildings/dwellings that are covered by the Fair Housing Act, and gives a brief discussion of the different types of disabilities.

[3]CFR = Code of Federal Regulations

Part Two: The Design Requirements of the Guidelines is a detailed, illustrated explanation of the seven requirements of the Fair Housing Accessibility Guidelines.

Part Three: The Appendix contains additional information that may be useful to anyone needing to be familiar with the design requirements of the Fair Housing Act. Included are a list of product resources, a list of selected references, a reprint of the Guidelines, and a reprint of the Supplemental Notice to the Guidelines.

Laws and Codes that Mandate Accessibility

Over the past two and a half decades, several statutes have been enacted at various levels of government that ensure nondiscrimination against people with disabilities, both in the design of the built environment and in the manner that programs are conducted. Even though this manual addresses the application of the Fair Housing Act and the Guidelines, certain dwellings, as well as certain public and common use areas, may be covered by several of the laws listed below. A brief synopsis of the landmark legislation follows to show where the Fair Housing Act fits into the overall history of accessibility legislation.

The Architectural Barriers Act (1968)

This Act stipulates that all buildings, other than privately owned residential facilities, constructed by or on behalf of, or leased by the United States, or buildings financed in whole or in part by the United States must be physically accessible for people with disabilities. The Uniform Federal Accessibility Standards (UFAS) is the applicable standard.

Section 504 of the Rehabilitation Act (1973)

Under Section 504 of the Rehabilitation Act of 1973 as amended, no otherwise qualified individual with a disability may be discriminated against in any program or activity receiving federal financial assistance. The purpose of Section 504 is to eliminate discriminatory behavior toward people with disabilities and to provide physical accessibility, thus ensuring that people with disabilities will have the same opportunities in federally funded programs as do people without disabilities.

Program accessibility may be achieved by modifying an existing facility, or by moving the program to an accessible location, or by making other accommodations, including construction of new buildings. HUD's final regulation for Section 504 may be found at 24 CFR Part 8. Generally, the UFAS is the design standard for providing physical accessibility, although other standards which provide equivalent or greater accessibility may be used.

The Fair Housing Act of 1968, as Amended

The Fair Housing Act provides equal opportunities for people in the housing market regardless of disability, race, color, sex, religion, familial status or national origin, regardless of whether the housing is publicly funded or not. This includes the sale, rental, and financing of housing, as well as the physical design of newly constructed multifamily housing. The Fair Housing Act is discussed in more detail in the next section, "General Provisions of the Fair Housing Act."

The Americans with Disabilities Act (1990)

The Americans with Disabilities Act (ADA) is a broad civil rights law guaranteeing equal opportunity for individuals with disabilities in employment, public accommodations, transportation, state and local government services, and telecommunications. Title III of the Act covers all private establishments and facilities considered "public accommodations," such as restaurants, hotels, retail establishments, doctors' offices, and theaters. People with disabilities must have equal opportunity in these establishments, both in terms of physical access and in the enjoyment of services. Title II of the ADA applies to all programs, services, and activities provided or made available by public entities. With respect to housing, this includes, for example, public housing and housing provided for state colleges and universities.

Under Title I of the ADA, employers may not discriminate in hiring or firing, and must provide reasonable accommodations to persons with disabilities, such as providing special equipment or training and arranging modified work schedules. A discussion of the relationship between the ADA and the Fair Housing Act appears on page 2 of the "Supplement to Notice of Fair Housing Accessibility Guidelines: Questions and Answers About the Guidelines" at Appendix C.

State and Local Codes

All states and many cities and counties have developed their own building codes for accessibility, usually based in whole or in part on the specifications contained in the major national standards such as ANSI and UFAS. Many states also have nondiscrimination and fair housing laws similar to the Fair Housing Act and the Americans with Disabilities Act.

When local codes differ from the national standard, either in scope or technical specification, the general rule is that the more stringent requirement should be followed. Many states also have provisions that a certain percentage (often 5%) of new multifamily housing must meet more stringent physical accessibility requirements than required under the Fair Housing Act. In such cases, both the state's mandated percentage of accessible units must be provided and all dwellings covered by the Fair Housing Act must meet the Guidelines.

General Provisions of the Fair Housing Act

The 1988 amendments to the Fair Housing Act extend to persons with disabilities and to families with children the same kinds of nondiscrimination protections afforded to persons based on race, color, religion, sex, and national origin. Thus, the Fair Housing Act protects persons with disabilities from discrimination in any activities relating to the sale or rental of dwellings, in the provision of services or facilities in connection with such dwellings, and in the availability of residential real estate related transactions.

The Fair Housing Act covers most types of housing. In some circumstances it exempts owner-occupied buildings with no more than four units, single-family housing sold or rented without the use of a broker, and housing operated by organizations and private clubs that limit occupancy to members.

The design and construction requirements of the Fair Housing Act and the Guidelines apply only to new construction of housing built for first occupancy after March 13, 1991. Those requirements are the focus of this manual; however, a brief discussion follows on the effect of the Fair Housing Act on policies and procedures in both new and existing multifamily housing developments.

The broad objective of the Fair Housing Act is to prohibit discrimination in housing because of a person's race, color, national origin, religion, sex, familial status, or disability. To ensure that persons with disabilities will have full use and enjoyment of their dwellings, the Fair Housing Act also includes two important provisions: one, a provision making it unlawful to refuse to make **reasonable accommodations** in rules, policies, practices, and services when necessary to allow the resident with a disability equal opportunity to use the property and its amenities; and two, a provision making it unlawful to refuse to permit residents with disabilities to make **reasonable modifications** to either their dwelling unit or to the public and common use areas, at the residents' cost.

Reasonable Accommodations

Under the Fair Housing Act, it is unlawful for any person to refuse to make reasonable accommodations in rules, policies, practices, or services when such accommodations may be necessary to afford a person with a disability equal opportunity to use and enjoy the dwelling. For example, in buildings with a "no pets" rule, that rule must be waived for a person with a visual impairment who uses a service dog, or for other persons who use service animals. In buildings that provide parking spaces for residents on a "first come, first served" basis, reserved parking spaces must be provided if requested by a resident with a disability who may need them. Sales material for apartments may need to be provided in a format so an individual with a visual disability may access the information.

Reasonable Modifications

When a resident wishes to modify a dwelling unit under the reasonable modification provisions of the Fair Housing Act, the resident may do so. The landlord/manager may require that the modification be completed in a professional manner under the applicable building codes, and may also require that the resident agree to restore the interior of the dwelling to the condition that existed before the modification, reasonable wear and tear excepted.

Landlords may not require that modifications be restored that would be unreasonable, i.e., modifications that in no way affect the next resident's "enjoyment of the premises." For example, in existing construction, a resident needs grab bars and pays to have the original wall reinforced with blocking between studs so grab bars can be securely mounted. It would be reasonable to require that the resident remove the grab bars at the end of the tenancy; however, it would be unreasonable to require that the blocking be removed since the reinforced wall would not interfere with the next resident's use and enjoyment of the dwelling unit and may be needed by some future resident.

However, if a resident who uses a wheelchair were to remove a kitchen base cabinet and mount a lowered countertop to a height suitable for his or her use, the landlord may condition permission on the resident agreeing to restore the cabinet to its original condition when the resident vacates the unit. On the other hand, if a resident who uses a wheelchair finds that the bathroom door in the dwelling unit is too narrow to allow his or her wheelchair to pass, the landlord must give permission for the door to be widened, at the resident's expense. The landlord may not require that the doorway be narrowed at the end of the resident's tenancy because the wider doorway will not interfere with the next resident's use of the dwelling.

Residents also may make modifications to the public and common use spaces. For example, in an existing development it would be considered reasonable for a resident who uses a wheelchair to have a ramp built to gain access to an on-site laundry facility. Modifications of this type are not required to be returned to their original condition. If a resident cannot afford such a modification, the resident may ask a friend to do his or her laundry in the laundry room, and the landlord must waive any rule that prohibits nonresidents from gaining access to the laundry room.

Regarding the cost of special modifications in new construction, builders or landlords are responsible only for meeting the design requirements specified by the Fair Housing Act. If a particular resident intends to buy a unit and needs additional modifications to meet the needs of his or her disability, then the resident may ask for such modification and the builder may not refuse. However, the resident is responsible for any extra cost that the modifications might create over and above what the original design would have cost.

The Scope of the Design and Construction Requirements of the Fair Housing Act

The accessibility requirements of the Fair Housing Act are intended to provide usable housing for persons with disabilities without necessarily being significantly different from conventional housing. The Fair Housing Act specifies certain features of accessible design and certain features of adaptable design. These basic design features are essential for equal access and to avoid future de facto exclusion of persons with disabilities, as well as being easy to incorporate into housing design and construction. These design features assist not only persons with disabilities but also other persons to use and enjoy all aspects of a residential development.[4]

Adaptable Dwelling Units

Covered dwelling units that meet the design requirements of the Guidelines are sometimes referred to as "adaptable dwelling units" or units that meet "certain features of accessible design." The Guidelines incorporate accessibility features that are both accessible and adaptable. Accessible elements and spaces are those whose design allows them to be used by the greatest number of users without being modified. For example, the requirement within the covered dwelling unit for "usable" doors, with a nominal clear opening of 32 inches, ensures that dwelling unit doors are not too narrow or impassable for any resident.

Adaptable/adjustable elements and spaces are those with a design which allows them to be adapted or adjusted to accommodate the needs of different people. The Fair Housing Act incorporates the adaptable/adjustable concept in bathroom walls by requiring that they contain reinforced areas to allow for later installation of grab bars without the need for major structural work on the walls.

Dwellings Covered by the Design Requirements

The design requirements apply to buildings built for first occupancy after March 13, 1991, which fall under the definition of "covered multifamily dwellings." See page 12 for a discussion of "first occupancy." Covered multifamily dwellings are:

1. all dwelling units in buildings containing four or more dwelling units if such buildings have one or more elevators, and
2. all ground floor dwelling units in other buildings containing four or more units.

To be a covered unit, all of the finished living space must be on the same floor, that is, be a single-story unit, such as single-story townhouses, villas, or patio apartments. Even though raised and sunken areas are permissible in covered dwelling units, there are limitations to their use and they are discussed in Chapter Four: "Accessible Route Into and Through the Covered Unit." Multistory dwelling units are not covered by the Guidelines except when they are located in buildings which have one or more elevators, in which case, the primary entry level is covered.

---

[4] House Report No. 711, 100th Congress, 2nd Session

Dwelling Units in Buildings with Elevator(s)

As is evident from the preceding discussion, the Fair Housing Act's definition of "covered multifamily dwellings" distinguishes between buildings with elevators and buildings without elevators. Thus, if a building has one or more elevators, all of the dwelling units in the building are covered.

There is one exception to this requirement, and that is when an elevator is provided only as a means of creating an accessible route to dwelling units on a ground floor. In that case, the elevator is not required to serve dwelling units on floors which are not ground floors, and the building is not considered to be a "building with one or more elevators" that would require all of the dwelling units to meet the requirements of the Guidelines. This concept is discussed more fully in Chapter 1: "Accessible Building Entrance on an Accessible Route," starting on page 1.21.

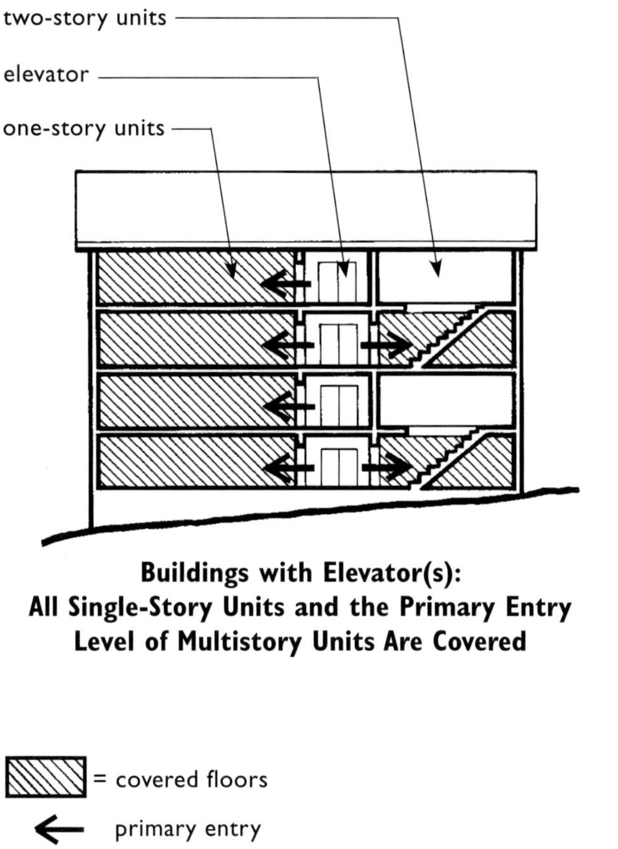

Buildings with Elevator(s): All Single-Story Units and the Primary Entry Level of Multistory Units Are Covered

Ground Floor Dwelling Units

The **ground floor** is defined as a floor of a building with a building entrance on an accessible route. The ground floor may or may not be at grade.

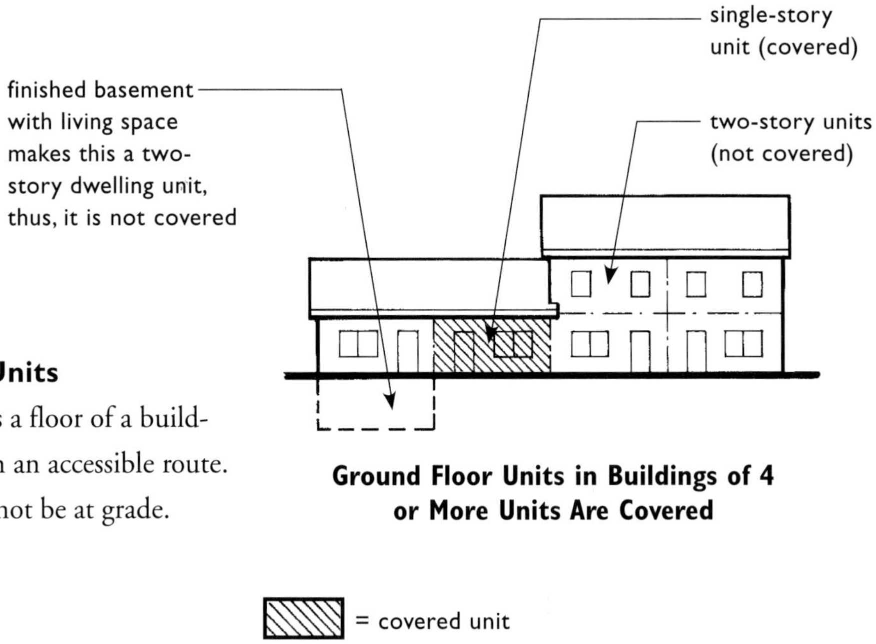

Ground Floor Units in Buildings of 4 or More Units Are Covered

The definition of **ground floor** further provides that where the first floor containing dwelling units in a building is above grade, all units on that floor must be served by a building entrance on an accessible route. This floor will be considered to be a ground floor.

If more than one story can be designed to have an accessible entrance on an accessible route, then each story becomes a ground floor and all units on those stories are covered. However, the Fair Housing Act and the Guidelines do not require that there be more than one ground floor. See Chapter 1: "Accessible Building Entrance on an Accessible Route" for more detailed discussion of covered ground floors.

Covered Dwelling Units Over Shops and Garages

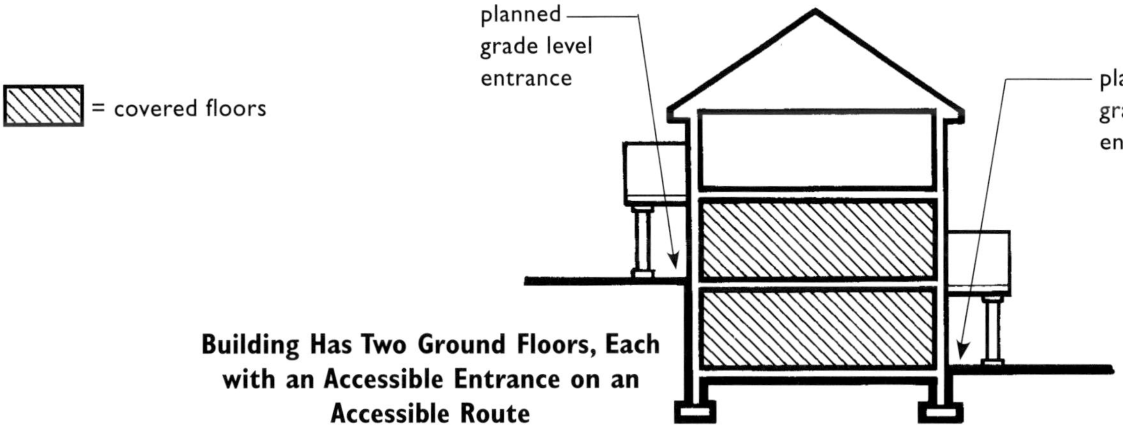

Building Has Two Ground Floors, Each with an Accessible Entrance on an Accessible Route

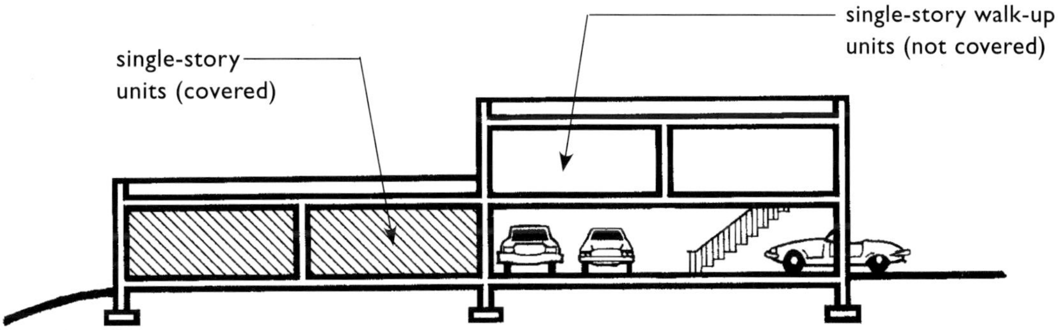

Dwelling Units on the Ground Floor Are Covered (the Guidelines Do Not Require that There Be a Second Ground Floor)

Examples of Covered Multifamily Dwellings

The Fair Housing Act does not distinguish between different forms of ownership when determining whether a unit or building is covered. Condominiums are covered by the Fair Housing Act even if they are pre-sold as a shell and the interior is designed and constructed by the buyer. All covered units must comply with the design and construction requirements of the Guidelines. Single-story townhouses are covered, as are other types of housing including vacation timeshare units, college dormitories, apartment housing in private universities, and sleeping accommodations intended for occupancy as a residence in a shelter.

Continuing care facilities or retirement communities are covered even when they include health care, provided the facility includes at least one building with four or more dwelling units. Whether a facility is considered a "dwelling" depends on whether the facility is to be used as a residence for more than a brief period of time. The operation of each continuing care facility must be examined on a case-by-case basis to determine whether it contains covered multifamily dwellings.

Buildings Separated by Firewalls or Covered Walkways

Dwellings built within a single structure but separated by a firewall are treated under the Fair Housing Act as a single building. For example, a structure containing two units on each side of a firewall would not be regarded as four two-unit buildings (and thus not covered by the Guidelines) but as a single eight-unit building.

In other situations where the dwelling units are connected, such as by stairs or a walkway that is structurally tied to the main body of the building, for purposes of the Guidelines, they are considered a single building and ground floor units in such buildings without elevators are covered.

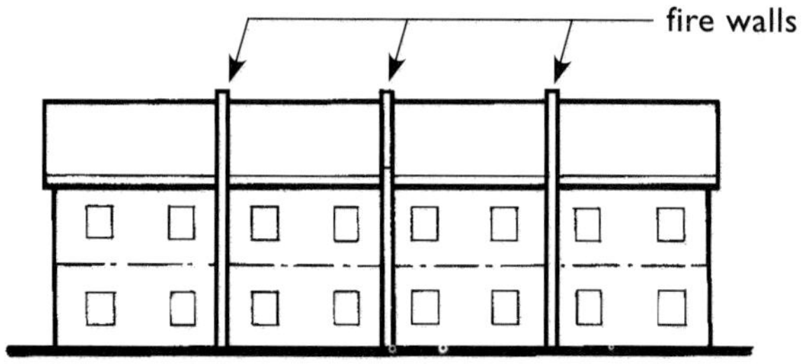

Building with Firewalls Is Treated as a Single Building

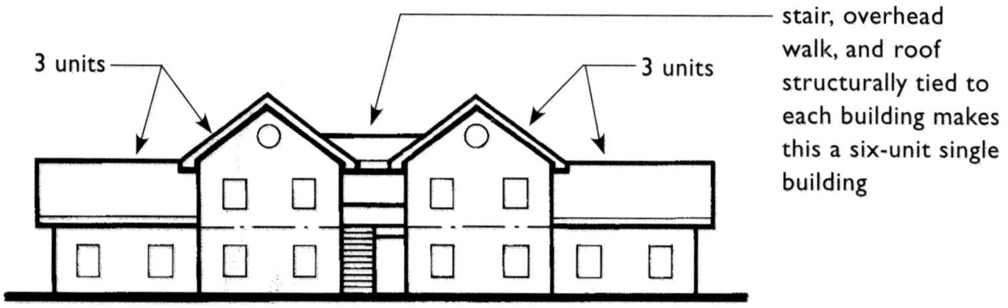

For Purposes of the Guidelines, Two Structurally Joined Buildings Are Treated as a Single Building

Building Conversions

If a building was used previously for a nonresidential purpose, such as a warehouse, office building, or school, and is being converted to multifamily housing, the conversion is not covered. The Fair Housing Act only applies to covered buildings for first occupancy after March 13, 1991. The regulations define "first occupancy" as "a building that has never before been used for any purpose."
See page 12 for additional discussion of "first occupancy."

New Construction Behind Old Facade

In cases where the facade of a building is preserved, but the interior of the building, including all structural portions of floors and ceilings is removed, and a new building is constructed behind the old facade, the building is considered a new building for the purposes of the Fair Housing Act. Thus, it is covered and must comply with the Guidelines.

Additions to Existing Buildings

When an addition is built as an extension to an existing building, the addition of four or more units is regarded as a new building and must meet the design requirements of the Guidelines.
If any new public and common use spaces are added, they are required to be accessible. If, for example, an apartment wing is added to an existing hotel, the apartments are covered by the Fair Housing Act.

Housing for Older Persons Is Covered

Housing built specifically for older persons is exempt from complying with the Fair Housing Act's prohibition against discrimination based on familial status (see 24 CFR 100.303 and 100.304). However, such housing is still subject to the Fair Housing Act's other requirements, including the design requirements for accessibility.

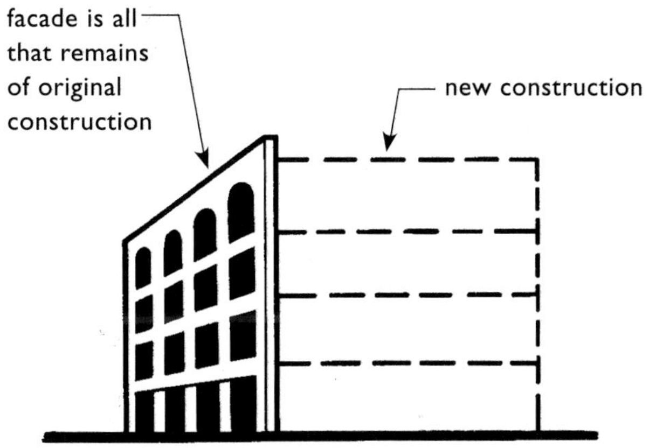

New Construction Behind Old Facade Is Covered

First Occupancy After March 13, 1991

The Fair Housing Act does not require any renovations to existing buildings. Its design requirements apply to new construction only – to covered multifamily dwellings that are built for first occupancy after March 13, 1991. First occupancy is defined as "a building that has never before been used for any purpose." See also "Definitions Used in the Guidelines," page 16.

A building is not subject to the design requirements of the Fair Housing Act if:

1. it was occupied on or before March 13, 1991,

– **or** –

2. the last building permit or renewal thereof was issued by a state, county, or local government on or before June 15, 1990.

For a building to be considered occupied, the following criteria must be met:

1. a certificate of occupancy must have been issued,

– **and** –

2. at least one dwelling unit actually must be occupied.

a. For a building containing **rental units**, this means that a resident has signed a lease and taken possession of a unit. The resident must have the legal right to occupy the premises, but need not have physically moved in yet.

b. For a building containing **for-sale units**, this means that a new owner has completed settlement and taken possession of a unit. The new owner must have the legal right to occupy the premises, but need not have physically moved in yet.

A certificate of occupancy, or the fact that units are being offered for sale but not yet sold, would not be an acceptable means of establishing occupancy. For a project consisting of several buildings which are constructed in phases spanning the March 13, 1991 date, first occupancy will be determined on a building-by-building basis.

The ANSI Standard, the Fair Housing Act, and the Guidelines

The Fair Housing Act requires certain features of accessible design for covered multifamily dwellings built for first occupancy after March 13, 1991. The Act and HUD's implementing regulations, as well as the final Fair Housing Accessibility Guidelines (the Guidelines) reference the 1986 ANSI A117.1 *American National Standard for Buildings and Facilities – Providing Accessibility and Usability for Physically Handicapped People* as an acceptable standard to meet when designing accessible elements, spaces, and features outside covered dwelling units.

The level of accessibility required by the Fair Housing Act is relatively high on the site and in common use areas where compliance with much of the ANSI Standard is required. Accessibility is less stringent within the dwelling units where only specific features outlined in the Guidelines are required. In some instances, the specification is a modification of the related ANSI section, and in other instances the Guidelines substitute specifications.

The Guidelines state in the "Purpose" Section that the Guidelines are to provide technical guidance on designing dwelling units that are in compliance with the Fair Housing Act, and are not mandatory. Rather, the Guidelines provide a safe harbor for compliance with the accessibility requirements of the Act.

The "Purpose" Section also states, "Builders and developers may choose to depart from these Guidelines and seek alternate ways to demonstrate that they have met the requirements of the Fair Housing Act." However, it is recommended that, if a designer or builder chooses to follow an accessibility standard other than the 1986 ANSI A117.1 Standard, or a more recent version of the ANSI A117.1, such as the 1992 CABO/ANSI, that care be taken to ensure the standard used is at least equivalent to or stricter than the 1986 ANSI A117.1 Standard.

Note: Whenever this Manual states the ANSI Standard or the ANSI A117.1 Standard "must be followed," it means the 1986 ANSI A117.1 Standard or an equivalent or stricter standard.

The Guidelines

The design requirements of the Guidelines to which new buildings and dwelling units must comply are presented in abridged form below. Dwelling units are not subject to these requirements only in the rare instance where there are extremes of terrain or unusual characteristics of the site. Such instances are discussed in detail in Chapter One: "Accessible Building Entrance on an Accessible Route."

Requirement 1

Accessible Building Entrance on an Accessible Route: Covered multifamily dwellings must have at least one building entrance on an accessible route, unless it is impractical to do so because of terrain or unusual characteristics of the site. For all such dwellings with a building entrance on an accessible route the following six requirements apply.

Requirement 2

Accessible and Usable Public and Common Use Areas: Public and common use areas must be readily accessible to and usable by people with disabilities. See Chapter Two.

Requirement 3

Usable Doors: All doors designed to allow passage into and within all premises must be sufficiently wide to allow passage by persons in wheelchairs. See Chapter Three.

Requirement 4

Accessible Route Into and Through the Covered Dwelling Unit: There must be an accessible route into and through the dwelling units, providing access for people with disabilities throughout the unit. See Chapter Four.

Requirement 5

Light Switches, Electrical Outlets, Thermostats and Other Environmental Controls in Accessible Locations: All premises within the dwelling units must contain light switches, electrical outlets, thermostats and other environmental controls in accessible locations. See Chapter Five.

Requirement 6

Reinforced Walls for Grab Bars: All premises within dwelling units must contain reinforcements in bathroom walls to allow later installation of grab bars around toilet, tub, shower stall and shower seat, where such facilities are provided. See Chapter Six.

Requirement 7

Usable Kitchens and Bathrooms: Dwelling units must contain usable kitchens and bathrooms such that an individual who uses a wheelchair can maneuver about the space. See Chapter Seven.

Definitions Used in the Guidelines

This is the complete list of definitions used in the Guidelines, excluding a definition for "handicap" and "controlled substance." See Appendix B of this manual for a reprint of the Guidelines, which contains the complete list. Two additional definitions, taken from the regulations and a Guideline Requirement, are provided below. They are so noted with the definition.

Accessible
when used with respect to the public and common use areas of a building containing covered multifamily dwelling units, means that the public or common use areas of the building can be approached, entered, and used by individuals with physical disabilities. The phrase "readily accessible to and usable by" is synonymous with accessible. A public or common use area that complies with the appropriate requirements of ANSI A117.1-1986, a comparable standard, or these Guidelines is "accessible" within the meaning of this paragraph.

Accessible route
means a continuous and unobstructed path connecting accessible elements and spaces in a building or within a site that can be negotiated by a person with a severe disability using a wheelchair, and that is also safe for and usable by people with other disabilities. Interior accessible routes may include corridors, floors, ramps, elevators, and lifts. Exterior accessible routes may include parking access aisles, curb ramps, walks, ramps, and lifts. A route that complies with the appropriate requirements of ANSI A117.1-1986, a comparable standard, or Requirement 1 of these Guidelines is an "accessible route." In the circumstances described in Requirements 1 and 2, "accessible route" may include access via a vehicular route.

Adaptable dwelling units
when used with respect to covered multifamily dwellings, means dwelling units that include the features of adaptable design specified in 24 CFR 100.205(c) (2)-(3).

ANSI A117.1 - 1986
means the 1986 edition of the American National Standard for buildings and facilities providing accessibility and usability for physically disabled people.

Assistive device
means an aid, tool, or instrument used by a person with disabilities to assist in activities of daily living. Examples of assistive devices include tongs, knob-turners, and oven-rack pusher/pullers.

Bathroom
means a bathroom which includes a water closet (toilet), lavatory (sink), and bathtub or shower. It does not include single-fixture facilities or those with only a water closet and lavatory. It does include a compartmented bathroom. A compartmented bathroom is one in which the fixtures are distributed among interconnected rooms. A compartmented bathroom is considered a single unit and is subject to the Act's requirements for bathrooms.

Building
means a structure, facility, or portion thereof that contains or serves one or more dwelling units.

Building entrance on an accessible route
means an accessible entrance to a building that is connected by an accessible route to public transportation stops, to parking or passenger loading zones, or to public streets or sidewalks, if available. A building entrance that complies with ANSI A117.1 -1986 (see Requirement 1 of these Guidelines) or a comparable standard complies with the requirements of this paragraph.

Clear
means unobstructed.

Common use areas
means rooms, spaces, or elements inside or outside of a building that are made available for the use of residents of a building or the guests thereof. These areas include hallways, lounges, lobbies, laundry rooms, refuse rooms, mail rooms, recreational areas, and passageways among and between buildings. See Requirement 2 of these Guidelines.

Covered multifamily dwellings
or covered multifamily dwellings subject to the Fair Housing Amendments means buildings consisting of four or more dwelling units if such buildings have one or more elevators, and ground floor dwelling units in other buildings consisting of four or more dwelling units. Dwelling units within a single structure separated by firewalls do not constitute separate buildings.

Dwelling unit
means a single unit of residence for a household of one or more persons. Examples of dwelling units covered by these Guidelines include: condominiums, an apartment unit within an apartment building, and other types of dwellings in which sleeping accommodations are provided but toileting or cooking facilities are shared by occupants of more than one room or portion of the dwelling. Examples of the latter include dormitory rooms and sleeping accommodations in shelters intended for occupancy as a residence for homeless persons.

Entrance
means any exterior access point to a building or portion of a building used by residents for the purpose of entering. For purposes of these Guidelines, an "entrance" does not include a door to a loading dock or a door used primarily as a service entrance, even if nondisabled residents occasionally use that door to enter.

Finished grade
means the ground surface of the site after all construction, levelling, grading, and development has been completed.

First occupancy
means a building that has never before been used for any purpose. (Definition found in regulations at 24 CFR 100.201)

Ground Floor
means a floor of a building with a building entrance on an accessible route. A building may have one or more ground floors. Where the first floor containing dwelling units is above grade, all units on that floor must be served by a building entrance on an accessible route. This floor will be considered a ground floor.

Loft
means an intermediate level between the floor and ceiling of any story, located within a room or rooms of a dwelling.

Multistory dwelling unit
means a dwelling unit with finished living space located on one floor and the floor or floors immediately above or below it.

Powder room
A room containing a toilet and a sink. (Definition found in Requirement 6 of the Guidelines.)

Public use areas
means interior or exterior rooms or spaces of a building that are made available to the general public. Public use may be provided at a building that is privately or publicly owned.

Single-story dwelling unit
means a dwelling unit with all finished living space located on one floor.

Site
means a parcel of land bounded by a property line or a designated portion of a public right of way.

Slope
means the relative steepness of the land between two points and is calculated as follows: The distance and elevation between the two points (e.g., an entrance and a passenger loading zone) are determined from a topographical map. The difference in elevation is divided by the distance and that fraction is multiplied by 100 to obtain a percentage slope figure. For example, if a principal entrance is ten feet from a passenger loading zone, and the principal entrance is raised one foot higher than the passenger loading zone, then the slope is $1/10 \times 100 = 10\%$.

Story
means that portion of a dwelling unit between the upper surface of any floor and the upper surface of the floor next above, or the roof of the unit. Within the context of dwelling units, the terms "story" and "floor" are synonymous.

Undisturbed site
means the site before any construction, levelling, grading, or development associated with the current project.

Vehicular or pedestrian arrival points
means public or resident parking areas, public transportation stops, passenger loading zones, and public streets or sidewalks.

Vehicular route
means a route intended for vehicular traffic, such as a street, driveway, or parking lot.

Disability Types and Implications for Design

Types of Disabilities

Most people will, at some time during their life, have a disability, either temporary or permanent, which limits their ability to move around in and use the built environment. In fact, more than one in five Americans aged 15 and over have some type of disability; problems with walking and lifting are the most common. Not until fairly recently have the needs of people with disabilities been given adequate attention. The passage of the Fair Housing Act is another step in the process to create a built environment where people with disabilities can move freely in society as do persons who have no disability.

According to the "Statistical Report: the Status of People with Disabilities," compiled by the President's Committee on Employment of People with Disabilities, published in 1994[5] :

- 48.9 million Americans are persons with disabilities;
- 32 million Americans are age 65 or over;
- 3.3 million Americans are 85 and older, and this number is projected to grow by 100%, to over 6 million by 2010;
- 70% of all Americans will, at some time in their lives, have a temporary or permanent disability that makes stair climbing impossible;
- 8,000 people survive traumatic spinal cord injuries each year, returning to homes that are inaccessible;
- 17 million Americans have serious hearing disabilities;
- 8.1 million Americans have vision disabilities;
- 27 million Americans have heart disease and reduced or limited mobility.

There are hundreds of different disabilities and they manifest themselves in varying degrees. One person may have multiple disabilities while another may have a disability whose symptoms fluctuate. Most standards and design criteria are based on the needs of people defined by one of the following four general categories:

1. Mobility Disabilities

This category includes people who use wheelchairs and those who use other mobility aids.

Wheelchair Users

People with severe mobility disabilities use either a power-driven or manually operated wheelchair or, the more recent development, the three-wheeled cart or scooter to maneuver through the environment. People who use wheelchairs have some of the most obvious access problems. They include maneuvering through narrow spaces, going up or down steep paths, moving over rough or uneven surfaces, making use of toilet and bathing facilities, reaching and seeing items placed at conventional heights, and negotiating steps or changes in level at the entrance to a dwelling unit.

The design and construction requirements of the Fair Housing Act and the Guidelines focus primarily on the spatial needs of people who use wheelchairs because those needs are met more easily in the initial construction phase of a building project. This section provides basic information on the spatial requirements for an average seated adult

[5]Based on the census report *Americans With Disabilities* 1991/1992, published January 1994

in a stationary position and the space necessary to execute the two most common turns typically described in accessibility standards. The specifications given here are based on the A117.1 - 1986 ANSI Standard (see ANSI 4.2, 4.3, and 4.4).

Clear Floor Space: The minimum clear floor space required to accommodate a single, stationary wheelchair is 30 inches by 48 inches. For an approach to an object, counter, or control, depending upon the object, the user may position his or her chair either parallel or perpendicular to the object. These two types of approaches are discussed in more detail in Chapters Five and Seven.

Turning Spaces: The space required for a person using a wheelchair to make a 180-degree turn is a circle with a diameter of 60 inches. Alternatively, a person can make a T-shaped turn, similar to a three-point turn in a car, at the intersection of a hall or in a room where some of the space necessary to perform the turn may be under a desk, table, or countertop.

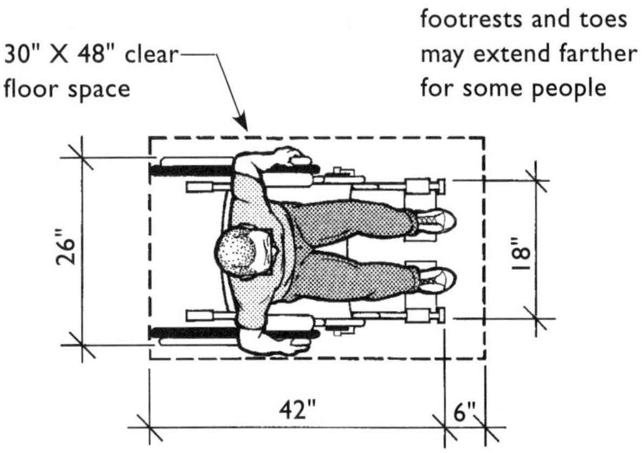

Space Allowances and Approximate Dimensions of Adult-Sized Wheelchairs

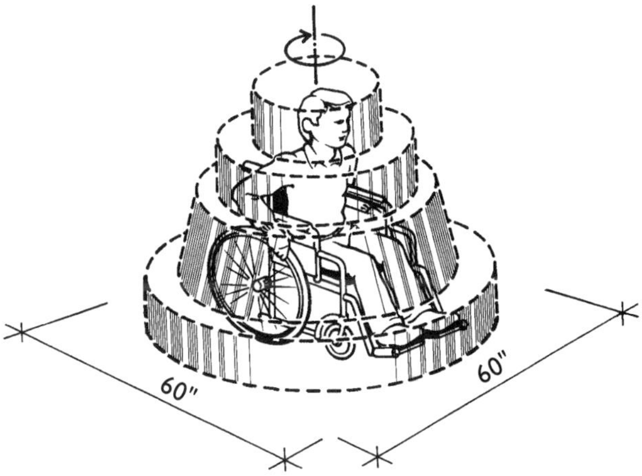

Pivoting Turn Space

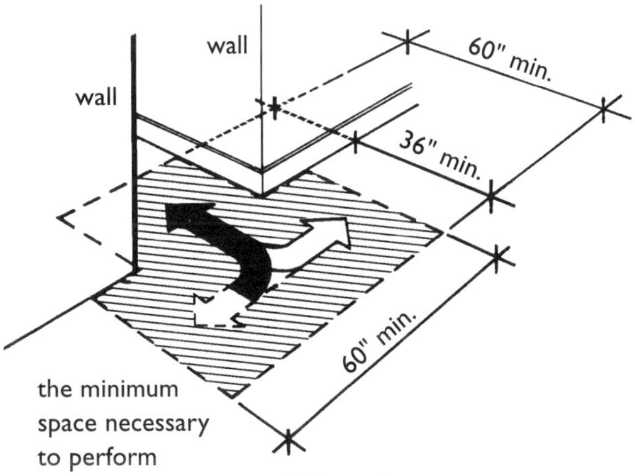

T-Turn Space

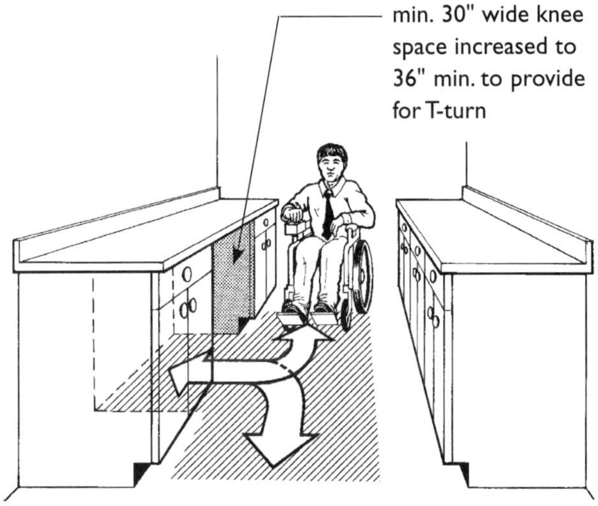

T-Turn within a Knee Space

Ambulatory Mobility Disabilities

This category includes people who walk with difficulty or who have a disability which affects gait. It also includes persons who do not have full use of arms or hands, or who lack coordination. Persons who use crutches, canes, walkers, braces, artificial limbs, or orthopedic shoes are included in this category. Activities that may be difficult for people with mobility disabilities include walking, climbing steps or slopes, standing for extended periods of time, reaching, and fine finger manipulation.

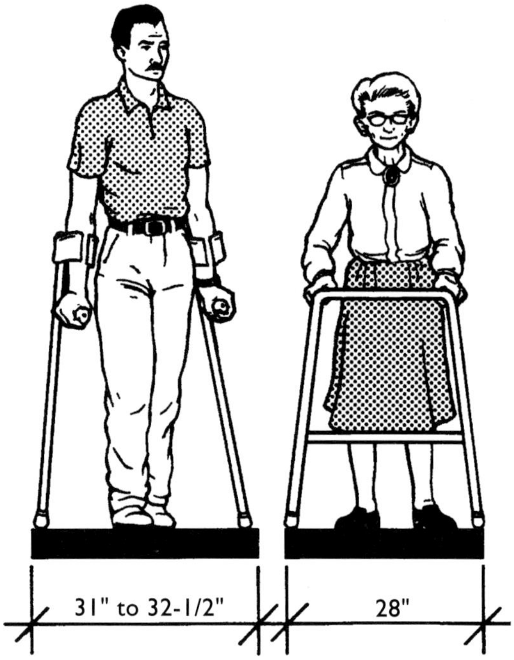

Space Necessary for Adults Using Crutches or Walker

2. Visual Disabilities

This category includes people with partial vision or total vision loss. Some people with a vision disability can distinguish light and dark, sharply contrasting colors, or large print, but cannot read small print, negotiate dimly lit spaces, or tolerate high glare. Many people who are blind depend upon their sense of touch and hearing to perceive their environment and communicate with others. Many use a cane or have a service animal to facilitate moving about.

Minimum Space Necessary for Person with a Service Animal

3. Hearing Disabilities

People with partial hearing often use a combination of speech reading and hearing aids which amplify the available sounds. Echo, reverberation, and extraneous background noise can distort hearing aid transmission. People who are deaf and who rely on lip reading for information must be able to see clearly the face of the individual who is speaking. Those who use sign language to communicate also may be adversely affected by poor lighting. People who are hard of hearing or deaf may have difficulty understanding oral communication and receiving notification by equipment that is exclusively auditory such as telephones, fire alarms, public address systems, etc.

4. Cognitive Disabilities and Other Hidden Conditions

People with cognitive and learning disabilities may have difficulty using facilities, particularly where the signage system is unclear or complicated. In addition to people with permanent disabilities, there are others who may have a temporary condition which affects their usual abilities. Broken bones, illness, trauma, or surgery – all may affect a person's use of the built environment for a short time. Frequently, people have diseases of the heart or lungs, neurological diseases with resulting lack of coordination, arthritis, or rheumatism that may reduce physical stamina or cause pain. Reduction in overall ability is also experienced by many people as they age. People of extreme size or weight often need special accommodation as well.

Enforcement

Under the Fair Housing Act, discrimination includes a failure to design and construct covered multifamily dwellings in a manner which includes the specific features of accessible design delineated in the Act. Thus, responsibility for complying with the law rests with any and all persons involved in the design and construction of covered multifamily dwellings. This means, for example, that if a complaint is filed, the complaint could be filed against all persons involved in the design and construction of the building, including architects, builders, building contractors, the owner, etc.

HUD has the responsibility for enforcement of the Fair Housing Act. The Fair Housing Act provides that an aggrieved person may, not later than one year after an alleged discriminatory housing practice has occurred or terminated, file a complaint with the Secretary of HUD. The Secretary, on the Secretary's own initiative, also may file such a complaint. With respect to the design and construction requirements, complaints could be filed at any time that the building continues to be in noncompliance, because the discriminatory housing practice – failure to design and construct the building in compliance – does not terminate.

Following the filing of the complaint, an investigation is conducted and completed within 100 days, unless impracticable to do so. During the period beginning with the filing of the complaint and ending with the filing of a charge or a dismissal by the Secretary, HUD will engage in conciliation.

If a charge of discrimination is issued after an investigation, an aggrieved person or a respondent may elect, in lieu of an administrative proceeding with HUD, to have the complaint decided in a civil action. An aggrieved person may bring a civil action in state or federal district court within two years after occurrence or termination of an alleged discriminatory housing practice.

If an administrative law judge finds that a respondent has engaged in or is about to engage in a discriminatory housing practice, the administrative law judge will order appropriate relief. Such relief may include actual and compensatory damages, injunctive or other equitable relief, attorney's fees and costs, and may also include civil penalties ranging from $10,000 for the first offense to $50,000 for repeated offenses. In addition, in the case of buildings which have been completed, structural changes could be ordered, and an escrow fund might be required to finance future changes.

With respect to the design and construction requirements, HUD may encourage, but cannot require, states and units of local government to include in their existing procedures for the review and approval of newly constructed covered multifamily dwellings, determinations as to whether the design and construction of such dwellings are consistent with the requirements of the Fair Housing Act, HUD's implementing regulations, and the Fair Housing Accessibility Guidelines.

HUD provides technical assistance to states and units of local government and other interested persons, in order to implement the design and construction requirements of the Fair Housing Act. Architects, designers and builders may contact HUD with questions, either by telephone or by letter. However, HUD is not required to, nor does the agency have a procedure for, review and approval of building plans to determine if they are in compliance. Technical assistance provided by HUD serves only as general interpretation of law and regulations and is not binding on the agency with respect to a specific case.

Some states have incorporated the requirements of the Fair Housing Act into their state laws. How this is done may differ from state to state. Some states, for example, have included the design and construction requirements as a part of the state law and simply incorporated HUD's Fair Housing Accessibility Guidelines by reference. Other states have drafted their own language to implement the design and construction requirements of the Fair Housing Act into the state building code. States which have incorporated the requirements of the Fair Housing Act into their state laws enforce those laws independently of the federal government. However, it should be noted that it is the state law that is being enforced. Such enforcement will not preclude any individual from exercising his or her right to file a complaint with HUD under the Fair Housing Act, or from filing a private lawsuit; nor does it preclude HUD from conducting a Secretary-initiated complaint.

The Fair Housing Act does not invalidate or limit any law of a state or local government that requires dwellings to be designed and constructed in a manner that affords persons with disabilities greater accessibility than the requirements of the Fair Housing Act. Likewise, the Fair Housing Act does not invalidate or replace other federal laws which require greater accessibility in certain housing, such as Section 504 of the Rehabilitation Act of 1973 or the Architectural Barriers Act of 1968.

The following is a list of HUD enforcement offices. Architects, builders and other users of this manual are encouraged to contact these and other HUD Fair Housing field offices for technical assistance as needed.

New England
U. S. Department of Housing
and Urban Development
Thomas P. O'Neill, Jr. Federal Building
10 Causeway Street, Room 308
Boston, Massachusetts 02222-1092
(617) 994-8300
Connecticut, Maine, Massachusetts, New Hampshire, Rhode Island, Vermont

New York/New Jersey
U. S. Department of Housing
and Urban Development
26 Federal Plaza
New York, New York 10278-0068
(212) 264-1290
New Jersey, New York

Mid-Atlantic
U. S. Department of Housing
and Urban Development
The Wanamaker Building
100 Penn Square East
Philadelphia, Pennsylvania 19107-3390
(215) 656-0647
Delaware, District of Columbia, Maryland, Pennsylvania, Virginia, West Virginia

Southeast/Caribbean
U. S. Department of Housing
and Urban Development
Five Points Plaza
40 Marietta Street
Atlanta, Georgia 30303-3388
(404) 331-5140
Alabama, Florida, Georgia, Kentucky, Mississippi, North Carolina, South Carolina, Tennessee, Puerto Rico, Virgin Islands

Midwest
U. S. Department of Housing
and Urban Development
77 West Jackson Boulevard
Chicago, Illinois 60604-3507
(312) 353-7776
Illinois, Indiana, Minnesota, Michigan, Ohio, Wisconsin

Southwest
U. S. Department of Housing
and Urban Development
801 North Cherry Street
Fort Worth, Texas 76113-2905
(817) 978-5900
Arkansas, Louisiana, New Mexico, Oklahoma, Texas

Great Plains
U. S. Department of Housing
and Urban Development
Gateway Tower II, 400 State Avenue
Kansas City, Kansas 66101-2406
(913) 551-6958
Iowa, Kansas, Missouri, Nebraska

Rocky Mountain
U. S. Department of Housing
and Urban Development
First Interstate Tower North
633 17th Street
Denver, Colorado 80202-2349
(303) 672-5434
Colorado, Montana, North Dakota, South Dakota, Utah, Wyoming

Pacific/Hawaii
U. S. Department of Housing
and Urban Development
Phillip Burton Federal Building
450 Golden Gate Avenue
P. O. Box 36003
San Francisco, California 94102-3448
(415) 436-6569
Arizona, California, Hawaii, Nevada, Guam, American Samoa

Northwest/Alaska
U. S. Department of Housing
and Urban Development
Federal Office Building
909 First Avenue, Suite 200
Seattle, Washington 98104-1000
(206) 220-5170
Alaska, Idaho, Oregon, Washington

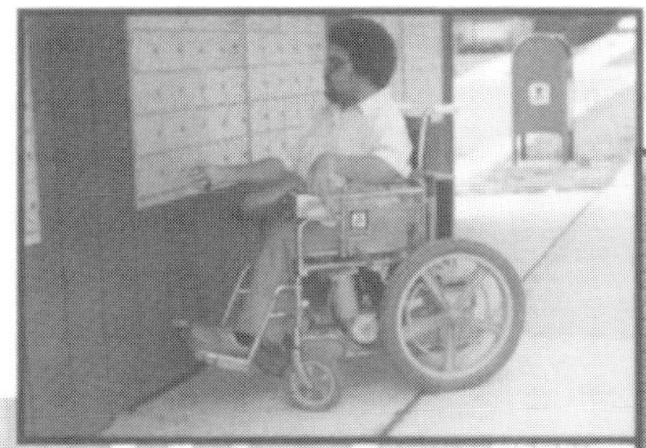
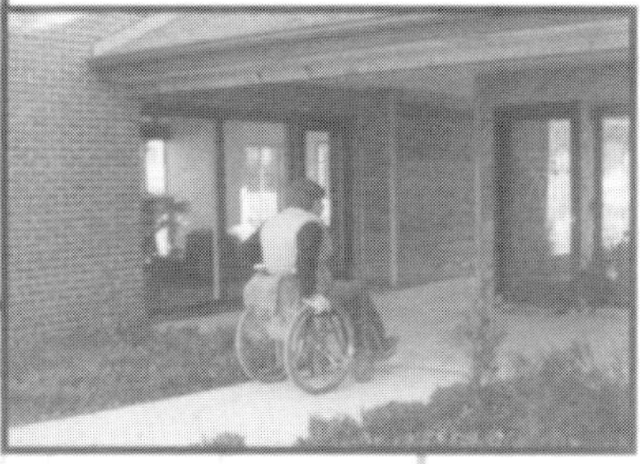

Part Two

Design Requirements of the Guidelines

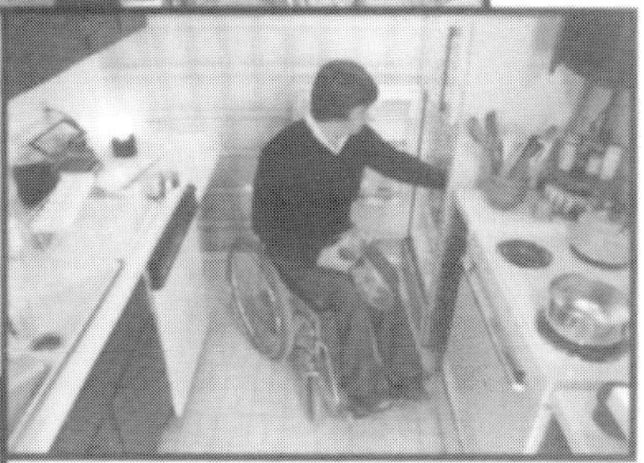

Chapter One:

REQUIREMENT 1

Accessible Building Entrance on an Accessible Route

1

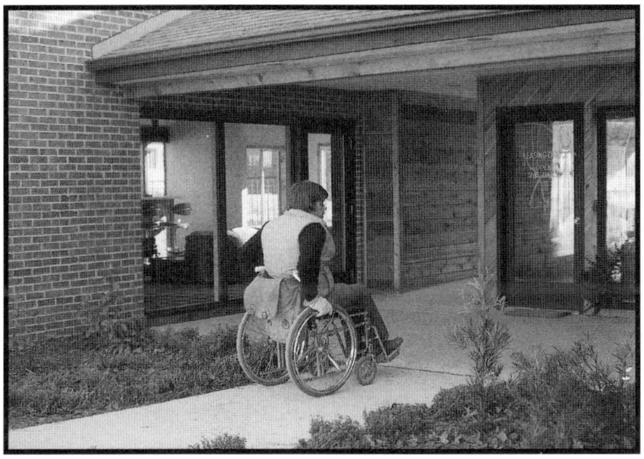

"...covered multifamily dwellings shall be designed and constructed to have at least one building entrance on an accessible route unless it is impractical to do so because of terrain or unusual characteristics of the site."
Fair Housing Act Regulations, 24 CFR 100.205

Definitions from the Guidelines

Accessible route. A continuous unobstructed path connecting accessible elements and spaces in a building or within a site that can be negotiated by a person with a severe disability using a wheelchair, and that is also safe for and usable by people with other disabilities. Interior accessible routes may include corridors, floors, ramps, elevators and lifts. Exterior accessible routes may include parking access aisles, curb ramps, walks, ramps, and lifts. A route that complies with the appropriate requirements of ANSI A117.1 – 1986, a comparable standard, or Section 5, Requirement 1 of these guidelines is an "accessible route." In the circumstances described in Section, 5, Requirements 1 and 2, "accessible route" may include access via a vehicular route.

Building. A structure, facility or portion thereof that contains or serves one or more dwelling units.

Building entrance on an accessible route. An accessible entrance to a building that is connected by an accessible route to public transportation stops, to parking or passenger loading zones, or to public streets or sidewalks, if available. A building entrance that complies with ANSI A117.1 – 1986 or a comparable standard complies with the requirements of this paragraph.

Entrance. Any exterior access point to a building or portion of a building used by residents for the purpose of entering. For purposes of these guidelines, an "entrance" does not include a door to a loading dock or a door used primarily as a service entrance, even if nonhandicapped residents occasionally use that door to enter.

Finished grade. The ground surface of the site after all construction, levelling, grading, and development has been completed.

Site. A parcel of land bounded by a property line or a designated portion of a public right of way.

Slope. The relative steepness of the land between two points and calculated as follows: The distance and elevation between the two points (e.g., an entrance and a passenger loading zone) are determined from a topographical map. The difference in elevation is divided by the distance and that fraction is multiplied by 100 to obtain a percentage slope figure. For example, if a principal entrance is ten feet from a passenger zone, and the principal entrance is raised one foot higher than the passenger loading zone, then the slope is 1/10 x 100 = 10%.

Undisturbed site. The site before any construction, levelling, grading, or development associated with the current project.

Vehicular or pedestrian arrival points. Public or resident parking areas, public transportation stops, passenger loading zones, and public streets or sidewalks.

Vehicular route. A route intended for vehicular traffic, such as a street, driveway, or parking lot.

Introduction

The Fair Housing Accessibility Guidelines (the Guidelines) define covered multifamily dwellings as **1.** those buildings consisting of four or more units if such buildings have one or more elevators and **2.** ground floor units in other buildings having four or more units. The Guidelines do not specify the total number of entrances a building must have nor where they must be positioned. However, the Guidelines do stipulate that each covered building on a site must have at least one accessible entrance on an accessible route. It is expected that most sites can and should be made accessible, i.e., an accessible route can be provided to entrances of covered dwellings; therefore, it is also expected that covered dwelling units will be provided on all building sites, including those where steep slopes, rock outcroppings, marshy areas, and similar conditions exist.

The requirements of the Fair Housing Act are outlined in the Act itself and in the implementing regulations issued by the U.S. Department of Housing and Urban Development (HUD). Section 100.205 (a) of these regulations states: "Covered multifamily dwellings for first occupancy after March 13, 1991, shall be designed and constructed to have at least one building entrance on an accessible route unless it is impractical to do so because of the terrain or unusual characteristics of the site."

Requirement 1 of the Guidelines presents guidance on designing an accessible building entrance on an accessible route. Requirement 1 also provides tests to assist a developer of buildings that do not have one or more elevators to determine when an accessible entrance is impractical because of extreme terrain or unusual characteristics of the site. See impracticality tests pages 1.40 through 1.55. Units where entrances are impractical do not have to meet the other design requirements; the tests, therefore, can alter the number of units on a site that must comply.

The language of the Fair Housing Act itself does not provide an exception for site impracticality; however, as HUD notes in the preamble to its regulations, "the legislative history makes it clear that Congress was 'sensitive to the possibility that certain natural terrain may pose unique building problems.'"[6] In applying the site impracticality tests, architects and builders should keep in mind that in enforcement proceedings under the Fair Housing Act, it is the person(s) who designed and constructed the building(s) who has the burden of establishing that site impracticality existed.

Accessible routes and accessible entrances may occur in the course of any design project. They also may not occur and be expensive to include later if a careful approach to site design is not conducted. Deliberate manipulation of the grade to avoid the requirements of the Fair Housing Act is regarded as a discriminatory housing practice and must be avoided. This chapter offers methods and strategies to assist designers and builders to more efficiently provide accessible entrances and routes for all sites.

[6] House Report No. 100-711, page 27

Early Planning for Accessible Routes at Entrances

The language of the Fair Housing Act requires covered multifamily dwellings to be **designed** and constructed in a manner that incorporates certain features of accessible and adaptable design. The Act specifically includes the design process, thereby recognizing that changes will need to be made in the way buildings are designed in order to assure accessibility.

Planning for accessibility should be an integral part of the design process in multifamily housing developments. This is particularly crucial in the early stages of planning when major decisions are being made about the overall design of the site. The location and orientation of buildings, parking areas, loading zones, and other elements have a major impact on the ease with which accessibility can be achieved in a finished development. This is especially important on sloping sites where careful initial planning can eliminate the need for major earthwork and the construction of elaborate ramps, bridges, lifts, or elevators to provide accessibility.

Attempts should be made to set the entrance floor levels of buildings at or close to ground levels to eliminate or minimize changes in level that may require steps or ramps. Often this may be accomplished by making use of fill dirt which has been excavated from other parts of the building site to alter the ground levels at appropriate places.

Since people generally arrive at buildings by a private car, bus, or taxi, the location of vehicle arrival points is critical. Passenger drop-off points and parking areas for people with disabilities should be located close to building entrances and at levels which do not necessitate climbing steep slopes to reach the entrance floor level.

The path of travel to and placement of site amenities, such as outside mailboxes, refuse disposal areas, swimming pools, clubhouses, and sports facilities should be given careful consideration early in the planning process. The intent of the Fair Housing Act is that people with disabilities be able to reach and use such amenities.

In this manual, the ANSI Standard A117.1 - 1986 is referenced as the accessibility standard for compliance in much of public and common use space of multifamily housing developments. The Guidelines themselves cite the ANSI A117.1 - 1986 Standard (*the American National Standard for Buildings and Facilities – Providing Accessibility and Usability for Physically Handicapped People*). Although referenced, the ANSI specifications are not mandated. Any ANSI citation in this manual refers to the 1986 ANSI A117.1 Standard and should be understood to mean that compliance with ANSI or any other similar accessibility standard that is equal to or more stringent than the ANSI A117.1 (1986) Standard would fulfill the requirements of the accessibility provisions of the Fair Housing Act.

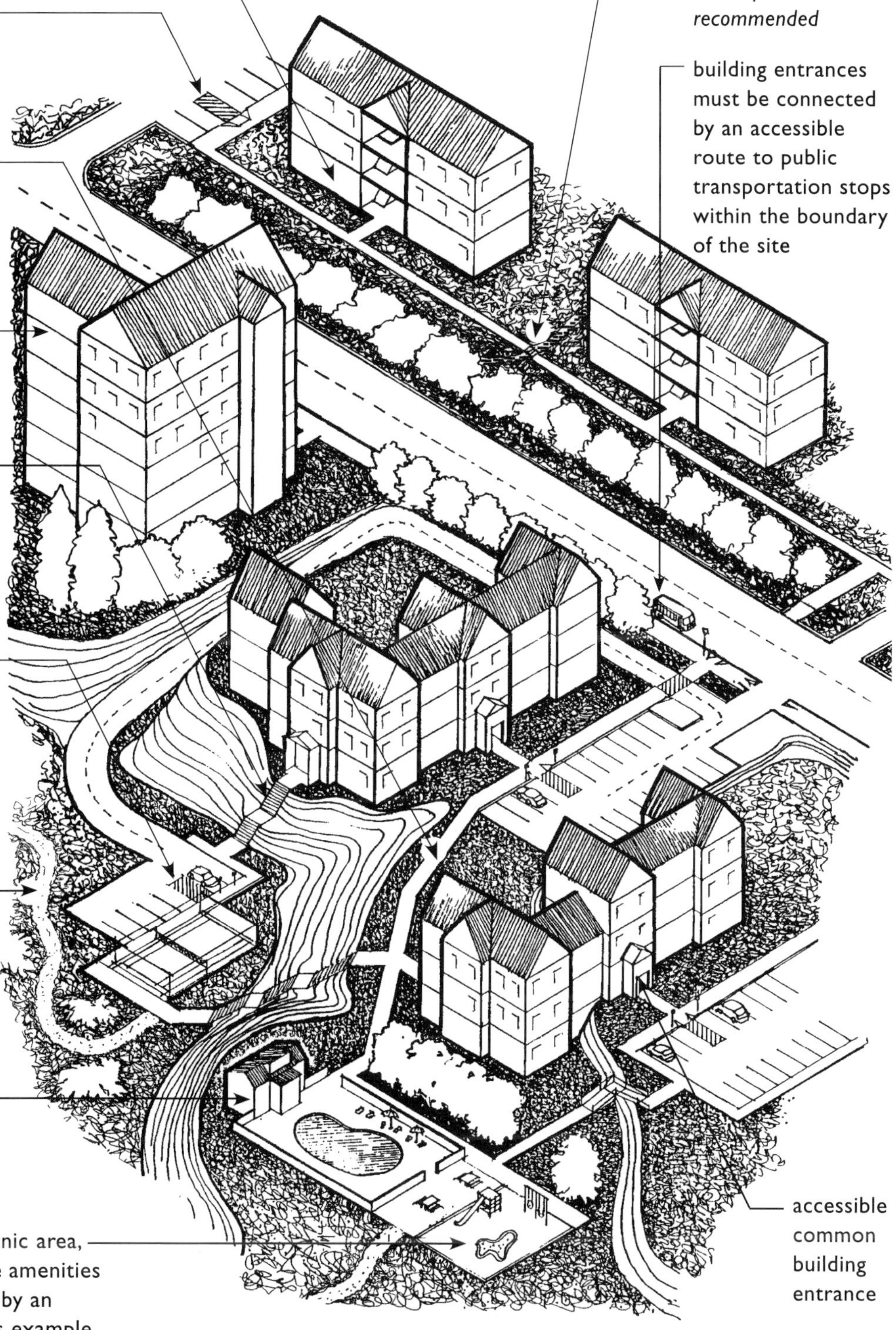

Careful Site Analysis and Building Placement in the Planning Stage of a Housing Development Makes Accessible Entrances Easier to Provide

What is an Accessible Route ?

An accessible route is a continuous, unobstructed path through sites and buildings that connects all accessible features, elements, and spaces. It is the critical element that allows the successful use of any site or building by a person with a disability. Such a route is safe for someone using a wheelchair or scooter and also is usable by others.

Accessible routes on a site may include parking spaces, parking access aisles, curb ramps, walks, ramps, and lifts. Accessible routes within buildings may include corridors, doorways, floors, ramps, elevators, and lifts. Specifications for accessible routes are found in ANSI 4.3. Certain elements of accessible routes which must be given careful attention are:

- width of route
- ground and floor surfaces
- headroom
- protruding objects
- slope of route
- cross slope
- curb ramps
- lift/elevator design

These elements are discussed in detail in Part Two, Chapter 2.

Stairs and Accessible Routes

Stairs are not an acceptable component of an accessible route because they prevent use by people using wheelchairs and others who cannot climb steps. ANSI specifications for accessible stairs (4.9) make stairs safer and more usable by mobility impaired people who can climb stairs.

Route with No Abrupt Change in Level to Provide Access to Dwelling Units and Site Amenities

When stairs are installed along routes that are required to be accessible, there must be an alternative way to get between levels. If the alternative way is an elevator or lift, the stairs do not need to comply with ANSI 4.9. If the alternative way is a ramp, the stairs must comply with ANSI 4.9. When an accessible route consists of both a ramp and stairs, it is best if they are located in close proximity so people who can use only one of the two (such as the ramp), need not travel an unreasonable additional distance.

Walks on Accessible Routes

Walks that are part of accessible routes become ramps when their slope exceeds 5% (1 in 20). Handrails are not required on walks with slopes between 0% and 5%, but they are required on those steeper than 5% and up to 8.33% (1 in 12). Slopes steeper than 8.33% are not usable by most people with disabilities and cannot be considered part of an accessible route. Handrail requirements for walks differ, depending upon which buildings the walks connect. This is addressed in the following sections.

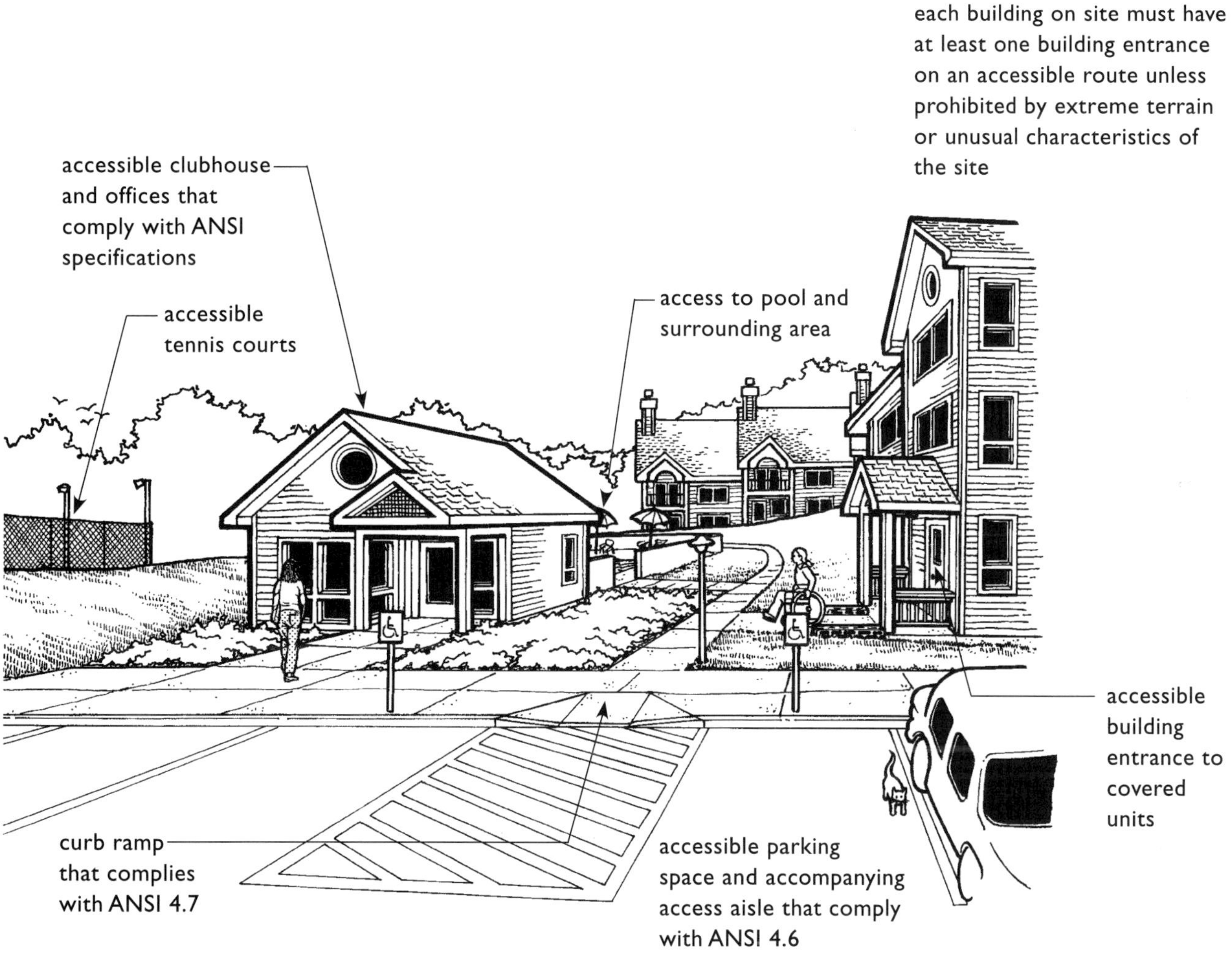

Where Are Accessible Routes Required on Sites?

Accessible Route from Site Arrival Points to Accessible Building Entrances

The Guidelines require that an accessible route be provided from public transportation stops, accessible parking spaces, accessible passenger loading zones, and public streets or sidewalks to accessible building entrances unless it is impractical to do so as determined by application of the site tests specified in Requirement 1(site impracticality due to terrain or unusual site characteristics, see page 1.38). Because these walkways are required to be accessible, handrails, as per ANSI, must be provided when the slope of the walk is between 5% (1 in 20) and 8.33% (1 in 12).

Accessible Routes and Walks Between Accessible Buildings and Site Facilities

The Guidelines require accessible routes to connect buildings containing covered dwelling units (those with one or more elevators and ground floors of other buildings, except two-story townhouses) and accessible facilities, elements, and spaces on the same site. The Guidelines do not require accessible routes, walks, or paths between buildings containing only covered dwelling units unless the route is also part of a required accessible route. For example, if a building also contains a facility such as a laundry that is shared by two buildings, then an accessible route must be provided between the two buildings.

If no portion of the finished grade of a route between two buildings that contain only dwelling units exceeds 8.33% (1 in 12), it is recommended that the route be made accessible. Such voluntary accessible walks must meet the same specifications as an accessible route except that handrails, commonly required on accessible routes when their slope exceeds 5% (1 in 20), are not required.

Accessible Site Facilities on Accessible Routes

The Guidelines require accessible and usable public and common use areas. All facilities, elements, and spaces that are part of public and common use areas must meet ANSI 4.1 through 4.30 and must be on an accessible route from covered dwelling units. Such facilities might include outside mailboxes, site furnishings, outside storage areas, refuse disposal areas, playing fields, amphitheaters, picnic sites, swimming pools and sun decks, tennis courts, clubhouses, playgrounds, gazebos, parking areas, sidewalks, and all or part of nature trails and jogging paths.

Where multiple recreational facilities of the same type are provided at the same location on the site (e.g., tennis courts), not all but a "sufficient" number of the facilities must be accessible to ensure an equitable opportunity for use by people with disabilities. Whenever only one of a type of recreational facility is provided at a particular location on the site, it must be accessible and connected by an accessible route to the covered dwelling units. (See Chapter 2: "Accessible Public and Common Use Spaces.")

Use of Vehicles for Access to Site Facilities

When the finished grade exceeds 1 in 12 or other physical barriers (natural or man made) or legal restrictions, all of which are outside the control of the owner, prevent the installation of an accessible pedestrian route between covered dwellings and some public or common use site facilities; the Guidelines allow for automobiles to be used for access if certain conditions are met. When such a vehicular route is used as an alternative method to achieve accessibility:

1. the required parking at covered dwelling units must be provided, and

2. an appropriate number of additional accessible parking spaces on an accessible route must be provided at each facility that is otherwise unreachable by means of an accessible pedestrian route. For a complete discussion of parking requirements, see Chapter 2: "Accessible and Usable Public and Common Use Areas."

Careful planning and strategic location of accessible parking spaces and curb ramps around dwelling units and amenities will help give continuity between vehicular and pedestrian accessible routes. Accessible parking spaces and curb ramps are recommended at all on-site amenities to give residents choices in how to reach them, even those served by accessible pedestrian routes. This is especially important where accessible routes are very long and where parts or all of the route have maximum allowable slopes of 1 in 12 (1:12), which are difficult or impossible for many people to use.

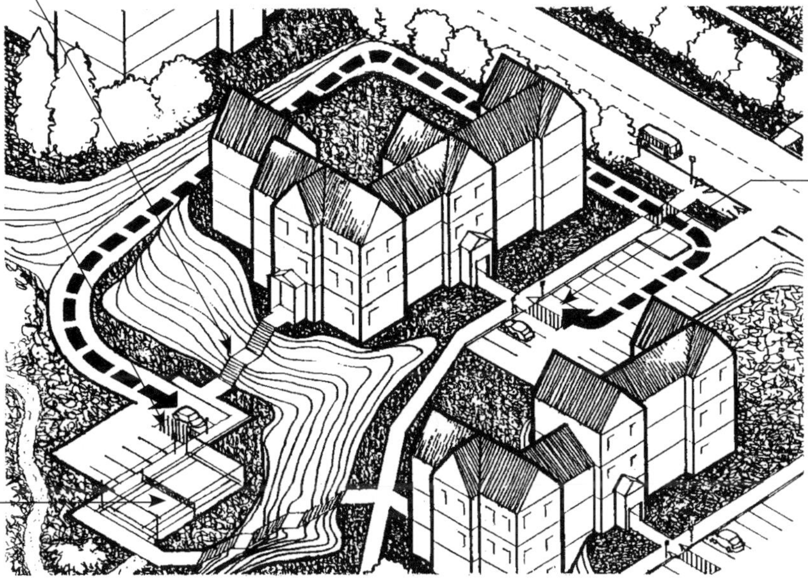

In Some Circumstances, Site Access by Vehicle May Be Acceptable

Accessible Entrances

All buildings containing covered dwelling units and separate buildings containing public and common use spaces, such as clubhouses, must have at least one accessible building entrance on an accessible route, unless it is impractical to do so as determined by applying the site impracticality tests provided in the Guidelines; see pages 1.38 through 1.58. Entrances into individual dwellings on an interior accessible route are referred to in the Guidelines as "entries." These entries and the entries to dwelling units having separate exterior ground floor entrances will be discussed in Chapter 3: "Usable Doors." The Guidelines establish three requirements for an accessible building entrance.

Accessible Building Entrance on an Accessible Route

The building entrance must be connected by an accessible route to public transportation stops, to accessible parking and passenger loading zones, and to public streets or sidewalks.

Primary Use

The accessible (common use) entrance must be one which is typically used by residents and/or guests for the purpose of entering the building. Service doors or loading docks cannot serve as the only accessible entrance to buildings, even if residents occasionally use such a door for entering the building.

Building Entrance Design Features

The entrance door itself must be usable by people with disabilities. Detailed specifications to achieve this are given in ANSI 4.13. Accessible building entrances are considered public and common use spaces and, unlike unit entrances, must meet the ANSI requirements on both sides of the door; see the next page.

Main factors which must be addressed are:

- minimum clear width of open doorway 32 inches,
- low or no threshold,
- clear maneuvering space inside and outside the door,
- force needed to open the door,
- accessible door hardware, and
- safe door closing speed.

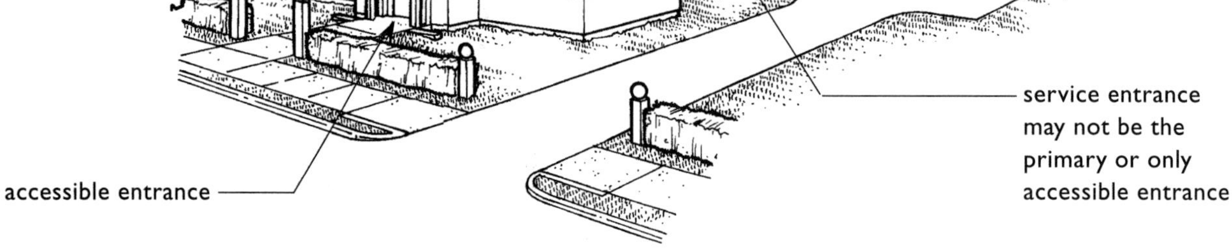

Accessible Primary Use Entrance

good general illumination

weather protection

high intensity lighting focused at locks for people with low vision

color contrast between door and frame

clear, readable, high contrast signage

door closer with safe sweep period (ANSI 4.13.10)

view window (or wide angle peep hole in door)

lever or other easy-to-use door hardware (ANSI 4.13.9)

maneuvering space next to latch side of door (ANSI 4.13.6)

clear width of open doorway min. 32" (ANSI 4.13.5)

low force to open door (ANSI 4.13.11)

adequate slope to prevent ice build-up

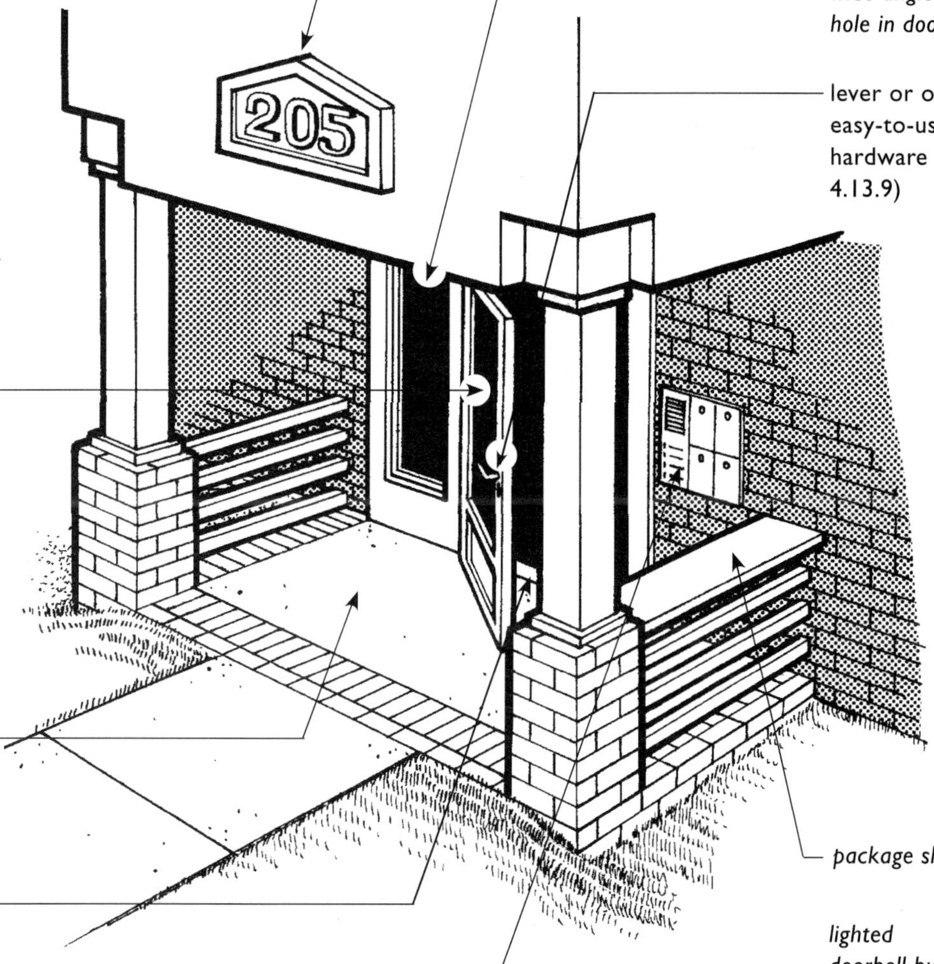

package shelf

low or no threshold (ANSI 4.13.8)

lighted doorbell buttons

Call and mail boxes within reach of a seated person.

Call boxes should be equipped with both visual and audible signals so as to be usable by both hearing and non-hearing people.

Design of Accessible Building Entrances

Notes in italic type are recommendations only and are not required by ANSI or the Guidelines. All recommended features are helpful to people with and without disabilities.

Site Planning for Accessible Entrances on Accessible Routes

The ease of establishing an accessible route at building entrances can be radically affected by the type of construction used and the placement and positioning of the building on the site. These factors should be considered along with others essential to successful early planning and design of a housing complex.

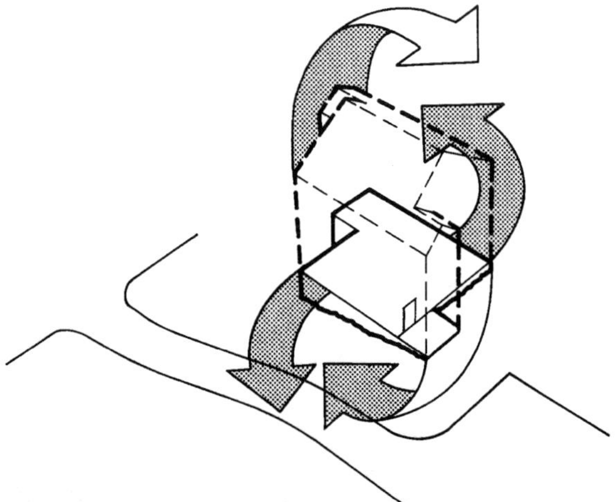

Rotate, Flip, or Redesign Floor Plan to Place Entrance as Close to Grade as Possible

Careful Building Placement

Regardless of the type of construction, the way in which a building is located on a site will affect accessibility at entrances. If entrances exist at locations where the floor level is close to the ground, accessibility will be easier and less expensive to provide. Sometimes plans can be rotated or flipped to bring entrances closer to grade. Entrances and parking often can be relocated to maximize use of existing grades. In some cases, the best solution is to redesign the proposed floor plan to place entrances at or as near grade as possible.

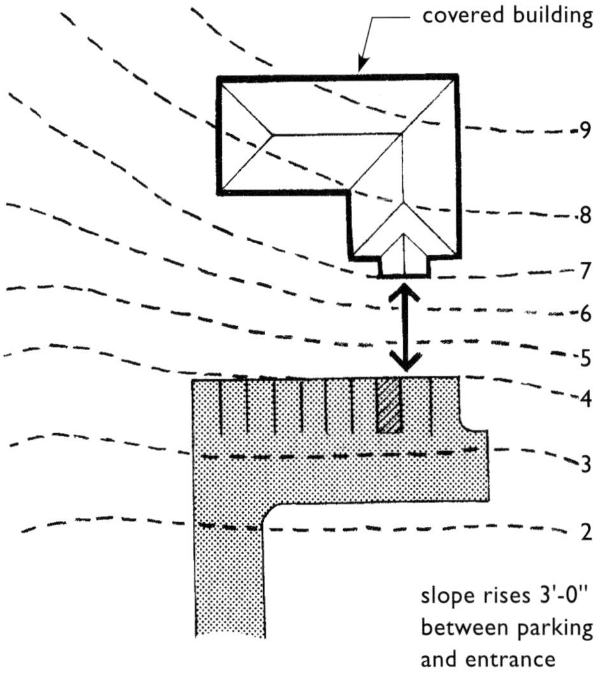

Current Position of Parking Lot Makes Accessible Route Difficult or Impossible to Provide

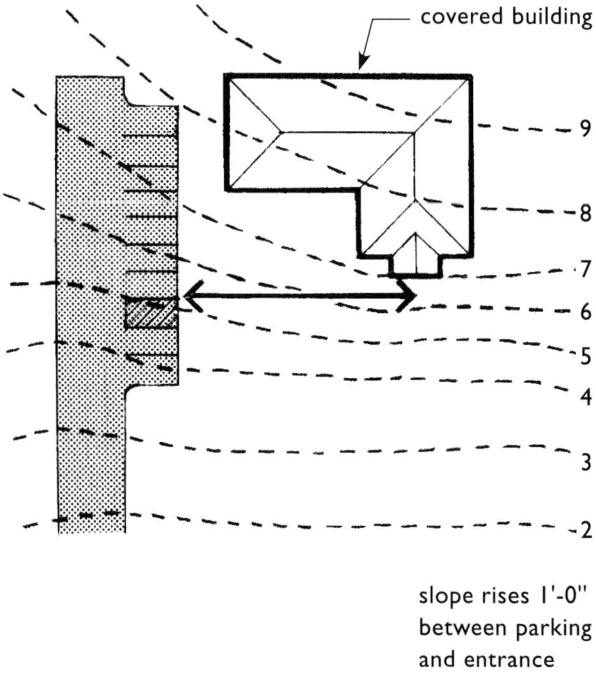

Reorientation of Parking Area to Achieve Accessible Route

Earthwork and Site Grading

It is often possible to create accessible routes to entrances by means of earthwork and the grading of sites. On sloping sites, fill can be added or the land can be cut and graded to place the building entrance at ground level.

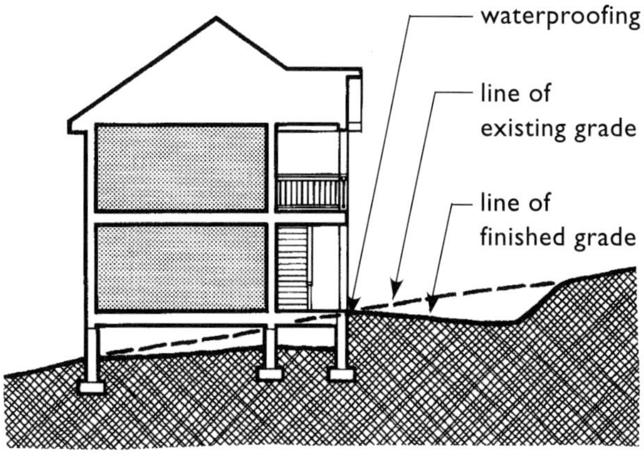

Earth Cut Site Grading

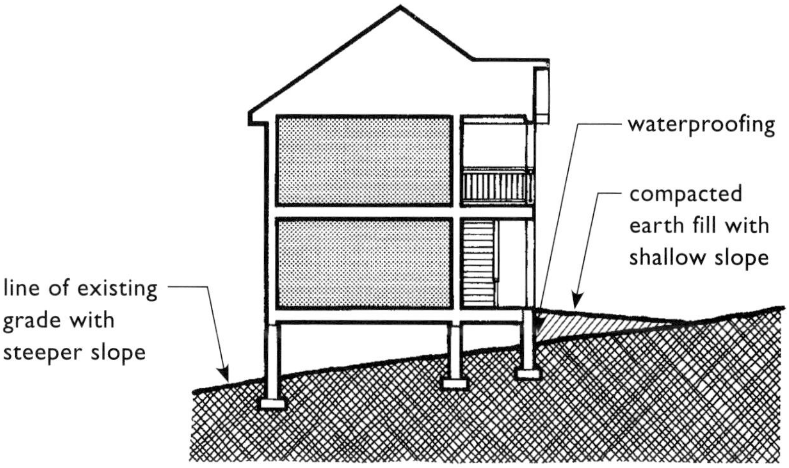

Earth Fill at Entrance

Bridges and Elevated Walks

Bridges or elevated walkways may be a good solution to providing an accessible route to an entrance on a sloping site, particularly where the building is approached from an uphill location. Combinations of techniques can be used on some sites to provide accessible entrances on more than one level. Bridges usually can be made level and thus easy and safe for everyone.

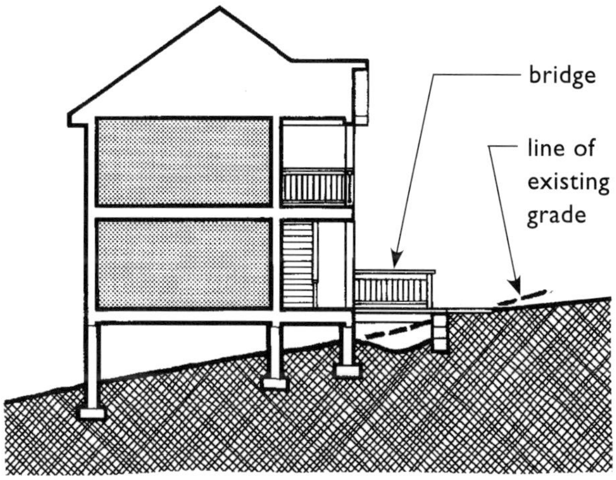

Bridges to Uphill Locations on Sloping Sites

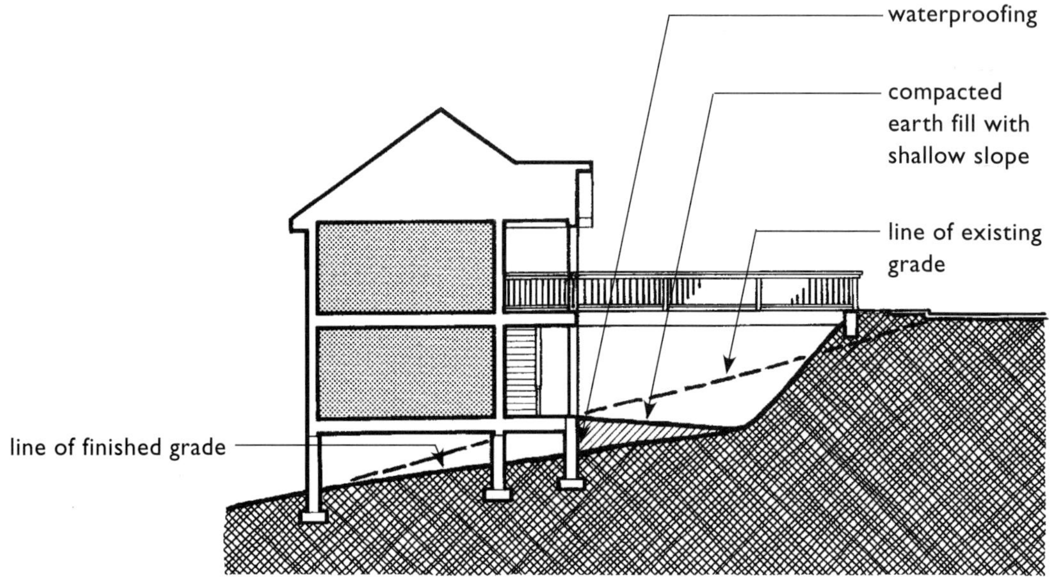

Combination Earth Cut and Accessible Bridge/Walk to Entrances

Earth Berms and Bridges

On flat or irregular sites an accessible route to an above grade entrance might be created by providing a low retaining wall, an earth berm, and a bridge. There are several advantages to this method. The retaining wall is held several feet away from the foundation forming a moat that allows drainage and ventilation to occur at the foundation and eliminates the need for additional waterproofing. The bridge from the retaining wall to the floor of the building can be level. The sloping walk on the berm, if kept flush with the earth and less than 1:20 slope, will not require handrails, thus eliminating the awkward sloping appearance of access ramps and their handrails. Plants on and around the berm and in the moat create an attractive landscaped garden entrance rather than an "access ramp."

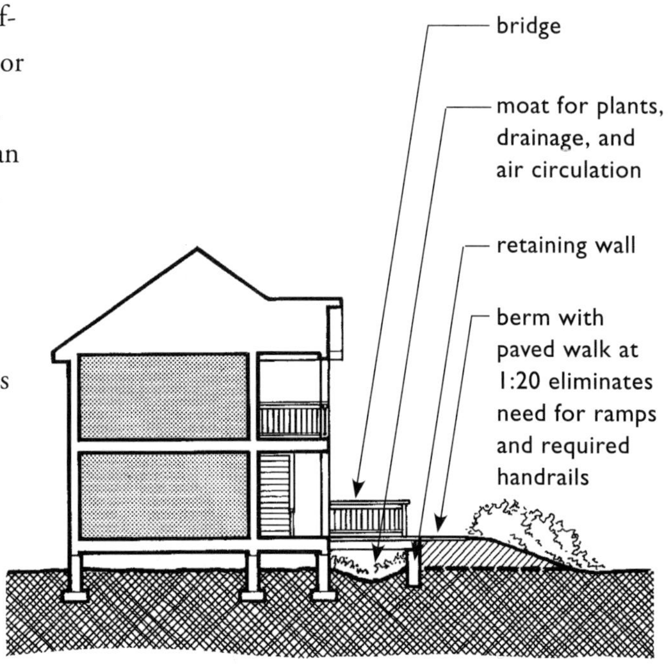

Earth Berm and Bridge

In this site configuration a ramp provides the accessible route from several possible site arrival points to the building entrance. Often a ramp can be combined with stairs and a planter to create attractive entrances that serve the needs of a wide range of people.

ground floor units are covered in this building without elevator(s)

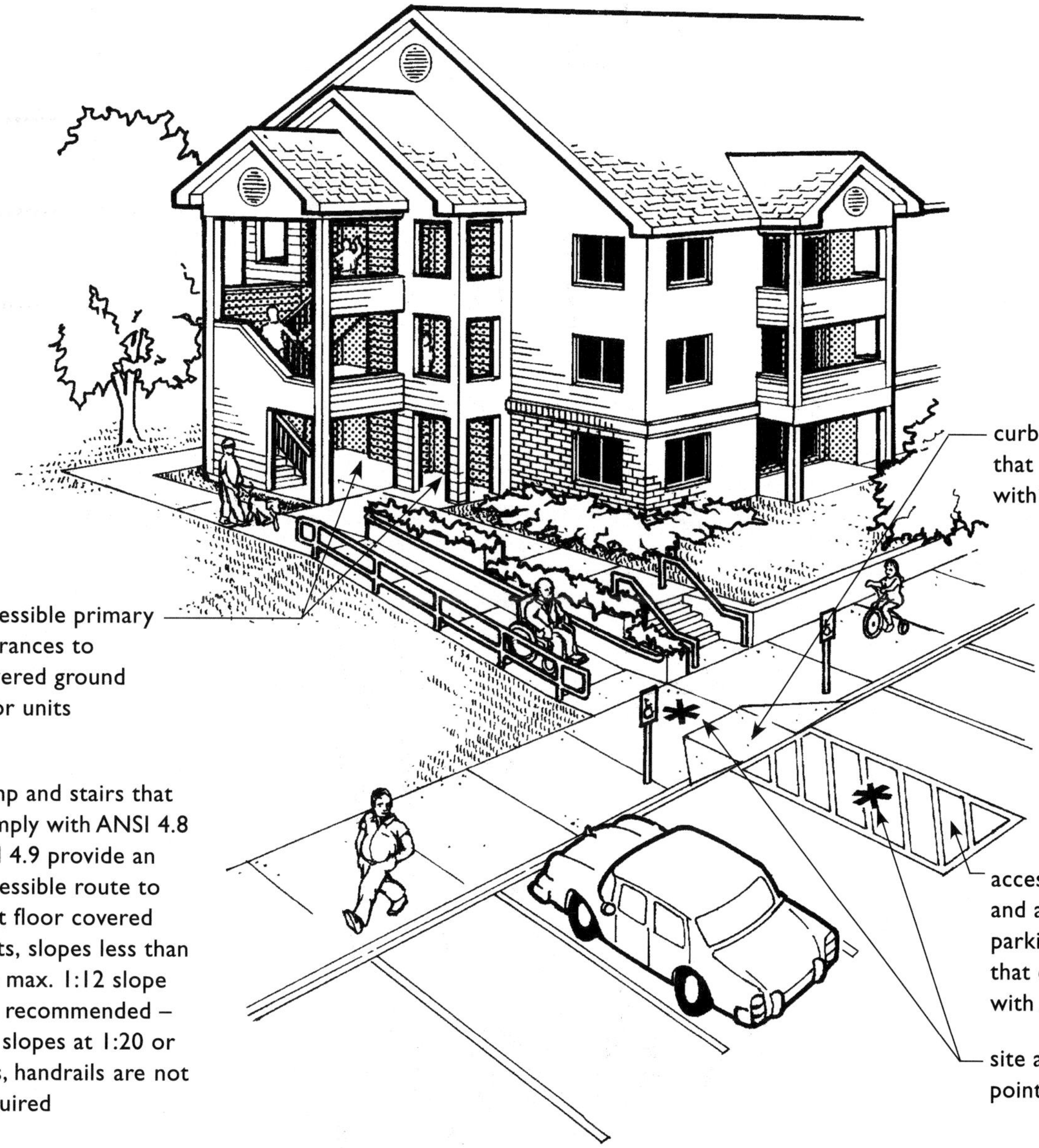

curb ramp that complies with ANSI 4.7

accessible primary entrances to covered ground floor units

ramp and stairs that comply with ANSI 4.8 and 4.9 provide an accessible route to first floor covered units, slopes less than the max. 1:12 slope are recommended – for slopes at 1:20 or less, handrails are not required

access aisle and accessible parking spaces that comply with ANSI 4.6

site arrival points

Site Grading with Combined Ramp and Stairs to Create Access to First Floor Units

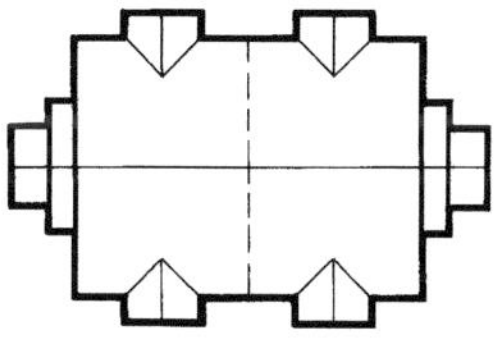

Key Plan
4 Units on Each Floor

In this site configuration the parking for the building is divided between two levels, with the accessible parking provided on the upper level. This solution creates the possibility of an accessible route, with little or no slope, to the building entrance and may reduce the required amount of earthwork necessary for a larger parking lot on the upper level that would serve the entire building.

buildings without one or more elevators, only ground floor units are covered

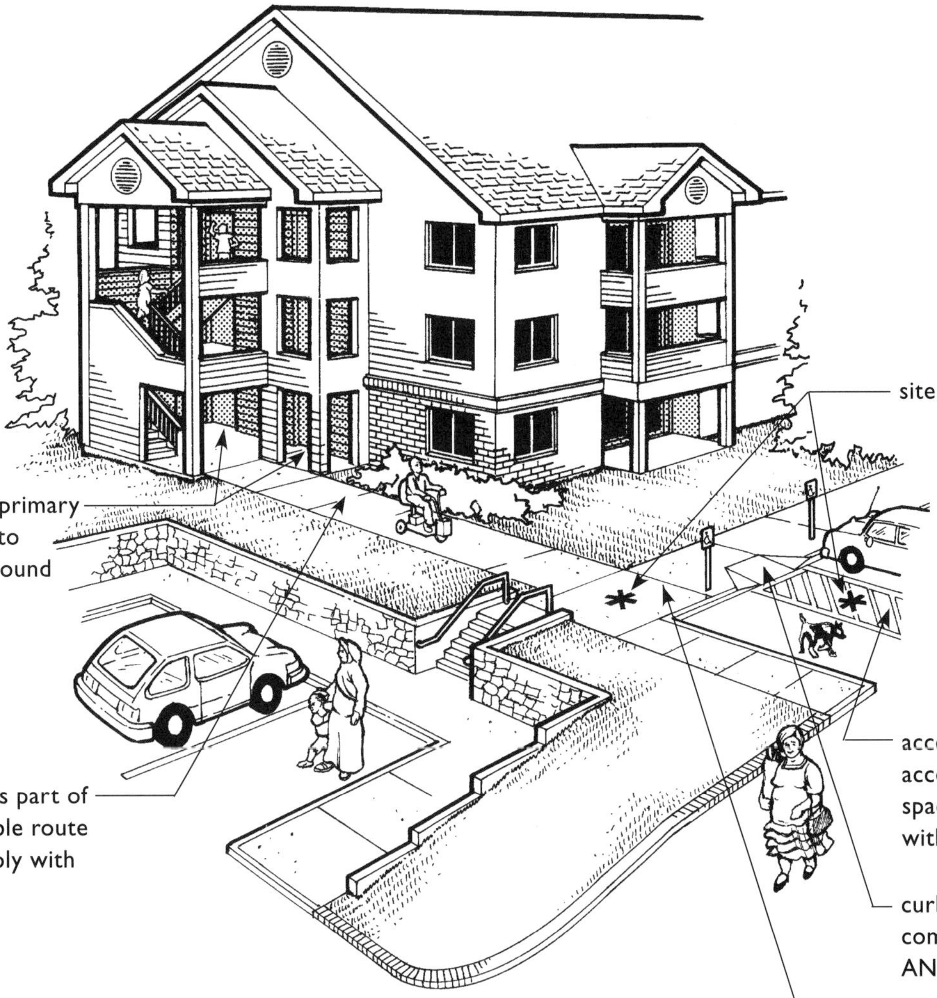

Earthwork and Site Grading to Achieve Access to Ground Floor Units

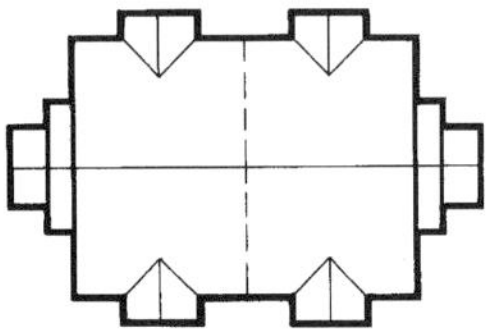

Key Plan
4 Units on Each Floor

In this site configuration a combination of level walkway and bridge is used to create an accessible route to the units on the second floor. On such sloping sites, bridges can provide convenient, safer, and direct access to the upper level.

Access by level bridge and walk provides an accessible route from site arrival points to entrance of two covered units on the second floor level on this side of the building.

stairs down to two lower level units and up to two top floor units

Accessible route from lower level site arrival point to the accessible ground floor entrances to two covered units on the lower level ground floor at the far end of the building.

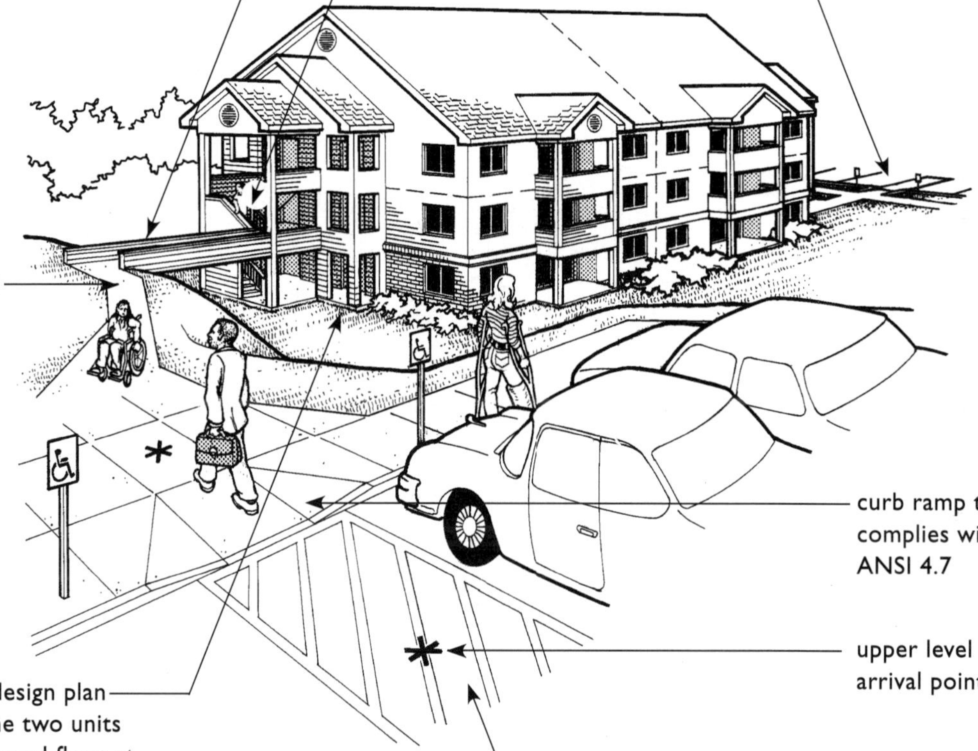

this walk is part of an accessible route and must comply with ANSI 4.3

curb ramp that complies with ANSI 4.7

upper level site arrival point

If the resulting design plan was such that the two units on the lower ground floor at the near end of the building were on an accessible route, those units would also be covered.

access aisle and accessible parking that comply with ANSI 4.6

Bridge to Achieve Access to Second Floor Units

this building has four dwelling units on each floor with separate unit entrances and stairs at each end

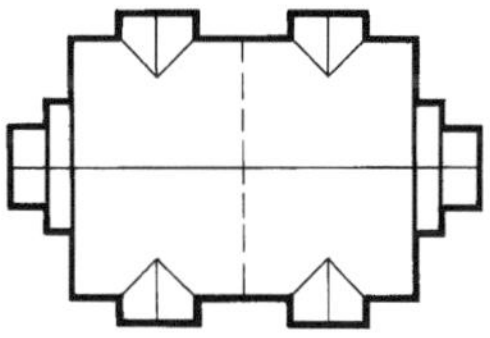

Key Plan
4 Units on Each Floor

In this site configuration an ordinary site feature, a bridge over a stream, has been integrated with a level walkway to create an accessible route to the ground floor units of the building.

Bridge to Achieve Access to Ground Floor Units

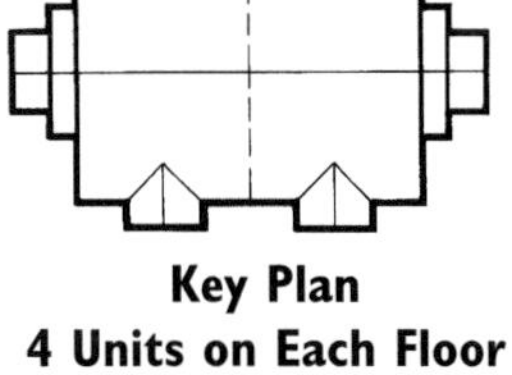

Key Plan
4 Units on Each Floor

accessible route from site entry points via the exterior elevator to the primary entrance of each dwelling unit

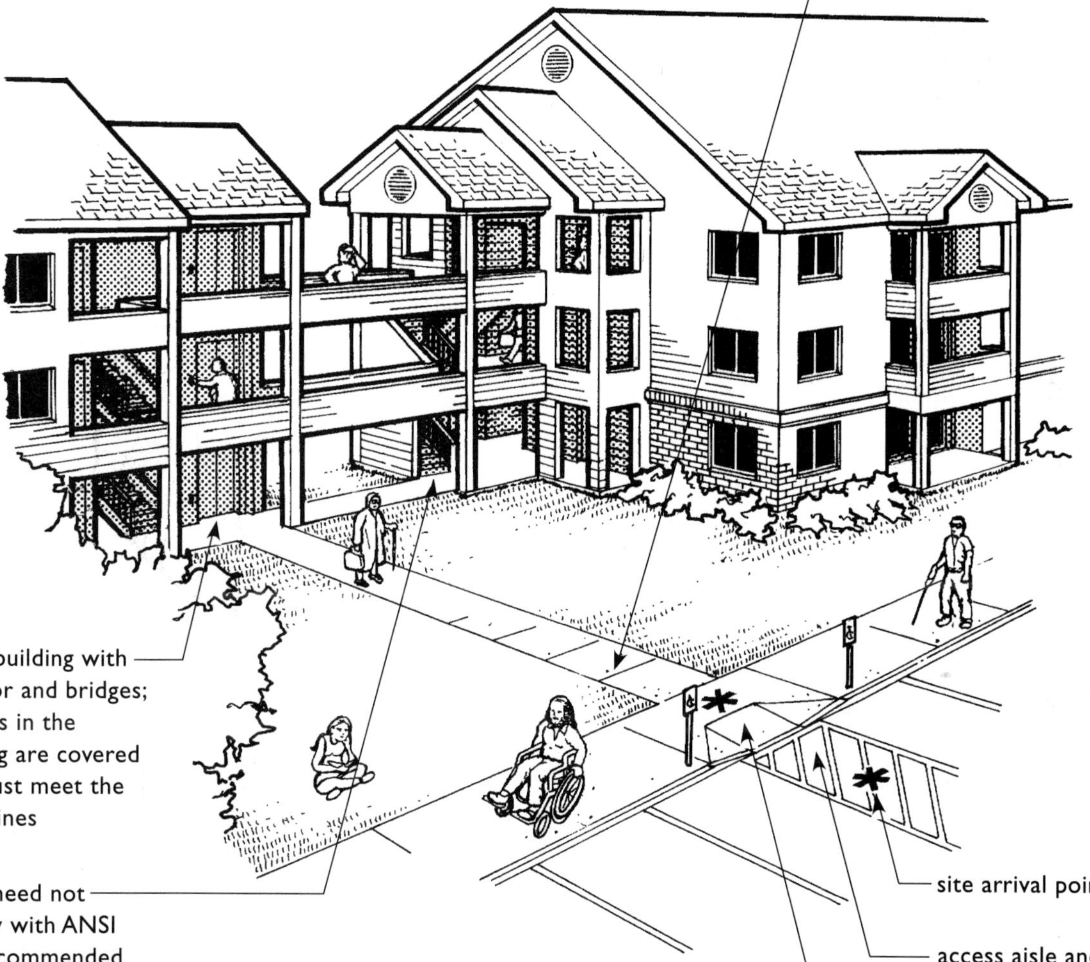

single building with elevator and bridges; all units in the building are covered and must meet the Guidelines

stairs need not comply with ANSI 4.9, recommended compliance for safe egress

site arrival point

access aisle and accessible parking spaces that comply with ANSI 4.6

curb ramp that complies with ANSI 4.7

Building with Exterior Elevator
(All Units are Covered)

elevator

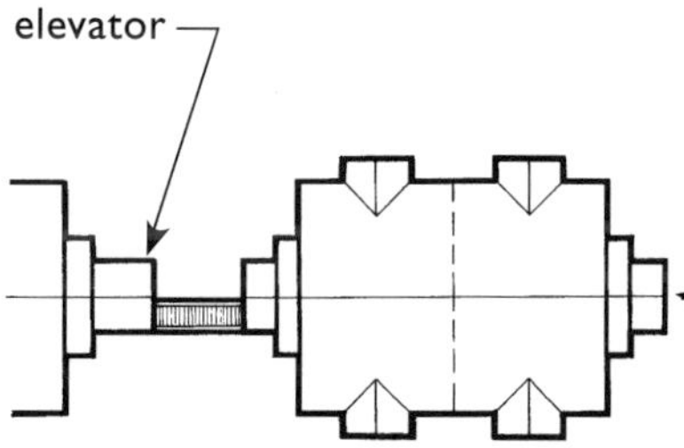

this building has four units on each floor, each with primary entrances on a central double-loaded corridor

Key Plan
4 Units on Each Floor

Covered Dwelling Units and Their Accessible Entrances

In buildings containing multiple dwelling units, common use exterior entrances and individual exterior entrances to ground floor units are required by the Guidelines to be accessible, unless it is impractical to do so as determined by one of the site impracticality tests discussed in the next section on pages 1.38 through 1.58.

It is expected that all multifamily buildings will have covered dwelling units. However, the configuration of the building; the location of the entrances; the determination of which is the ground floor(s) (there can be more than one); the placement, origin, and destination (range) of elevators; and site impracticality will affect which units in multifamily buildings are covered and where or how accessible entrances are provided. This section of the manual discusses coverage and accessible exterior entrances in

1. buildings having one or more elevators,
2. buildings with separate ground floor entrances to dwelling units, and
3. buildings with common entrances.

Entrances to covered dwelling units from interior halls, corridors, or accessible common use spaces are discussed in Chapter 3: "Usable Doors."

Based on the legislative history of the Fair Housing Act, it is expected that **only** extreme conditions of a site may make it impractical to provide an accessible route to entrances of some covered dwelling units. The Guidelines allow, in some instances, the number of covered units to be reduced where such impracticality can be demonstrated. Requirement 1 of the Guidelines includes two site impracticality tests that can be used to determine if an accessible route at a required entrance is impractical due to extreme terrain or site conditions. The tests are referenced in this section and their applications are described in detail on pages 1.38 to 1.58 of this chapter.

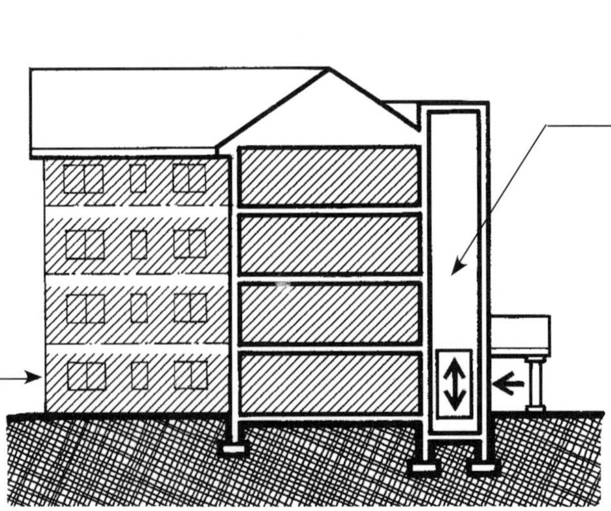

In Buildings with One or More Elevators: (Elevator Buildings) All Units are Covered

Buildings with Elevators

All dwelling units are covered in buildings having one or more elevators and one or more common entrances. The Guidelines require that such buildings with elevators (elevator buildings) have at least one accessible entrance on an accessible route, regardless of the terrain or unusual characteristics of the site. In other words, site impracticality as defined in the tests discussed on pages 1.38 through 1.58 is not allowed for "buildings having one or more elevators."

The rationale for disallowing site impracticality for such buildings includes the assumption that a building having elevators is a mid- to high-rise building and that all floors are accessible via the elevators. In addition, it is expected that the site work performed when building such elevator buildings generally results in a finished grade that would make an accessible route into and through the building practical. For a building to meet the Fair Housing Act definition of a "building having one or more elevators" (elevator building), it must have at least one elevator that travels from an entrance level to a floor containing dwelling units that is above or below a "ground floor." If such an elevator is planned, it must go to all floors that contain dwelling units. Thus, it is not acceptable to provide elevator service to some floors or units and not others.

In the building shown in the upper right column on this page, the elevator only goes to the first and second floors containing dwelling units. This is unacceptable because the elevator is going to a floor other than a ground floor (floor two), therefore, floors three and four also must have access via the elevator.

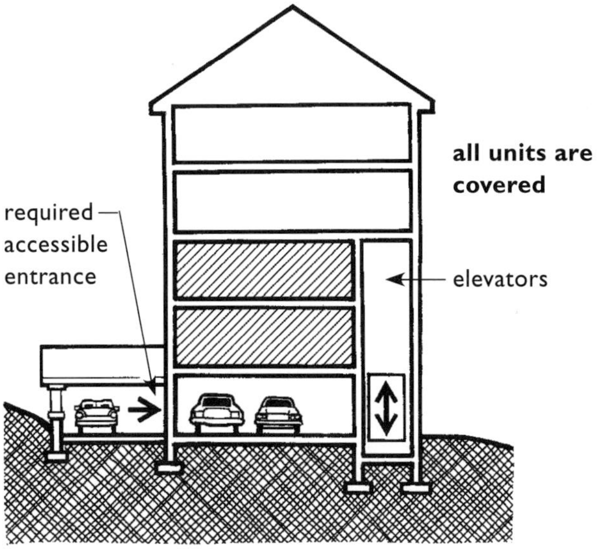

✕ Termination of Elevator as Shown in this Building is NOT Acceptable

when an elevator provides access to dwelling units other than dwelling units on a ground floor, it becomes a "building with one or more elevators" and the elevator must go to all floors and all dwelling units are covered

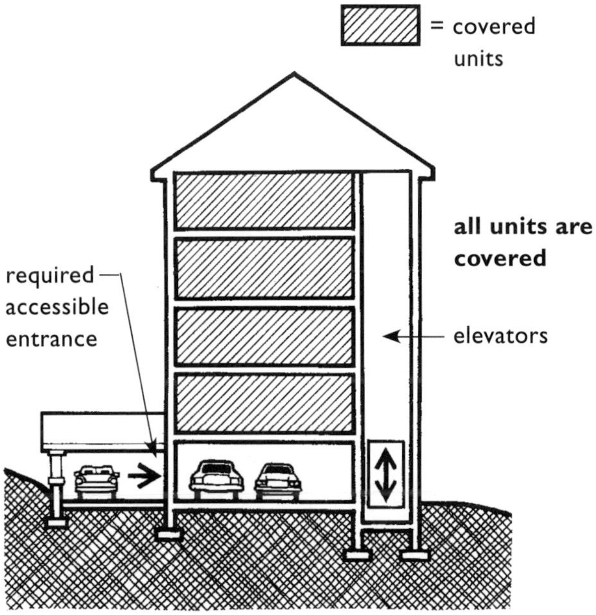

Elevators Must Provide Access to All Dwelling Units in Elevator Buildings

In the example to the right, if the elevator stops at floors other than just one, the building is classified as a building with one or more elevators (an elevator building), and the elevator must have a stop at the second and fourth floors. Floor three is not required to have a stop since it contains only second floors of two-story dwelling units. Note: most building codes require buildings over three stories to have elevators. All such buildings are covered by the Guidelines.

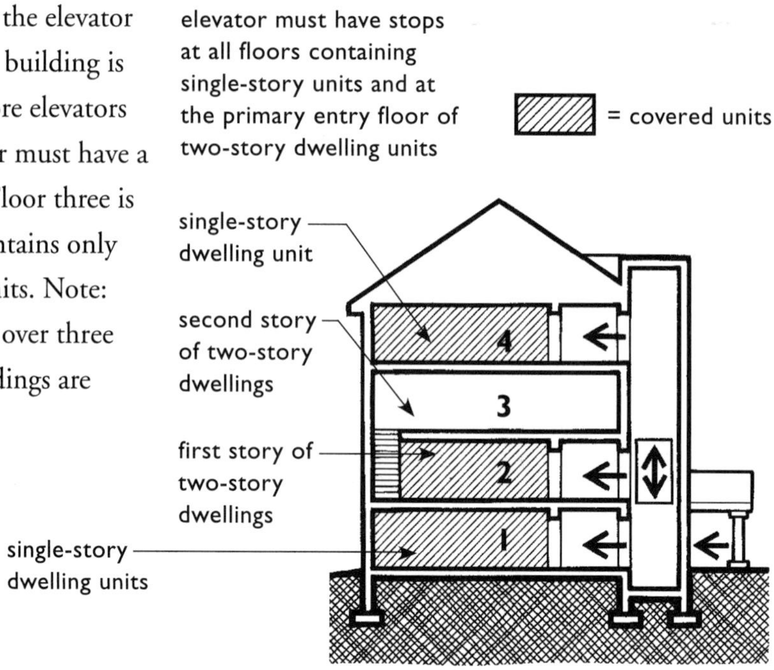

Elevators Must Provide Access to Primary Entry Floors of Two-Story Dwellings in Elevator Buildings

If an elevator in or at one building is connected to other buildings via overhead walks or bridges, the connectors must be accessible and all the connected buildings are covered.

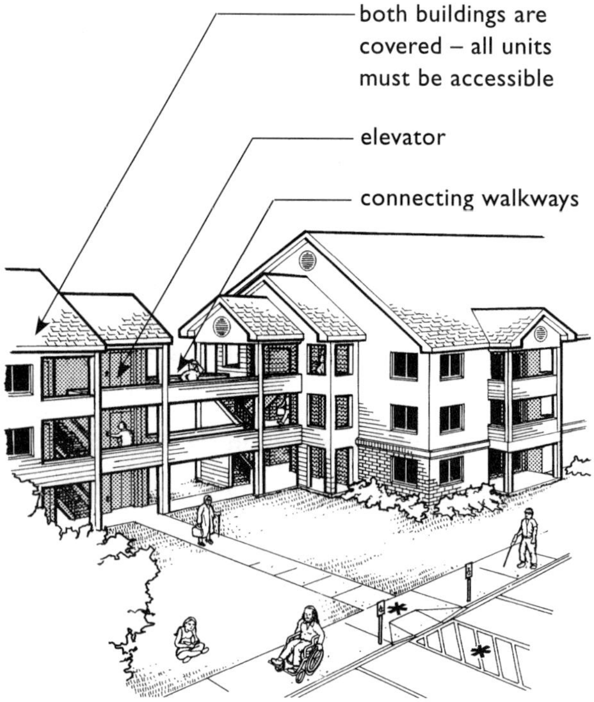

A Central Elevator Serving a Building with Two Wings

Free-Standing Elevators for Site Access Do Not Create Elevator Buildings

Free-standing elevators not connected to buildings serve as part of an accessible route from one site level to another and do not have any effect on the building's status as an elevator or nonelevator building.

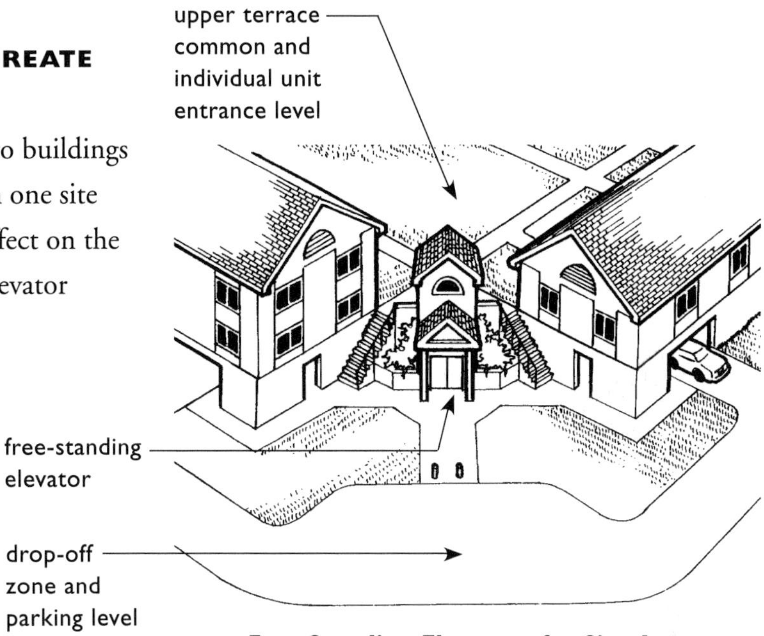

Free-Standing Elevators for Site Access Do Not Create Elevator Buildings

Buildings Not Having Elevators

In buildings not having elevators, only ground floor dwelling units are covered and each dwelling unit must be on an accessible route and meet Requirements 3-7.

Buildings not having elevators must have at least one accessible entrance on an accessible route, unless prohibited by extreme terrain or unusual site characteristics. See site impracticality section, page 1.38. Note, in buildings either with or without elevators, more than one accessible entrance may be required when:

1. there is more than one ground floor,
2. there is a split-level ground floor, or
3. units are clustered on the ground floor and each cluster has a separate entrance.

These situations are covered on the next several pages.

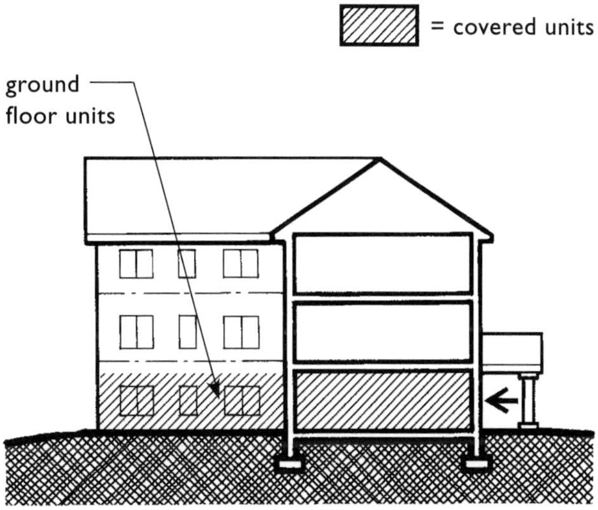

In Buildings Not Having Elevators (Nonelevator Buildings) Only Ground Floor Units Are Covered

In some circumstances the "ground floor" units that are covered may not actually be at grade level. For example, when common use spaces such as parking, meeting rooms, shops, etc. occupy the floor at grade, the first floor containing dwelling units above or below that level will be the designated "ground floor" for purposes of the Guidelines. All dwelling units on such levels must meet Requirements 3-7 and be on an accessible route.

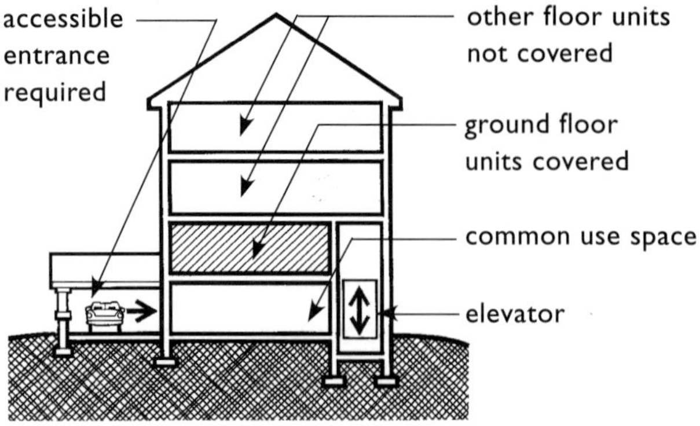

Elevator to First Floor of Dwelling Units Above Grade or Entrance Level Does Not Make a Building with One or More Elevators (a Covered Elevator Building)

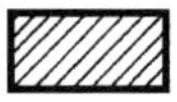

It is important to note that some buildings may contain an elevator and not be considered a "building having one or more elevators" for purposes of the Guidelines. For example, when an elevator travels from a garage or other entry level not containing dwelling units only to a "ground floor" containing dwelling units, these "ground floor" units are covered; however, the building is not a "building having one or more elevators" (elevator building) and the elevator is not required to travel to all floors.

If a building elevator is provided only as a means of creating an accessible route from parking to dwelling units on a ground floor, the building is not considered an elevator building. In this case, the dwelling units on the "ground floor," plus one of each type of public and common use area, must comply with the Guidelines.

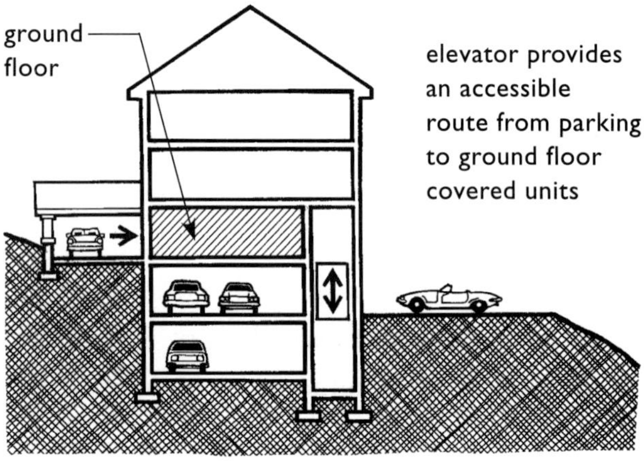

Elevators for Access to Ground Floor Units Do Not Make an Elevator Building

Buildings Having Connected Elevator and Non-Elevator Wings

Buildings having multiple wings of different configurations may have to provide more than one entrance and possibly more than one elevator. If any wing has an elevator, all of the units in the building are covered and must be on an accessible route.

In the example below, a single building has two wings, one of which has an elevator. A lobby or similar public and common use space connects the wings and serves both wings. All the units in the building are covered, therefore, the building either must have an additional elevator serving the two-story wing, or an alternative means of access to the dwelling units on the second floor of the two-story wing. In addition, since the two wings share the common use entrance, lobby, and related amenities, such as mailboxes, reception desk, etc., there must be an interior accessible route between the lobby and the two-story wing. In this example, an accessible route has been created from the second floor of the five-story wing to the second floor of the two-story wing by means of a covered walkway, thereby providing the necessary access.

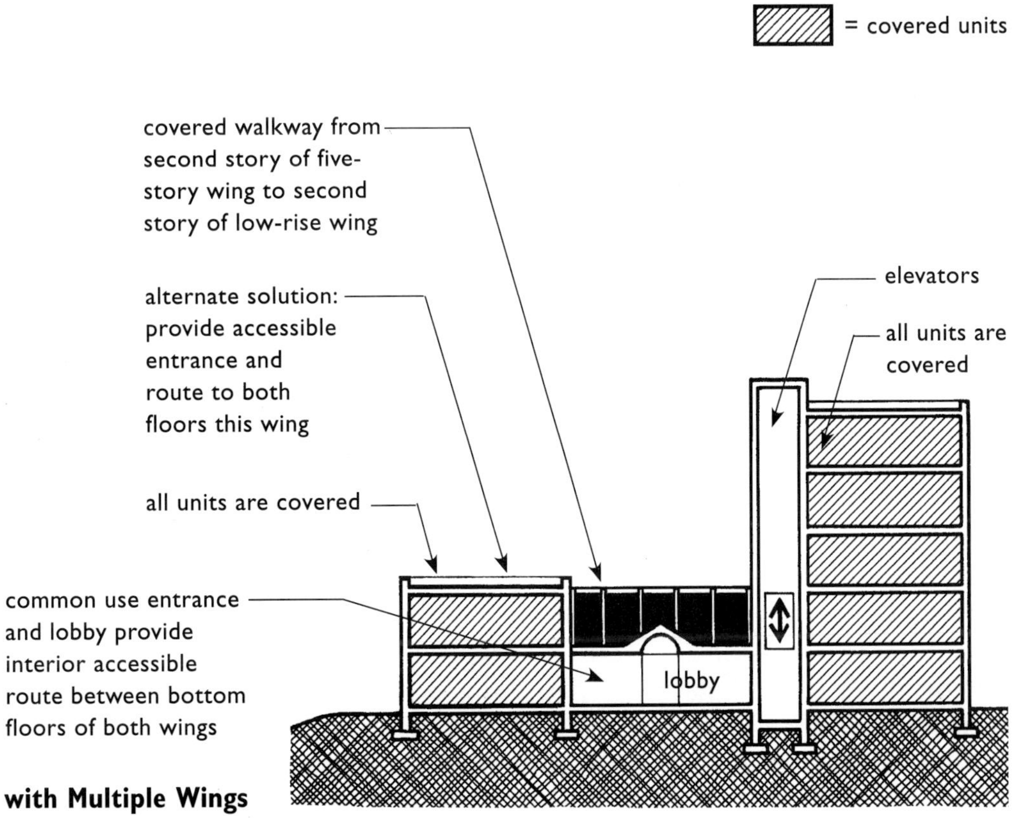

Buildings with Multiple Wings

Buildings with Separate Exterior Unit Entrances

Buildings with Separate Exterior Ground Floor Unit Entrances

Where a building has ground floor units, each with its own exterior entrance, the Guidelines provide that each of these ground-floor units shall:

1. have an accessible entrance,
2. be on an accessible route, and
3. meet all other design requirements of the Guidelines.

The only exception applies to ground floor units where terrain or unusual characteristics of the site make an accessible entrance on an accessible route impractical.

The example below is a single non-elevator building on a site and has multiple entrances. Regardless of which site impracticality test is used, a minimum of 20% of the ground floor units must be accessible, and possibly more, based on the results of the test. The individual building test was used, and resulted in site impracticality at Unit #5. The site was not impractical for Units #1 and #2, and therefore, those units must be made accessible. Two out of three units = 66%, so the minimum of 20% has been satisfied, and no additional ground floor units must be made accessible. See site impracticality on page 1.38.

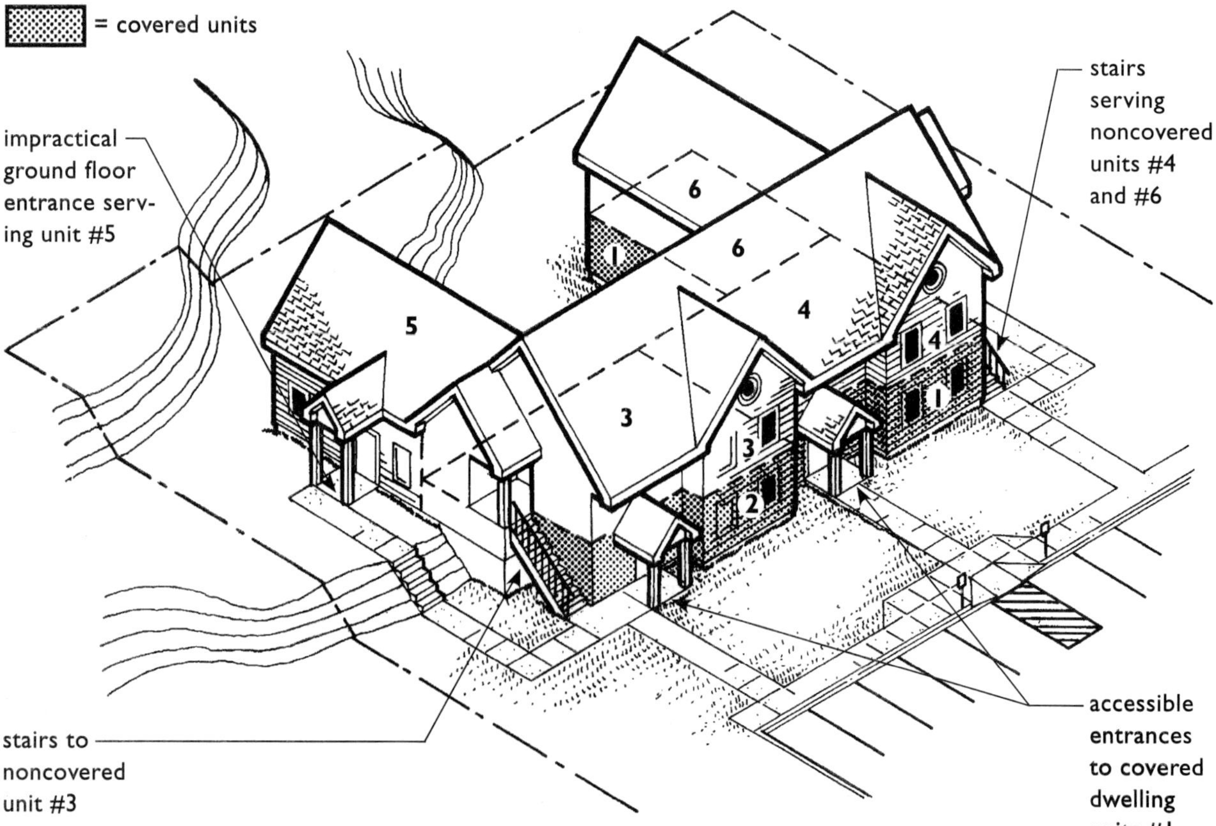

Ground Floor Units with Separate Entrances Are Covered

Buildings with Separate Ground Floor Unit Entrances on Two or More Ground Floors

Where a building has ground floor units with their own individual entrances on two or more ground floors, the Guidelines provide that each of these entrances shall be an accessible entrance on an accessible route. The only exception to this applies to ground floor units where terrain or unusual characteristics of the site make an accessible entrance impractical, see site impracticality tests, page 1.38.

Since entrances were planned on both ground floors and all ground floor units are covered, each must have an accessible entrance on an accessible route and meet the other design requirements of the Guidelines.

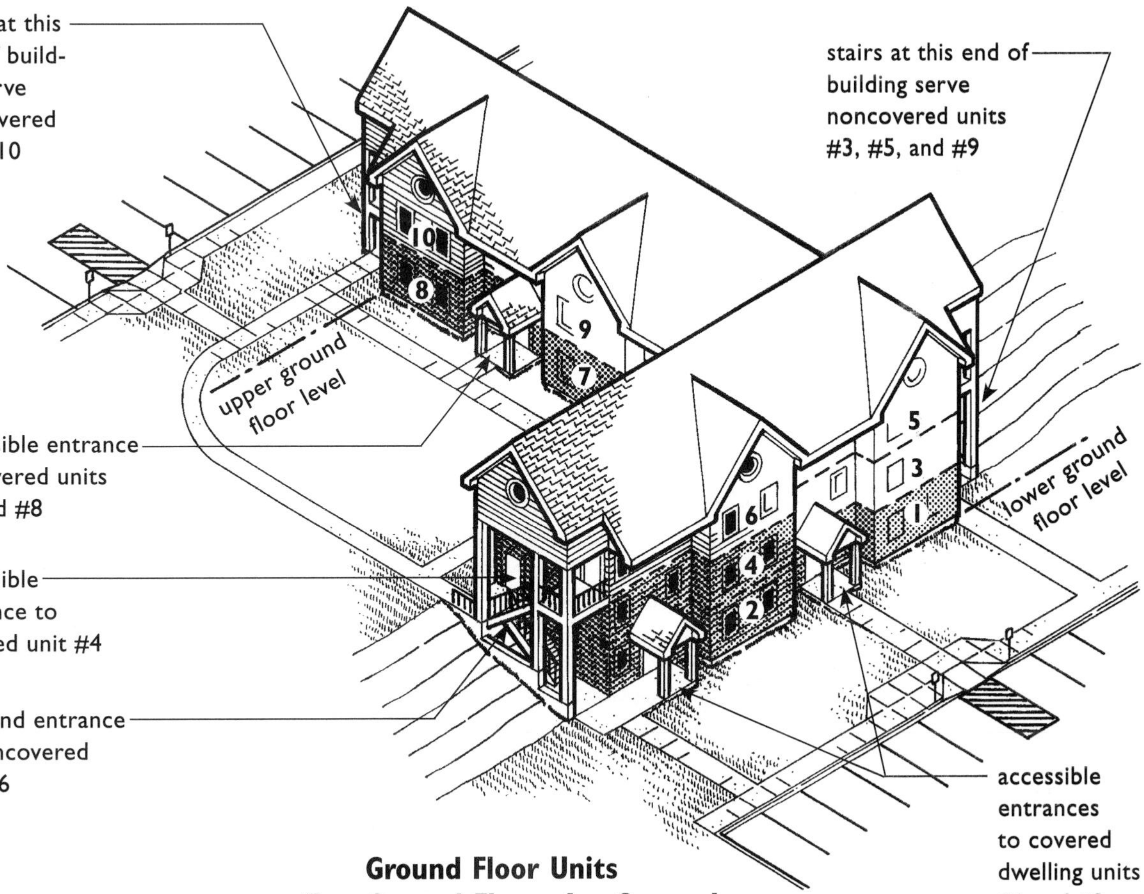

Ground Floor Units on Two Ground Floors Are Covered

Buildings with Separate Unit Entrances Having Split-Level Approaches

Apartments with split-level approaches to their entrances typically cannot provide an accessible route from parking or other pedestrian arrival points to either lower or upper level primary entrances. Redesign is necessary to ensure an accessible building entrance on an accessible route to ground floor units. Note, however, that simply adding an accessible route to the secondary, rear entry is not acceptable as that results in "back door" access. See the first illustration and Solution One.

In Solution Two, regrading and the addition of a bridge provides access to the upper level, making that level the ground floor. Because no primary entrance was planned at the rear of the lower level units, and since there is no requirement to have more than one ground floor, an accessible route is not required to those units.

=covered units

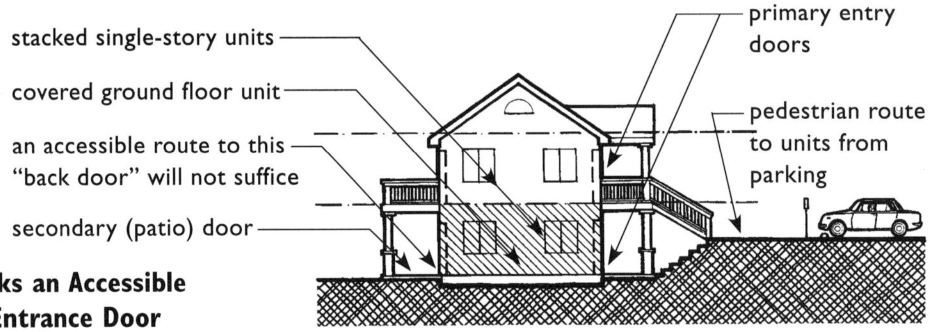

X

NOT Acceptable – Lacks an Accessible Route to a Primary Entrance Door

Solution One: Reorient Ground Floor Plan to Reverse Entrances

Solution Two is for a building having single-story units on each floor. Note, however, that if multistory units are stacked over the single-story units, then the building is still covered, and access to the single-story units would be required, as shown in Solution One.

If the units are one story, either level could be designated as the ground floor. If two-story townhouses are stacked over one-story units on grade, the building is still covered. Access must be provided to the lower units.

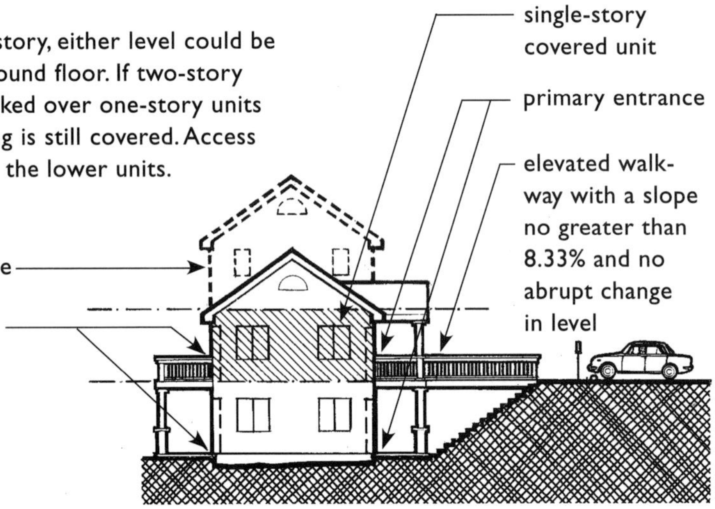

Solution Two: Regrade and Add Bridge from Parking to Second Story Entrance

Buildings with Separate Ground Floor Unit Entrances Over Private Garages (Carriage Units)

Carriage House Units

Carriage houses in which the garage footprint is used as the footprint for the remaining floor or floors of the units are not required to meet the design and construction requirements. (See December 16, 1991 memorandum from Frank Keating at back of Appendix C.)

If buildings containing carriage units have one or more units at grade level with an entrance on an accessible route, the grade level unit establishes a ground floor for the building and is covered. There is no requirement for there to be more than one ground floor nor for other units in the building on the second or elevated floor to be accessible.

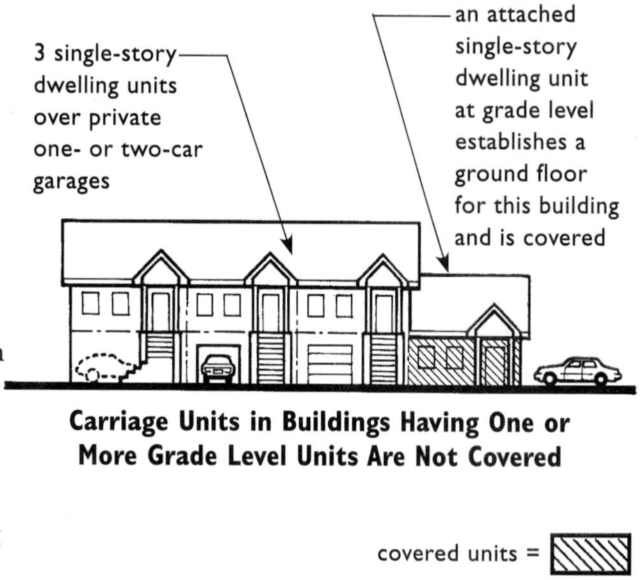

Carriage Units in Buildings Having One or More Grade Level Units Are Not Covered

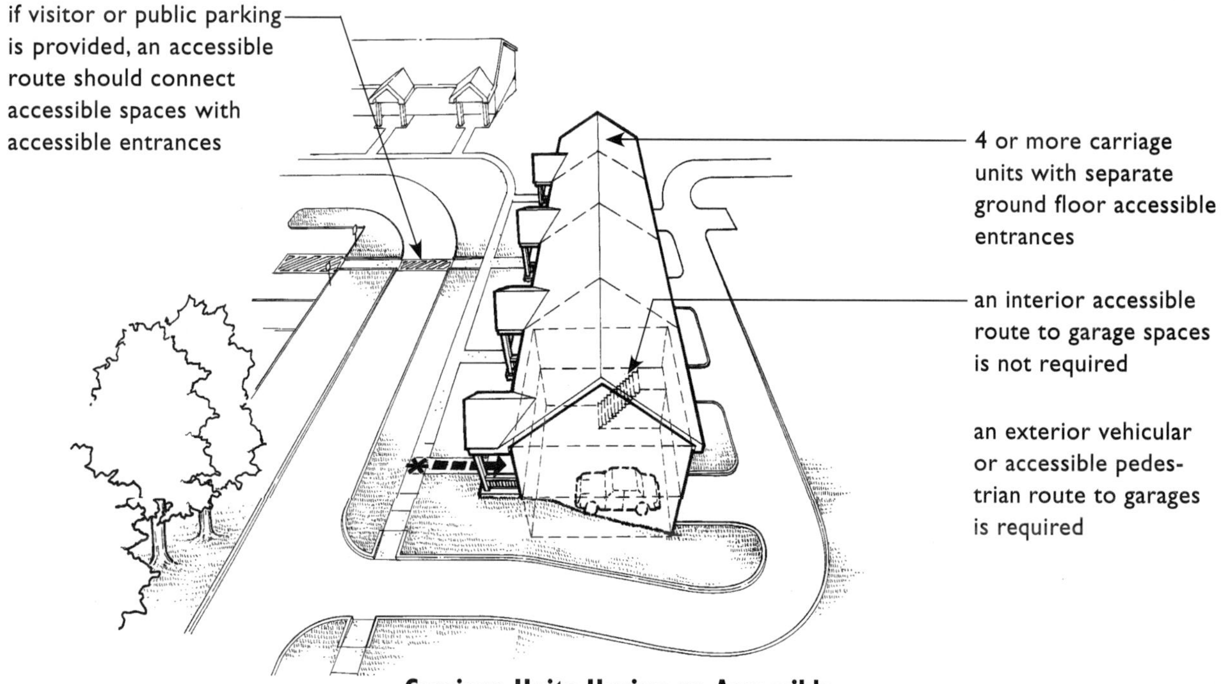

Carriage Units Having an Accessible Route to an Entry Are Covered

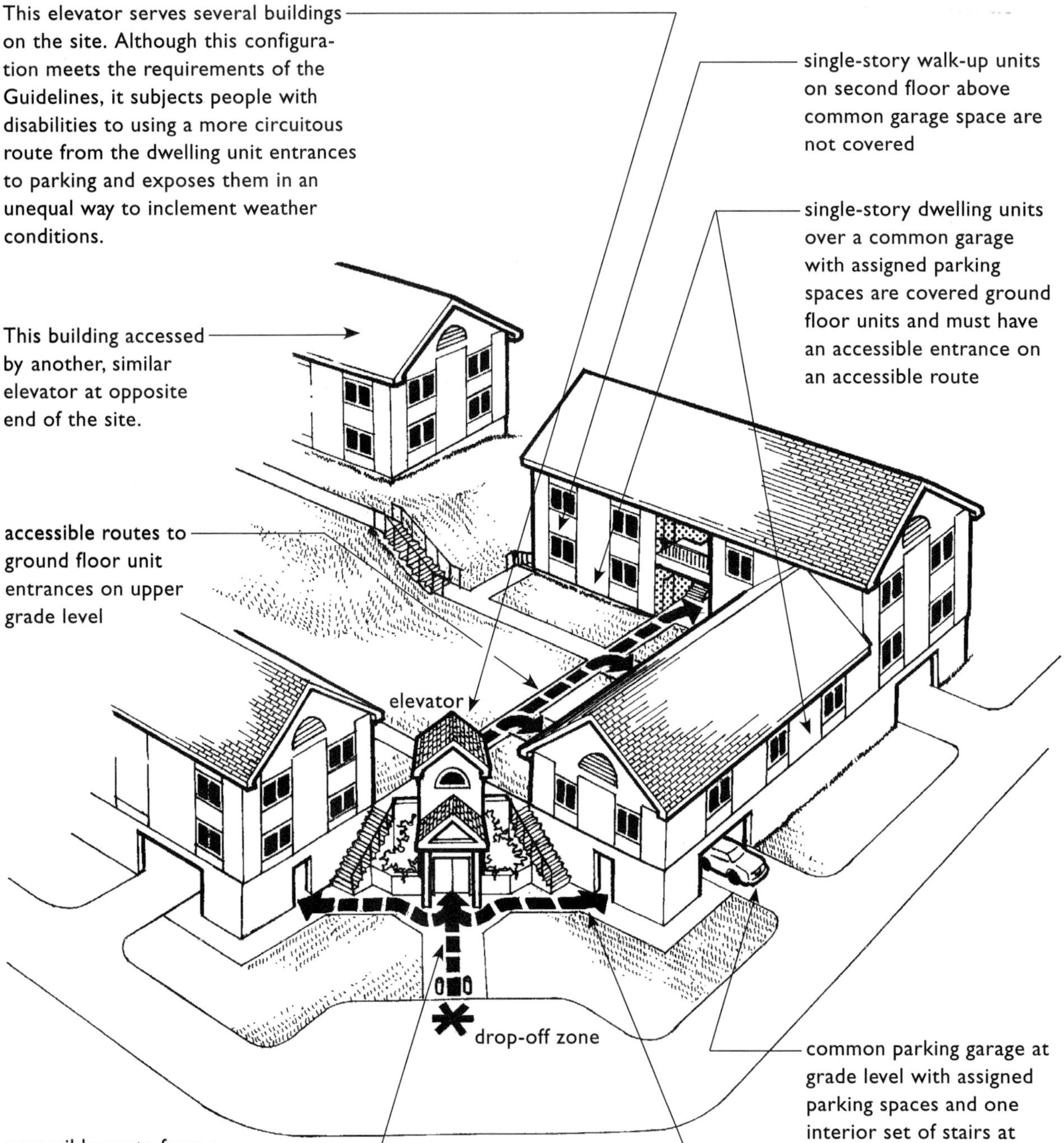

Single-Story Ground Floor Dwelling Units with Separate Entrances Over Common Use Parking Garages

elevator to create an accessible route from parking to ground floor does not make these elevator buildings

Buildings with Common Entrances

Buildings with Ground Floors Over Shops or Garages

Where the first floor containing dwelling units in a building is above grade, all units on that floor are covered and must be served by a building entrance on an accessible route. This floor will be considered a ground floor, thus making dwelling units over retail stores, garages, or other common use spaces covered units.

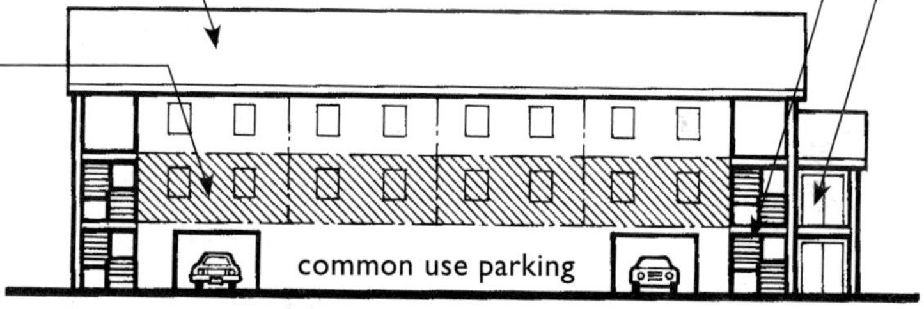

Note: if the elevator is also taken to the next level, the building becomes a building with one or more elevators and all floors and units must comply.

Walk-Up Dwelling Units Over Garages, Shops, and Other Public or Common Use Spaces Are Covered

If one or more single-story dwelling units with an accessible entrance on an accessible route are located at grade level in buildings otherwise having public or common use parking or shops at grade level, a new grade level ground floor is established and only the grade level units are covered.

One or More Grade Level Accessible Units Establishes a Ground Floor and Eliminates Need for Accessible Routes to Units Over Garages or Shops

= covered units

Buildings with One or More Common Entrances

When a building has one or more common entrances, the Guidelines provide that at least one of these entrances shall be accessible and shall be on an accessible route to **all** dwelling units in buildings with one or more elevators, and to all ground floor units in nonelevator buildings. Examples of how this applies to specific buildings and sites follow. The only situation where an accessible entrance is not required is when there is a single building with a single entrance on a site with no elevator, and the terrain or unusual characteristics of the site make the provision of an accessible route to the entrance impractical. See site impracticality, page 1.38.

This is a single building on a site. It has two common entrances and an elevator serving multiple floors. Because it is a building with one or more elevators (an elevator building), all units in the building are covered, and at least one common entrance must be accessible and on an accessible route from a public street or sidewalk or other pedestrian arrival point, regardless of the terrain or unusual characteristics of the site; site impracticality tests do not apply for elevator buildings.

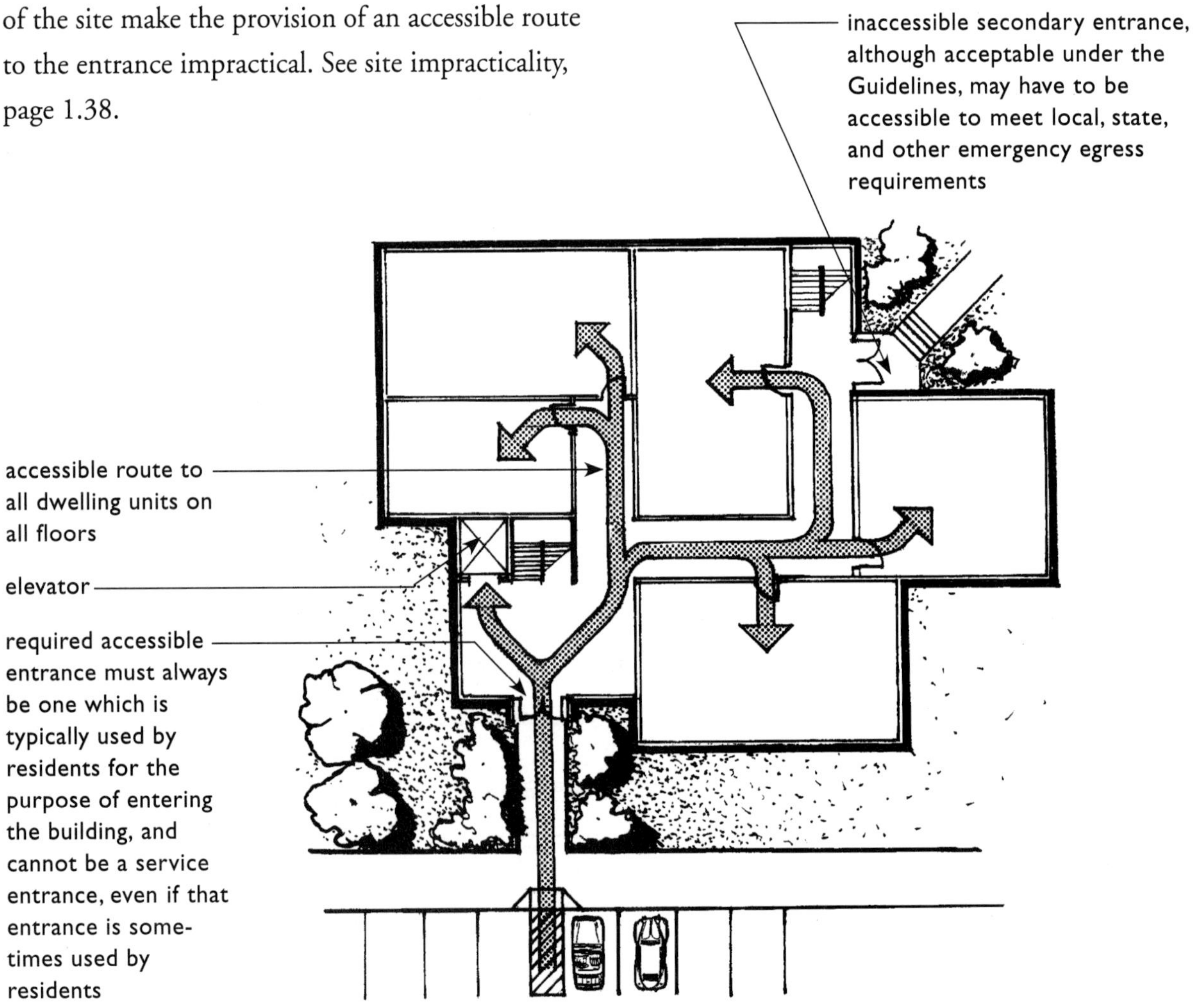

Buildings with Common Entrances

Buildings with Common Entrances and a Single Ground Floor

When a building has a single ground floor and more than one common entrance, at least one entrance must be accessible. This accessible entrance should be the primary entrance and must provide an interior accessible route to all ground floor units in the building. If an interior accessible route does not connect the primary entrance to all ground floor units, additional entrances on accessible routes are necessary to reach the additional ground floor units.

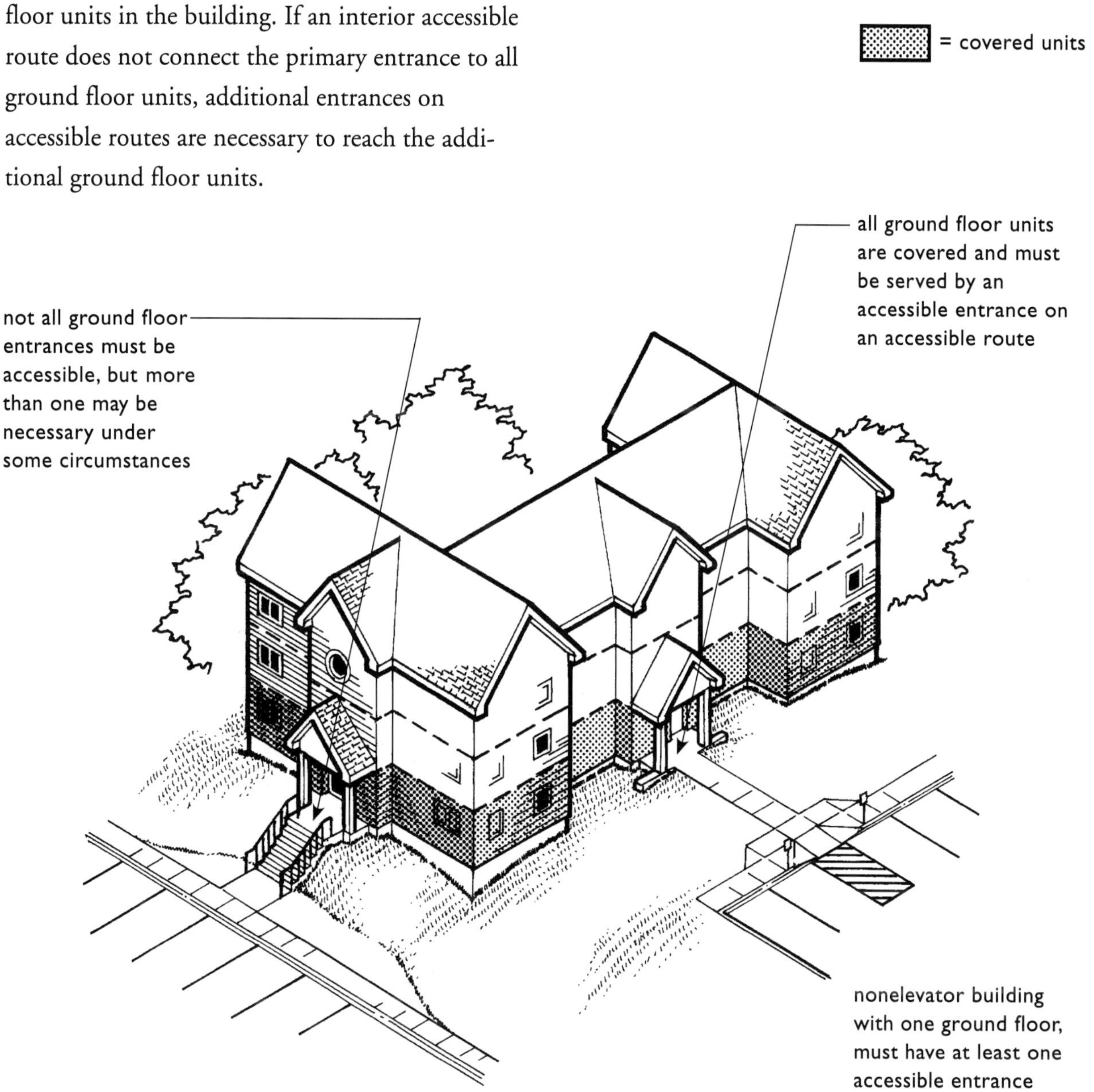

Common Entrances in Buildings with a Single Ground Floor

Buildings with Common Entrances and Clustered Dwelling Units

Where dwelling units are clustered in a building, each cluster which has its own entrance or entrances shall have at least one accessible entrance providing access to all ground floor units in the cluster.

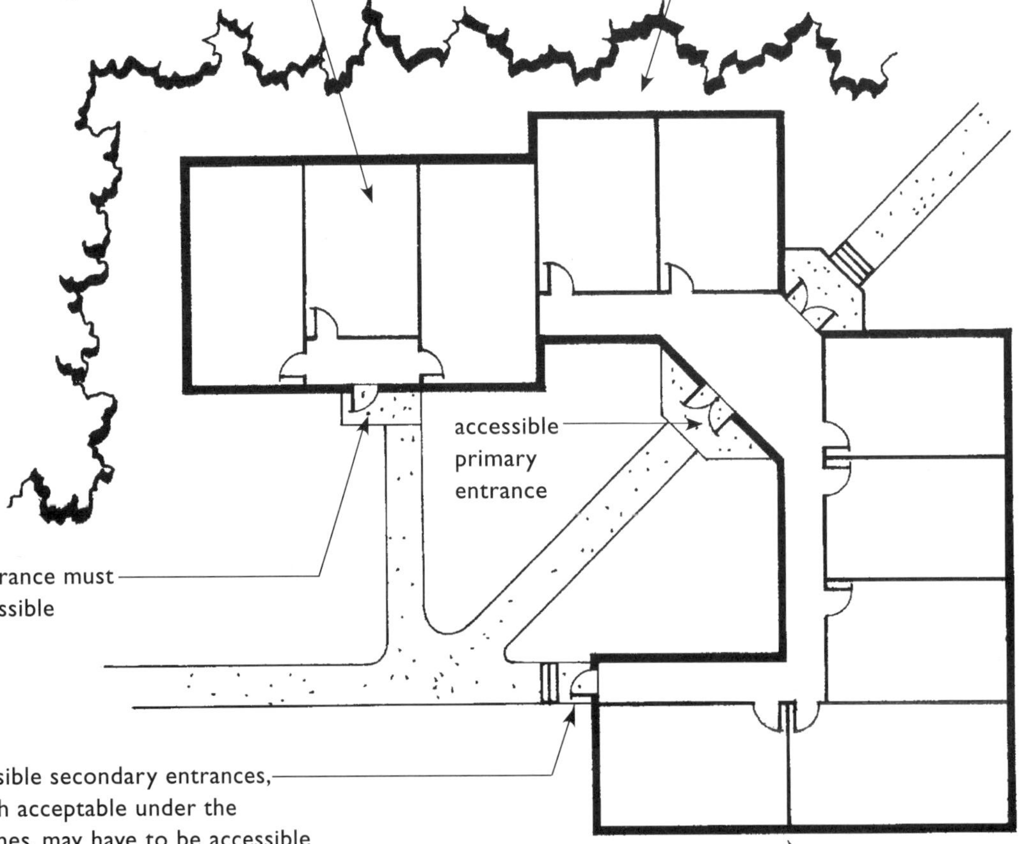

Common Entrances at Clustered Dwelling Units

Buildings with Split-Level Ground Floors

Split-level floors of less than a full story in height are not separate floor levels and are considered to be one ground floor. Covered ground floor units on each level must have entry doors on an accessible route connecting to at least one accessible common use building entrance and at least one of each type of common use facility or feature, such as mail rooms, laundries, vending areas, etc. Since steps and stairs cannot be part of an accessible route, changes in level on covered floors must be accomplished by means of ramps, lifts, or elevators.

If an accessible route, in lieu of or in addition to steps or stairs, is provided between levels, the route must not be remote, hidden, circuitous, or require people with disabilities to travel excessively long distances to arrive at the same point as others. Finally, the accessible route between levels must be readily available to all residents and visitors and not be locked or require keys, attendants, or special services or permits for use.

If an accessible route is not provided between covered floor levels, each level must have its own accessible common use entrance on an accessible route; any common use facilities or features provided on one level must also be available on an accessible route on each other level.

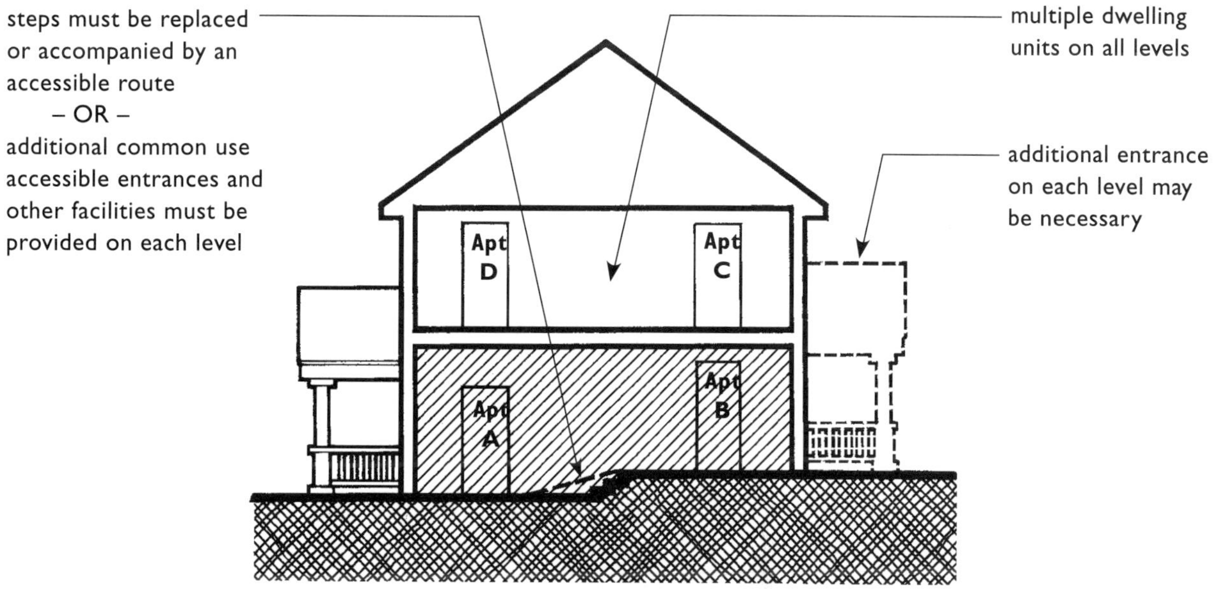

Split-Level Ground Floor Regarded as Single Ground Floor

Buildings with Common Entrances and More than One Ground Floor

In building designs that are planned to have more than one ground floor, an entrance on each ground floor is required to be accessible unless site conditions make it impractical to provide an accessible route to each entrance. See page 1.38 for site impracticality. In this illustrated example, the planned location of parking and sidewalks (that would serve as the pedestrian and vehicular arrival points) is close to the planned entrances, with only minor changes in level between the arrival points and the floor level of the building at the planned entrances, therefore, it is practical to make the planned entrances accessible. Because the common entrances are accessible via an accessible route, all the dwelling units served by each entrance are covered dwelling units and must meet the requirements of the Guidelines.

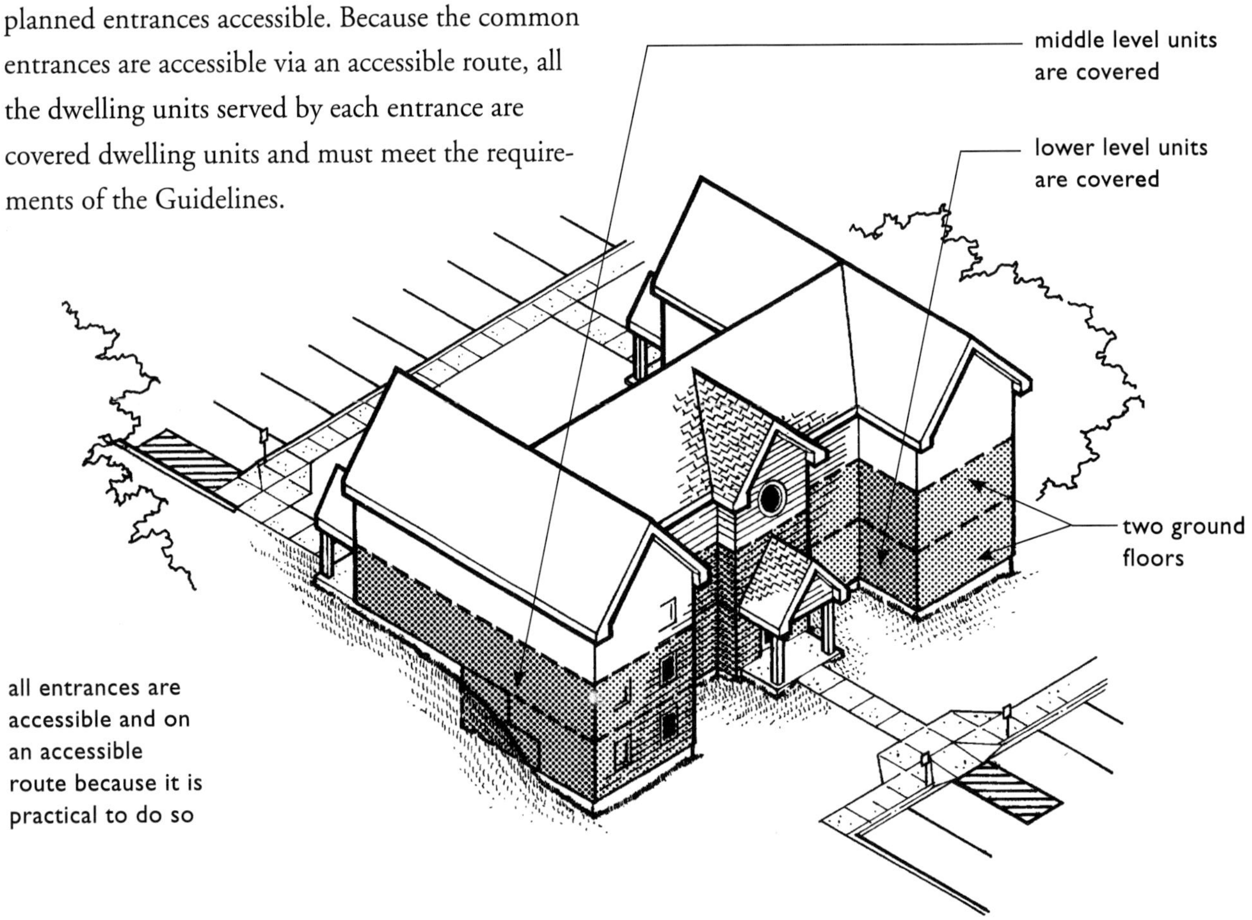

Common Entrances at Buildings with More Than One Ground Floor

Building Floors Having Common Entrances Served by Elevated Walkways

When a developer plans an elevated walkway from a pedestrian or vehicular arrival point to the building entrance and the walkway has a slope of 10% or less, that floor shall be considered a ground floor. The dwelling units on that floor are covered and the site is not considered impractical. Since the walkway meets the 10% slope criterion, it is practical to provide an accessible route to the entrance, and the slope of the walkway must be reduced to 8.33% maximum.

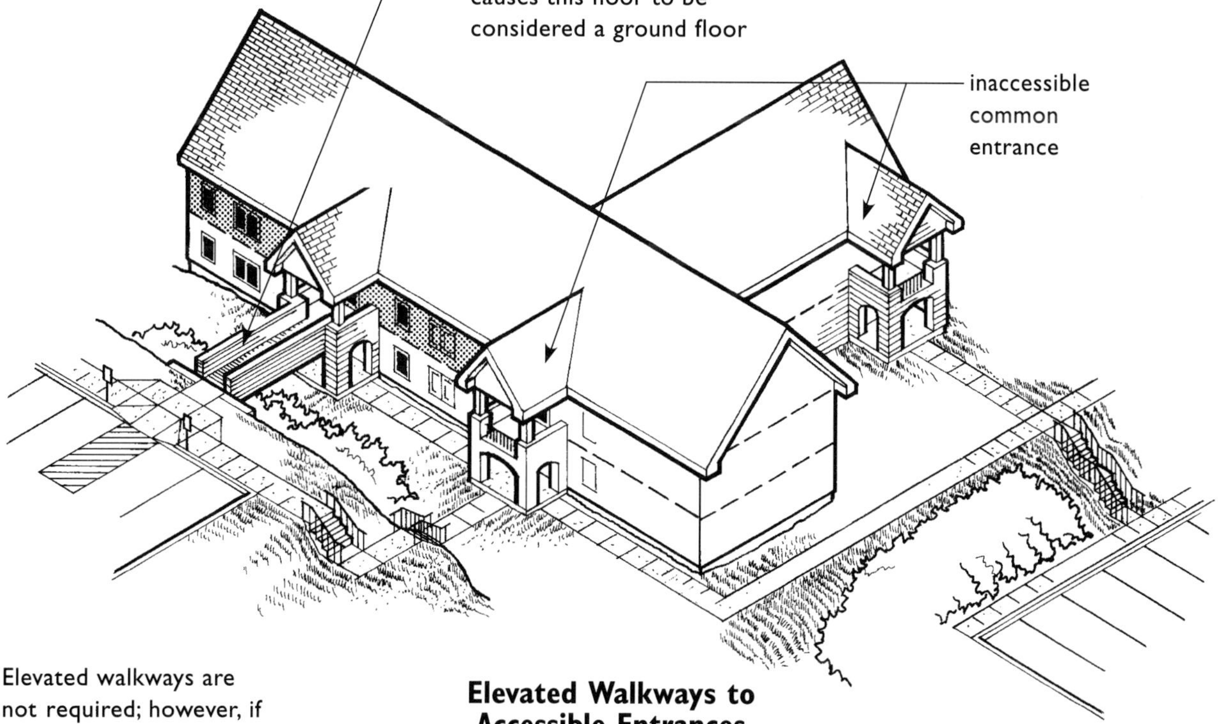

Elevated Walkways to Accessible Entrances

Elevated walkways are not required; however, if one is planned and its slope is no greater than 10%, then the slope must be reduced to 8.33% maximum and the dwelling units on that floor shall be accessible.

SITE IMPRACTICALITY

INTRODUCTION

HUD's regulations implementing the Fair Housing Act state:

> Covered multifamily dwellings for first occupancy after March 13, 1991 shall be designed and constructed to have at least one building entrance on an accessible route unless it is impractical to do because of the terrain or unusual characteristics of the site. [24 CFR 100.205(a)].

The Fair Housing Act itself does not contain an impracticality exception; however, the preamble to HUD's regulations explains as follows: "Congress did not intend to impose an absolute standard that all covered multifamily dwelling units be made accessible without regard to the impracticality of doing so. Even though the statute itself does not contain an impracticality standard the legislative history makes it clear that Congress 'was sensitive to the possibility that certain natural terrain may pose unique building problems'." Thus, the regulations and the Guidelines recognize that certain site conditions may make it impractical to make all ground floor units accessible in buildings that do not have an elevator due to the difficulty of providing an accessible route to the building entrance or to individual dwelling unit entrances. The Guidelines provide tests for determining site impracticality, which are discussed beginning on page 1.40.

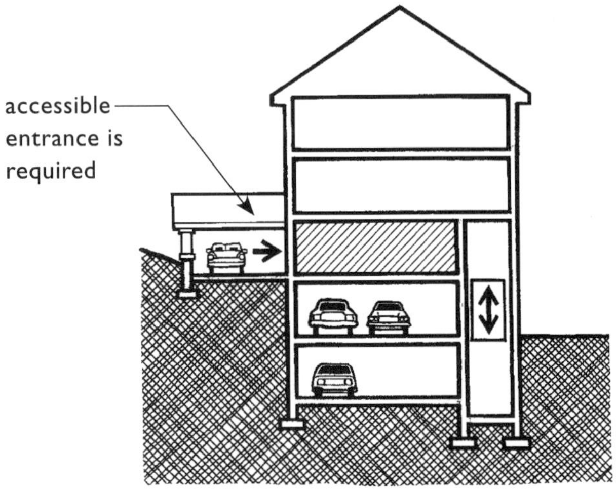

Elevator From Garage to Covered Ground Floor Units

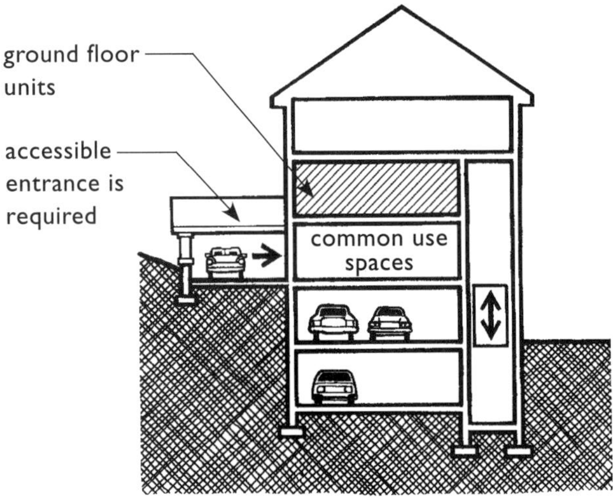

Elevator From Garage Levels to Ground Floor Units Above Common Use Grade Level Floor

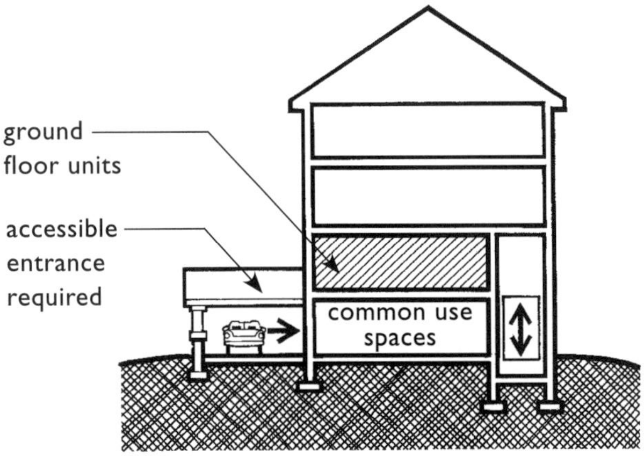

Elevator From Grade Level Common Use Spaces to Covered Ground Floor Units Above

Elevators from garages or grade levels to ground floors need not serve other floors and only the ground floor dwelling units must meet the design requirements of the Guidelines.

Buildings With Elevators, Including Those Having Elevators Only for Access to Covered Ground Floor Units, Cannot Claim Site Impracticality

If an elevator provides access to any floors other than a ground floor, then it must go to all floors in the building and all units in the building must meet the design requirements of the Guidelines.

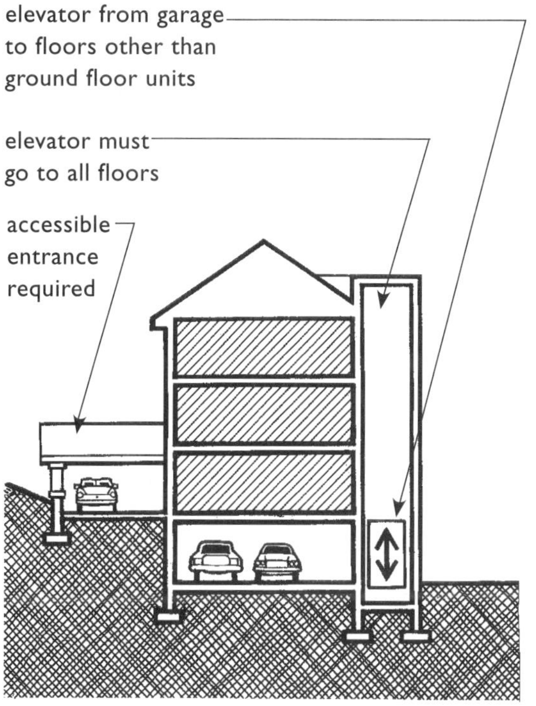

Buildings with One or More Elevators Cannot Claim Site Impracticality

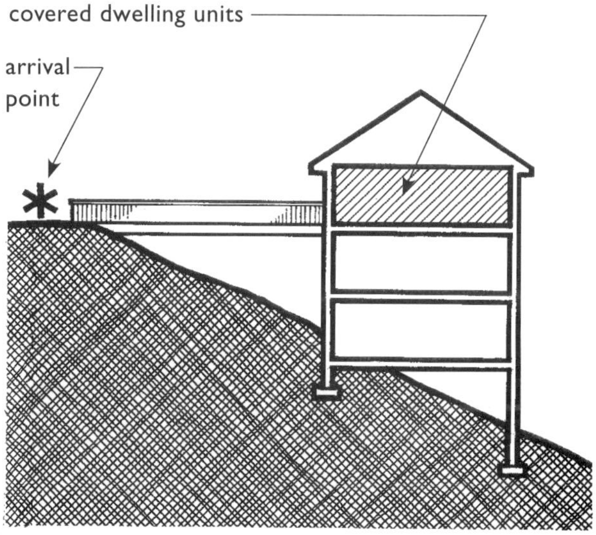

Buildings Served by a Planned Elevated Walkway Cannot Claim Site Impracticality

Building Types Where Site Impracticality Is Not Allowed

The Guidelines address the regulatory provision for site impracticality discussed above in Requirement 1, Accessible Building Entrance on an Accessible Route. The Guidelines **do not allow site impracticality for certain buildings.** These buildings are:

1. Buildings with one or more elevators – These buildings are covered and must have at least one entrance on an accessible route regardless of terrain or other characteristics of the site.
2. Buildings where an elevator is provided solely as a means of access to units on a ground floor – These buildings are covered and all ground floor units must be accessible. However, this type of building is not treated as an elevator building where all of the units in the building are covered. For a full explanation of buildings with elevators, see pages 1.20 through 1.25.
3. Buildings that have an elevated walkway – Site impracticality is not allowed for buildings where an elevated walkway is planned between a building entrance and a vehicular or pedestrian arrival point and the planned walkway has a slope no greater than 10%. The 10% criterion only determines whether making the entrance is practical. Once this criterion is met, the slope would have to be reduced to a maximum of 8.33 %.

These building types for which site impracticality is not permitted are illustrated on this page and 1.38.

Site impracticality is not allowed where the entrance to the building is provided by an elevated walkway between the building entrance and an arrival point with a planned slope no greater than 10%. By meeting the 10% slope criterion, it is considered practical to provide an accessible route, and the slope must be reduced to 8.33% maximum.

SITE IMPRACTICALITY TESTS FOR SITES WITH DIFFICULT TERRAIN

The Guidelines provide **two tests to determine site impracticality** based upon difficult terrain conditions, the **Individual Building Test** and the **Site Analysis Test**.

Since buildings with one or more elevators and those served by a planned elevated walkway cannot claim site impracticality, the site impracticality tests apply only to other types of buildings on sites having extreme terrain or unusual characteristics. The tests will help determine the actual number of units that must meet the Guidelines on such sites.

The tests differ and their application will be affected by the number of buildings on the site, the number of planned entrances, the slope of the land, and the distance between key points on the planned site. Unusual site characteristics, including such conditions as federally designated flood plains or coastal high hazard areas where it is required to raise the floor level of buildings above a base flood elevation, also have an impact on the number of covered dwelling units. Each of the tests follow the Guidelines and conclude with a minimum required number of accessible units.

The **Individual Building Test** accepts as inaccessible, because of site impracticality due to terrain, all ground floor units in which the elevation difference between the undisturbed site grade and the proposed finished site grade from arrival points and the planned building entrance is over 10% when measured in a straight line. If either the undisturbed slope or the proposed finished slope, measured in a straight line, is 10% or less, then site impracticality due to terrain does not exist and the developer must provide an accessible route to the particular entrance being measured.

The **Site Analysis Test** measures the total buildable area of undisturbed or natural grade having an existing slope before grading less than 10% (**Step A**). The area of less than 10% slope is expressed as a percentage of the total site area less any restricted use areas such as wetlands or flood plains. The percentage establishes the minimum percentage of ground floor units to be made accessible (**Step B**) subject to the additional requirement of **Step C**. **Step C** requires that, in addition to the percentage established in **Step B**, all ground floor units in a building or ground floor units served by a particular entrance shall be made accessible if the entrance to the units is on an accessible route, defined as a walkway with a slope between the planned entrance and a pedestrian or vehicular arrival point that is no greater than 8.33%.

Which Tests Apply to Which Sites

The tests relate to different buildings and site conditions. It is important to remember before discussing the test applications that they are not applicable to buildings having one or more elevators (elevator buildings) because they already are covered and all units in them must meet the requirements of the Guidelines, and they must have at least one entrance on an accessible route regardless of terrain or other characteristics of the site. None of the buildings described in the following explanation of test applications are elevator buildings; nor are they served by an elevated walkway between a building entrance and an arrival point.

Sites Where Only the Individual Building Test May be Used

For sites with difficult terrain which have a single building with only one common entrance on the site, the individual building test **must** be used. If the results of this test determine that it is impractical to make that entrance accessible, then the building is not required to be accessible and none of the ground floor units are covered. This is the only circumstance under which an entire site may not be covered.

Sites Where Either Test May be Used

Either test may be used for building sites having multiple buildings or a single building with more than one common entrance. When the Individual Building Test is applied to such sites it must be calculated for each building and each building entrance separately.

The 20% Rule

For those sites where **either** the Individual Building Test or the Site Analysis Test may be used, the Guidelines set a **minimum** percentage of ground floor units, which serves as a starting point even before the tests are applied. This minimum is 20%. Thus, for those sites where either test may be used, there never will be a situation where less than 20% of the units are required to comply with the Guidelines; in most cases the tests will result in a much larger percentage of units required to be accessible. Keep in mind that this 20% minimum cannot be used as a maximum. The results of the test, depending on which test is used, will determine the maximum number of units required to be accessible.

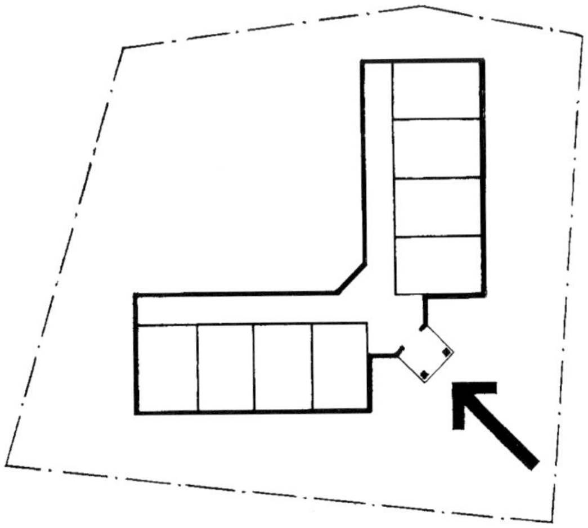

Single Building on a Site with One Common Entrance

Note: The following examples apply only to buildings that do not have one or more elevators (elevator buildings). Buildings having one or more elevators must be accessible regardless of site conditions.

- one building
- 4 or more units
- 1 entrance

- **must** use the Individual Building Test

A site with a single building with one common entrance may not be required to be accessible if the site is impractical and application of the Individual Building Test determines impracticality at this entrance.

Example of Potentially Impractical Site Based on Terrain and Application of Individual Building Test

Note: The following examples apply only to buildings that do not have one or more elevators (elevator buildings). Buildings having one or more elevators must be accessible regardless of site conditions.

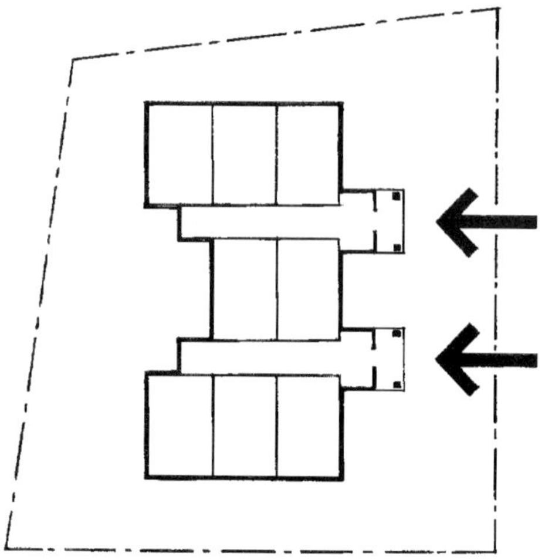

Single Building with Multiple Entrances on a Site

- single building on a site
- 4 or more units
- 2 or more entrances
- **may** use either the Individual Building Test or the Site Analysis Test

A minimum 20% of ground floor units must comply with the requirements of the Guidelines, plus an additional number determined by application of one of the tests. In addition, if any entrance is made accessible to meet either the 20% minimum or the percentage resulting from the test:
all units served by that entrance must comply.

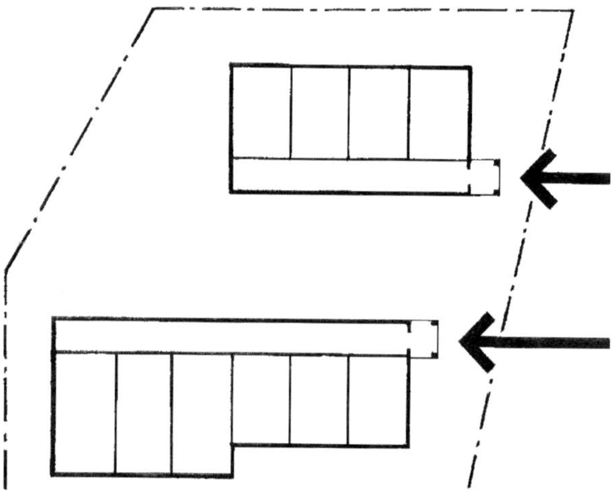

Multiple Buildings on a Site

- multiple buildings an a site
- 4 or more units in each building
- I or more entrances

- **may** use either the Individual Building Test or the Site Analysis Test

A minimum 20% of ground floor units must comply with the requirements of the Guidelines, plus an additional number determined by application of one of the tests. In addition, if any entrance is made accessible to meet either the 20% minimum or the percentage resulting from the test:
all units served by that entrance must comply.

Examples of Potentially Impractical Sites Based on Terrain and Application of Site Impracticality Tests

INDIVIDUAL BUILDING TEST

The Individual Building Test **must** be used to analyze a site with a single building with one common entrance and also may be used for all other sites. The Individual Building Test, unlike the Site Analysis Test, does not have to be certified by a professional licensed engineer, landscape architect, or surveyor; but it should be calculated on a topographic map with two-foot (or less) contour intervals.

For it to be considered impractical to provide an accessible route to any building or individual dwelling unit entrance, the slope between the pedestrian arrival points and the planned entrances must meet both of the following two conditions (quoted directly from the Guidelines):

STEP A. the slopes of the undisturbed site measured between the planned entrance and all vehicular or pedestrian arrival points within 50 feet of the planned entrance exceed 10%; and

STEP B. the slopes of the planned finish grade measured between the entrance and all vehicular or pedestrian arrival points within 50 feet of the planned entrance also exceed 10%.

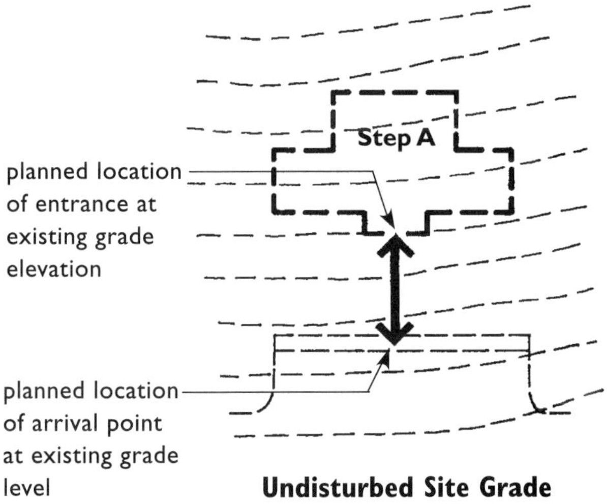

Undisturbed Site Grade Measurement

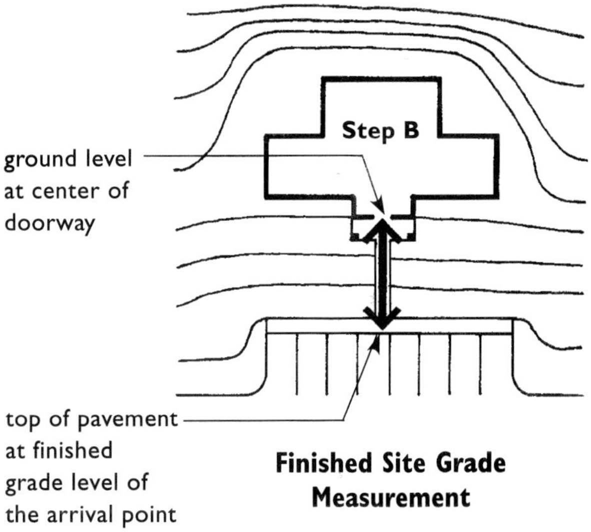

Finished Site Grade Measurement

If the slope of both the undisturbed site and the planned finished grade between the building entrance and pedestrian arrival points does not exceed the 10% slope criterion, then it is considered practical to provide an accessible route with a maximum slope of 8.33% to the building or dwelling unit entrance. The entrance, thus, must be accessible and the unit(s), plus the public and common use spaces in the building served by the entrance, must comply with the design requirements of the Guidelines. The 10% slope criterion determines whether it is practical to provide an accessible route from a pedestrian arrival point to the building or dwelling unit entrance. It is not meant to imply that 10% is the acceptable slope for an accessible route.

INDIVIDUAL BUILDING TEST: EXAMPLE ONE

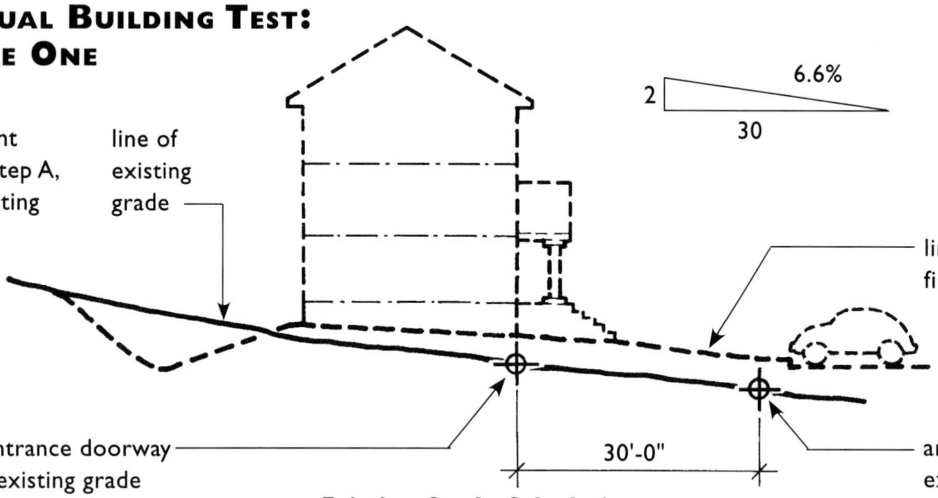

Existing Grade Calculation

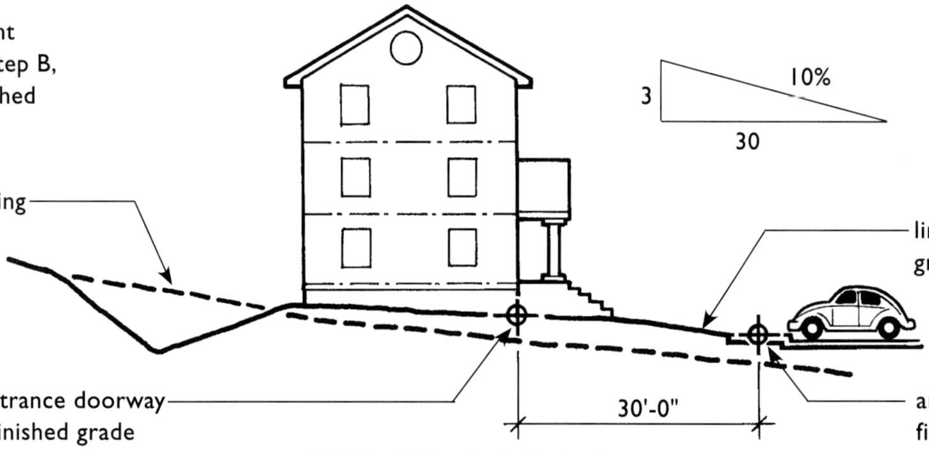

Finished Grade Calculation

Individual Building Test: Example One

both calculations do not exceed 10%; therefore, the developer must provide an accessible route to the entrance and all units on the ground floor served by the entrance are covered

Vehicular or pedestrian arrival points include public or resident parking areas, public transportation stops, passenger loading zones, and public streets or sidewalks. In applying the test, all arrival points within the radius of 50 feet must be reviewed and not just a direct line to the closest arrival point. As shown in the diagram below, a 30-foot line to the closest arrival point has a slope of more than 10%, while a 45-foot line to a farther point has a slope of less than 10%. An accessible building entrance on an accessible route is, therefore, practical and the entrance must be accessible.

If there are no vehicular or pedestrian arrival points within 50 feet, the slope must be calculated to the closest arrival point beyond 50 feet. For sidewalks, the closest point to the planned entrance is taken at the point where a public sidewalk entering the site intersects with a sidewalk leading to the entrance.

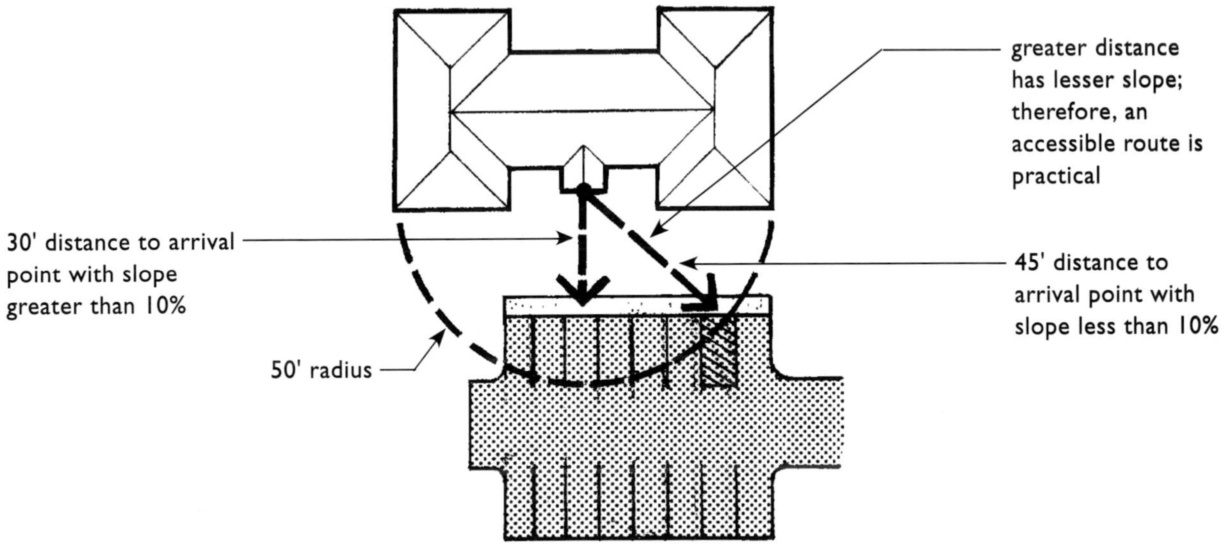

All Arrival Points within 50 Feet Must Be Considered

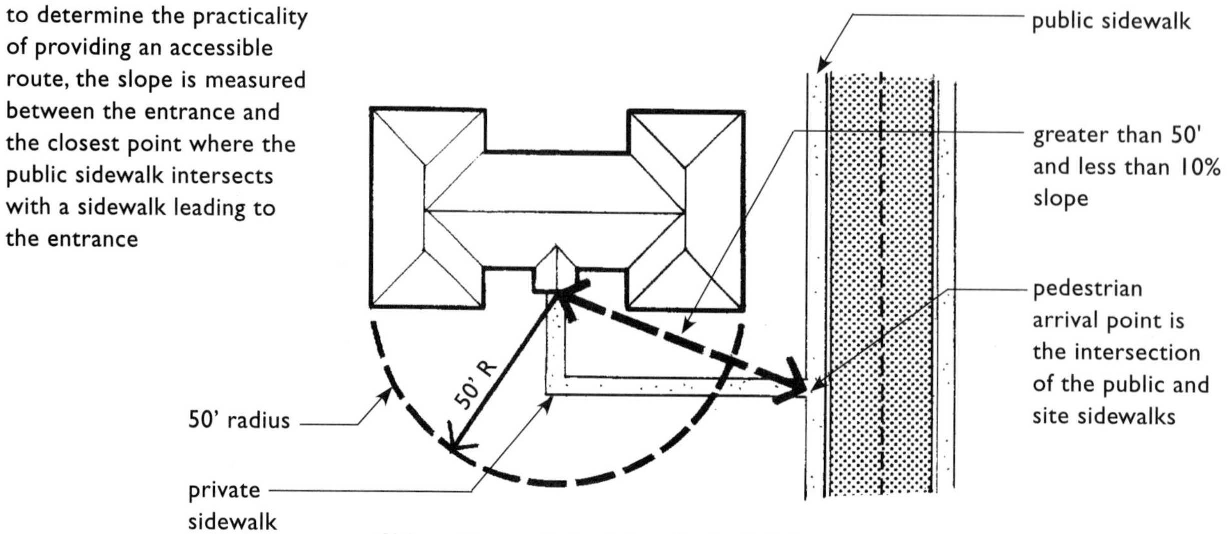

Sidewalks as Pedestrian Arrival Points
(Closest Arrival Point Is Outside 50-Foot Range)

In the case of resident parking areas, the closest point to the planned entrance will be measured from the entry point to the parking areas that are located closest to the planned entrance.

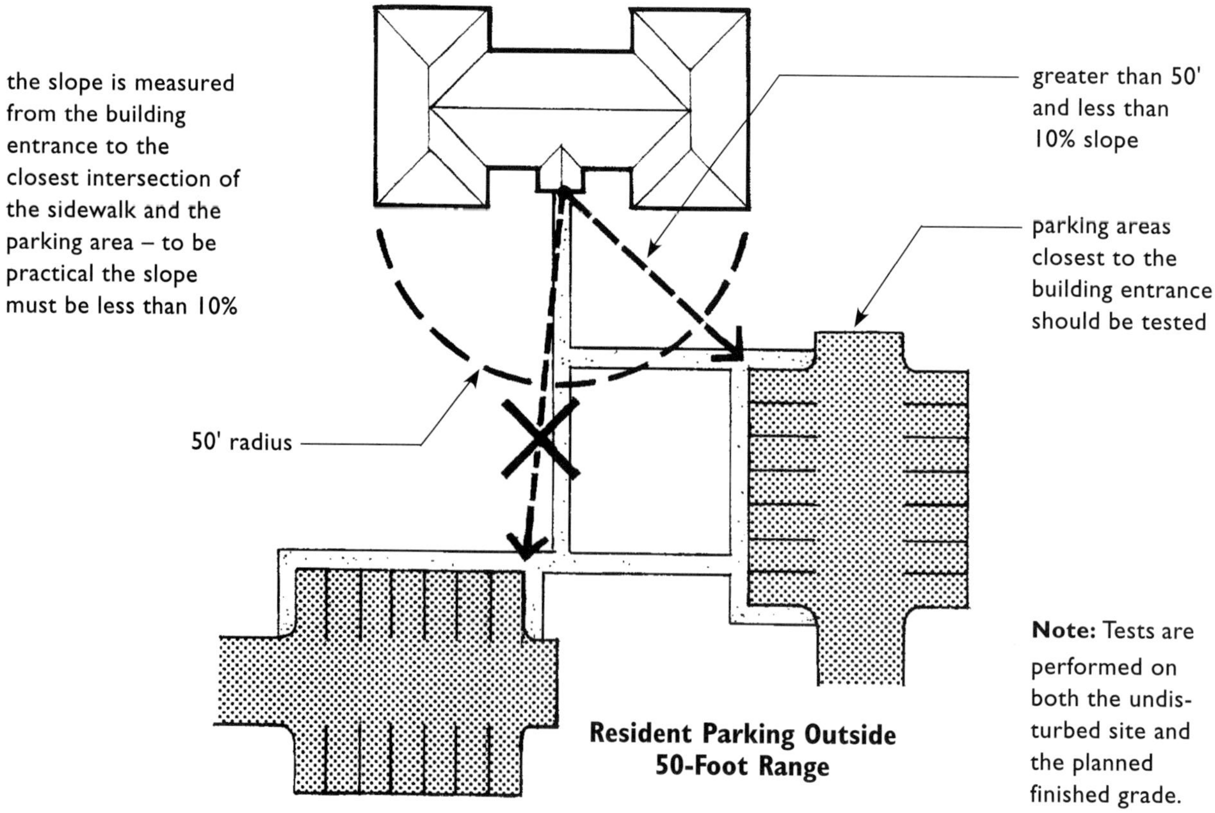

Resident Parking Outside
50-Foot Range

Note: Tests are performed on both the undisturbed site and the planned finished grade.

In some buildings the Individual Building Test may need to be applied to each entrance. The following pages contain illustrations explaining the application of this test at different site conditions.

Individual Building Test: Example Two

For buildings having **more than one planned common entrance** on a ground floor, the Individual Building Test must be conducted for each entrance. Even if both entrances prove to be impractical, 20% of the ground floor units still must meet the requirements of the Guidelines; and the developer must change the entrance in whatever way necessary to provide an accessible route to these units. Once the accessible route and entrance is provided, all ground floor units served by the accessible entrance must comply. However, only one entrance is required to be accessible and on an accessible route.

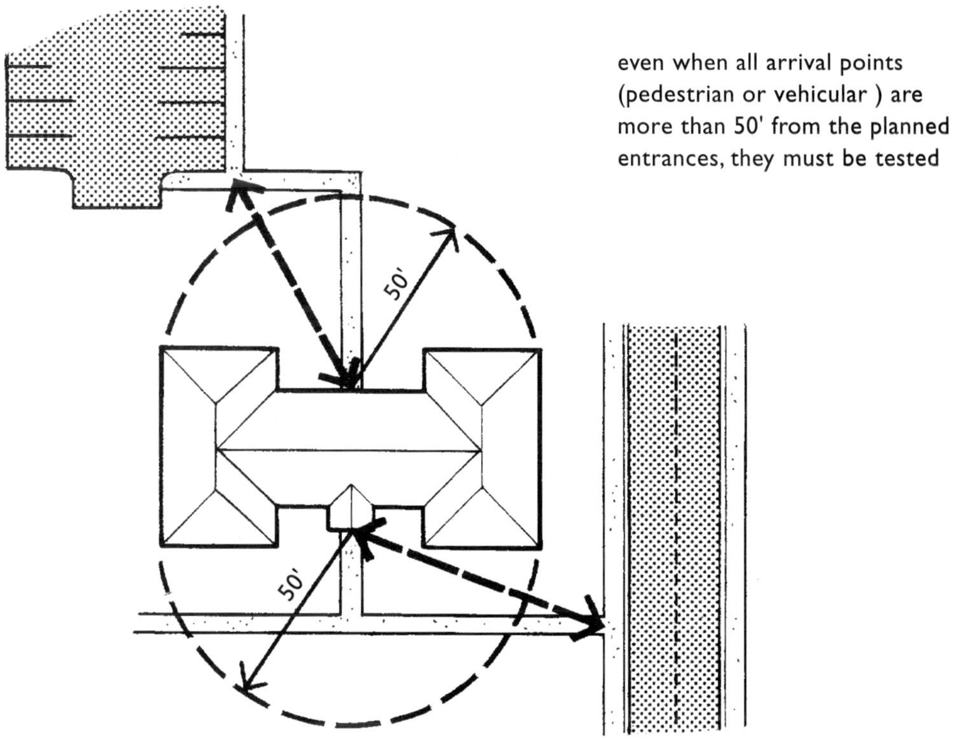

**Individual Building Test:
Example Two
Buildings with More than One Planned Common Entrance on a Ground Floor**

Individual Building Test: Example Three

For buildings having **more than one planned common entrance on more than one ground floor** the Individual Building Test is applied to each entrance.

The site arrival points within 50 feet of each entrance for both the existing and finished grade do not exceed 10%; therefore, all entrances are practical. Since all entrances are practical, units on both floors are covered and must comply with the requirements of the Guidelines. The entrance on the lower floor level and at least one of the entrances on the upper floor level must be on an accessible route unless the two entrances on the upper level serve different sets of clustered units, in which case both upper level entrances must be on an accessible route.

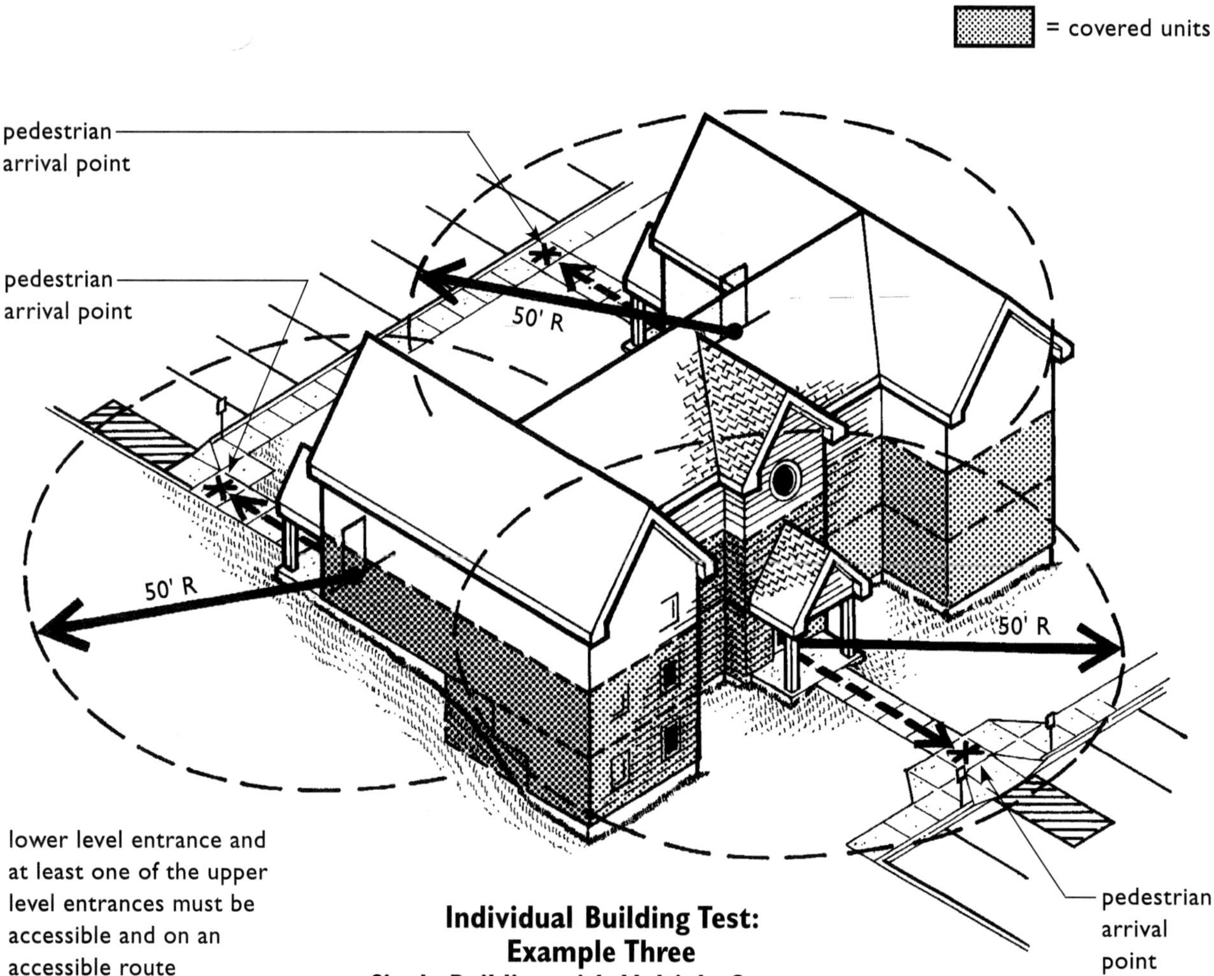

Individual Building Test: Example Three
Single Building with Multiple Common Entrances on Two Ground Floors

Individual Building Test: Example Four

There is a site arrival point within 50 feet of each planned entrance. The slopes from the existing and finished grade for the two upper level entrances do not exceed 10%, but the slopes for the lower level entrance do.

It is impractical to provide an accessible route from parking to the entrance on the lower ground floor. However, a secondary and nonrequired walk system is planned (dotted lines). It would connect the lower level entrance to the upper level arrival points and to other on-site buildings, amenities, and arrival points. The walk would not exceed a 1:20 slope and would therefore be an accessible route. If the walk is installed, the lower level entrance would be on an accessible route and the units on the lower level floor also would be covered.

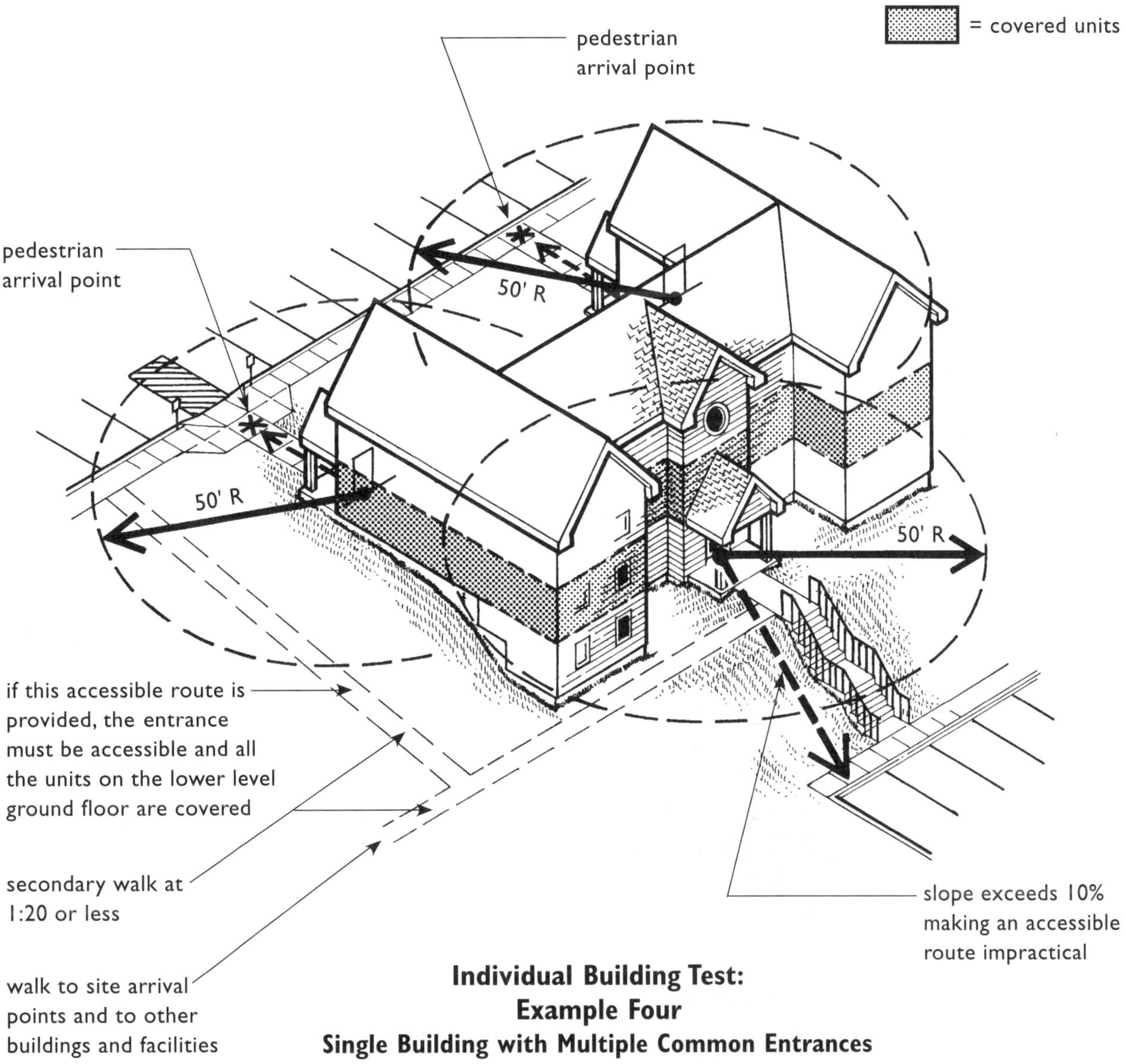

Individual Building Test:
Example Four
Single Building with Multiple Common Entrances
Lower Ground Floor Units May Be Covered

Individual Building Test: Example Five

Vehicular Route Provides Access to Building Entrances

There is a single nonelevator building on a site having one common entrance, so the Individual Building Test is used to evaluate the practicality of providing an accessible route from the arrival points to the planned entrance. The closest arrival point is the sidewalk beside the driveway that curves up a slope to a flat area in front of the entrance (point A). The slopes from the entrance to arrival point A are less than 10%, but no parking is provided. The slopes between the entrance and all other vehicular and pedestrian arrival (point B) are greater than 10%, making it impractical to provide an accessible pedestrian route from the parking lot to the building entrance.

This is still a covered building since an accessible route is possible from the entrance to the sidewalk in front of the building. Because it is impractical to install an accessible pedestrian route from the parking area, an acceptable alternative is to provide access via a vehicular route. However, necessary site provisions, such as parking spaces and curb ramps, must be provided on an accessible route to 2% of the covered dwelling units.

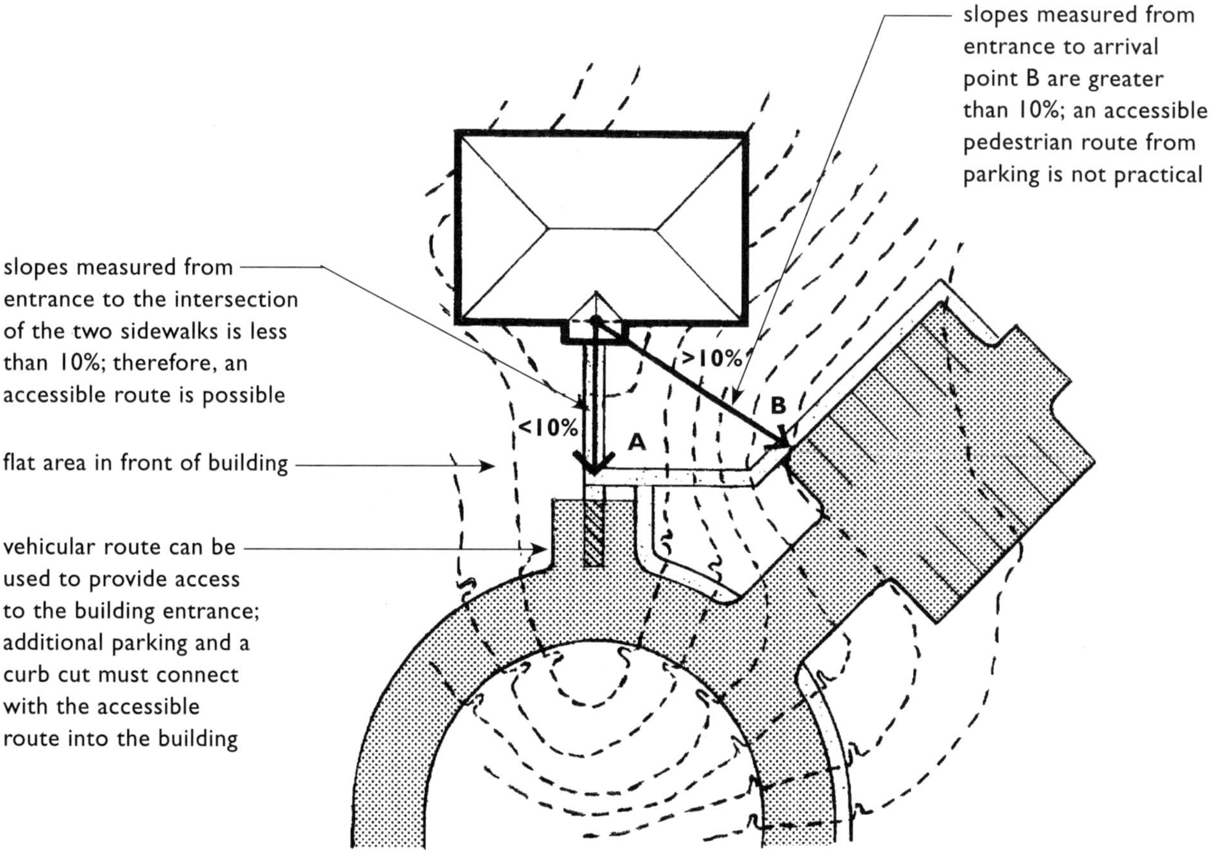

Individual Building Test:
Example Five
Vehicular Route May Be Used to Provide Access to Buildings Containing Dwelling Units

Site Analysis Test

This test may be used to analyze the site for a multifamily housing development containing multiple buildings without elevators, or a single nonelevator building with multiple entrances. The methodology for this test is significantly different from the Individual Building Test. It requires an analysis of the site to determine the number of required units which must be on an accessible route and which must meet the design requirements of the Guidelines. After this calculation is completed, the site is laid out and the minimum number of covered units must be provided. A third step which analyzes the placement of required units, accessible routes, and accessible entrances is then performed. This step is used to identify any additional units that can and therefore must be made to comply. Where the site contains multiple buildings, all the covered units should not be clustered in one building, but, as much as the site allows, should be dispersed throughout all the buildings. To perform the Site Analysis Test the following steps must be taken:

Step A

Calculate the percentage of total buildable area of the undisturbed site with a natural grade less than 10% slope.

1. Obtain a Survey Map: Obtain a topographic survey map of the undisturbed site with 2-foot contour intervals. The map must show precise boundaries of the site as well as areas where building is not allowed, such as floodplains, wetlands, setbacks, easements, or other restricted use areas.

2. Measure the Total Buildable Area: Measure the total area on which building is allowed, i.e., the area of the lot or site where a building can be located in compliance with applicable codes and zoning regulations. The "Total Buildable Area" is the total area of the site minus any restricted use areas.

3. Complete a Slope Analysis: Do a slope analysis of the total buildable area and mark on the topographic survey all those areas which have a slope of 10% or less. Calculate the combined area of site with slopes less than 10%. The slope determination shall be made between each successive 2-foot contour interval. **The accuracy of the slope analysis must be certified by a professional licensed engineer, architect, landscape architect, or surveyor.**

Step B

Calculate percentage of accessible units.

Calculate the percentage of total buildable area of the undisturbed site with a natural grade less than 10%. This percentage is the minimum percentage of ground floor units which must be made accessible. See sample site on page 1.52.

For example, if the total buildable area is 125,000 square feet and the area with slopes of less than 10% is 100,000 square feet, then the minimum percentage of units to be accessible is 80%.

$$\frac{\text{Area with slope} < 10\%}{\text{Total buildable area}} = \frac{100{,}000}{125{,}000} = 80\%$$

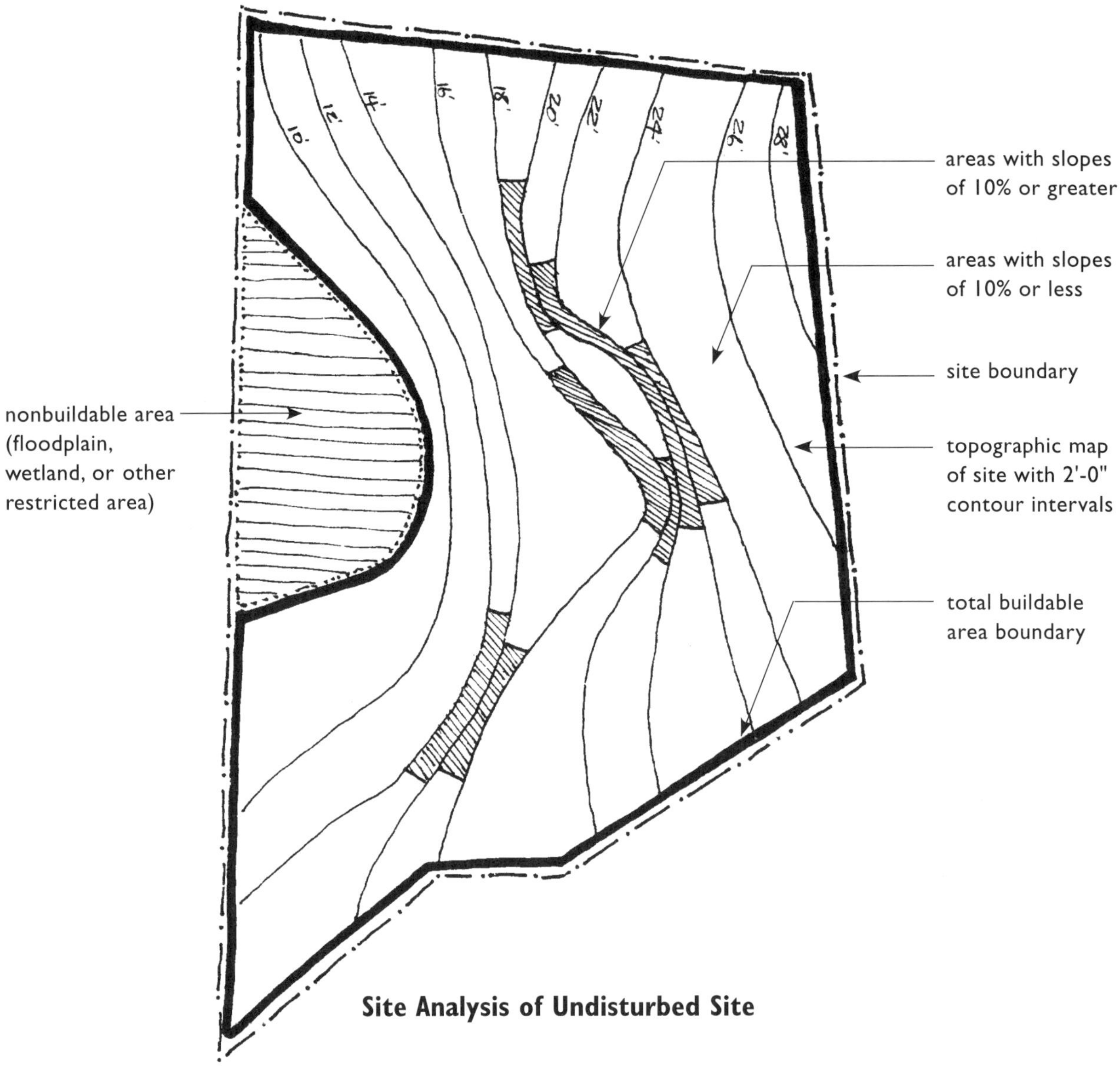

Site Analysis of Undisturbed Site

Step C

Additional Covered Units

In addition to the number of units required by the preceding analysis, **all ground floor units** must meet the design requirements of the Guidelines if they are served by a planned building entrance which is on an accessible route, i.e., on a walkway having a slope no greater than 8.33% between the planned entrance and a vehicular or pedestrian arrival point. This requires the builder/developer to review the site plan a second time to determine if additional accessible routes and/or entrances have been created that will increase the number of covered accessible units. Whenever accessible routes or entrances have been created to provide access to the minimum required number of units, any additional units that may be served by those entrances also must meet the requirements of the Guidelines.

Applying the Site Analysis Test

Calculating the Required Number of Covered Units

There are three nonelevator buildings on a site. Two have 16 units, 4 on the lowest ground floor level and 6 on each of the other floors. The third building has 12 units, 6 on each floor. Performing **Step A** of the site analysis test reveals that 75% of the buildable area has a slope of less than 10%. Therefore, 75% of the total number of ground floor units must meet the requirements of the Guidelines and be on an accessible route.

Buildings One and Two have two ground floors, while Building Three has only one ground floor. The total number of ground floor units for the development is 26. Seventy-five percent of 26 = 20 (19.5 rounded up) ground floor units that are covered (**Step B**). The covered units should be dispersed on the site among the three buildings.

To provide the required number of units the developer/builder chooses to place the covered units on the only ground floor in Building Three and on the upper ground floor of Buildings One and Two, where accessible entrances on accessible routes can be provided most easily. The number of units on these floors totals 18, which is 2 units **less** than the 20 that are needed to meet **Steps A and B**.

To meet the requirement for 20 accessible units, the developer/builder has the option of providing the 2 additional units on the second ground floor of either Building One or Two. In this example, the builder places the additional 2 required units on the lower ground floor of Building One, and provides the required accessibility by regrading and adding a ramp to the lower level entrance. Additionally, under **Step C**, since the lower level entrance is now on an accessible route, all the units on that floor become covered units and the entire ground floor must comply. As a result, the total number of covered units is 22.

Positioning Covered Units on a Building Site

It is permissible under the Site Analysis Test to select in which buildings and on which floors covered units will be placed; however, in a multiple building development, all the covered units should not be located in a single building. Covered units should be dispersed between buildings and, if possible, among all the ground floors. However, if the required number of covered units is less than the total number of units on a floor, all the units on that floor become covered units because the required units are served by an accessible route and entrance.

Step A
Topographic analysis:
Area < 10% slope = 75%
Ground floor units to comply = 75%

Step B
Total Ground Floor Units = 26
x 75%
Covered Units = 20

Step C
After distribution of required units, total count of 20 covered ground floor units is raised to 22.

Two more units are added to lower ground floor of Building #1 and an accessible route is provided to meet the required 20. Two remaining units on that floor become covered units because all ground floor units served by an accessible route are covered units.

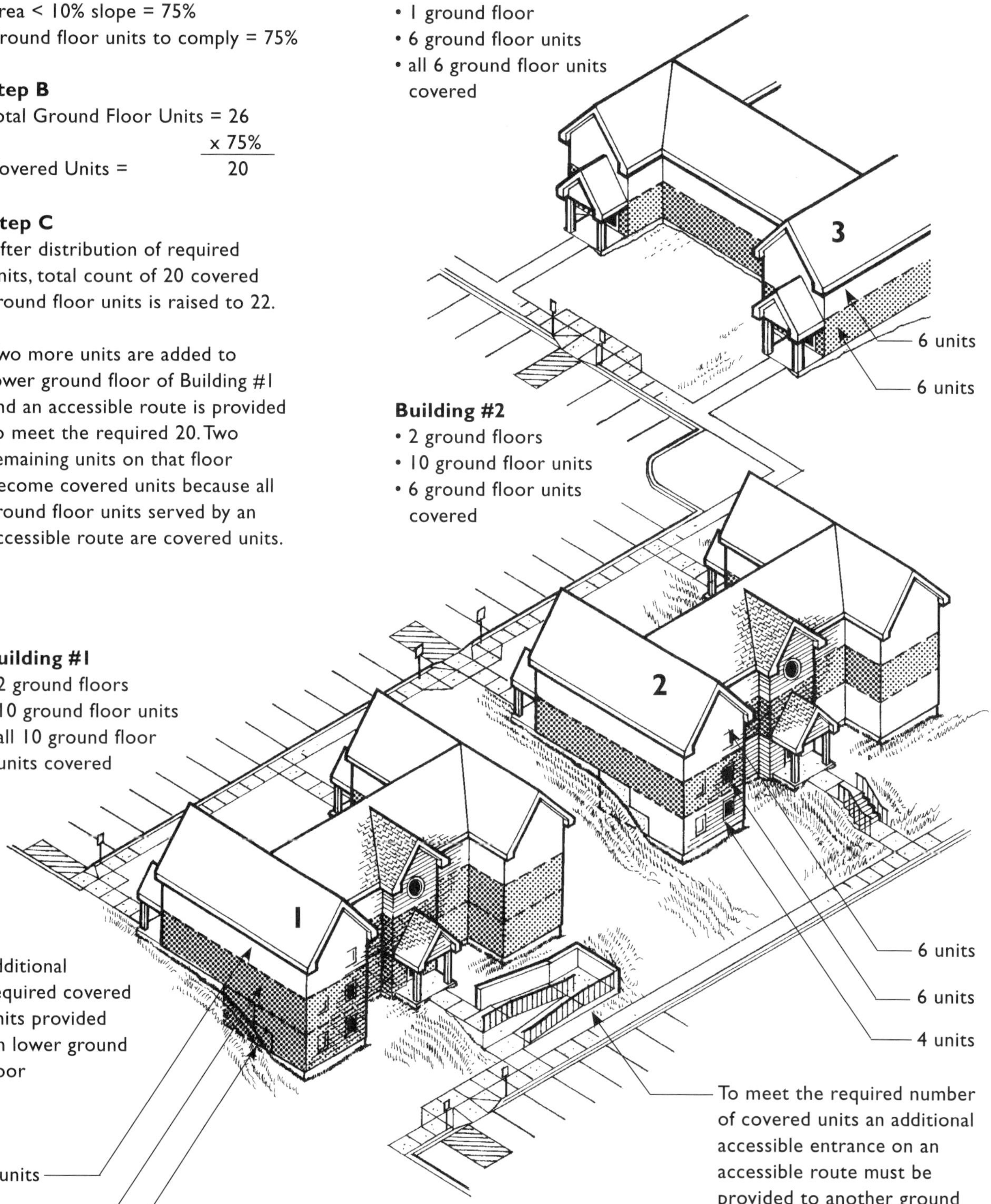

Site Analysis Test:
Example One
The Number of Covered Units

Accessible Routes May Dictate Additional Covered Units

If the Site Analysis Test indicates a particular percentage of required covered units and the project has a larger number, all of which are on accessible routes, the larger number are covered and must meet the design requirements of the Guidelines.

Ten three-story nonelevator buildings are planned for a site, each having eight ground floor units for a total of 80 units. **Steps A and B** of the site analysis test show 60% (or 48) of the ground floor units must comply. During planning the developer places these 48 required units in six of the ten buildings, selecting the six buildings where providing accessibility is easily achieved. However, after the site planning is completed, application of **Step C** shows that all ten buildings have entrances on an accessible route, i.e., a walkway with a slope between the planned building entrances and a pedestrian or vehicular arrival point that is no greater than 8.33%. Therefore, all ground floor units in each building (or 80 units) must meet the Guidelines.

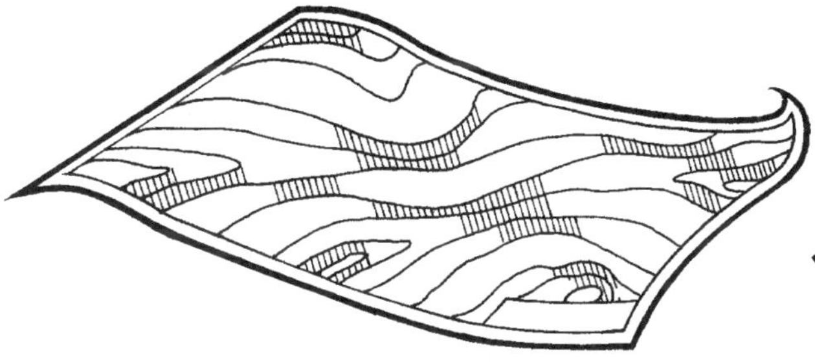

Steps A and B of the site analysis reveals 60% of ground floor units are covered

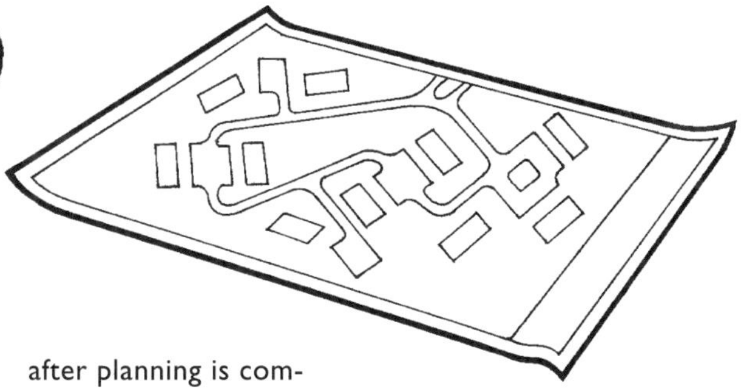

after planning is completed **Step C** of the test requires all buildings to have entrances on an accessible route; therefore, 100% of ground floor units are covered

Site Analysis Test: Example Two Additional Covered Units

Sites with Unusual Characteristics

Certain sites are subject to laws or codes which specify that the lowest floor of a building or the lowest structural member of the lowest floor must be raised to a specified level. Examples of such sites are those located in a federally designated flood-plain or coastal high-hazard area, where buildings must be raised to a level at or above the base flood elevation.

When these circumstances result in **Step One**, a difference in grade elevation exceeding 30 inches

– **and** –

Step Two, a slope exceeding 10% between a building entrance and all vehicular and pedestrian arrival points within 50 feet of the entrance (or to the closest one if none are within 50 feet), then an accessible route to that building entrance is considered impractical. Therefore, the building would not be subject to the accessibility requirements of the Fair Housing Act.

The heavy dotted line between the door threshold and the arrival point in the following illustrations is a measuring and slope determination line only. It is not intended to represent the surface of a ramp or walk. The slope and the length of this line simply will determine whether or not the building entrance is required to be on an accessible route. Once that determination is made, the developer/builder can design any system of ramps, walks, lifts, or other method of providing the necessary access.

The entrances shown in these examples may be either a common or an individual dwelling unit entrance. If the measuring and slope determination line shown has a vertical elevation change less than 30 inches and the slope is less than 10%, the entrance and the route to it must be accessible (meet the Guidelines) as well as the dwelling units on that ground floor.

Tree-save ordinances do not constitute an unusual site characteristic that necessarily would exempt a site from complying with the requirements of the Act. However, the Guidelines would not require that a site be graded in violation of a tree-save ordinance. If, however, access is required based on the final site plan, then installation of a ramp for access, rather than grading, could be necessary in some cases so as not to disturb the trees.

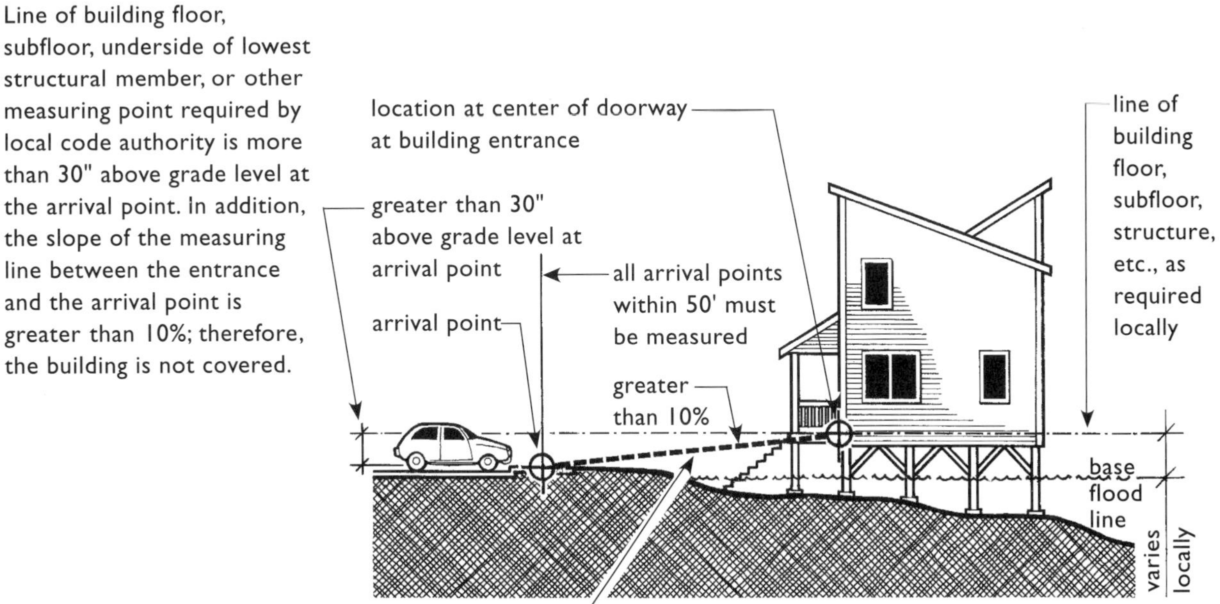

Building Meets Both Criteria for Exemption

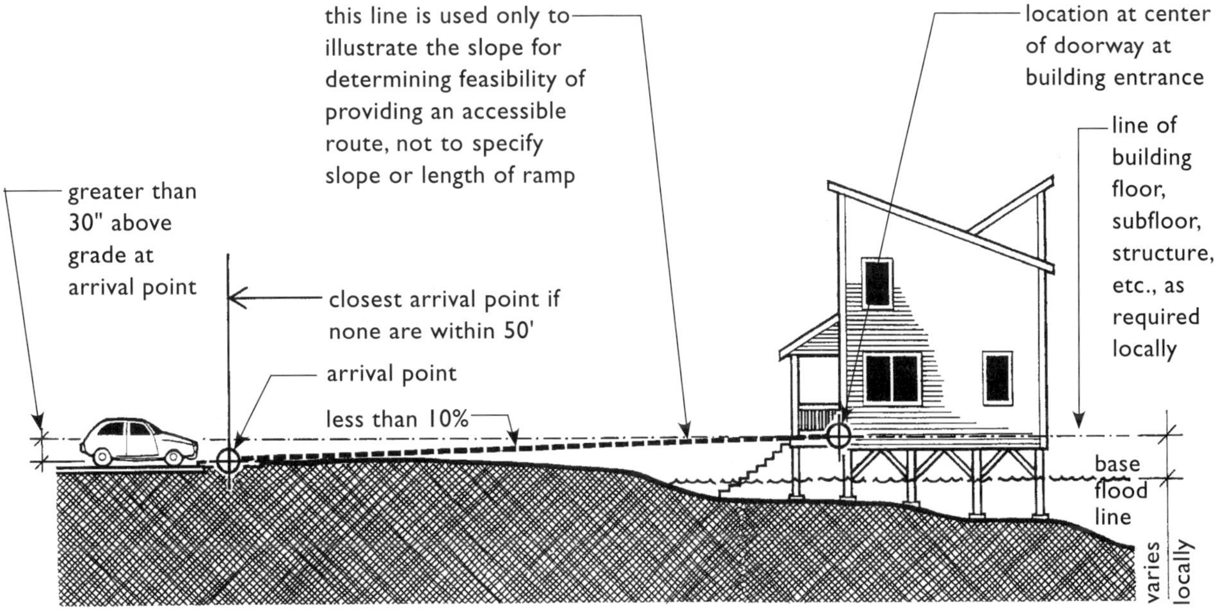

Building Must Comply With Requirements of the Guidelines

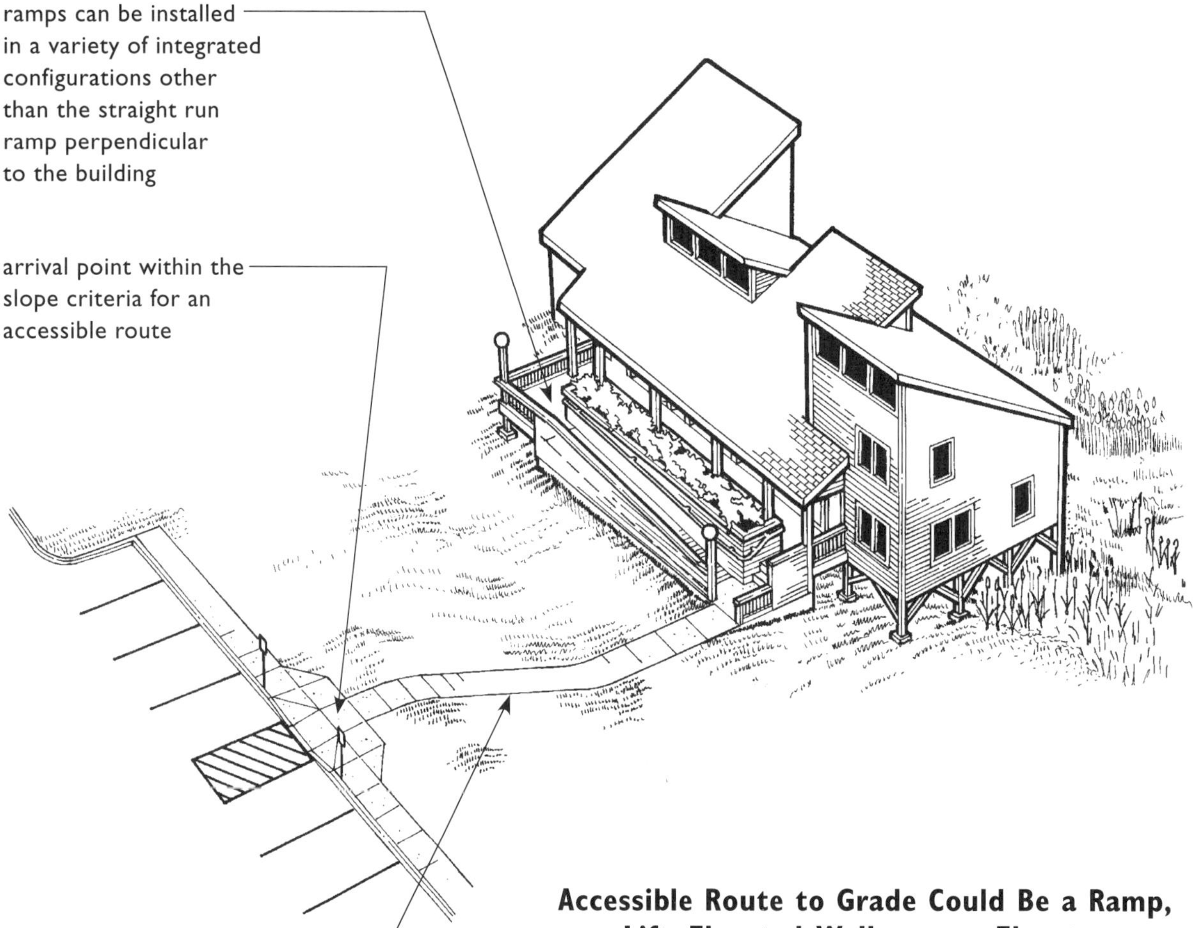

Accessible Route to Grade Could Be a Ramp, Lift, Elevated Walkway, or Elevator

Chapter Two:

Requirement 2

Accessible and Usable Public and Common Use Areas

2

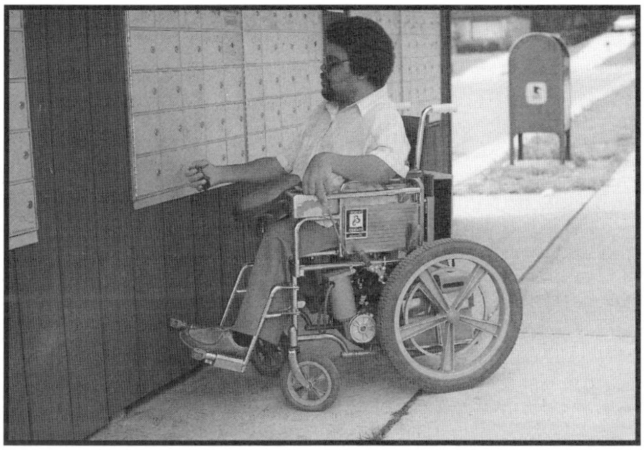

"...covered multifamily dwellings with a building entrance on an accessible route shall be designed in such a manner that the public and common use areas are readily accessible to and usable by handicapped persons."

Fair Housing Act Regulations, 24 CFR 100.205

Definitions from the Guidelines

Accessible. When used with respect to the public and common use areas of a building containing covered multifamily dwellings, means that the public or common use areas of the building can be approached, entered, and used by individuals with physical handicaps. The phrase "readily accessible to and usable by" is synonymous with accessible.
A public or common use area that complies with the appropriate requirements of ANSI A117.1 – 1986, a comparable standard or these guidelines is "accessible" within the meaning of this paragraph.

Common Use Areas. Rooms, spaces, or elements inside or outside of a building that are made available for the use of residents of a building or the guests thereof. These areas include hallways, lounges, lobbies, laundry rooms, refuse rooms, mail rooms, recreational areas, and passageways among and between buildings.

Public Use Areas. Interior or exterior rooms or spaces of a building that are made available to the general public. Public use may be provided at a building that is privately or publicly owned.

INTRODUCTION

The Fair Housing Accessibility Guidelines (the Guidelines) require public and common use areas and facilities in covered multifamily housing developments to be accessible to people with disabilities so they may benefit from and enjoy the amenities present in the housing development in which they live. Public and common use areas that must be accessible include, but are not limited to, such spaces and elements as selected on-site walks, parking, corridors, lobbies, drinking fountains and water coolers, swimming pool decks or aprons, playgrounds, rental offices, mailbox areas, trash rooms/refuse disposal areas, lounges, clubhouses, tennis courts, health spas, game rooms, toilet rooms and bathing facilities, laundries, community rooms, and portions of common use tenant storage.

The Guidelines require an accessible route (see page 2.15) to public and common use spaces, but not all features or elements within that space may be required to be accessible. The scoping provisions, or "where," "when," and "how many" elements and spaces must be accessible, will be addressed throughout this chapter. For example, where multiple recreational facilities are provided, the Guidelines do not require that each amenity be accessible, but rather that "sufficient numbers" be accessible to provide equitable use by people with disabilities.

In general, however, if each building on a site has its own trash room, lounge area, laundry room, game room, etc., then each of these in each building must be on an accessible route and comply with the applicable portions of an appropriate accessibility standard since they serve different buildings. For an overview of the scoping requirements refer to the illustrations on pages 2.8 through 2.11 and to the chart, taken from the Guidelines, entitled "Basic Components for Accessible and Usable Public and Common Use Areas or Facilities," reprinted on the next page.

Federal Register / Vol. 56, No. 44 / Wednesday, March 6, 1991 / Rules and Regulations 9505

BASIC COMPONENTS FOR ACCESSABLE AND USABLE PUBLIC AND COMMON USE AREAS OR FACILITIES

Accessible element or space	ANSI A117.1 section	Application
1. Accessible route(s)	4.3	Within the boundary of the site: (a) From public transportation stops, accessible parking spaces, accessible passenger loading zones, and public streets or sidewalks to accessible building entrances (subject to site considerations described in section 5). (b) Connecting accessible buildings, facilities, elements and spaces that are on the same site. On-grade walks or paths between separate buildings with covered multifamily dwellings, while not required, should be accessible unless the slope of finish grade exceeds 8.33% at any point along the route. Handrails are not required on these accessible walks. (c) Connecting accessible building or facility entrances with accessible spaces and elements within the building or facility, including adaptable dwelling units. (d) Where site or legal constraints prevent a route accessible to wheelchair users between covered multifamily dwellings and public or common-use facilities elsewhere on the site, an acceptable alternative is the provision of access via a vehicular route so long as there is accessible parking on an accessible route to at least 2% of covered dwelling units, and necessary site provisions such as parking and curb cuts are available at the public or common use facility.
2. Protruding objects	4.4	Accessible routes or maneuvering space including, but not limited to halls, corridors, passageways, or aisles.
3. Ground and floor surface treatments	4.5	Accessible routes, rooms, and spaces, including floors, walks, ramps, stairs, and curb ramps.
4. Parking and passenger-loading zones	4.6	If provided at the site, designated accessible parking at the dwelling unit on request of residents with handicaps, on the same terms and with the full range of choices (e.g., surface parking or garage) that are provided for other residents of the project, with accessible parking on a route accessible to wheelchairs for at least 2% of the covered dwelling units: accessible visitor parking sufficient to provide access to grade-level entrances of covered multifamily dwellings: and accessible parking at facilities (e.g., swimming pools) that serve accessible buildings.
5. Curb ramps	4.7	Accessible routes crossing curbs.
6. Ramps	4.8	Accessible routes with slopes greater than 1:20.
7. Stairs	4.9	Stairs on accessible routes connecting levels not connected by an elevator.
8. Elevator	4.10	If provided.
9. Platform lift	4.11	May be used in lieu of an elevator or ramp under certain conditions.
10. Drinking fountains and water coolers	4.15	Fifty percent of fountains and coolers on each floor, or at least one, if provided in the facility or at the site.
11. Toilet rooms and bathing facilities (including water closets, toilet rooms and stalls, urinals, lavatories and mirrors, bathtubs, shower stalls, and sinks.)	4.22	Where provided in public-use and common-use facilities, at least one of each fixture provided per room.
12. Seating, tables, or work surfaces	4.30	If provided in accessible spaces, at least one of each type provided.
13. Places of assembly	4.31	If provided in the facility or at the site.
14. Common-use spaces and facilities (including swimming pools, playgrounds, entrances, rental offices, lobbies, elevators, mailbox areas, lounges, halls and corridors, and the like.)	4.1 through 4.30	If provided in the facility or at the site: (a) Where multiple recreational facilities (e.g., tennis courts) are provided sufficient accessible facilities of each type to assure equitable opportunity for use by persons with handicaps. (b) Where practical, access to all or a portion of nature trails and jogging paths.
15. Laundry rooms	4.32.6	If provided in the facility or at the site, at least one of each type of appliance provided in each laundry area, except that laundry rooms serving covered multifamily dwellings would not be required to have front-loading washers in order to meet the requirements of § 100,205(c)(1). (Where front loading washers are not provided, management will be expected to provide assistive devices on request if necessary to permit a resident to use a top loading washer.)

Reprint of "Basic Components" chart from the Guidelines. The application column gives guidance on scoping: how many of what kind located where.

Scope of ANSI and the ADA in Public and Common Use Spaces

Application of ANSI A117.1 - 1986

The Fair Housing Act references the ANSI A117.1 Standard *(American National Standard for Buildings and Facilities: Providing Accessibility and Usability for Physically Handicapped People)* as an acceptable means of complying with the design requirements of the Act. However, the Act does not exclusively require following ANSI A117.1. The Fair Housing Act regulations of the U.S. Department of Housing and Urban Development (HUD) adopt the ANSI Standard, but specify the 1986 version of the ANSI A117.1 Standard. Likewise, the Guidelines reference specific portions of the 1986 ANSI A117.1 Standard.

The Guidelines are to provide technical guidance and are not mandatory. They provide a safe harbor for compliance with the accessibility requirements of the Act.

The "Purpose" section in the Guidelines states that "Builders and developers may choose to depart from these guidelines and seek alternate ways to demonstrate that they have met the requirements of the Fair Housing Act." If an accessibility standard other than the ANSI A117.1 Standard is followed, care must be taken to ensure the standard used is at least equivalent to or stricter than the 1986 ANSI A117.1 Standard. See also the ANSI Standard discussion in the Introduction on page 13.

The Guidelines, in some instances, modify the ANSI specifications and, in other instances, substitute specifications. The illustrations in this chapter provide an overview of many of the key requirements for public and common use areas.

When designing these areas it is essential to refer to the 1986 ANSI A117.1 Standard specifications 4.1 through 4.31, as appropriate (or an equivalent or stricter standard), for detailed dimensional design specifications for each required accessible element or space.

Note: When this Manual states the ANSI Standard or the ANSI A117.1 Standard "must be followed" it means the 1986 ANSI A117.1 Standard or an equivalent or stricter standard.

ANSI Technical Specifications for Accessible Elements and Spaces

4.1 Basic Components
4.2 Space Allowances and Reach Ranges
4.3 Accessible Route
4.4 Protruding Objects
4.5 Ground and Floor Surfaces
4.6 Parking Spaces and Passenger Loading Zones
4.7 Curb Ramps
4.8 Ramps
4.9 Stairs
4.10 Elevators
4.11 Platform Lifts
4.12 Windows
4.13 Doors
4.14 Entrances
4.15 Drinking Fountains and Water Coolers
4.16 Water Closets
4.17 Toilet Stalls
4.18 Urinals
4.19 Lavatories, Sinks, and Mirrors
4.20 Bathtubs
4.21 Shower Stalls
4.22 Toilet Rooms, Bathrooms, Bathing Facilities, and Shower Rooms
4.23 Storage
4.24 Grab Bars, and Tub and Shower Seats
4.25 Controls and Operating Mechanisms
4.26 Alarms
4.27 Detectable Warnings
4.28 Signage
4.29 Telephones
4.30 Seating, Tables, and Work Surfaces
4.31 Auditorium and Assembly Areas

Public and Common Use Areas not Covered by the Guidelines

Where a newly constructed development consists entirely of buildings of four or more **multistory dwelling units without elevators** (e.g., two-story townhouses), the development is not required to comply with the Fair Housing Act or the Guidelines. Since there are no covered multifamily dwellings on the site, no public and common use areas anywhere on the site are required to be accessible. Note, however, that the Americans with Disabilities Act (ADA) of 1990 may apply. See the discussion of the ADA in the next column.

However, in housing developments of two- or three-story walk-up buildings where the ground floor dwelling units are single-story, all the ground floor units are covered (unless site impracticality can be claimed, see Chapter 1: "Accessible Building Entrance on an Accessible Route") and must be on an accessible route with accessible entrances. Since an accessible route does not go to the upper floors, then the stairs up to those dwelling units, and the halls, corridors, and entry doors on the upper floors are not covered by the requirements of the Guidelines.

Of course, public and common use facilities must be accessible and cannot be located on upper floors of buildings which do not have an elevator(s), unless similar facilities also are located on the ground floor. For example, it would not be acceptable to have a common use trash room on the second floor of a building and not have one on the ground floor of the same building.

Impact of the Americans with Disabilities Act (ADA) on Public and Common Use Spaces

The dwelling units of private multifamily housing developments generally are not required to meet the accessibility provisions of the Americans with Disabilities Act Accessibility Guidelines (ADAAG). However, some public and common use spaces such as rental offices and sales offices are considered "public accommodations" under Title III of the ADA because, by their nature, they are open to people other than residents and their guests. They, therefore, must comply with the ADA requirements in addition to all applicable requirements of the Fair Housing Act.

Other buildings and amenities in a housing development, such as laundry buildings and recreational facilities (clubhouses, swimming pools, spas, game rooms, and exercise rooms), will be covered by the ADA **only** if they are available for use by people other than residents and their guests. If such facilities are made available to the public only periodically, such as for a festival or seasonal event, they must comply with the ADA during the event.

Fortunately the ANSI and the ADAAG have similar technical specifications for most features. However, there are some differences in scope and technical requirements. For example, the ADAAG requires designated parking spaces for vans. For more discussion of this, see page 2.20 "Access Aisles." Since this document presents the ANSI specifications cited in the Fair Housing Act, the reader is advised to consult ADAAG only when public and common use facilities are to be available to the general public.

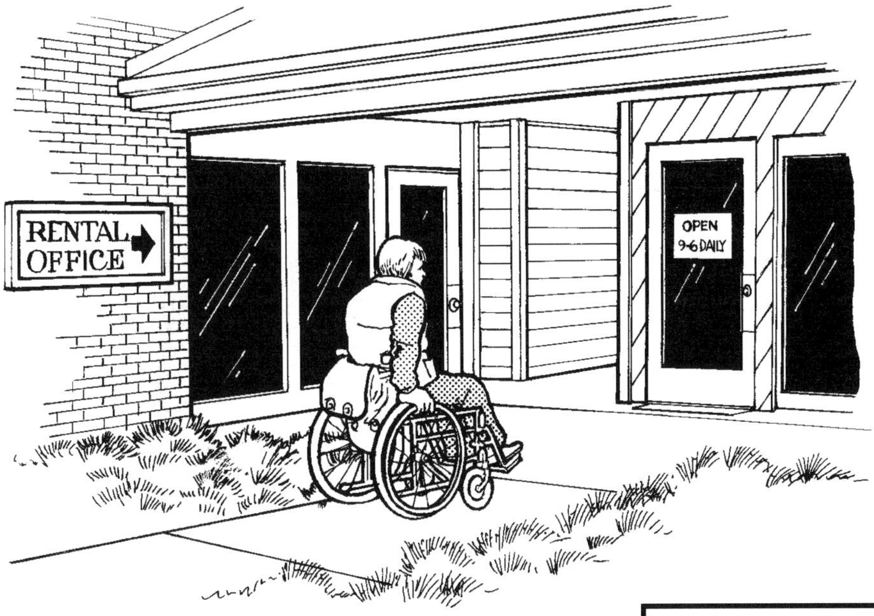

> **Public and Common Use Space Covered by the ADA**
>
> Places of public accommodation subject to the requirements of Title III of the ADA include: 1. places of lodging, 2. establishments serving food or drink, 3. places of exhibition or entertainment, 4. places of public gathering, 5. sales or rental establishments, 6. service establishments, 7. stations used for specified public transportation, 8. places of public display or collection, 9. places of recreation, 10. places of education, 11. social service center establishments, and 12. places of exercise or recreation. **28 CFR Part 36, Section 36.104. Definitions**

Multiple Recreational Facilities

Where multiple recreational facilities of the same type are provided at the same location on the site (e.g., tennis courts), not all but a "sufficient" number of the facilities must be accessible to ensure an equitable opportunity for use by people with disabilities. It is recommended that all recreational facilities be accessible when the site is relatively flat and this can be easily achieved. Whenever only one of a type of recreational facility is provided at a particular location on the site, it must be accessible and connected by an accessible route to the covered dwelling units. In instances where each building or cluster of buildings is served by its own recreational facility e.g., a swimming pool, then the facility must be on an accessible route from the covered dwelling units.

In the case of recreational facilities, special equipment and features are not required by the Guidelines. For example, play areas for children and swimming pool aprons must be accessible and meet ANSI specifications for all commonly constructed elements, but special mechanical pool lifts or wheelchair accessible play equipment are not required. The Guidelines do not require an accessible route (ramp or lift) down into the water at pools.

Example: Accessible Site Features for a Multifamily Housing Development Covered by the FHA Guidelines

1. accessible passenger loading zone, see ANSI 4.6
2. accessible bus shelter (pedestrian arrival point) on an accessible route, see drawing on page 1.6
3. accessible resident and visitor parking, see page 2.23
4. ramp from upper level of site with tennis court to lower level with clubhouse is part of a required accessible route and must meet ANSI 4.8 Ramps
5. both pools must be on an accessible route that continues around the apron (access into water not required) since they serve separate buildings containing covered dwelling units
6. all or a portion of jogging trails must be accessible where practical; this trail is accessible from this point to bridge (smooth, level, paved surface with no abrupt change in level); beyond bridge, trail is inaccessible
7. van accessible space, see page 2.13, note 16

8'-0" access aisle for van parking at rental/sales office, see pages 2.6 and 2.20, "Access Aisles"

since accessibility is provided at tennis court at playground/clubhouse, this public and common use facility may remain on an inaccessible walk

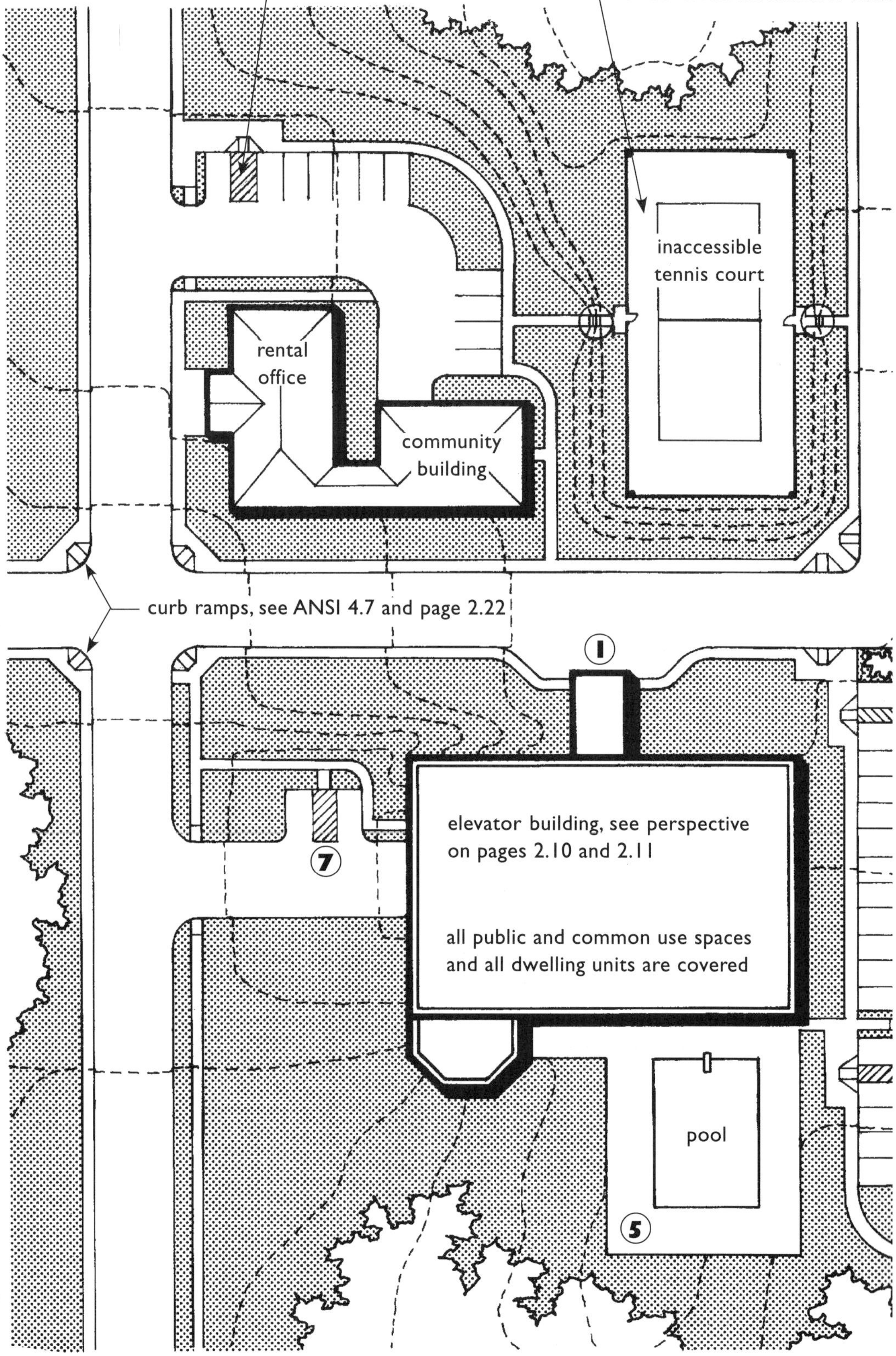

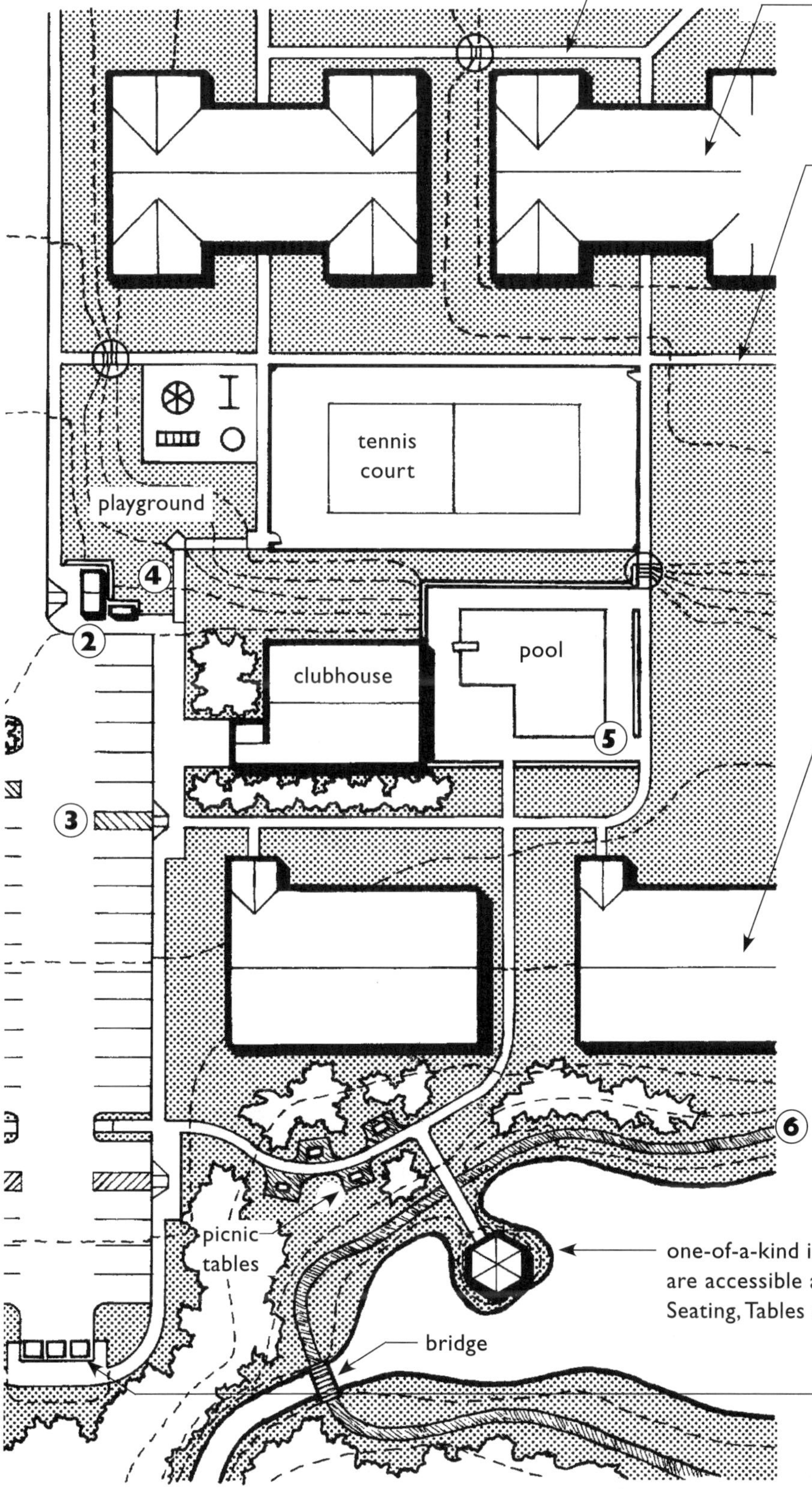

inaccessible walk between buildings containing only covered dwelling units

three-story buildings without elevator(s), ground floor units are covered

inaccessible walk allowed since accessible site amenities are linked by alternate accessible route to buildings containing covered dwelling units

Whenever multiple recreational facilities are provided, sufficient accessible facilities of each type must be provided to assure equitable opportunity for use by people with disabilities.

buildings without elevator(s), ground floor units are covered

- stairs along inaccessible walks
- accessible route
- jogging trail
- parking access aisle (part of accessible route)

one-of-a-kind island gazebo and the four picnic tables are accessible and on an accessible route, see ANSI 4.30 Seating, Tables and Work Surfaces

trash facility serving covered dwelling units on an accessible route with at least one dumpster being accessible, see page 2.16

Example: Common Use Accessible Spaces and Elements on an Accessible Route

See pages 2.12 and 2.13 for notes keyed to the numbers located at specific elements and spaces.

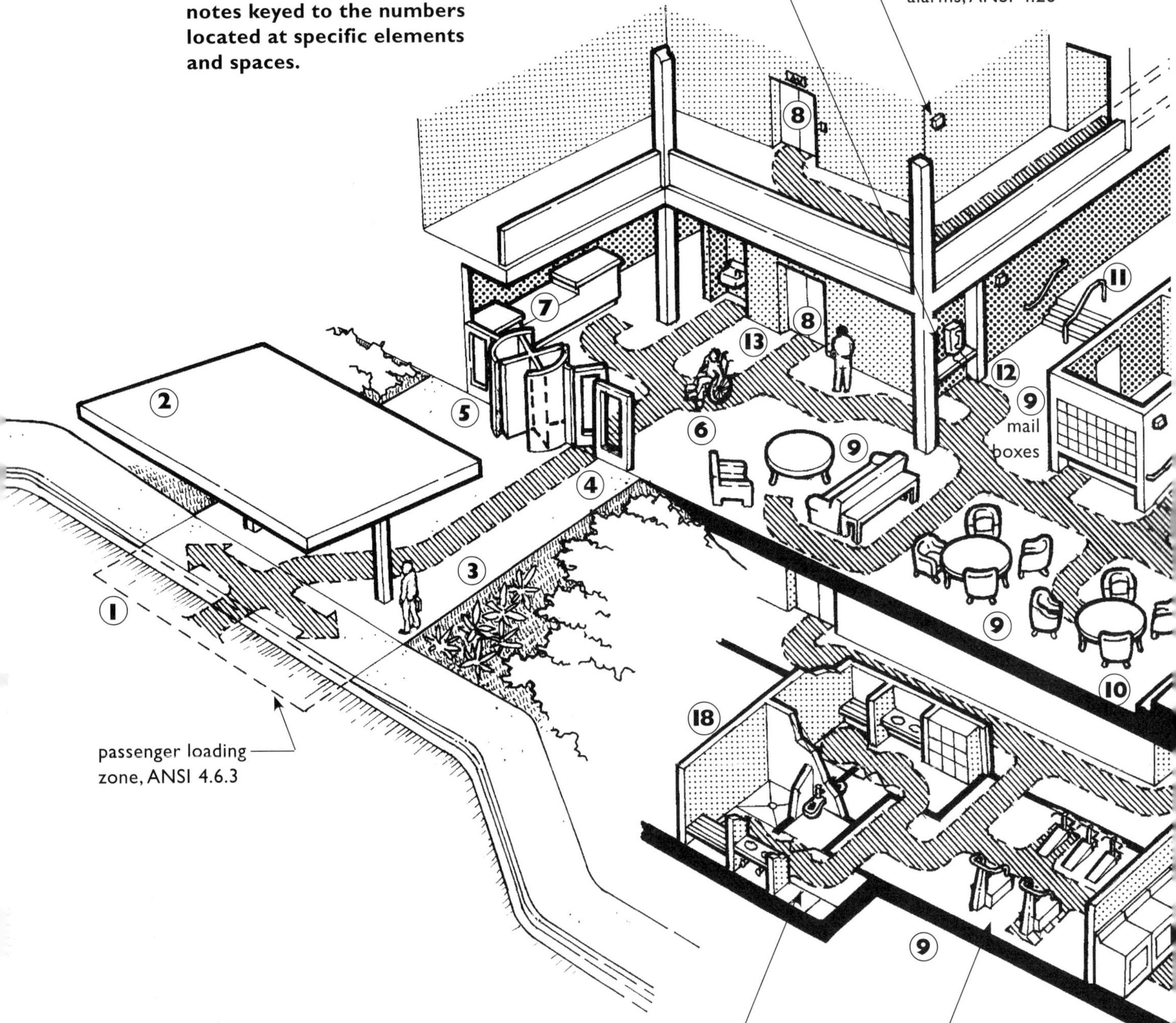

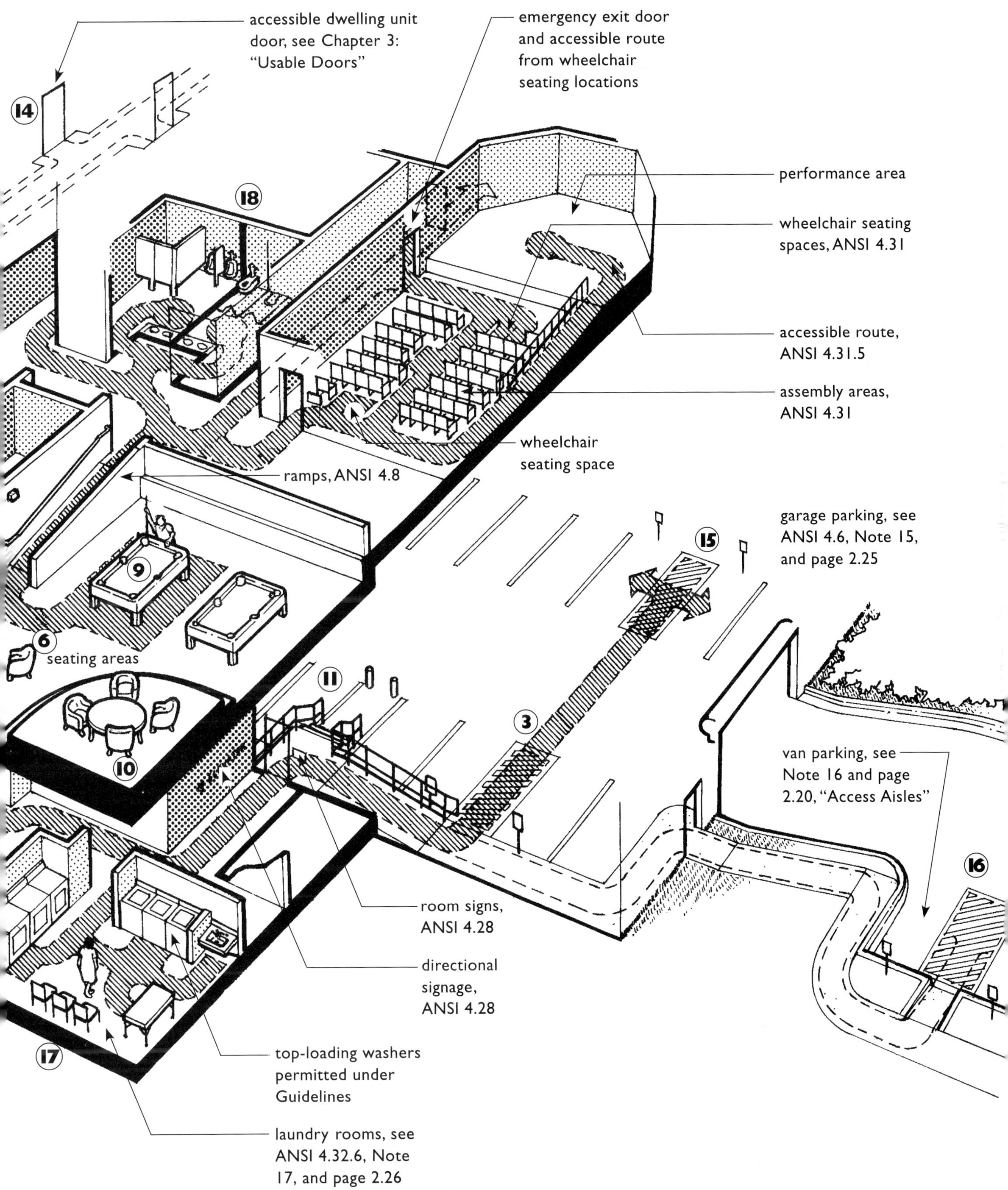
accessible dwelling unit door, see Chapter 3: "Usable Doors"
emergency exit door and accessible route from wheelchair seating locations
14
18
performance area
wheelchair seating spaces, ANSI 4.31
accessible route, ANSI 4.31.5
assembly areas, ANSI 4.31
wheelchair seating space
ramps, ANSI 4.8
garage parking, see ANSI 4.6, Note 15, and page 2.25
15
9
6
seating areas
11
3
10
van parking, see Note 16 and page 2.20, "Access Aisles"
16
room signs, ANSI 4.28
directional signage, ANSI 4.28
top-loading washers permitted under Guidelines
17
laundry rooms, see ANSI 4.32.6, Note 17, and page 2.26

The following numbered notes are keyed to the perspective "Example: Common Use Accessible Spaces and Elements on an Accessible Route" appearing on pages 2.10 and 2.11. Each note contains selected technical design references and explanations based on the FHA Guidelines and the ANSI A117.1 - 1986.

1

Passenger Loading Zones. Passenger loading zones must have a large clear pedestrian access aisle connected by an accessible route to accessible building entrances. They also must have sufficient headroom to clear buses or vans with high roofs. See ANSI 4.6 and Notes 2 and 3 below.

2

Overhanging Objects. Roofs, tree limbs, or other elements that overhang passenger loading zones must be kept high enough to clear buses or vans with high roofs. See ANSI 4.6.

3

Accessible Route. Accessible routes must connect accessible transportation stops, parking spaces, passenger loading zones, and public streets and sidewalks within the boundaries of the site to accessible entrances. See ANSI 4.3, Note 6, and page 2.15.

4

Accessible Entrance. Doors along accessible routes must meet ANSI 4.13. See also Chapter 1: "Accessible Building Entrance on an Accessible Route."

5

Revolving Doors. Revolving doors generally cannot meet the requirements of ANSI 4.13, and, therefore, cannot be the only means of passage at an accessible entrance or on an accessible route.

6

Accessible Route. An accessible route must connect accessible building or facility entrances with accessible spaces and elements within the building or facility, including adaptable (or covered) dwelling units. See also ANSI 4.3, Note 3, and page 2.15.

7

Reception Desk. Accessible reception desks are not specifically described in ANSI. This common use facility must be accessible to people with disabilities and should comply with the applicable specifications of ANSI 4.1 - 4.31. See also Note 9.

8

Elevators. All elevators, if provided, must comply with ANSI 4.10.

9

Multiple Elements, Features, or Spaces. Whenever one of a type of element, feature, or space is provided for public or common use of residents, it must be on an accessible route and meet the applicable specifications of ANSI. Whenever multiple features or facilities are provided, sufficient accessible features of each type must be provided to assure equitable opportunity for use by people with disabilities.

When ANSI does not contain specifications for the specific facility or feature in question, then related human factors and performance specifications must be used to achieve accessibility. Such specifications include, but are not limited to, 4.2 Space Allowances and Reach Ranges, 4.3 Accessible Route, 4.4 Protruding Objects, 4.5 Ground and Floor Surfaces, and 4.25 Controls and Operating Mechanisms.

10

Raised or Sunken Floor Areas. Small raised or sunken floor areas within a single space or room not connected by an accessible route may be allowed, provided that any facilities or elements on the raised or lowered area also are provided on the main or accessible floor area in the same room or space. In many building codes raised areas, such as mezzanines, are limited to a maximum of 33-1/3 percent of the floor area of the space in which they are located. This seems to be a reasonable limiting percentage for a cumulative total of the entire inaccessible raised and lowered floor areas. The majority of all facilities or elements must be on the accessible floor area and be served by an accessible route. The raised or sunken area must not prevent an accessible route from serving other accessible areas, facilities, or elements; it must not require people with disabilities to take a circuitous route or travel an inordinate additional distance to reach the accessible space.

11

Stairs Along Accessible Routes. A properly designed ramp is considered to be an acceptable part of an accessible route. However, since some users are safer on stairs than on ramps, it is best if stairs are provided in combination with ramps. This is especially true when they are located along an accessible route connecting levels not connected by an elevator. Such stairs are required to meet the ANSI requirements since they will be used by people with particular disabilities for whom steps are easier to traverse than ramps. See page 2.17 for further discussion of stairs along accessible routes.

12

Protruding Objects. The corridor space is an accessible route and like all accessible routes and maneuvering areas, it must be free of hazardous protruding objects that project from walls and posts and are dangerous to someone who is inobservant or a person with a visual impairment. See ANSI 4.4 Protruding Objects and page 2.18.

13

Drinking Fountains and Water Coolers. Where drinking fountains or water coolers are provided, 50 percent on each floor, or at least one, must be on an accessible route and comply with ANSI 4.15.

14

Doors to Covered Units. Doors to adaptable (or covered) dwelling units must meet ANSI 4.13 on the exterior or public and common use side, but need only meet Guidelines Requirement Three: Usable Doors on the inside. See Chapter 3: "Usable Doors."

15

Parking. Where parking is provided on a multifamily building site, accessible parking spaces on an accessible route are required for residents and visitors. To comply with the Guidelines, such spaces must meet the ANSI 4.6 specifications for parking. The accessible parking that serves a particular building should be located on the shortest possible accessible circulation route to an accessible entrance of the building.

16

Van Parking. The Guidelines do not require special van parking, but they do require headroom over passenger loading zones for vans. ANSI accessible parking spaces, when located in parking garages, may or may not have sufficient headroom to accommodate vans. Also, the 60-inch access aisle specified in ANSI is not wide enough for vans with side-mounted lifts. For these reasons, it is recommended, where accessible parking is located in garages not having headroom equal to that required by ANSI at loading zones, additional supplemental designated van parking spaces be placed outdoors and furnished with an 8-foot (96 inches) wide access aisle and an accessible route to the garage or other entrances of the building.

17

Laundry Rooms. Where laundry rooms are provided for common use of residents, at least one of each type of appliance provided in each laundry area must be accessible, see ANSI 4.32.6. Note, however, front-loading machines are not required. The accessible route into the room must adjoin a clear floor space to permit a person using a wheelchair to make a parallel or forward approach (see page 5.5) to at least one of each type of appliance, i.e., washing machines, dryers, and soap dispensers. If related features are provided in laundry rooms, such as wash sinks, tables, and storage, at least one of each type must be accessible and comply with applicable ANSI specifications. See page 2.26.

18

Toilet Rooms, Bathrooms, Bathing Facilities, and Shower Rooms. Where toilet rooms and bathing facilities are provided for public use or common use of residents, at least one fixture of each type provided must be accessible per room. See page 2.28 and ANSI 4.22. If related features are provided, such as lockers, at least one of each type must be accessible and comply with applicable ANSI specifications including 4.2 Space Allowances and Reach Ranges, 4.25 Controls and Operating Mechanisms, and 4.23 Storage.

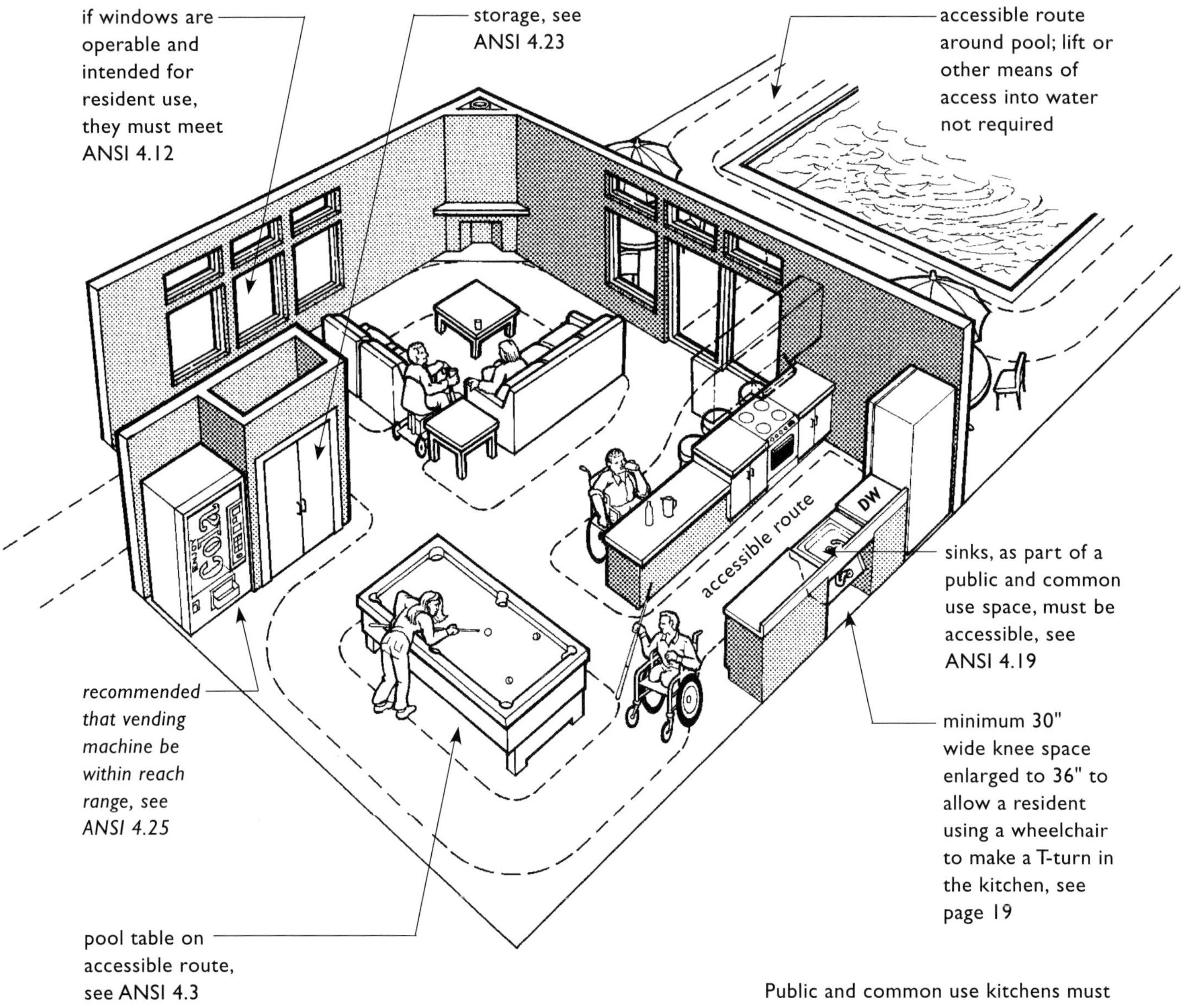

Accessible Elements and Features of a Public and Common Use Clubhouse

Public and common use kitchens must be usable and at least meet the requirements in the Guidelines for kitchens. If preferred, the requirements for kitchens in ANSI 4.32 could be followed.

Notes in italic type are recommendations only and are not required by ANSI or the Guidelines. All recommended features are helpful to people with and without disabilities.

Selected Topics on Accessible Public and Common Use Spaces and Facilities

The following is additional explanatory text and illustrations describing selected topics related to accessible public and common use spaces and facilities covered by the Guidelines.

Accessible Route

An accessible route is a path that is at least 36 inches wide, smooth, as level as possible, and without hazards or obstructions. Within the boundary of the site, an accessible walk or route on a site must connect public transportation stops, accessible parking spaces, accessible passenger loading zones, and public streets and sidewalks to accessible building entrances. Such accessible walks and routes are subject to site constraints discussed in Chapter 1: "Accessible Building Entrance on an Accessible Route." In addition, an accessible route must connect accessible buildings with public and common use site amenities. The accessible route links all accessible elements and features on a site and within a building, making it possible for people with a wide range of disabilities to maneuver safely and use a facility successfully.

Exterior accessible routes include but are not limited to parking access aisles, passenger loading zones, curb ramps, crosswalks at vehicular ways, walks, ramps, and lifts. See Chapter 1: "Accessible Building Entrance on an Accessible Route" for additional discussion of accessible routes on sites. As the accessible route continues into a building, it may include corridors, doorways, floors, ramps, elevators, lifts, and clear floor space at fixtures. Accessible routes also may include sky walks, tunnels, garages, and parts of many public and common use spaces. ANSI 4.3 contains complete technical specifications for accessible routes, including width, headroom, surface texture, slope, changes in level, doors, and egress in emergencies.

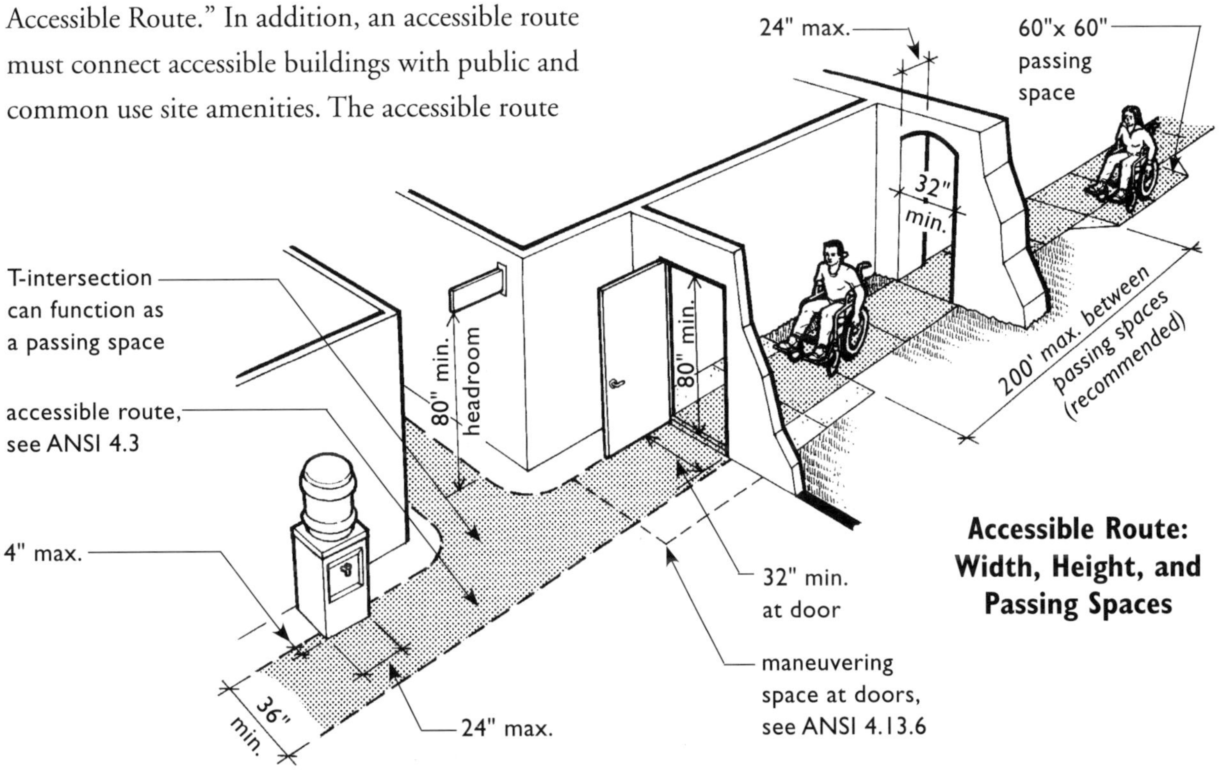

Accessible Route: Width, Height, and Passing Spaces

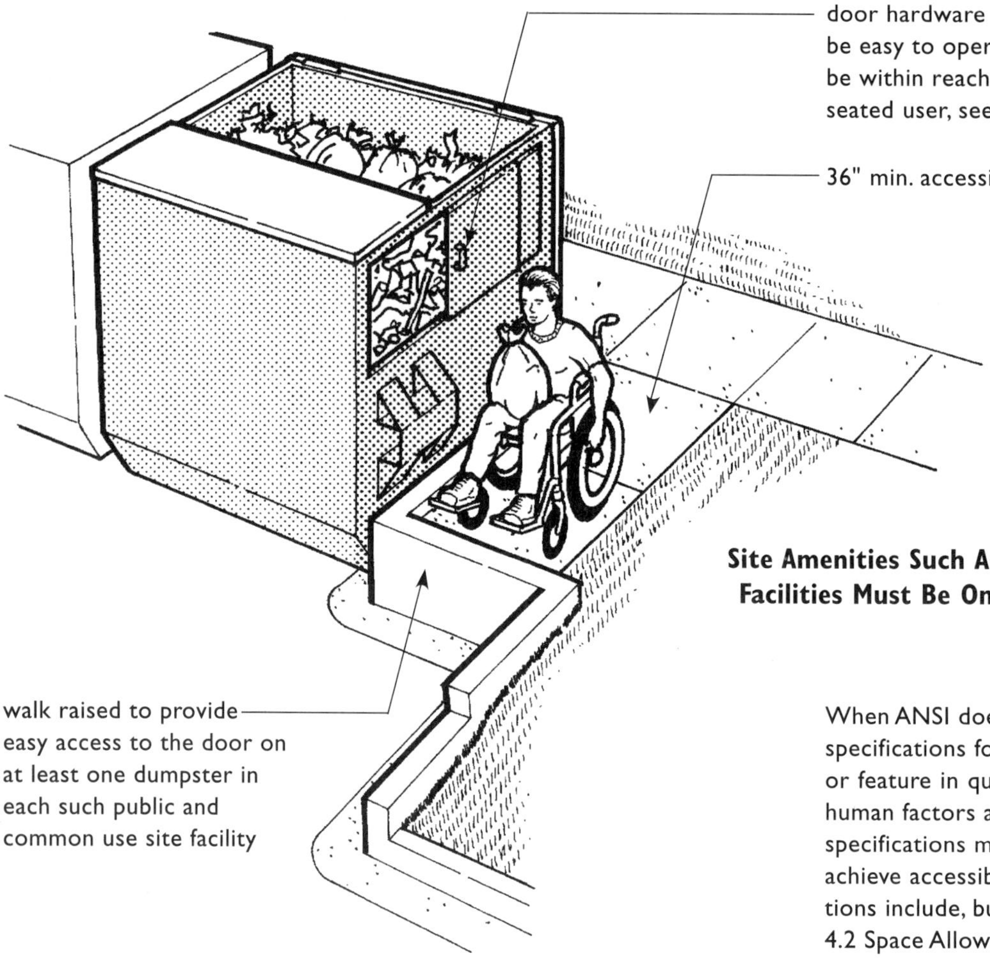

Site Amenities Such As Tenant-Use Trash Facilities Must Be On Accessible Route

When ANSI does not contain specifications for the specific facility or feature in question, related human factors and performance specifications must be used to achieve accessibility. Such specifications include, but are not limited to, 4.2 Space Allowances and Reach Ranges, 4.3 Accessible Route, 4.4 Protruding Objects, 4.5 Ground and Floor Surfaces, and 4.25 Controls and Operating Mechanisms.

Walks Exempt from Accessible Route Requirements

On-grade walks between separate buildings containing only covered dwelling units are not required to be accessible. However, if the grade of walks between buildings containing only dwelling units does not exceed 8.33%, it is recommended that these walks meet the requirement for accessible routes and not be interrupted by steps. If these walks are made accessible, handrails will not be required on any part of the walk where the slope is between 5% and 8.33%.

It is important to note, however, that if walks between buildings containing only covered dwelling units are also part of a required accessible route–for example, if the walk serves as the route to a common use facility located nearby--then the route would be required to be accessible. (See page 1.8, "Accessible Routes and Walks Between Accessible Buildings and Site Facilities.")

Stairs and Accessible Routes

By definition and ANSI 4.3.8 Changes in Level, a stair can never be part of an accessible route, i.e., a stair can never interrupt or be part of the path of an accessible route. Elevators, ramps, and mechanical lifts, however, can be part of an accessible route. In view of the fact that some users have difficulty walking on ramps and are safer using appropriately designed stairs, it is always best that stairs be placed adjacent to or nearby ramps that are used to provide an accessible route between levels not served by elevators.

The ANSI and the Guidelines "Application" charts both state "stairs on accessible routes connecting levels not connected by an elevator" must comply with ANSI 4.9 Stairs. However, the preamble to the Guidelines states "stairs are subject to the ANSI Standard only when they are located **along** an accessible route not served by an elevator." Therefore, "along" and "on" are interpreted to have the same meaning, especially given the definition of an accessible route that states a stair cannot be part of an accessible route. Thus, "along" and "on" are intended to mean either "adjacent to" or "nearby."

Nearby in this case means within the same area or within sight of the accessible route or at an unseen location indicated by directional signage. See the example in the illustration below.

In buildings that do not have elevator(s), the Guidelines do not require stairs serving floors above or below the ground floor to meet the ANSI standard. It should be noted, however, that any applicable state or local law or code that sets a stricter standard, may require the stairs to be accessible.

For example, if the local building code has adopted the 1986 ANSI A117.1 Standard, then ANSI 4.9.1 would be applicable. ANSI 4.9.1 states, "Stairs that are required as a means of egress and stairs between floor levels not connected by an elevator shall comply with 4.9." Because most stairs in nonelevator buildings are provided either to connect floors not connected by an elevator or are stairs required as a means of egress, this would mean that virtually all stairs, including monumental or decorative stairs, would have to comply. Therefore, it is important to check state or local laws for their applicability to stairs.

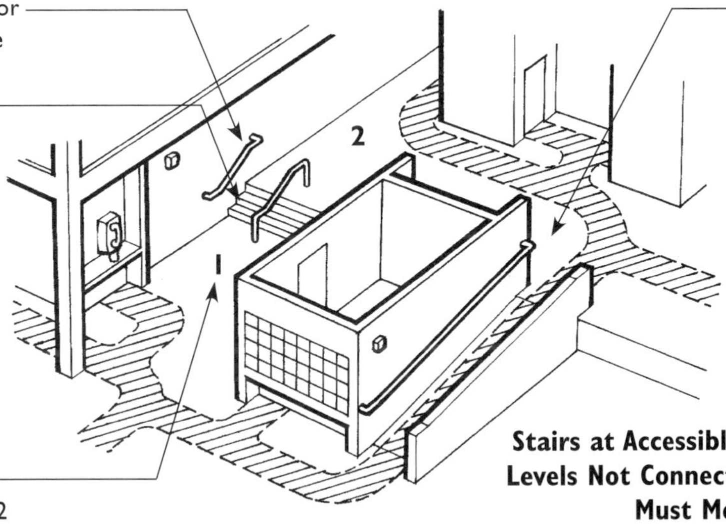

Stairs at Accessible Routes Between Levels Not Connected By an Elevator Must Meet ANSI

Protruding Objects

Many people with visual impairments use a long cane for guidance. The cane is used to follow a "shoreline" such as the edge of a sidewalk or a curb or, indoors, the baseboard of a wall. The cane, when swept ahead of the user, also detects obstacles in the path. Objects which protrude from walls or hang from overhead are not detectable and are, therefore, hazardous because a person with a visual disability can not avoid running into them.

Detectable items are obstacles that can be maneuvered around.

There must always be a 36-inch wide accessible route around any obstacle. Large wall-mounted items such as fire extinguishers and telephone enclosures must be recessed, set in alcoves, or designed so they have structures extending close to the floor, no higher than 27 inches, and within the long cane detectable area.

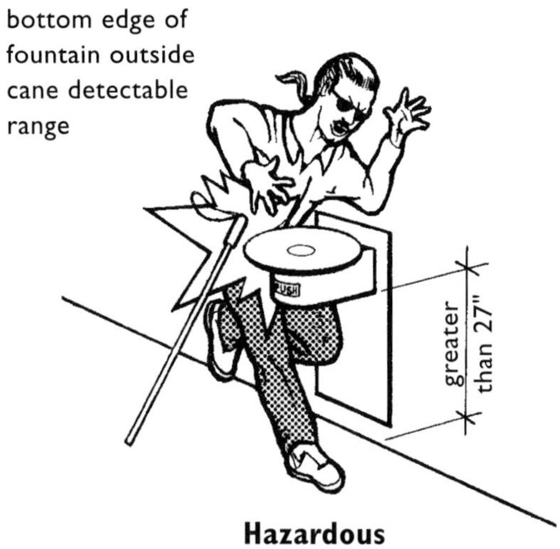

Hazardous Protruding Objects

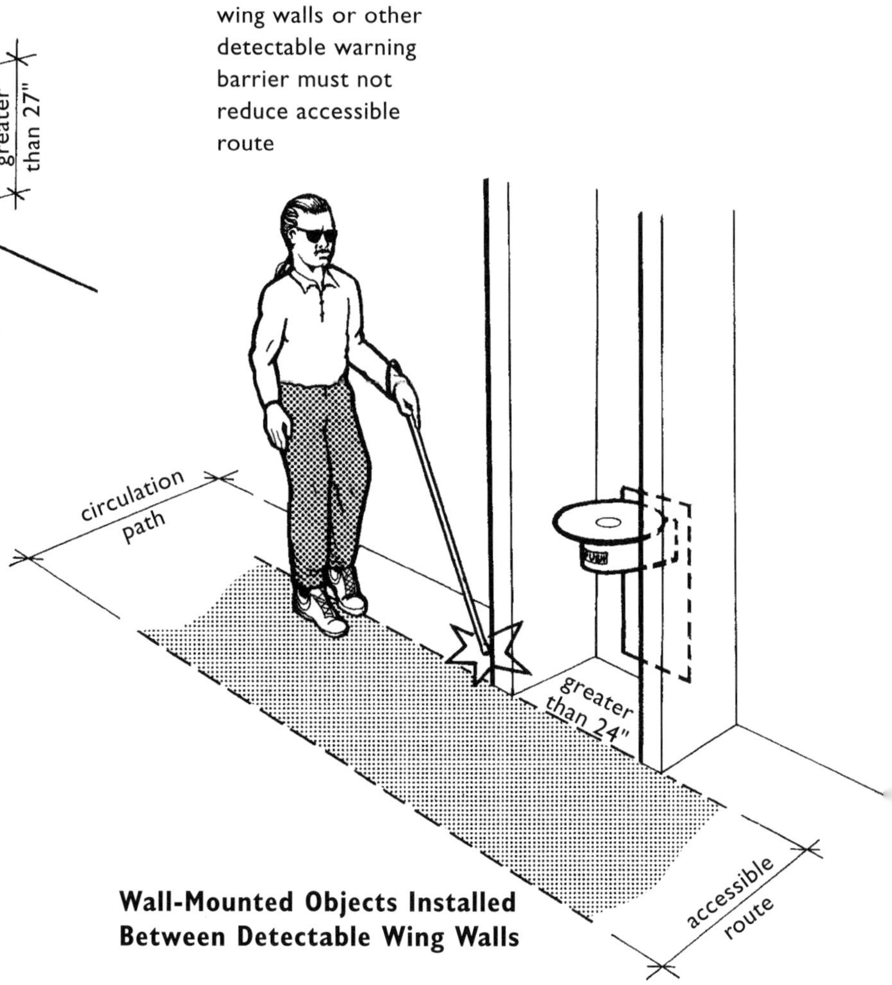

Wall-Mounted Objects Installed Between Detectable Wing Walls

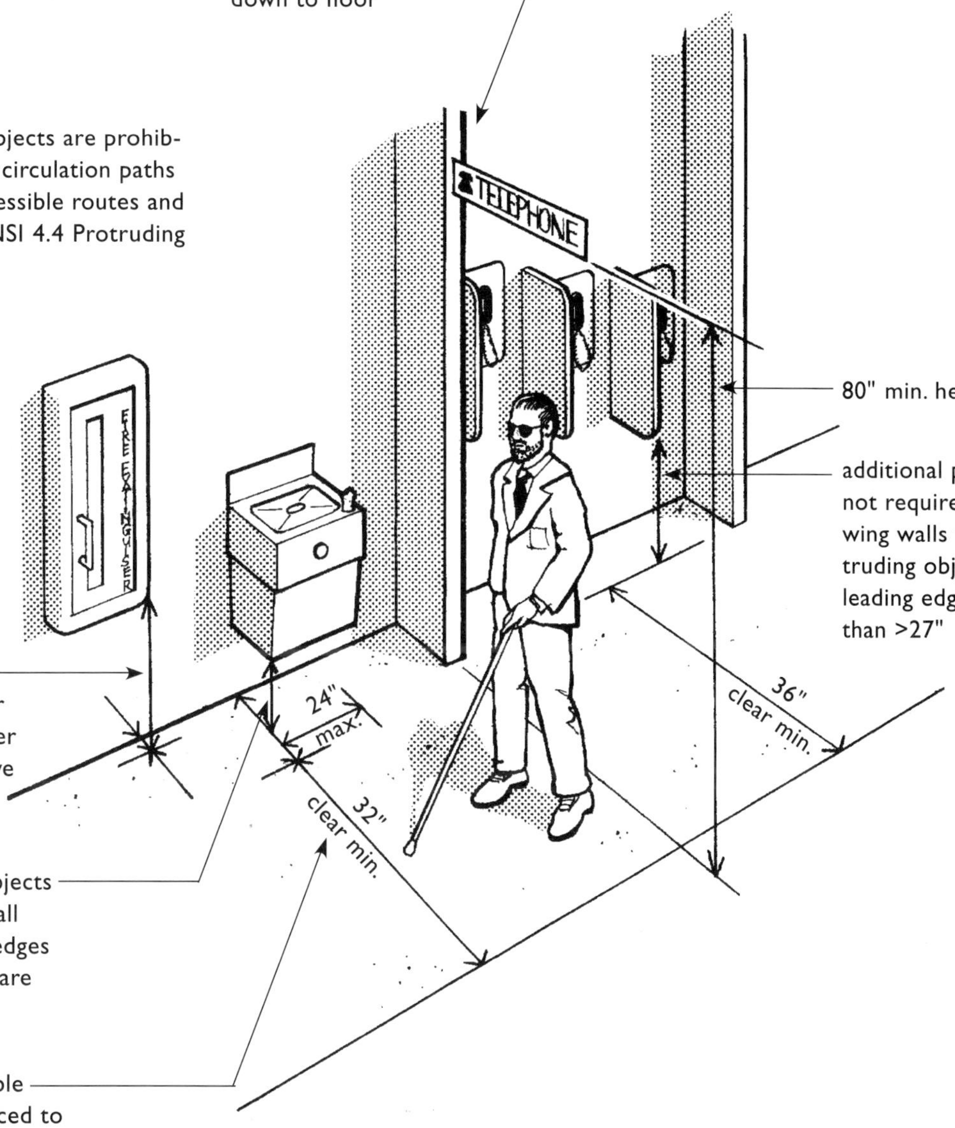

Wall-Hung and Other Commonly Found Items in Public and Common Use Spaces Located so They Are Not Hazardous Protruding Objects

Accessible Parking on an Accessible Route

When parking is provided on a residential site, accessible parking spaces on an accessible route must be provided for residents and visitors. Accessible parking spaces must meet the requirements for parking in ANSI 4.6 and be located on the shortest possible accessible circulation route to an accessible entrance, subject to site considerations in Chapter 1.

Access Aisles. Parking spaces must be wide enough to allow people using wheelchairs or mobility aids to move between cars and to enter cars or vans. Accessible parking spaces must be at least 96 inches wide and have an adjacent access aisle that is 60 inches wide. This 60-inch access aisle is regarded as a minimum, and although it is adequate for people using wheelchairs who can transfer into and out of cars, it is too narrow for safe and comfortable use for people who drive vans. The Guidelines do not require nor specify the size of van-accessible access aisles. The only nationally accepted design standard that contains such a specification is the Americans with Disabilities Act Accessibility Guidelines (ADAAG), which specify that a van parking access aisle must be at least 96 inches wide and is required at sales and rental offices. See page 2.6.

Curb Ramps. Curb ramps are transitions between roads, parking areas, access aisles, and sidewalks that allow a pedestrian route to remain accessible to people who use wheelchairs and other mobility aids, see ANSI 4.7. Curb ramps are a necessity for people with mobility impairments but are a hazard to people who are blind who use the curb as a "cue" to know when they are entering the street. The ANSI Standard requires a texture on curb ramp surfaces to make them detectable. These textures often do not provide enough of a cue and a person with a visual impairment may inadvertently enter the street. Locating curb ramps out of the usual line of pedestrian flow and "shorelines" (edge between sidewalk and grass or other cane detectable surface) is one solution to this problem. See drawing at the bottom of page 2.22.

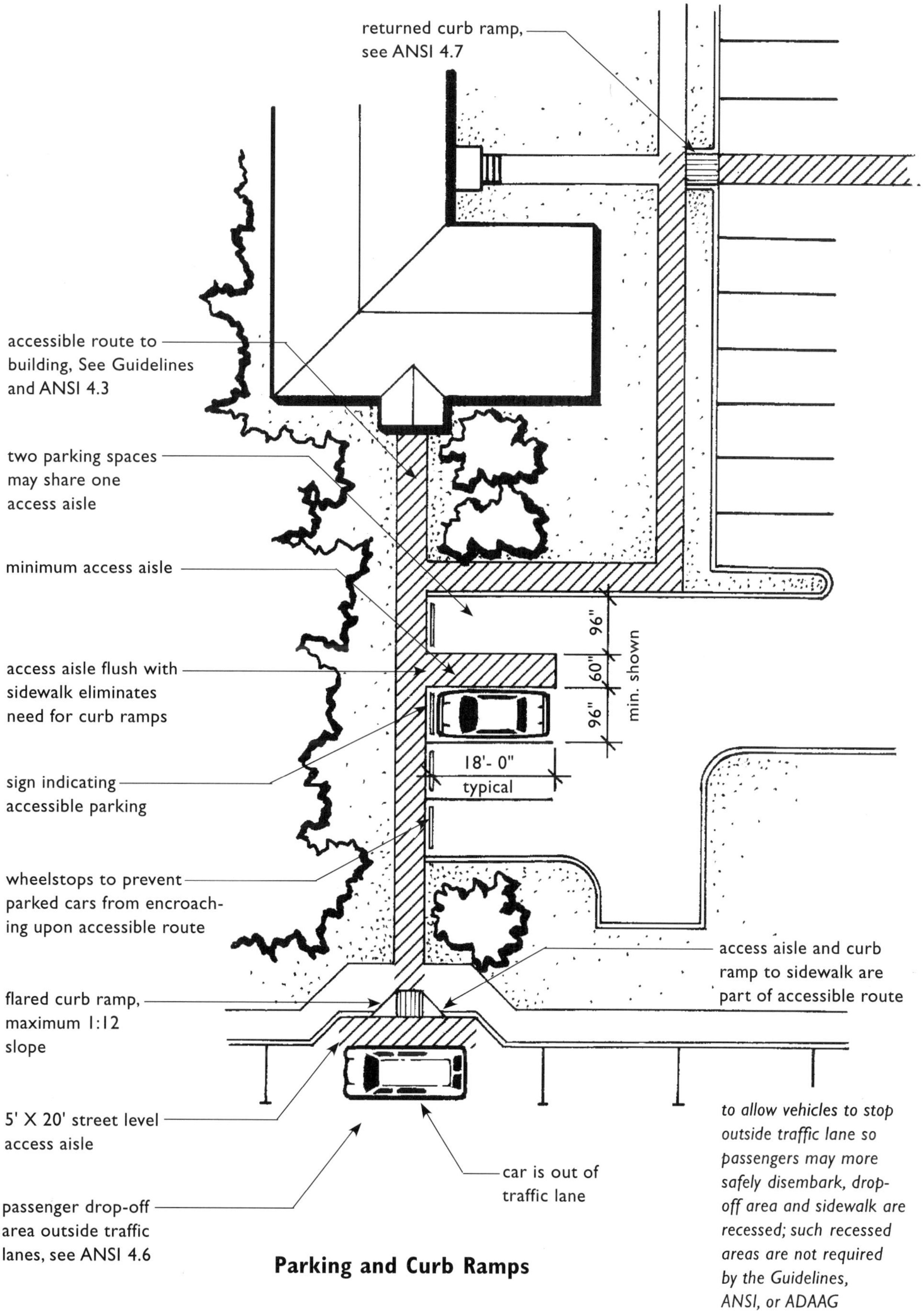

Parking and Curb Ramps

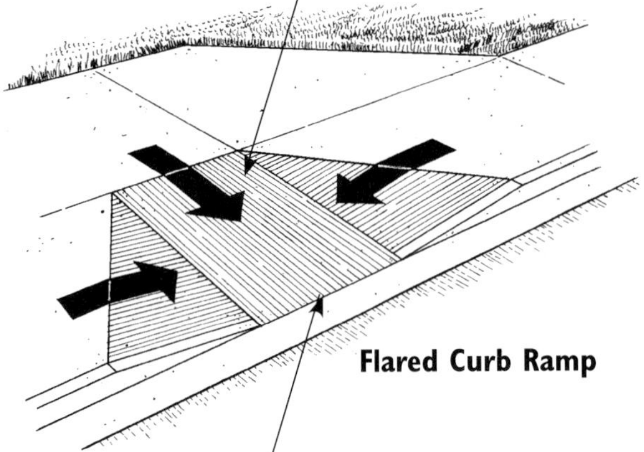

Flared Curb Ramp

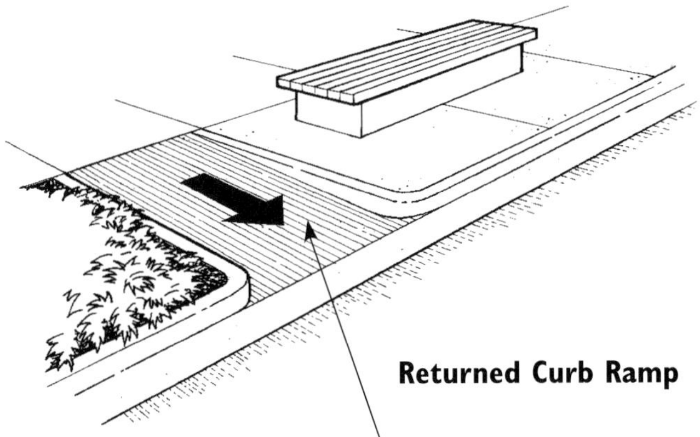

Returned Curb Ramp

The "flared curb" ramp is safest and allows people to enter the ramp directly or from a side angle. This design is best used where pedestrians are likely to walk across the ramp.

The "returned curb" ramp has the curb "turned back" the full depth of the ramp. This design can be a tripping hazard to pedestrians and should be used only where adjacent plant beds or other features will prevent approach from the sides.

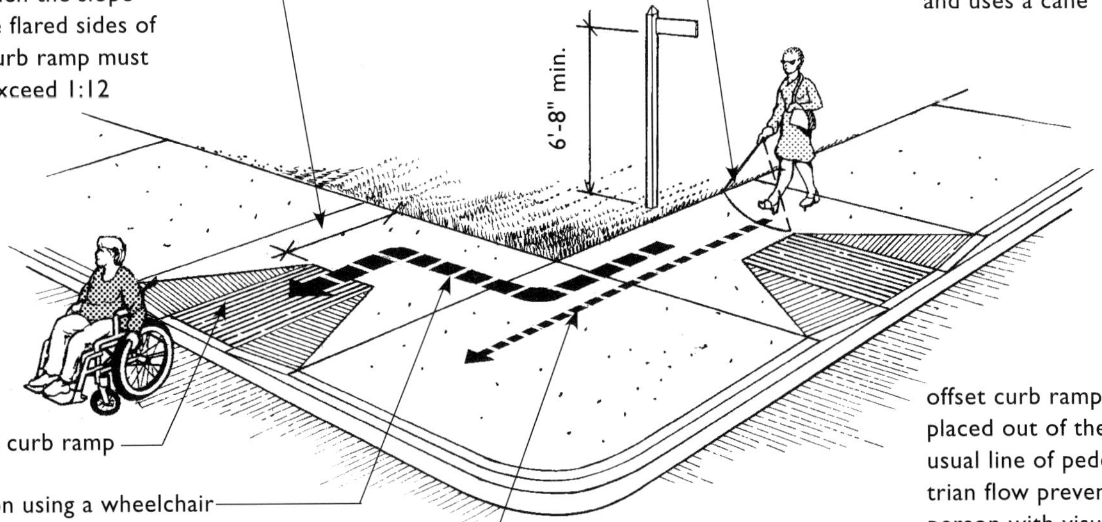

Offset Curb Ramps

Types of Curb Ramps

Resident Accessible Parking

Minimum Number. The Guidelines provide that a minimum of two percent of the parking spaces serving covered dwelling units be made accessible and be located on an accessible route. For example, if 100 units are covered, then a minimum of two accessible spaces is required.

100 x 2% = 2

If the development provides different types of parking, such as surface parking, garage, or covered spaces, at least one of each must be made accessible. Since many people with disabilities require more time to get in and out of vehicles, covered parking is especially important; therefore, where covered parking is provided, such covered parking must include at least one, and preferably more than one, accessible parking space. Accessible covered surface parking may be substituted for garage parking if the latter is not accessible. While the total number of spaces required to be accessible is only two percent, at least one space for each type of parking must be made accessible even if this number exceeds two percent.

Many state or local codes may require a greater percentage of accessible parking spaces for both residents and visitors. Builders/developers must follow the local or state code whenever it is stricter. Note also that accessible spaces benefit a wide range of users, residents and visitors with disabilities, residents carrying packages, families with strollers, movers, and delivery personnel.

Requested Parking Spaces. If buyers or renters request an accessible space at the time of first sale or rental, it may be necessary to provide additional accessible parking spaces if the two percent are already reserved. These must be offered on the same terms and with the full range of choices offered other residents, i.e., surface, garage, or covered parking. If the spaces that make up the two percent count are not being used by residents with disabilities, such space(s) may be moved to a resident requested location near a building or unit entrance. These new parking spaces must be on an accessible route including curb ramps.

Number of Accessible Parking Spaces

For Residents
- 2% of parking spaces serving covered dwelling units
- minimum of one at each site amenity

For Visitors, When Visitor Parking Is Provided
- a sufficient number of spaces to provide access to grade level entrances of covered multifamily dwellings
- minimum of one at sales/rental office

Parking at Public and Common Use Facilities

If parking spaces are available at a facility, such as a swimming pool, then at least one accessible parking space must be provided and be on an accessible route. A specific number or percentage of spaces is not defined in the Guidelines; however, to provide equitable use of facilities by people with disabilities, parking should be provided in accordance with the local code, or, at a minimum, at least one accessible parking space must be provided at each facility serving buildings containing covered dwelling units.

The Guidelines allow a vehicular route as an alternative to an accessible pedestrian route between dwellings and accessible public or common use site amenities when the site conditions are deemed extreme or where other physical barriers or legal restrictions prevent the installation of an accessible pedestrian route. See page 1.9 for additional discussion of "Use of Vehicles for Access to Site Amenities." When use of a vehicle is the only means for a person with a mobility disability to reach a facility, it is recommended that more than one accessible parking space on an accessible route to the facility be provided. Since there is no accessible pedestrian route, it is important to provide ample parking at such public and common use facilities that may be accessed only via a vehicular route. If a person who uses a wheelchair must drive to a site facility, he or she should not be further inconvenienced and frustrated by finding the only accessible space already occupied.

Visitor Accessible Parking

If visitor parking is provided, accessible parking spaces for visitors also must be provided. The Guidelines do not specify a number or percentage of accessible visitor spaces, but provide that such parking must be "sufficient" to provide access to grade level entrances of covered multifamily dwellings. To allow people with disabilities to visit and have access to such entrances on an equitable basis, it is recommended that accessible visitor spaces be dispersed throughout the site, and that several spaces be provided at a building with large numbers of dwelling units.

Impractical Sites

Where site conditions make it impractical to provide an accessible route from the designated general parking area to a building containing covered dwelling units, accessible parking spaces at a minimum of two percent of the covered dwelling units must be provided on an accessible route to the entrance. It is strongly recommended that every effort be made to provide this parking from an adjacent location. If visitor parking is provided, there also must be accessible parking spaces on an accessible route for use by visitors. See Chapter 1: "Accessible Building Entrance on an Accessible Route," and the illustration on page 1.50 of that chapter.

Clearances for Covered Parking

If a project provides detached parking garages for assignment or rental to its tenants, it is considered public and common use parking. In the "Supplemental Questions and Answers," item 14 (see Appendix), it is suggested that at least two percent of the garages should be at least 14'-2" wide and the passage door for the vehicle should be at least 10'-0" wide. The width of such garages would be adequate for cars, but to provide sufficient space for a van, it is recommended that the width be increased to between 16 and 18 feet. The door width of the garage could remain the same.

Neither the Guidelines nor ANSI give specifications for vertical clearance in parking garages or at other sheltered parking to accommodate vans. However, ANSI does give specifications for vertical clearance of 108 inches at accessible passenger loading zones. The ADAAG specifies 98 inches of vertical clearance for van parking and 114 inches of clearance at accessible passenger loading zones. The dimensions shown below are a compilation of available figures from commonly accepted accessibility standards that may be used to assist the building industry when planning to provide covered van parking. Such parking is not required by the Guidelines nor ANSI.

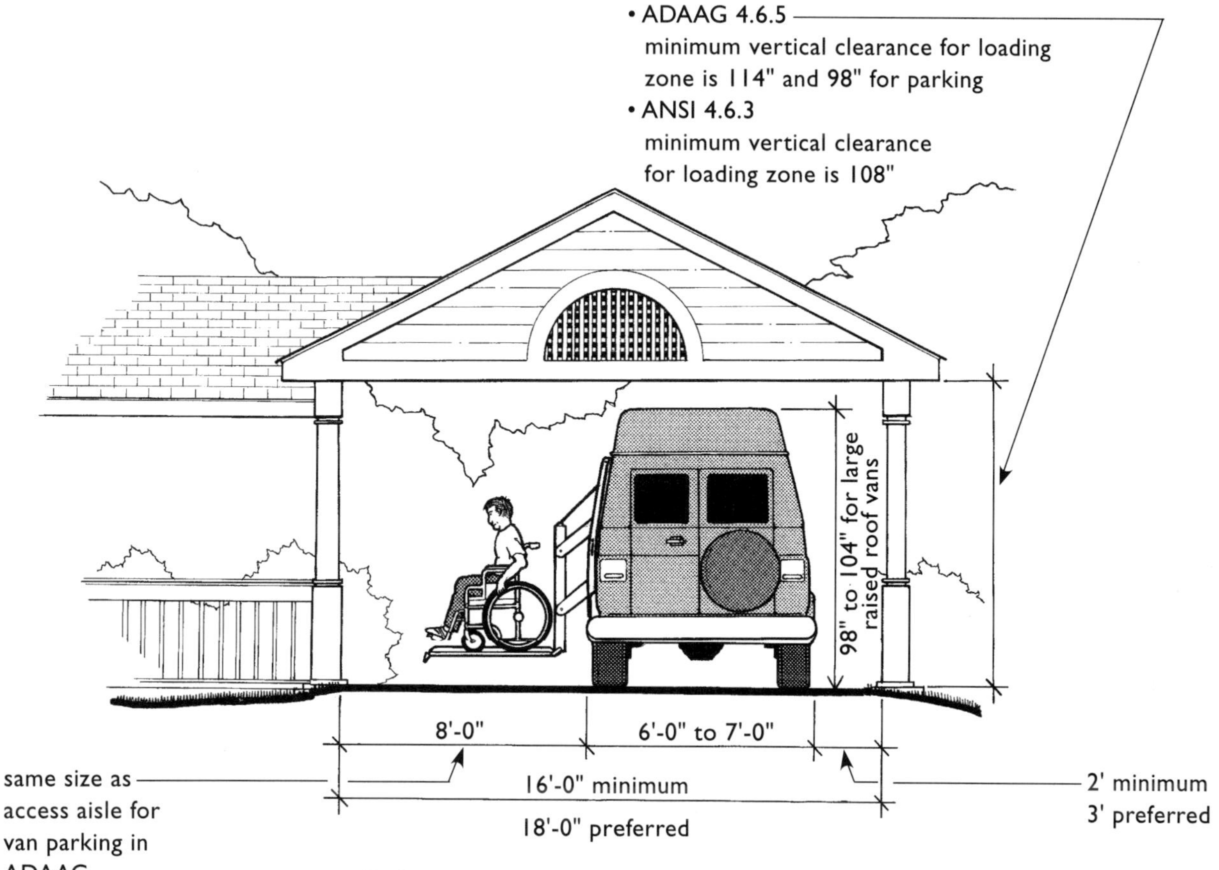

Reference Dimensions for Vertical and Horizontal Clearances for Raised Roof Van with Lift Extended

Laundry Rooms

Where common use laundry rooms are provided, at least one of each type of appliance provided in each laundry area must be accessible and be on an accessible route, see ANSI 4.32.6. Such appliances include washing machines, dryers, soap dispensers, and any related features such as wash sinks, tables, and storage areas.

Where there are laundry rooms that serve each floor of an elevator building, each laundry room must be accessible. Likewise, where there is one laundry room on a ground floor in each building, each must be accessible. In the rare situation where there is a laundry room on the ground floor of a building and another located in the basement, it is acceptable to have only the ground floor laundry room accessible.

Front-loading washing machines are not required in common use laundry rooms if management, upon request, provides assistive devices (reachers) to enable a resident to use a top-loading washer. However, for people who use wheelchairs, front-loading washers generally are easier to reach into than top-loading machines.

Top-loading machines with rear-mounted controls should not be installed on elevated pads that place the top of the cabinet and the controls beyond the reach range of a seated user. Dryers with either side-hinged or bottom-hinged doors may be installed in public and common use laundry rooms. Dryers with side-hinged doors usually are easier to reach into than those with bottom-hinged doors which, when open, obstruct floor space in front of the dryer.

The washer and dryer must have controls (including coin slots) within the reach range of a seated user. Since the Guidelines permit the installation of stacked washers and dryers, this same requirement for controls applies to at least one of these stacked units. Controls should be operable with one hand and not require tight grasping, pinching, or twisting of the wrist. If they can be operated with a closed fist they would work well for most users. See ANSI 4.25 Controls and Operating Mechanisms.

It is possible that management will be requested to provide, in addition to the grabbers, a knob turner that would allow someone with limited grasp to operate washer/dryer controls more easily. See Product Resource List in Appendix A, under "Assistive Devices" for manufacturers that carry knob turners in addition to reachers/grabbers.

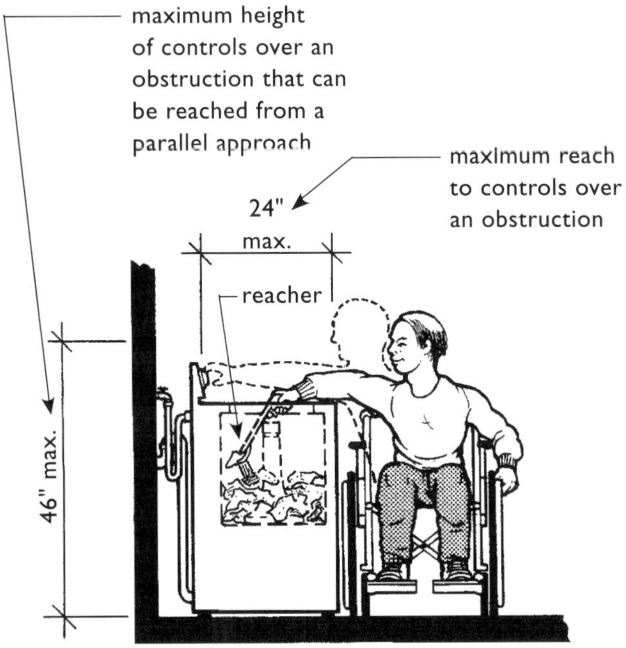

Use of Top-Loading Machine Made Possible With Assistance of a Mechanical Reacher

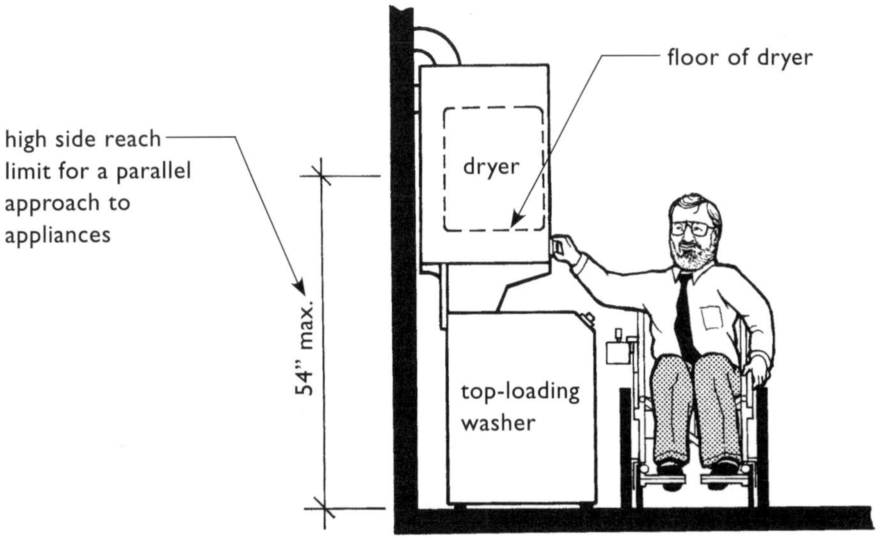

Stacked Washer/Dryer Unit with Dryer and All Controls Within Reach Range of Seated User

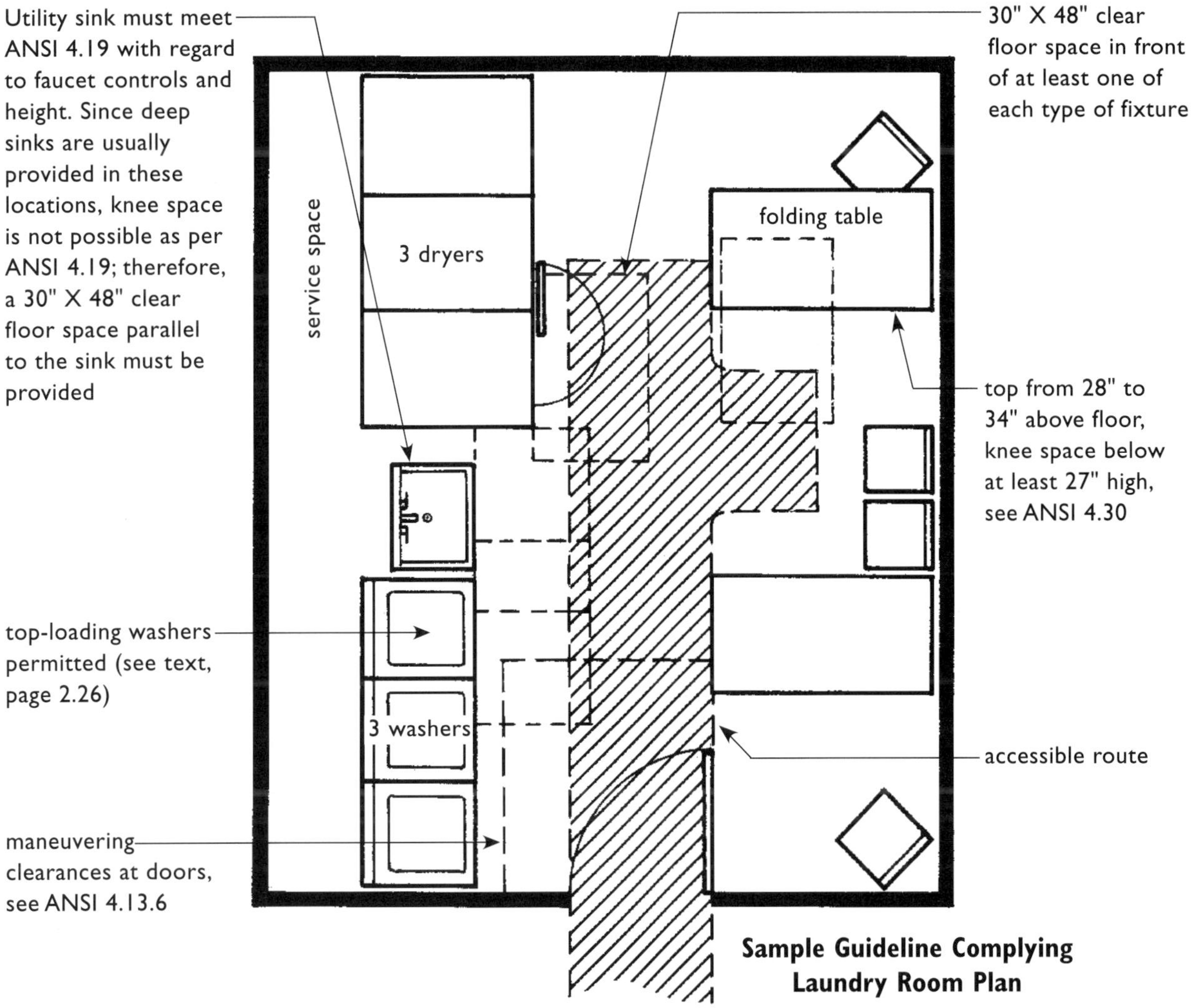

Sample Guideline Complying Laundry Room Plan

Toilet Rooms, Bathrooms, Bathing Facilities, and Shower Rooms

The Guidelines require that all toilet rooms and bathing facilities in all public and common use facilities must be on an accessible route and at least one of each fixture type in each room or space must be accessible. The ANSI Standard addresses the types of fixtures and their mounting heights, the types of controls, and the amount of clear floor space required at accessible fixtures. These specifications, combined with clearances for doors and turning spaces for wheelchairs, determine the minimum toilet room requirements. See ANSI 4.22 Toilet Rooms, Bathrooms, Bathing Facilities, and Shower Rooms.

Toilet and bathing facilities that are required to be accessible include shower/dressing rooms located on the site for use of residents and their guests in addition to such spaces as common use public toilet rooms. Although neither the Guidelines nor the ANSI contain specifications for shower/dressing rooms, such as those which may serve a swimming pool, the applicable sections of ANSI for similar components apply in these spaces and must be provided.

Three Types of Toilet Stalls. The ANSI Standard allows considerable flexibility in the size and layout of toilet rooms. There are three types of accessible toilet stalls for use by people with different disabilities. The narrow stall is 36 inches wide and varies in length, depending on whether it has a floor-mounted or wall-hung toilet fixture. This stall was originally intended for people who walk with difficulty, many of whom use crutches and braces and who need grab bars to steady themselves when sitting down and standing up. Such people generally have good upper body strength, a characteristic not always true of people who use wheelchairs. This 36-inch wide stall, although space efficient, does not work well for many people who use wheelchairs.

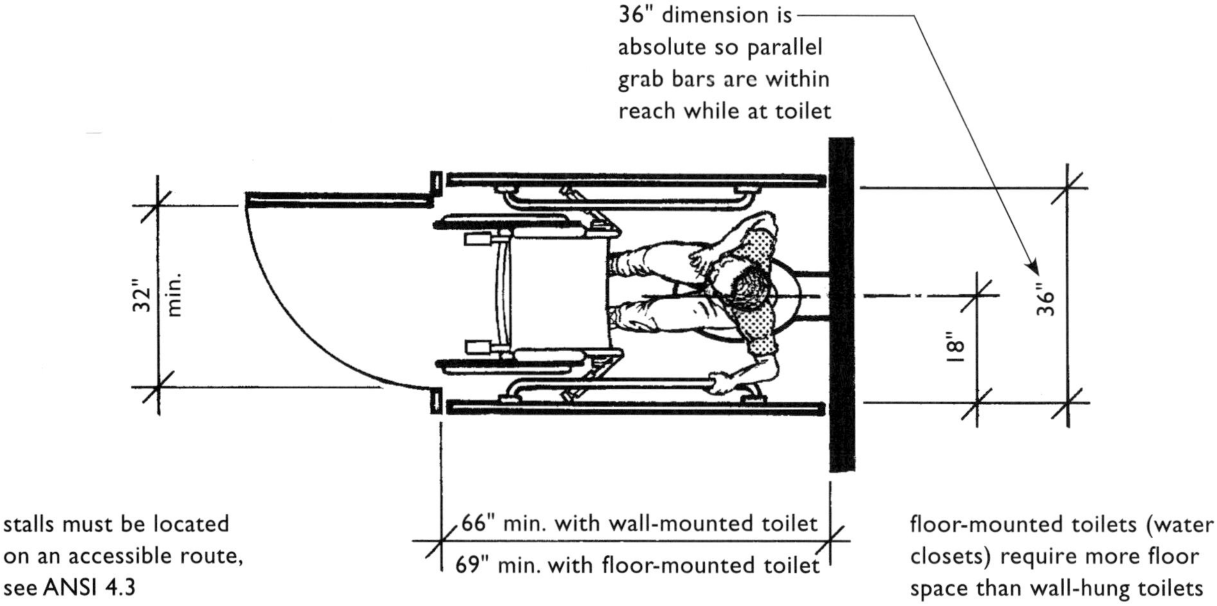

Alternate Stall 1: 36" Wide

The 60-inch wide stall is a significant improvement over the narrow one because it accommodates most users. The extra floor space allows a person who uses a wheelchair to maneuver into his/her own best position to transfer onto the toilet. It also allows space for an attendant, if needed, to assist a person with a disability.

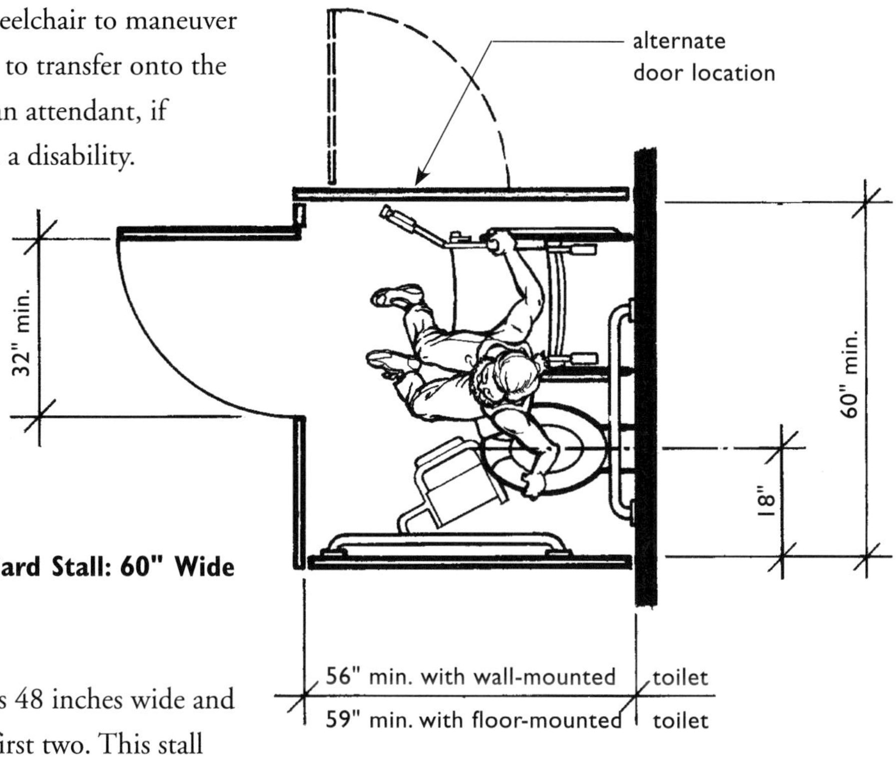

Standard Stall: 60" Wide

The third ANSI stall is 48 inches wide and is a compromise between the first two. This stall offers slightly more flexibility in the manner it is used by people with disabilities than the 36-inch wide stall. Since it cannot be used the same way as either of the others, it is limited in its usefulness. Often it is designed into renovation projects where sufficient space for the 60-inch stall is not available.

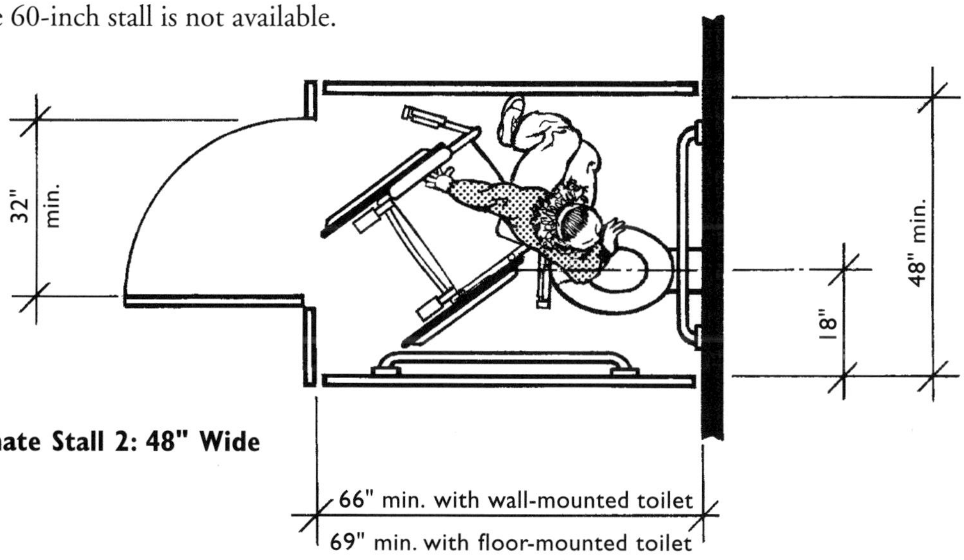

Alternate Stall 2: 48" Wide

Sample plans of toilet rooms and shower/dressing rooms are presented to offer examples of how fixtures and elements can be combined into modest efficient spaces that comply with the ANSI.

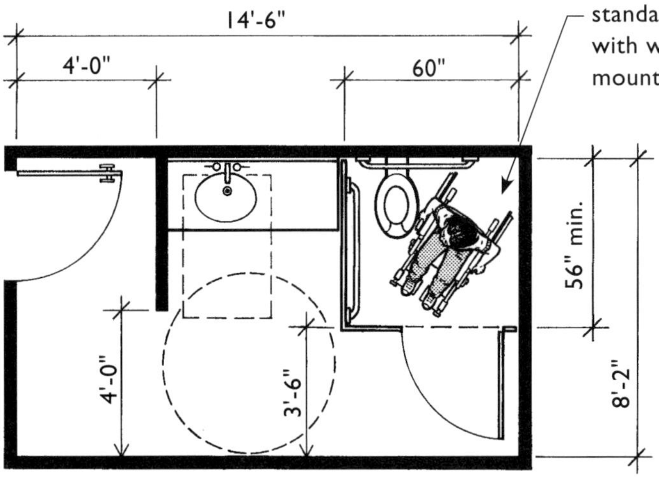

Small Toilet Room with Single Standard Stall
Scale 3/16"=1'-0"

By repositioning the partition layout, additional space can be added to the toilet compartment to provide more maneuvering space without adding additional square footage to the room.

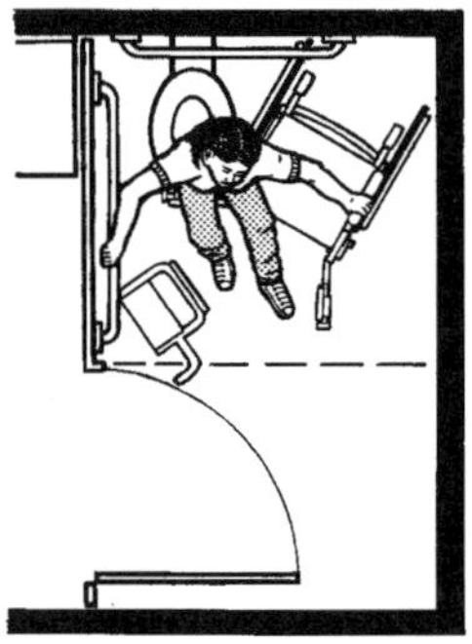

Standard Alcove or "End of Row" Stall
Scale 3/16"=1'-0"

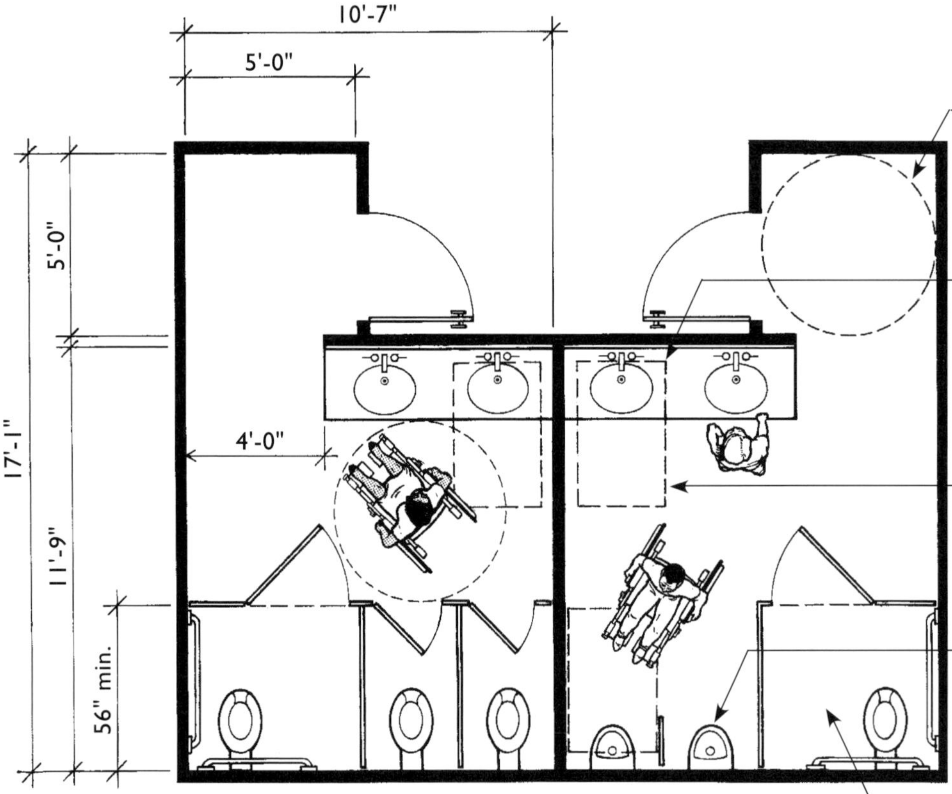

Larger Public and Common Use Toilet Room
Scale 3/16"=1'-0"

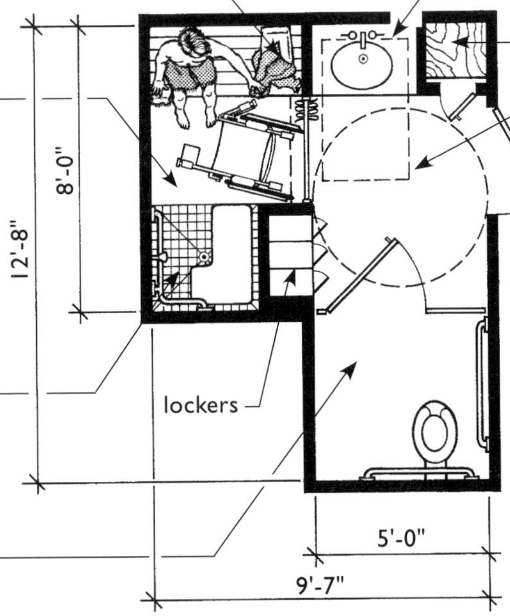

Some lockers must be accessible. When ANSI does not contain specifications for the specific facility or feature in question, related human factors and performance specifications must be used to achieve accessibility. Such specifications include, but are not limited to, 4.2 Space Allowances and Reach Ranges, 4.3 Accessible Route, 4.4 Protruding Objects, 4.5 Ground and Floor Surfaces, and 4.25 Controls and Operating Mechanisms.

Small Toilet/Dressing Room
with 36-Inch x 36-Inch Transfer Shower
Scale 3/16"=1'-0"

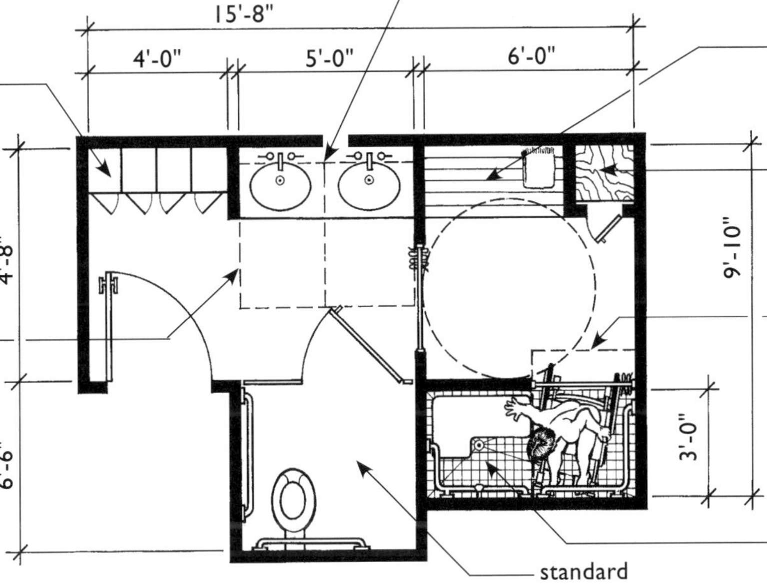

Small Toilet/Dressing Room
with Combination Roll-in/Transfer Shower
Scale 3/16"=1'-0"

Chapter Three:

Requirement 3

Usable Doors

3

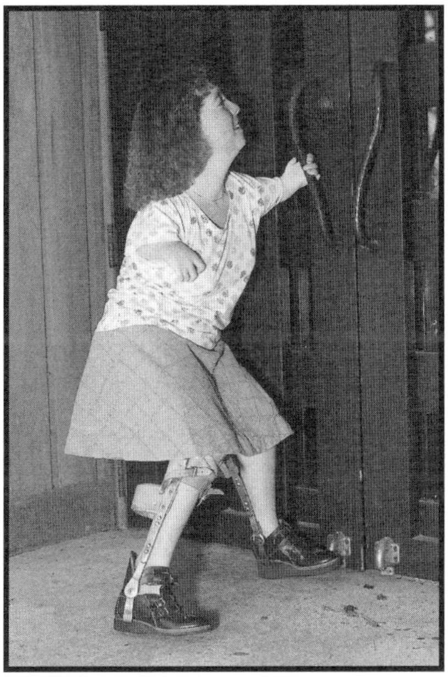

"...covered multifamily dwellings with a building entrance on an accessible route shall be designed in such a manner that all the doors designed to allow passage into and within all premisies are sufficiently wide to allow passage by handicapped persons in wheelchairs."

Fair Housing Act Regulations, 24 CFR 100.205

◆ **accessible doors** (in public and common use spaces and on public side of dwelling unit entry door)
- must provide 32" minimum clear width
- must meet ANSI 4.13 Doors

● **usable doors** (within interior of dwelling unit)
- must provide 32" nominal clear width (see page 3.5)
- have no additional requirements except low or no threshold, see Chapter Four: "Accessible Route Into and Through the Covered Unit"

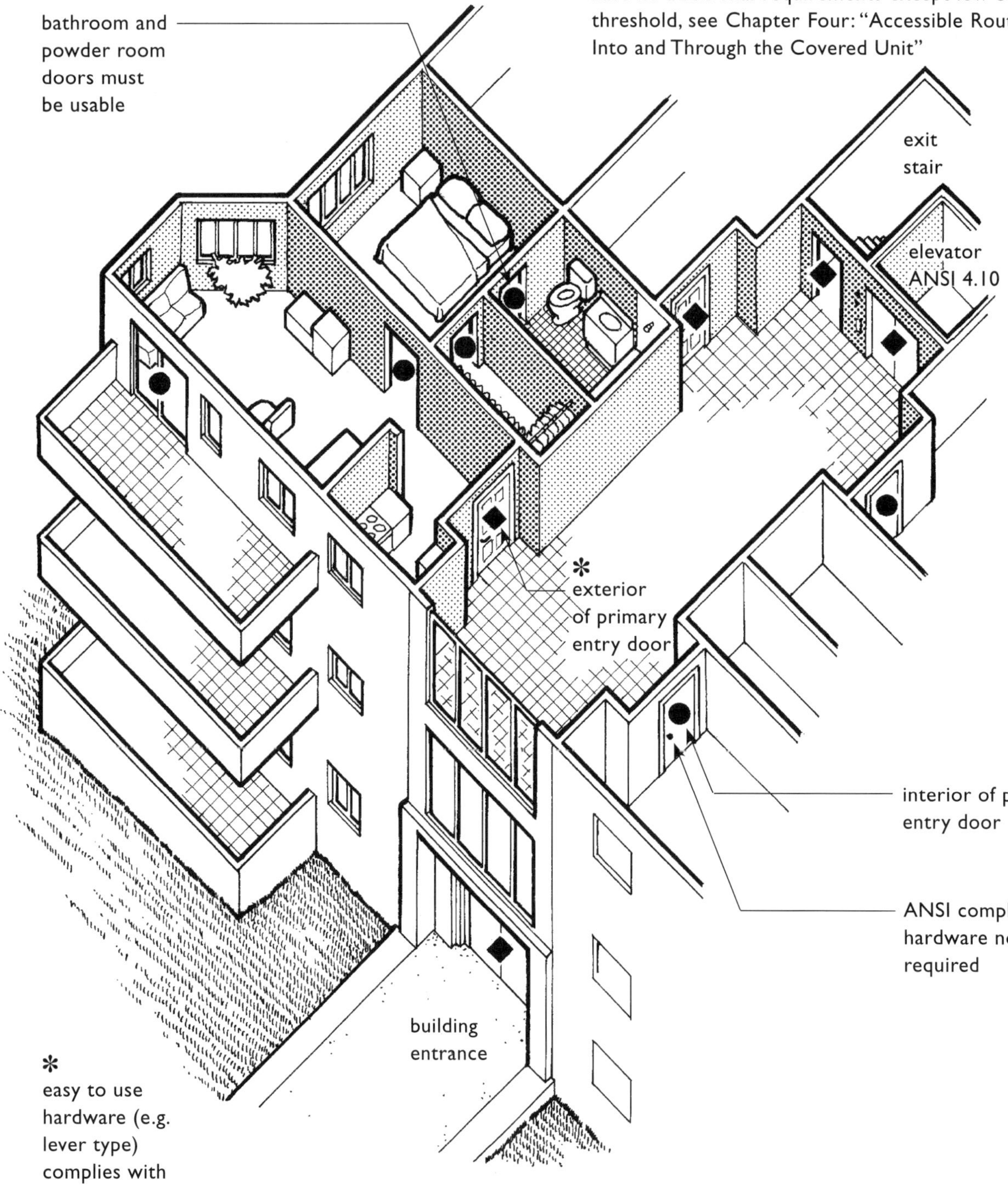

Accessible and Usable Doors in Buildings Containing Covered Dwelling Units

Introduction

The regulations for the Fair Housing Act state that **all** doors "designed to allow passage into and within all premises are sufficiently wide to allow passage by...persons in wheelchairs." The Fair Housing Act Guidelines (the Guidelines) apply the requirements to doors that are part of an accessible route in public and common use areas of multifamily housing developments, as well as doors into and within covered dwelling units.

The Fair Housing Act and the Guidelines cover all doors designed to allow passage into and within all premises. However, doors in public and common use areas and primary entry doors of covered dwelling units must meet more stringent requirements for accessibility than doors that are located inside each dwelling unit. Therefore, to clarify this difference, this chapter refers to doors in public and common use areas and primary entry doors of covered dwelling units as **accessible doors**. Doors which are interior to the dwelling unit and which are subject to less stringent requirements for accessibility are referred to as **usable doors.**

Accessible doors must meet the ANSI 4.13 requirements for clear width, maneuvering clearances, thresholds, hardware, and opening force. Accessible doors are:

1. Doors that are part of an accessible route in public and common use spaces. They include, but are not limited to, doors residents use to enter buildings and doors into and within clubhouses, public restrooms, laundry rooms, and rental offices.

2. Primary entry doors to covered dwelling units – exterior side only. Entry doors may open from a corridor or lobby or can be private individual entry doors accessed directly from the outside.

Usable doors are doors within the dwelling unit intended for user passage and must be usable in terms of clear opening width. Doors within the unit are not required to meet the ANSI 4.13 Doors requirements for maneuvering clearances, hardware, and opening force; but because an accessible route must be provided within the unit, thresholds must be low or nonexistent, see Chapter Four: "Accessible Route Into and Through the Covered Dwelling Unit."

Usable doors include all secondary exterior doors at dwelling units that open onto private decks, balconies, and patios. Usable doors also include all passage doors within the covered dwelling unit, such as doors between rooms, doors into walk-in closets, and doors into utility/storage rooms or rooms that contain washers and dryers. Not covered are doors to small closets such as linen closets which typically have shelves within easy reach. Also not covered are access doors to small mechanical closets dedicated specifically to furnaces or hot water heaters.

In addition, the Guidelines also require that usable doors be provided to areas of the dwelling that may not be accessible at the completion of construction, such as an unfinished basement or a garage attached to a single-story dwelling unit (in the latter case, another door is used for the accessible entrance). Usable doors at these locations will allow people with mobility impairments to modify their unit later to provide accessibility to these areas, such as installing a ramp from the dwelling unit into the garage. Usable doors also are important for people with walkers or crutches so they may have improved access to such areas.

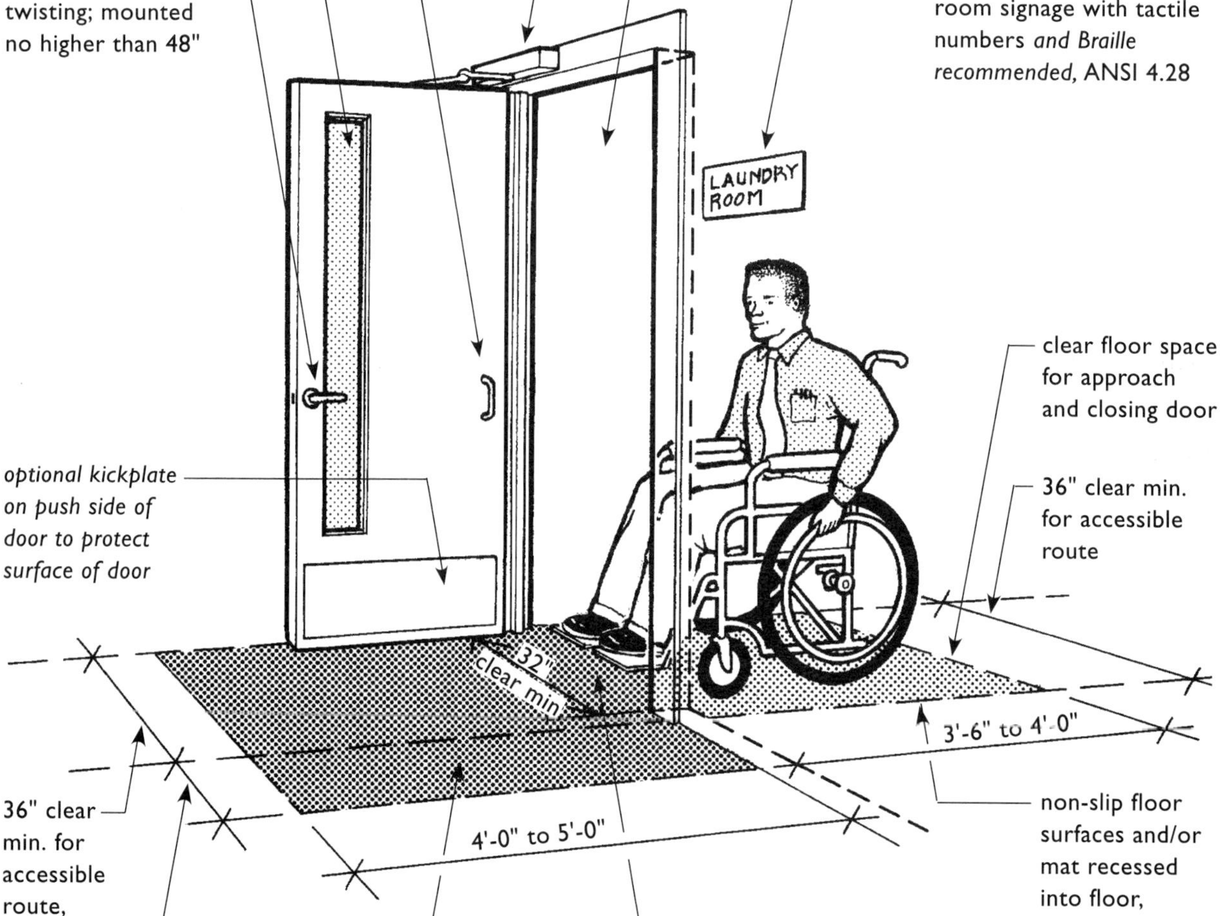

Features of ANSI Complying Accessible Doors

ANSI 4.13

Notes in italic type are recommendations only and are not required by ANSI or the Guidelines.

Doorway Width and Depth

Doorway Clear Opening

The commonly used hinged, folding, or sliding doors installed in the standard manner provide a passage width that is reduced by both the door standing in the doorway and door stops, if present. Thus, the available passage width is less than the size of the door.

Accessible doors in public and common use spaces and primary entry doors of dwelling units must provide a clear opening of **32 inches minimum**. This means the clear opening must not be less than 32 inches, but it may be more. The Guidelines allow **usable doors** (secondary exterior doors and doors that allow passage within the dwelling unit) to be a **nominal 32 inches** clear width. Usable doors are intended to provide 32 inches of clear width. But because of normal installation practices, adjacent conditions, variation in products such as hinges, and thicknesses of available materials, the doorway may vary from the 32-inch clear width by a nominal or small amount. Tolerances of 1/4 inch to 3/8 inch are considered an acceptable range for usable doors. This tolerance does not apply to accessible doors.

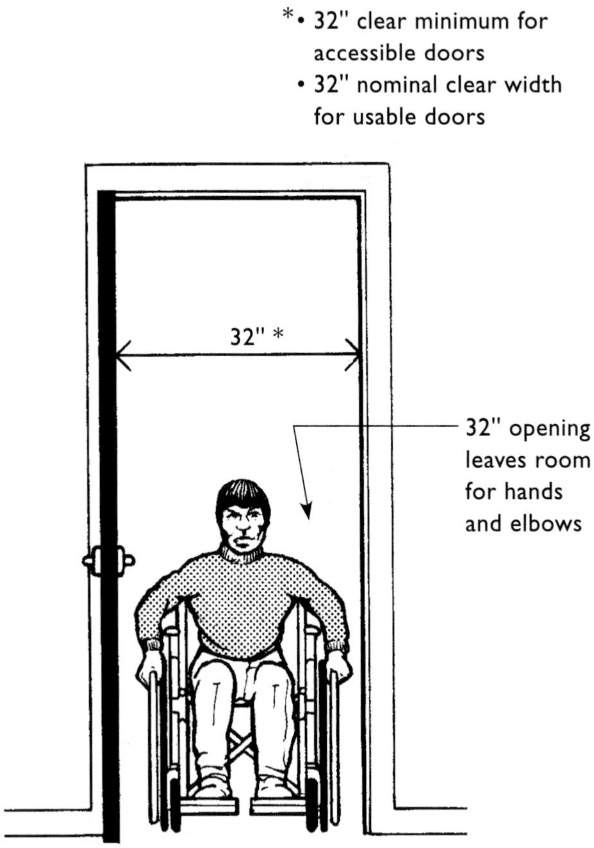

Doorway Clear Opening

Doorway Depth

In both public and common use spaces and within dwelling units, the wall thickness of all cased openings must be no greater than 24 inches if the width of the doorway or passage is the minimum 32 inches. Doorways with a depth greater than 24 inches must be widened to provide the 36-inch minimum clear width for an accessible route.

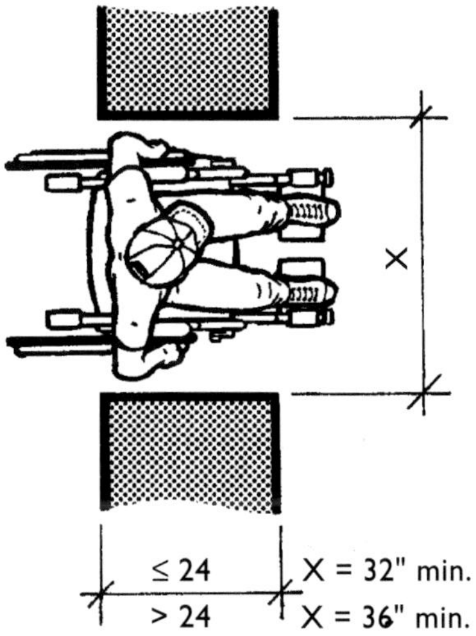

Doorway Depth

Types of Doors

Hinged Doors, Single-Leaf

At hinged doors the 32-inch opening is measured from the stop on the latch side jamb to the face of the door when standing in a 90-degree open position. Because the door, when open, remains in the doorway, the size of door used for the main entry door must be wide enough so that when open 90 degrees, it provides 32 inches minimum clear width. Main entry doors to dwelling units may be thicker than doors used within the unit, often making it necessary to install a door wider than 34 inches at the main entry. (In addition, most building codes require a 36-inch door at the main entry.) Within the dwelling unit, a 34-inch wide door, hung in the standard manner, is considered a usable door because it provides an "acceptable" nominal 32-inch clear opening of at least 31-5/8 inches clear.

Accessible hinged doors in public and common use spaces may be equipped with push bar or panic type hardware even though the bar may protrude into the 32-inch clear width. The hardware should be mounted high enough (approximately 36 inches minimum above the floor) to allow sufficient room for people pushing themselves in manual wheelchairs to get through the doorway without catching their arms, shoulders, or clothing on the panic hardware. In no case may the bar extend more than 4 inches from the door because it then becomes a hazardous protruding object, see ANSI 4.4 Protruding Objects.

In the interior of dwelling units it is possible for residents or landlords to adapt the nominal 32-inch clear opening to create a wider and more usable doorway by installing offset or swing-clear hinges, by removing the lower portion

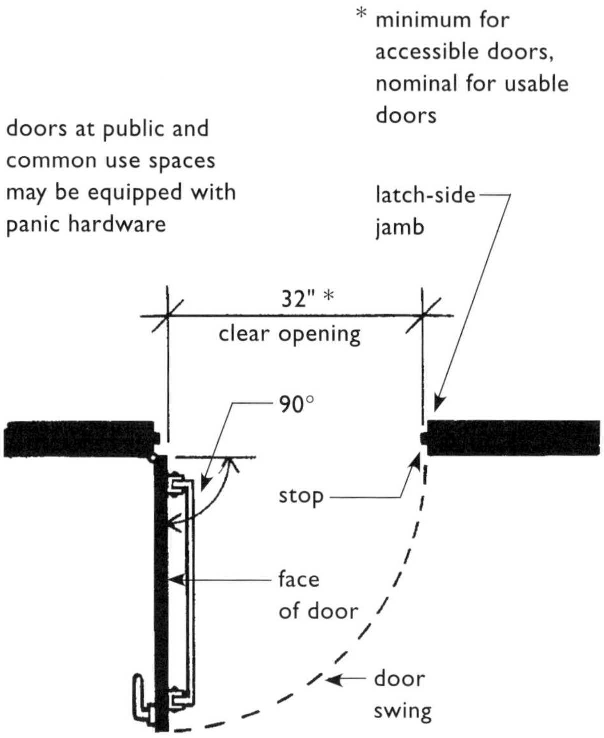

Measuring Clear Width at Hinged Doors

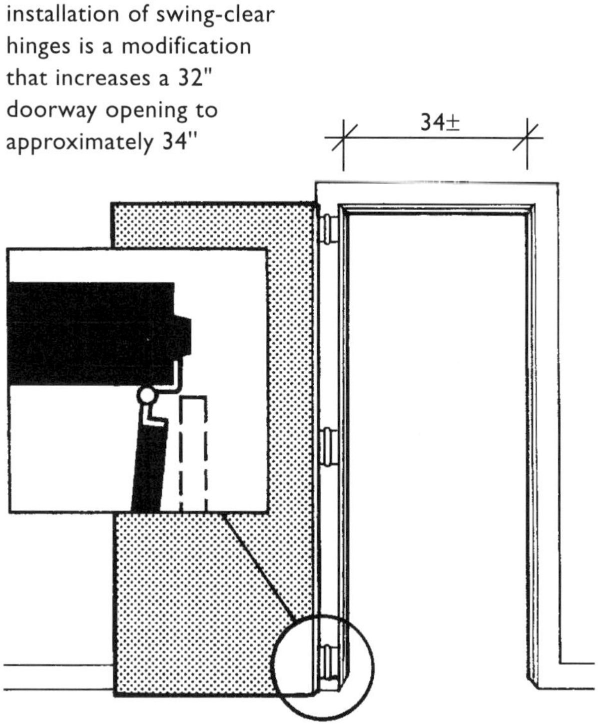

Use of Swing-Clear Hinges

of the door stop, or by doing both. With standard hinges, a door, when open, remains in the door opening; swing-clear hinges allow a door to swing completely out of the doorway and increase the clear opening of the doorway. See Product Resource List, Appendix A, for manufacturers of swing-clear hinges. Builders are cautioned that they may not install a 32-inch wide door (which effectively yields a 30 to 30-1/2 inch opening) and expect residents to make modifications later to bring the door up to the 32-inch nominal width required at the time of initial construction.

Hinged Doors, Double-Leaf

Two narrow, double-leaf doors (two hinged doors) mounted in a single frame may be slightly more difficult to open and close than a single door. Double-leaf doors can be a useful choice where space for the door swing is limited and where doors are likely to stand open. If narrow double-leaf doors are used, the nominal 32-inch clear opening must be maintained between door faces when in a 90-degree open position. Where larger double-leaf doors are installed, and if only one leaf is active, that leaf must be usable, i.e., provide the nominal 32-inch clear opening.

Pocket, Sliding, and Folding Doors

Pocket, sliding (e.g., automatic sliding doors at a main entrance), and folding doors may be installed in public and common use areas and at those times must meet the technical requirements of ANSI 4.13 Doors. The following discussion will focus on this category of doors when installed within dwelling units.

Unlike hinged doors, pocket, sliding, and folding doors, encroach little or not at all upon clear floor space and may, therefore, be an advantage when planning small rooms. This category of doors has additional features pertaining to the amount of space the door occupies within the doorway and the type of hardware installed. Hardware on interior dwelling unit doors is not covered by the Guidelines; however, recommendations are made to increase ease of use of the hardware, and thus the door.

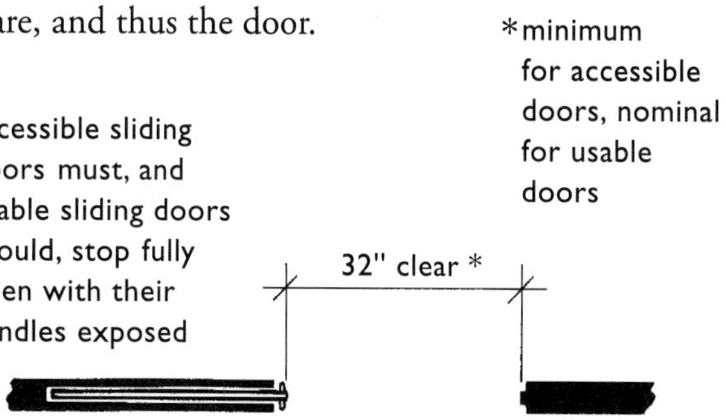

Clear Width at Sliding/Pocket Door

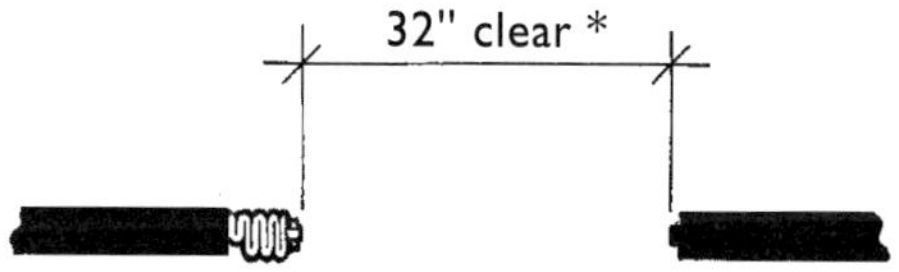

Clear Width at Accordion-Fold Door

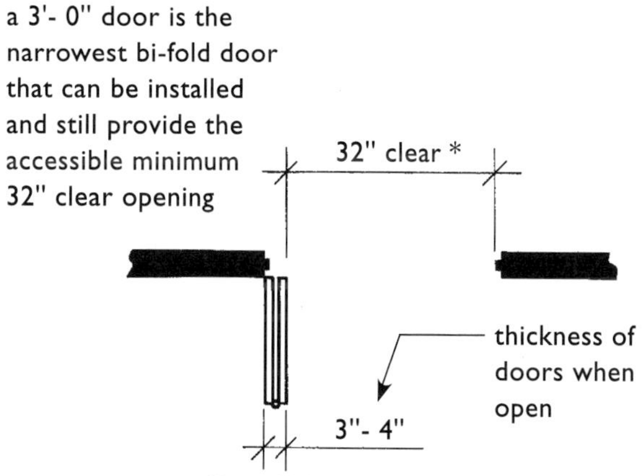

Clear Width at Bi-Fold Door

Pocket Doors. The traditional handle and latch installed in pocket doors are difficult for many people to operate because the hardware is recessed into the face of the door so the door can slide completely into the wall pocket. If carefully monitored, it may be possible to install a 32-inch wide pocket door that yields a nominal 32-inch clear opening; however, without modifying the door hardware, the door is still difficult to open and close.

Lacking complete control of variables such as the specific manufacturer's design of the door track assembly, the builder's installation method, the decision to install door stops (which vary in thickness), and other field conditions, it is recommended that pocket doors wider than 32 inches be installed. If a 36-inch wide door is installed, residents may make the following simple modifications later so the door is easier to operate: add loop handles on the door and a stop at the floor to prevent the door from sliding so far into the wall pocket that the handle is tight against the door jamb. This ensures that when the door is in the open position the handle will remain exposed and 32 inches will remain clear for passage.

Notes in italic type are recommendations only and are not required by ANSI or the Guidelines.

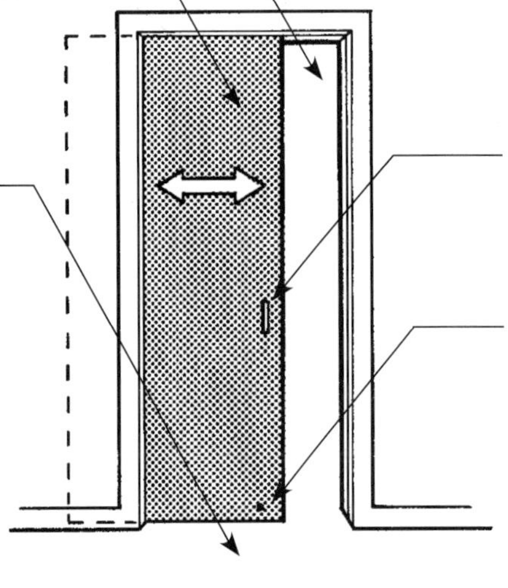

Usable Sliding/Pocket Door

Sliding Doors. Interior sliding doors are generally used as closet doors since they avoid problems caused by door swings. If installed, each panel or door must provide a nominal clear opening of at least 32 inches. It is recommended that loop handles be installed rather than the more common recessed finger cups. Exterior sliding doors are discussed on page 3.10.

Folding Doors. Folding doors typically found in dwelling units are either accordion or bi-fold. They are made up of two or more attached or hinged panels that fold together when opened. When either type of door is in the open position, the clear opening is reduced by the thickness of the folded door. Considering this, the smallest doorway in which either a bi-fold assembly or accordion type door assembly can be installed is 36 inches.

To improve the ease of use of bi-folding doors, loop handles can be installed in the recommended locations as shown in the adjacent drawing. Magnet catches and latches on accordion-folding doors often are difficult to line up with the receiving end of the catch for people with any hand or grasp limitation.

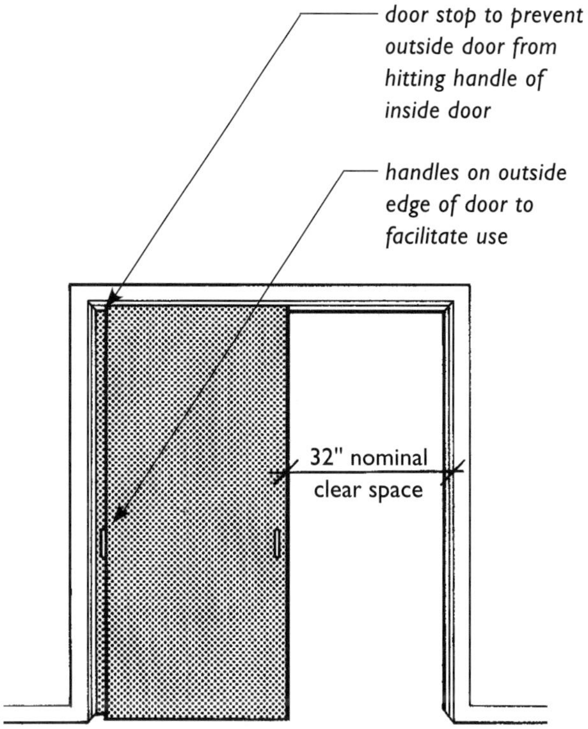

Usable Sliding Door

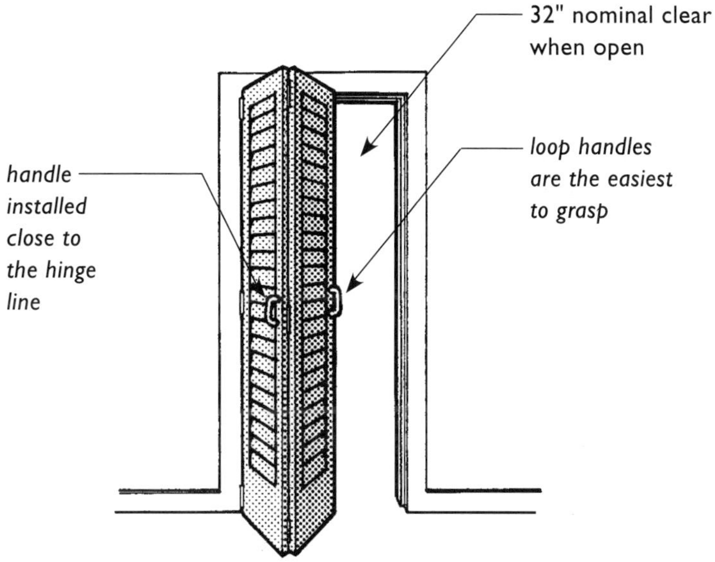

Usable Folding Door

Notes in italic type are recommendations only and are not required by ANSI or the Guidelines.

Dwelling Unit Doors

Primary Entry Door

The exterior of the primary entry door of covered dwelling units is part of public and common use spaces, therefore, it must be on an accessible route and be accessible, i.e., meet the ANSI requirements of 4.13 Doors. This is true both of entry doors opening off interior corridors internal to a building containing multiple dwelling units, and of separate exterior ground floor dwelling unit entrances.

Because primary entry doors to covered units must be on an accessible route, thresholds at these doors must be no higher than 3/4 inch and must be beveled with a slope no greater than 1:2. See additional discussion of thresholds and accessible route at dwelling units on page 4.12.

Secondary Exterior Doors

All secondary exterior doors from the same or different rooms that provide passage onto exterior decks, patios, or balconies must be usable. For example, if a deck is served by French doors or other double-leaf doors, and if only one leaf is active, that leaf must be usable, i.e., provide a nominal 32-inch clear opening. If both leaves are active, one leaf would not have to provide a nominal 32-inch clear opening as long as both leaves, when open, do provide the nominal 32-inch clear opening.

Since an accessible route must be provided throughout the unit, thresholds at secondary exterior doors also are limited to a maximum height of 3/4 inch. However, secondary doors that exit onto exterior decks, patios, or balcony surfaces are allowed to have a 4-inch maximum step (or more if required by local building code) to prevent water infiltration at door sills only if the exterior surface is constructed of an impervious material such as concrete, brick, or flagstone. If the exterior surface is a pervious material such as a wood deck that will drain adequately, the decking must be maintained to within 1/2 inch of the interior floor level. See Chapter Four: "Accessible Route Into and Through the Covered Dwelling Unit."

Sliding glass doors are often installed as secondary exterior doors. The Guidelines state that "the nominal 32-inch clear opening provided by a standard 6-foot sliding patio door assembly is acceptable." Unfortunately, many of the standard 6-foot sliding glass door assemblies yield only a 28-1/2-inch maximum clear opening in the full open position. Note: 28-1/2 inches is not an acceptable 32-inch nominal dimension. Builders and product specifiers must carefully select door assemblies that yield the 32-inch nominal clear opening (a clear opening from 31-5/8 to 32 inches or more). Some economy suppliers have 6-foot sliding glass doors that will meet the required width. Other assemblies on the market larger than 6 feet also provide the required width. See Product Resource List, Appendix A.

Accessible Primary Entry Door at Covered Dwelling Unit
See ANSI 4.13 Doors

Notes in italic type are recommendations only and are not required by ANSI or the Guidelines. All recommended features are helpful to people with and without disabilities.

Where sliding glass doors are used, it also may be necessary to modify the threshold either by sinking the frame into the floor, or by adding a beveled edge. See Chapter Four: "Accessible Route into and Through the Covered Unit" for additional discussion of thresholds along accessible routes. Locks and latches on sliding glass doors are often difficult to operate for someone with any hand limitation. Although not required by the Guidelines, but because sliding glass door hardware is more difficult to modify at a later time if needed than hardware on hinged doors, it is recommended that locks be installed that can be raised and lowered with a closed fist or that require no finger manipulation. When sliding glass doors are being selected, doors with loop handles or large blades to push or pull against are the easiest to use.

In some parts of the country construction or building code requirements may restrict the size of window or door openings placed in exterior walls. Where it is necessary to have a 5-foot wide maximum opening or if a standard 6-foot wide sliding door assembly does not provide adequate passage width, a passage door must still be provided that will yield the 32-inch nominal clear width. One suggested solution is to install a 36-inch wide full glass swinging door coupled with an appropriate width sidelight to provide equivalent or similar glass area for natural light and view.

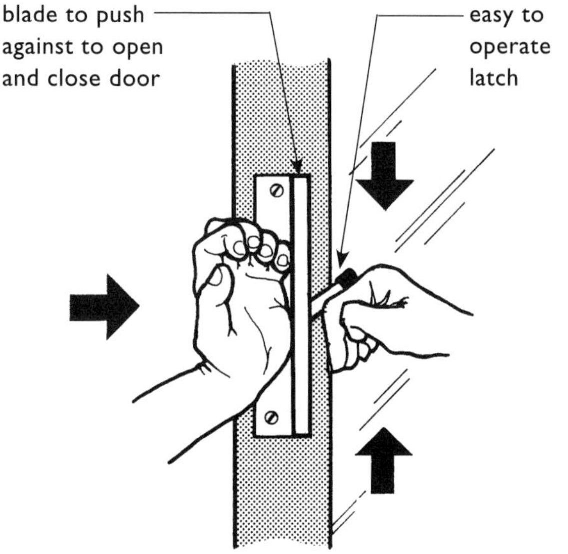

Sliding Glass Door Hardware that Requires No Twisting, Turning, or Fine Finger Manipulation to Operate Recommended

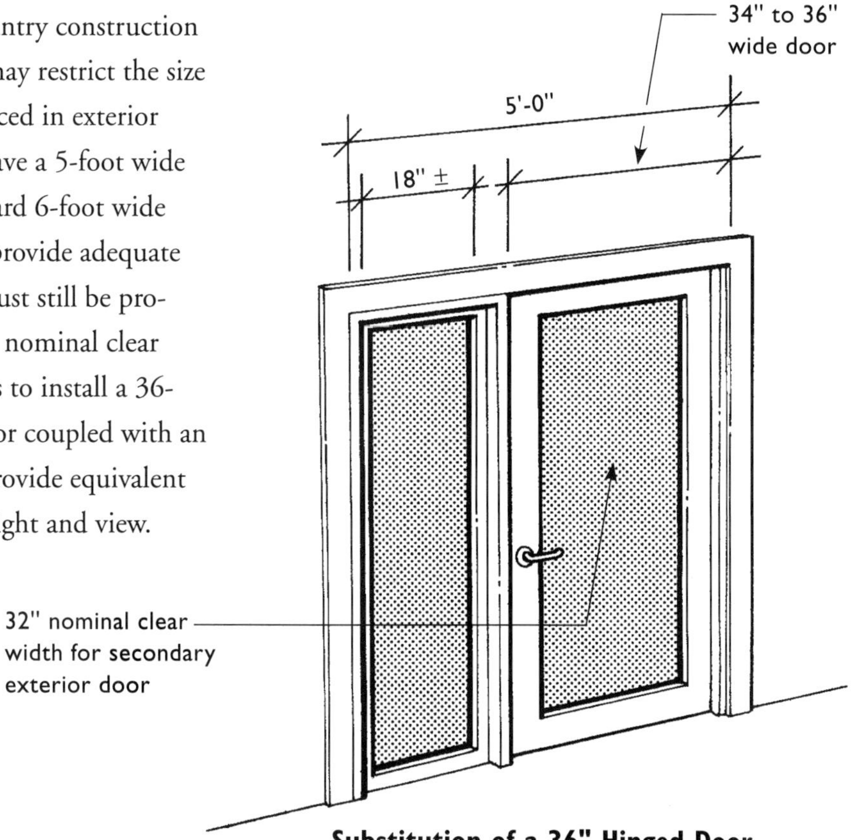

Substitution of a 36" Hinged Door Plus Sidelight When a 5' or 6' Sliding Door Assembly Cannot Provide a 32" Door Opening

Doors In Series or Double Door Vestibule

Doors in a series are not typically part of an individual dwelling unit but are used at entrances to buildings. As such they are part of public and common use spaces and subject to the design specifications found in ANSI 4.13 Doors. However, where doors in a series are provided as part of a dwelling unit (to form an air lock when extremes of climate exist or to create a privacy vestibule), the requirements of an accessible route into and through the dwelling unit would apply.

If a vestibule is too small, people using mobility aids may get trapped and not be able to open the second door and exit the vestibule. For this reason, even though doors on the interior of the unit only must be usable (or have a 32-inch nominal clear width) the distance between the doors must be sufficient to allow users to maneuver to get the second door open and pass through. This is especially critical for safe egress in emergency situations. Guidance can be found at ANSI 4.13.7.

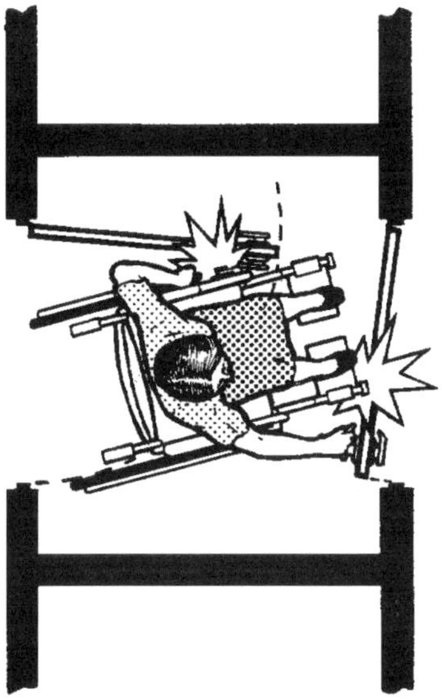

Inadequate Space in Vestibule

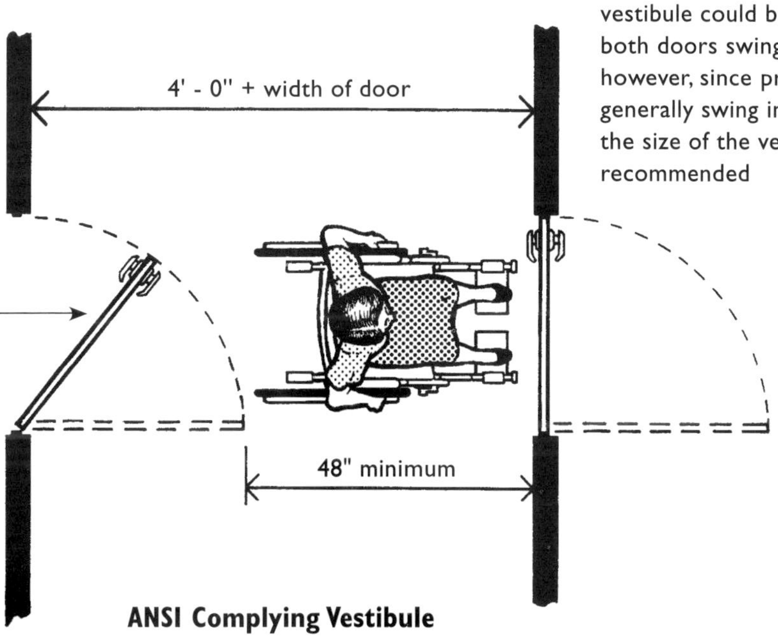

ANSI Complying Vestibule

CLOSET DOORS

Closets that require users to pass through the doorway to reach the contents must have doors that provide at least 32 inches nominal clear opening. Closets that permit the user to access the contents from outside the closet have no door width specifications whatsoever.

Closets for hanging clothes are usually 24 inches deep and of variable width. Small clothes and linen closets should be no more than 48 inches long to avoid dead space at the ends that is difficult or impossible for most users to reach, seated or standing, even if a 34-inch door is installed.

If wider closets are provided it is best that doors be double (hinged or bi-folding preferred) to provide maneuvering space and clear view of contents. If "walk-in" closets are planned, they must have usable doors to provide adequate space for passage of a person using a wheelchair.

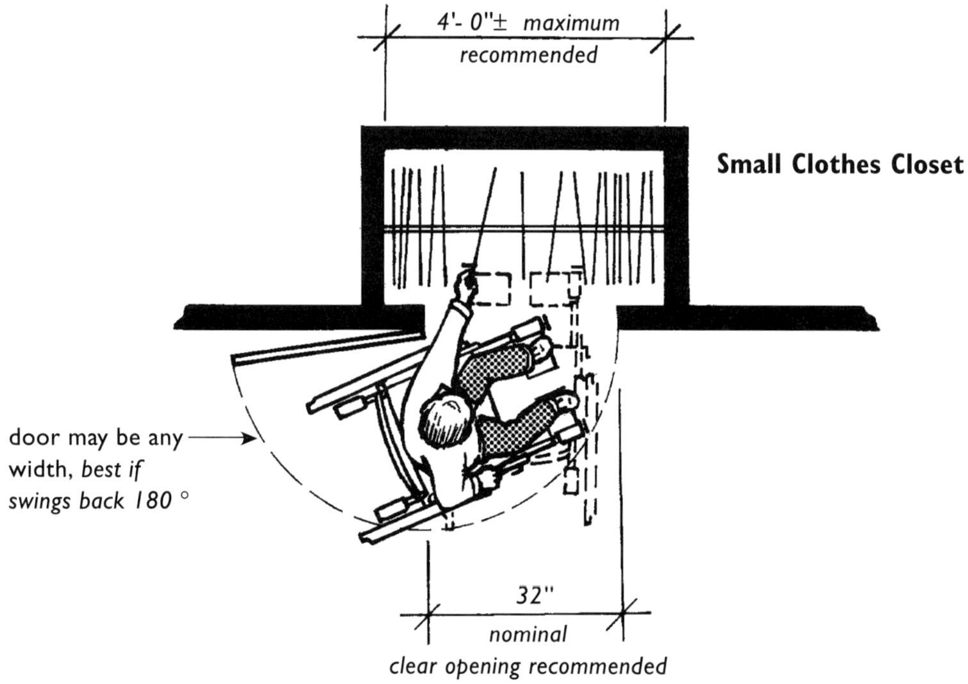

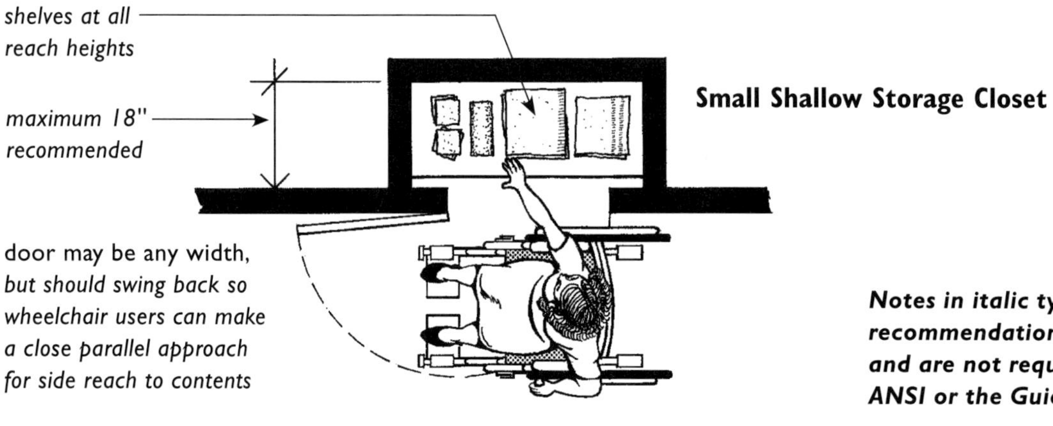

Notes in italic type are recommendations only and are not required by ANSI or the Guidelines.

Wide Closet with Wide Doorway Easy for Everyone to Use

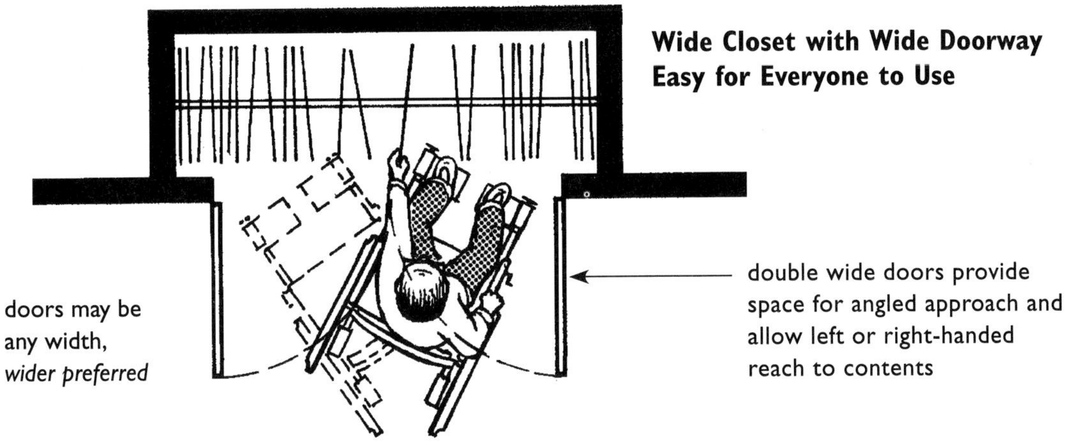

Double Folding Doors Also Allow Good Access to Closet Contents for All Users

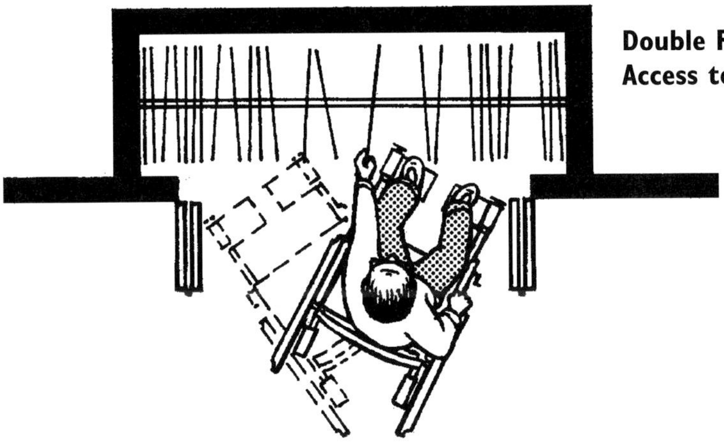

Minimum Suggested L-Shaped Walk-In Closet with Usable Door

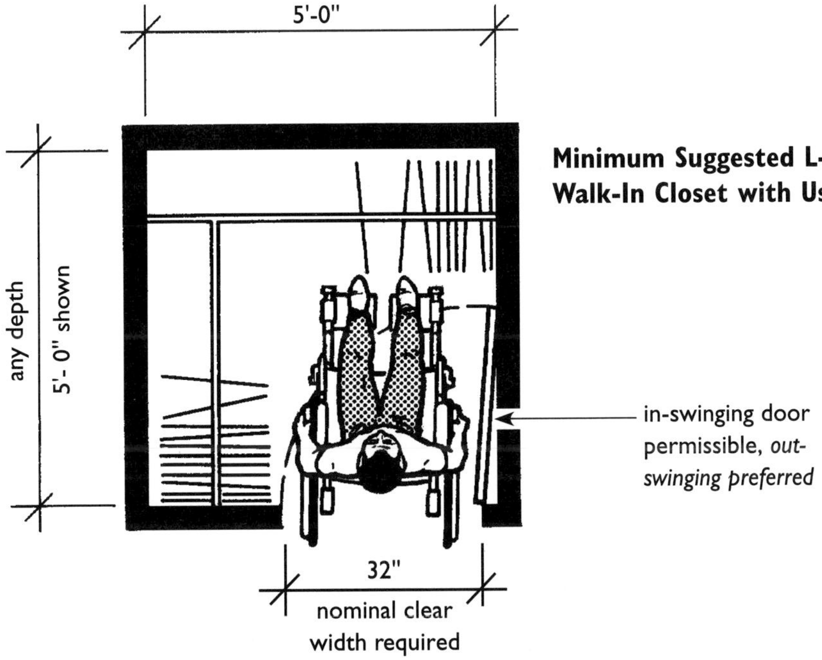

Notes in italic type are recommendations only and are not required by ANSI or the Guidelines.

Chapter Four:

Requirement 4

Accessible Route into and Through the Covered Unit

4

"...covered multifamily dwellings with a building entrance on an accessible route shall be designed and constructed in such a manner that all premises within covered multifamily dwelling units contain an accessible route into and through the covered dwelling unit."

Fair Housing Act Regulations, 24 CFR 100.205

Definitions from the Guidelines

Loft. An intermediate level between the floor and ceiling of any story, located within a room or rooms of a dwelling.

Multistory dwelling unit. A dwelling unit with finished living space located on one floor and the floor or floors immediately above or below it.

Single-story dwelling unit. A dwelling unit with all finished living space located on one floor.

Story. That portion of a dwelling unit between the upper surface of any floor and the upper surface of the floor next above, or the roof of the unit. Within the context of dwelling units, the terms "story" and "floor" are synonymous.

Introduction

The Fair Housing Accessibility Guidelines (the Guidelines) specify that an accessible route be provided into and throughout the entire covered dwelling unit. The accessible route must pass through the main entry door, continue through all rooms in the unit, adjoin required clear floor spaces at all kitchen appliances and all bathroom fixtures, and connect with all secondary exterior doors.

Unlike public and common use areas, where a fully accessible route that complies with ANSI A117.1 - 1986, or an equal or more strict accessibility standard is required, the Guidelines designate specific elements of an accessible route that must be provided. The accessible route must be **1.** sufficiently wide and **2.** lacking in abrupt changes in level so residents with disabilities (and/or their guests with disabilities) can safely use all rooms and spaces, including storage areas and, under most circumstances, exterior balconies and patios that may be part of their dwelling unit. See page 4.11 for exception at balconies and patios constructed of impervious materials.

An accessible route is not required into a basement or garage. However, doors from the interior of the dwelling unit to an unfinished basement or a garage attached to a single-story dwelling unit must be "usable"; see Chapter 3: "Usable Doors." Providing an accessible route and a usable door in these circumstances will allow a resident to make later modifications, such as installing a ramp from the dwelling unit into the garage, thereby increasing usability of the unit.

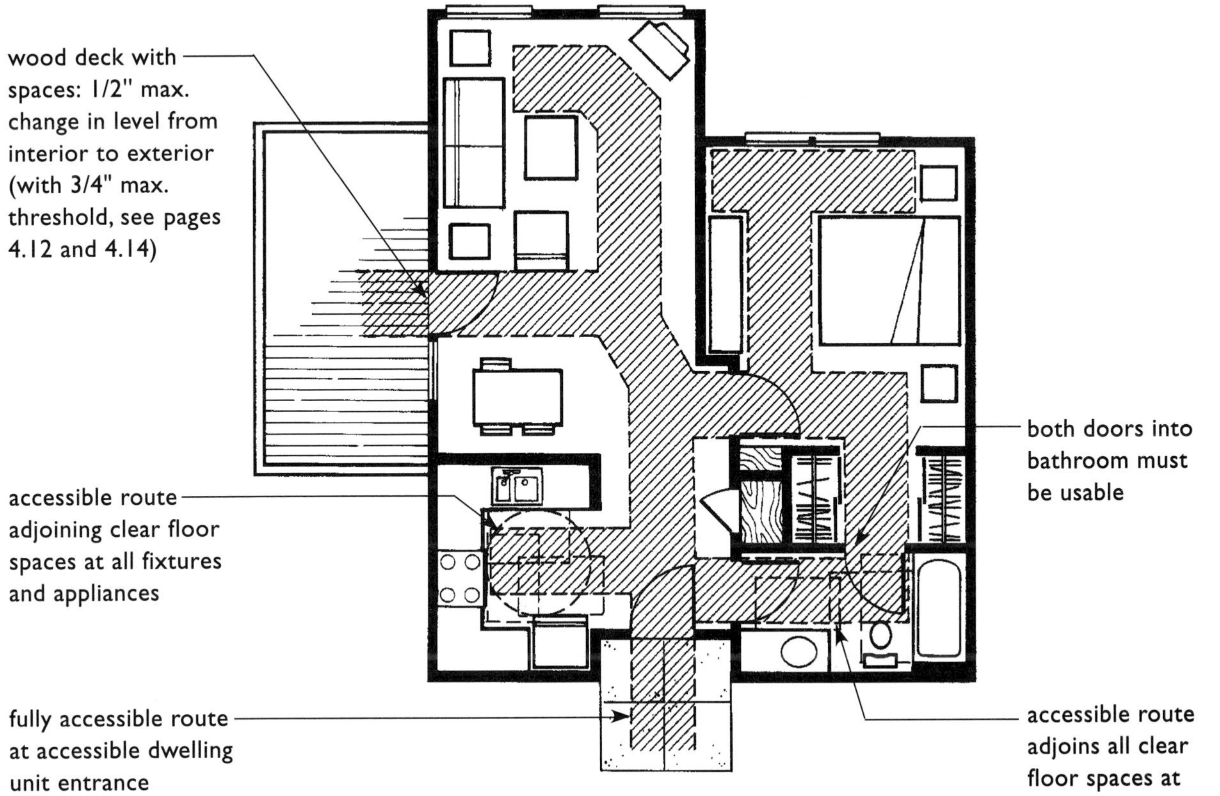

36-Inch Wide Minimum Accessible Route Through Dwelling Unit

Accessible Route

Width

The 36-inch wide fully accessible route as described in Chapters 1 and 2 must connect with the clear floor space outside the primary entry door of each covered dwelling unit. As the accessible route passes into the unit it may be reduced to 32 inches minimum clear width at the door. Throughout the unit the accessible route must be 36 inches wide or wider, except as it passes through passage doors, where it may be reduced to 32 inches nominal clear width. See Chapter 3: "Usable Doors."

When specifications for accessible routes are presented in most accessibility standards they contain provisions for minimum height or headroom. The Guidelines, with respect to the interiors of dwelling units, do not include a specification for headroom. Protruding objects also are not addressed within the interior of the dwelling unit, but they should be avoided in all cases.

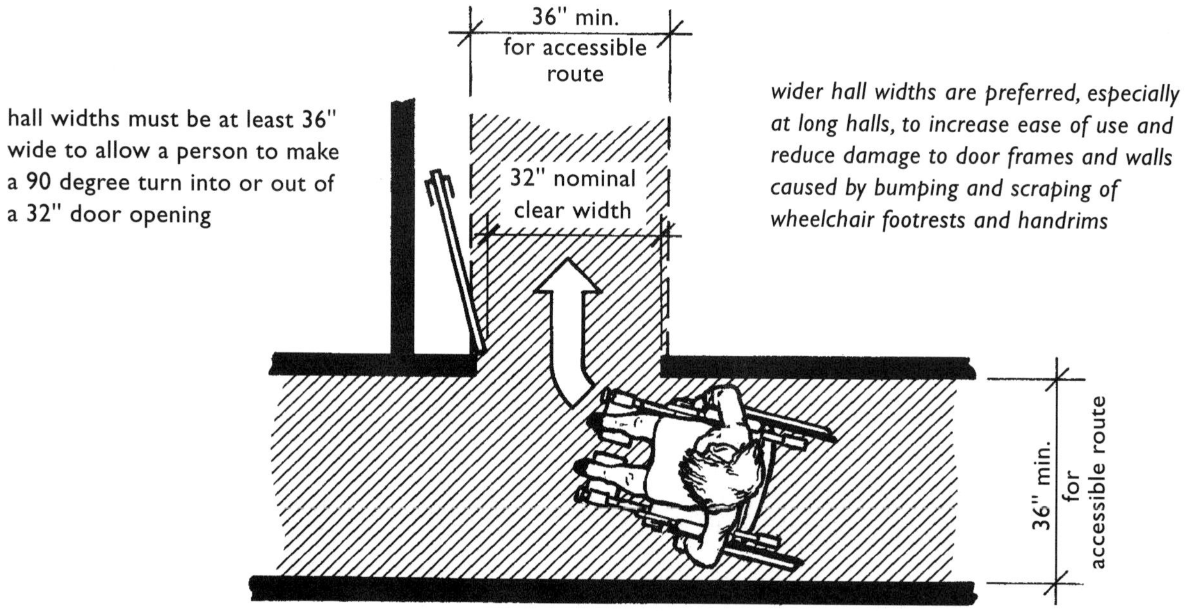

Minimum Width of Accessible Route

Changes in Level

Within single-story dwelling units (and on the primary entry level of multistory dwelling units in buildings with elevators) the maximum vertical floor level change is 1/4 inch, except when a tapered threshold is used, the maximum height is 1/2 inch. Even small abrupt changes of level in the surface of an accessible route pose a tripping hazard for many people and can be a significant obstacle for people using wheelchairs. People who walk wearing braces and/or who have difficulty maintaining balance are particularly susceptible to catching their toes on small changes in level.

Small abrupt changes in level occur most frequently at floor material changes and at door thresholds. Within the interior of the dwelling unit, thresholds should not be used or they should be thin and installed flush with the flooring surface. If a threshold must be used, it must not have a level change more than 1/4 inch without being beveled or tapered. When a tapered threshold is used, the level change may be a maximum of 1/2 inch. If an interior door threshold represents a change in level greater than 1/2 inch, it must be ramped and must slope at 1 inch in 12 inches maximum (1:12). Thresholds at exterior doors are addressed on page 4.12.

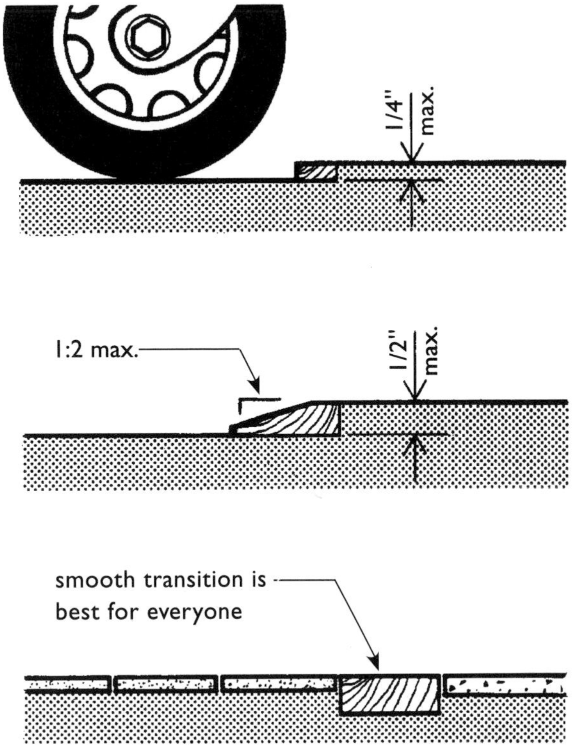

Small Changes in Level Along Accessible Routes

Special Design Features

Single-story dwelling units are not prohibited from having specific design features, such as a split-level entry, a sunken living room, or a loft area; but the Guidelines do contain restrictions for each of these. Where a single-story dwelling unit has such a design feature, all portions of the unit, except the loft or the sunken or raised area, must be on an accessible route, i.e., the accessible route must be continuous throughout the dwelling unit and not be interrupted by the design feature.

The Guidelines specify that kitchens and all bathrooms, including powder rooms, must be on an accessible route; therefore, no part of kitchens or bathrooms may be located in a raised or sunken area unless an accessible route can be provided to that area. However, a wet bar on a loft or in a sunken area that is not equipped with an accessible route is permissible since the wet bar is not a part of a kitchen. The combination of both a loft and a sunken area within the same dwelling unit prohibits residents with mobility impairments from using a significant percentage of their units and is thus not permitted under the Guidelines.

Split-Level Entries

A split-level entry foyer, where the foyer is on one level and the remainder of the unit is down a few steps, does not exempt the unit from coverage by the Fair Housing Act. The entry is critical to providing an accessible route into and through the dwelling unit; therefore, an accessible route to the lower area must be provided by a ramp with a maximum slope of 1:12 or other means of access. It is recommended that the ramp comply with the other ramp requirements of ANSI A117.1 - 1986 or an equal or more strict accessibility standard. See ANSI 4.8.

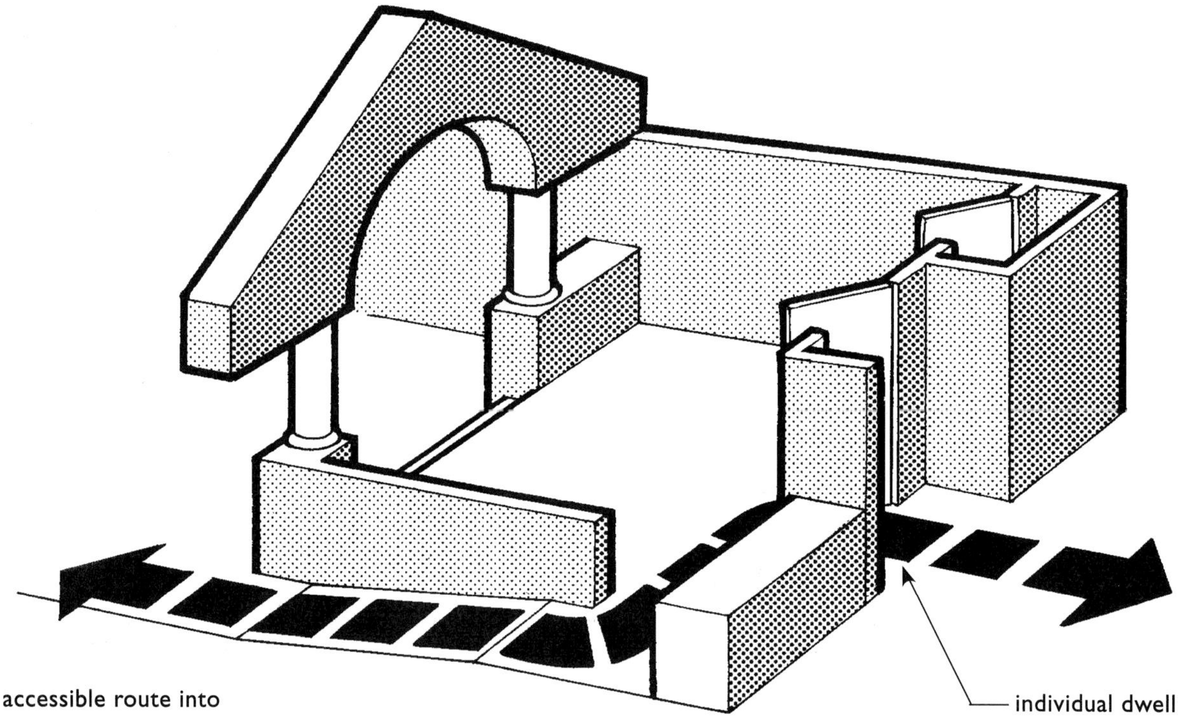

Units with Split-Entry Foyers Are Covered

Lofts

Dwelling units containing a loft are distinguished from multistory units in that a loft is open to the surrounding space and does not exceed 33-1/3 percent of the floor area of the room in which it is located. Each story (or floor) in a multistory unit is enclosed and contains finished living space with its own ceiling and floor. See "Accessible Routes in Multistory Dwelling Units" on page 4.9.

Because a loft is an intermediate level between the floor and ceiling of the unit, it is not considered a second story. Therefore, a dwelling unit with a loft is a single-story unit covered by the Guidelines. Since all primary or functional living spaces must be on an accessible route, secondary living spaces, such as a den, play area, or an additional bedroom are the only spaces that can be on a loft unless an accessible route can be taken to the loft.

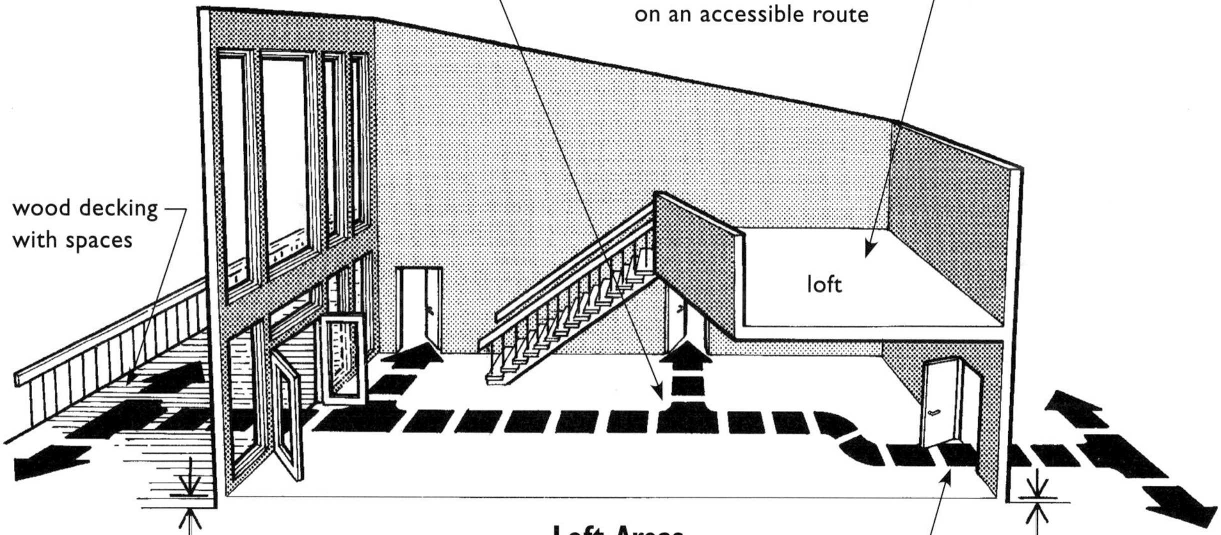

Loft Areas

Raised or Sunken Areas

A raised or sunken area is usually limited to a few steps maximum and has less of a change in level than a loft. These "special design features" may not contain a functional space in its entirety. For example, the entire living room must not be sunken; however, an auxiliary feature such as a second sitting area could have several steps down to that level that is not served by an accessible route.

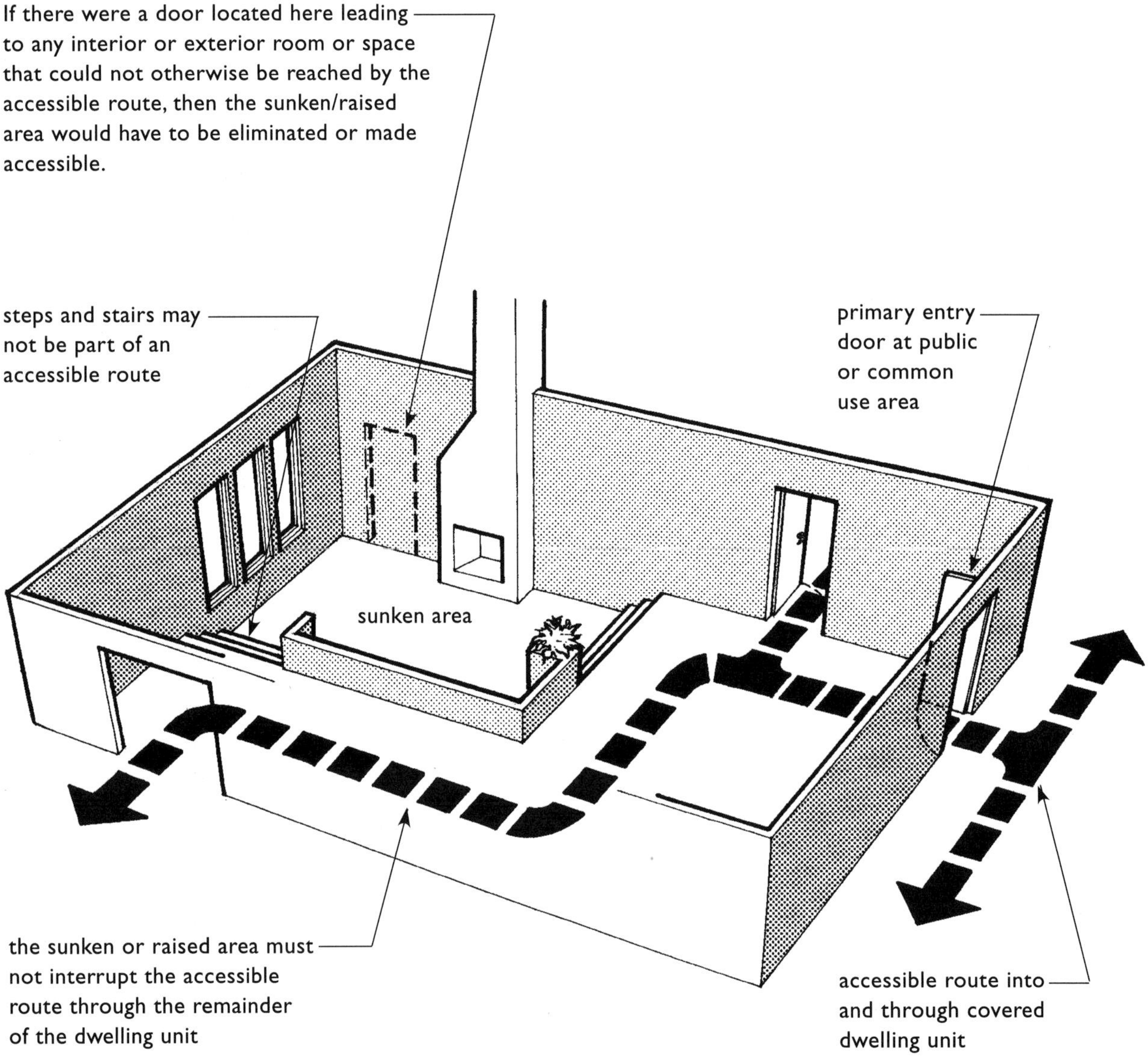

Living/Dining Room with Sunken Area

Accessible Routes in Multistory Dwelling Units

"Multistory dwelling unit" is defined in the Guidelines as a unit "with finished living space located on one floor and the floor or floors immediately above or below it." Multistory dwelling units in buildings without one or more elevators are not covered by the Fair Housing Act; however, when multistory dwelling units are in buildings with elevators, the dwelling unit is covered and the story that is served by the building elevator must be the primary entry to the unit and must meet the requirements of the Guidelines. Where the primary entry level of a covered multistory dwelling unit contains either a raised or sunken area, that floor level is subject to the same requirements as discussed at "Lofts" and "Raised and Sunken Areas."

Even though many people with significant mobility impairments may choose not to live in such a unit, multistory units, where the primary entry level meets the Guidelines, allow people with disabilities to visit with friends and relatives who may choose to live in a unit with more than one floor. A resident with a disability may choose to live in such a unit and add a lift at his or her own expense.

In multistory units the story that is served by the elevator must:

1. be the primary entry to the unit,

2. comply with Requirements 3 through 7 of the Guidelines for all rooms located on the entry floor level, and

3. contain a usable bathroom or powder room.

If there is both a bathroom and a powder room on the entry level of a multistory unit, then the bathroom must meet Requirement 7 of the Guidelines and the powder room needs to meet only Requirements 3, 4, and 5 of the Guidelines. In cases where only a powder room is provided on the entry level, it is treated as a bathroom and must: **1.** be on the accessible route, **2.** have a door with a 32-inch nominal clear width, **3.** meet the maneuvering and clear floor space requirements at toilets and lavatories, **4.** allow the user to enter the room, close the door, use the facilities, and reopen the door to exit, **5.** have reinforcing around the toilet for future installation of grab bars, and **6.** have switches, outlets, and controls in accessible locations. See page 7.38 and powder room plans starting on page 7.81.

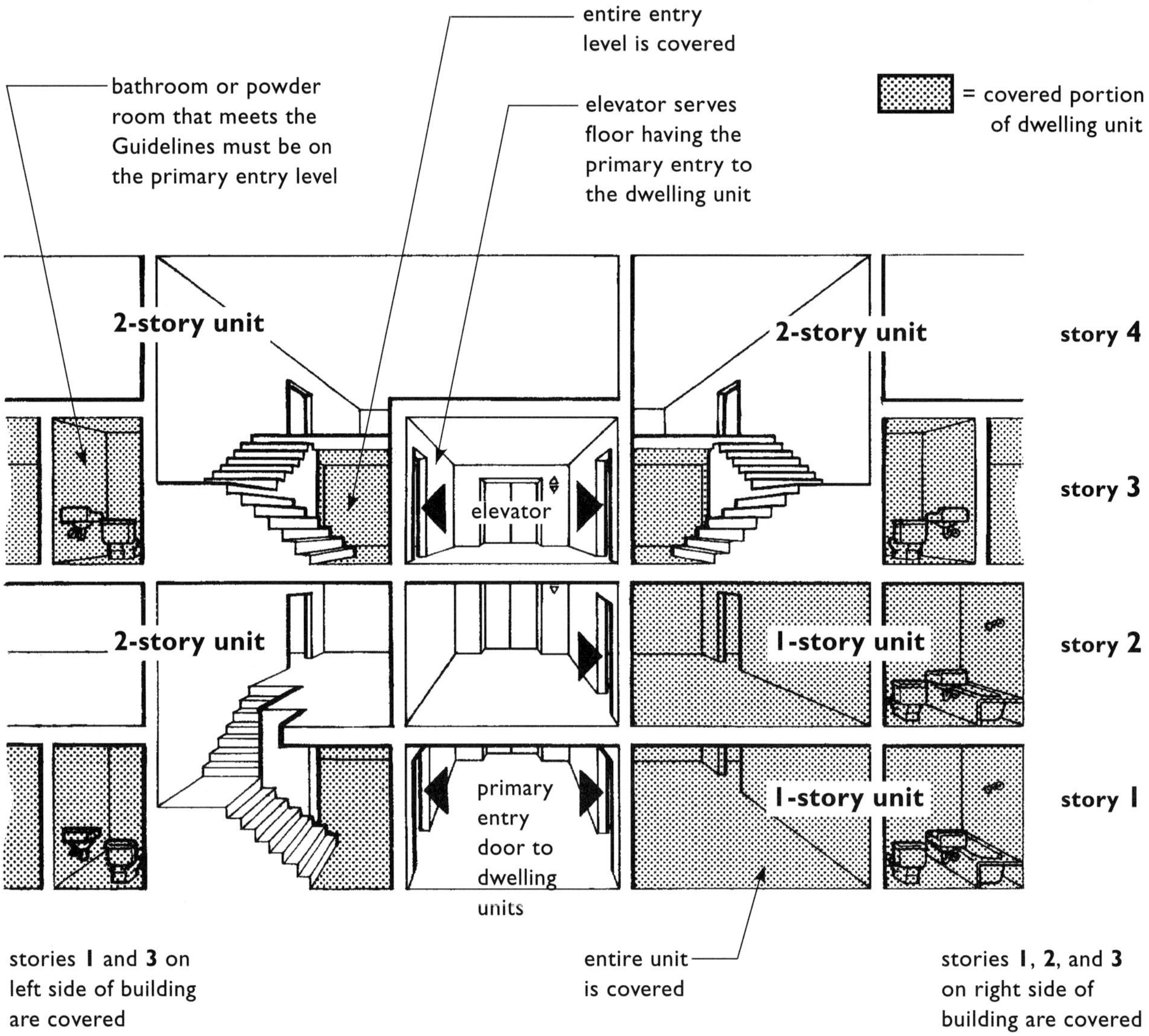

Single-Story Units and the Primary Entry Level of Multistory Units in Buildings with One or More Elevators Are Covered

Thresholds and Accessible Routes at Exterior Doors

The Guidelines allow the change in level between the interior floor level of the dwelling unit and an outside surface or platform to vary somewhat, depending upon **1.** whether the door is a primary or secondary door and **2.** the construction material of the outside landing surface. If the primary entry door to a dwelling unit has direct exterior access, the landing surface outside the door, as part of the accessible route, must be level with the interior floor, unless the landing is constructed of an impervious material, such as concrete; in which case, the landing may be up to 1/2 inch (but no more than 1/2 inch) below the interior floor of the dwelling unit. However, to prevent water damage, the finished surface outside the primary entry door may be sloped at a maximum of 1/8 inch for every 12 inches.

When a secondary exterior door exits onto decks, patios, or balcony surfaces constructed of impervious materials, the accessible route may be interrupted. In this case, the outside landing surface may be dropped a maximum of 4 inches below the floor level of the interior of the dwelling unit (or lower if required by local building code) to prevent water infiltration at door sills. If the exterior surface is constructed of pervious material, such as a wood deck that will drain adequately, that surface must be maintained to within 1/2 inch of the interior floor level. Note: When measuring the distance between the floor inside and the outside surface, the interior floor level must be calculated from the finished floor and not from the subfloor. If carpet is to be installed, the measurement should be calculated with a fully compressed carpet and, if present, the pad. In addition to the above changes in floor level, the Guidelines specify the maximum height for the door threshold, which is discussed on page 4.12.

Maximum Allowable Height Difference Between Interior Floor Level and Exterior Floor Level

level difference	at primary entry door
0"	pervious construction (e.g., wood decking with spaces)
1/2"	impervious construction (e.g., concrete, brick, or flagstone)
level difference	**at secondary door**
1/2"	pervious construction
4"	impervious construction

Thresholds at Exterior Doors

The concept of an accessible route is intended to ensure the maintenance of a continuous path of travel with no abrupt changes in level so people with disabilities who use wheelchairs or scooters and those who walk are not impeded. However, changes in level are inevitable at exterior doors because thresholds and changes in level are needed to control and/or prevent water infiltration.

The Guidelines allow limited changes in levels at exterior doors along accessible routes. In addition to the change in floor level between the interior floor and exterior landing discussed on page 4.11, the Guidelines specify that thresholds at these exterior doors, including sliding door tracks, shall be no higher than 3/4 inch. The Guidelines further state that changes in level at these locations must be beveled with a slope no greater than 1:2.

In the case of primary entry doors where the exterior landing surface is impervious, the exterior landing surface is permitted to be below the finish floor level by 1/2 inch. Therefore, the Guidelines allow an overall change in level of 1-1/4 inch on the exterior side of the primary entry door. Note, however, as already stated, these changes in level must be beveled with a slope no greater than 1:2. See the first illustration below.

Exterior door thresholds of 3/4 inch, even when beveled, can be extremely difficult to navigate for some persons who use wheelchairs, and the additional change in level when outside landing surfaces are impervious adds to this difficulty. Because of this, it is recommended that other solutions be considered which both provide for less of a change in level at the door threshold and also are designed to prevent water infiltration. One such solution is to use a threshold that rises a maximum of 1/4 inch on the inside and drops 3/4 inch at a slope of 1:2 at the exterior. See illustration two below. An even better solution is to bring the exterior surface up to the same level as the interior floor using an interlocking threshold. See illustration 3.

The illustrations on pages 4.13 through 4.14 offer design details of door thresholds that meet the requirements of the Guidelines as well as recommended door thresholds that provide for lesser changes in level while still preventing water infiltration to the dwelling unit.

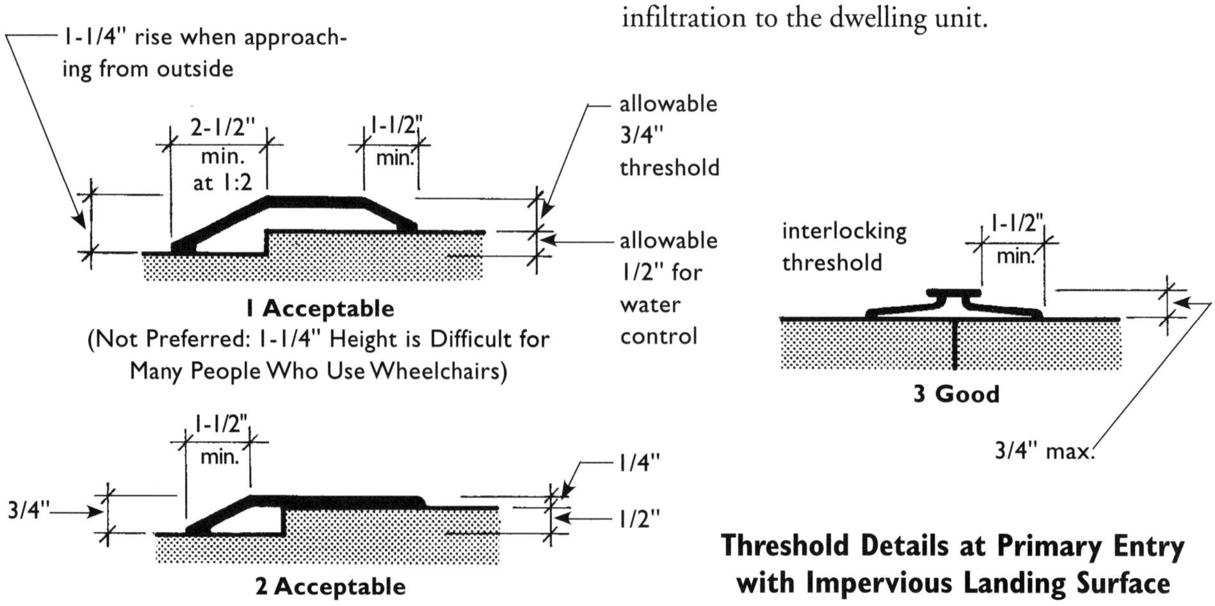

Threshold Details at Primary Entry with Impervious Landing Surface

Swinging Primary Entry Door at Concrete Landing

showing allowable changes in level at primary entry doors with direct exterior access onto concrete or other impervious landing surface where 1/2-inch maximum changes in level are permitted.

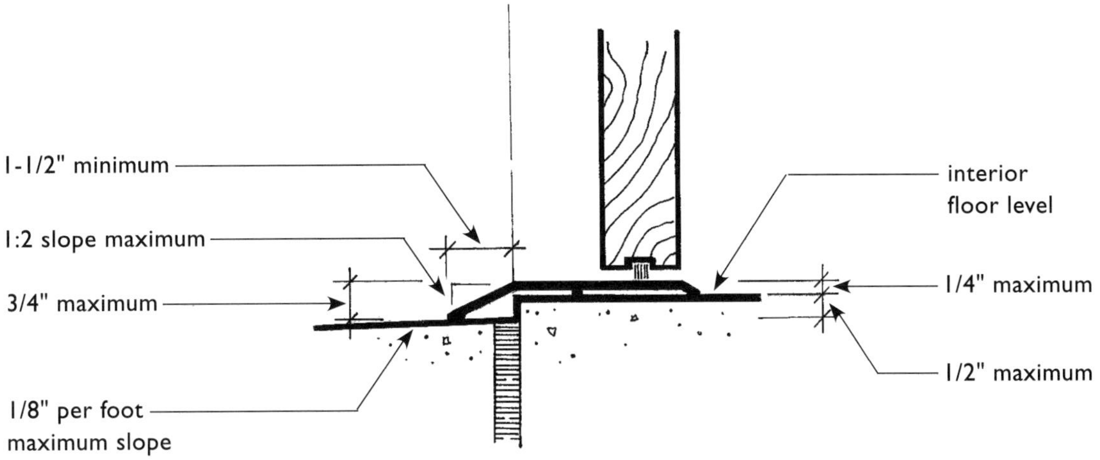

Swinging Secondary Door at Concrete Landing

showing allowable changes in level at exterior swinging doors onto concrete or other impervious landing surface where 4-inch changes in level are permitted.

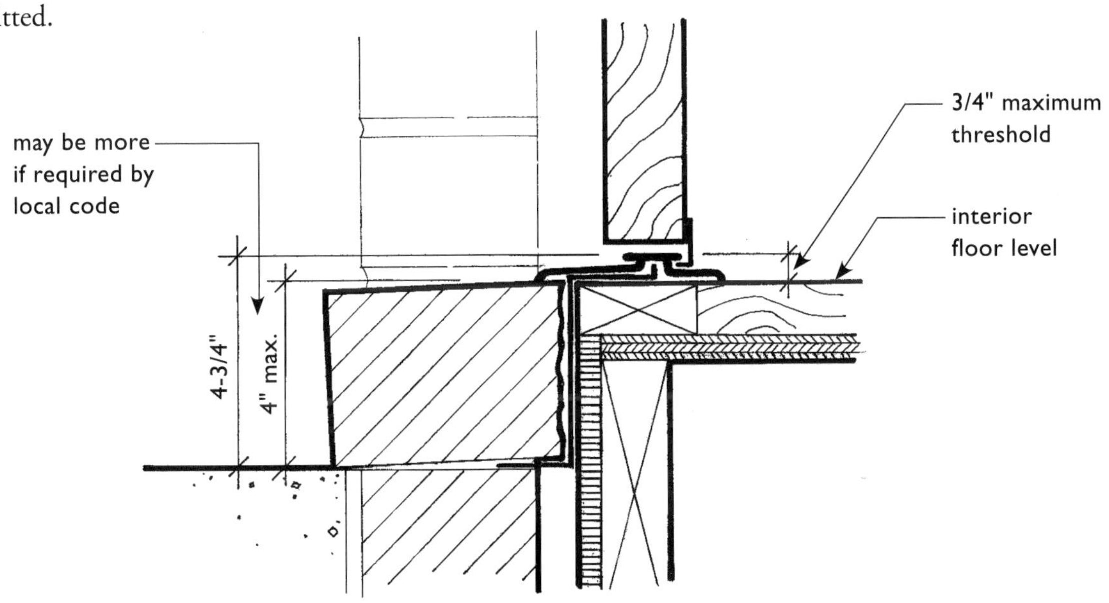

Sliding Secondary Door at Wood Deck

showing allowable changes in level at exterior sliding glass doors to balcony or patio where 1/2-inch maximum changes in level are permitted.

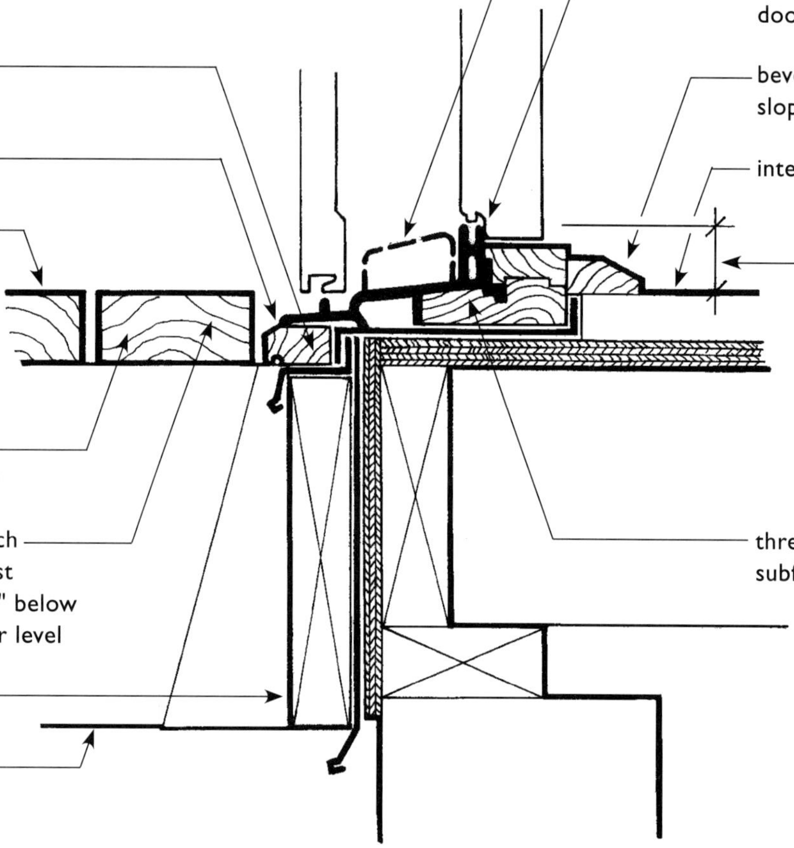

Sliding Secondary Door at Concrete Landing

showing allowable changes in level at exterior sliding glass doors to balcony or patio where 4-inch changes in level are permitted.

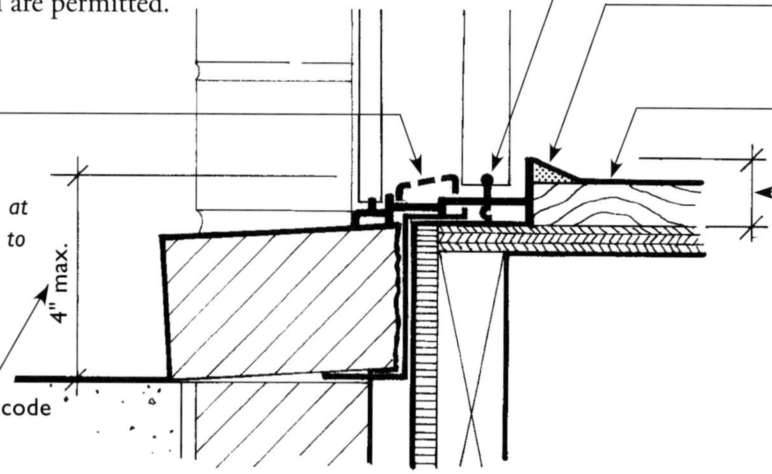

Notes in italic type are recommendations only and are not required by ANSI or the Guidelines.

Accessible Route onto Balcony Constructed of Concrete, Brick, or Flagstone May Be Interrupted by a 4-Inch Step

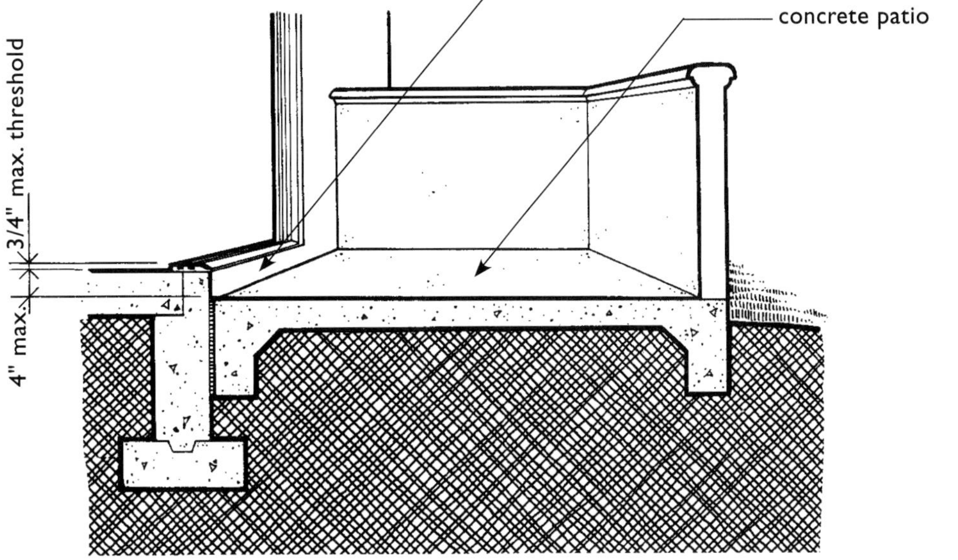

Notes in italic type are recommendations only and are not required by ANSI or the Guidelines.

Accessible Route onto Balcony Created with the Addition of a Raised Platform (Added by the Resident)

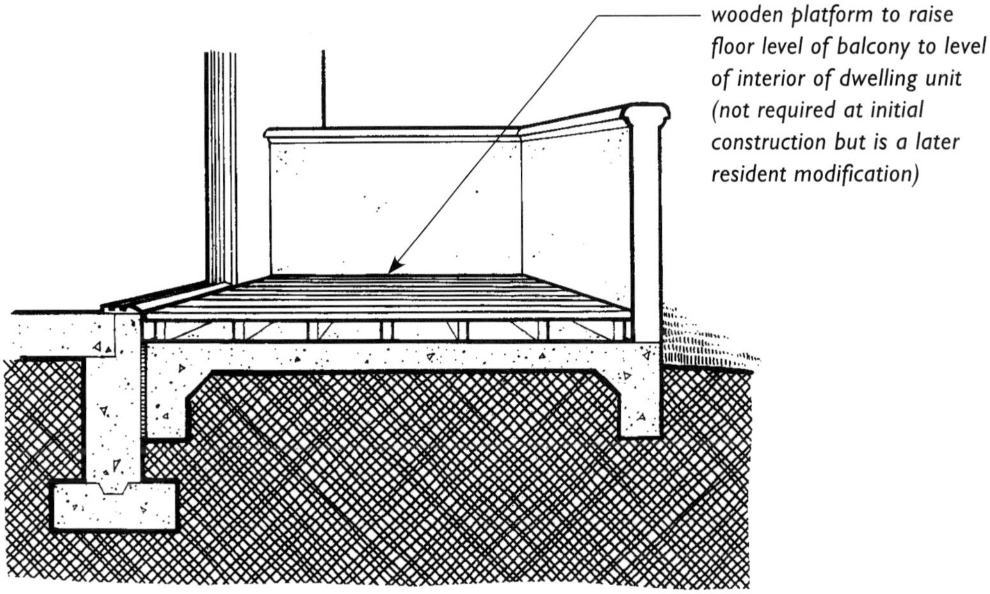

Chapter Five:

REQUIREMENT 5

Light Switches, Electrical Outlets, Thermostats, and Other Environmental Controls in Accessible Locations

5

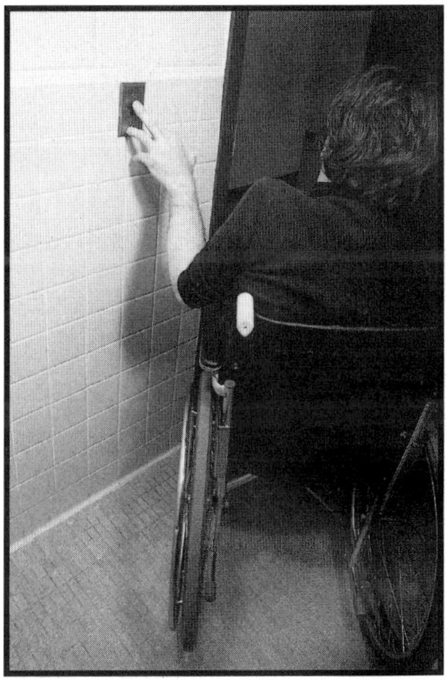

"...covered multifamily dwellings with a building entrance on an accessible route shall be designed and constructed in such a manner that all premises within covered multifamily dwelling units contain light switches, electrical outlets, thermostats and other environmental controls in accessible locations."

Fair Housing Act Regulations, 24 CFR 100.205

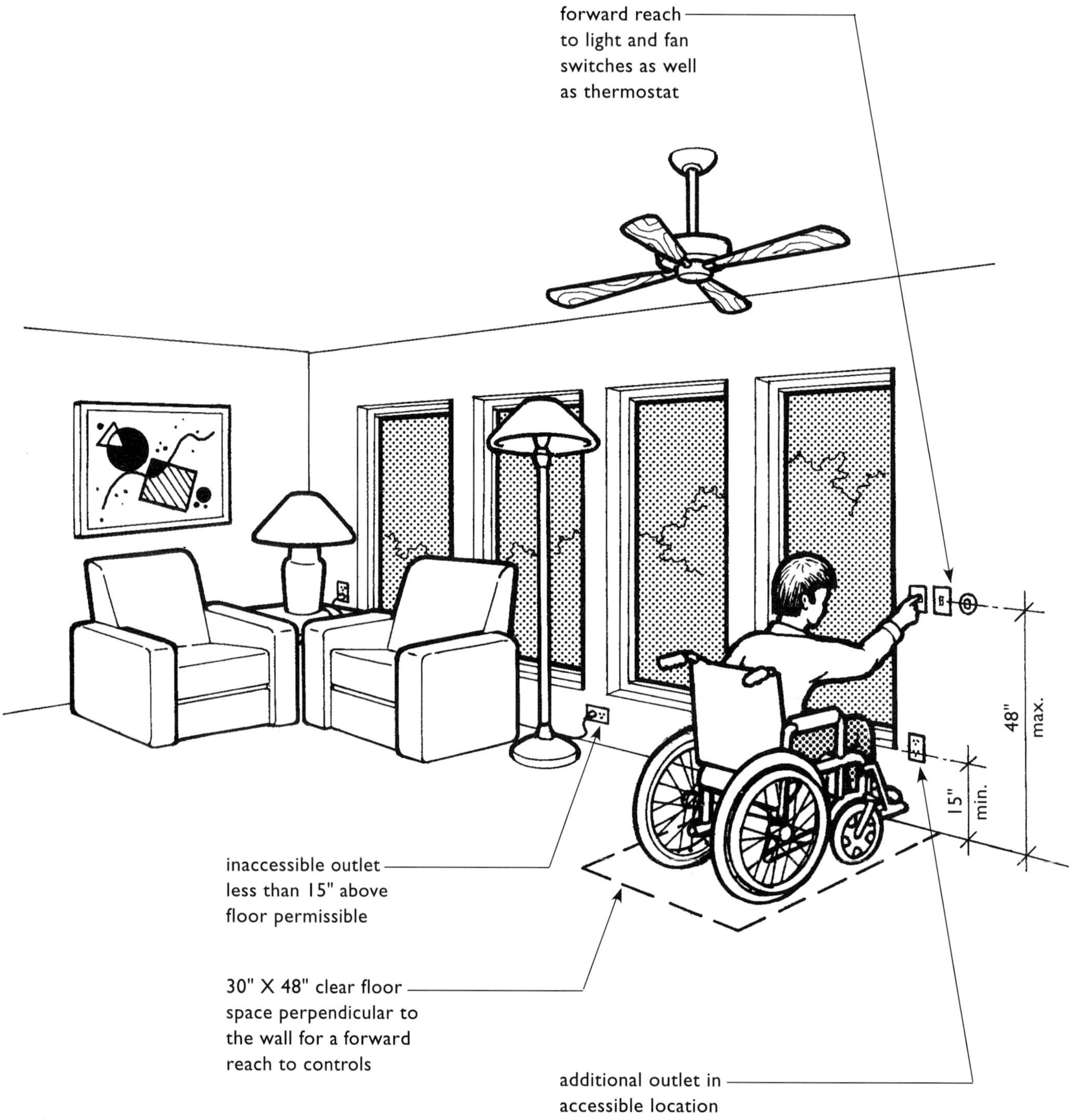

All Covered Switches, Outlets, and Controls Operated on a Frequent Basis Must be in Accessible Locations

Introduction

The ANSI specifications for accessible controls and operating mechanisms require a clear floor space to allow an approach by a person using a wheelchair, specify the height of the operable portion of the control, and require little or no force be exerted to operate the control. The Fair Housing Accessibility Guidelines (the Guidelines) do not require controls to be fully accessible but specify that light switches, electrical outlets, thermostats and other environmental controls, which are operated on a regular or frequent basis in the daily use of a dwelling unit, be in accessible locations.

The Guidelines' specifications for accessible locations, based on the ANSI (A117.1 - 1986) Standard, address where to position controls and outlets to be within the reach range of a seated user. Force and type of motion required to operate controls are not covered by the Guidelines.

Controls and Outlets Subject to the Requirements of the Guidelines

Environmental controls such as thermostats and other heating, air-conditioning, and ventilation mechanisms including ceiling fans and electrically operated skylights must be positioned in accessible locations, as must **light switches** and **electrical outlets** for each room. All these covered controls and outlets must be in accessible locations, with a few exceptions.

The Guidelines allow, for example, controls or outlets that do not satisfy the requirements, if comparable controls or outlets in accessible locations are provided within the same area. Comparable controls or outlets are those that perform the same function. For example, floor outlets (which are inaccessible) or outlets mounted in the corner of kitchen counters are permitted under the Guidelines, provided other outlets are available to serve the same space or area.

Controls and outlets not covered by the Guidelines include circuit breakers or electrical outlets dedicated to individual appliances such as refrigerators, built-in microwave ovens, washing machines, and dryers because neither circuit breakers nor these outlets are accessed frequently by residents. Appliance controls are not required to be in accessible locations because the Fair Housing Act is not intended to regulate the design of appliances.

Thus, when appliance controls are built into or are located on the appliance itself, they are not considered to be covered controls. Range or washing machine controls need not be within the reach range of seated users, although certainly it is preferred that such controls be within reach. Range hood fan and light controls, when mounted on the hood, are part of an appliance and are, therefore, not covered. However, if the range hood fan and light are wired to a separate switch on a wall or any location other than on the hood, range, or cooktop, then the control must be in an accessible location.

Garbage disposals do not fall under any of the categories of covered controls. The operating switch for a garbage disposal is not mounted on the appliance itself but is wired to another location. Although not a covered control, since garbage disposals are used frequently and since it is relatively simple to place operating switches for garbage disposals in accessible locations, it is recommended that it be done.

Emergency interrupt switches to mechanical systems such as furnaces or hot water heaters also are not covered by the Guidelines. However, it is recommended that such switches be in locations that can be reached from a seated position. Even when the mechanical system is located behind a narrow door in a small closet dedicated specifically to that purpose, it is recommended that the interrupt switch be positioned so it can be reached from outside the closet by a person using a wheelchair.

Switches, Outlets, and Controls Covered by the Guidelines

Covered

- light switches for controlling all room lights
- electrical outlets
- environmental controls
  thermostats and controls for other heating, air-conditioning, and ventilation systems

Not Covered

- circuit breakers
- appliance controls
- outlets dedicated for specific appliances

Accessible Locations

The Guidelines contain height specifications for wall-mounted controls and outlets based upon the reach ranges of seated people given in the ANSI Standard. Typically ANSI and other accessibility standards present reach ranges for both forward and side reaches: **1.** where the user must reach over an obstruction, and **2.** where the user's approach is not restricted by an obstruction. One of these positions, a side reach from a parallel position without an obstruction, requires a 48-inch long clear floor space parallel and close to the wall so a user can get close enough to reach controls and switches. Once a dwelling unit is furnished, sufficient room to execute such a parallel approach usually is not available; thus this specification was omitted from the Guidelines.

To accommodate all users in situations where there may or may not be a built-in counter, base cabinet, or other obstruction to interfere with reach, the Guidelines include specific requirements for mounting controls and switches so a person using a wheelchair can execute: **1.** a forward reach with no obstruction, **2.** a forward reach over an obstruction, and **3.** a side reach over an obstruction.

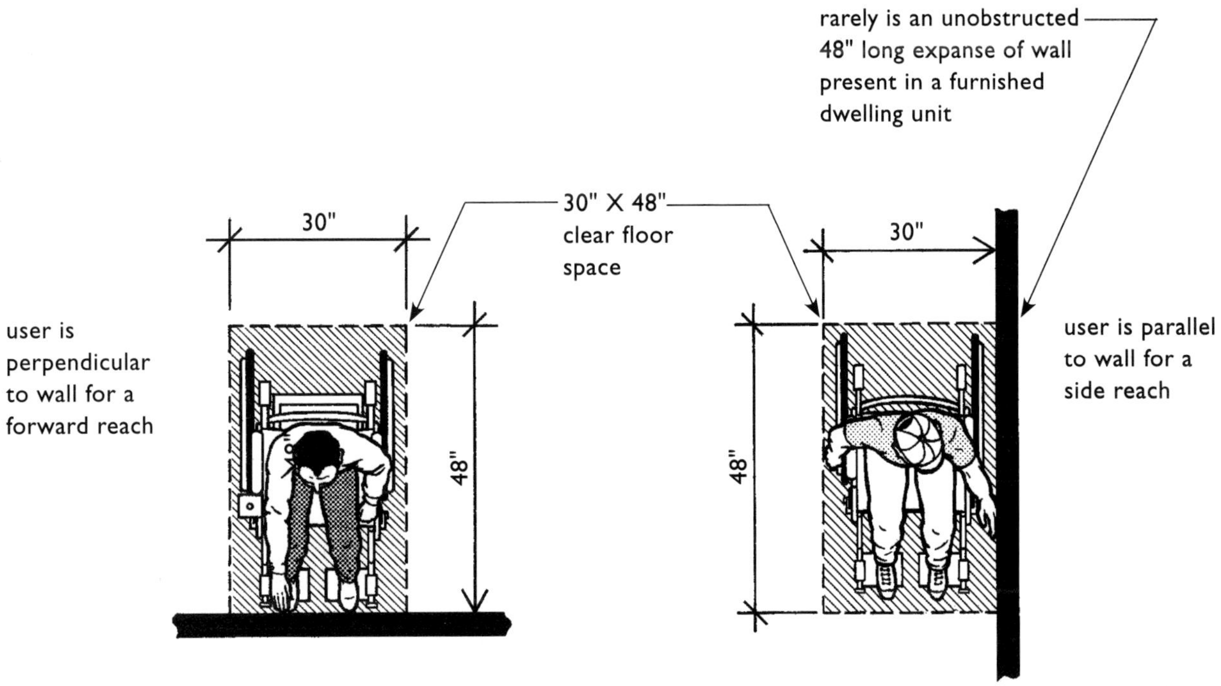

Forward Reach From a Perpendicular Approach Included in Guidelines

Side Reach from a Parallel Approach Not Included in Guidelines

Forward Reach with No Obstruction

Where there are no obstructions to interfere with the reach of a person using a wheelchair, controls and outlets may be mounted in a range from 15 to 48 inches above the floor. There must be a clear floor space of 30 inches x 48 inches perpendicular to the wall, adjoining a 36-inch wide accessible route, to allow a person using a wheelchair to approach and get into position to execute a forward reach to the control or outlet. See Chapter 4: "Accessible Route into and Through the Covered Dwelling Unit."

Thermostats and other controls that must be read pose additional considerations. Even though people using wheelchairs may be able to execute a forward reach of 48 inches at a clear wall, they may have difficulty seeing the small numerals and indicators generally found on thermostats. A person using a wheelchair, when positioned perpendicular to a wall, must lean forward over his or her feet and knees making it difficult to get close enough to read small type. Therefore, it is critical that thermostats and similar controls that must be read are mounted at or lower than 48 inches above the floor.

Forward Reach Over an Obstruction

Controls and outlets may be positioned above obstructions (e.g. built-in shelves and countertops) and still be mounted in locations that are accessible. A minimum 30-inch wide clear knee space as deep as the reach distance, adjoining a 36-inch wide accessible route, must be available below the counter/obstruction to allow a person using a wheelchair to pull up and execute a forward reach over the obstruction.

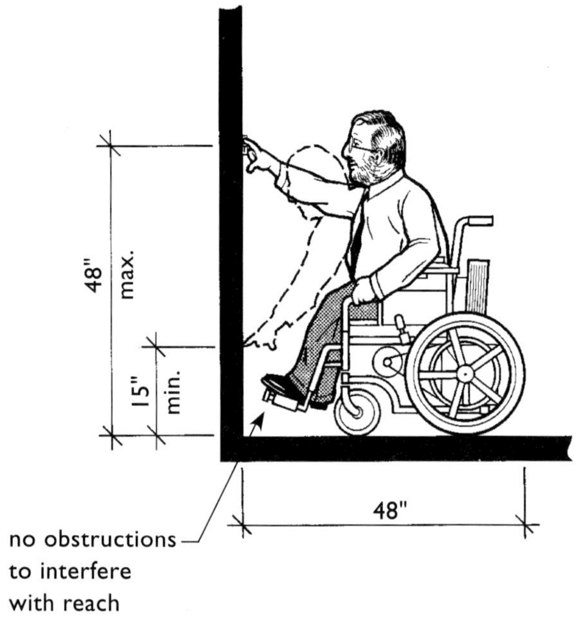

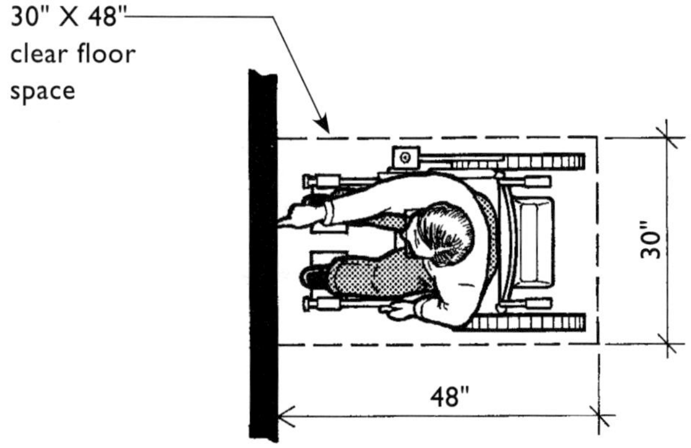

High and Low Forward Reach Limits From a Perpendicular Approach

For obstructions extending from 0 to 20 inches from the wall the maximum height for a control or outlet over the obstruction is 48 inches above the floor. Deeper shelves, extending 20 to 25 inches from the wall, reduce the maximum mounting height of controls and outlets to 44 inches. Controls and outlets mounted over obstructions extending further than 25 inches are outside the reach range of people using wheelchairs and are not considered to be in accessible locations. However, HUD allows an industry tolerance of 1/2 inch to permit the installation of standard countertops that may project from the back wall for a maximum dimension of 25-1/2 inches.

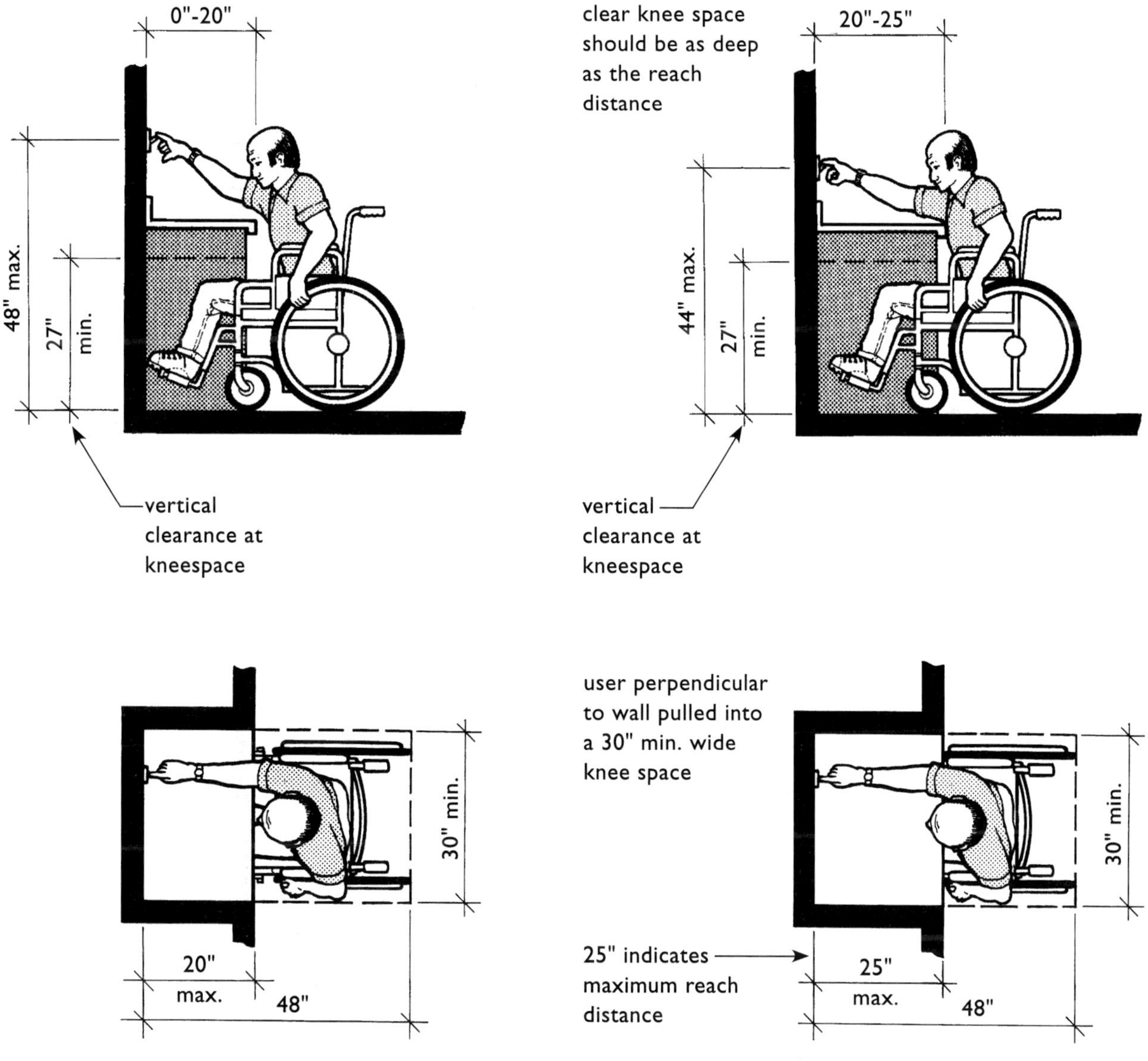

Maximum Forward Reach
(From a Perpendicular Approach) over an Obstruction

Side Reach Over an Obstruction

To reach controls and outlets mounted over base cabinets which lack knee space, a person using a wheelchair must be able to approach the cabinet from a position parallel to the cabinet and execute a side reach. This parallel position is made up of a 30-inch x 48-inch clear floor space adjoining a 36-inch wide minimum accessible route. When executing a side reach over a cabinet, the upper limit of the range is reduced to 46 inches.

Cabinet depth is limited to 24 inches. HUD permits use of a standard 24-inch deep cabinet with an additional extension of 1 to 1-1/2 inches for countertops for a maximum depth of 25-1/2 inches. If a built-in shelf, cabinet, or other obstruction must be deeper than 25-1/2 inches, then any switches, outlets, and controls that must be in accessible locations are not permitted to be installed over such deep surfaces.

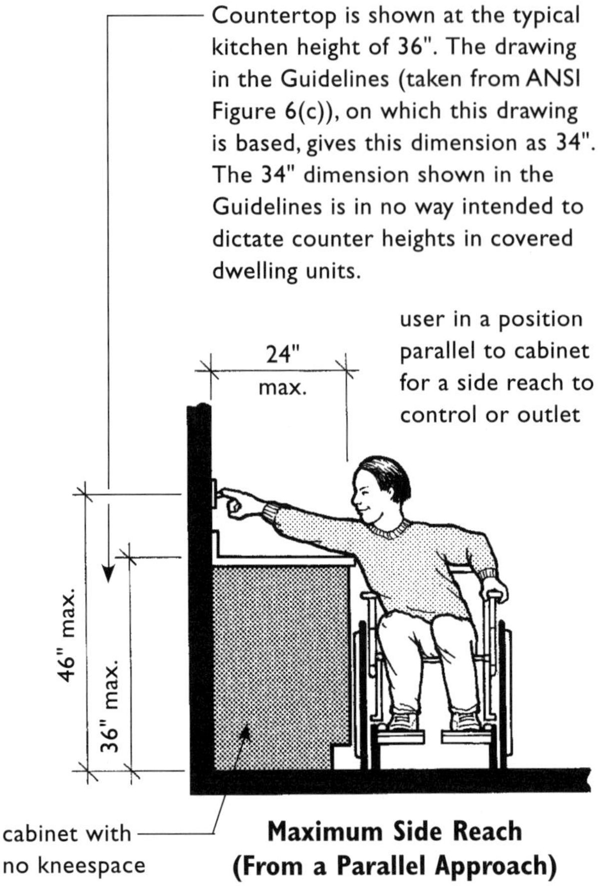

Maximum Side Reach (From a Parallel Approach) Over an Obstruction

Mounting Locations for Outlets

For accessible controls and outlets, all operable parts must be within the ranges specified above. When electrical outlets are installed horizontally or vertically, duplex outlets must have both receptacles within the reach range. Measurements are made as illustrated below.

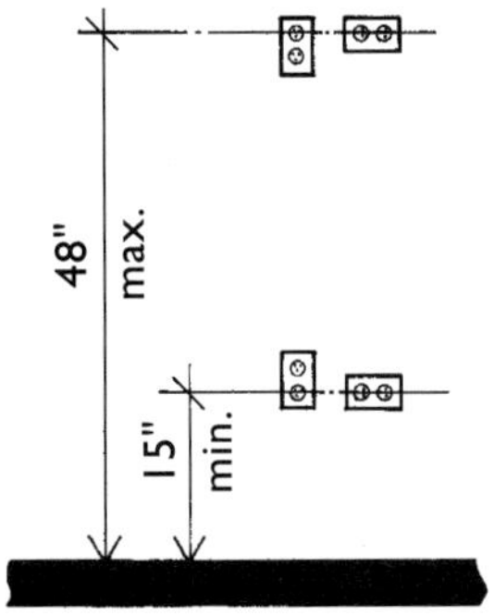

Mounting Height for Outlets

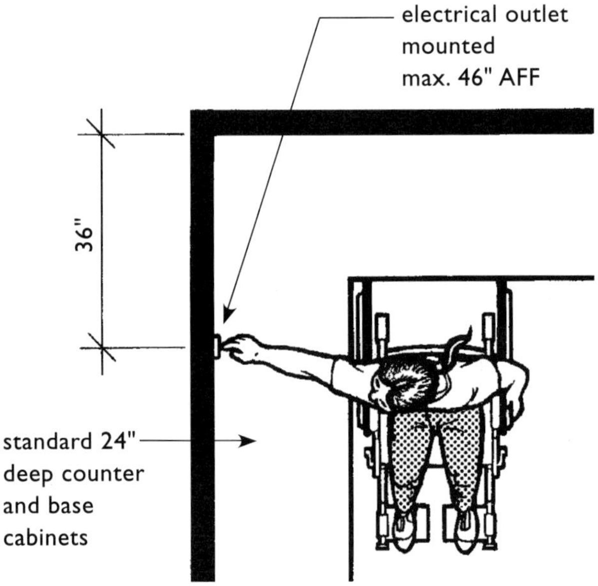

Electrical Outlets on Walls Over Cabinets Must Be a Minimum of 36" from a Corner

Recommendations for Increased Accessibility

The Guidelines do not specify that controls and switches installed in dwelling units be accessible in terms of ease of operation, but that they be in accessible locations. For anyone specifying building products and appliances and wishing to enhance the accessibility of dwelling units, the following is a brief discussion of the types of switches and controls that increase usability for people with disabilities, as well as other persons who may experience hand limitations.

The most universally usable switches are rocker switches, toggle switches, and touch type electronic switches because they can be operated by a single touch, require little force, and do not require gripping, twisting, or fine finger dexterity.

Lever controls are generally usable by people with disabilities because they do not require grasping or significant force, and in some instances, their shape may double as an integral pointer to indicate the control's position. For people with limited strength or hand dexterity, smooth round knobs are especially difficult, as are controls that must be pushed down and turned at the same time.

Poor Choice

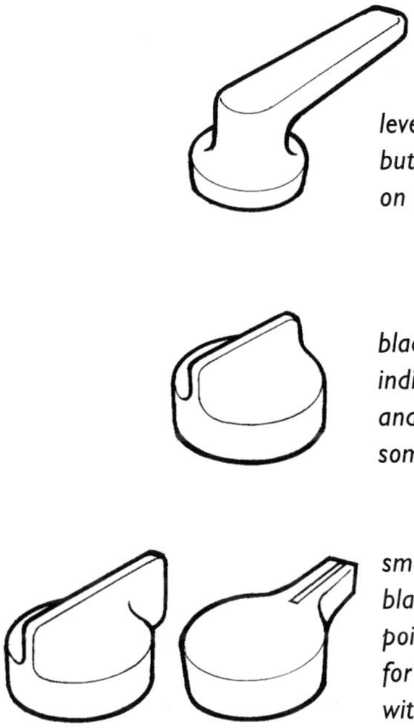

Better Control Choices

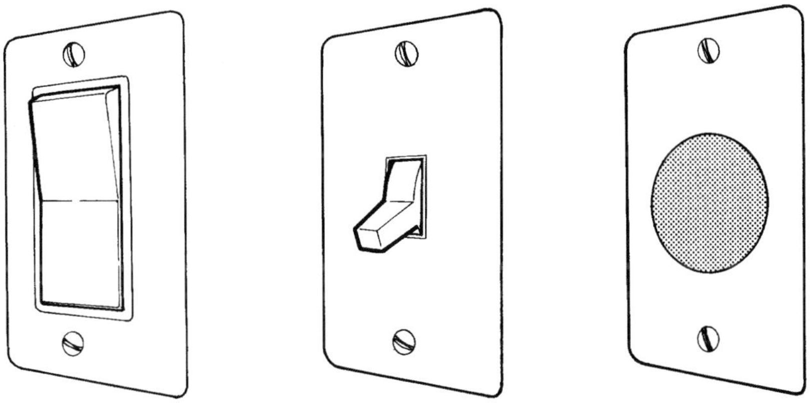

Switches Most People Can Operate

Chapter Six:

Requirement 6

Reinforced Walls for Grab Bars

6

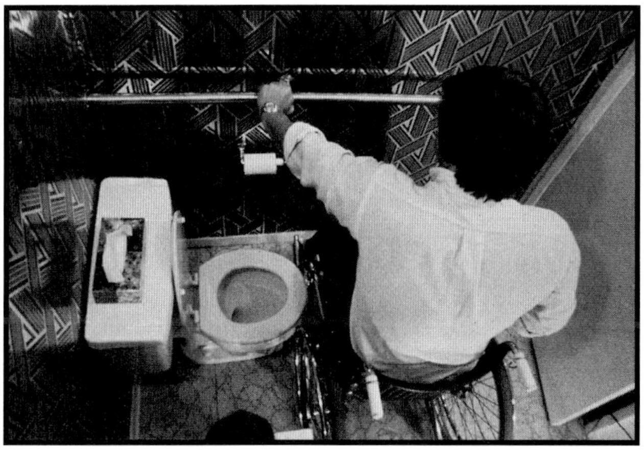

"...covered multifamily dwellings with a building entrance on an accessible route shall be designed and constructed in such a manner that all premises within covered multifamily dwelling units contain reinforcements in bathroom walls to allow later installation of grab bars around toilet, tub, shower stall and shower seat, where such facilities are provided."

Fair Housing Act Regulations, 24 CFR 100.205

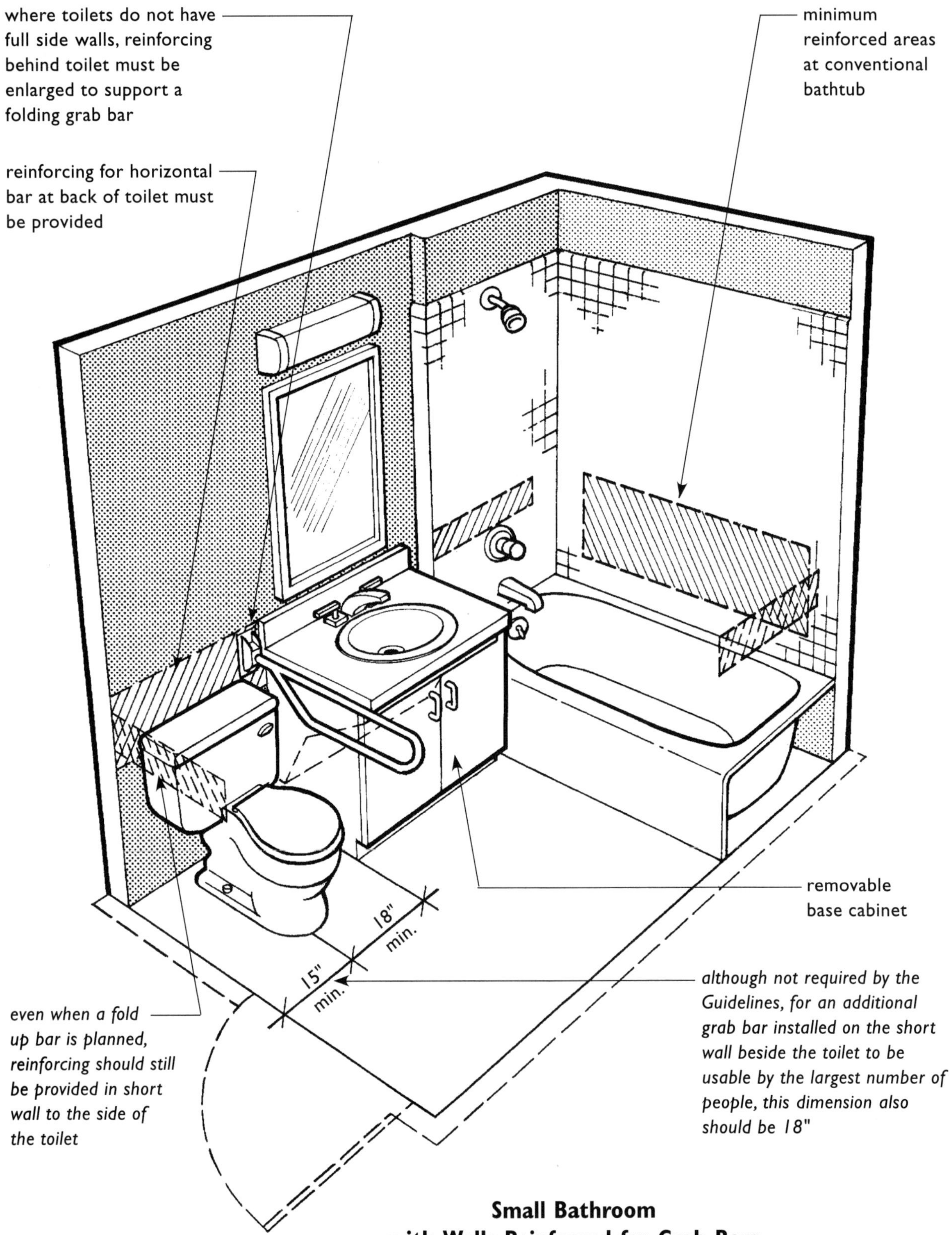

Small Bathroom
with Walls Reinforced for Grab Bars

Introduction

The Fair Housing Accessibility Guidelines (the Guidelines) do not require that grab bars be installed in bathrooms. However, the Guidelines do require that bathroom walls be sufficiently strong to allow for later installation of grab bars for resident use. This requirement applies to all bathrooms, and also to powder rooms when the powder room is the only toilet facility on the entry level of a multistory dwelling unit in an elevator building (see page 4.9). Reinforcing methods are discussed later in this chapter.

Grab bars are critical for many people with mobility impairments to be able to safely transfer on and off the toilet. Safety for everyone is greatly increased by the addition of grab bars at bathtubs and showers. The Guidelines do not prescribe the type or size of grab bars, nor the structural strength they must exhibit. The Guidelines state only that the necessary reinforcement must be placed "to permit the later installation of appropriate grab bars." HUD encourages builders to look at the 1986 ANSI A117.1 Standard, or an equivalent or stricter standard, or their state or local building code in planning for or selecting appropriate grab bars.

It is recommended that building owners and managers permanently mount directions for installation of grab bars in every dwelling unit where applicable. The type of construction should be described, where reinforcing is located, and suggestions made for the most effective method for installing grab bars. These notices could be laminated to the inside of a linen closet door or to the inside of a utility or water heater/furnace door.

Reinforcing for Grab Bars at Toilets

The Guidelines specify that reinforcing at least 6 inches wide by 24 inches long, capable of supporting grab bars, be provided behind and beside toilets. These minimal areas to be reinforced are adapted from the 1986 ANSI A117.1 Standard. However, the reinforcing should be both longer and wider so sufficient solid material is available to mount grab bars of differing lengths, mounting configurations, and designs. In fact, the Guidelines encourage longer reinforcing, as shown in the Guidelines Figure 3, "Water Closets in Adaptable Bathrooms," where the preferred length of 42 inches for side wall reinforcing is given.

Grab bars, to be within the ranges presented in most accessibility standards, are mounted so their centerline is 33 inches to 36 inches above the floor. If the bottom of the reinforced area is at 32 inches, and a resident chooses to mount a bar at 33 inches, the mounting plates will extend below the reinforced area by 1/2 inch or more. To avoid a weak and unsafe connection, it is critical that reinforcing be enlarged.

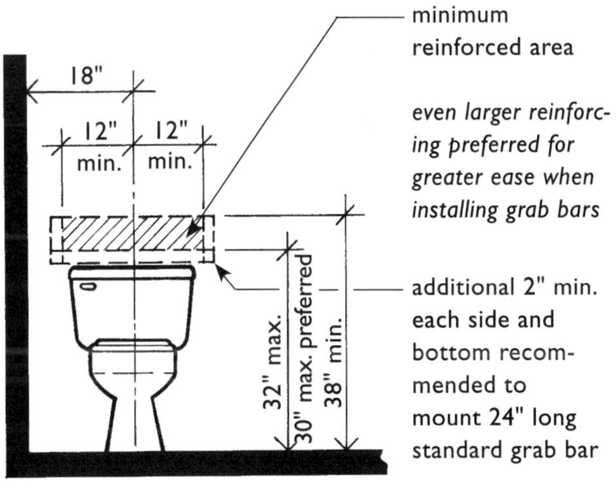

Minimum Reinforcing Behind Toilets Located Beside a Wall

The leading edge of the reinforcing beside the toilet should be positioned at least 36 inches from the back wall to accommodate a bar that is a minimum of 24 inches long. If the reinforcing starts 6 inches from the back wall then the 24 inches of reinforcing should be increased to 30 inches minimum. Whenever a toilet is next to a wall that allows for a longer area of reinforcing (42" is preferred), the longer area should be reinforced.

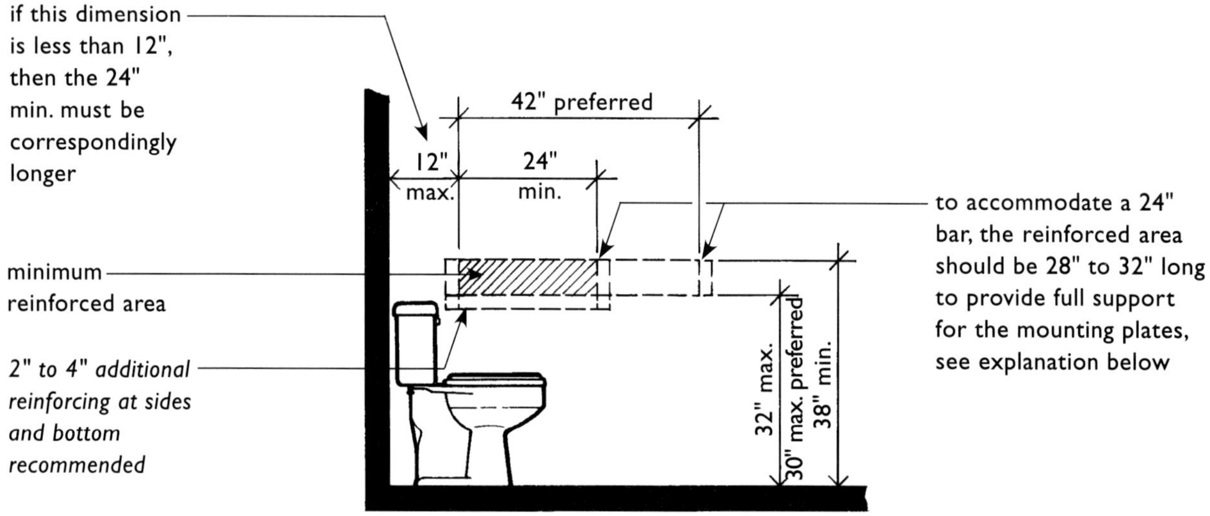

Minimum Reinforcing to the Side of Toilets

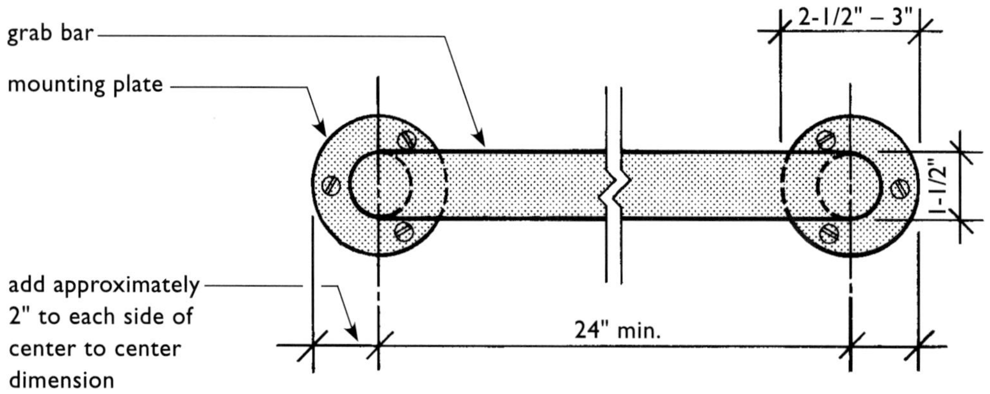

Escutcheon Plates
Extend Beyond the Given Grab Bar Length

Toilets positioned beside a wall offer the highest degree of safe use since a grab bar can be mounted to the side of the toilet. The dimensions describing the distance from the center of the toilet to a side wall and to the nearest fixture or obstruction on the opposite side have been adapted from the ANSI Standard. The 18 inches from the centerline of the toilet to the wall is an absolute measurement and will accommodate a grab bar and the shoulders of a person seated on the toilet. The Guidelines provide for a 15-inch minimum dimension on the nongrab bar side, which is more lenient than ANSI (which requires 18 inches minimum).

In small bathrooms where the door is located in the side wall immediately adjacent to the toilet, full length reinforcing as specified in the Guidelines may not be possible without enlarging the room. While a short grab bar is not preferred, it does work for some people.

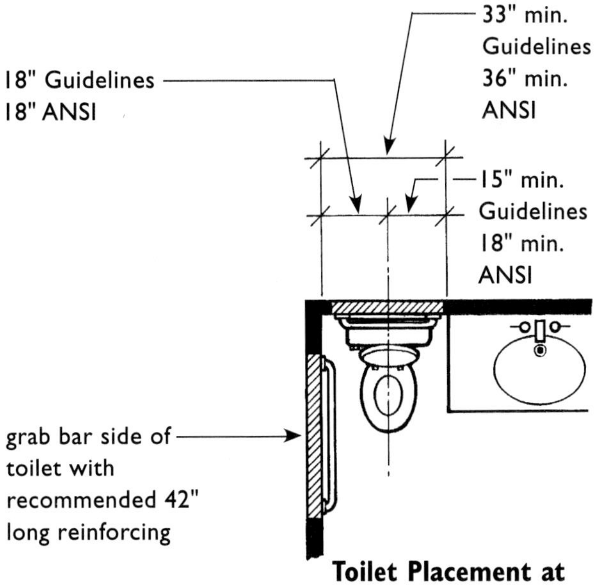

Toilet Placement at Adjoining Walls and Fixtures

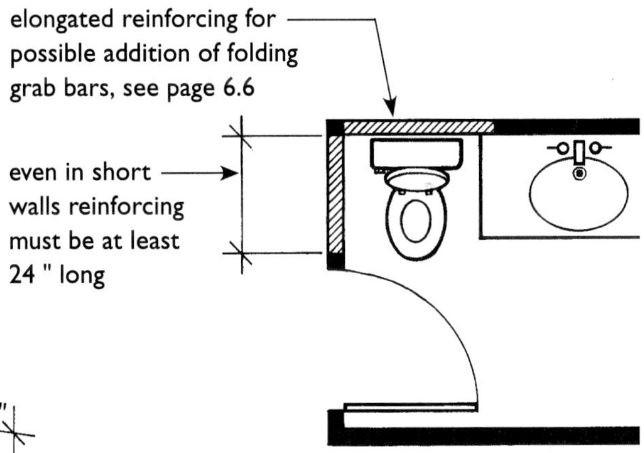

Reinforcing Beside Toilet Shorter Because Door is Located on Same Wall

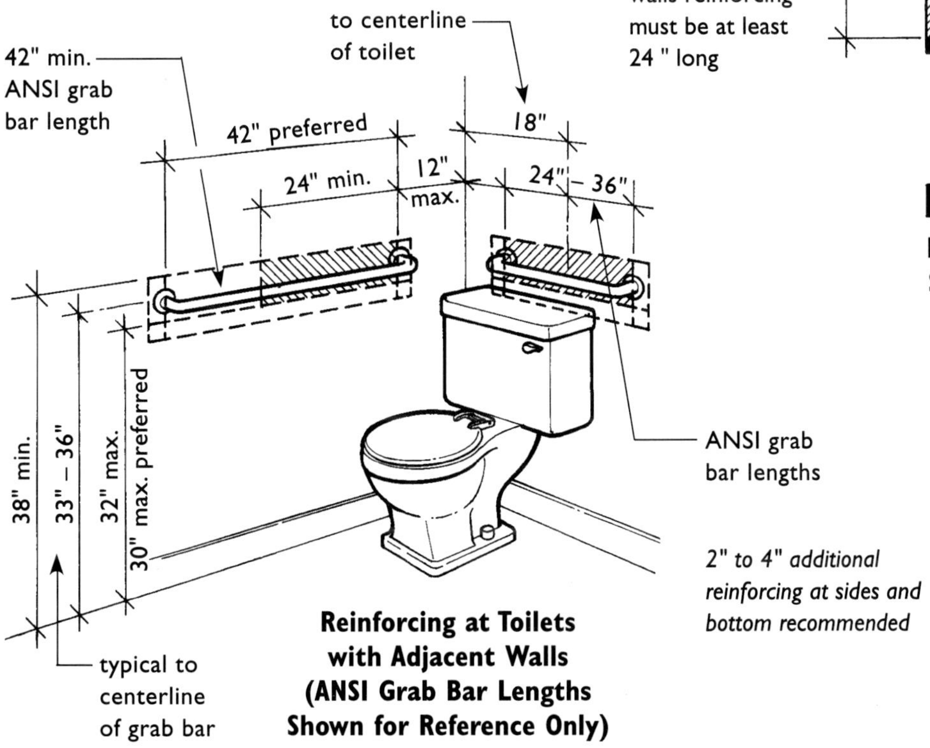

Reinforcing at Toilets with Adjacent Walls (ANSI Grab Bar Lengths Shown for Reference Only)

Folding and Floor-Mounted Grab Bars at Toilets

The Guidelines permit the installation of folding wall-mounted, floor-mounted or wall and floor-mounted grab bars where it is not possible to install "appropriate" wall-mounted ANSI, or similar, complying grab bars. This is particularly relevant when there is no wall or a very short wall adjacent to the toilet.

A wide variety of alternative folding grab bars are available. One of the most versatile is the bar that may be pulled down for support and folded out of the way when not needed. Although not quite as stable as the bar that is securely mounted to a wall at both ends, it provides reasonable support for some people.

Reinforcing for such folding grab bars must be substantial because of their cantilevered design. See the top illustration in the right column. For a grab bar to be floor-mounted or be hinged and mounted on the wall behind the toilet, larger areas of reinforcing in walls will be necessary and care must be taken to provide for the types of bars that will not encroach upon the necessary clear floor space at fixtures.

It is recommended that reinforcing for all types of folding grab bars be done strictly as recommended by manufacturers. Information about the exact size and location of reinforcement, and the type and size of bars the reinforcement is engineered to accommodate, should be included in the residents' information suggested on page 6.3. See Product Resource List in Appendix A for sources of fold-up grab bars.

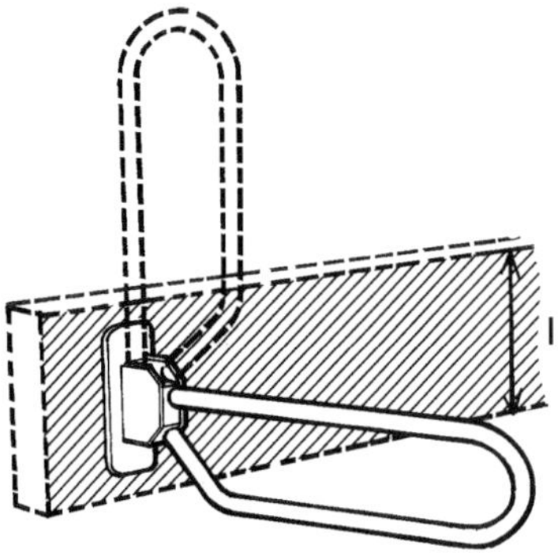

Wall-Mounted Fold-Up Grab Bar

Floor-mounted fold-up grab bars, because of the stresses exerted upon them, will require an extremely secure floor connection. In frame construction, if access to the underside of the floor is available (i.e., from a crawl space or basement), necessary blocking or other reinforcing might be installed at the time the bar is installed. On concrete floor systems additional reinforcing may or may not be necessary. In either case the advice of the manufacturer and/or a professional structural engineer should be followed.

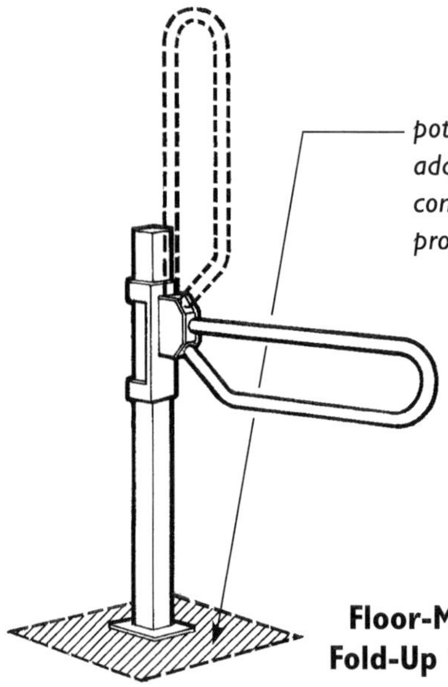

Floor-Mounted Fold-Up Grab Bar

When a toilet is positioned in the room away from a side wall, grab bars must be mounted on the wall behind the toilet or be floor mounted. Reinforcing should be long and wide enough so a folding bar can be installed and, when lowered into position for use, its centerline is 15-3/4 inches from the centerline of the toilet. This dimension is consistent with the requirement that 18 inches be provided from the centerline of the toilet to the wall when that wall is to be equipped with a grab bar.

Advance planning will be necessary to determine on which side of the toilet a folding grab bar will be placed so the necessary 18 inches of space and additional reinforcing can be shifted to the grab bar side of the toilet. Although not required, it is recommended that the toilet be centered in a 36-inch space rather than the 33-inch space specified for usable bathrooms in the Guidelines. Adequate reinforcing could then run the full length behind the toilet to allow fold-up bars to be installed on either side, depending upon the needs and desires of the resident.

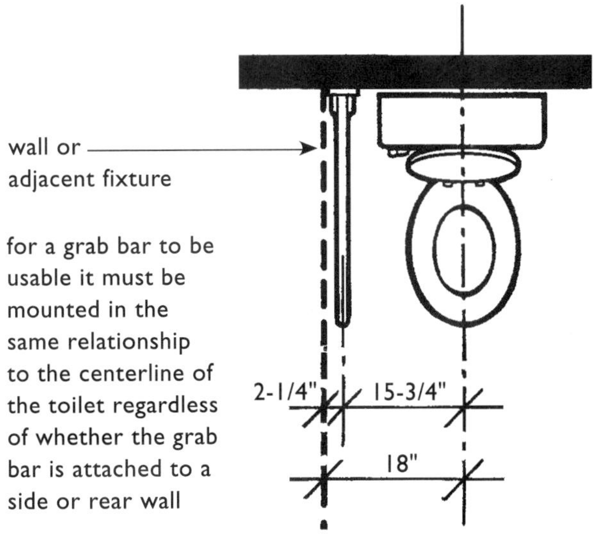

Grab Bar Placement

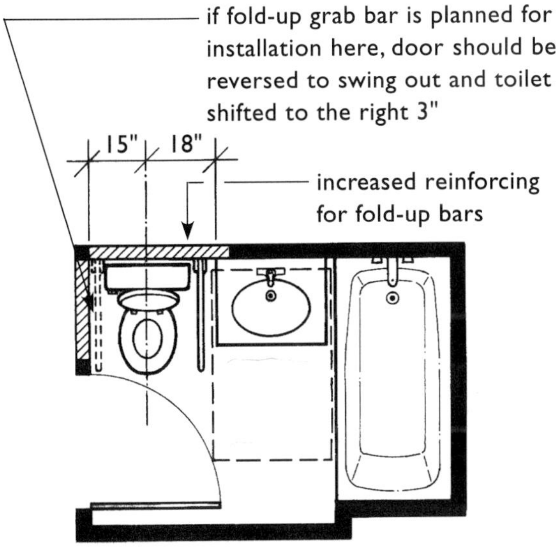

Toilet Between Lavatory and Short Wall

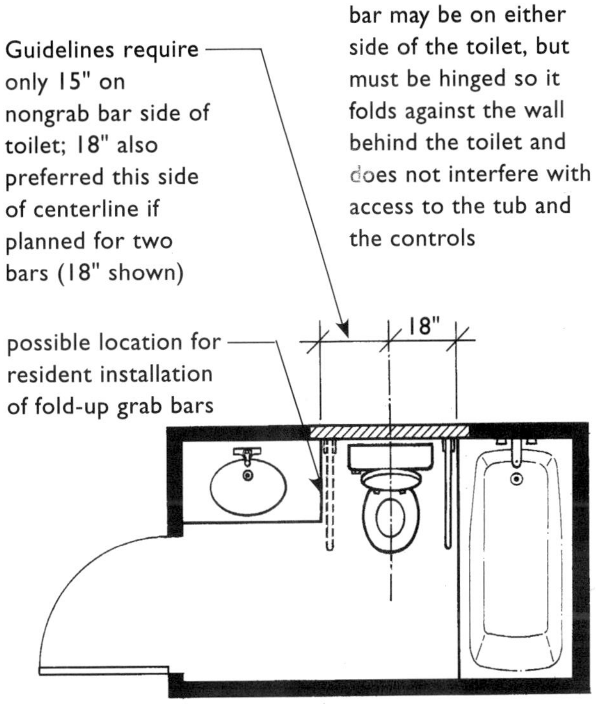

Toilet Between Tub and Lavatory

Recommended Locations for Fold-Up Grab Bars

Fixed floor and wall-mounted grab bars also can be installed where toilets are not adjacent to full length walls. This type of installation will require little if any additional reinforcing but is a poor choice because the grab bars tend to block access to adjacent fixtures. The fixed floor mount encroaches on clear floor space and interferes with wheelchair maneuvering.

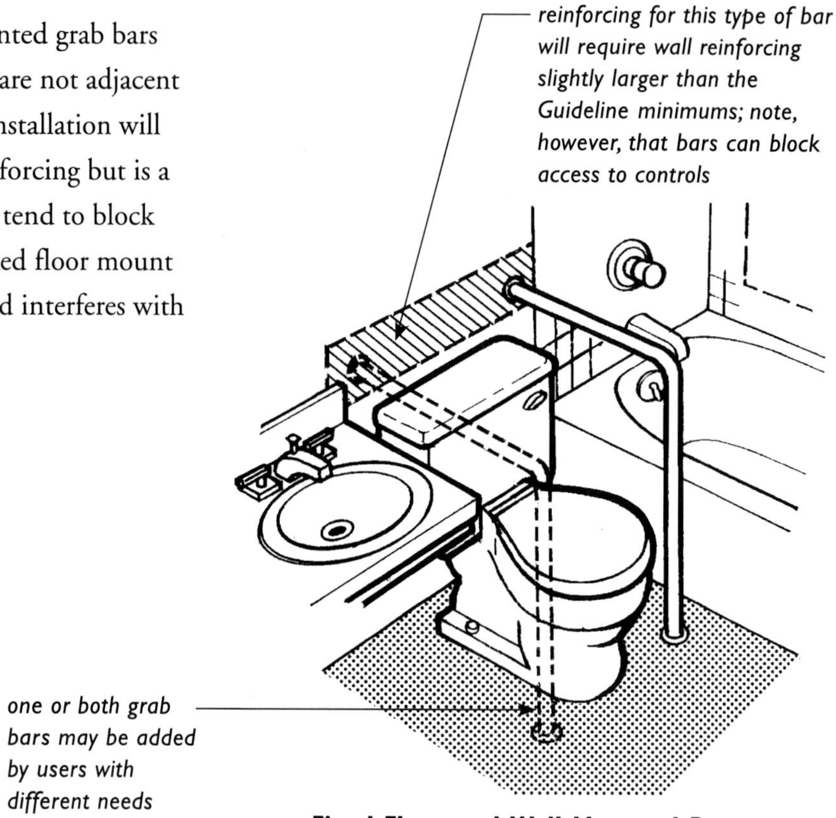

Fixed Floor and Wall-Mounted Bars Not a Good Choice for Many People

REINFORCING FOR GRAB BARS AT CONVENTIONAL BATHTUBS

At conventional bathtubs the Guidelines specify wall reinforcing for grab bars as shown in the accompanying illustrations. The intent is to make it easy for a resident to install grab bars similar to those specified in ANSI A117.1 or other equal accessibility standard or code.

For the same reasons as discussed at toilets, the reinforced areas specified at the head and foot of tubs should be enlarged to provide full support for mounting plates and horizontal bars at the lowest position of 33" above the room floor. The enlarged reinforced areas are shown here as recommended additional reinforcing.

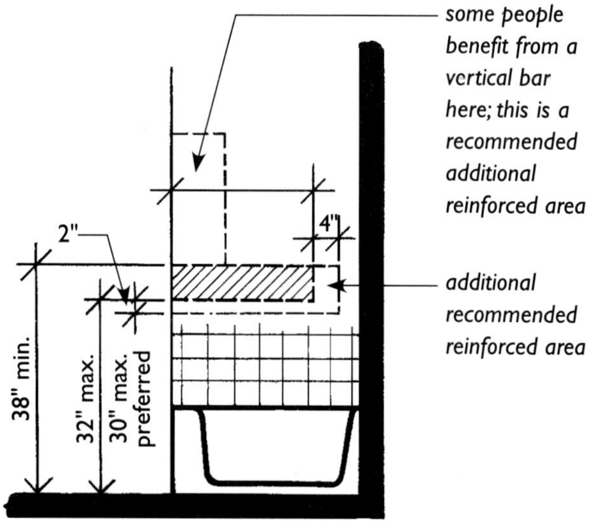

Foot (Control Wall)

Reinforced Areas Required by the Guidelines at Conventional Bathtubs

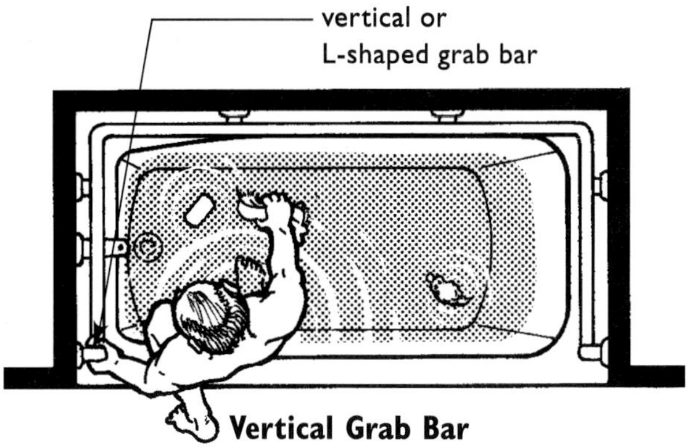

Vertical Grab Bar Provides Support for Ambulatory Users

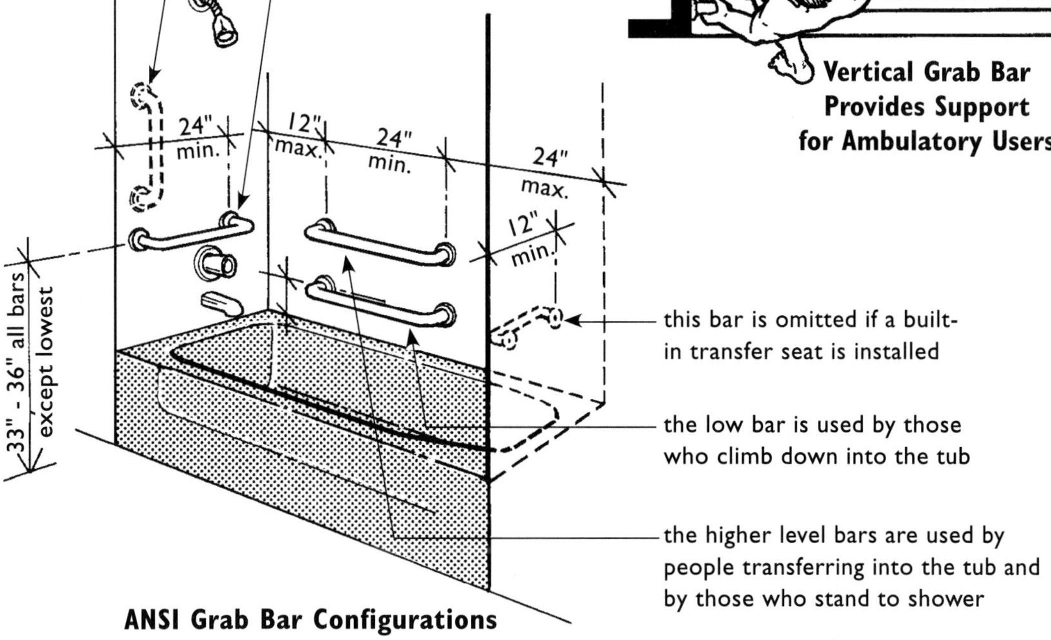

ANSI Grab Bar Configurations at Conventional Tubs (for Reference Only)

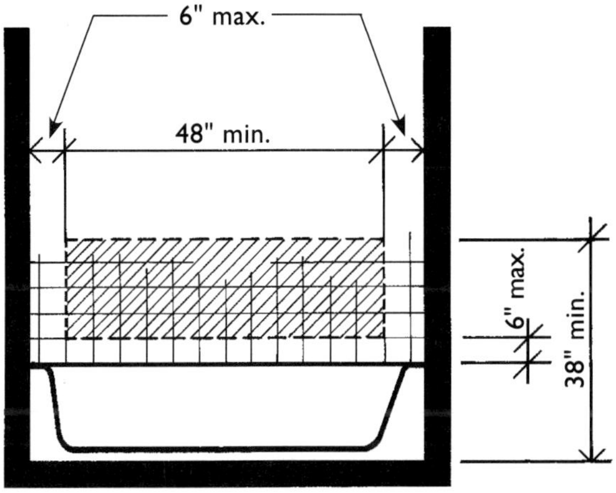

Back Wall

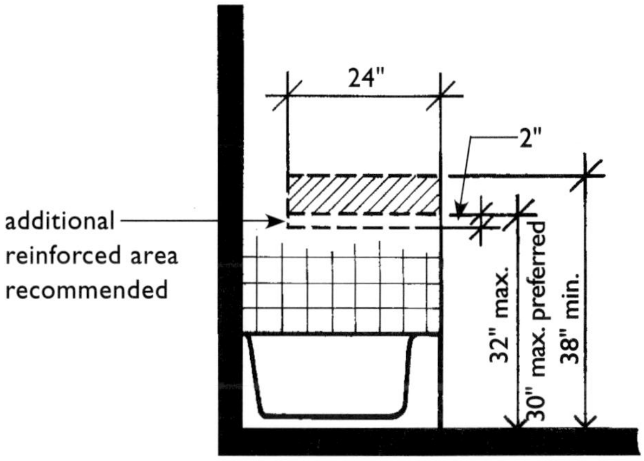

Head

Reinforced Areas Required by the Guidelines at Conventional Bathtubs

Reinforcing for Grab Bars at Non-Conventional Bathtubs

The Guidelines do not limit the size or proportion of bathtubs or showers to the configurations shown. Bathtubs may have shelves or benches at either end, or may be installed without surrounding walls, provided alternative methods for mounting grab bars are made. For example, a sunken bathtub placed away from walls could have reinforced areas in the floor for installation of floor-mounted grab bars. Whenever walls are adjacent to raised or sunken tubs, reinforcing should be provided that closely matches the sizes given at conventional bathtubs.

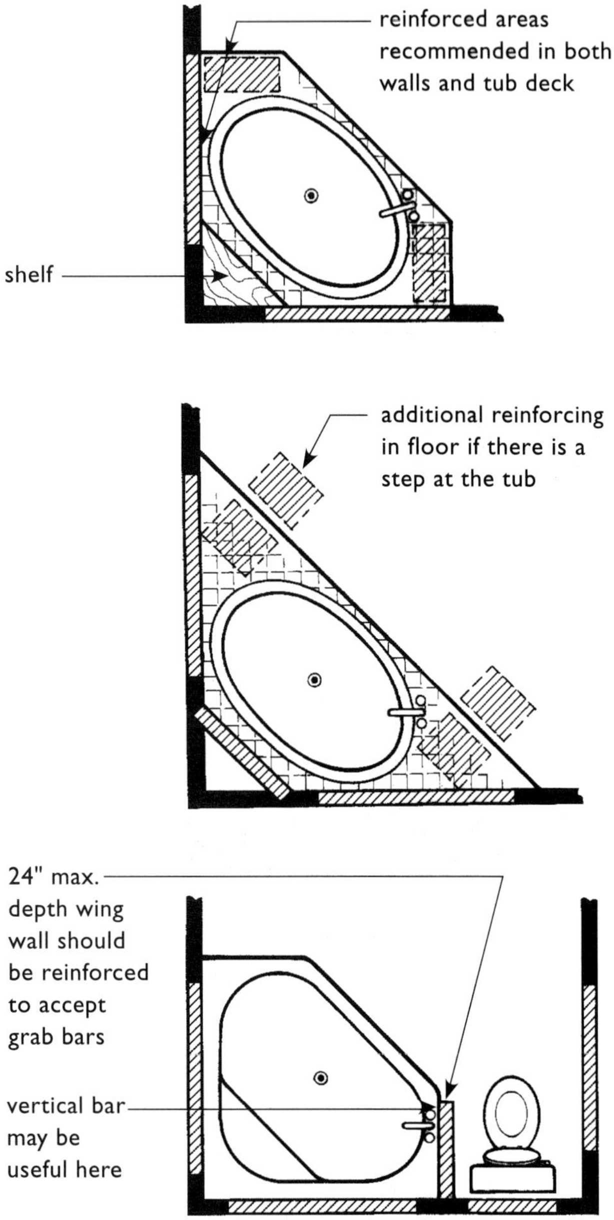

Recommended Reinforcing for Grab Bars at Raised or Sunken Tubs

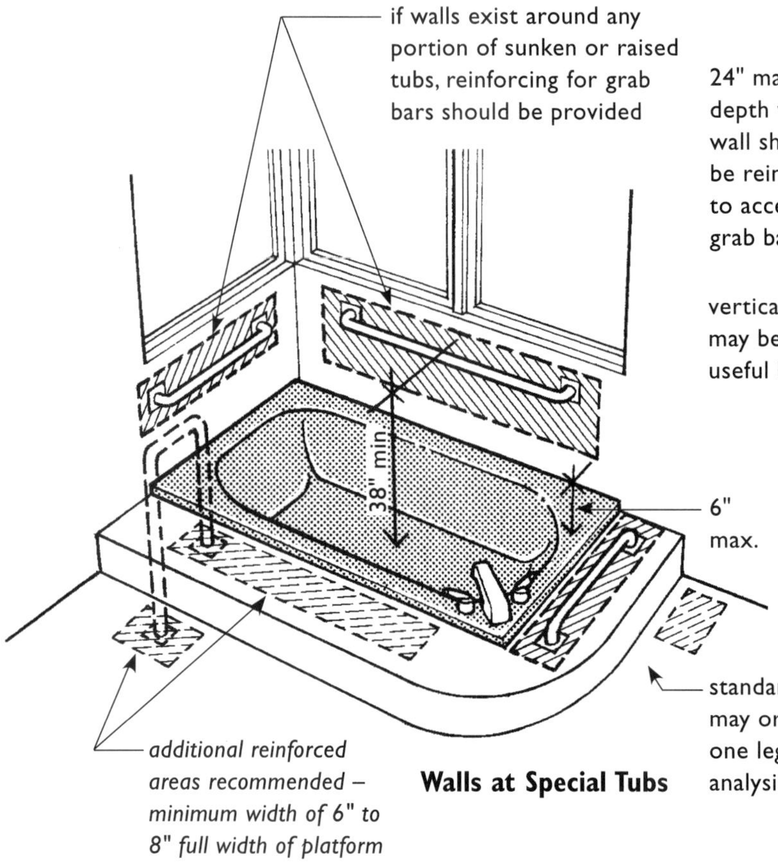

Walls at Special Tubs

Floor-Mounted Grab Bars at Special Bathtubs

On open sides of raised tubs having decks at tub rim level and at floors surrounding sunken tubs, the deck and other designated floor areas should be reinforced so they are structurally capable of receiving floor-mounted grab bars. The floor or deck must provide secure anchorage and such bars should withstand a 250 pound load applied in any direction and at any point. Although not required, any grab bar installation should be able to meet or exceed ANSI 4.24 Grab Bars.

Floor-mounted bars in these installations may be from 18 inches to 36 inches above the tub rim. Some have a braced double-footed mount as shown here.

If designated reinforced floor areas are to be provided, their size should be comparable in length to those required for conventional bathtubs, or proportionally longer if the bathtub is larger than a conventional bathtub. The width of the reinforcing may well need to be wider than other reinforced areas for sufficient strength and space to accept the braced double-footed mounts described above.

The size and exact location of designated reinforced floor areas should be included in the permanent affixed tenant information for installing grab bars recommended at the beginning of this chapter. The builder/owner/manager also may want to include in that information the height, type of fasteners, type of bar and mount, or even the model number and manufacturer of the bars upon which the adequacy of the structure was engineered.

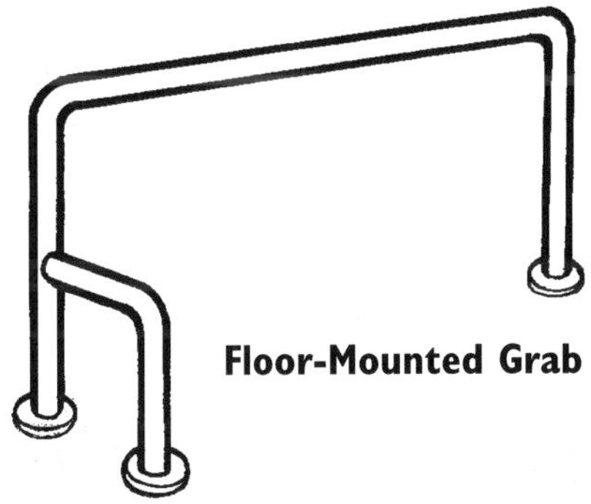

Floor-Mounted Grab Bar

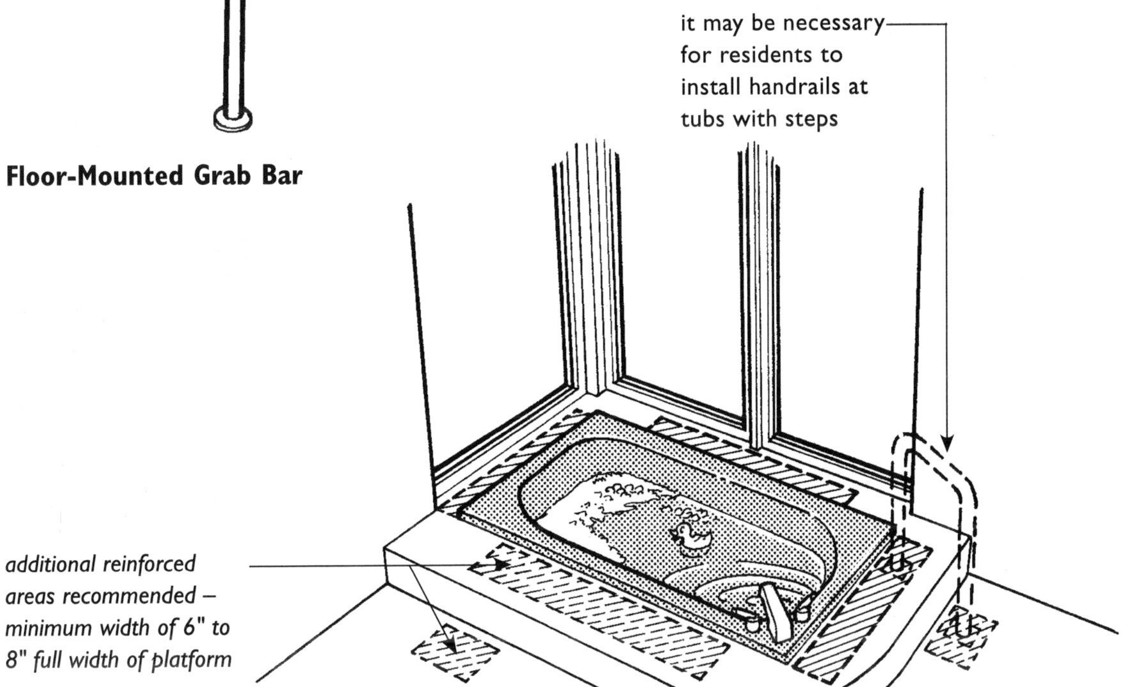

No Structural Walls at Special Tubs

Reinforcing for Grab Bars and Seats at Showers

In glass shower stalls, only those walls that are solid construction, i.e., wood or metal studs with gypsum wallboard and/or tile or solid masonry, must have reinforced areas. Glass walls are not required to be reinforced, nor are shower stalls required to have the waterproof pan or floor seal pierced to receive screws/bolts for floor-mounted grab bars.

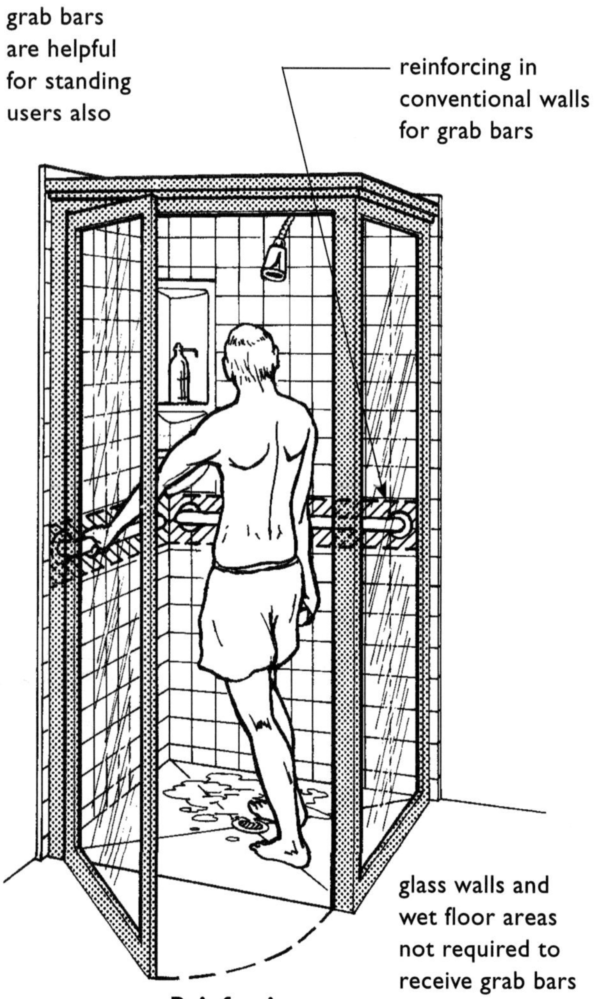

Reinforcing in Glass-Walled Shower Stalls

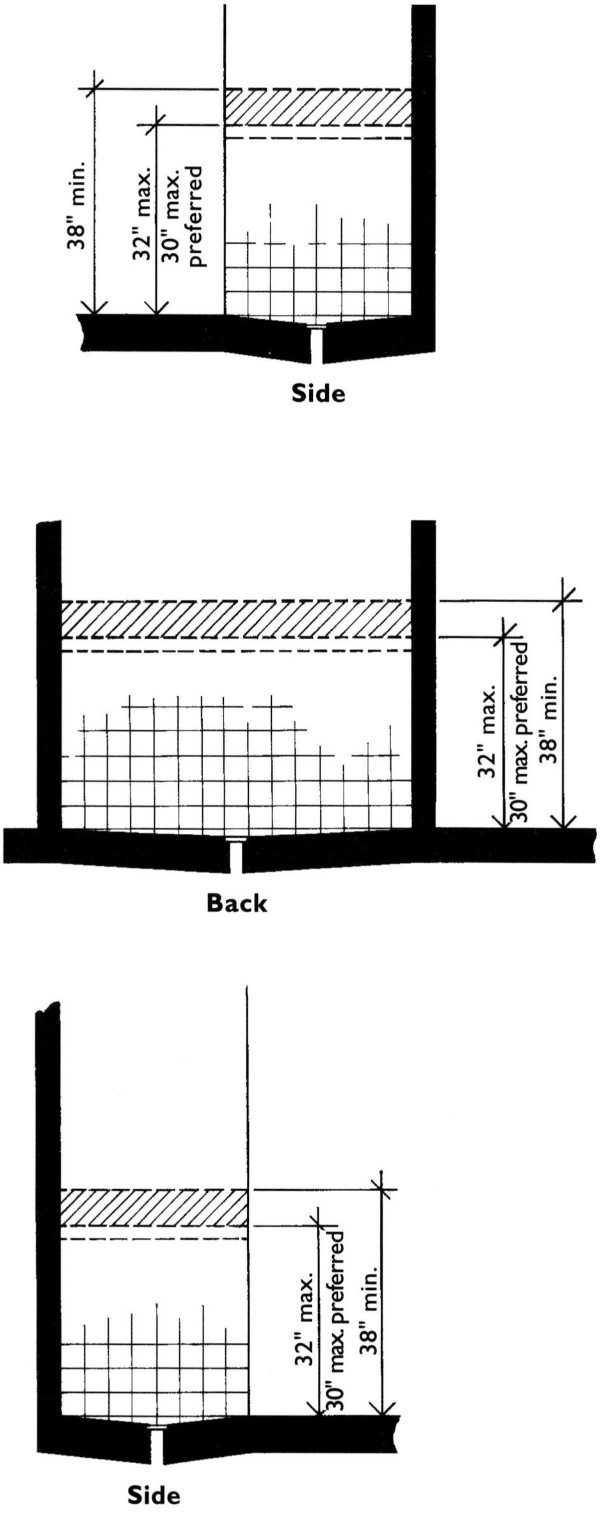

Minimum Reinforcing for Grab Bars in Showers

Shower stalls in covered dwellings may be any size or configuration unless they are the only bathing fixture provided in the dwelling unit or on the entry level of a multistory dwelling in a building with one or more elevators. (See clear floor space at shower stalls in Chapter 7, Part B: "Usable Bathrooms.") Reinforcing for grab bars must be at the height shown in the illustrations on the preceding page and extend the full width of both side walls and the back wall. If shower walls curve, reinforcing must still be provided.

Because of the commonly accepted need to install horizontal grab bars between 33 and 36 inches above the floor, it is recommended that this reinforcing be enlarged so the bottom edge is 30 inches above the floor as explained previously at toilets and tubs.

There are certain situations where the shower stall is required to have reinforcing for later installation of a wall-hung bench seat. When this is required is addressed in Part B of Chapter 7, "Usable Bathrooms." Reinforcing is required in a shower stall that measures a nominal 36 inches x 36 inches. The reinforcing is located on the wall opposite the controls and must run the full width of the stall, starting at the floor, to a minimum height of 24 inches.

HUD encourages builders to refer to the ANSI Standard or local codes for specifications on grab bars and wall-hung shower benches. The ANSI specified shower seat is an excellent design for safe use by people with disabilities. The builder should attempt to locate several manufacturers and size the reinforced area for the seat to accommodate more than one model. See Product Resource List in Appendix A. Information detailing reinforced areas and location, as well as product choices, should be included in the permanently affixed resident information recommended at the beginning of this chapter.

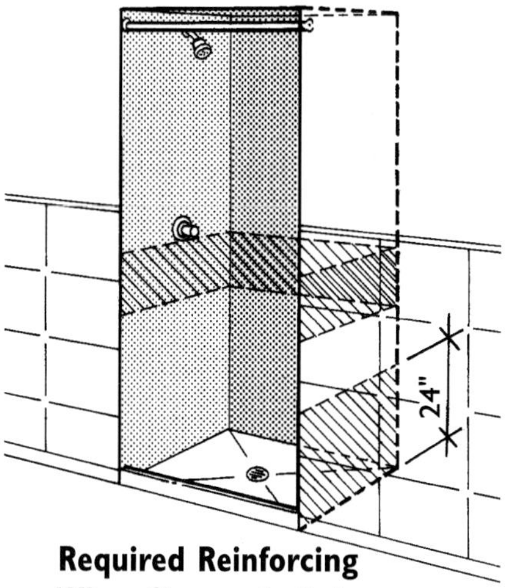

Required Reinforcing When Shower is Only Bathing Fixture

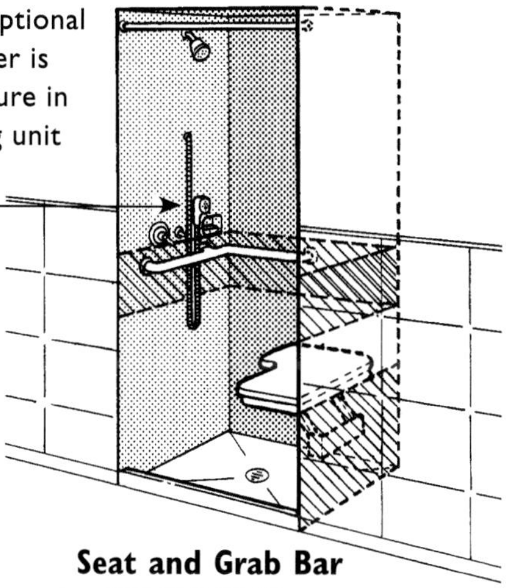

Seat and Grab Bar in 36" X 36" Shower

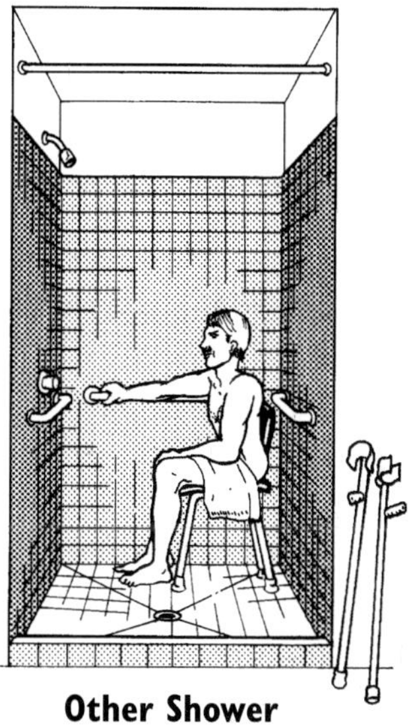

Other Shower Configurations Permitted

Recommended Reinforcing Methods

The Guidelines do not prescribe the type of material to use or methods for providing reinforcement at bathroom walls. Grab bar reinforcing may be accomplished in a variety of ways, some of which are suggested below.

Limited Area Reinforcing with Solid Wood Blocking

Stud Wall. In wood frame construction, the mounting area for grab bars can be reinforced by installing solid wood blocking either between or "let into" the studs and fastening the blocking securely to the studs. In either way, the solid wood reinforcing is installed flush with the face of the stud so finish materials can be applied to the studs and blocking in the normal manner.

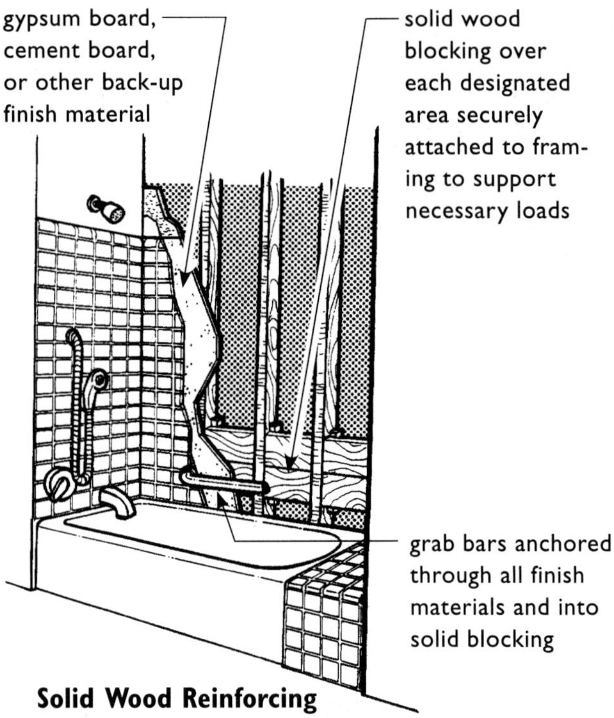

Solid Wood Reinforcing on Wood Stud Walls

Molded Fixtures. Fiberglass and acrylic bathtubs and showers with integral wall panels are common in both new construction and remodeling. The panels alone are too thin to support grab bars, and because they do not touch the stud wall except at the top, there is a space between the panel and the stud wall. To attach grab bars to these surfaces, an area of solid wood blocking or other solid substance must be installed in the cavity between the fiberglass or acrylic wall and the wall.

Since the space between the panels and the stud wall gets narrower as it approaches the top of the panels where they are fastened to the studs, this blocking must be cut to fit snugly in the space between the studs and the panel. The blocking must contact the plastic panel over the entire reinforced area.

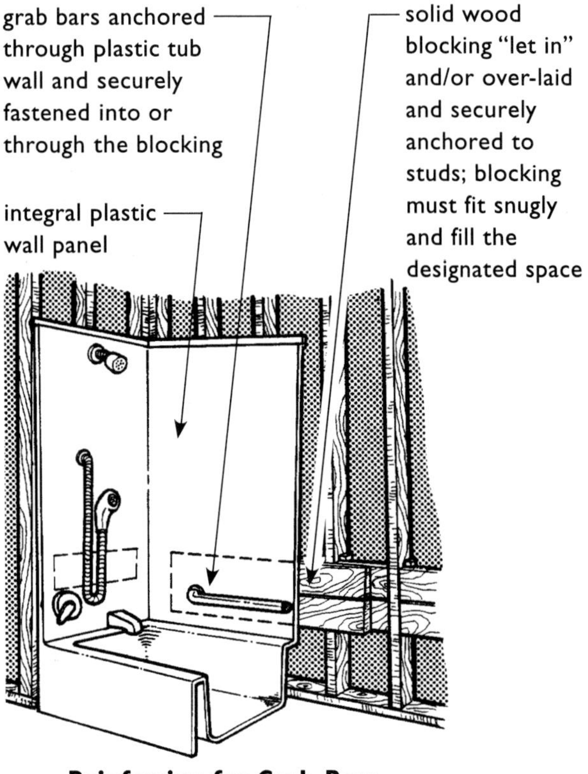

Reinforcing for Grab Bars Behind Fiberglass or Acrylic Tub and Shower Surrounds

Some fiberglass and acrylic tubs, showers, and wall sections are now made with reinforcing already in the walls to stiffen the fixture. If the reinforced fiberglass or acrylic wall is not specifically labeled as built for grab bars and meeting the ANSI load requirements, then additional reinforcing may need to be installed.

Whole Wall or Large Area Reinforcing with Plywood

Although the location and the limited size of the wall areas that must be reinforced are specified by the Guidelines, it may be necessary or desirable to extend the reinforcing over a larger area or throughout the entire wall. Some people may want to locate grab bars in areas other than those specified in the Guidelines and other accessibility standards. Other people may have difficulty finding the minimum reinforced wall areas concealed inside a finished wall and install the grab bars in an unreinforced area. A larger reinforced area provides greater flexibility in placement and easier installation of grab bars.

Heavy plywood applied to the studs over a larger area can support grab bars and provide a base for the installation of finish materials such as ceramic tile or plastic wall panels. Plywood can be applied to the face of studs or "let in." In either case the plywood must be of sufficient thickness and should be securely attached to withstand the forces specified in ANSI 4.24, or an equivalent or stricter standard. Anchors for securing the grab bars to the reinforced walls should be through-the-wall type or another type capable of meeting the ANSI force requirements.

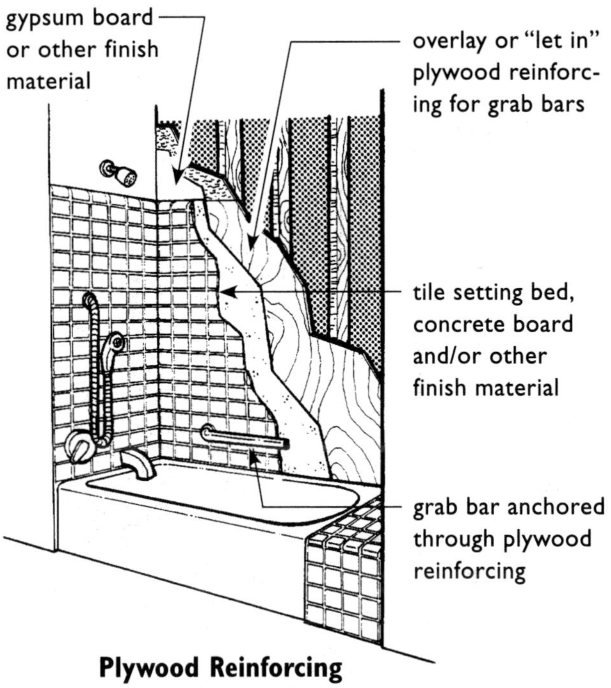

Plywood Reinforcing on a Wood or Metal Stud Wall

Because of standard stud spacing, reinforced areas often will have to be longer than specified to support necessary blocking.

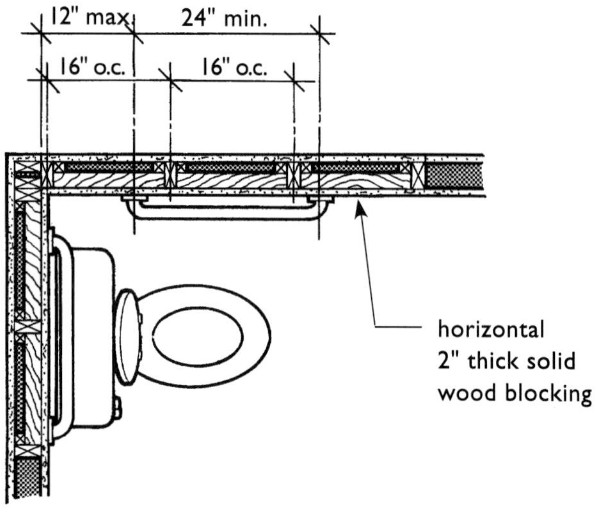

Plan View of Extended Horizontal Blocking Between Conventional Wood Studs

Additional vertical studs can be placed at ends of each specified reinforced area. This method is more expensive, difficult to install accurately, and more difficult to find after construction. It provides less flexibility in bar placement and is more likely to result in a weak connection.

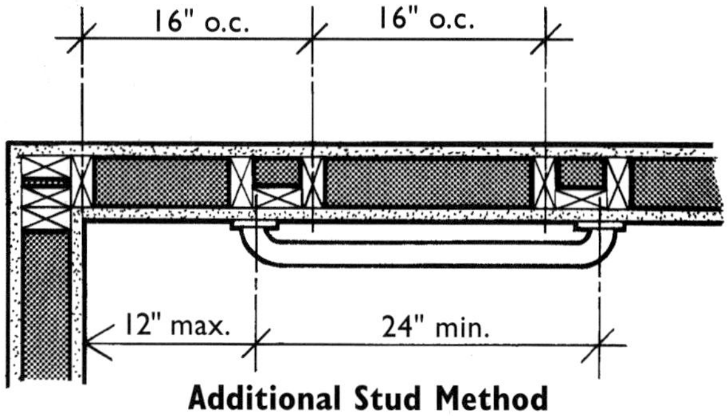

Additional Stud Method of Reinforcing for Grab Bars

A manufactured, formed metal reinforcing plate can be spot welded or screwed to studs.

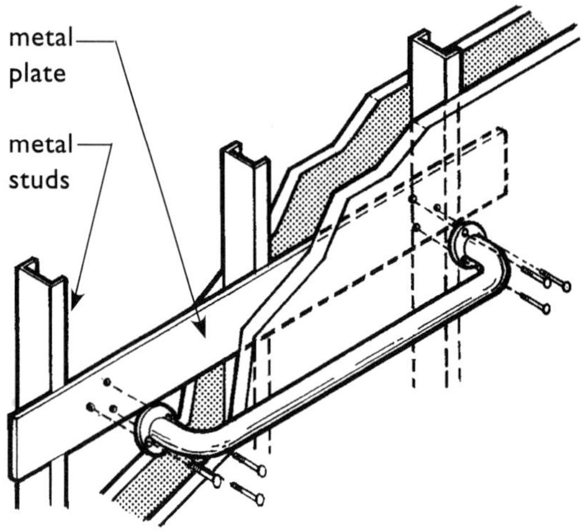

Reinforcing at Metal Studs

Chapter Seven:

Requirement 7

Usable Kitchens and Bathrooms

- **Part A:** Usable Kitchens
- **Part B:** Usable Bathrooms

7

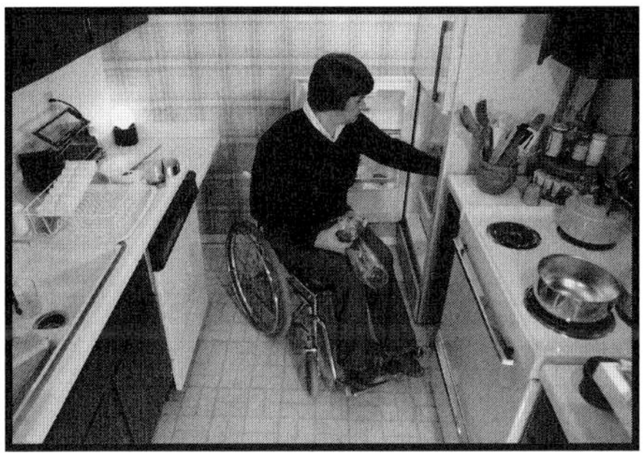

■ PART A: Usable Kitchens

7a

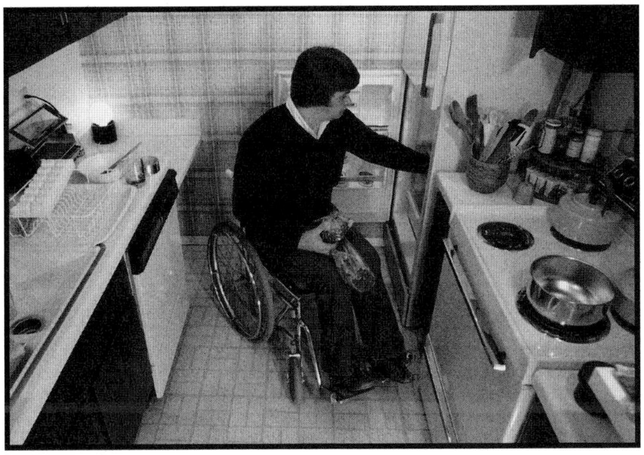

"...covered multifamily dwellings with a building entrance on an accessible route shall be designed and constructed in such a manner that all premises within covered multifamily dwelling units contain usable kitchens...such that an individual in a wheelchair can maneuver about the space."

Fair Housing Act Regulations, 24 CFR 100.205

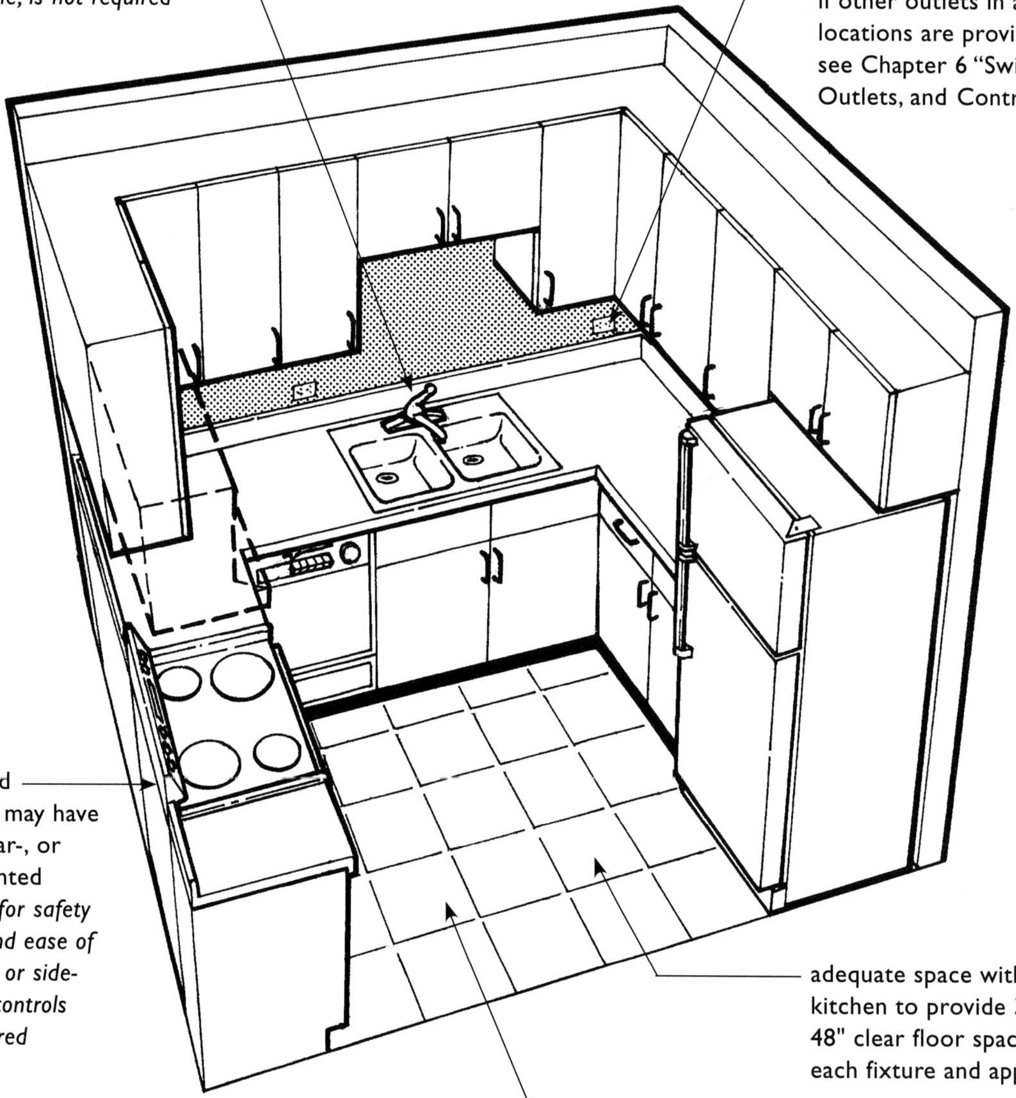

Notes in italic type are recommendations only and are not required by ANSI or Guidelines.

Guideline Specifications for Kitchens

Introduction

Kitchens that comply with the Fair Housing Accessibility Guidelines (the Guidelines) can be designed to look and function like conventional kitchens typically found in multifamily housing. The Guidelines specify that three specific requirements must be provided to allow people who rely on mobility aids to "use" the kitchen. "Usable" kitchens, as specified in the Guidelines, are not necessarily "accessible" kitchens, but they do provide maneuvering space for a person who uses a wheelchair, scooter, or walker to approach and operate most appliances and fixtures.

The Guidelines 1) specify minimum clear floor spaces at fixtures and appliances, 2) define minimum clearance between counters, and 3) provide additional specifications when a U-shaped kitchen is planned. Wheelchair turning spaces, described in accessibility standards, are not required in kitchens that meet the Guidelines, except in some U-shaped kitchens, see page 7.9.

Additional supplemental design information, presented in italic type, is offered for designers/builders who may wish to increase the accessibility of dwelling units. This supplemental information is not required by HUD, the Fair Housing Act, or the Guidelines.

Clear Floor Space at Fixtures and Appliances

The Guidelines specify that a 30-inch x 48-inch clear floor space be provided at each kitchen appliance or fixture, and that each of these clear floor spaces adjoin the accessible route that must pass into and through the kitchen. It is anticipated that in any conventional kitchen plan, the overlapping of the minimum 36-inch wide accessible route with the clear floor spaces at all fixtures and appliances provides the necessary maneuvering space to make it possible for a person using a mobility aid to approach, and then position himself or herself close enough to use the fixture safely.

The clear floor space must be positioned either parallel or perpendicular to and centered on the appliance or fixture, i.e., the clear floor space must have its centerline aligned with the centerline of the fixture or appliance. This centered position is most critical at corners where an appliance may have to be pulled away from the corner to allow a full centered approach. The two types of approaches and where they are necessary are described on the following pages.

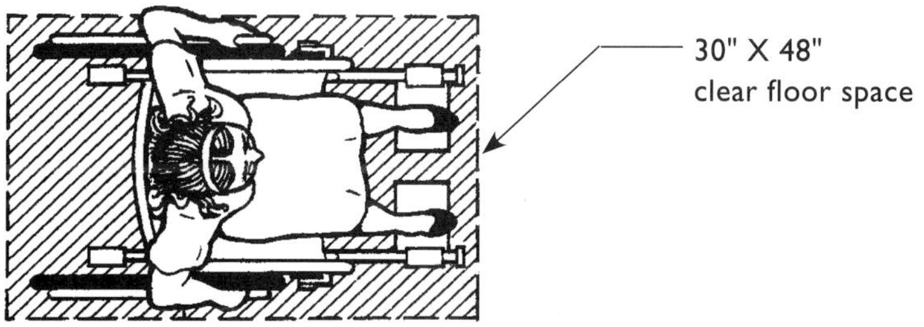

Clear Floor Space for Wheelchair Parking at Appliances and Fixtures

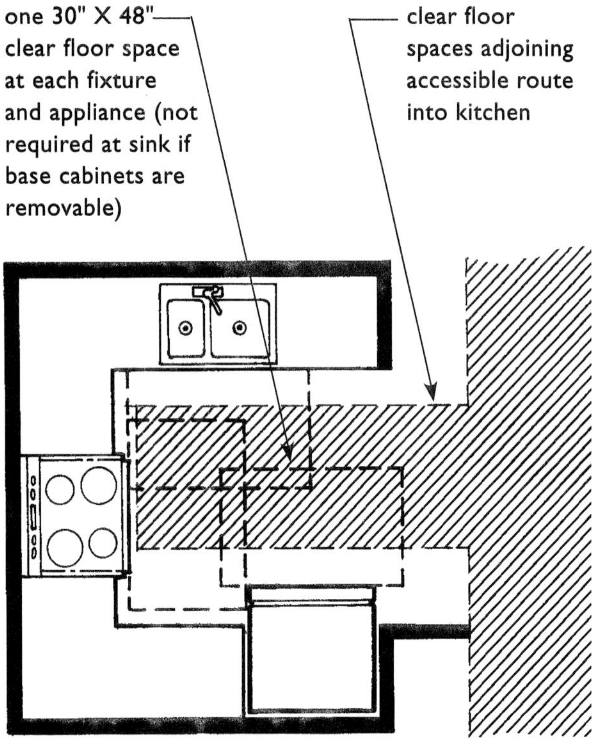

Overlapping Clear Floor Spaces and Accessible Route Provide Maneuvering Space

Clear Floor Space at Ranges, Cooktops, and Sinks

Unless knee space is provided, space to execute a parallel approach must be provided at ranges, cooktops, and sinks. The clear floor space in this parallel orientation allows the wheelchair user to make a close side approach permitting safer and easier reach to controls and cooking surfaces. A forward approach, on the other hand, is difficult and unsafe, especially when controls are located at the back, because it requires seated users to lean forward over their feet and knees to reach not only hot pots and pans but the controls as well. See pages 7.11 through 7.16 for required clear floor space at cooktop or sink when knee space is provided.

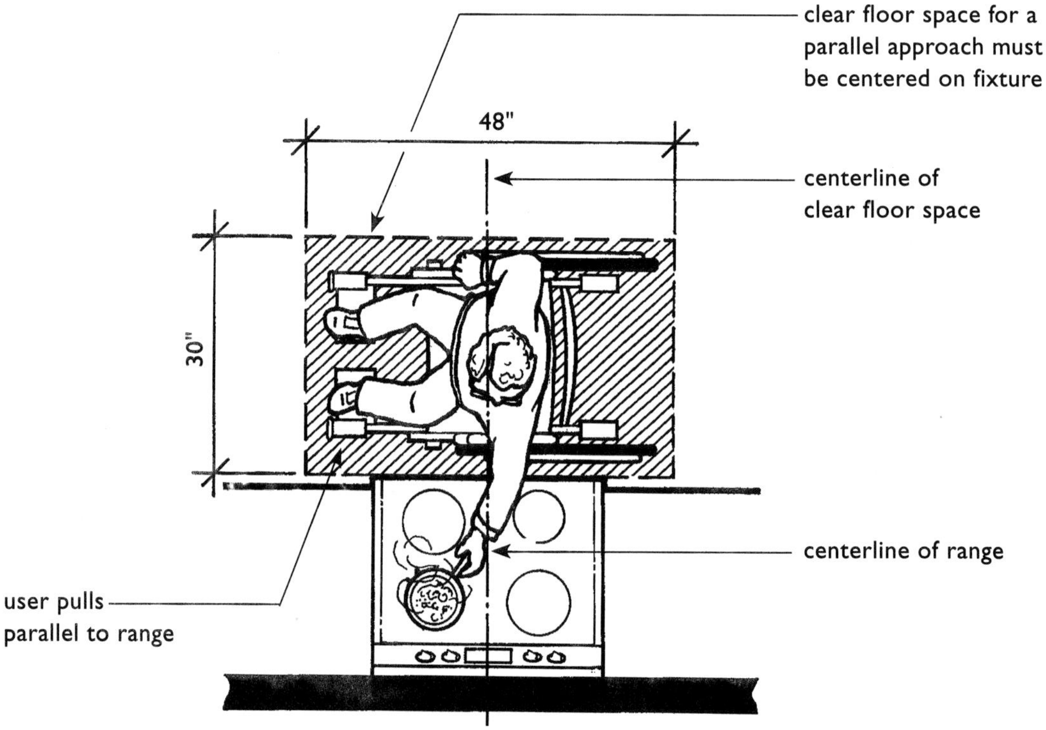

Space for Parallel Approach Required at Range and Cooktop

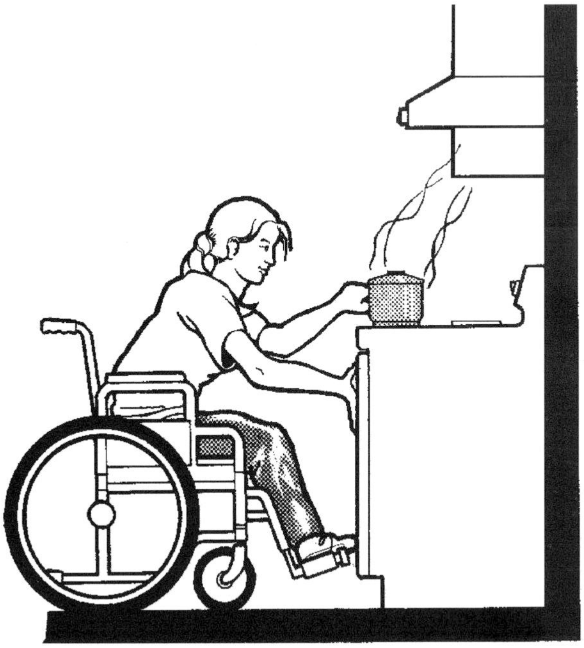

Forward Approach at Range is Difficult and Unsafe

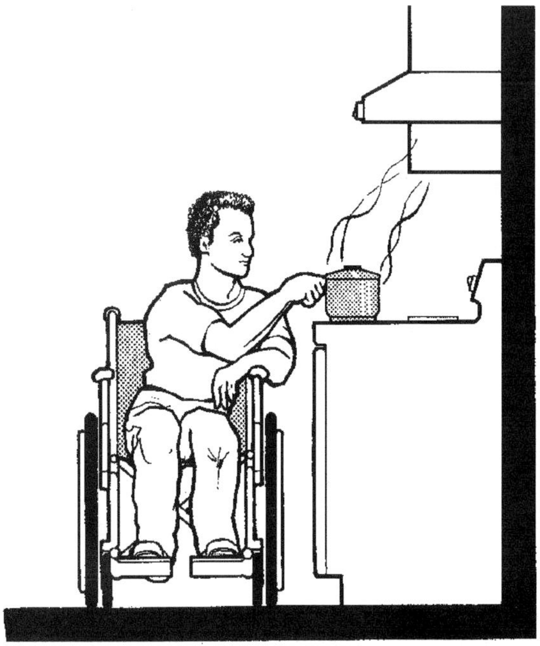

Parallel Approach to Range Specified in Guidelines

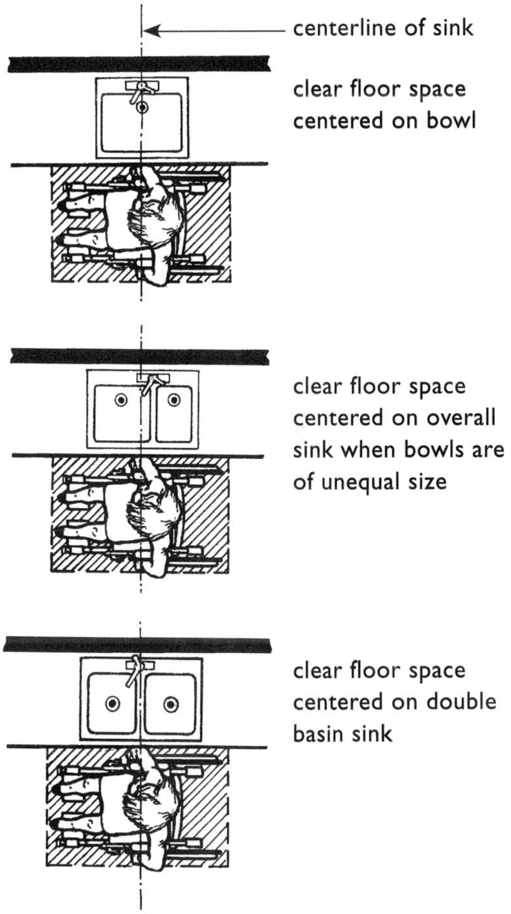

Space for Parallel Approach Required at Sinks

A **parallel** approach also must be provided at sinks so a seated user can reach down into the bowl. A forward approach with kneespace below the sink may be required in some very small U-shaped kitchens. See page 7.11.

The parallel clear floor space at sinks, as at ranges and cooktops, must be centered on the bowl or appliance. At single bowl sinks the centerline of the clear floor space must align with the centerline of that bowl. Where there are multiple bowl sinks the clear floor space must be centered on the overall sink itself.

Faucets usually are placed at the center of or within six inches of the center of the sink, regardless of the number of basins. Since the clear floor space is centered on the sink, users are still afforded access to faucet controls.

Clear Floor Space at Ovens, Dishwashers, Regrigerators, Freezers, and Trash Compactors

The 30-inch x 48-inch clear floor space oriented in either one of two positions—parallel or perpendicular—is required at the oven, dishwasher, refrigerator, freezer, and trash compactor. Wall-mounted and microwave ovens, like ovens in ranges, also must have either a parallel or perpendicular clear floor space adjacent to the appliance.

Even though this group of appliances has operable doors that require the user to be able to get out of the way of the door swing, for purposes of design and room layout the clear floor space must be centered on the appliance itself. However, the clear floor space for the specific appliance and the clear floor space for adjacent appliances and fixtures, combined with the 36-inch wide accessible route into the room, provide the functional space necessary to open a door and maneuver close to the appliance to be able to reach into it.

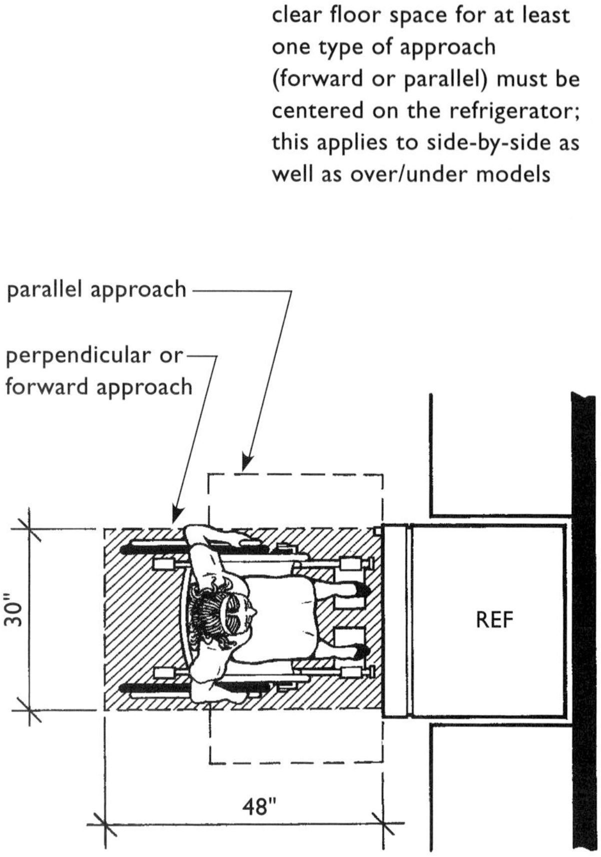

Space for Either a Forward or Parallel Approach Must be Provided

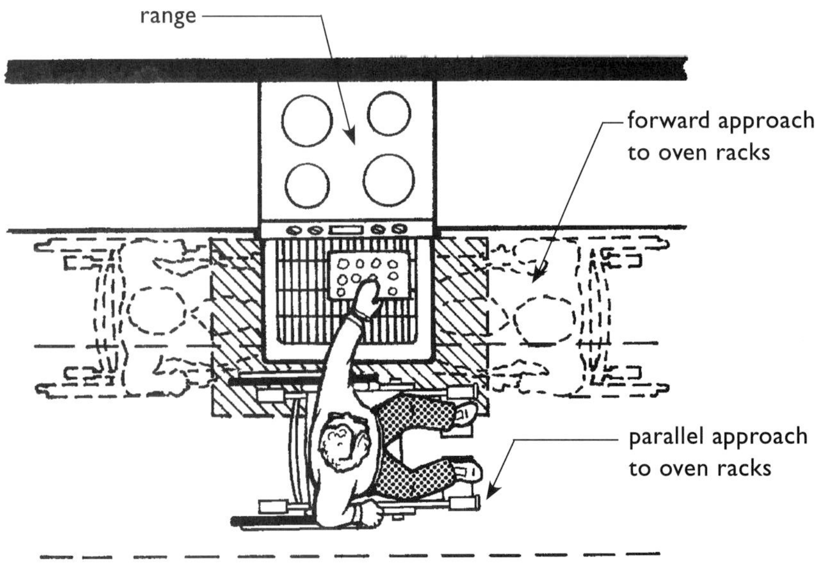

Functional Use of Oven Could Be From Any One of These Positions

Clearance Between Counters and All Opposing Elements

The Guidelines require a clearance of at least 40 inches between all opposing base cabinets, countertops, appliances, and walls. The 40-inch clearance is measured from any countertop or the face of any appliance (excluding handles and controls) that projects into the kitchen to the opposing cabinet, countertop, appliance, or wall.

Refrigerators vary greatly in depth and may extend up to eight inches beyond cabinet faces. Standard free-standing and drop-in ranges may project up to three inches. Appliance depths (excluding door handles) must be included when calculating the 40-inch clearances.

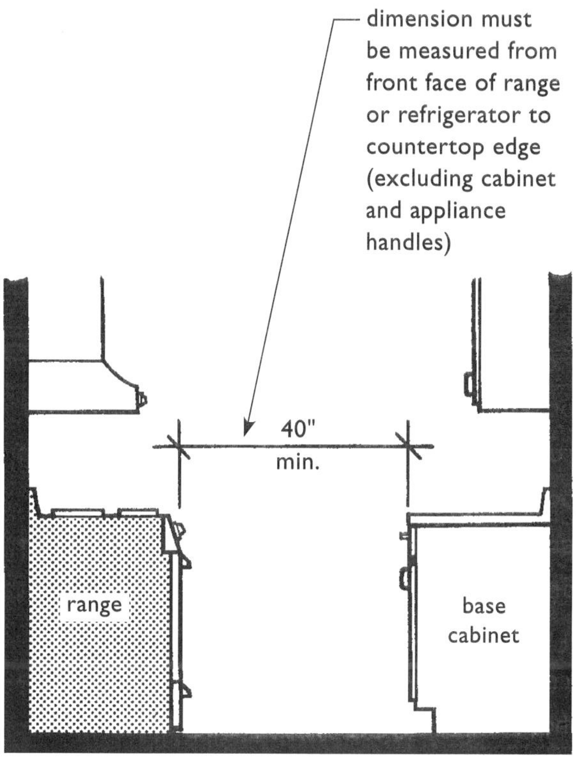

Minimum Clearance between Range and Opposing Base Cabinet

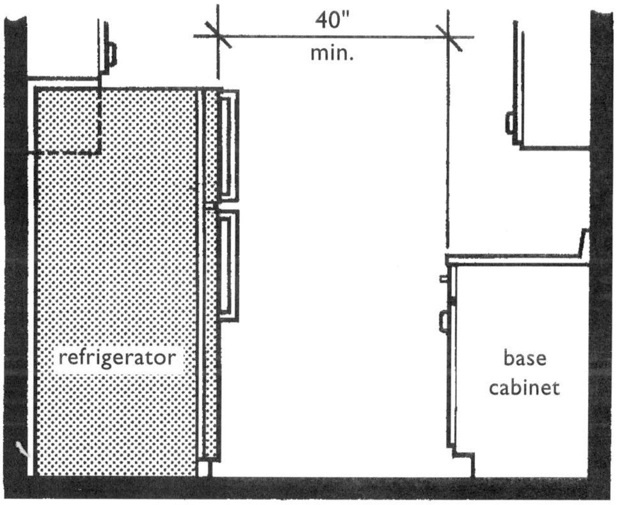

Minimum Clearance between Refrigerator and Opposing Base Cabinet

In a narrow kitchen the 40-inch minimum clearance provides an additional five inches on either side of the required clear floor space of 30 inches x 48 inches at each fixture or appliance, so a user in a wheelchair can maneuver as close as possible to appliances or fixtures. A narrow kitchen such as the one shown to the right meets the Guidelines and is usable, but may be difficult for many people using wheelchairs. Its narrow corridor design requires a user in a wheelchair to exit the kitchen to turn around.

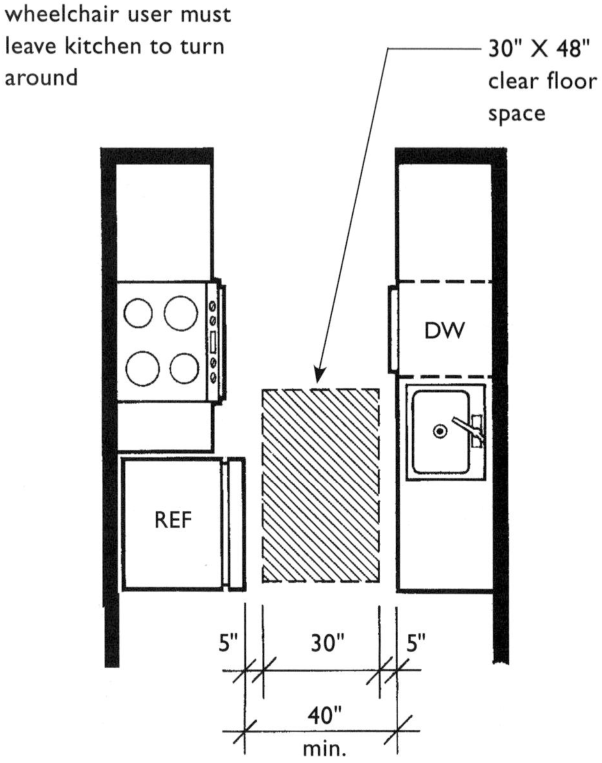

40" Minimum Clearance Between all Counters, Base Cabinets, Appliances, and Walls

In more elaborate kitchens where an island is planned, the 40-inch clearance must be maintained between the face of the island and all opposing features. Even though an accessible route for a 90-degree turn around an obstruction is 36 inches, to ensure sufficient space for maneuvering within the kitchen, the Guidelines require that the minimum clearance of 40 inches be maintained.

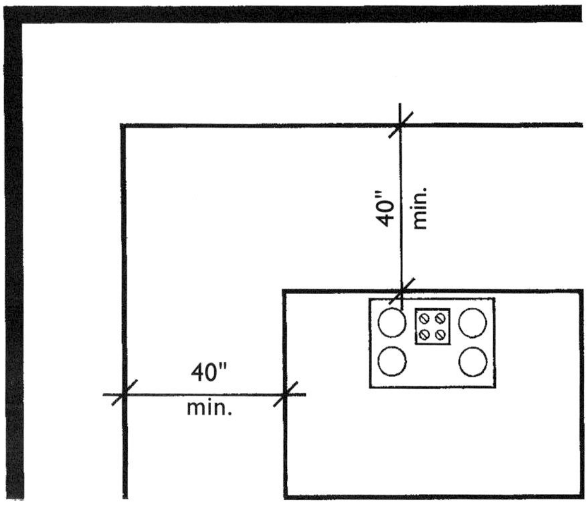

40" Must Be Maintained Between Island and all Opposing Features

U-Shaped Kitchens

A 60-inch diameter turning circle is required in a U-shaped kitchen that has a sink, range, or cooktop at its base. This turning diameter is necessary to provide adequate maneuvering space for a person using a wheelchair to approach and position themselves parallel to the appliance or fixture at the base of the U. Any appliances, such as refrigerators and ranges (excluding door handles), that project beyond countertops and cabinets must not encroach upon this 60-inch diameter turning space.

In addition to the turning space, the kitchen must be arranged so there is a 30-inch x 48-inch clear floor space for a parallel approach centered on the sink, range, or cooktop. The centerline of the fixture or appliance must be aligned with the centerline of the clear floor space.

When a sink, even a standard single basin sink, is at the bottom of the U and a dishwashing machine is planned to be included adjacent to the sink, the distance between the legs of the U must be greater than 60 inches to allow for a full centered approach at the sink. See the lower plan in the right column.

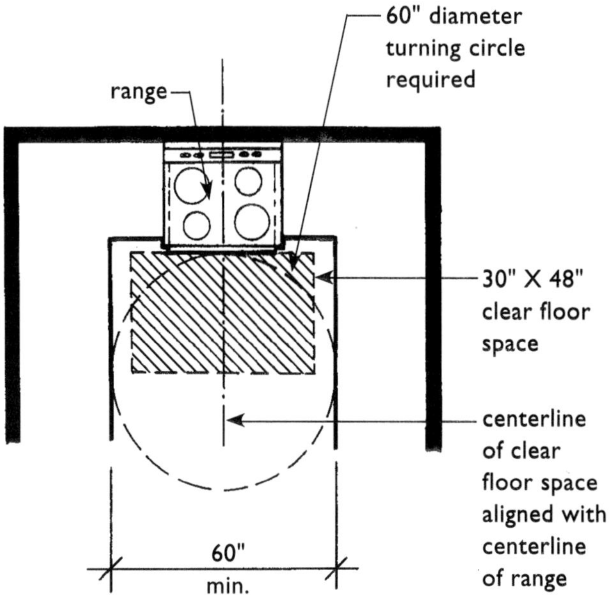

60" Diameter Turning Circle when Sink (Only), Cooktop, or Range is at Bottom of U-Shaped Kitchen

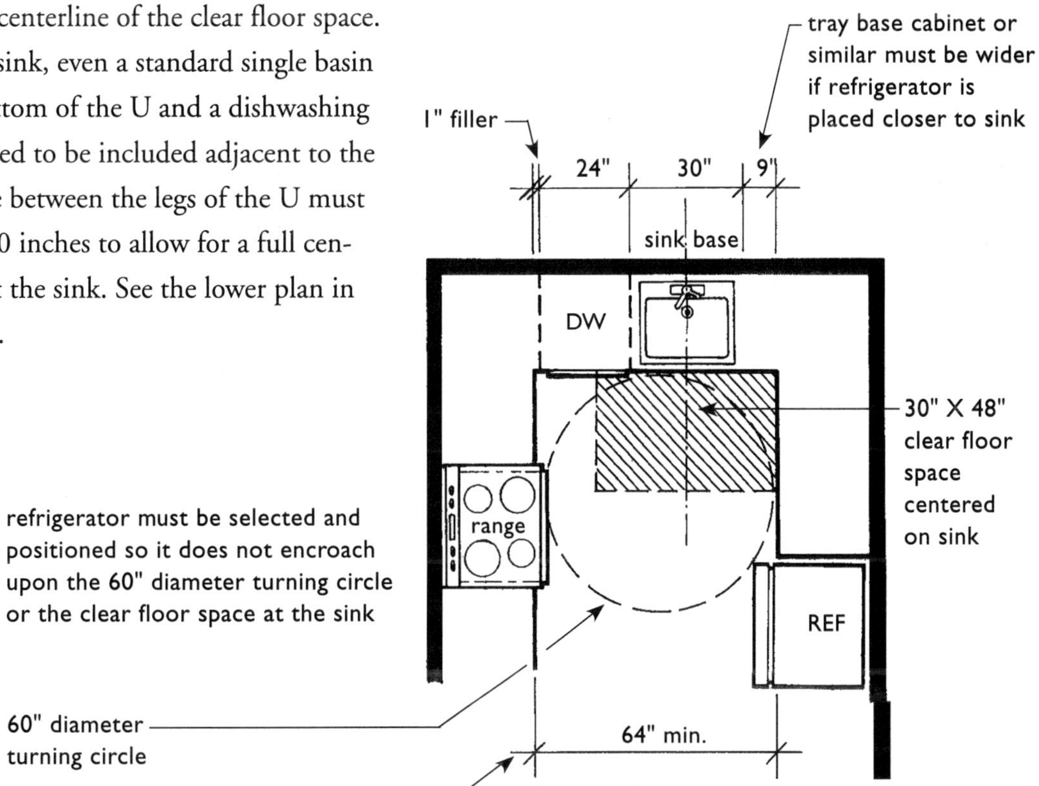

Sink and Dishwasher at Bottom of U-Shaped Kitchen Increases Room Width

In the lower plan on page 7.9, the refrigerator is pulled away from the sink and beyond the turning circle. Since a refrigerator may not overlap the five-foot turning space, if the refrigerator must be located closer to the sink, the distance between the legs of the U must be increased.

To reduce the need for additional floor space, and because clear floor space at appliances and fixtures may overlap, the clear floor space at the sink can serve as the clear floor space for a forward approach to dishwasher racks when they are pulled out of the dishwasher. Even though the dishwasher door would rest on the feet of the user, the required clear floor spaces are provided and the kitchen complies with the maneuvering requirements of the Guidelines.

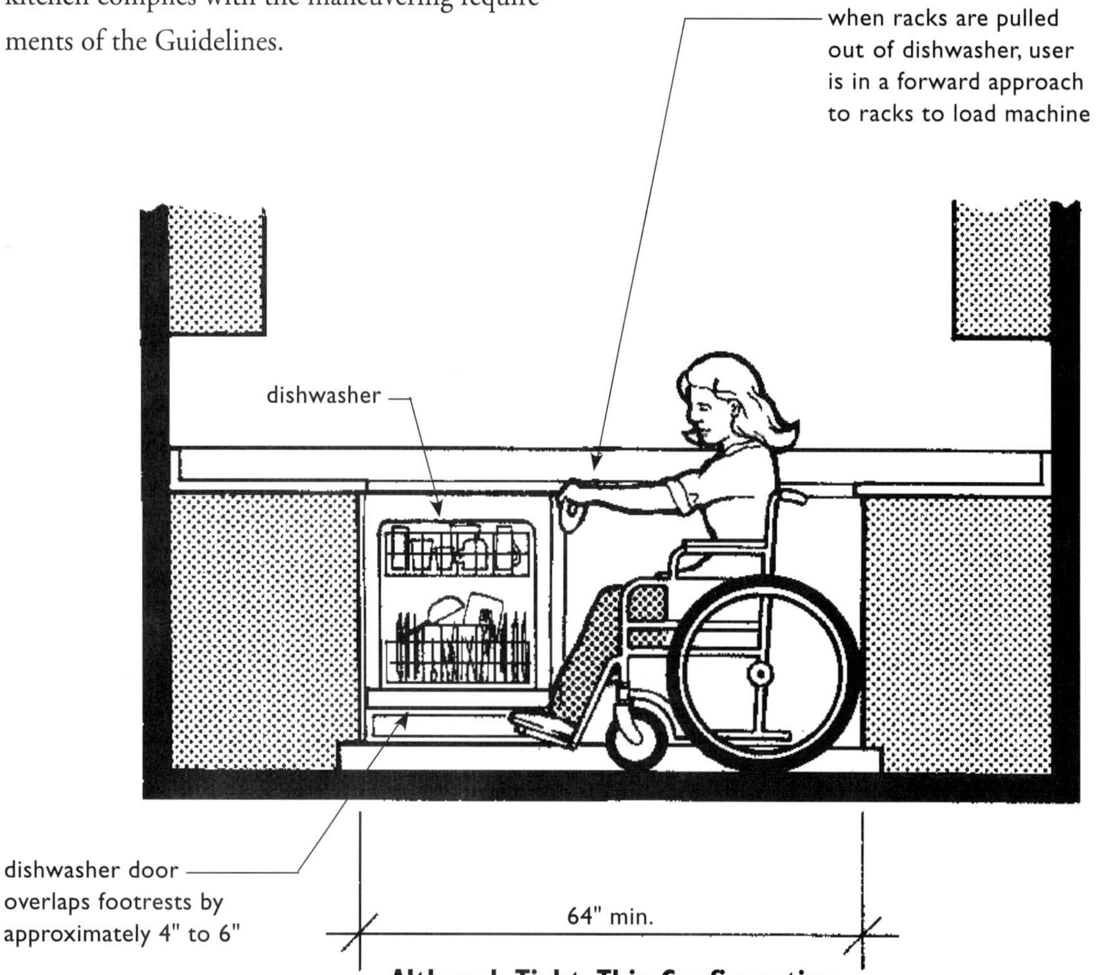

Although Tight, This Configuration Generally Is Usable

An Exception

The Guidelines permit U-shaped kitchens with a sink or cooktop at the base of the U to have less than 60 inches between the legs of the U only when removable base cabinets are provided under the cooktop or sink. A clearance of at least 40 inches is required. Since knee space cannot be provided below a range, kitchens with a range at the base of the U must have the 60-inch minimum turning diameter.

Once the base cabinet is removed, the resulting knee space allows a person using a wheelchair to pull up under the feature to reach controls and perform cooking/cleaning functions. A note of caution: knee space beneath cooktops provides essential maneuvering space for seated people, but it also creates a greater risk from hot food spilled in the lap. If cooktops are to be provided with knee space below, although not required, it is suggested that they be placed in lowered or adjustable height counter segments so they can be used more easily and safely by people using wheelchairs. Knee space configurations are shown on pages 7.14 and 7.15.

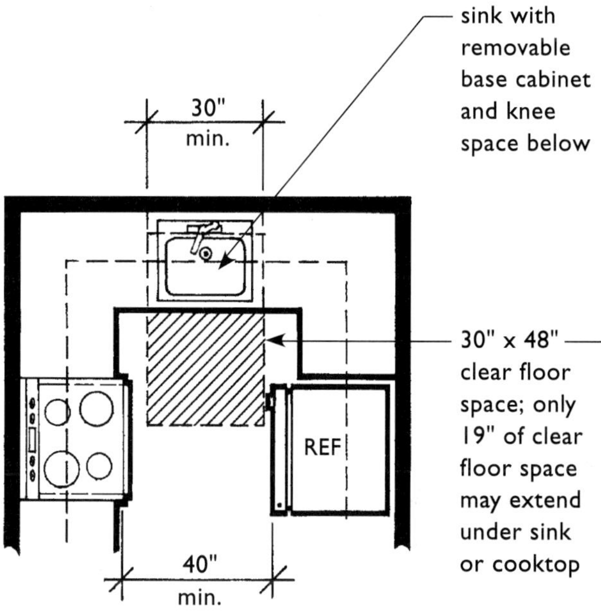

Sink at Base of Narrow U-Shaped Kitchen

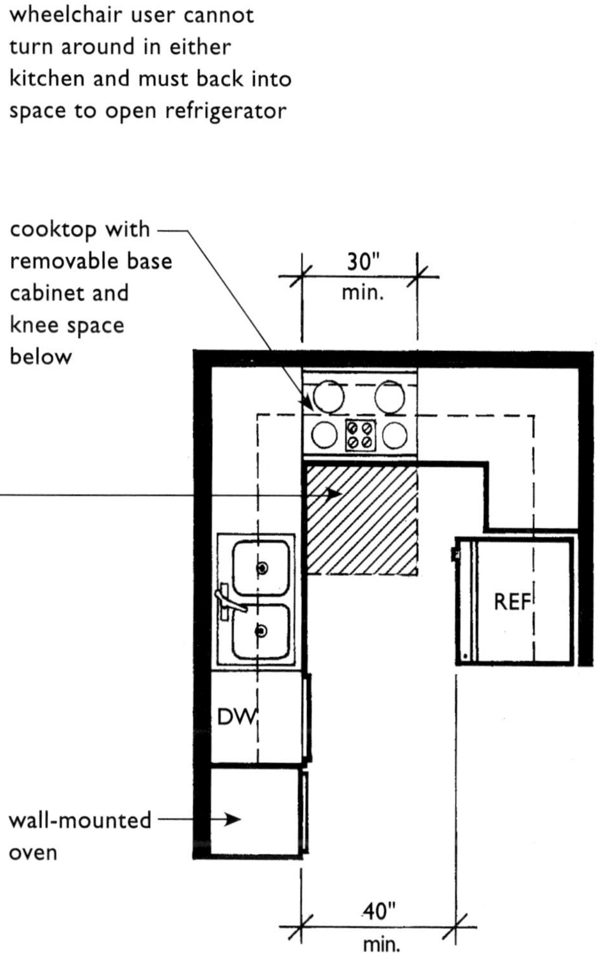

Cooktop at Base of Narrow U-Shaped Kitchen (Not Allowed for a Range)

Removable Base Cabinets

Narrow U-shaped kitchens, where knee space must be provided below sinks or cooktops, can appear identical to those kitchens which lack this additional feature since knee space can be concealed by a removable base cabinet. When a potential resident or owner needs the knee space it can be provided quickly and easily. Specifications for knee space are based on the Guidelines' requirements for bathrooms and ANSI 4.19 and 4.32. See also pages 7.14 - 7.15 and 7.52.

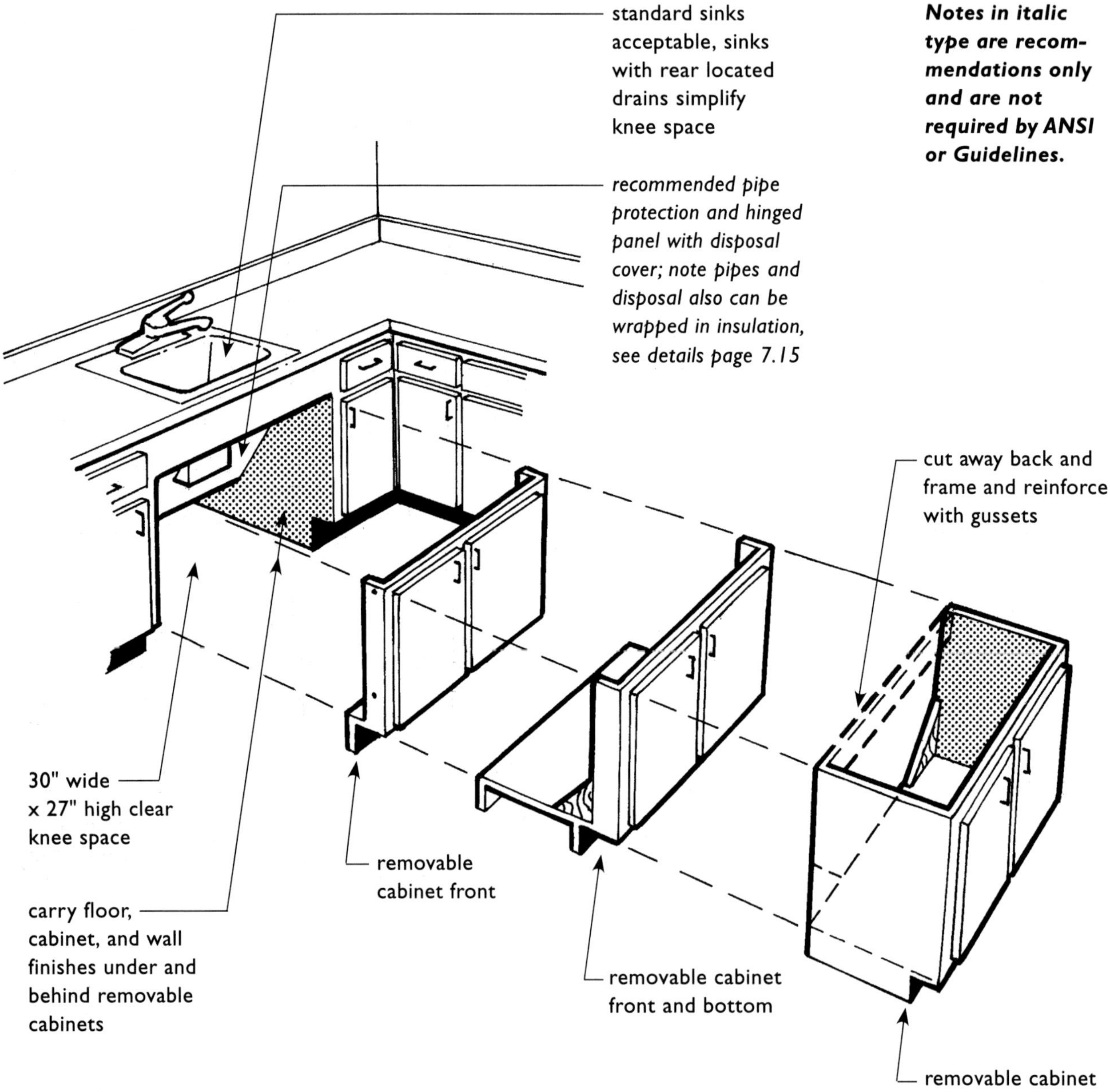

Possible Removable Cabinet Options for Required Knee Spaces at Sinks or Cooktops in Narrow (Less Than 60" Wide) U-Shaped Kitchens

The Guidelines require that the floor, walls, and cabinet faces of knee space be finished during initial construction so no other work is necessary when the base cabinet is removed. When sinks or cooktops are installed at the bottom of a narrow U-shaped kitchen, regardless of whether the knee space is exposed or concealed by a removable cabinet, hot pipes or exposed sharp edges should be insulated or enclosed at the time of initial construction. Protection methods are addressed on page 7.14 "Knee Space and Pipe Protection."

There are no kitchen cabinet manufacturers that currently offer "removable base cabinets" in their standard lines. The methods for providing removable cabinets presented here are some of the possible solutions. Of those shown, the removable cabinet front is likely to be the easiest to accomplish based upon current manufacturing processes. However, the resident may need to reinstall the cabinet at a later date, therefore, storage needs to be considered. It is recommended that instructions regarding proper storage be taped to the inside of the cabinet, as well as reinstallation instructions, if applicable. Other similar design options include removable cabinet floor and bottom, or, with some modification of rear supports, removal of the entire cabinet. This last option requires the counter to be installed independent of the base cabinet, with storage of the removable portion of the cabinet again a consideration.

Use of swinging retractable cabinet door hardware provides another excellent method to conceal knee space because the doors are self-storing and no part of the cabinet has to be removed or stored at another location. A special combination hinge allows the doors to swing open in a traditional manner and, when desired, allows the doors to be pushed back into the cabinet.

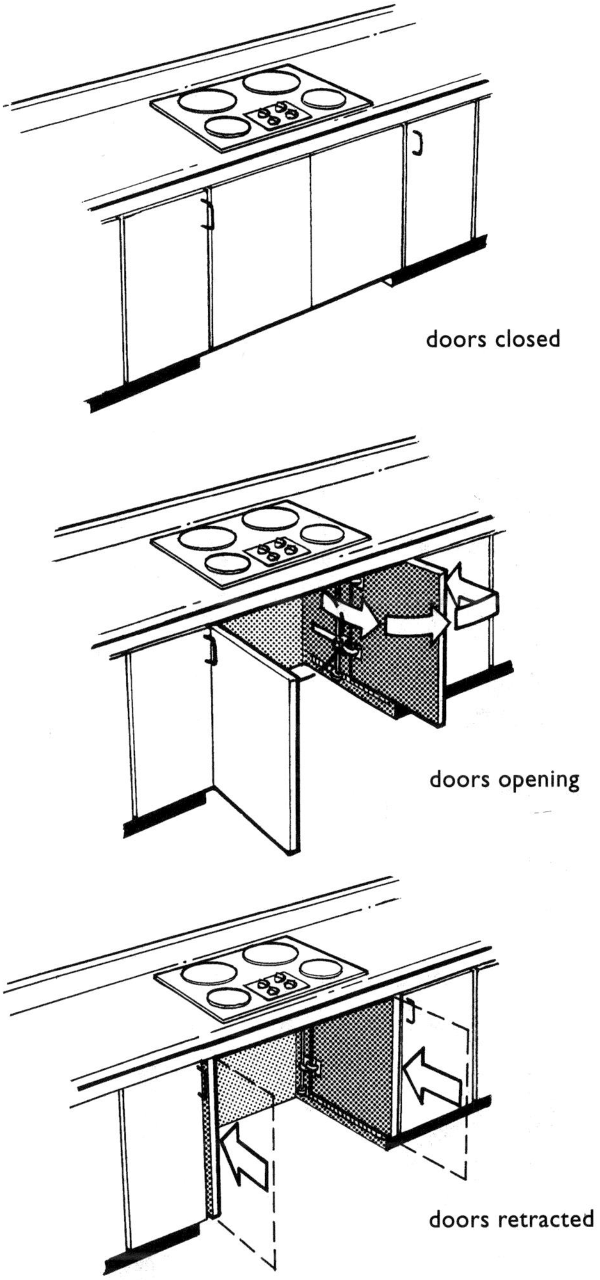

Use of Self-Storing Door Hardware to Expose Knee Space

Knee Space and Pipe Protection

Where knee spaces are provided below sinks and cooktops, protecting seated users from burns and abrasions is strongly recommended. While the Guidelines do not specify such protection, the two most common design standards on accessibility (ANSI A117.1, 1986 and UFAS) require that the bottom of cooktops and sink supply lines and drain pipes be insulated or enclosed. Many people who use wheelchairs or scooters have limited sensation in their legs and cannot feel that they are touching a hot pipe or sharp edge and may be unaware that a serious injury has occurred. In addition, the need for protection from burns is an important safety consideration for all persons.

Pipes at sinks may be wrapped with insulation, but each time the plumbing is serviced the insulation must be removed and reinstalled. If the pipes are rewrapped using the original insulation (which may have lost much of its adhesion) the resulting application often is ineffective or the insulation may be left off entirely.

A more aesthetic and practical method for pipe protection is the installation of a removable panel over the plumbing. This panel shields the seated user and hides the plumbing from view. If such a panel is installed it should not inhibit access by encroaching upon the knee space. The panel should be hinged or otherwise removable so the pipes can be serviced easily.

The dimensions for the knee space itself must be 30 inches wide (minimum) and should be 27 inches high (minimum). Since there is no specific ANSI figure delineating the requirements for knee space clearance beneath sinks or cooktops in dwelling units, the accompanying illustrations may be used as guidance when providing knee space beneath removable base cabinets. The pipe protection panel is patterned after the ANSI Figure 31 for Lavatory Clearances. See also ANSI 4.32.5.5 Sinks and 4.32.5.6 Ranges and Cooktops.

Notes in italic type are recommendations only and are not required by ANSI or Guidelines.

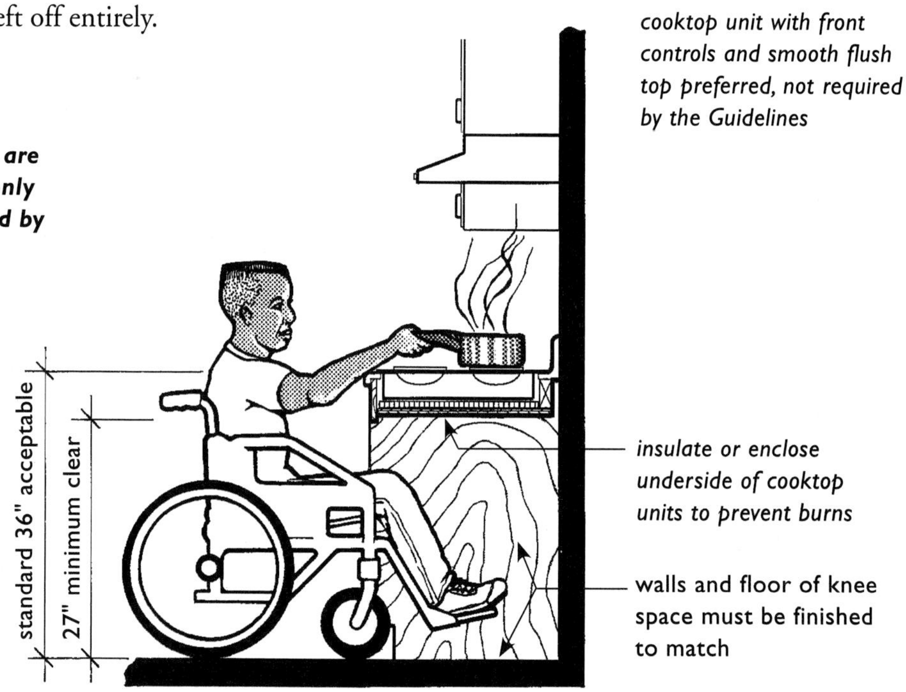

Cooktop with Knee Space Below

Knee Space at Sink with Pipe Protection Panel

sinks with rear located drain are not required but are a significant advantage when creating usable knee space

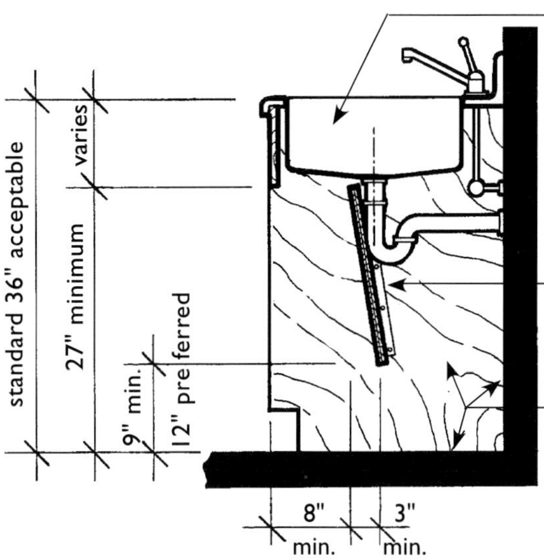

Knee Space at Sink with Wrapped Pipes

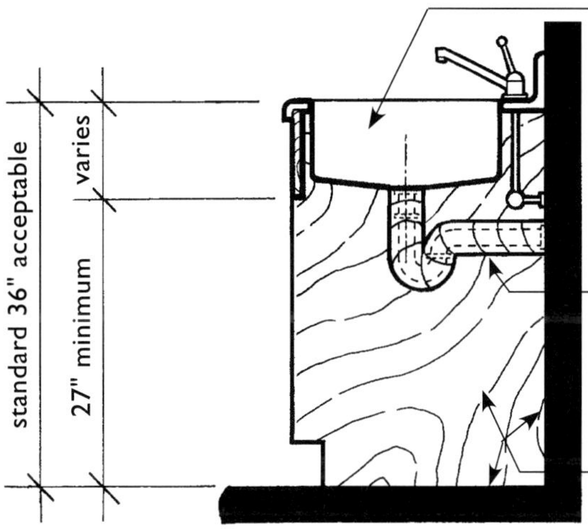

Knee Space at Sink with Garbage Disposal and Pipe Protection Panel

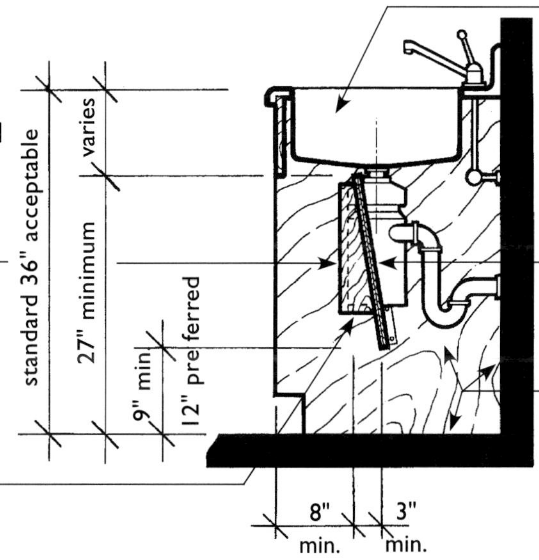

shallow basin sink and rear drain, although not required by the Guidelines, greatly improve access by wheelchair user

lever hardware, although preferred, is not required

knee spaces must have walls and floor surfaces finished

plumbing and other elements should be covered by a removable pipe protection and appearance panel, or be wrapped with padded insulating material, see details page 7.15

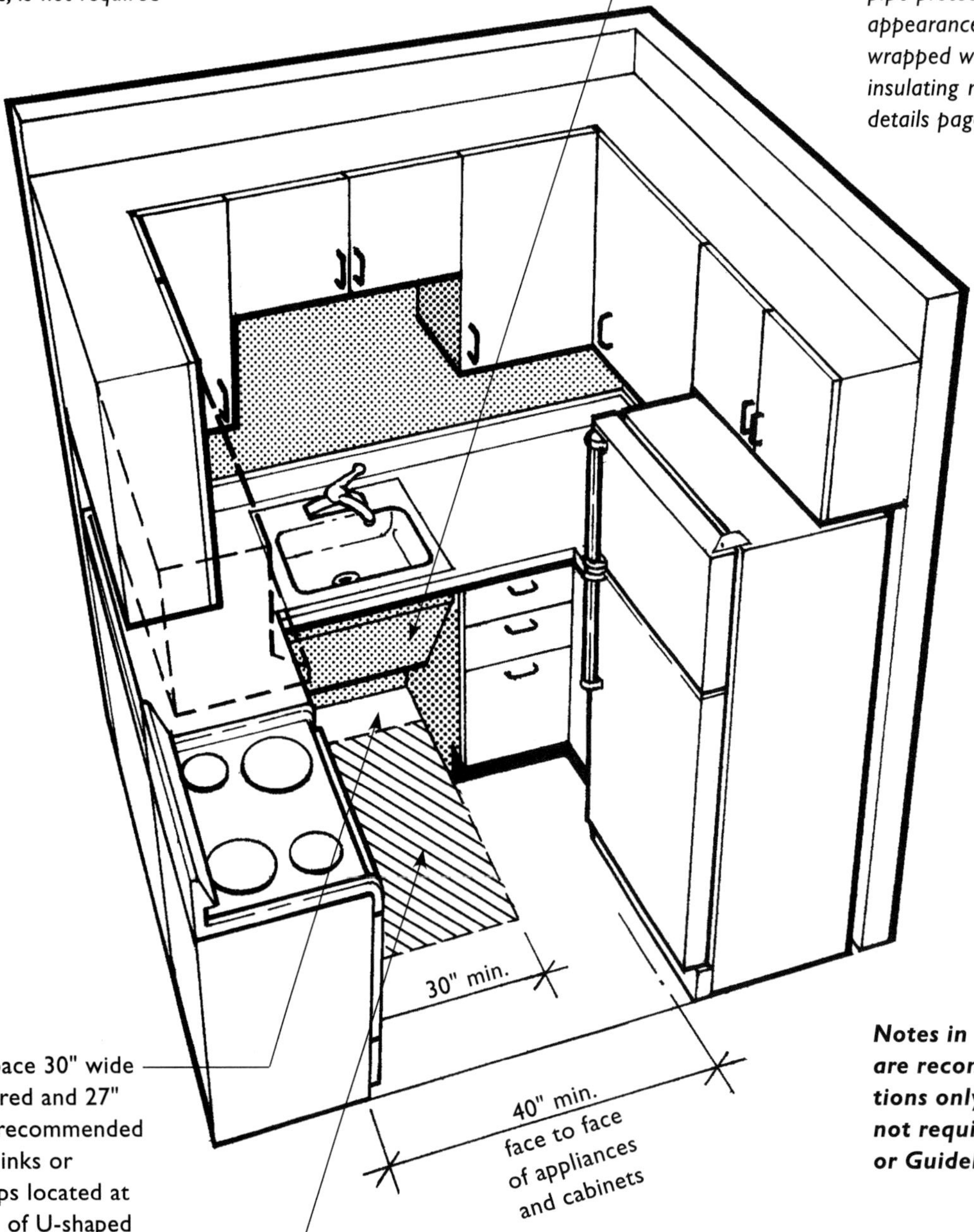

knee space 30" wide is required and 27" high is recommended under sinks or cooktops located at bottom of U-shaped kitchens when the U is less than 60" wide

30" X 48" min. clear floor space; must not extend more than 19" into knee space

Notes in italic type are recommendations only and are not required by ANSI or Guidelines.

Knee Space at Narrow U-Shaped Kitchens

PANTRIES

Shallow storage closets, such as pantries, may have doors that do not provide a 32-inch clear width since they do not require the user to pass through the door to reach the contents. However, at walk-in pantries that must be entered to reach the stored items, the doorway must provide a 32-inch nominal clear opening. Shelving is not addressed by the Guidelines; however, it is recommended that it be provided at a variety of levels.

In the small walk-in pantry (below left), if wheelchair users enter the pantry facing the contents, they must back out of the space. In the larger walk-in pantry (below right), if the first shelf is placed at two feet above the floor, a wheelchair user could turn around in the pantry and exit facing out.

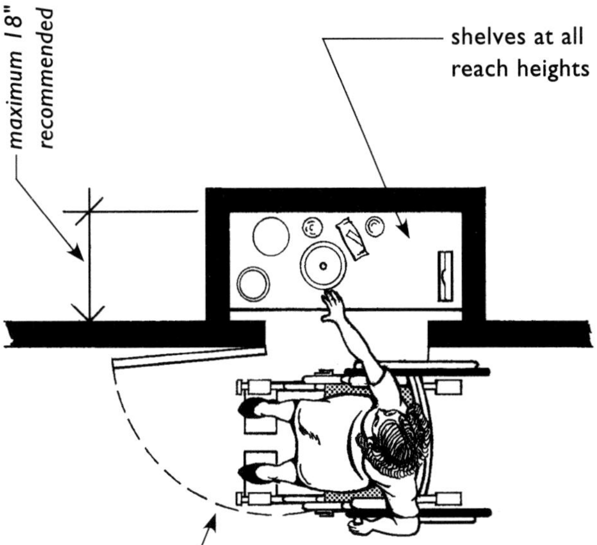

Small Shallow Pantry

Notes in italic type are recommendations only and are not required by ANSI or Guidelines.

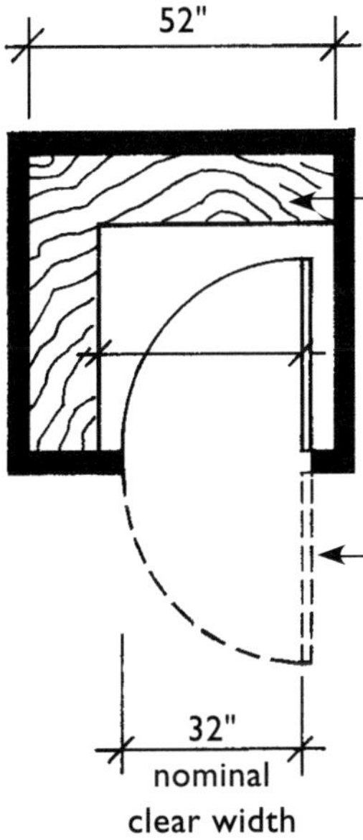

Small Walk-In Pantry

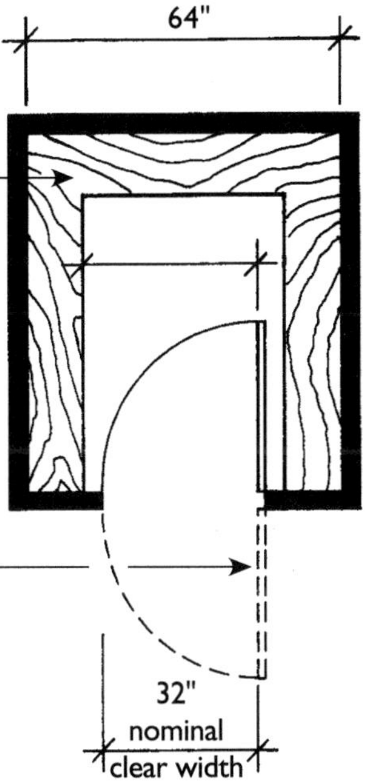

Larger Walk-In Pantry

Recommendations for Increased Accessibility

At Wall Ovens

Wall-mounted ovens, like ovens in ranges, must have either a parallel or forward clear floor space adjacent to the appliance. When a single wall-mounted oven is installed, it is recommended that the bottom of the oven be mounted at or near counter height so a seated user could reach over a potentially hot door and, at a minimum, pull out the bottom oven rack. Controls also should be within the reach of a seated user.

If double ovens are installed, a wheelchair user must be able to execute a parallel or a forward approach at the appliance. At least one oven interior and its controls, even though appliance controls are not covered by the Guidelines, should be within the reach range of a seated person. *See page 5.5 for reach ranges.*

bottom of oven should be positioned so lowest oven rack is at or near countertop height

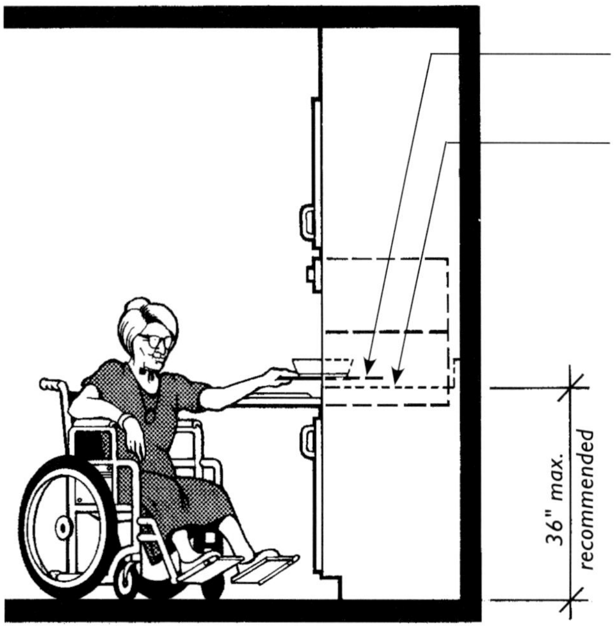

36 Inches to Bottom of Single Wall-Mounted Oven

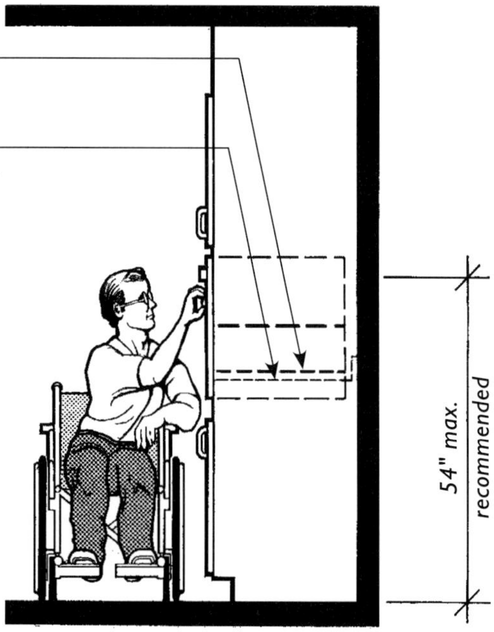

54 Inches Recommended Reach to Controls at Single Wall-Mounted Oven

At Laundry Equipment

The Guidelines do not require washers and dryers in individual dwelling units to be accessible, which also means that they are not required to have 30-inch x 48-inch parallel clear floor spaces positioned in front of them. *However, when located in the kitchen along a row containing other appliances, it is recommended that space be provided for a parallel approach to each machine. The Guidelines permit the installation of stacked washers and dryers. It is recommended that the controls be within the reach of seated users; see the illustration in the upper right column.*

If the washer and dryer are located behind doors or are in a separate utility room, clear floor spaces in front of the machines are not required. However, if the door to the utility room is intended for user passage, the door must provide a 32-inch nominal clear opening. When laundry equipment is located in a common use area, it must conform to the requirements for accessible public and common use facilities, see page 2.26. Note: Non-italic type indicates a requirement of the Guidelines.

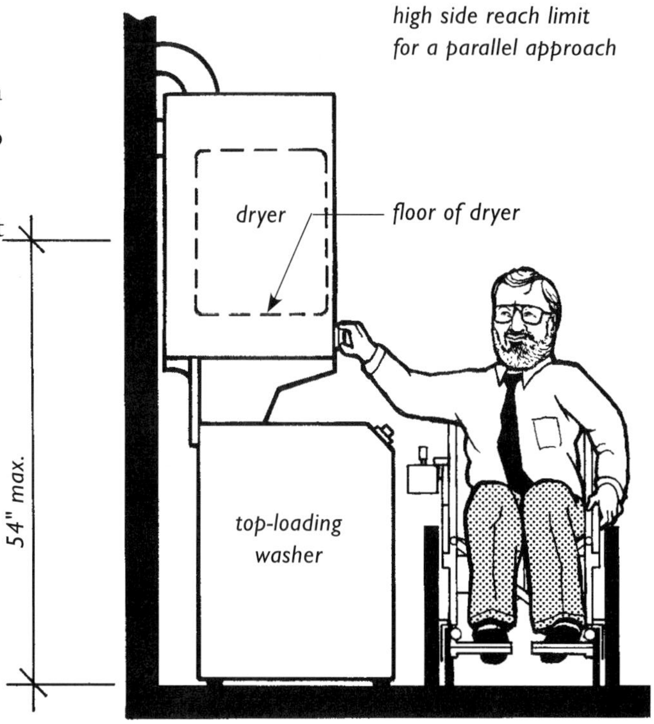

Stacked Washer/Dryer Unit with Dryer and All Controls Within Reach Range of Seated User

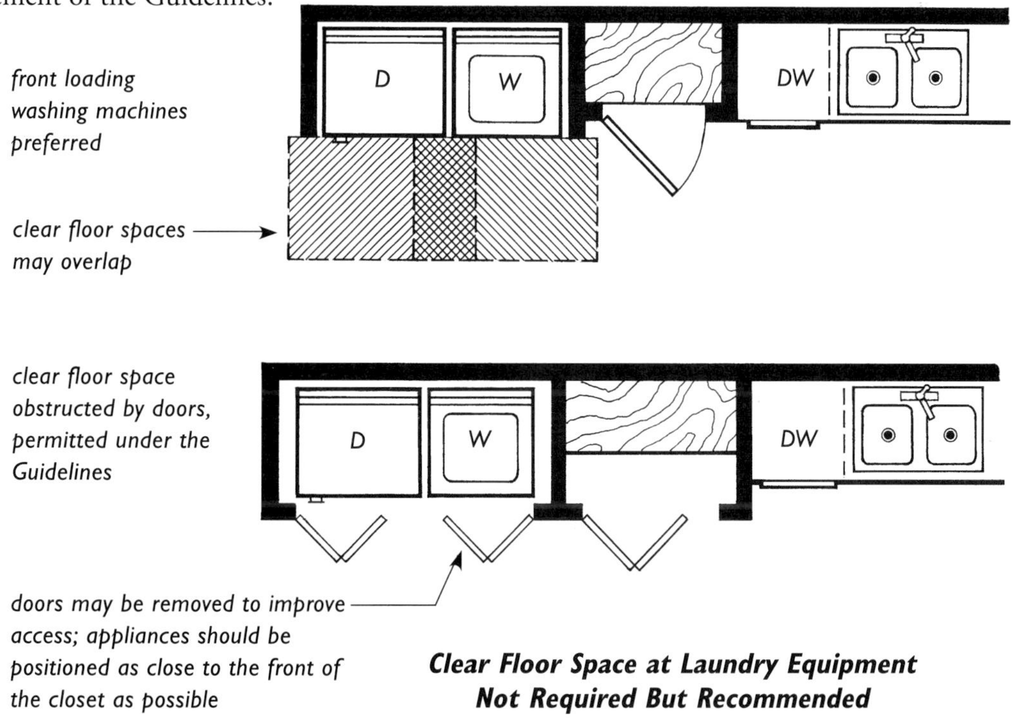

Clear Floor Space at Laundry Equipment Not Required But Recommended

At Other Appliances and Fixtures

While not required by the Guidelines, careful consideration should be given to the selection of other appliances and fixtures installed in kitchens so potential residents who may currently, or in the future, have a physical limitation may more completely use and enjoy their dwelling.

A partial list of additional considerations for kitchens:

- *ranges and cooktops with controls that are front- or side-mounted and have click stops to indicate heat settings,*
- *vent hoods with controls mounted at or near countertop level,*
- *shallow sink basins with rear-mounted drains when removable base cabinets are provided,*
- *lever or blade type handle faucets and controls,*
- *revolving/extending semicircular shelves for corner base cabinet storage.*

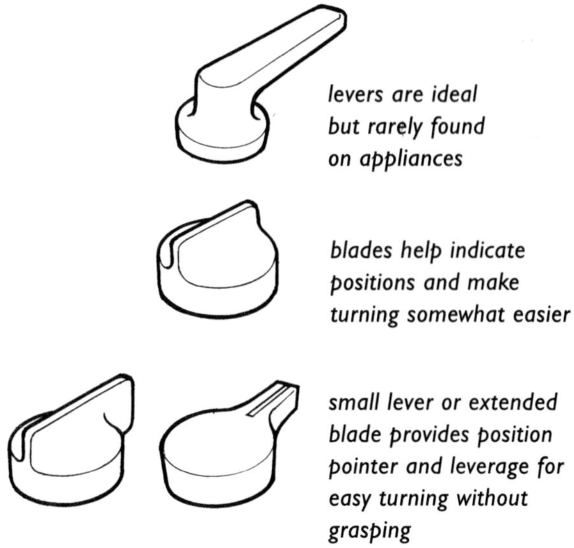

Preferred Control Choices

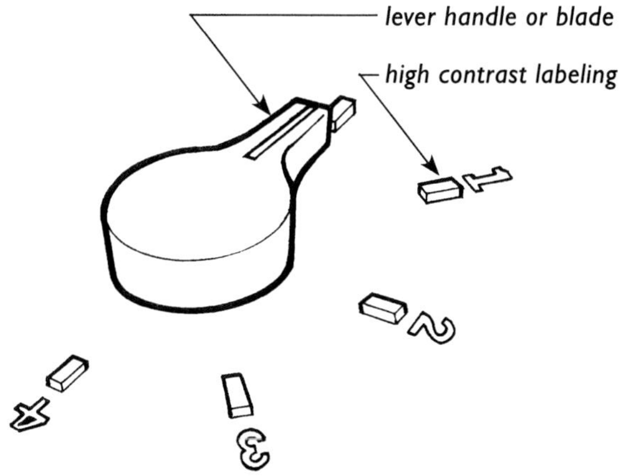

Ideal Control Knob

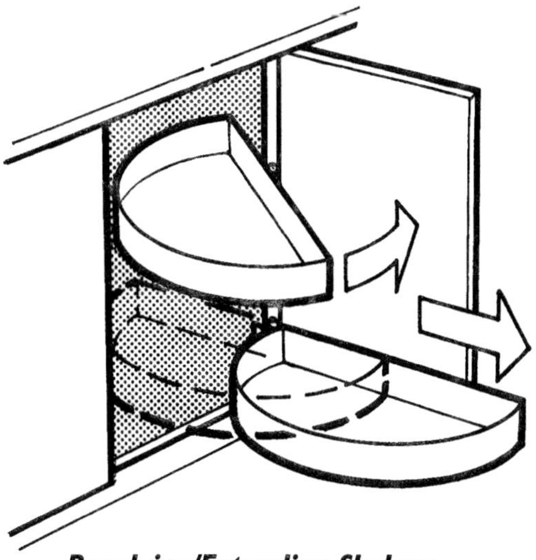

Revolving/Extending Shelves at Corner Base Cabinets Are an Advantage for All Users

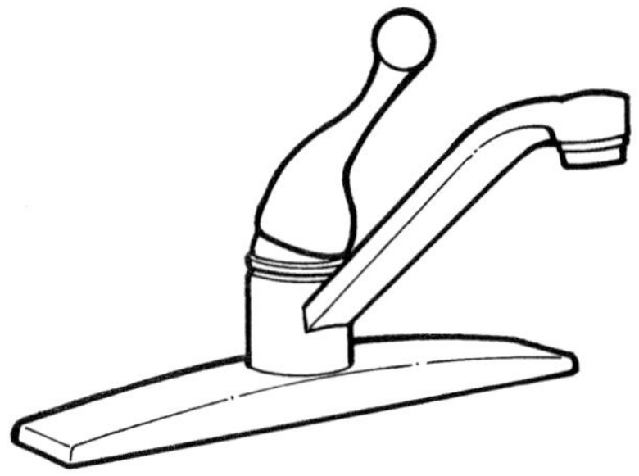

Lever Handles on Faucets Are Easy for Most People to Operate

Examples of Kitchen Floor Plans that Comply with the Guidelines

The plans presented on the following pages are examples of "usable" kitchens that comply with the Fair Housing Accessibility Guidelines (the Guidelines). They range from very small to larger, more elaborate kitchens but are only a small sampling of the layouts possible. The plans are neither required nor even suggested as ideal examples. They are included to illustrate typical applications or interpretations of specific requirements of the Guidelines under various circumstances.

The plans may be used as resource material and planning guides when developing new multi-family housing designs. Conventional industry standard fixture and appliance sizes have been used consistently when developing these plans. It is important to allow sufficient space for any fixtures that may be larger than those shown here. Although designers should rely upon the dimensions indicated and not scale off the drawings, all plans in this section are reproduced at 1/4 inch scale.

The plans are presented in pairs, with the first plan showing fixture and appliance placement and key dimensions, such as aisle widths, that are required by the Guidelines. The second plan gives the overall room dimensions which are offered for comparison purposes only and are not required by the Guidelines. The second plan also shows clear floor spaces adjoining individual appliances and fixtures and describes their use, and, to give the reader the "real" space that appliances occupy, appliance doors are shown in their open position.

Text and notes presented in *italic* type are comments or recommendations and are not required by the Guidelines.

Very Small Parallel Wall Kitchen (Without Dishwasher)

In this kitchen design, walls may not continue across either open end because they would obstruct clear floor spaces required at each appliance. Although discouraged because maneuvering space would be severely restricted, the sink end could be closed if a removable cabinet that conceals a minimum 30-inch wide knee space is provided under the sink; 36-inch wide knee space is preferred.

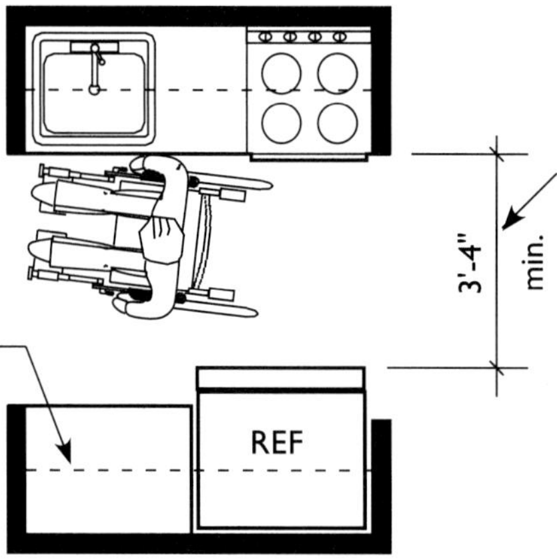

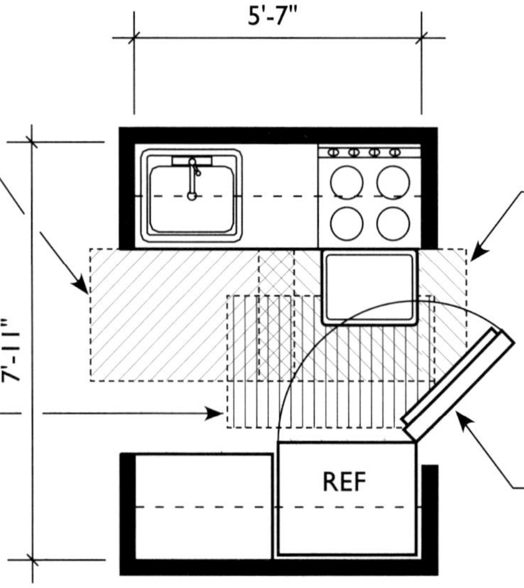

Parallel Wall Kitchen

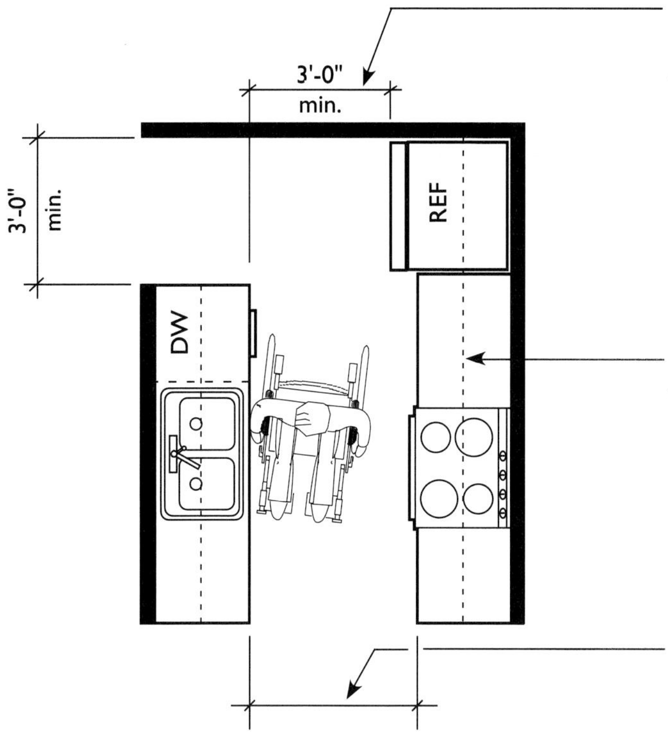

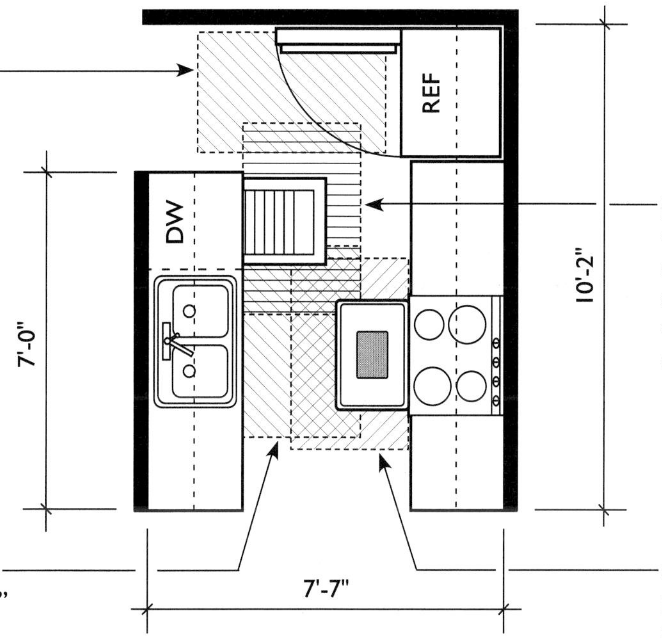

Narrow U-Shaped Kitchen (Without Dishwasher)

sink or cooktop in this location must have removable cabinet to provide knee space below

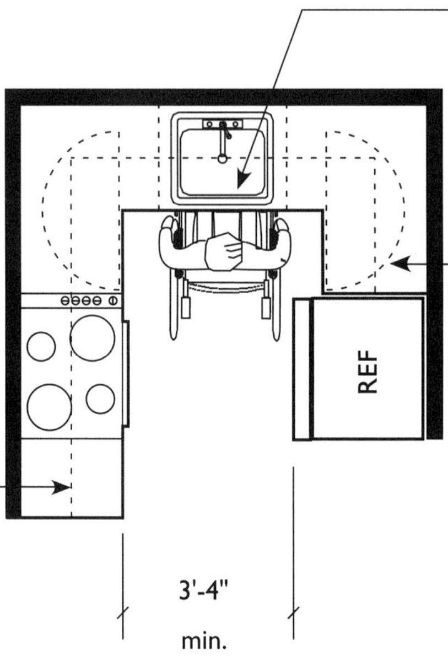

although not required by the Guidelines, this optional rotating/sliding cabinet storage maximizes use of difficult to reach space for all users (see page 7.20)

indicates overhead cabinets

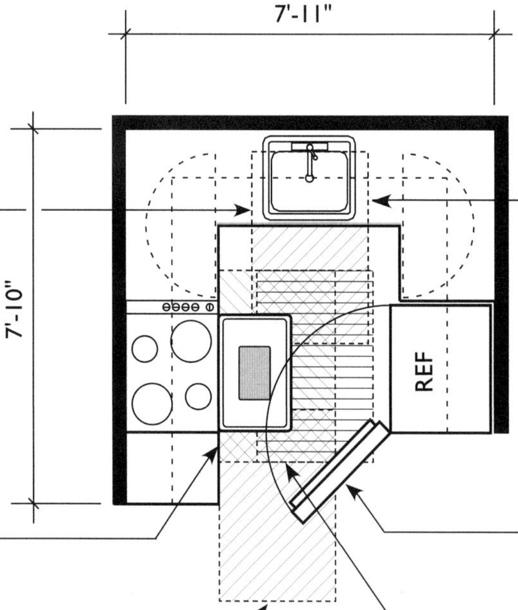

knee space under sink must be a minimum of 30" wide; removable base cabinets may be used if permanent knee space is not desired

clear floor space for forward approach may extend a maximum of 19" into knee space

clear floor space for parallel approach to range cooking surface

although not required, it is preferred that refrigerator door swings back 180 degrees to permit close parallel approach

A typical oven door projects 20" when fully open and must be fairly close to fully open to pull out lower rack. Enough floor area must be available for a clear floor space in this location to permit a "forward" approach to oven racks when pulled out of the oven.

clear floor space for parallel approach to refrigerator

Wider U-Shaped Kitchen

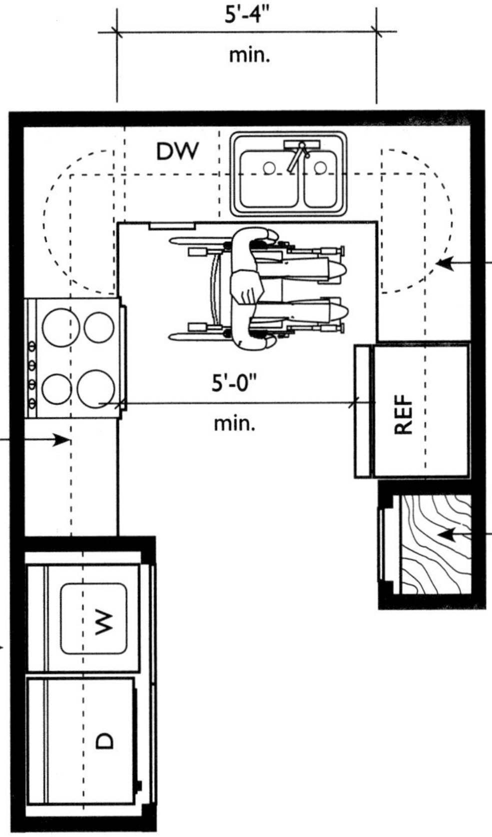

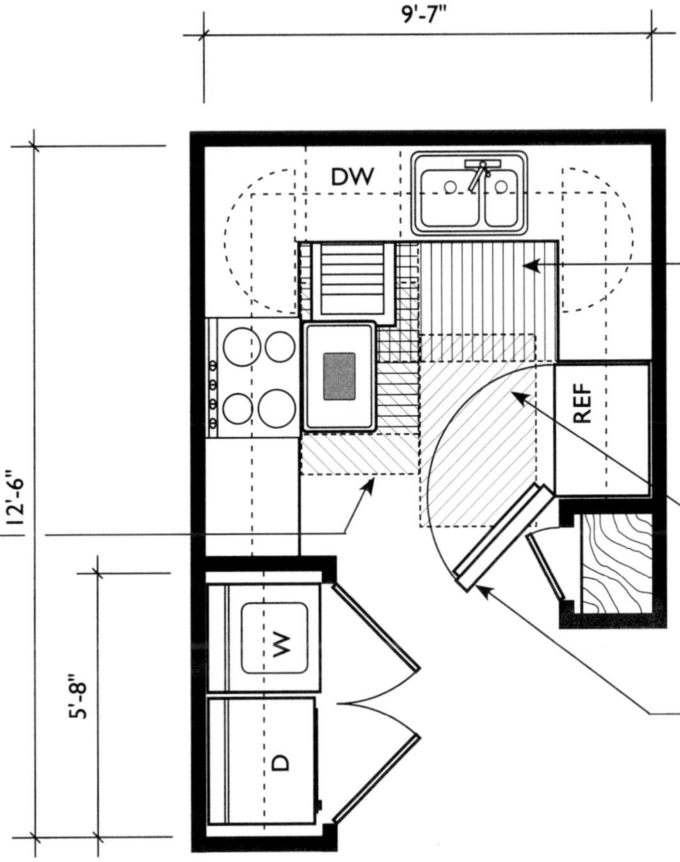

Parallel Wall Kitchen

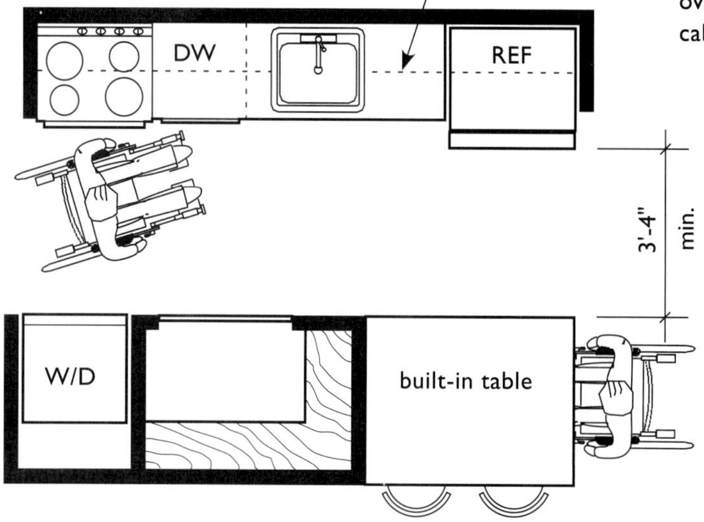

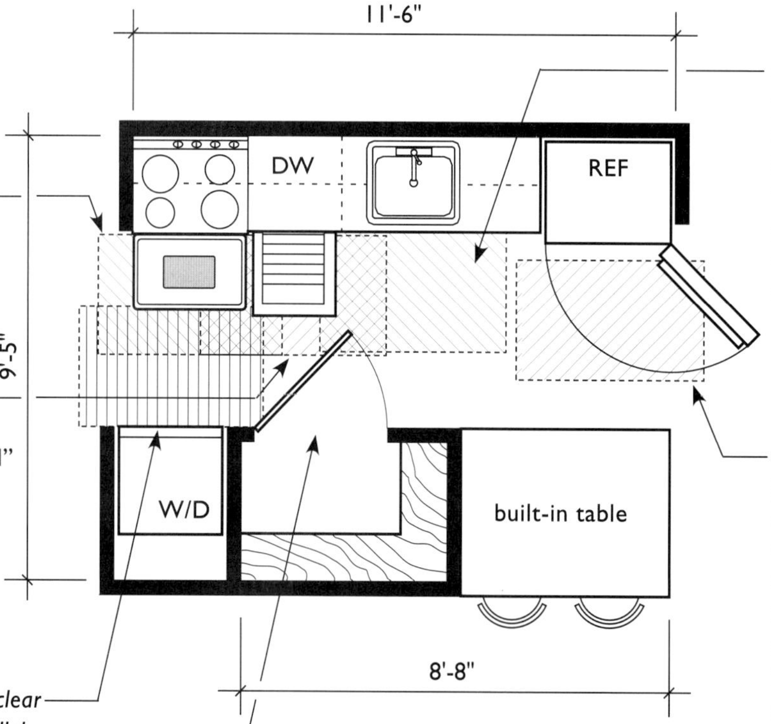

Small L-Shaped Kitchen

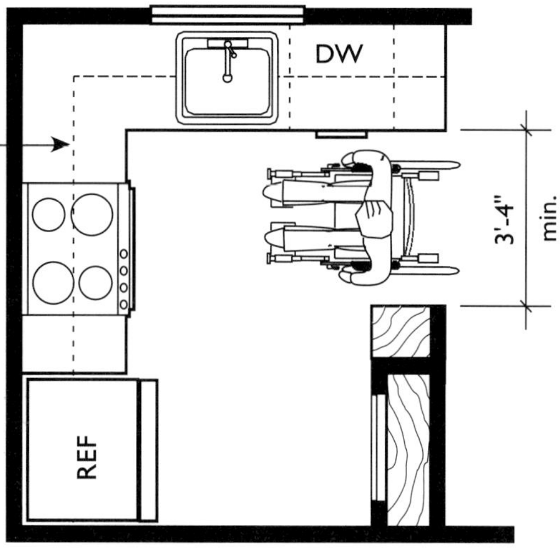

indicates overhead cabinets

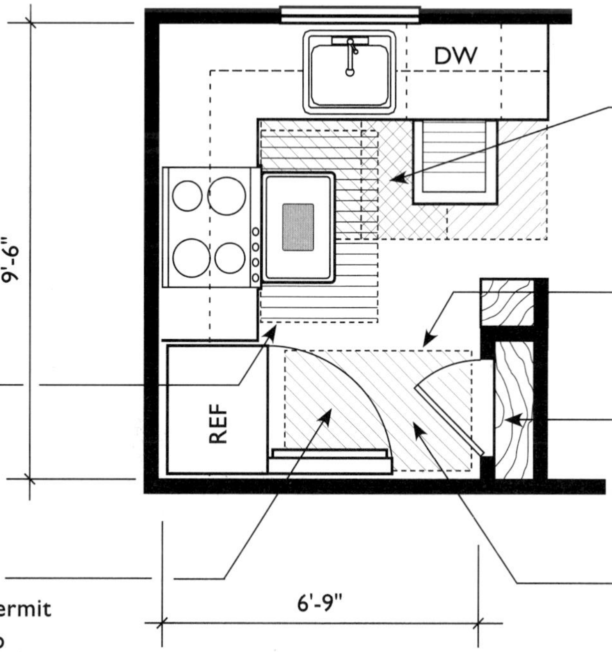

parallel approach centered on sink permits a "forward" approach to dishwasher baskets when they are pulled out of the dishwasher

both forward and limited parallel approach to pantry permitted

parallel approach to range cooktop

because pantry is shallow, door may be less than 32" nominal clear width

sufficient space in front of the refrigerator to permit a "forward" approach to oven racks when they are pulled out of the oven

forward approach to refrigerator

Larger L-Shaped Kitchen

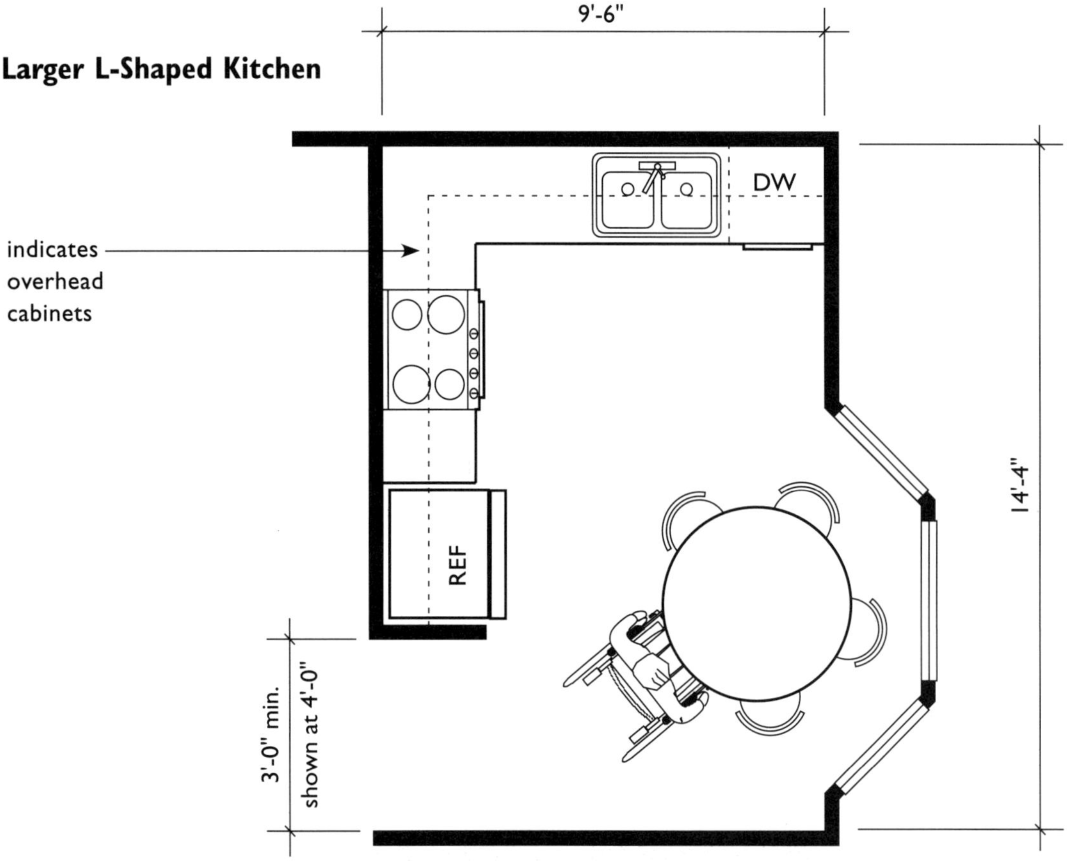

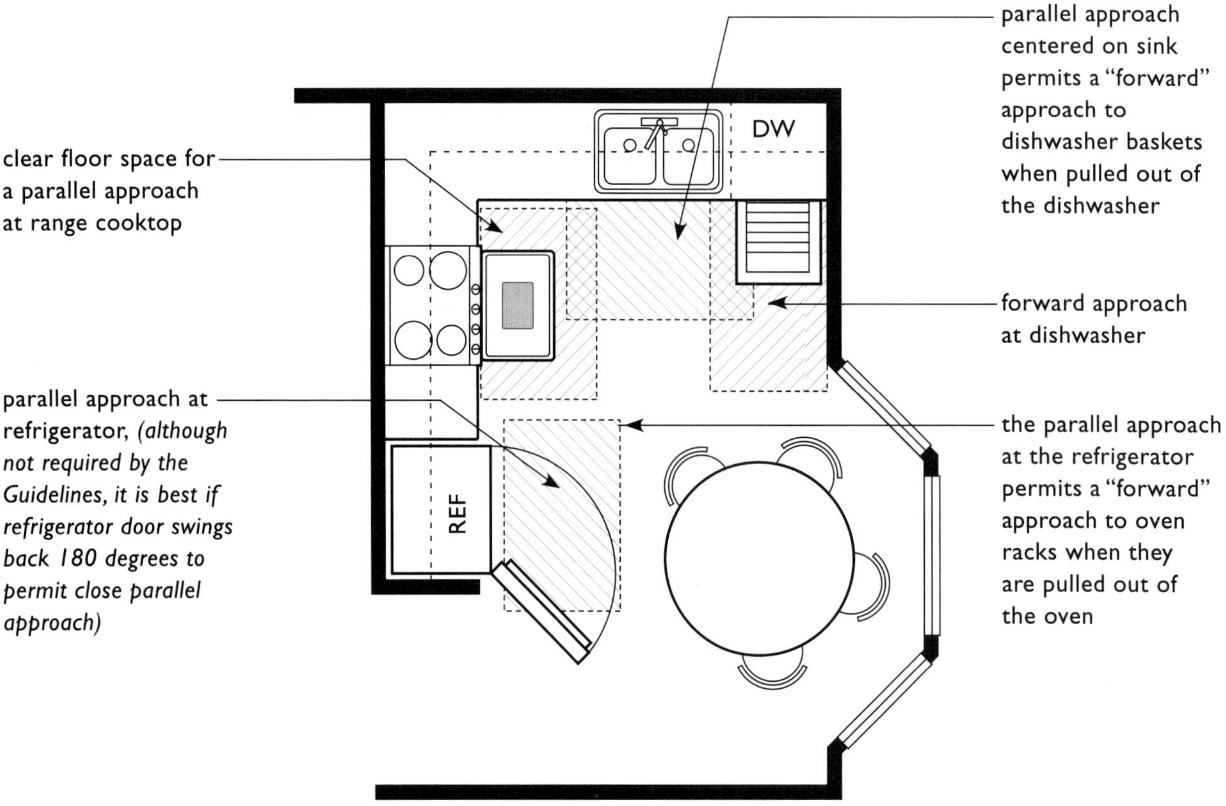

Broken U-Shaped Kitchen

If a corner position with knee space below is being considered for either the sink or cooktop, it is preferred that the sink be located in the corner, as opposed to the cooktop. This is because a cooktop with knee space below at the standard 36-inch height of a kitchen countertop is dangerous for seated users.

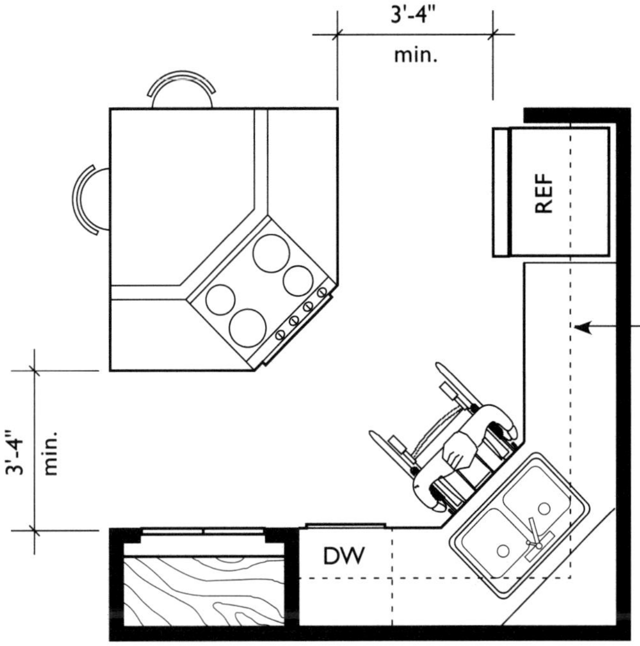

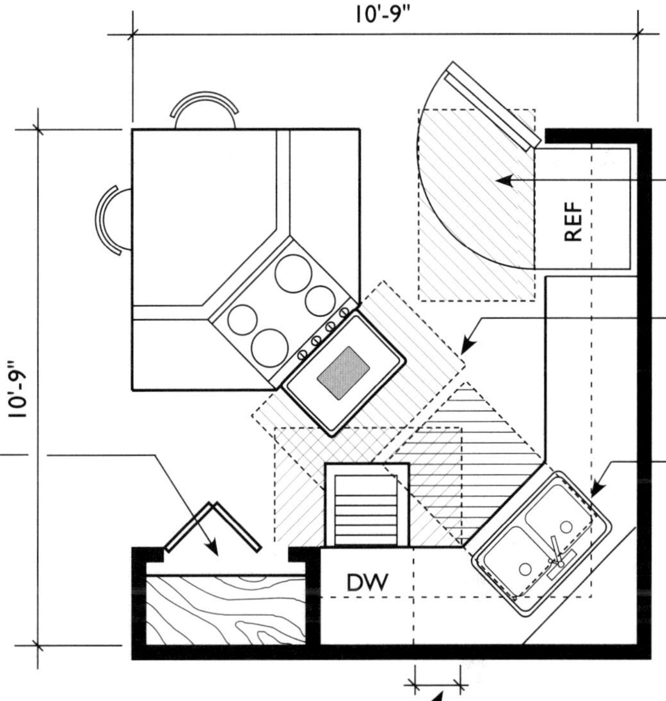

Spacious U-Shaped Kitchen

While this kitchen has an overall "U" shape, it functions like a parallel wall kitchen with two points of entry and exit and allows close parallel approach to the fixture at the base of the "U".

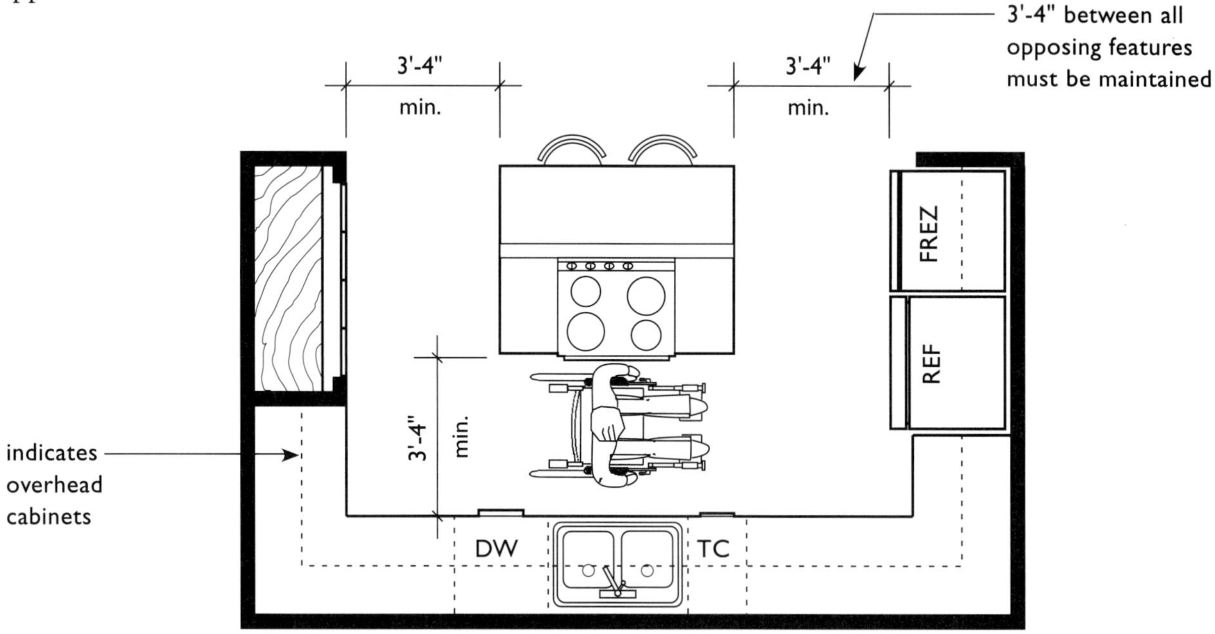

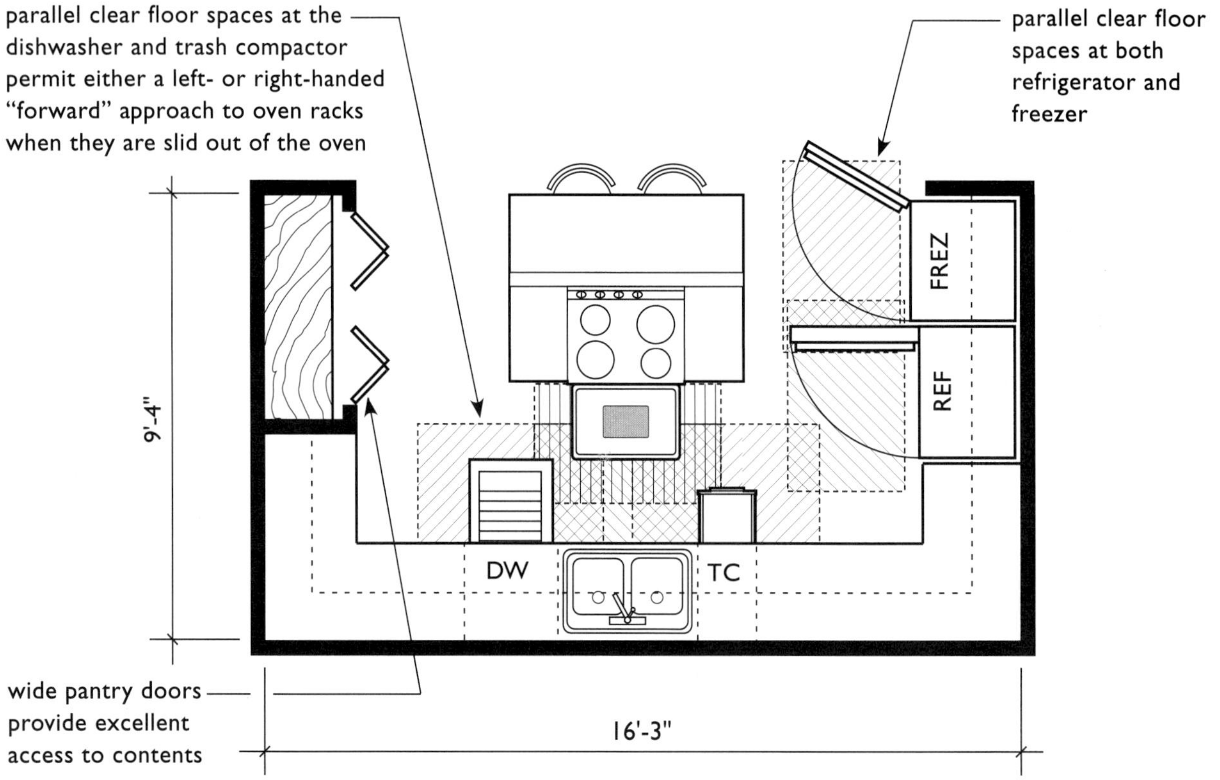

■ **PART B:** Usable Bathrooms

"...covered multifamily dwellings with a building entrance on an accessible route shall be designed and constructed in such a manner that all premises within covered multifamily dwelling units contain usable ...bathrooms such that an individual in a wheelchair can maneuver about the space."

Fair Housing Act Regulations, 24 CFR 100.205

Definitions from the Guidelines

Bathroom. A bathroom which includes a water closet (toilet), lavatory (sink), and bathtub or shower. It does not include single-fixture facilities or those with only a water closet and lavatory. It does include a compartmented bathroom. A compartmented bathroom is one in which the fixtures are distributed among interconnected rooms. A compartmented bathroom is considered a single unit and is subject to the Act's requirements for bathrooms.

Powder Room. A room with only a water closet (toilet) and lavatory (sink). (Definition found in Requirement 6.)

Introduction

The Fair Housing Accessibility Guidelines (the Guidelines) provide specifications for bathroom design that make it possible for people who use mobility aids, and who, heretofore, could not even get into conventional bathrooms in multifamily housing, to now use such facilities. Though not fully accessible, when designed to comply with the Guidelines, these "usable" bathrooms provide a person who uses a wheelchair or scooter or who may use a walker or other mobility aid with a bathroom that has enough maneuvering space to allow the person to enter, close the door, use the fixtures, and exit. In some cases, a resident with a disability will find it necessary to make additional modifications to meet his or her specific needs.

In covered multifamily housing, bathrooms that meet the definition in the Guidelines for a bathroom must then meet the specifications outlined in the Guidelines for usable bathrooms. The Guidelines distinguish between bathrooms and powder rooms and provide different specifications (see definitions on facing page).

Usable bathroom specifications include:

1. an accessible route to and into the bathroom with a nominal 32-inch clear door opening (Requirements 3 and 4),
2. switches, outlets, and controls in accessible locations (Requirement 5),
3. reinforced walls to allow for the later installation of grab bars around the toilet, tub, and shower stall; under certain conditions provisions for reinforcing must be made in shower stalls to permit the installation of a wall-hung bench seat (Requirement 6),
4. maneuvering space within the bathroom to permit a person using a mobility aid to enter the room, close and reopen the door, and exit (Requirement 7), and
5. maneuvering and clear floor space within the bathroom to permit a person using a mobility aid to approach and use fixtures; fixture dimensions and placement are specified only under certain conditions (Requirement 7).

Powder rooms, except as noted below, are only subject to the following specifications:

1. they must be on an accessible route with a nominal 32-inch clear door opening (Requirements 3 and 4) and
2. they must have switches, outlets, and controls in accessible locations (Requirement 5).

There is an **exception**, however, with respect to multistory dwelling units in buildings with one or more elevators. The level served by the building elevator must be the primary entry level for the dwelling unit and there must be either a usable bathroom or a usable **powder room** on the entry level. If there is both a bathroom and a powder room, then the bathroom would be required to be usable and meet Requirements 3 through 7 of the Guidelines. In cases where only a powder room is provided, then it must meet, in addition to Requirements 3, 4, and 5, the applicable provisions of Requirements 6 (Reinforced Walls) and 7 (Maneuvering and Clear Floor Spaces) of the Guidelines. The chart on page 7.35 summarizes the requirements for usable bathrooms and usable powder rooms.

Accessible route, usable doors, controls in accessible locations, and reinforced walls for later installation of grab bars are covered in other chapters of this manual. Maneuvering and clear floor space requirements are explained in the first part of this chapter, followed by a presentation of a variety of bathroom floor plans that comply with the requirements of the Guidelines.

Two Bathroom Specifications

To satisfy the maneuvering and clear floor space requirements for usable bathrooms, Requirement 7 of the Guidelines gives two sets of specifications to design bathrooms, referred to in this manual as Specification A and Specification B. Although not the only difference between the two specifications, a bathroom designed to meet Specification B has greater access to the bathtub than a bathroom designed to meet Specification A. The two specifications and their differences will be described in the following discussions of maneuvering and clear floor space requirements.

How Many Bathrooms and Fixtures Must Comply with the Guidelines?

In dwelling units containing more than one bathroom, if Specification A is selected as the basis for designing a bathroom, all bathrooms in the dwelling unit also must comply with the A Specifications. If Specification B is selected, only one bathroom in the dwelling unit must meet those requirements; all other bathrooms in the dwelling unit must be on an accessible route (Requirement 4), have doors with a nominal 32-inch clear opening (Requirement 3), have switches, outlets, and controls in accessible locations (Requirement 5), and have reinforced walls around toilets, tubs, and shower stalls (Requirement 6). However, maneuvering space as specified in the Guidelines' Requirement 7 is not required in other bathrooms within the dwelling unit when one bathroom is designed to meet the B Specifications.

However, any powder room provided in a dwelling unit, regardless of which set of specifications the bathroom(s) meets, is still subject to Requirements 3 (Usable Doors), 4 (Accessible Route), and 5 (Controls in Accessible Locations). The exception that requires certain powder rooms also to meet Requirements 6 (Reinforcing) and 7 (Maneuvering and Clear Floor Space) is discussed on page 7.33.

In bathrooms where several of each type of fixture are provided, e.g., a separate shower and tub or two lavatories, **all fixtures** must be usable in Specification A bathrooms while only **one** of each type of fixture must be usable by a person with a disability in a Specification B bathroom.

Which Bathroom Should Meet the Requirements of the Guidelines?

When a builder or developer is deciding whether to use the A or B Specifications when designing bathrooms, it is important to consider the number of bathrooms in the dwelling unit. If there is only one bathroom, the builder may follow the Specifications for either A or B. However, while not required by the Guidelines, it is recommended that Specification B, which provides the higher level of accessibility, be used.

In multiple bathroom dwelling units the issue is somewhat more complex. If the B Specification is selected for use in a two-bathroom dwelling, which bathroom should comply? The master or the hall bathroom? If the hall bathroom is selected to be the usable bathroom and the family member who has a disability would normally occupy the master bedroom, then he or she would have to go down the hall to that bathroom. If, on the other hand, the master bath is the usable bathroom and the family member with a disability is one of the children, then it will be necessary for the child to continually enter the master bedroom suite.

Where there are two or more bathrooms, the ideal situation would be to have at least one bathroom meet Specification B, and the other bathrooms meet Specification A. However, it is acceptable under the Guidelines to have only one bathroom meet Specification B, and the other bathrooms meet Requirements 3, 4, 5, and 6 of the Guidelines, but not Requirement 7. This discussion is advisory only.

Bathroom Requirements for Covered Dwelling Units

All bathrooms as defined in the Guidelines must:

1. be on an accessible route (Requirement 4),
2. have 32-inch nominal clear width doorways (Requirement 3),
3. have switches, outlets, and controls in accessible locations (Requirement 5),
4. have reinforcing around toilets, tubs, and showers (Requirement 6), and
5. meet Requirement 7, Specification A or B:

Specification A

If Specification A is used it applies to all bathrooms, and all fixtures in those bathrooms must be usable.

Specification B

If Specification B is used, it applies to one bathroom, and only one of each type of fixture must be usable; additional bathrooms in the unit are exempt **only** from maneuvering and clear floor space requirements at fixtures.

Powder Room Requirements for Covered Dwelling Units

Powder rooms must:

1. be on an accessible route (Requirement 4),
2. have 32-inch nominal clear width doorways (Requirement 3), and
3. have switches, outlets, and controls in accessible locations (Requirement 5).

Exception

When the powder room is the only toilet facility on the entry level of a multi-story unit in a building with one or more elevators, it must, in addition to Requirements 3, 4, and 5, **meet the reinforcing specifications of Requirement 6 and the maneuvering and clear floor specifications of Requirement 7.**

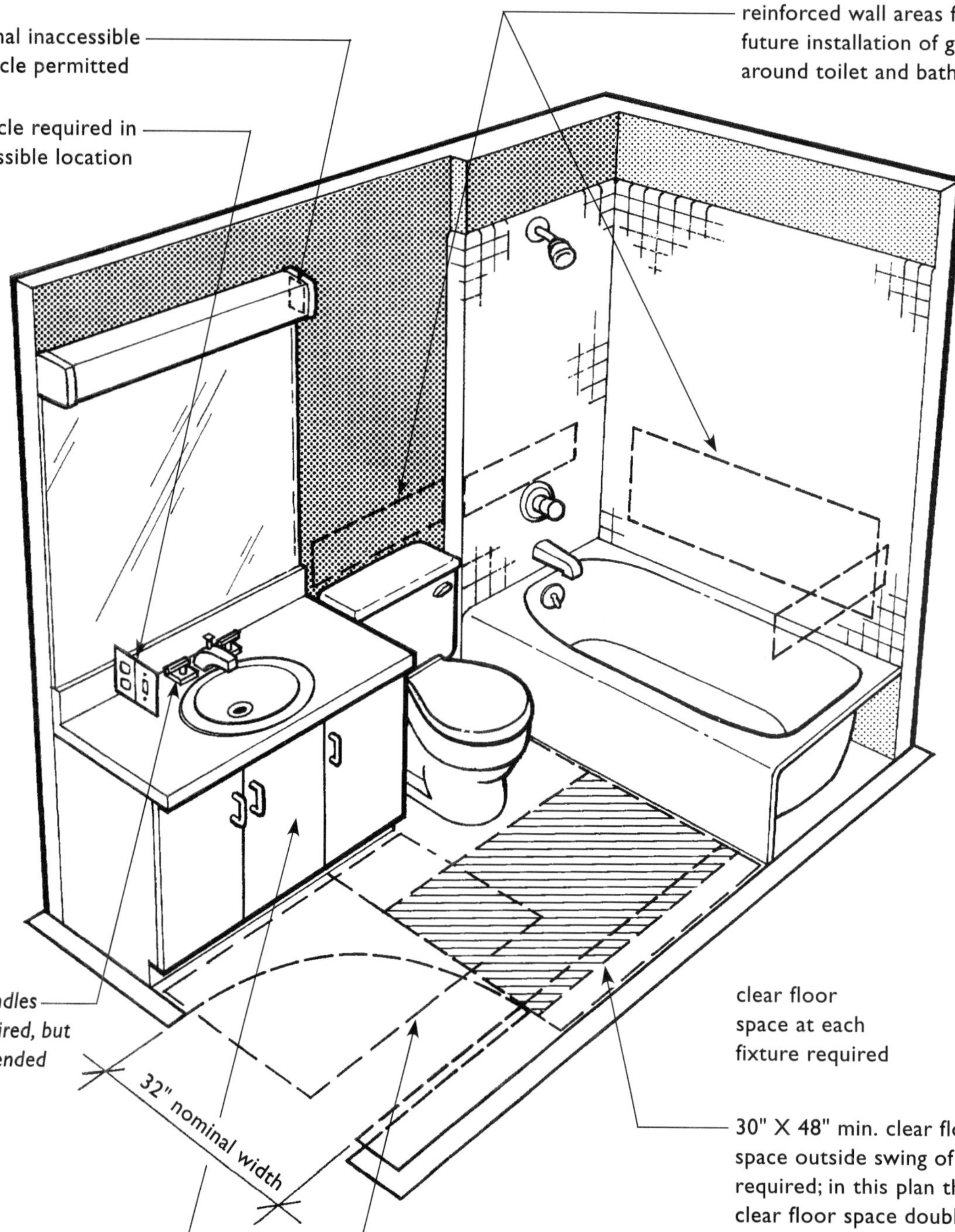

Example "A" Bathroom
9'-4" X 5'-2"
(See plan page 7.66)

Notes in italic type are recommendations only and are not required by the Guidelines.

reinforced wall areas for future installation of grab bars around toilet and bathtub

additional inaccessible receptacle permitted

specifically designated clear floor space at bathtub allows greater access to the bathtub and its controls, see page 7.55

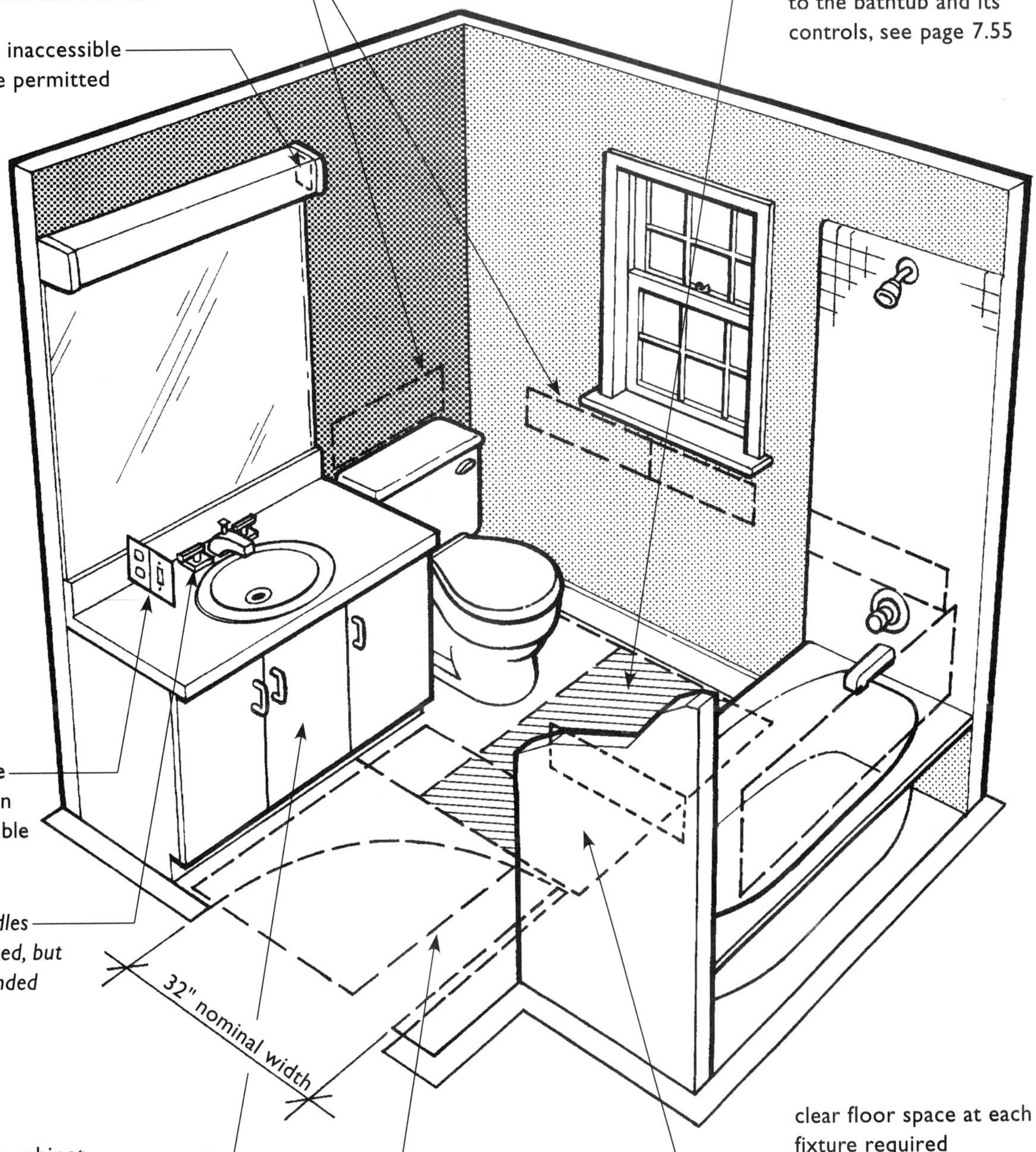

receptacle required in an accessible location

lever handles not required, but recommended

fixed base cabinet acceptable since parallel approach centered on basin is possible

30" X 48" clear floor space for parallel approach

clear floor space at each fixture required

30" X 48" min. clear floor space outside swing of door required

Example "B" Bathroom
Greater Access to Bathtub
6'-10" X 7'-9"
(Similar to Plan on Page 7.67)

Notes in italic type are recommendations only and are not required by the Guidelines.

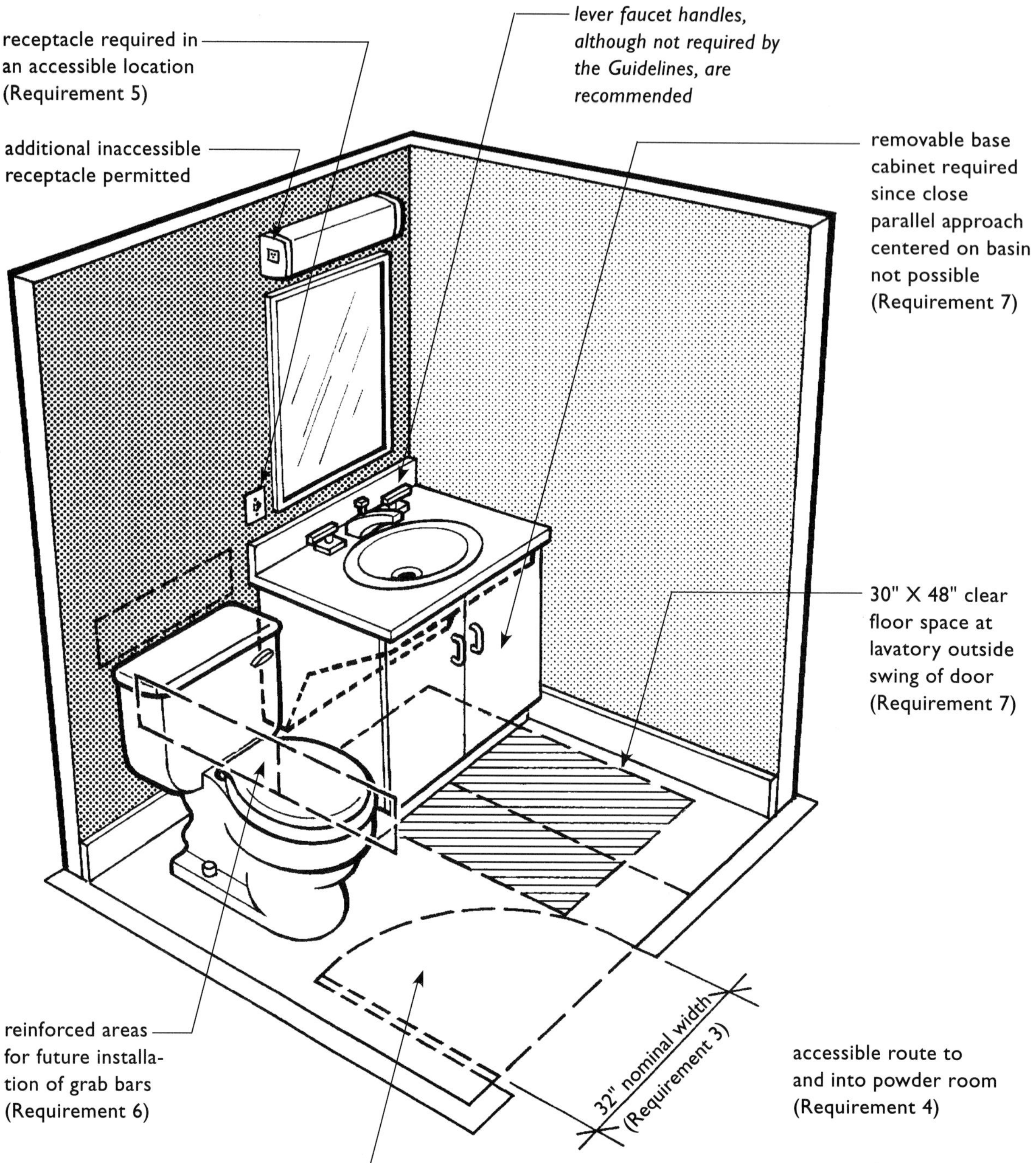

Notes in italic type are recommendations only and are not required by the Guidelines.

Usable Powder Room
5'-6" X 5'-8"
(See Plan Page 7.81)

Powder Room in Single-Story Dwelling Unit Must Meet Only Requirements 3, 4, and 5

Powder Room Must Meet Requirements 3, 4, 5, 6, and 7 When It Is the Only Toilet Facility on the Entry Level of a Multistory Unit in a Building with One or More Elevators

Maneuvering Space in Bathrooms

The Guidelines offer two different wordings for the maneuvering space requirements for bathrooms complying with Specification A and Specification B. When applied, the requirements yield almost identical results. Neither Specification requires that the space for a five-foot circular turn or a T-turn (see page 19) be available so a user in a wheelchair would have the space necessary to turn around in the bathroom. However, there are very specific clear floor space requirements that have been adapted from the ANSI A117.1 - 1986 Standard to make it possible for many people with mobility disabilities to be able to use bathrooms designed to meet the requirements of the Guidelines.

When the maneuvering space requirements of both Specification A and B are analyzed carefully, the primary difference is that a clear floor space must be provided adjacent to the foot of the tub in Specification B bathrooms to increase access to the bathtub and the bathtub controls. To assist the reader in understanding the other differences in the two specifications, this manual will describe in detail bathroom elements and features as required by the Guidelines.

Both Specification A and Specification B Bathrooms Require the Following:

1. A 30-inch x 48-inch clear floor space outside the swing of the door as it is closed. In bathrooms where the door swings out of the room all the clear floor spaces at fixtures still must be provided. In addition, the user must be able to reopen the door to exit.

2. Usable bathroom fixtures. Making bathroom fixtures usable in both Specification A and B bathrooms involves providing certain clear floor space dimensions at each fixture and meeting certain requirements for the shower if the shower is the only bathing facility in the covered dwelling unit. In addition, Specification B sets additional requirements for bathroom fixtures such as providing clear floor space at the bathtub in a manner that allows greater access to the bathtub and meeting certain specifications on the installation of vanities and lavatories.

The maneuvering space necessary for usable bathrooms is thus made up of the combination of the designated clear floor spaces at fixtures and the presence of clear floor space outside the swing of the door. Clear floor spaces may overlap each other and the maneuvering space also may include knee or toe space under lavatories or toilet bowls. See the illustration at the top of page 7.40.

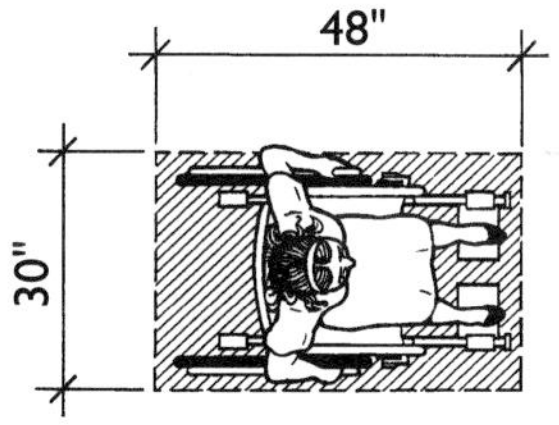

Minimum Clear Floor Space for Person Using a Wheelchair

The Guidelines contain no requirements for location or type of controls except in Specification B bathrooms, the controls must be located at the foot of the tub. There generally are no fixture specifications, except size of showers when they are the only bathing fixture in the unit and when knee space must be provided under lavatories. If the bathroom has sufficient space to allow a parallel approach centered on the lavatory, then standard base cabinets may be used below a lavatory. If not, a removable vanity cabinet is required so necessary knee space for a forward approach is available at the lavatory.

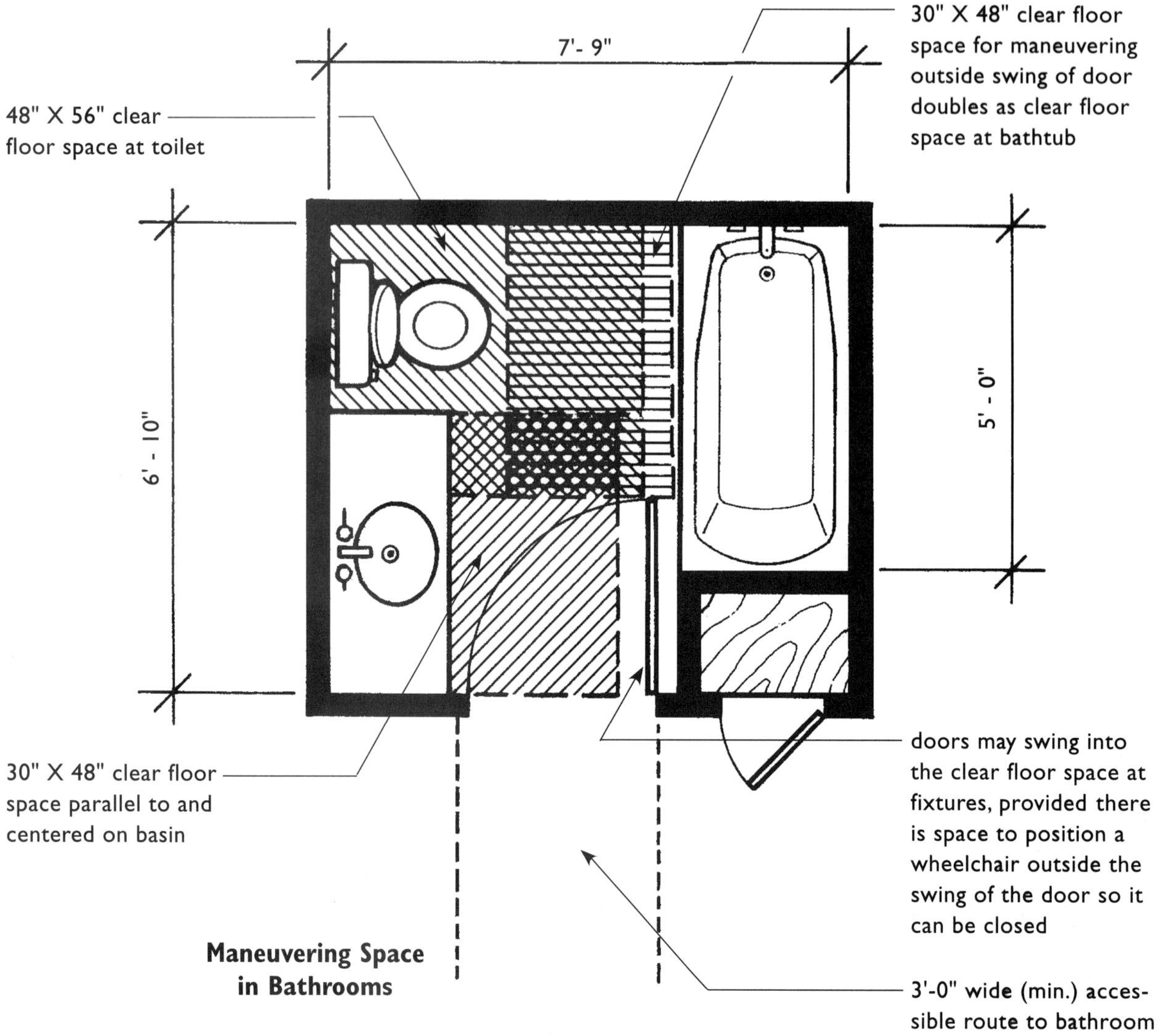

Maneuvering Space in Bathrooms

Clear Floor Space at Toilet Fixtures

The clear floor space at toilets varies in size and is larger than the clear floor space for wheelchairs shown at other fixtures. Different amounts of clear floor space must be maintained around a toilet fixture depending upon the direction of approach, either front or side, to allow ease of use by persons using wheelchairs.

Many people who use wheelchairs are unable to stand while transferring from a wheelchair to the toilet. Some people can transfer to and from the toilet from only one side. Others can complete right, left, or front transfers. The technique used depends on which approach is most familiar, easiest, and safest to complete.

The unobstructed clear floor space required by the Guidelines allows a wheelchair user to approach the toilet and transfer onto the fixture using a variety of independent and assisted transfer techniques. The transfer techniques most commonly used are the forward, perpendicular, diagonal, reverse diagonal, and parallel. Whenever possible, it is best to position the toilet to allow forward, perpendicular, and diagonal approaches.

Forward Approach
(Front Transfer)

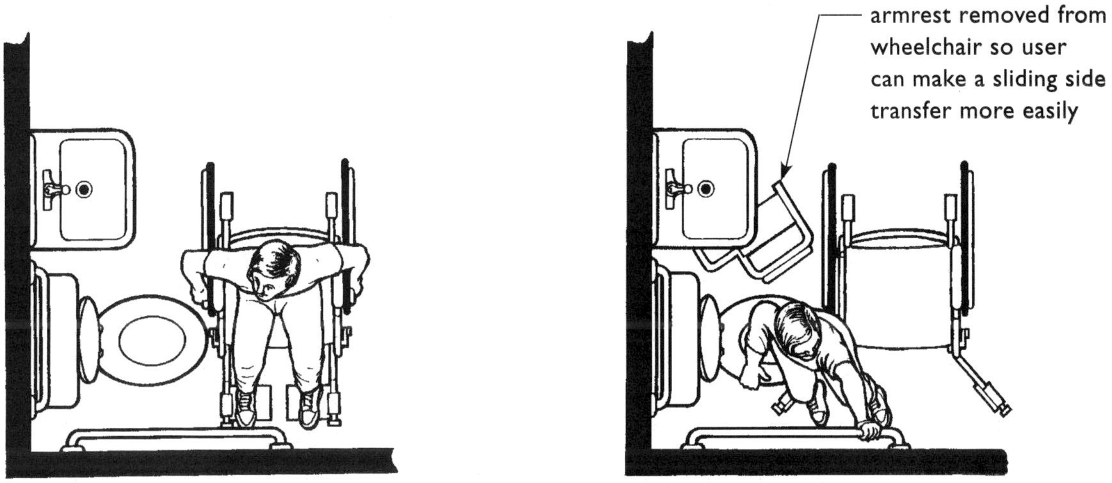

Perpendicular Approach
(Side Transfer)

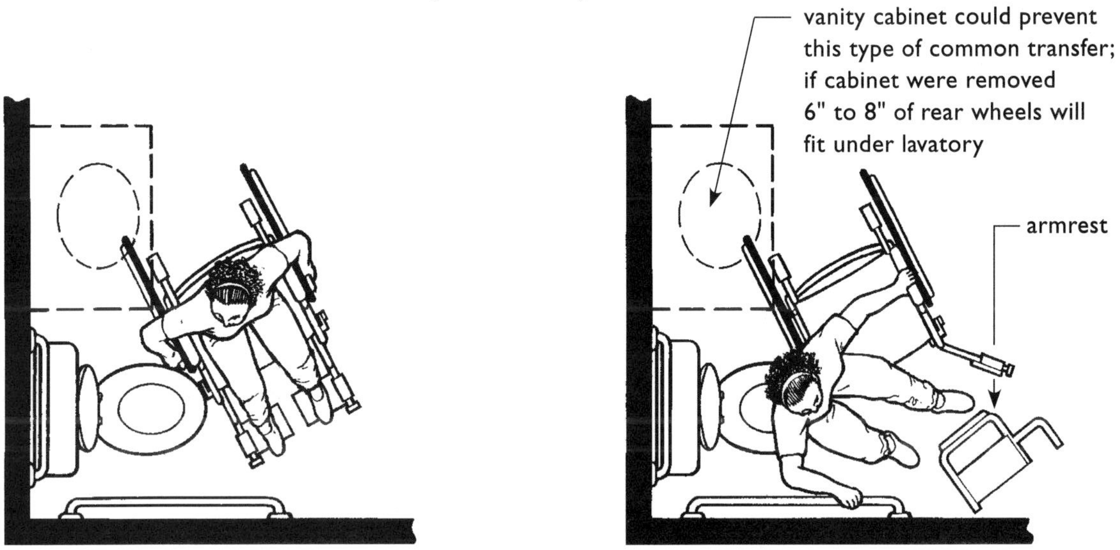

Diagonal Approach
(Probably Most Frequently Used Unassisted Transfer Technique)

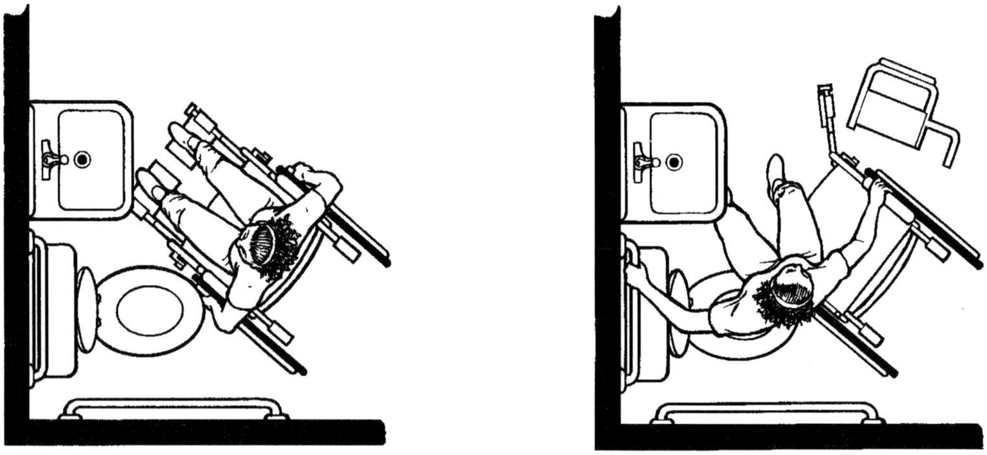

Reverse Diagonal Approach
(Diagonal Transfer)

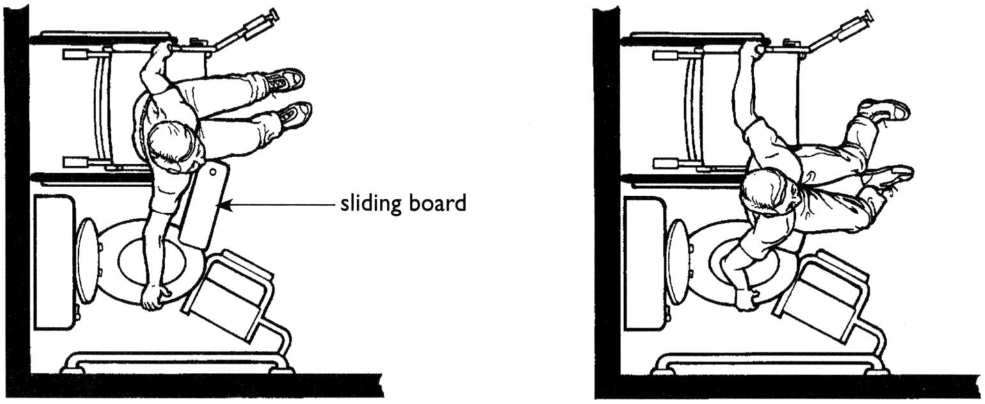

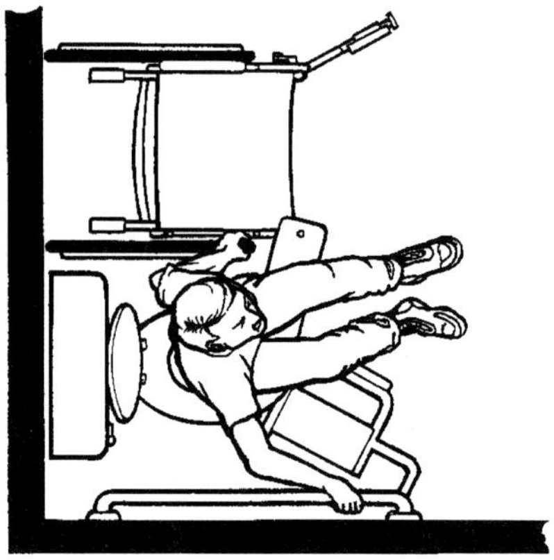

Parallel Approach
(Side Transfer Using Sliding Board)

One of Three Clear Floor Spaces Required in Both A and B Bathrooms

When planning both Specification A and B bathrooms, one of the following three clear floor spaces must be provided at toilets to allow people using wheelchairs and walkers to maneuver, approach the seat, and make a safe transfer onto the toilet. The clear floor space dimensions are to be applied or superimposed over a plan during the design process to determine if space requirements at toilets are being met.

In the plans shown below to illustrate the clear floor space options at toilets, the arrows pointing in toward the clear floor space are indicating the direction of approach to the toilet by a person using a wheelchair. In plans one and two, the incomplete box at the right of the toilet may be either a wall-hung lavatory or a countertop lavatory. Depending upon the placement of the other bathroom fixtures and the clearances in that room, any vanity cabinet may be fixed or may be required to be removable.

The Guidelines allow a countertop lavatory, with either a removable or fixed base cabinet, to be a maximum depth of 24 inches. A wing or privacy wall also may overlap the clear floor space; however, it, too, is restricted to a length of 24 inches and must be at least 33 inches from the opposite wall. In a compartmented bathroom, the 33-inch dimension would have to be increased. See the example on page 7.71.

In terms of accessibility or usability of the toilet, from left to right, diagram number one offers a middle level of usability, number two offers the lowest level, and number three, the highest.

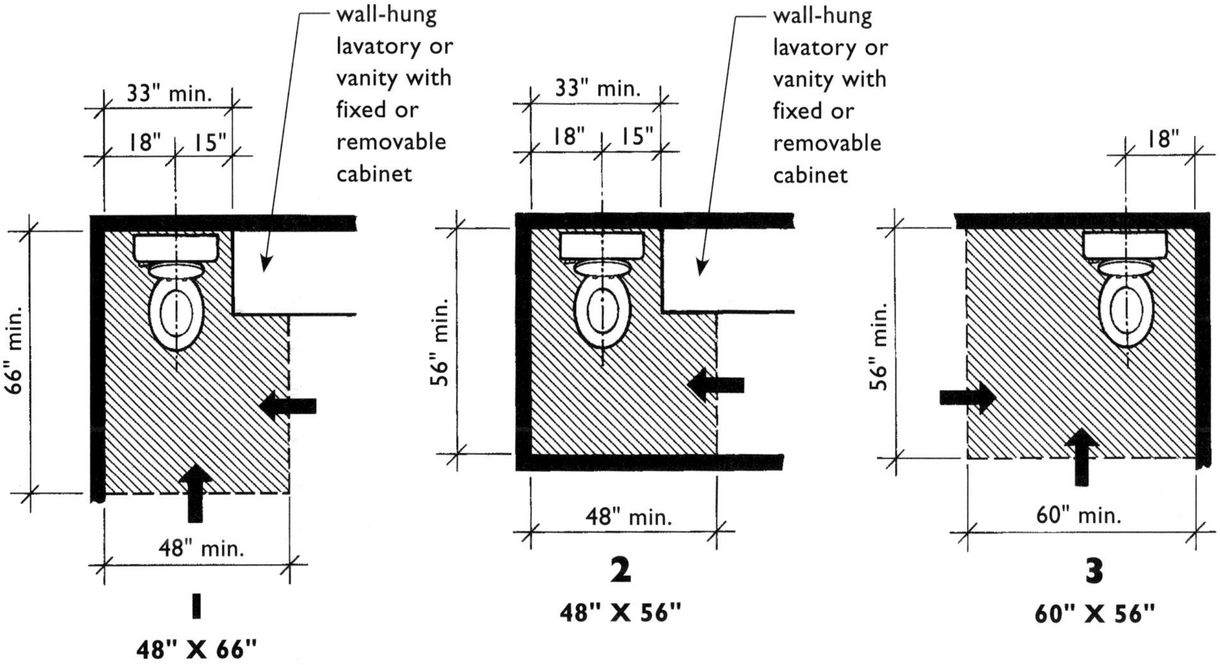

Clear Floor Space at Toilets
(One of the Three Must be Provided in "A" and "B" Bathrooms)

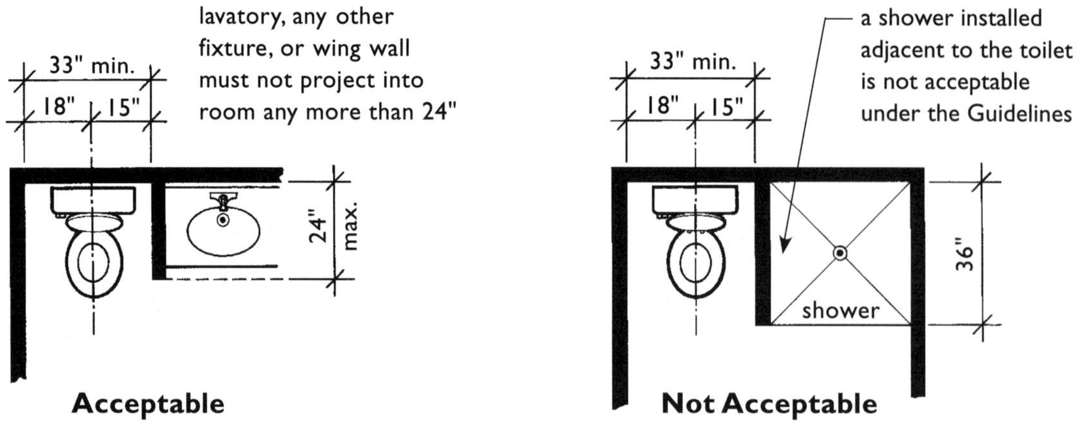

Some Features May Overlap Clear Floor Space at Toilet

48-Inch X 66-Inch Clear Floor Space

To provide space for a forward approach when a lavatory is adjacent to the toilet, the clear floor space must be a minimum of 66 inches long. The door is located opposite the toilet to provide the maneuvering space necessary to execute a forward approach to the toilet (see bottom right illustration).

The user may slide the wheelchair footrests under the toilet bowl or will swing them to either side of the toilet to pull in closer to the bowl to execute a front transfer. The space for a perpendicular approach is actually wider than in clear floor space number two. An added benefit of the 48-inch x 66-inch clear floor space is that a limited version of the commonly used diagonal approach to the toilet also is possible.

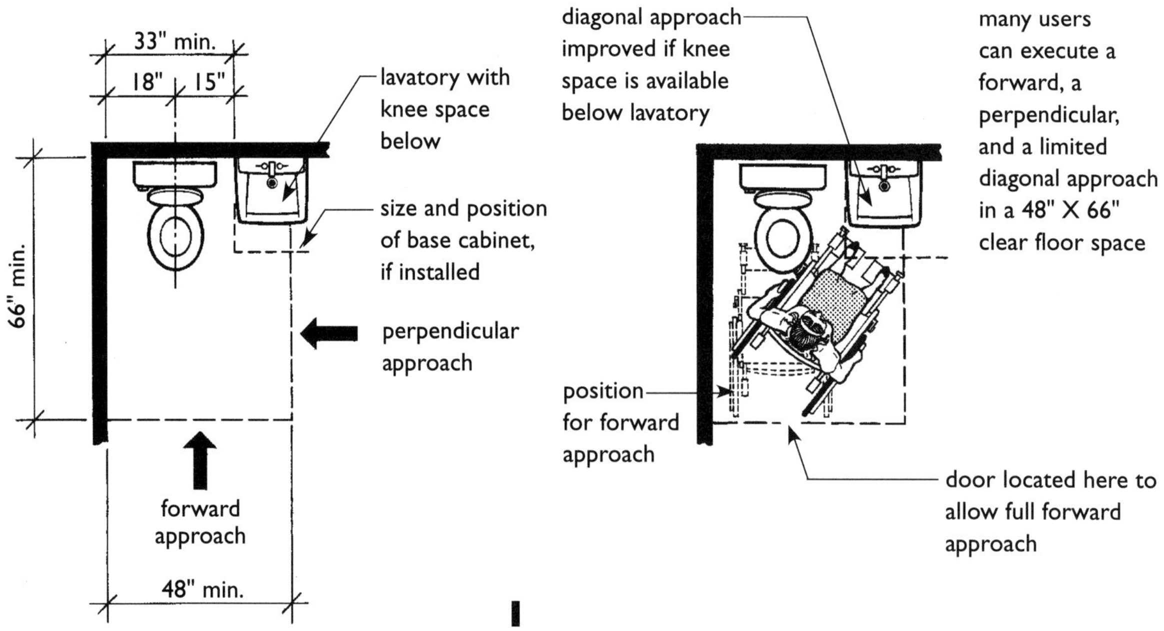

48" X 66" Clear Floor Space
(with Overlapping Lavatory)

48-Inch X 56-Inch Clear Floor Space

The 48-inch x 56-inch clear floor space enclosed on three sides is the minimum space in which a person using a wheelchair will be able to get close enough to make a side or perpendicular approach to the toilet. The 48-inch dimension is consistent with the length of the minimum clear floor space for wheelchairs. A person wishing to make a right transfer will approach the toilet head on as shown in the lower right illustration, or depending upon preference, the user may wish to back into the clear floor space to execute a left transfer.

The 56-inch dimension may allow some users to angle their wheelchair slightly to execute a safer transfer onto the toilet. This angled position is improved if the lavatory is open below. The Guidelines do not require that this additional maneuvering space be provided for access to toilets, but it can be accomplished with the installation of a lavatory with a removable base cabinet. As much as six to nine inches of the large wheels on a manual wheelchair (somewhat less for power wheelchairs) can be positioned under the lavatory. Removable base cabinets are required in other situations and will be discussed in the next section on "Clear Floor Space at Lavatories." See page 7.47.

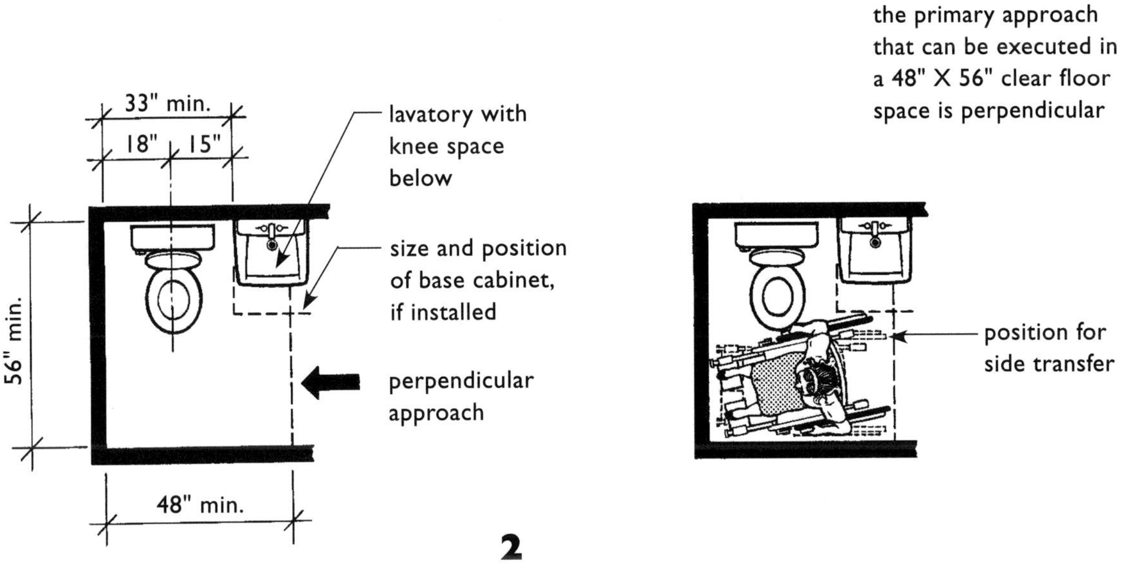

2
48" X 56" Clear Floor Space
(with Overlapping Lavatory)

60-Inch X 56-Inch Clear Floor Space

This clear floor space, minus the lavatory, is the same length as at toilet clear floor space number two, but its width is increased by 12 inches. Its shape and size permit a large variety of transfer positions to be assumed by someone using a wheelchair or scooter, including parallel, perpendicular, and diagonal approaches. However, a forward approach as shown at clear floor space number one is not possible unless the depth of this space is increased to 66 inches. The 60-inch x 56-inch clear floor space has added value in that it has sufficient space so someone could assist a person using a wheelchair in making a transfer.

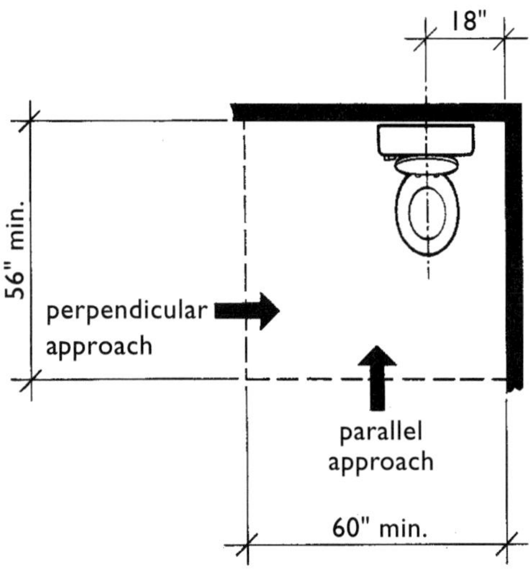

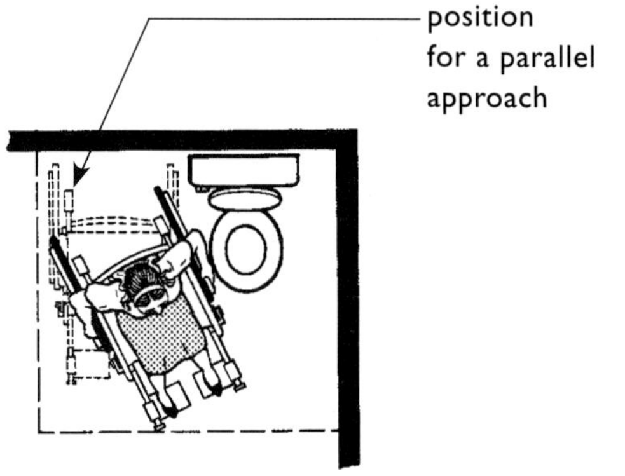

3
60" X 56" Clear Floor Space
(with No Overlapping Elements)

Clear Floor Space at Lavatories

A 30-inch x 48-inch clear floor space is required at the lavatory so a person who uses a wheelchair or scooter can get close enough to the basin and controls to use the fixture. When knee space is not provided for a forward approach, this 30-inch x 48-inch clear floor space must be parallel to the cabinet or counter front and centered on the basin.

Either a countertop lavatory with a vanity cabinet or a wall-hung lavatory may be installed in Specification A and B bathrooms. There are no specifications for control location or type nor for drain location. The lavatory type and width, plus the available maneuvering space in the room, determines whether or not a vanity cabinet must be removable.

To economize on floor space the basin may be offset so the length of the countertop may be less than 48 inches. In 36-inch wide countertops, the basin may be offset provided it remains centered on the required 48-inch long clear floor space.

If a lavatory must be installed where space does not permit a close parallel approach with the 30-inch x 48-inch clear floor space centered on the basin, the centerline of the basin must be at least 15 inches from an adjoining wall or fixture. It must have knee space at least 30 inches wide to allow a user to execute a forward approach into clear floor space beneath the fixture.

Knee space must be provided below narrow lavatories lacking this parallel and centered approach, because, if not, the user must make an awkward and often impossible, painful twisting motion over the side of the wheelchair to reach the faucet handle that is positioned somewhat behind one shoulder. In addition, it is difficult from this position to wash both hands, lean over the basin to clean teeth, etc. Information on removable base cabinets and knee space is given on page 7.49.

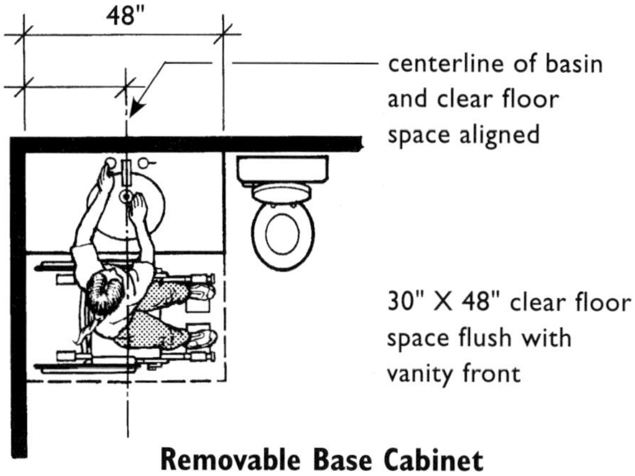

Removable Base Cabinet Not Required Because Clear Floor Space Centered on Basin (Applicable in A and B Bathrooms)

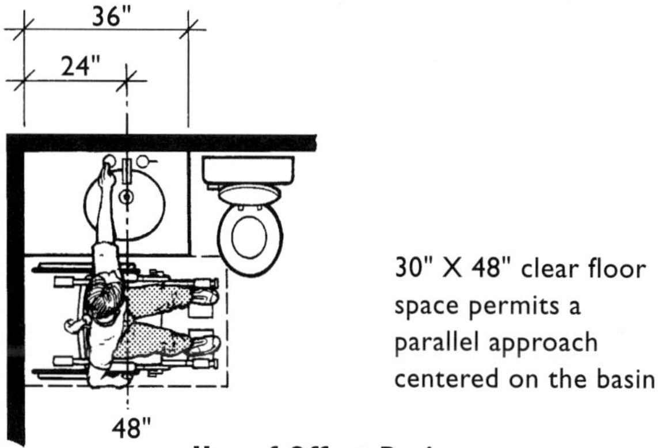

Use of Offset Basin to Reduce Lavatory Length (Applicable in A and B Bathrooms)

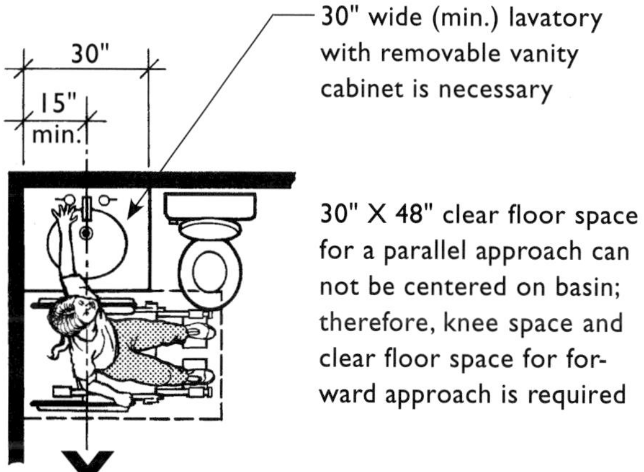

X Not Acceptable for Parallel Approach

Removable Base Cabinet Must Be Provided Because Clear Floor Space Can Not Be Centered (Required in A and B Bathrooms)

Double Basin and Pedestal Lavatories

It is also possible to install double basin lavatories and pedestal lavatories so they meet the requirements of the Guidelines. Countertops for double basin lavatories vary in length and may be as short as 60 inches.

Where two basins are planned for installation in a 60-inch long countertop, and especially where obstructions such as a wall and bathtub (as shown in the illustration at right) enclose the available maneuvering space, a forward approach with a removable vanity cabinet should be used. However, in this illustration the countertop is 72 inches long and the person using a wheelchair can be parallel and centered on the basin.

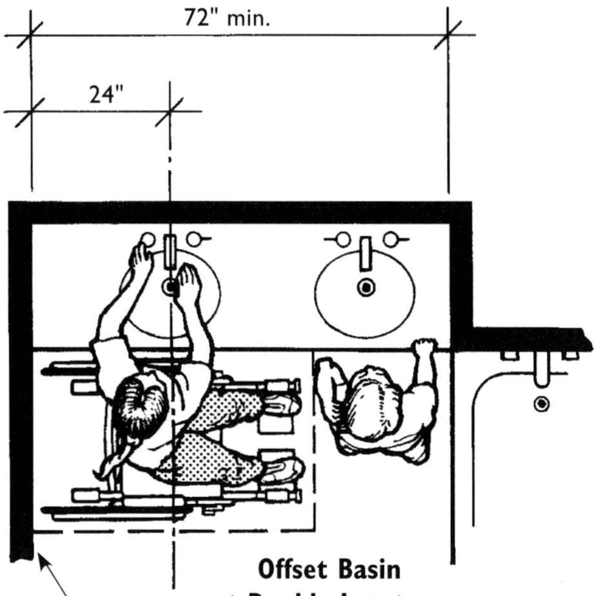

Offset Basin at Double Lavatory

Pedestal lavatories are manufactured with a variety of pedestal widths and depths. They can be installed in bathrooms covered by the Guidelines, provided a parallel approach centered on the basin can be made. Giving the appearance of having knee space, unlike a removable base cabinet where the knee space can be constructed to specific design parameters, pedestal lavatories have no removable element.

As they are currently manufactured, most pedestal lavatories do not provide adequate knee space to allow a user to make a head-on or forward approach. If pedestal lavatories are installed with the 30-inch x 48-inch clear floor space centered on the basin, a user may execute a variety of approaches. Angled approaches are possible provided adjacent fixtures do not interfere.

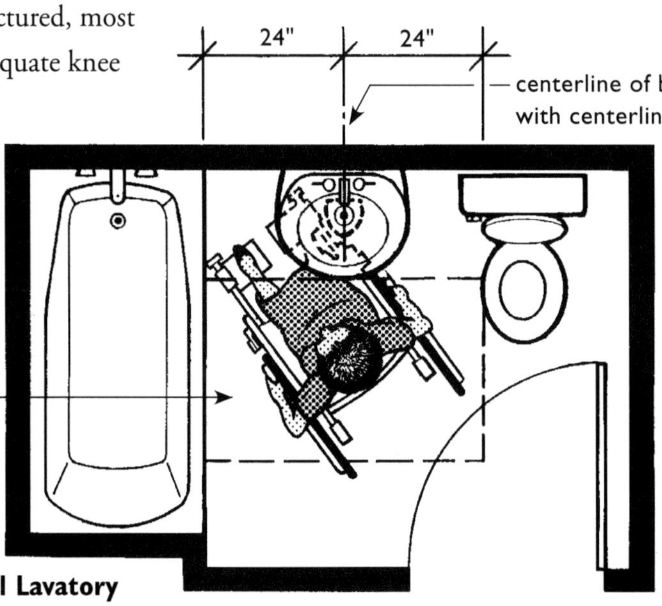

Usable Pedestal Lavatory

Removable Vanity Cabinets

Knee spaces are particularly important in bathrooms that are small and have limited maneuvering space. It is especially critical where a close parallel and centered approach cannot be provided at the lavatory basin. When knee space is necessary for a bathroom to be usable, that space must be provided at the time of initial construction. However, it may be concealed by a vanity cabinet that, when removed, will expose knee space. When the cabinet is in place a more common appearance is maintained and storage is provided. As in kitchens, finishes on the floor and walls in the knee space must be installed during initial construction so no additional finish work is required when the vanity cabinet is removed.

When a removable vanity cabinet is installed, the countertop and lavatory can be supported by wall-mounted brackets that fit inside the cabinet. These brackets are hidden when the base cabinet is in place; once the cabinet is removed, the brackets are exposed.

Unfortunately, removable vanity cabinets are not yet part of manufacturers off-the-shelf product lines. With growing demand, some of the commercial manufacturers are beginning to produce prototypes that should result, in the near future, in mass marketed lavatories with removable base cabinets.

Standard vanity cabinets may be modified and used as removable cabinets. The cabinet back or back supports may need to be cut down to clear the support system and to provide clearance for water lines, valves, and drain pipes. If the back of the cabinet is removed or significantly modified, the sides may have to be reinforced.

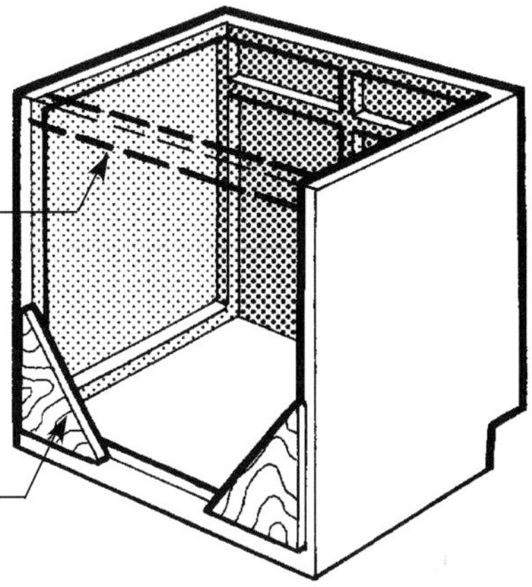

Standard Base Cabinet Modified to Be Removable

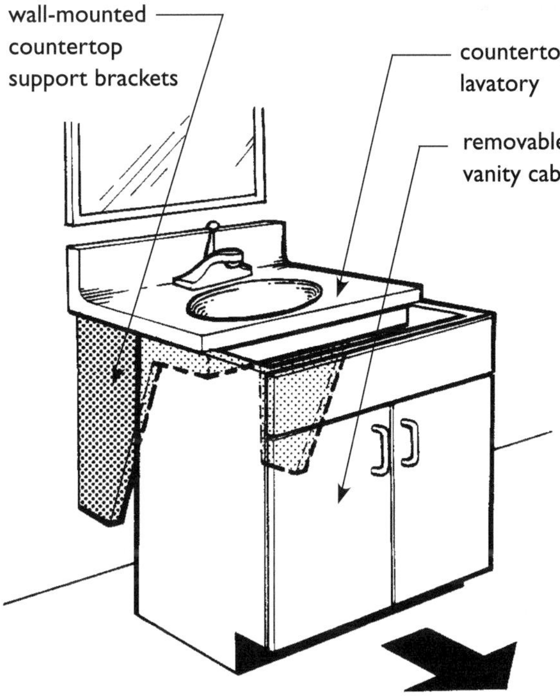

Removing Vanity Cabinet to Expose Knee Space

Any brackets used to support countertop lavatories should not interfere with maneuvering space within the bathroom; this is especially critical in small bathrooms where maneuvering space is at a minimum. The angled bracket shown in this series of illustrations is held away from the floor and is based on the ANSI knee space requirements. Use of a similarly designed bracket is strongly recommended.

Supports that are the full depth of the counter that go to the floor are discouraged at narrow lavatories but are acceptable for wider lavatories where it is assumed that more floor area will be available for maneuvering. Where supports extend to the floor, at least 30 inches must be provided between them to allow maneuvering space for a forward approach to the lavatory. This may require that some vanity cabinets be wider than 30 inches, so when the cabinet is removed and the concealed supports are exposed, 30 inches is provided between them.

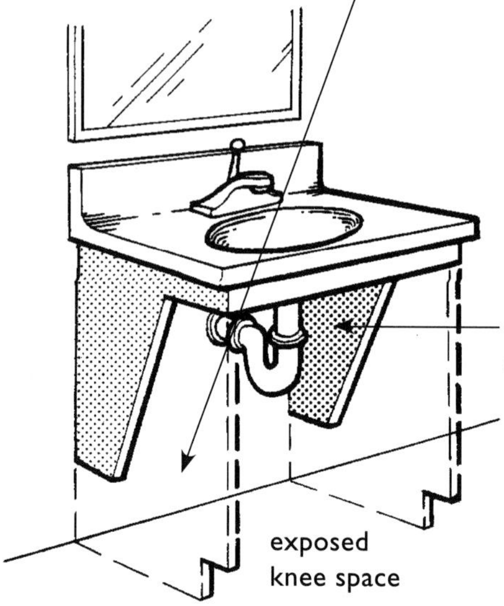

Exposed Knee Space Under Bracket-Supported Countertop Lavatory

Pipe Protection at Knee Space

Plumbing below the lavatory should be covered to prevent burns and abrasions. This can be done by using removable insulation to cover the hot water pipe and the drain, or by adding a fixed, one-piece cover.

The most economical method of providing protection from hot pipes and sharp surfaces is to wrap them with insulation. Although this solution is effective, it is often difficult to maintain the insulation; it may be removed when repairs are made and either is difficult to rewrap due to loss of adhesion or is not replaced at all.

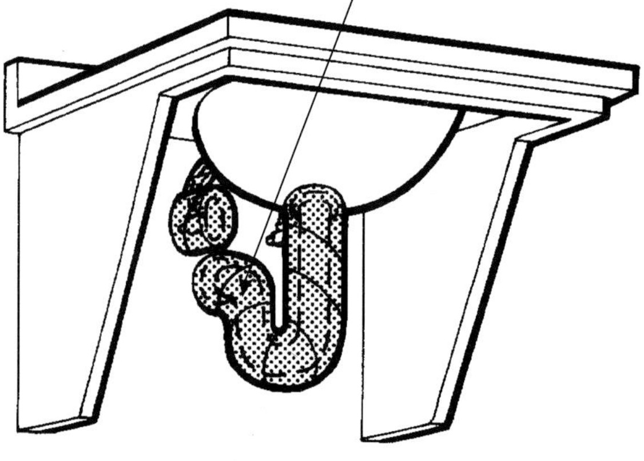

Lavatory with Removable Insulation Pipe Protection

A reasonably priced aesthetic and functional improvement is possible with the installation of a commercially available or custom-made pipe cover. These pipe covers should be designed and installed so they are easy to remove and replace when the drain trap or valves need repair.

For countertop lavatories, an appearance and protection panel that covers the water pipes and drain can be mounted directly to the support brackets. Such a panel can be removed easily to service pipes, and unlike wrapped insulation, retains a more aesthetically pleasing appearance. It is recommended that the insulation or protection be installed at the time of construction. The shape of the knee space influences the design of any pipe protection method and is considered in the next section.

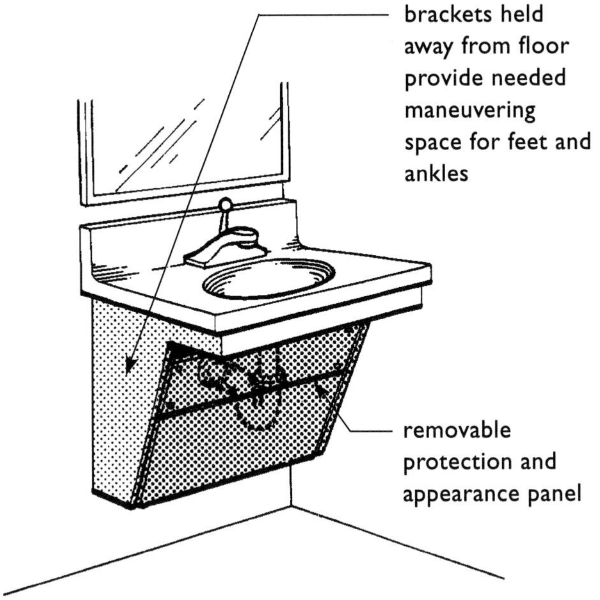

Countertop Lavatory with Wall Brackets and Appearance and Protection Panel

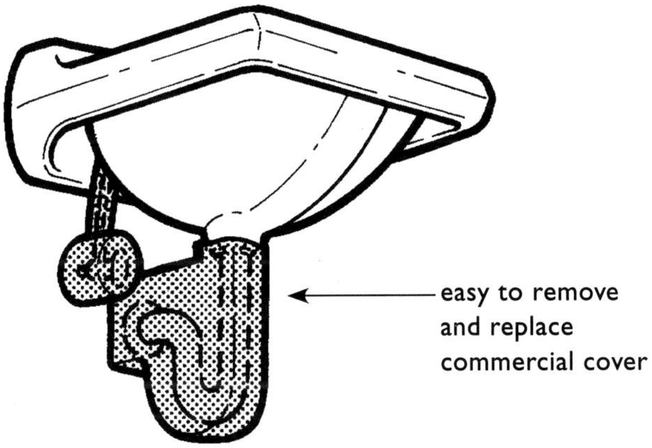

Lavatory with Removable Cover for Pipe Protection

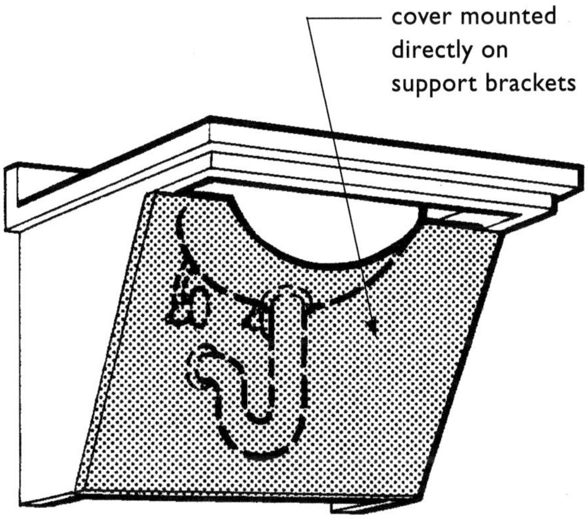

Preferred Appearance and Protection Panel

Knee Space Design

Knee space dimensions are specifically delineated in the Guidelines for lavatories in Specification B bathrooms. However, in Specification A bathrooms, "if parallel approach is not possible within the space, any cabinets provided would have to be removable to afford the necessary knee clearance for forward approach." [Guidelines Requirement 7 (2) (a) Note]

In Specification A bathrooms, knee space must be at least 17 inches deep, but only 19 of the 48 inches of clear floor space required for the perpendicular approach may extend under the lavatory. While the Guidelines do not provide further specifications for knee space, it is recommended that ANSI A117.1 be followed. The specific requirements given in the Guidelines for knee space in Specification B Bathrooms include: centerline of the fixture at least 15 inches from an adjoining wall or fixture, top of fixture rim a maximum of 34 inches above the floor, apron at least 27 inches above the floor, and kneespace at least 17 inches deep.

In both ANSI and the Specification B bathroom requirements, only 19 inches of the 30-inch x 48-inch clear floor space may extend under a lavatory. Seventeen inches is the minimum depth allowed for either a wall-hung or a countertop lavatory. This ensures that the basin extends sufficiently so a wheelchair user's feet do not strike the wall on which the fixture is mounted before his or her torso is close enough to the front of the lavatory to be able to reach the controls and use the basin.

The dimensions given in the Guidelines for Specification B bathrooms are consistent with those found in the ANSI Standard. They do not completely define the shape of the knee space, and it is recommended that builders/developers follow the ANSI Standard when knee space must be provided in either Specification A or Specification B bathrooms.

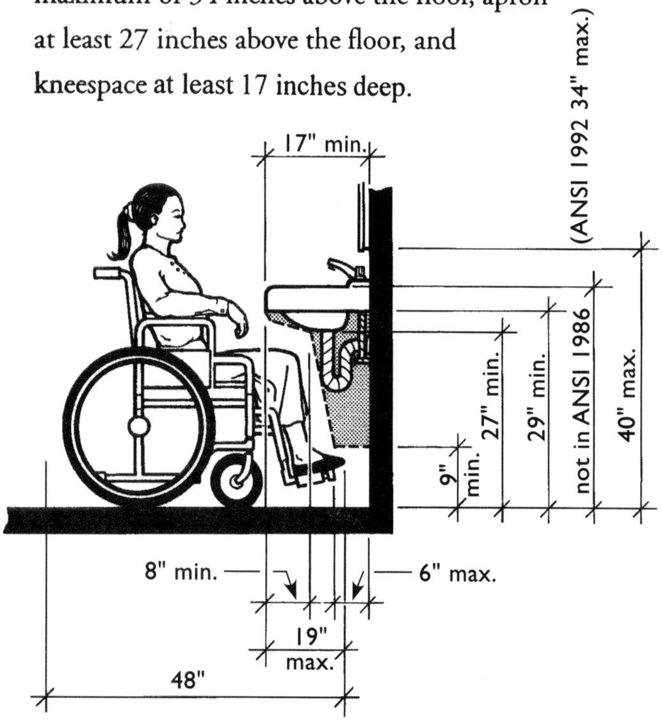

ANSI 1986 Requirements at Knee Space (Guidance for Knee Space in A Bathrooms)

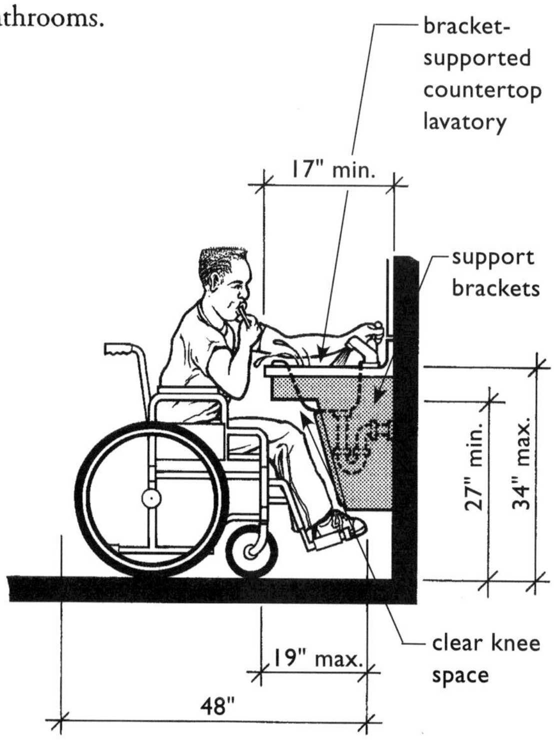

Knee Space at Lavatories that Meets the Requirements for B Bathrooms

Clear Floor Space at Bathtubs/Showers

The following discussion of bathtubs focuses on bathing fixtures that are a combination of bathtub and shower. It does not cover showers that are separate bathing fixtures; these will be addressed starting on page 7.56.

The Guidelines require that one of three different clear floor spaces be provided at bathtubs so people who use wheelchairs or scooters can get close enough to execute transfers into and out of bathtubs. The diagrams below, taken from the Guidelines, show the clear floor space requirements for bathtubs; numbers one and two apply to Specification A bathrooms and number three to Specification B bathrooms.

In all three clear floor spaces, the shaded areas must remain clear, except that in clear floor space diagram number 2, a lavatory that meets all applicable clear floor space requirements for lavatories may be located next to the toilet. In Specification A bathrooms, either a lavatory or a toilet may encroach upon the clear floor space next to the bathtub.

In clear floor space diagram number one, the arrow indicating direction of approach is relevant only if the lavatory is wall-hung and has knee space below. The user pulls forward into the knee space to transfer and/or operate controls, see illustration on the top of the next page.

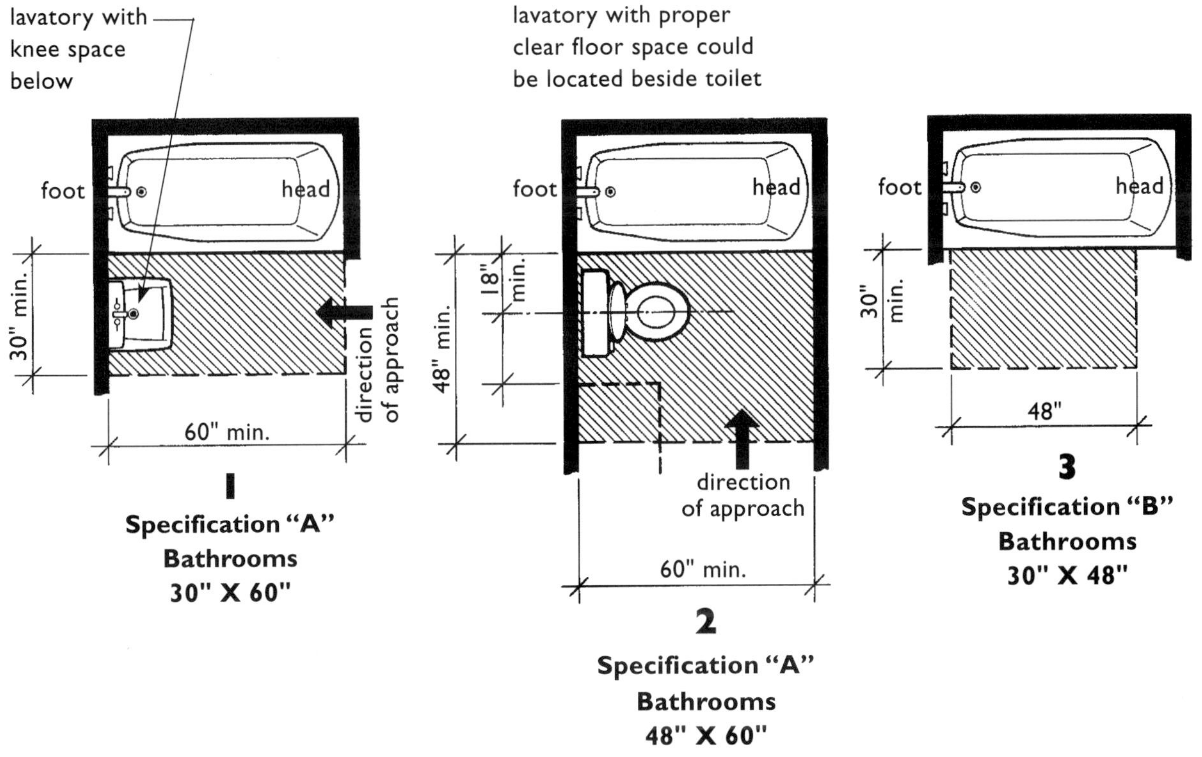

Clear Floor Space at Bathtubs/Showers
Shaded Areas Must Remain Unobstructed
(Taken from Guideline Figures 7(b) and 8)

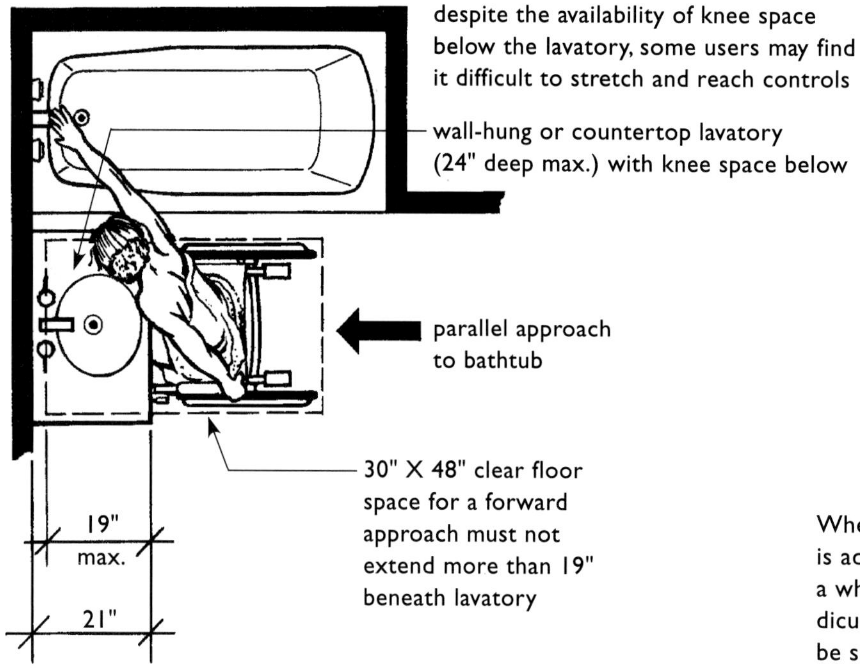

Parallel Approach to Bathtub at Lavatory with Knee Space
Permitted in Specification A Bathrooms

When a lavatory with vanity cabinet is adjacent to tub, a person using in a wheelchair must make a perpendicular approach to the tub rim to be sufficiently close to operate the controls. The user will have to remove footrests, place feet in tub, and execute a stretch which may be difficult for some people.

If a countertop lavatory with a vanity cabinet is located adjacent to the bathtub, a person using a wheelchair must be able to execute a close parallel approach centered on the basin. If the lavatory does not afford a full parallel approach to the basin, knee space and clear floor space for a forward approach are required, and any cabinets would have to be removable.

When the lavatory with vanity is adjacent to a bathtub, reach to the controls is possible only from a perpendicular approach which may be difficult for some wheelchair users. To improve access to controls, a resident who uses a wheelchair could have a new vanity with knee space installed or have controls repositioned closer to the tub rim.

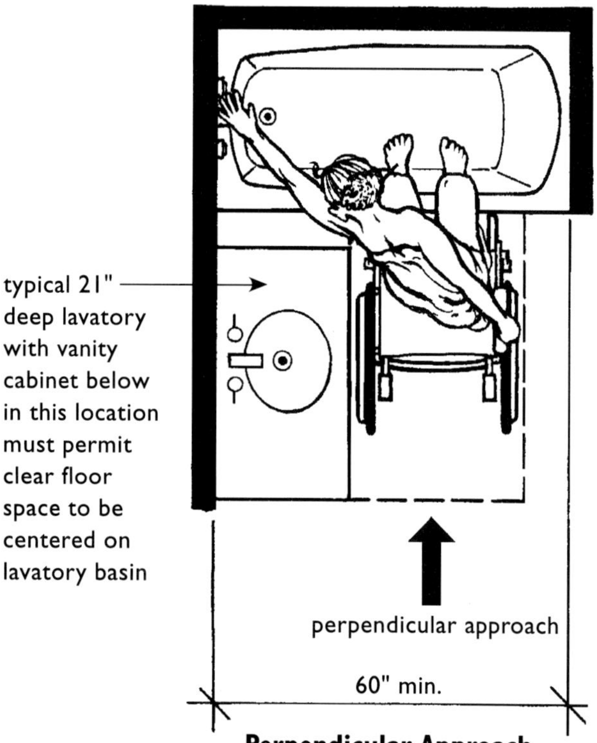

Perpendicular Approach to Bathtub at Vanity Cabinet
Permitted in Specification A Bathrooms Only

In **Specification A bathrooms**, the Guidelines also allow a toilet to occupy the space next to the bathtub. The approach by a person using a wheelchair is perpendicular to the bathtub. This arrangement of fixtures also makes it difficult to reach the controls, but reach can be improved if users can remove their footrests and position their feet in the tub to get closer to the tub rim.

A second option for some users is to transfer onto the toilet to reach the controls. The user then must transfer back into his or her wheelchair and maneuver to get sufficiently close to the bathtub rim to make a transfer down into the bathtub. Other users may add a bathtub seat that allows them to remain at the height of the tub rim while bathing. Transfers back into a wheelchair may be easier from a tub seat rather than from the floor of the bathtub, but this option does not allow the user to be immersed in water for a soaking bath.

In **Specification B bathrooms**, a 30-inch x 48-inch clear floor space is required adjacent to the bathtub to provide greater access for transferring into and out of the bathtub. The controls must be on the wall at the foot of the bathtub, as shown in the Guidelines' Requirement 7, Figure 8. The edge of the clear floor space should be flush with the control wall surface.

Neither a vanity cabinet nor a toilet may encroach on this clear floor space. However, a wall-hung lavatory with a depth of 17 to 19 inches and with knee space below is the only fixture that may overlap the clear floor space at bathtubs in Specification B bathrooms. A lavatory that is deeper than 19 inches only may be installed if it is recessed into the wall to allow the edge of the 30-inch x 48-inch clear floor space to begin flush with the control wall surface at the foot of the bathtub.

Toilets typically protrude into the room farther than vanity cabinets, making it necessary for a person using a wheelchair to perform, what may be for some people, a difficult stretch to operate tub controls.

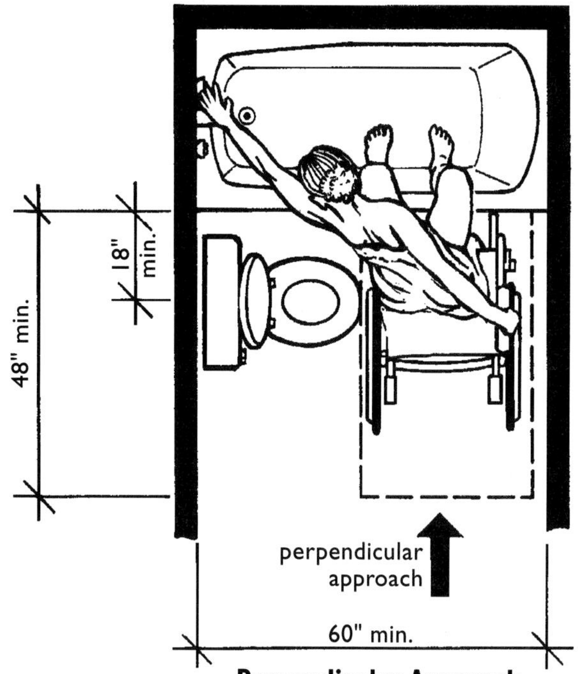

Perpendicular Approach to Bathtub at Toilet
Permitted in Specification A Bathrooms Only

The only permissible overlapping element is a 17" to 19" wall-hung lavatory with knee space below.

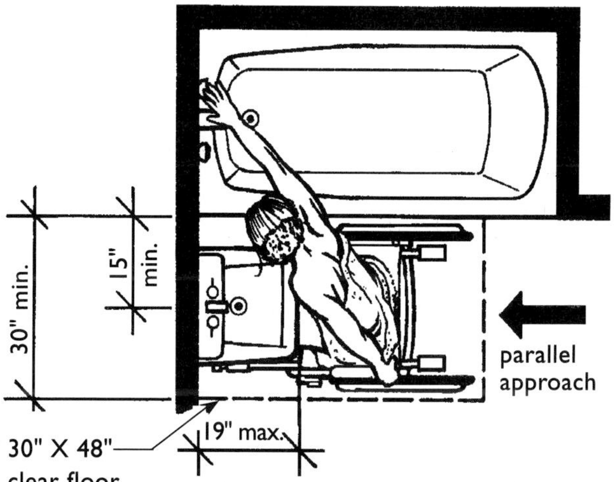

Parallel Approach at Bathtub with Small Wall-Hung Lavatory
Applies to Specification B Bathrooms Only

Clear Floor Space at Showers

Shower stalls in covered dwelling units may be of any size or configuration and are not limited to the 36-inch x 36-inch stall shown in the diagram on the right, taken from the Guidelines, that illustrates clear floor space requirements for showers. An exception regarding minimum stall size is made when a shower stall is the only bathing fixture in the covered dwelling unit; this is discussed on page 7.58.

A 30-inch x 48-inch clear floor space must be provided at shower stalls, parallel to the fixture and flush with the control wall. In 36-inch x 36-inch showers, the clear floor space must be positioned exactly as shown in the upper right diagram, with 12 inches offset behind the wall opposite the control wall. The Guidelines require this clear floor space beside the shower fixture primarily to ensure that adequate maneuvering space is available outside the stall for a person using a mobility aid to get sufficiently close to enter and exit the stall safely. The 36-inch x 48-inch shower in the center is generally not intended for use with a wall hung bench seat because a user seated on the bench could not reach the controls. However, because some users may elect to add their own seat, an additional 12 inches of clear floor space is, as well as reinforcing for such a seat, recommended (see page 6.13).

In Specification A bathrooms, where all fixtures must meet the Guidelines, if the room is equipped with both a bathtub and a separate shower, both fixtures must be provided with the required clear floor space. In Specification B bathrooms, only one bathing fixture must be provided with the required clear floor space. All shower stalls must have reinforced walls for later installation of grab bars (see Chapter 6). The Guidelines contain no specifications that limit the curb height, nor do they address control type or location.

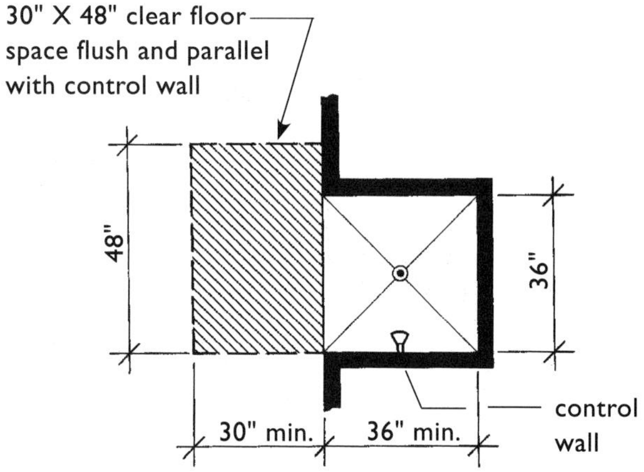

Guideline Requirements for Clear Floor Space at Showers

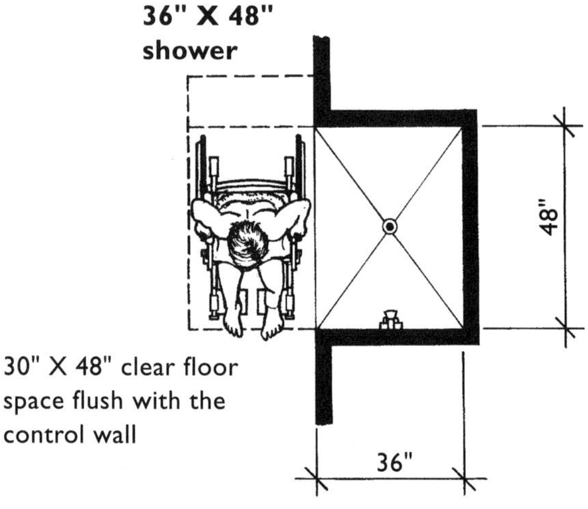

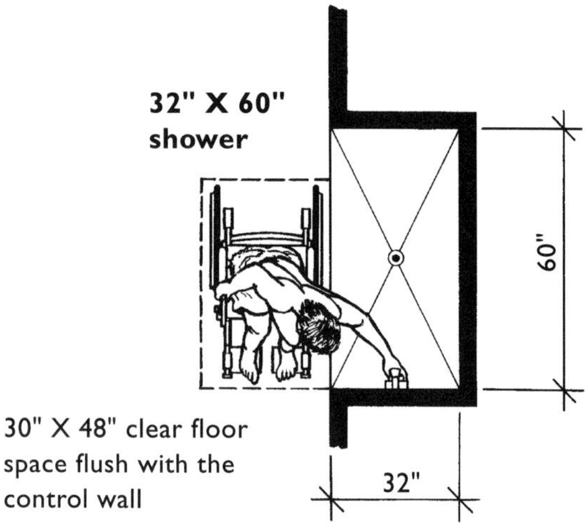

Other Shower Sizes Meet the Requirements of the Guidelines

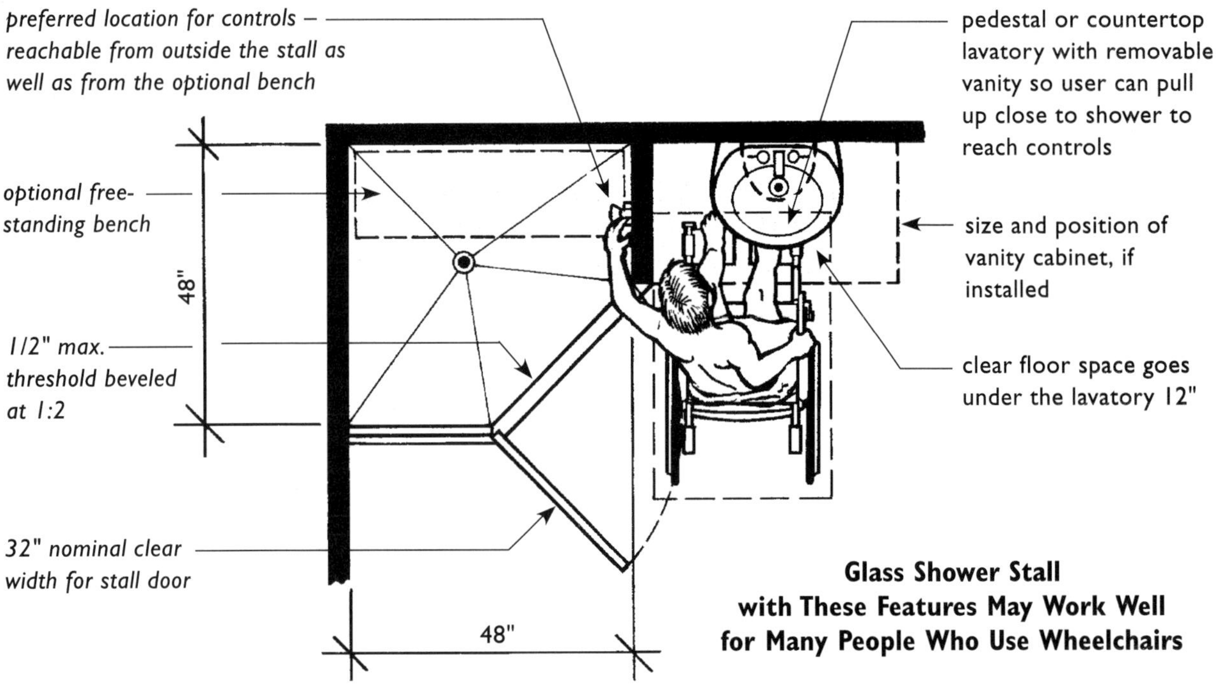

Glass Shower Stall with These Features May Work Well for Many People Who Use Wheelchairs

Fixtures that May Overlap Clear Floor Space at Showers

In both Specification A and B bathrooms, **no other fixture may overlap the clear floor space at showers** when the shower is only 36 inches long. However, if the shower is 42 inches long and a lavatory is mounted on the control wall beside the shower, it may overlap the clear floor space by six inches. The portion of the lavatory that overlaps the clear floor space must have knee space below or a removable vanity cabinet. Thirty-six inches of the stall entrance must always remain clear for maneuvering and transfers. These limitations ensure that if a wall-mounted transfer seat or a free-standing shower bench or stool is placed in the shower, sufficient space to make a transfer is available.

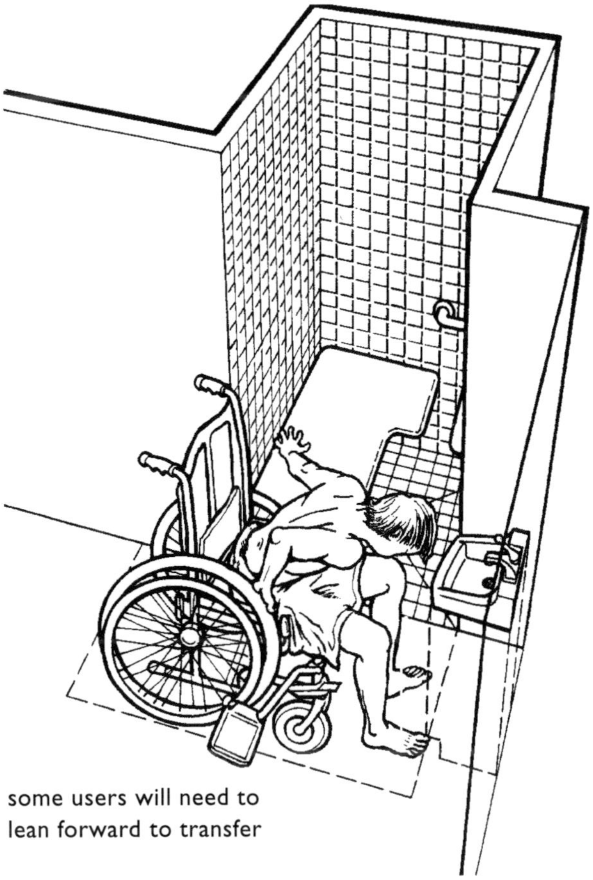

Lavatory Must Not Encroach on Clear Floor Space at 36-Inch X 36-Inch Shower

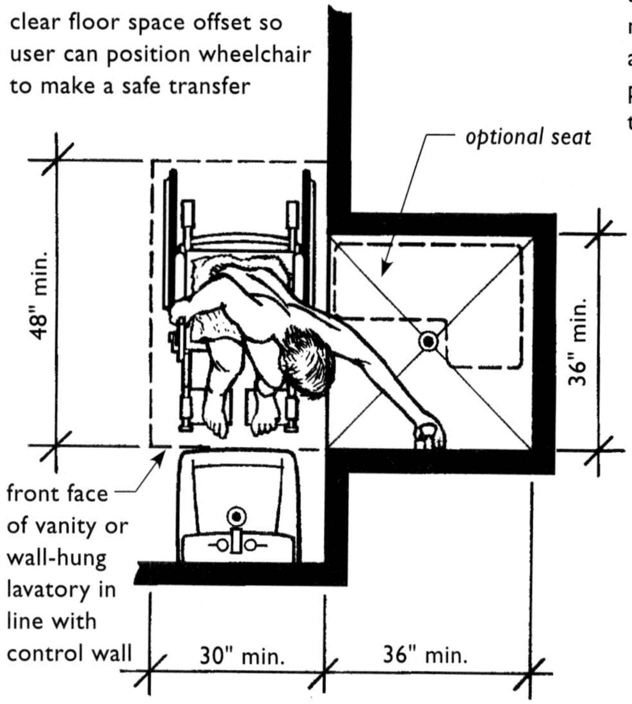

Lavatory at 36-Inch X 36-Inch Shower
Applicable in Specification A and B Bathrooms

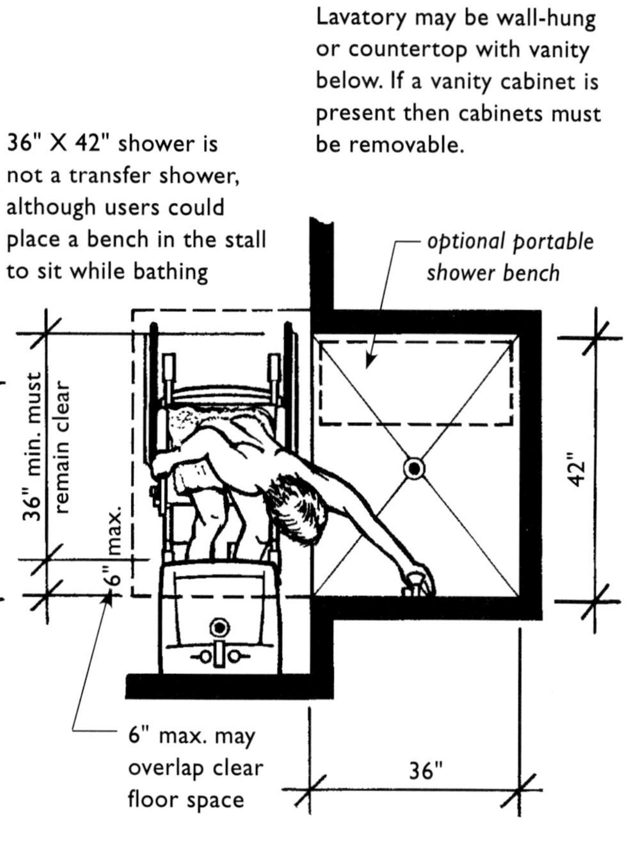

Lavatory at 36-Inch X 42-Inch Shower
Applicable in Specification A and B Bathrooms

Shower as Only Bathing Fixture

In both Specification A and B bathrooms, when a stall shower is the only bathing fixture in the covered dwelling unit it must be at least 36 inches x 36 inches in size. This also applies to any planned bathrooms on the primary entry level of covered multistory dwelling units in buildings with one or more elevators. Shower stalls of larger sizes and configurations are permitted, even when the shower stall is the only bathing fixture in the covered unit.

While reinforced walls for later installation of grab bars are required in all bathrooms, Specification A bathrooms do not require reinforcing to support a wall-mounted shower seat in the shower stall. However, it is strongly recommended that appropriate reinforcing for shower seats be installed in Specification A bathrooms. See Chapter 6: "Reinforced Walls for Grab Bars."

In Specification B bathrooms, however, in addition to the reinforcing required for grab bars, the shower stall must have reinforcing to allow for later installation of an optional wall-mounted seat in a shower stall measuring a nominal 36 inches square. By adding this requirement the Guidelines are setting the framework for a shower that could evolve into the ANSI accessible 36-inch x 36-inch transfer shower.

The 36-inch x 36-inch transfer shower with a low curb and L-shaped seat is a versatile and successful bathing fixture for people who use wheelchairs or have difficulty walking. If a seat is installed that can be folded up against the wall, an ambulatory user also can stand in the shower. The illustration below on the right shows the primary features found in a transfer shower. The 30-inch x 48-inch clear floor space beside the shower provides access to the control wall, and because it extends beyond the back of the stall, it allows a person using a wheelchair to position his or her chair in line with the wall-hung seat to make a safe sliding transfer.

Reinforcing for a shower seat is not required in stalls of larger sizes, e.g., 30 inches x 60 inches because the stall is so long that the user is not able to reach the controls from a seat at the opposite end of the stall. However, it is recommended that reinforcing be installed in stalls of different configurations and that thought be given to placing controls within reach of this potential seat as well as from outside the stall.

In Specification B bathrooms, when shower is only bathing fixture and is a nominal 36" X 36", it must have reinforcing for grab bars **and** a wall-mounted shower seat.

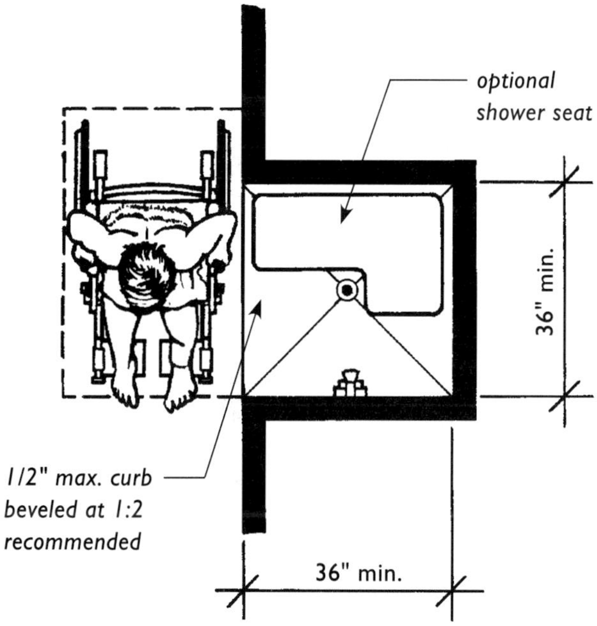

When Shower Stall Is the Only Bathing Fixture It Must Be at Least 36 Inches X 36 Inches

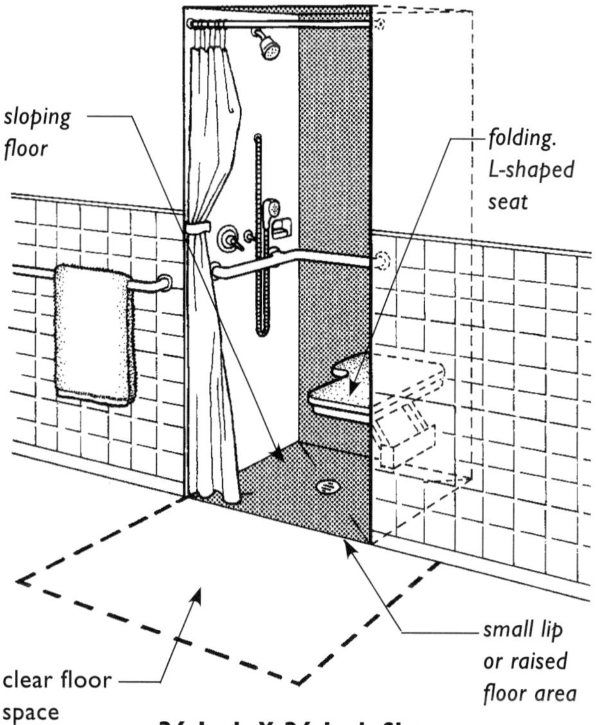

36-Inch X 36-Inch Shower with Folding Seat

Recommendations for Increased Accessibility

While the builder or developer of multifamily housing is not required to address all the design concerns faced by people with disabilities who may live in a development, there are certain aspects of bathroom design which should be considered when selecting fixtures.

Toilet Seat Height

There is no single seat height which would suit all users. Low toilet seats are difficult for people who have trouble getting up on their feet and for people who use wheelchairs who may be able to transfer onto the seat but not get back into their chairs without assistance. High seats may be difficult for some wheelchair users to get onto and for shorter people because their feet do not touch the floor, making it difficult to maintain balance.

ANSI 4.32.4.2 specifies that toilet seats in dwelling units "shall be at least 15 inches and no more than 19 inches measured to the top of the toilet seat." Standard toilets with 15-inch high seats are widely available in the marketplace and offer the best flexibility for adaptation for a wider range of people. For a user who may require that the seat be higher, it is relatively simple to install a seat spacer or thick seat. By contrast, to lower a toilet usually requires replacing the entire toilet fixture. It is recommended that standard low 15-inch toilets be installed in all dwelling units covered by the Guidelines.

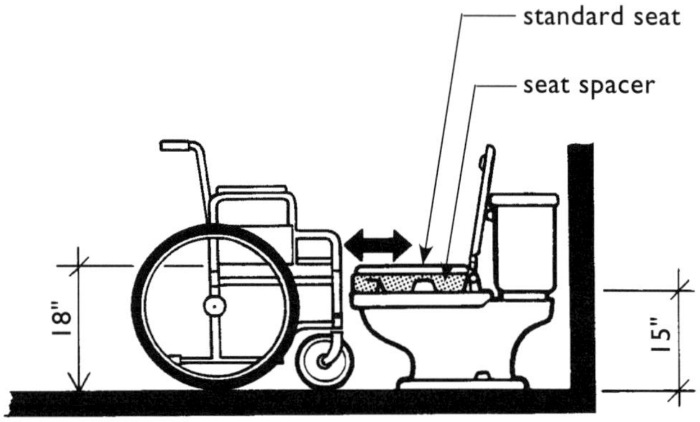

Elevated Seats at Conventional Toilets

Handles, Faucets, and Controls

Many people have difficulty using faucets and controls that require grasping and twisting of symmetrical shapes such as round, cylindrical, or square handles. It is preferable to install lever or blade handles which

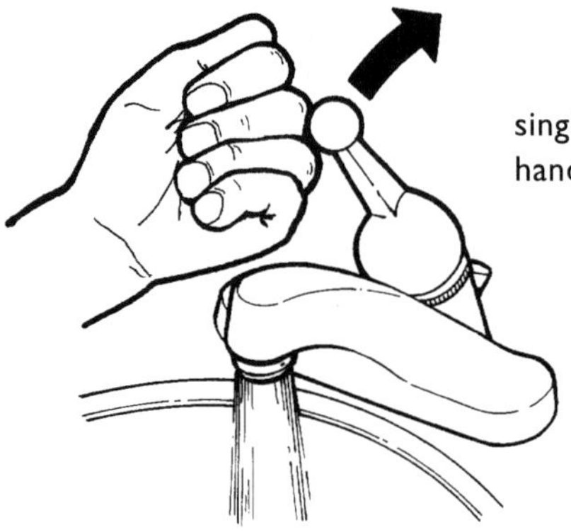

Ideal Faucet Control

can be used without gripping or twisting. If a faucet can be operated with a closed fist and requires less than five pounds of force to operate, then it is a usable control for most people with disabilities.

Control location also can greatly improve ease and safe use of the fixture. When bathtub controls are offset toward the outside of the bathing fixture, the need to bend and stretch to reach the controls from outside the fixture is greatly reduced - a help for any user with limited flexibility.

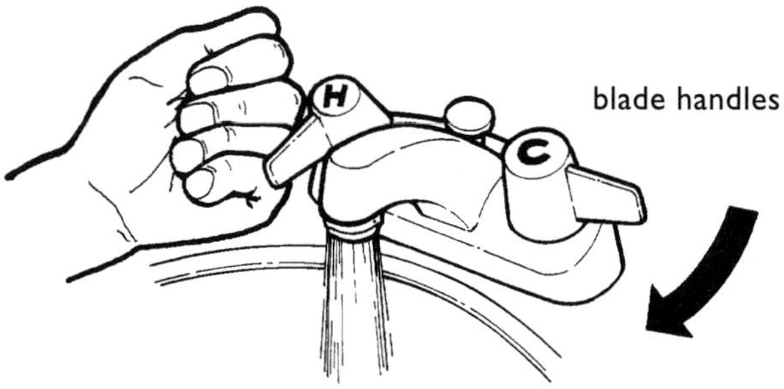

Another Usable Faucet Control

Preferred Offset Control Location

Auxiliary Handles at Doors

Suggestions to increase the accessibility and usability of bathrooms are made in the following section, "Example Bathroom Floor Plans that Comply with the Guidelines." One enhancement frequently highlighted is the installation of auxiliary handles on bathroom doors. Not required by the Guidelines, this additional hardware works well for many people with mobility impairments who have difficulty closing doors. With the installation of a second handle (such as a 4-inch loop handle similar to those used on drawers and kitchen cabinets) on the pull side of the door, near the hinge edge, the user is provided with an additional, and often easier, method of closing a door.

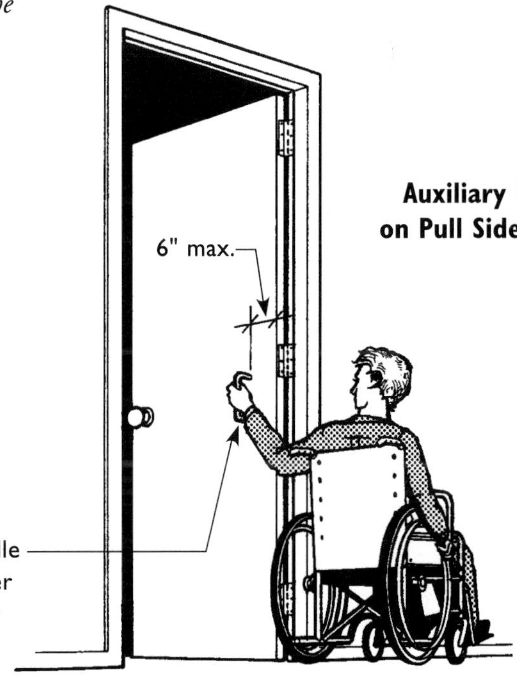

Auxiliary Handle on Pull Side of Door

Examples of Bathroom Floor Plans that Comply with the Guidelines

The plans presented on the following pages are examples of "usable" bathrooms and powder rooms that comply with either Specification A or Specification B or both. These plans are only a sampling of possible layouts that would conform to the specifications and are not intended to limit designers' options; certainly other layouts are feasible. The plans are neither required nor even suggested as ideal examples. They are included to illustrate typical applications or interpretations of specific requirements of the Guidelines under various circumstances.

The plans may be used as resource material and planning guides when developing new multifamily housing designs. Conventional industry standard fixture sizes have been used consistently when developing these plans.

The toilets used measure 29 inches from the back wall to the front edge of the bowl. As toilets vary in size, with some being as long as 30 inches, it is important to allow sufficient space for doors to clear the toilet bowl. Wall-hung lavatories are 19 inches deep and countertop lavatories with base cabinets below are 21 inches deep unless noted otherwise on the plans. Doors are 34 inches wide to provide the required nominal 32-inch clear opening. Rooms may need to be enlarged if a 36-inch door is installed. Bathtubs in the small bathrooms are 60 inches long and, along with showers, vary as the rooms become less conventional.

It is important to allow sufficient space for any fixtures that may be larger than those shown here. Although designers should rely upon the dimensions indicated and not scale off the drawings, all plans in this section are reproduced at 1/4-inch scale.

Some of the plans are more usable than others by people with disabilities and comments are included to describe where improvements could be made. The plans are divided according to bathing fixture type: bathtub/showers, showers, and multiple bathing fixtures. The plans are presented in pairs, with the first showing the overall room shape while the dimensioned plan describes the clear floor spaces at fixtures and indicates minimum wall and/or floor areas to be reinforced.

Text and notes presented in *italic* type are comments or recommendations and are not required by the Guidelines.

Bathrooms with Bathtub Bathing Fixture

"A" Bathroom with Bathtub

since parallel approach centered on basin not possible, cabinet below lavatory must be removable

no leg or support should be present on right outside corner so user can pull in under the lavatory

where a removable cabinet is provided below a countertop less than 32" in width, care must be taken to prevent support method or brackets from encroaching upon required kneespace, see page 7.50

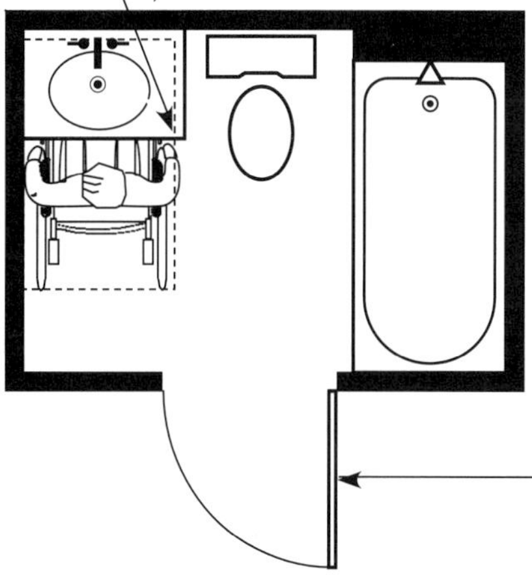

door must swing out (see note below)

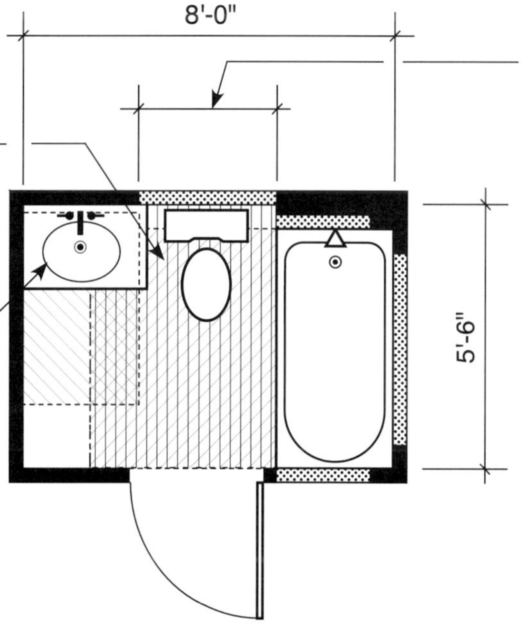

reinforcing must be located in this area to provide support for a drop-down grab bar or a floor-mounted bar similar to those shown on page 6.6; the bar must swing out of the way so access to the tub and controls is available

reinforcing may be required in floor depending on type of grab bars planned for

countertop lavatory with knee space below to allow forward approach to fixture

A person using a wheelchair would back into the room to use the bathtub but must be able to close the door and have an unblocked forward approach to the bathtub; therefore, to comply with the Guidelines, the door must swing out.

Legend: reinforcing in walls or floors for grab bars; min. clear floor space at each fixture; min. clear floor space outside swing of door

"A" Bathroom with Bathtub

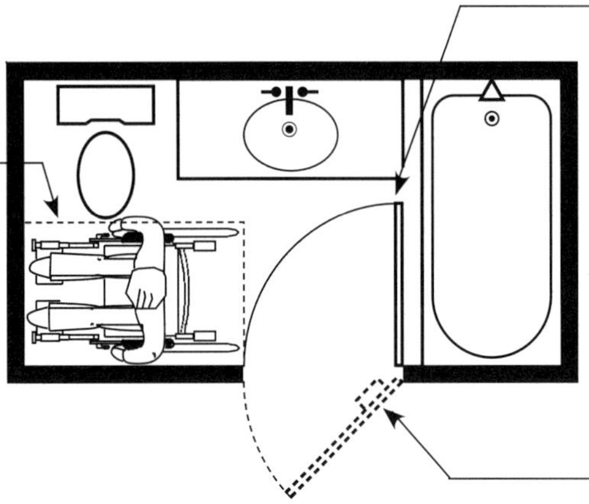

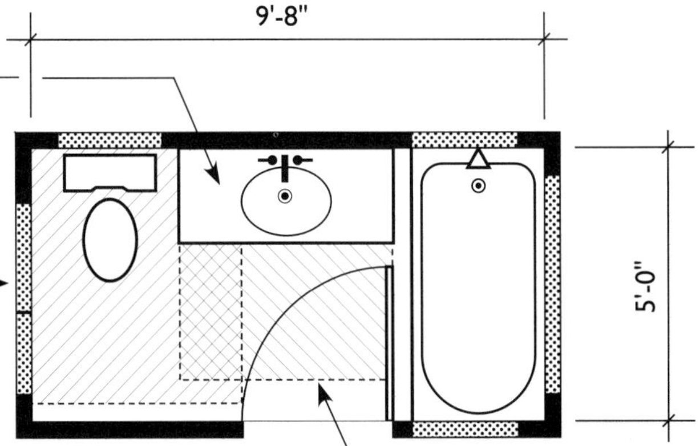

Legend: reinforcing in walls or floors for grab bars; min. clear floor space at each fixture; min. clear floor space outside swing of door

"A" Bathroom with Bathtub

The Guidelines do not require space for a five-foot turn or a T-turn in bathrooms; see page 7.39. In this bathroom, most persons using a wheelchair will not be able to turn around and may have to back into or out of the room. This, combined with the lack of space to the latch side of the door, makes this room difficult to use by many people. Therefore, it is recommended that the 5'-2" dimension be increased and/or that knee space be provided under the lavatory.

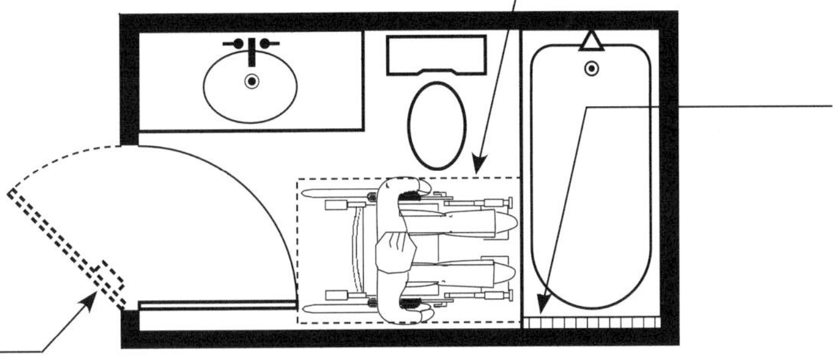

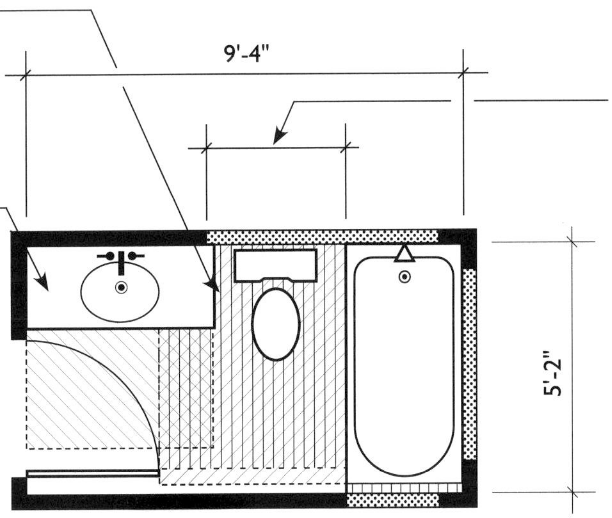

Legend: reinforcing in walls or floors for grab bars; min. clear floor space at each fixture; min. clear floor space outside swing of door

"B" Bathroom with Bathtub

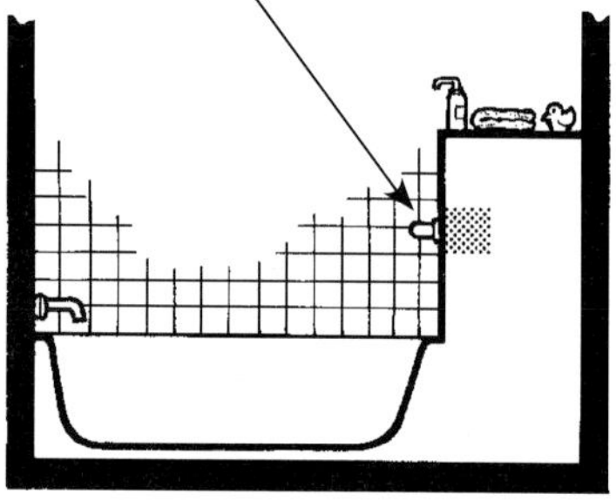

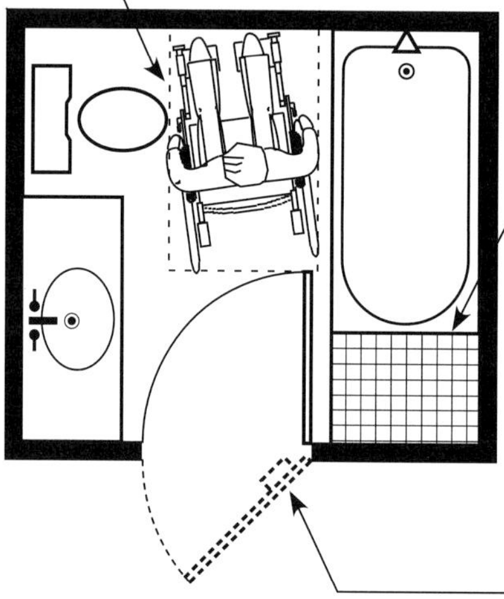

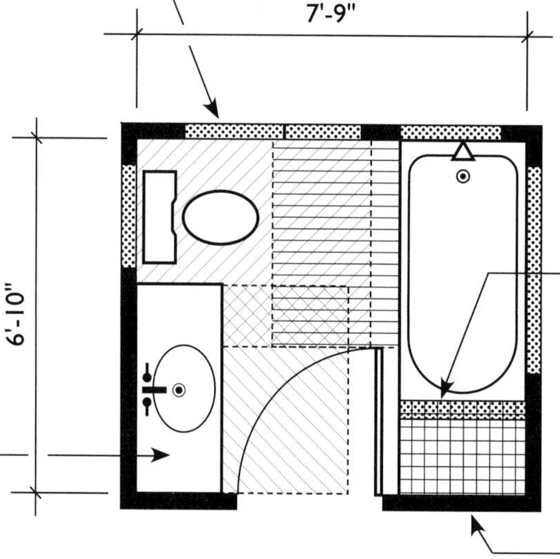

Legend: reinforcing in walls or floors for grab bars; min. clear floor space at each fixture; min. clear floor space outside swing of door

"B" Bathroom with Bathtub

Only 19 inches of the required 30-inch x 48-inch clear floor space can go under a lavatory. A deeper lavatory would require that the clear floor space be positioned away from the plumbing wall and closer to the tub, causing it to overlap with the door swing. If a deeper lavatory is desired the room must be lengthened.

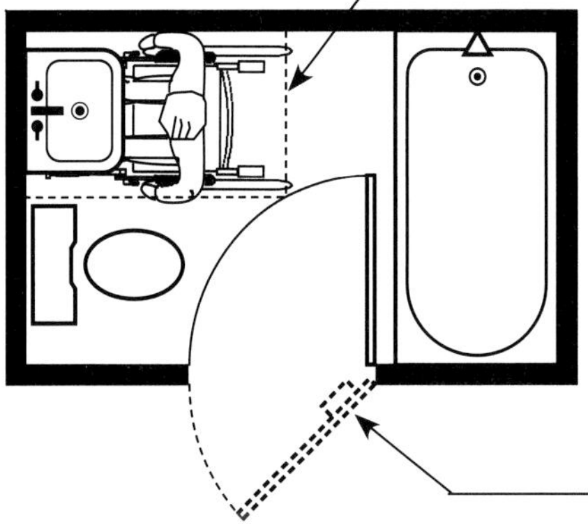

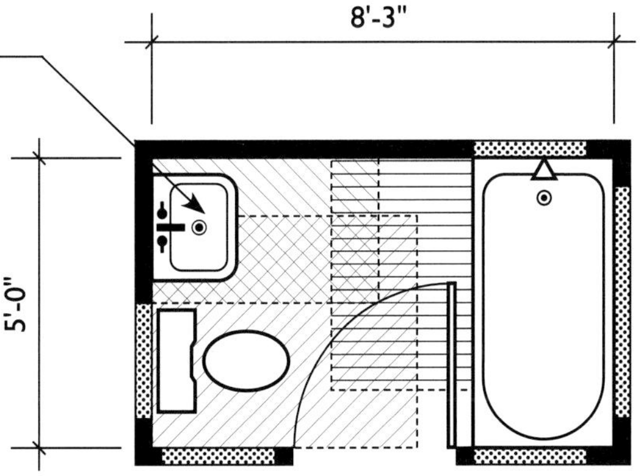

Legend: reinforcing in walls or floors for grab bars; min. clear floor space at each fixture; min. clear floor space outside swing of door

"B" Bathroom with Bathtub

because lavatory has no knee space below, to meet the Guidelines bathtub controls must be located on this wall

clear floor space for maneuvering outside swing of door

alternate door location

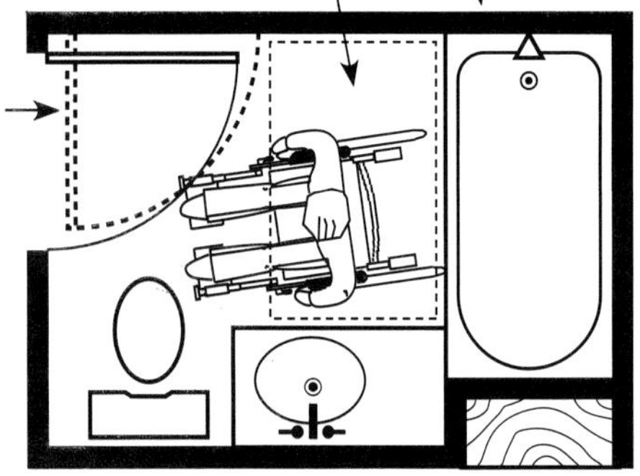

Option 1:
Plumbing on Opposite Walls
Lavatory With Base Cabinet Below
(No Knee Space)

end of knee space flush with bathtub control wall permits access to controls; because knee space is not the full depth, user must still be able to execute a parallel approach to lavatory

if lavatory has knee space below, bathtub controls can be located on a common plumbing wall

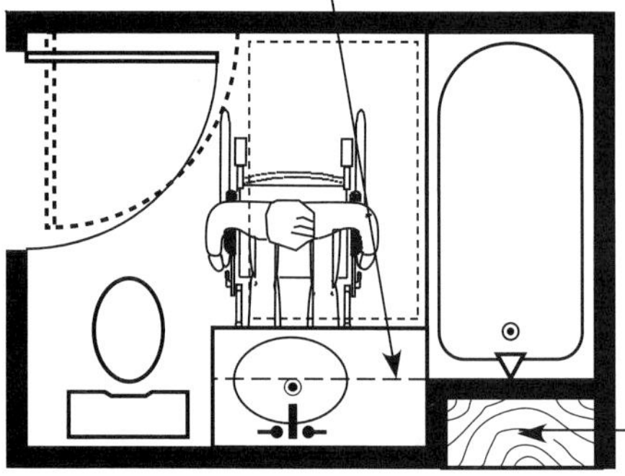

storage shelves

Option 2:
Plumbing on Common Wall
Lavatory With Shallow Knee Space

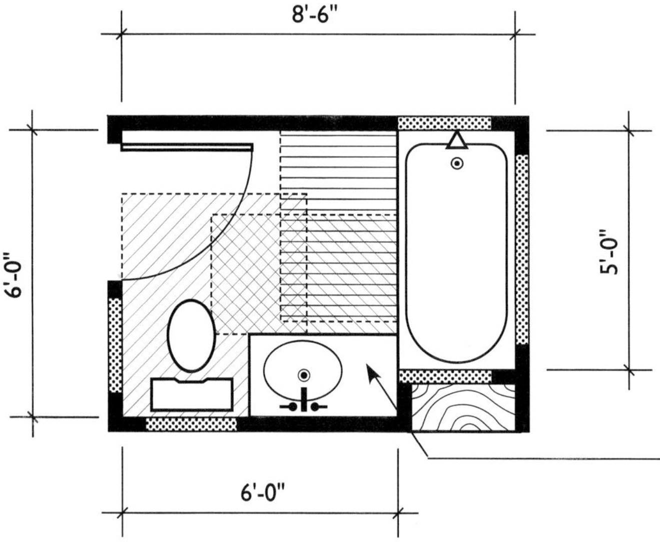

36" wide vanity with offset basin to permit parallel approach centered on basin

Legend: reinforcing in walls or floors for grab bars; min. clear floor space at each fixture; min. clear floor space outside swing of door

"B" Bathroom with Bathtub

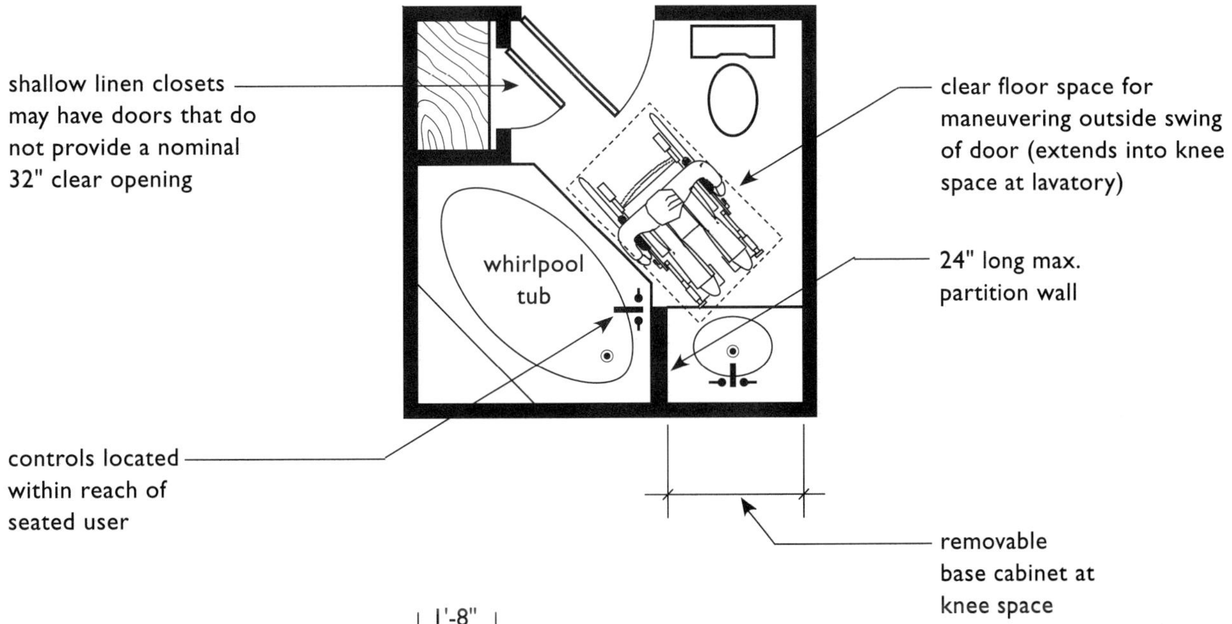

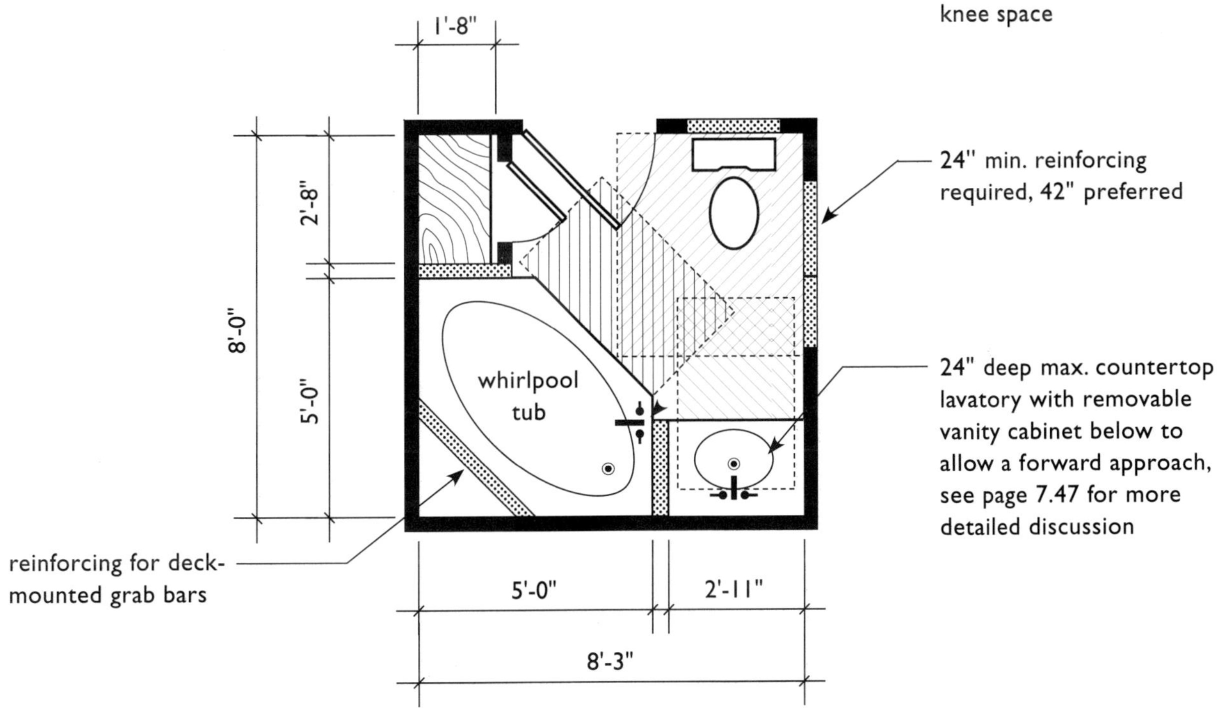

Legend: reinforcing in walls or floors for grab bars; min. clear floor space at each fixture; min. clear floor space outside swing of door

Compartmentalized "A" Bathroom with Bathtub

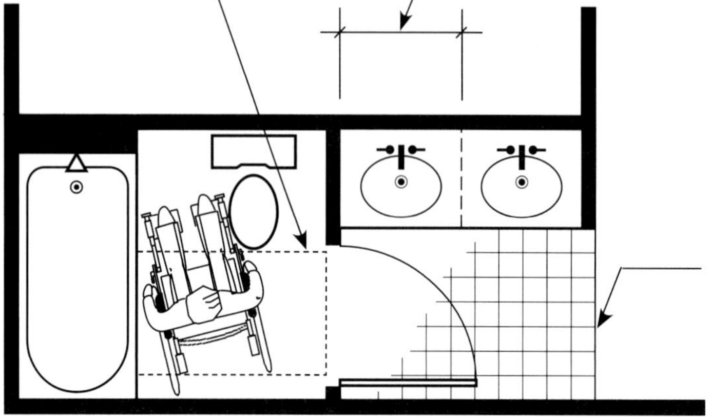

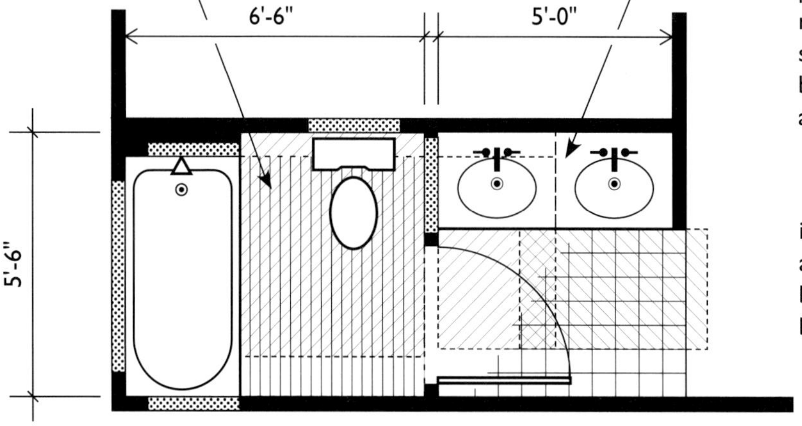

Legend: reinforcing in walls or floors for grab bars; min. clear floor space at each fixture; min. clear floor space outside swing of door

Bathrooms with Shower Bathing Fixture

"A" and "B" Bathroom with Shower

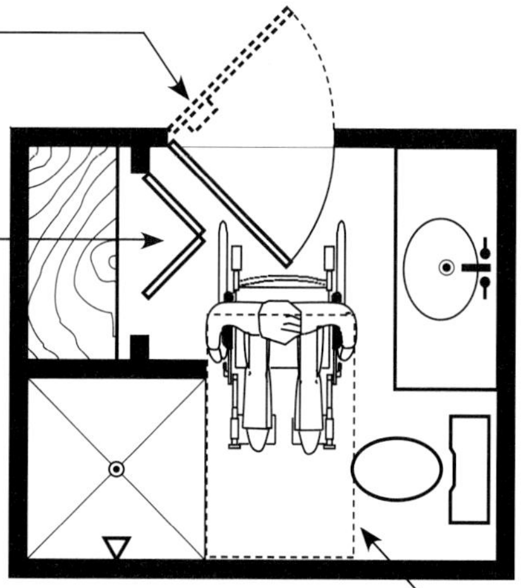

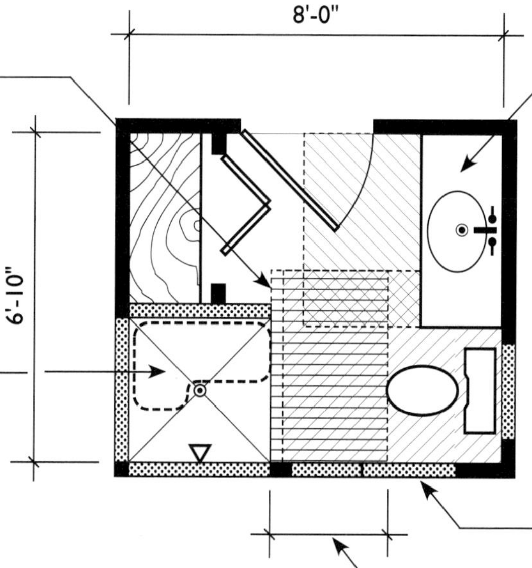

Legend: reinforcing in walls or floors for grab bars; min. clear floor space at each fixture; min. clear floor space outside swing of door

"A" and "B" Bathroom with Shower

clear floor space for maneuvering outside swing of door

while not required, access is improved if door swings out and an auxiliary door handle is installed

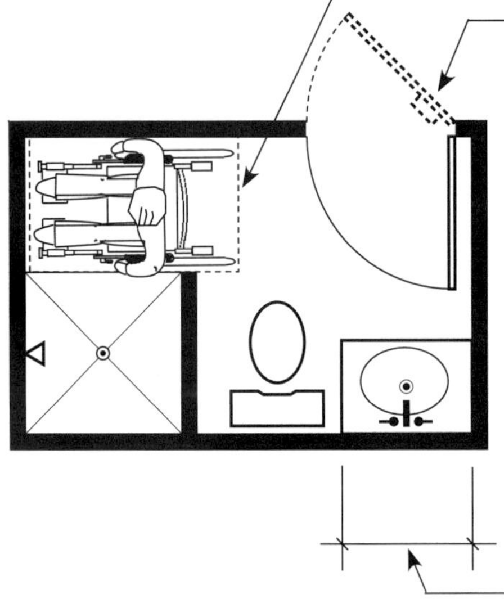

where a removable cabinet is provided below a countertop less than 32" in width, care must be taken to prevent support method or brackets from encroaching upon required knee space, see page 7.50

removable base cabinet at knee space

36" x 36" min. shower with clear floor space offset to provide access to optional seat

optional shower seat

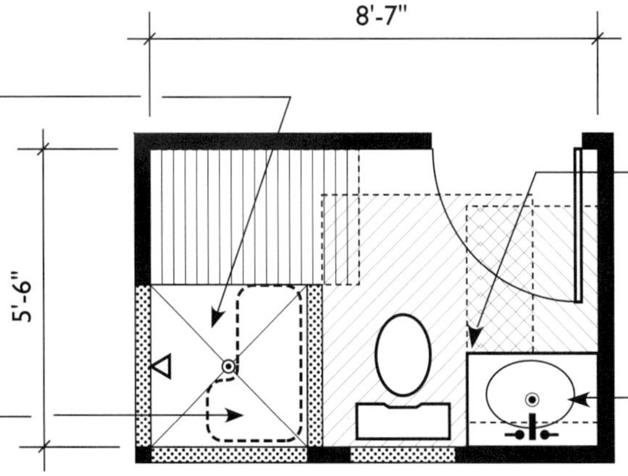

no leg or support should be present on left outside corner so user can pull in under the lavatory

30" wide countertop lavatory with knee space below to allow forward approach to fixture

Legend: reinforcing in walls or floors for grab bars	min. clear floor space at each fixture	min. clear floor space outside swing of door

"A" and "B" Bathroom with Shower

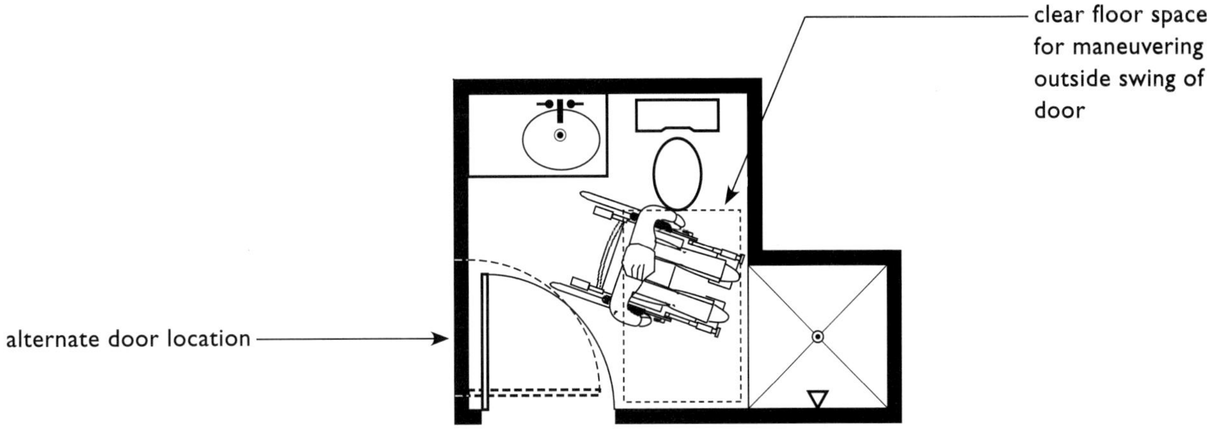

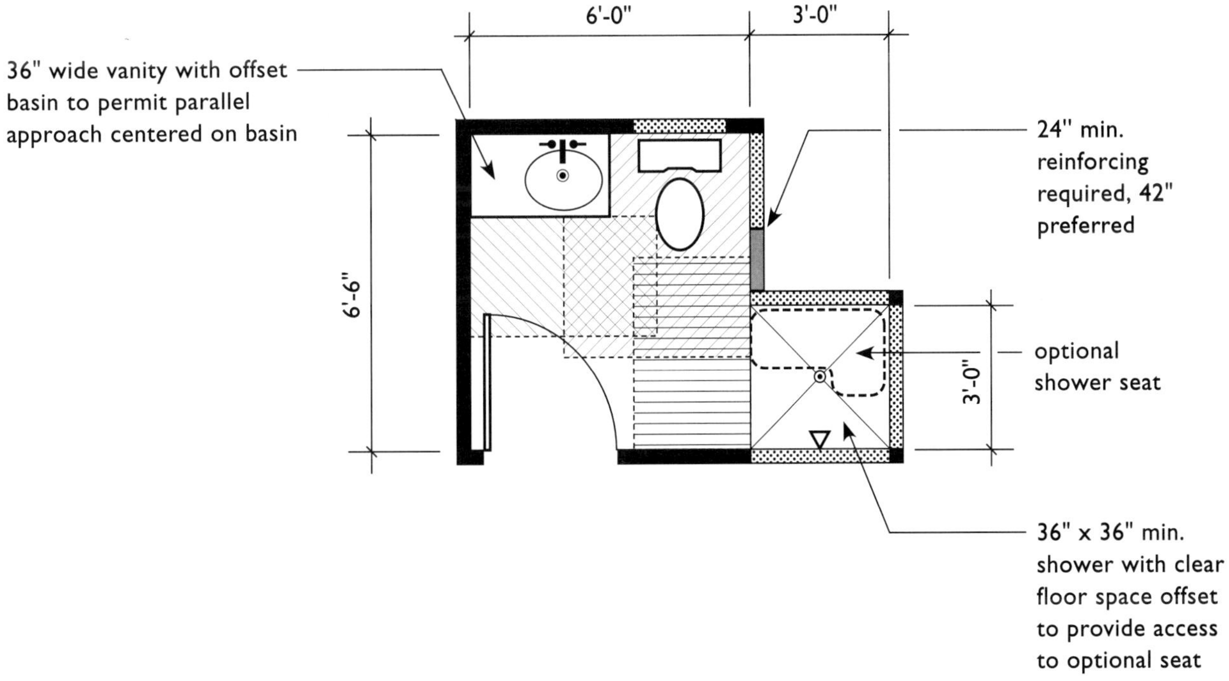

Legend: reinforcing in walls or floors for grab bars | min. clear floor space at each fixture | min. clear floor space outside swing of door

"A" and "B" Bathroom with Shower

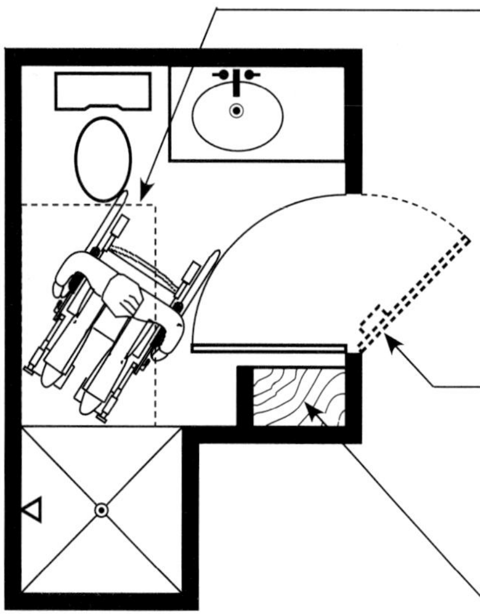

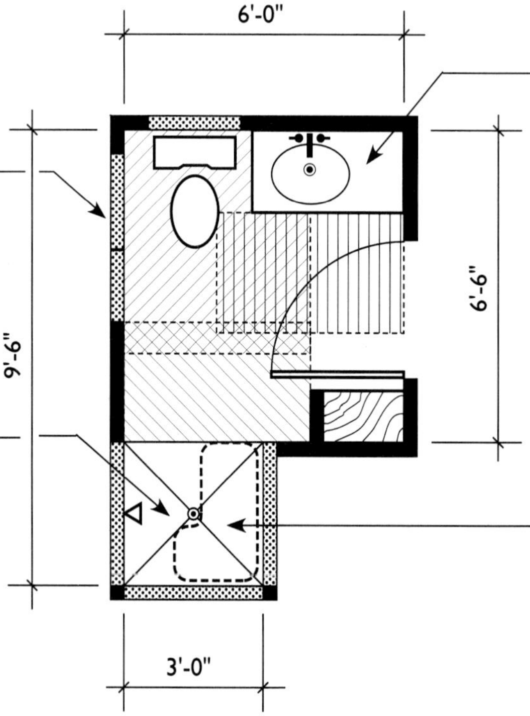

Legend: reinforcing in walls or floors for grab bars; min. clear floor space at each fixture; min. clear floor space outside swing of door

"A" Bathroom with Large Shower

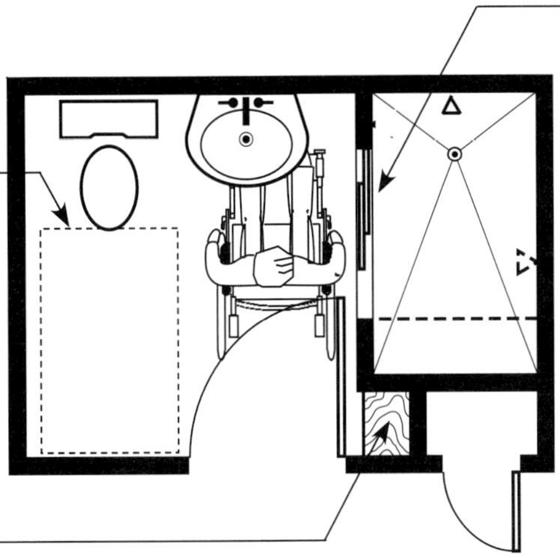

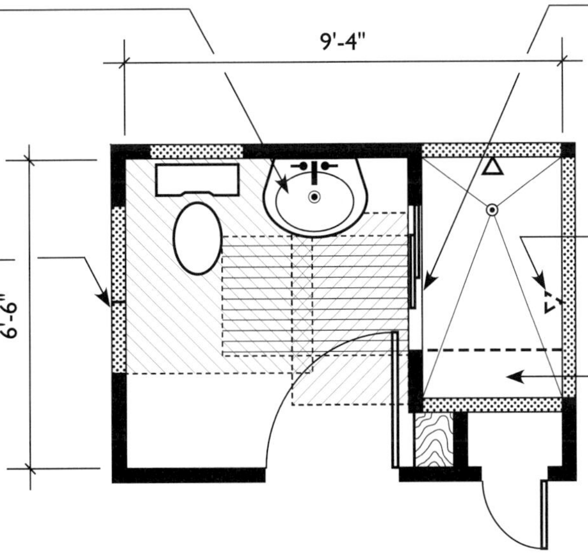

Legend: reinforcing in walls or floors for grab bars; min. clear floor space at each fixture; min. clear floor space outside swing of door

Single Room Occupancy Unit with Roll-In Shower

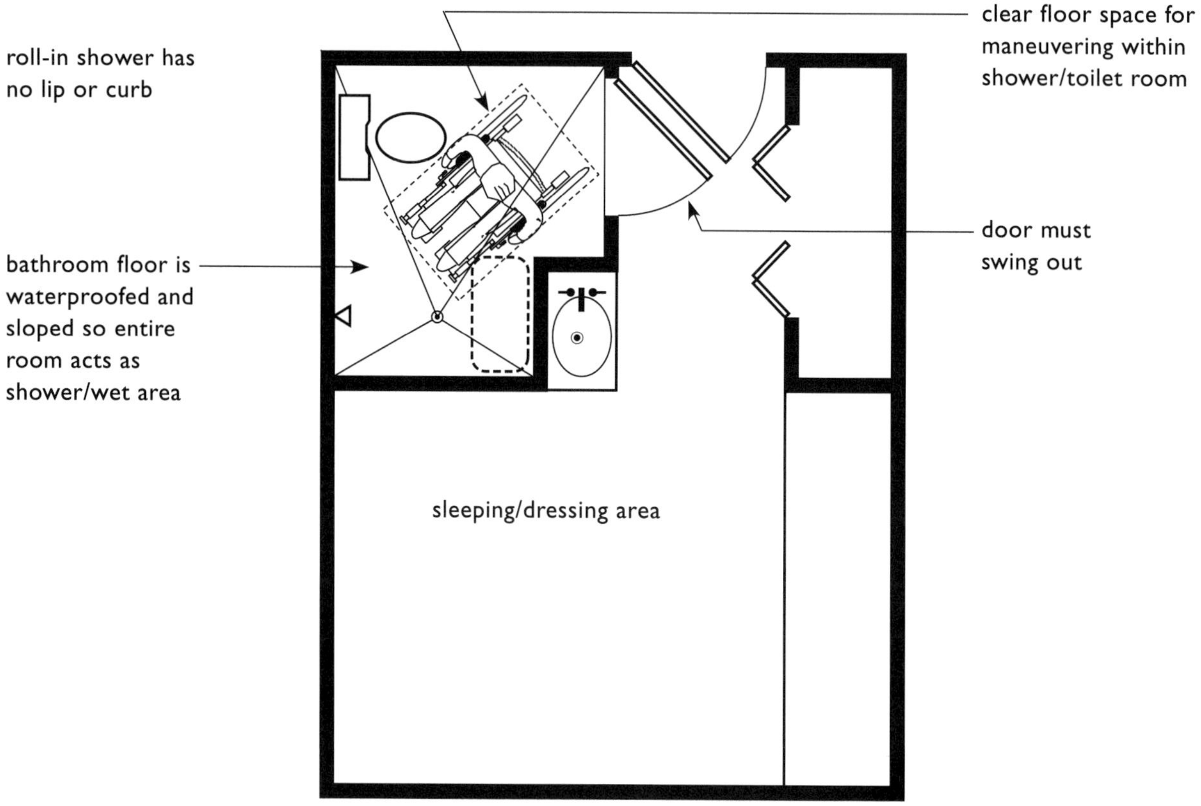

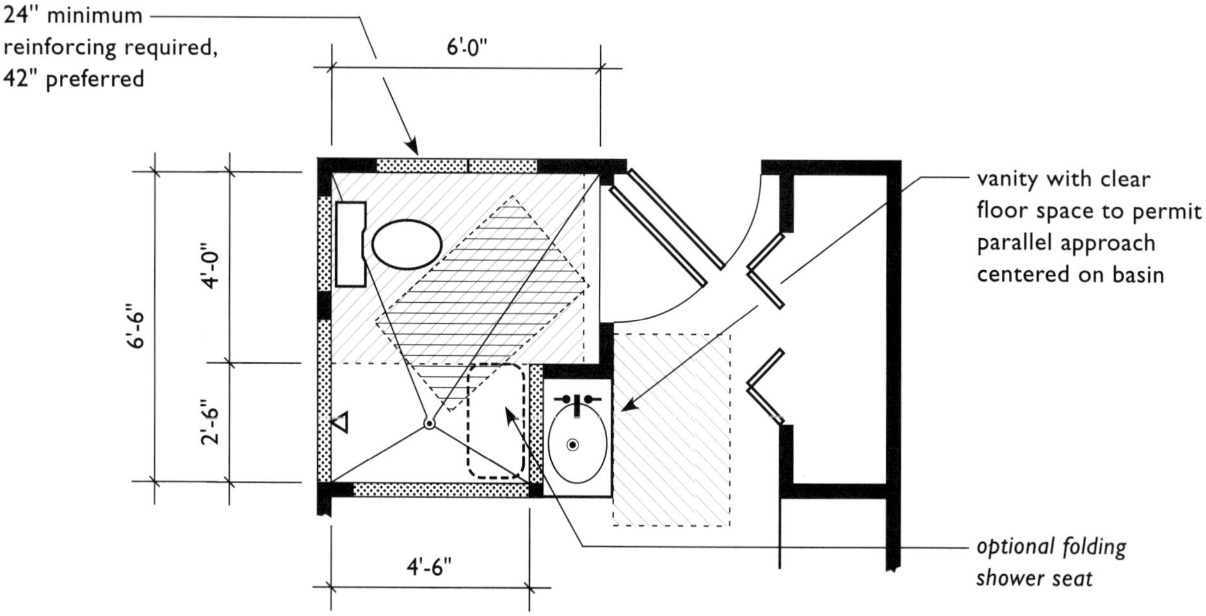

Legend: reinforcing in walls or floors for grab bars; min. clear floor space at each fixture; min. clear floor space outside swing of door

Bathrooms with Two Bathing Fixtures

"B" Bathroom with Two Bathing Fixtures (Accessible Shower/Inaccessible Bathtub)

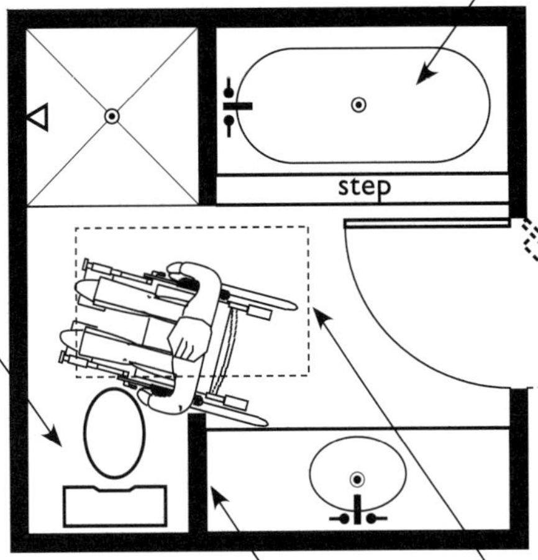

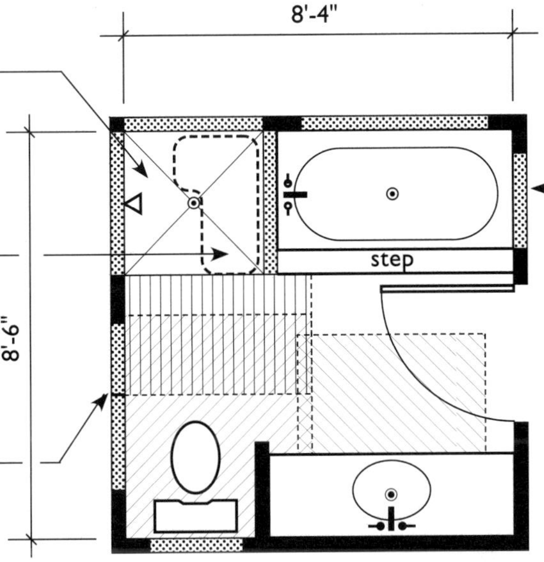

Legend: reinforcing in walls or floors for grab bars | min. clear floor space at each fixture | min. clear floor space outside swing of door

"A"and "B" Bathroom with Two Bathing Fixtures (Accessible Bathtub/Accessible Shower)

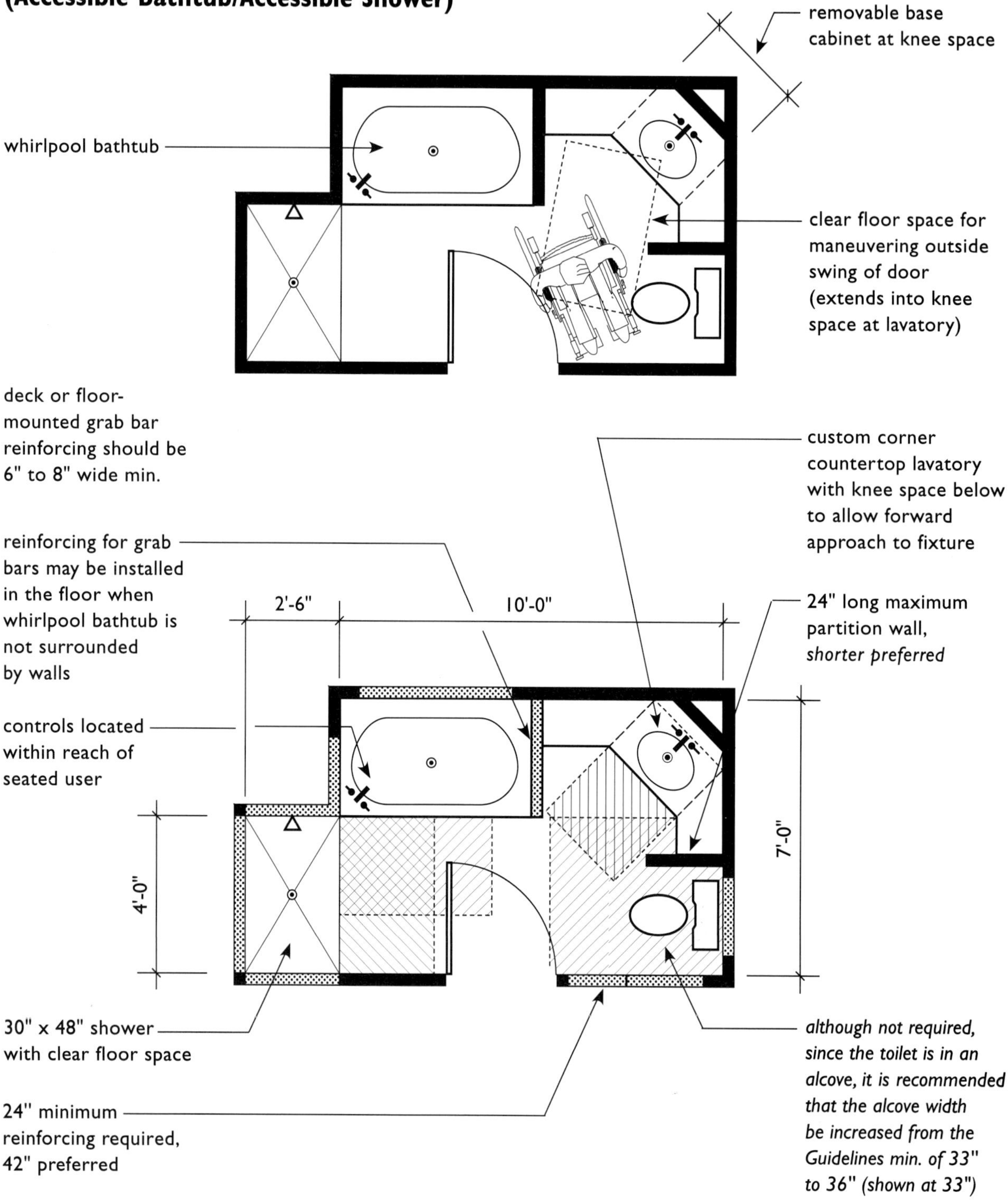

Legend: reinforcing in walls or floors for grab bars; min. clear floor space at each fixture; min. clear floor space outside swing of door

"B" Bathroom with Two Bathing Fixtures (Accessible Bathtub/Inaccessible Shower)

controls located within reach of seated user

linen closet doors may be less than 32" nominal clear width if user is not required to pass through the door to reach the contents

this room could be improved by omitting the closet to allow additional maneuvering space

some people using wheelchairs will have to leave the sliding door open in order to position their chair to make a transfer onto toilet

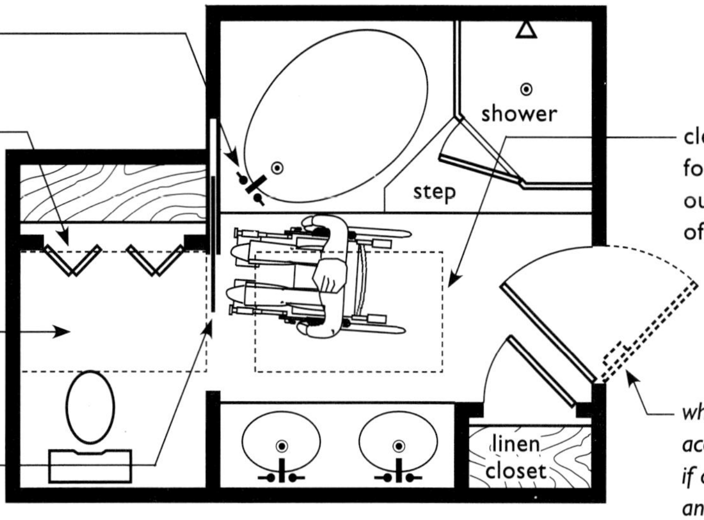

clear floor space for maneuvering outside swing of door

while not required, access is improved if door swings out and an auxiliary door handle is installed

grab bars can be deck-mounted if solid construction, wall-mounted if tub is prefabricated

deck or floor-mounted grab bar reinforcing should be 6" to 8" wide min.

inaccessible shower still must have reinforcing for grab bars

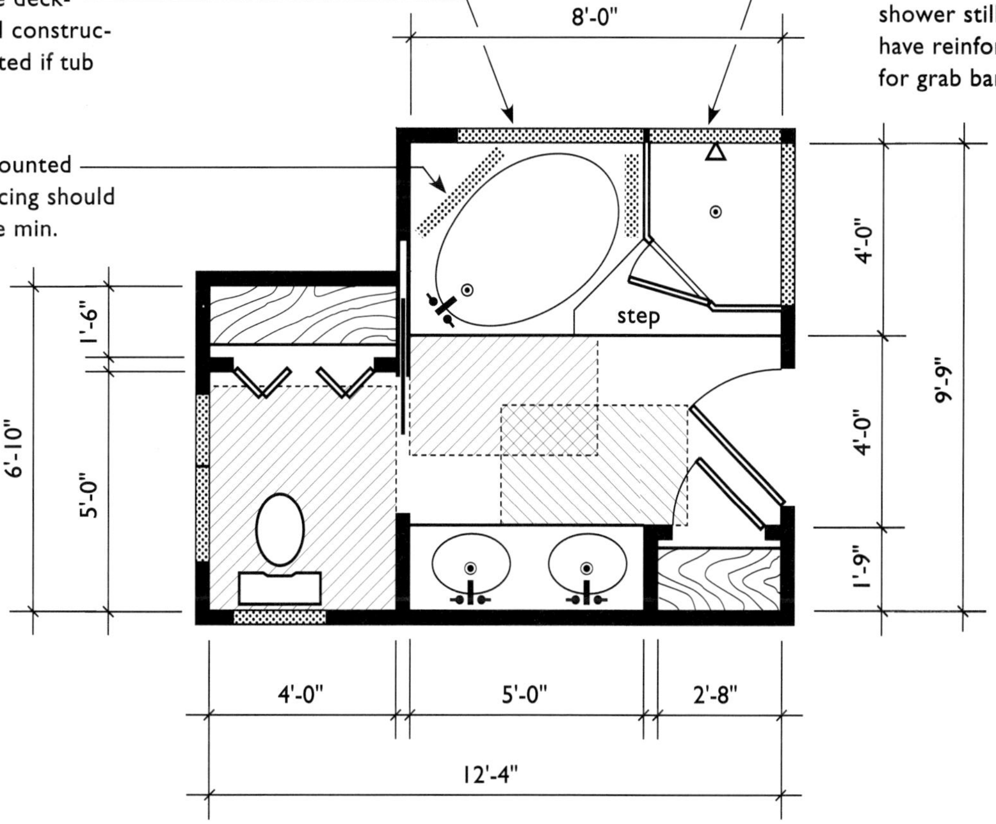

Legend: reinforcing in walls or floors for grab bars; min. clear floor space at each fixture; min. clear floor space outside swing of door

POWDER ROOMS

Powder rooms must meet the requirements for clear floor space at fixtures and reinforcing in walls only when they are on the accessible level of multistory units in buildings having one or more elevators.

removable base cabinet at knee space

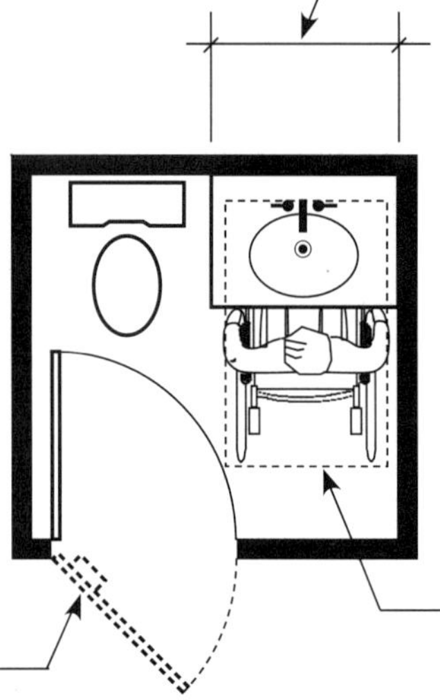

while not required, access is improved if door swings out and an auxiliary door handle is installed

clear floor space for maneuvering outside swing of door (extends into knee space at lavatory)

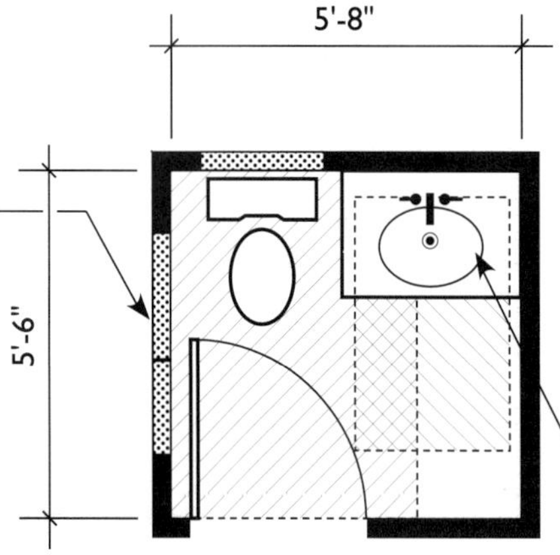

24" minimum reinforcing required, 42" preferred

where a removable cabinet is provided below a countertop less than 32" in width, care must be taken to prevent support method or brackets from encroaching upon required knee space, see page 7.50

24" deep countertop lavatory with knee space below to allow forward approach to fixture

Legend: reinforcing in walls or floors for grab bars; min. clear floor space at each fixture; min. clear floor space outside swing of door

Powder Room

Powder rooms must meet the requirements for clear floor space at fixtures and reinforcing in walls only when they are on the accessible level of multistory units in buildings having one or more elevators.

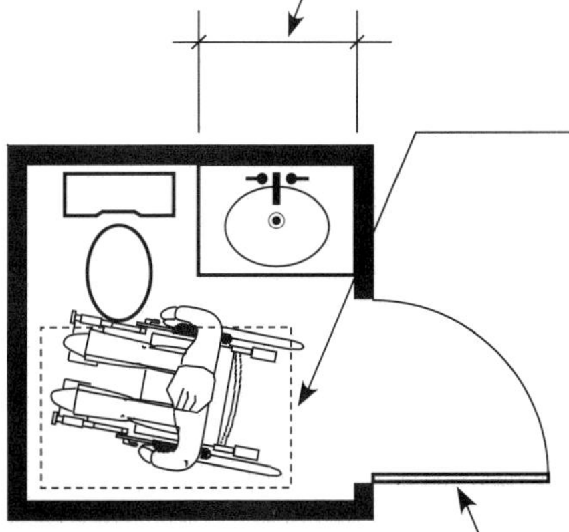

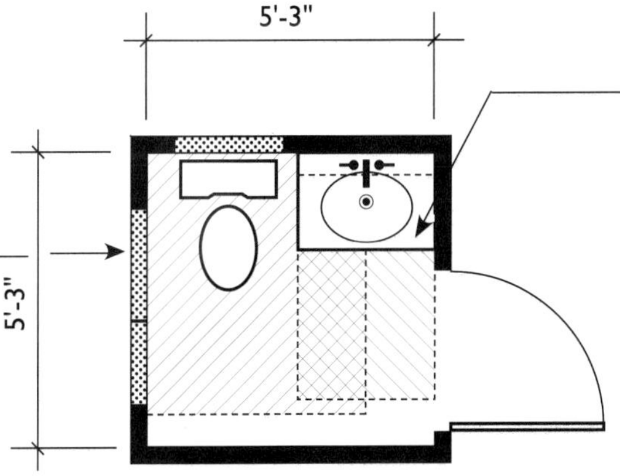

Legend: reinforcing in walls or floors for grab bars; min. clear floor space at each fixture; min. clear floor space outside swing of door

Powder Room

Powder rooms must meet the requirements for clear floor space at fixtures and reinforcing in walls only when they are on the accessible level of multistory units in buildings having one or more elevators.

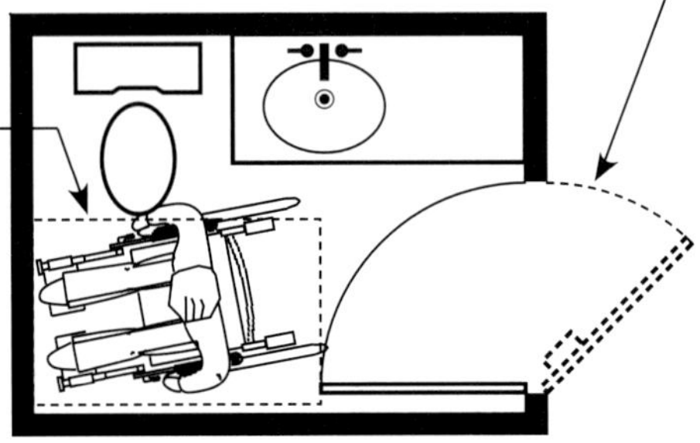

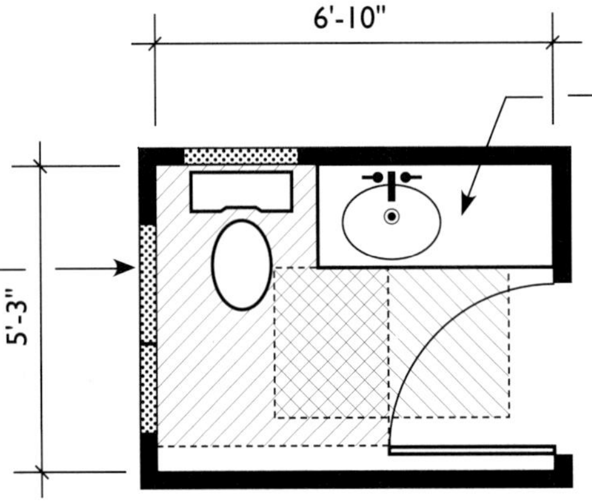

Legend: reinforcing in walls or floors for grab bars; min. clear floor space at each fixture; min. clear floor space outside swing of door

Powder Room

Powder rooms must meet the requirements for clear floor space at fixtures and reinforcing in walls only when they are on the accessible level of multistory units in buildings having one or more elevators.

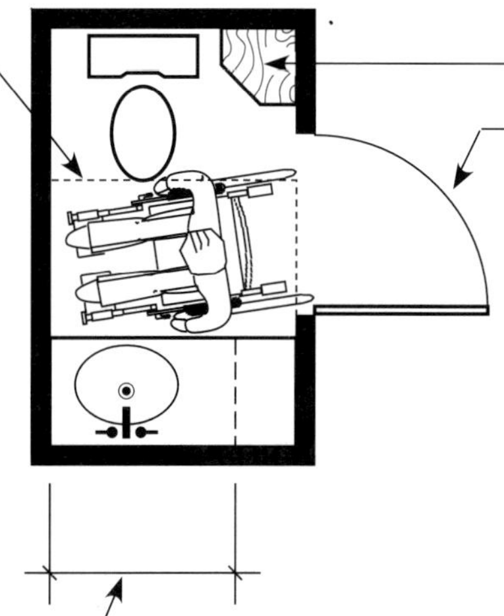

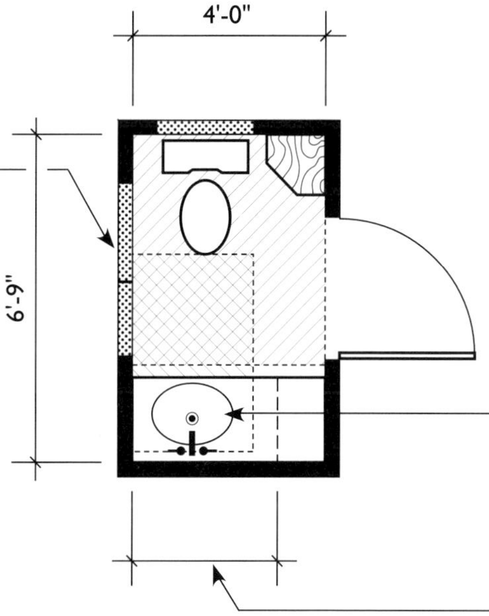

Legend: reinforcing in walls or floors for grab bars; min. clear floor space at each fixture; min. clear floor space outside swing of door

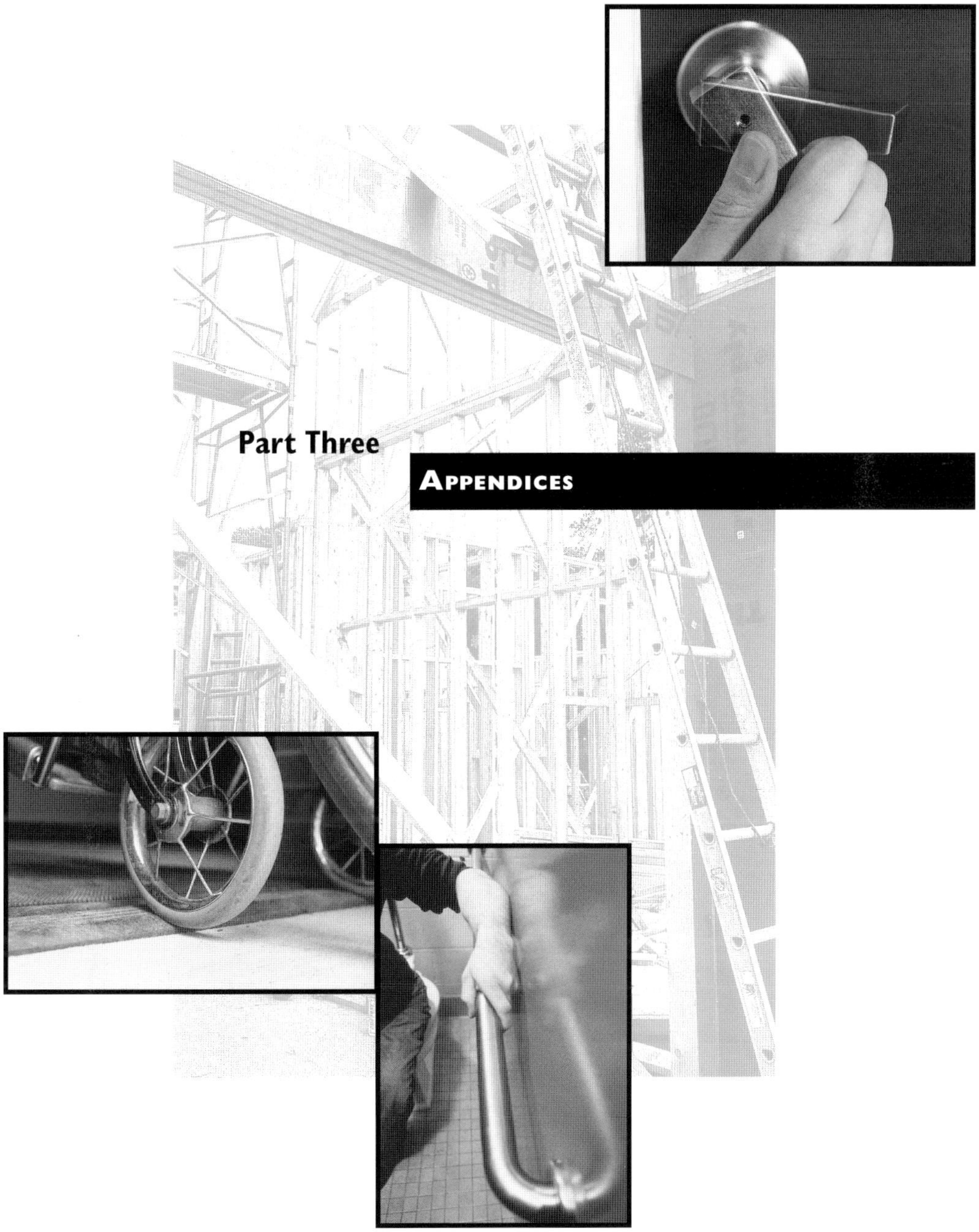

Part Three

APPENDICES

APPENDIX A

Product Resources
and Selected References

A

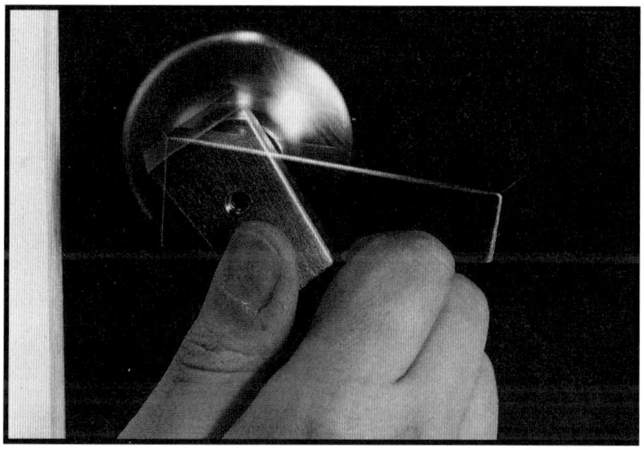

Product Resources

The following list of products is provided to assist owners/builders and potential residents to adapt Fair Housing covered units to suit individual needs and requirements. They are examples only and the list is not complete; other products with similar features also are available. No endorsement of the products or recommendation for use of the products is given nor implied.

Other compilations of building products are available, but few if any specifically address the issues exclusive to compliance with the Fair Housing Accessibility Guidelines. Going beyond the requirements of the Guidelines, the National Association of Home Builders Research Center publishes a *Directory of Accessible Building Products* in an effort to increase accessible housing for people with disabilities. The *Directory* is available from the NAHB Research Center, 400 Prince George's Boulevard, Upper Marlboro, Maryland, 20772-8731, phone: (301) 249-4000.

Few if any manufacturers presently offer "adaptable" or removable cabinets as part of their stock line. No individual cabinet manufacturers are cited in this product resource list; however, several have indicated that providing kitchen cabinets with removable fronts currently is possible using existing materials and methods.

Product Resource List

Appliances

G.E. Appliances
Appliance Park
Louisville, KY 40225
502-452-4311
(stacking front-loading coin operated residential dryers with front-mounted controls)

Sears, Roebuck, and Company
Sears Tower
Chicago, IL 60684
312-875-3000
(under-counter front-loading washers and dryers with front-mounted controls)

Note: Most companies have space saving and stacking models with front-mounted controls.

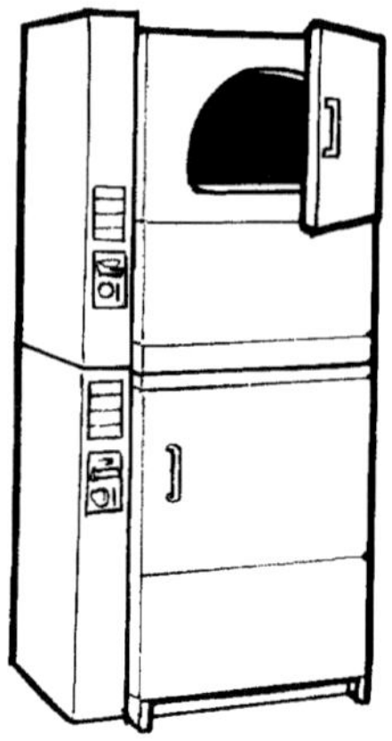

washers and dryers with front-mounted controls are more usable for everyone

Stacked Coin Operated Dryers

Assistive Devices

adaptAbility
P.O. Box 515
Colchester, CT 06415-0515
1-800-243-9232

Maddak, Inc.
6 Industrial Road
Pequannock, NJ 07440
201-628-7600

Sears, Roebuck, and Company
Sears Tower
Chicago, IL 60684
1-800-948-8800

reachers and grabbers can increase the reach for people who are short in stature, are seated, or have limited reach range

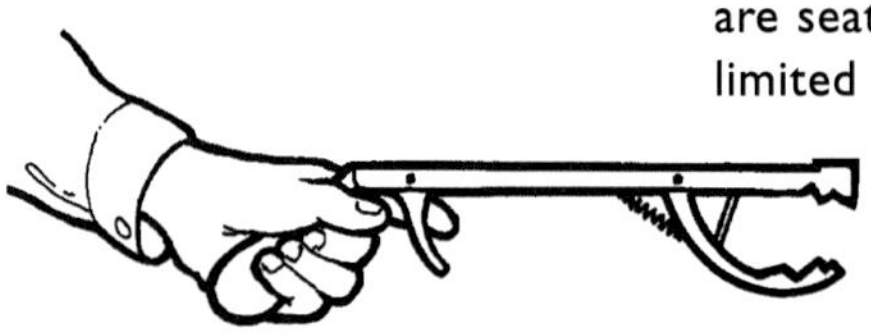

Grabber/Reacher

Bathroom Products

Grab Bars

Bobrick Washroom Equipment, Inc.
Northway 10 Industrial Park
Clifton Park, NY 12065
518-877-7444
(folding grab bars and reinforcing)

Bradley Corporation
Washroom Accessories Division
804 East Gate Drive
Mt. Laurel, NJ 08054
609-235-7420
(grab bar reinforcing)

Dryad Jebron
Suite 202
249 Ayer Road
Harvard, MA 01451
1-800-445-5388
508-772-4167
(colored and folding grab bars)

Elcoma Metal Fabricating Ltd.
1929-36 Street N.E.
Canton, Ohio 44705
216-588-8844
1-800-352-6625
(colored and folding grab bars and reinforcing)

Franklin Brass
Manufacturing Company
P.O. Box 5226
Culver City, CA 90231
213-306-5944
1-800-421-3375
(grab bar reinforcing)

Hewi, Inc.
6 Pearl Court
Allendale, NJ 07401
201-327-7202
(colored and folding grab bars)

Normbau
P.O. Box 548
Shepherdsville, KY 40165
502-538-7388
1-800-358-2920
(colored and folding grab bars)

Pressalit Inc.
1259 Rt. 46, Bldg. 2
Parsippany, NJ 07054
1-800-346-2380
201-263-8533
(colored and folding grab bars)

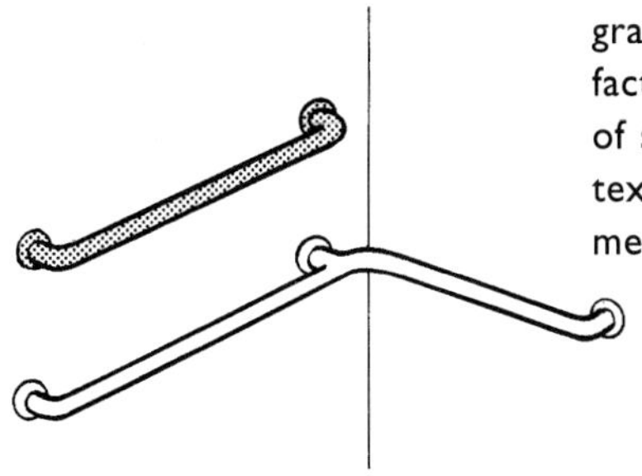

Standard Grab Bars

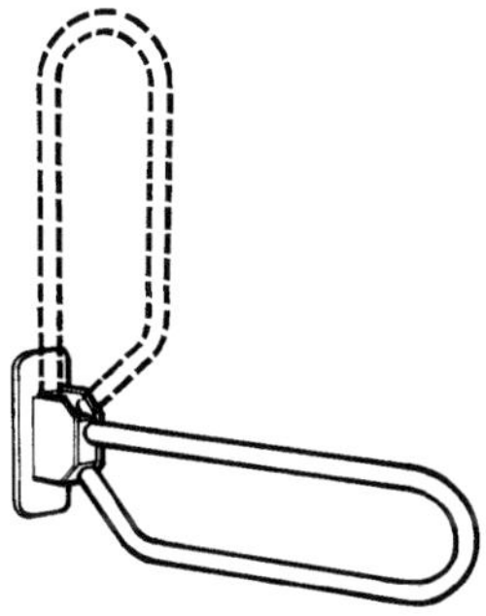

Folding Grab Bar

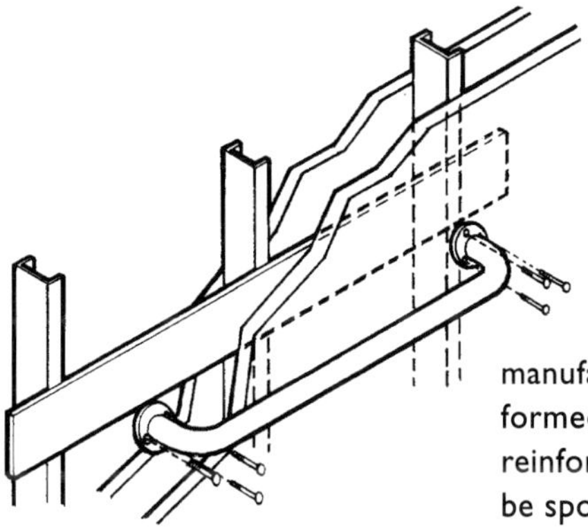

Reinforcing at Metal Studs

SafeTec International, Inc.
P.O. Box 23
Melbourne, FL 32902
407-952-1300
(colored grab bars)

Tubular Specialties Mfg., Inc.
13011 S. Spring Street
Los Angeles, CA 90061
1-800-421-2961
(colored and folding grab bars)

Lindo
1090 McCallie Avenue
Chattanooga, TN 37404
615-698-4200
(folding grab bars)

Hand-Held Shower Heads

Brass-Craft Mfg. Co.
27700 Northwestern Highway
Southfield, MI 48034
313-827-1100

Alsons
525 E. Edna Place
P.O. Box 311
Covina, CA 91723
818-966-1668

Moen Incorporated
377 Woodland Avenue
Elyria, OH 44036-2111
216-232-3341

Odine
Division of Interbath, Inc.
427 N. Baldwin Park Boulevard
City of Industry, CA 91746
818-369-1841

Grohe America
900 Lively Boulevard
Wood Dale, IL 60191
708-350-2600

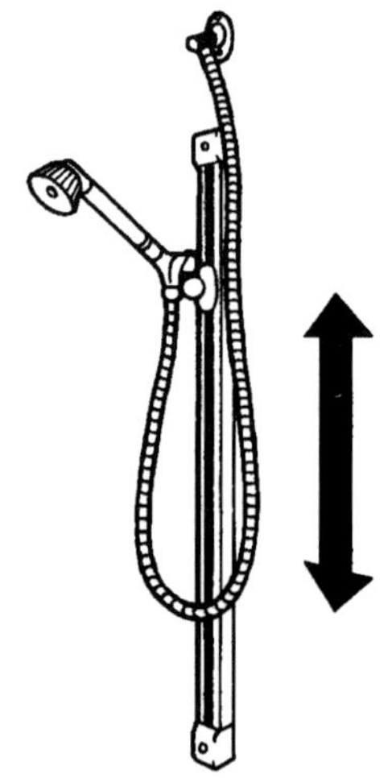

Hand-Held Shower Head On a Slide-Bar Mount

L-Shaped Shower Seats

Bobrick Washroom Equipment, Inc.
Northway 10 Industrial Park
Clifton Park, NY 12065
518-877-7444

Tubular Specialties Mfg., Inc.
13011 S. Spring Street
Los Angeles, CA 90061
1-800-421-2961

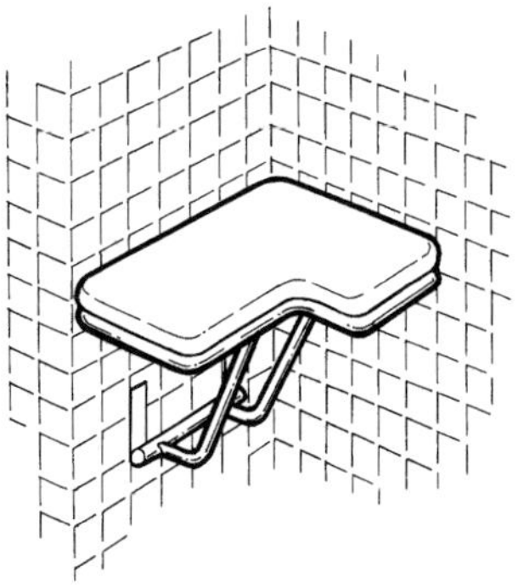

many L-shaped shower seats fold up, increasing available space in showers

L-Shaped Shower Seat

Manufactured Pipe Protection

I & S Insulation Co., Inc.
1819 So. Central Avenue, 38
Kent, WA 98032
206-859-1830

Truebro Inc.
P.O. Box 429
Ellington, CT 06029
203-875-2868

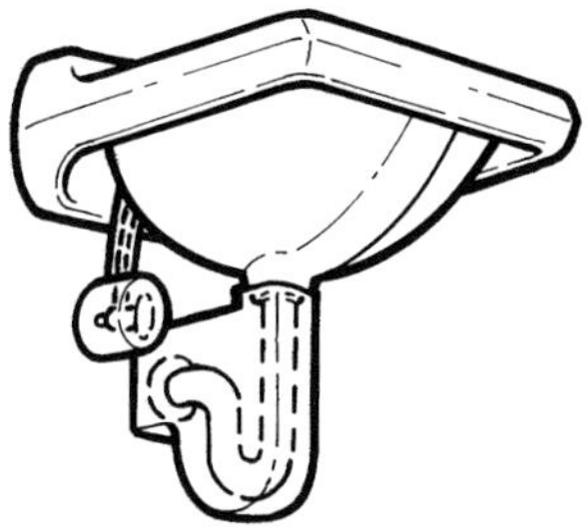

insulated pipe surround to protect seated users from burns and sharp edges

Manufactured Pipe Protection

Raised Toilet Seats

Beneke
P.O. Box 1367
Columbus, MS 39703
1-800-647-1042
601-328-4000

Church Seat Company
Sheboygan Falls, WI 53085
1-800-233-SEAT
414-467-2664

Olsonite
8801 Conant Avenue
Detroit, MI 48211
1-800-521-8266
313-075-5831

when standard low toilets are installed, raised toilet seats and spacers can be added to increase the height from 2" to 6" if necessary

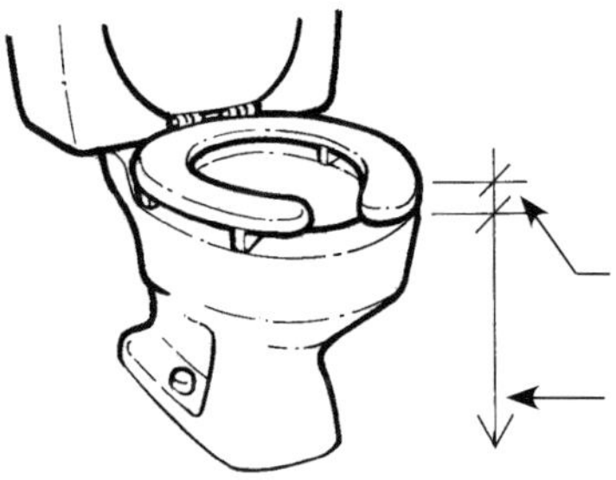

Raised Toilet Seat

Doors and Door Hardware

Accessible Thresholds

Stanley Hardware
P.O. Box 1840
New Britain, CT 06050
1-800-622-4393

National Guard Products, Inc.
540 North Parkway
P.O. Box 7353
Memphis, TN 38107
1-800-NGP-RUSH

Zero International, Inc.
415 Concord Avenue
Bronx, NY 10455-4898
1-800-635-5335
212-585-3230

Note: Most threshold companies have accessible thresholds.

Accessible Threshold

Add-On Lever Handles

Lindustries, Inc.
21 Shady Hill Road
Weston, MA 02193
617-235-5452

Extend Incorporated
P.O. Box 864
Moorhead, MN 56561-0864
218-236-9686

Schlage
2401 Bayshore Boulevard
San Francisco, CA 94134
415-467-1100

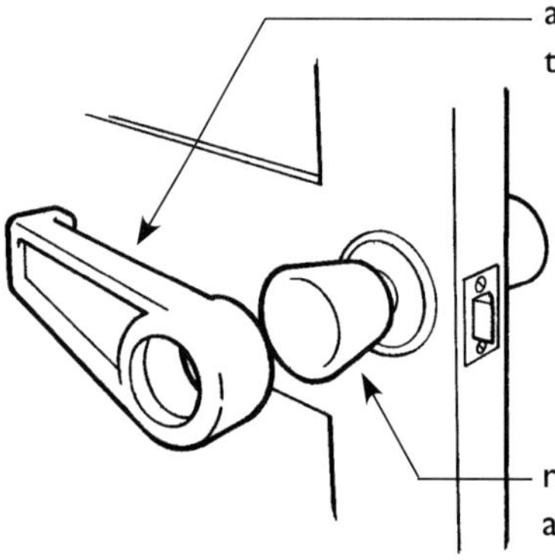

Add-On Lever Handle

Bi-Fold Door Hardware

Ezyfold
The Kiwi Connection
82 Shelburne Center Road
Shelburne, MA 01370
413-625-2854

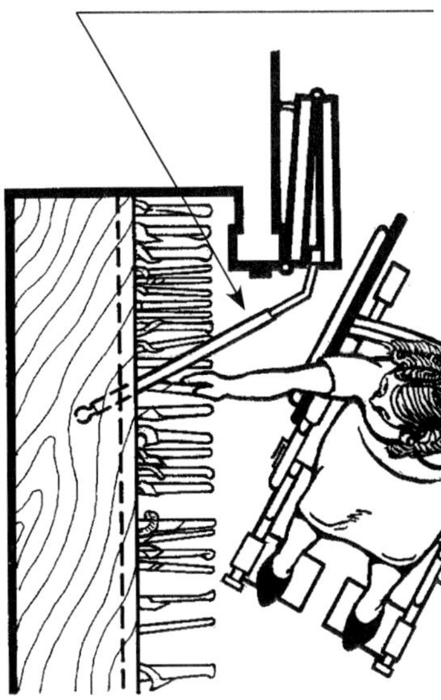

Bi-Fold Door Hardware

6'-0" Sliding Glass Doors with 32" Nominal Clear Opening

Bennings Building Products
210 Walser
Lexington, NC 27292
1-800-222-3861

Kolbe and Kolbe Millwork, Co., Inc.
1323 S. Eleventh Avenue
Wausau, WI 54401
715-842-5666
(no 6'-0" sliding door; do have 6'-6" door with nominal 33" clear width opening)

Moss Supply Company
5001 North Graham St.
Charlotte, NC 28213
1-800-438-0770

Note: While these doors provide the 32" nominal clear width, thresholds may need to be modified or altered to provide full access

Sliding Door with Nominal 32" Clear Opening

Swing-Clear Hinges

Stanley Hardware
P.O. Box 1840
New Britain, CT 06050
1-800-622-4393

Ply Gems Barrier Free
Philron Corporation
6948 Frankford Avenue
Philadelphia, PA 19135
215-331-3434

Mont-Hard Inc.
2415 Lifehaus Drive
New Braunfels, TX 78130
512-625-7795

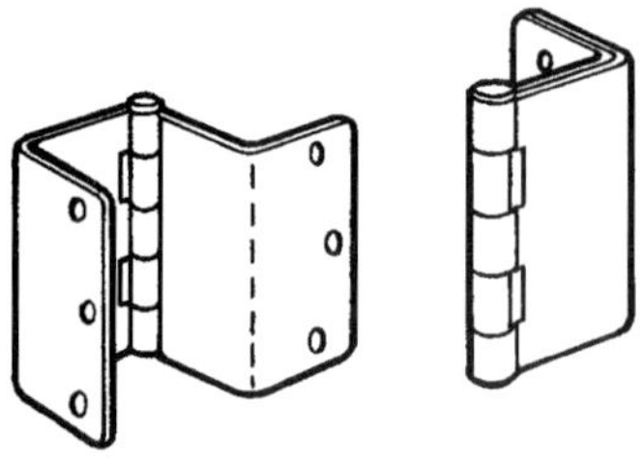

installation of swing-away hinges allows door to swing fully out of opening to increase the clear width of an existing door opening

Swing-Clear Hinges

Kitchen Storage

Revolving/Extending Shelves

Hafele America
203 Feld Avenue
P.O. Box 1590
High Point, NC 27261
910-889-2322

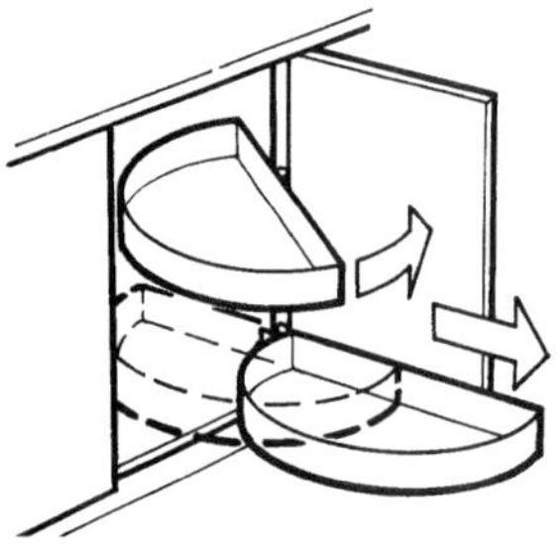

slide out shelves provide easy access for all users

Revolving/Extending Semicircular Shelves

Visual Signals and Alarms

HITEC Group Int'l., Inc.
P.O. Box 187
Westmont, IL 60559
708-963-5588
1-800-288-8303

Nutone
Madison and Red Bank Roads
Cincinnati, OH 45227-1599
513-527-5100

Aiphone Corporation
1700 130th Avenue. N.E.
P.O. Box 90075
Bellevue, WA 98009
206-455-0510
(video door signal)

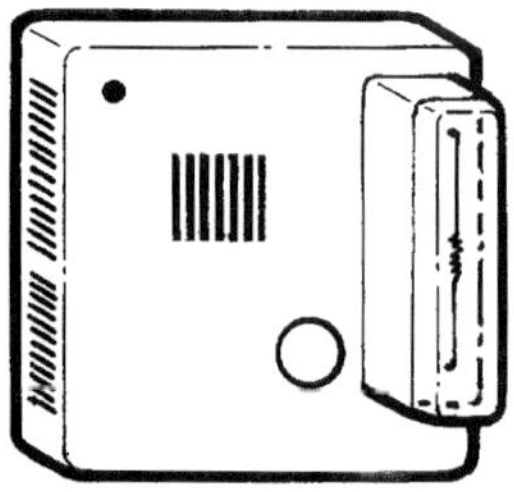

fire alarm with strobe light to alert people with hearing impairments

Visual and Audible Alarm

Selected References

American National Standards Institute (1986). *American National Standard for Buildings and Facilities - Providing Accessibility and Usability for Physically Handicapped People* (ANSI A117.1-1986). New York, NY. *

American National Standards Institute (1992). *Accessible and Usable Buildings and Facilities* (ANSI/CABO A117.1-1992). New York, NY. *

Barrier Free Environments, Inc. (1987). *Adaptable Housing.* Washington, DC: U.S. Department of Housing and Urban Development, Office of Policy Development and Research. **

Barrier Free Environments, Inc. (1991). *The Accessible Housing Design File.* New York, NY: Van Nostrand Reinhold Company.

Center for Accessible Housing (1992). *Technical Design Bulletin #1, Fair Housing Accessibility Guidelines Requirement 1: Analyzing Site Impracticality on Difficult Sites.* Raleigh, NC.

Davies, Thomas D. Jr., and Kim A. Beasley (1992). *Fair Housing Design Guide for Accessibility.* Washington, DC: Paralyzed Veterans of America, National Association of Home Builders, National Multi-Housing Council, and the National Apartment Association.

---

* Available from the American National Standards Institute, 1430 Broadway, New York, NY 10018, telephone: 1-212-642-4900

**Available from HUD USER, P. O. Box 6091, Rockville, MD 20850, telephone: 1-800-245-2691

Leibrock, Cynthia, with Susan Behar (1992). *Beautiful Barrier-Free: A Visual Guide to Accessibility.* New York, NY: Van Nostrand Reinhold Company.

Raschko, Bettyann Boetticher (1982). *Housing Interiors for the Disabled and Elderly.* New York, NY: Van Nostrand Reinhold Company.

Salmen, John P. S. (1985). *The Do-Able Renewable Home.* Washington, DC: American Association of Retired Persons.

Steven Winter Associates, Inc., Tourbier and Walmsley, Inc., Edward Steinfeld, and Building Technology, Inc. (1993). *Cost of Accessible Housing.* Washington, DC: Department of Housing and Urban Development, Office of Policy Development and Research. **

U.S. Department of Housing and Urban Development, Office of the Assistant Secretary for Fair Housing and Equal Opportunity. 24 Code of Federal Regulations (CFR) Chapter 1: Subchapter A.

Appendix I, *Final Fair Housing Regulations,* January 23, 1989.***

Appendix II, *Final Fair Housing Accessibility Guidelines,* March 6, 1991.***

Appendix III, *Preamble to the Final Fair Housing Accessibility Guidelines,* March 6, 1991.***

Appendix IV, *Fair Housing Accessibility Guidelines, Questions and Answers, Supplement to the Notice,* June 28, 1994. ***

U.S. Department of Housing and Urban Development, Office of the Assistant Secretary for Fair Housing and Equal Opportunity (1992). Washington, DC. *HUD Accessibility Seminars Workbook.*

Wylde, Margaret, Adrian Baron-Robbins, and Sam Clark (1994). *Building for a Lifetime: The Design and Construction of Fully Accessible Homes.* Newtown, CT: the Taunton Press.

** Available from HUD USER, P.O. Box 6091, Rockville, MD 20850, telephone: 1-800-245-2691

*** Available from HUD Distribution Center, 451 Seventh Street S.W., Washington, D.C. 20410, telephone: 1-800-767-7468

Appendix B

Fair Housing Accessibility Guidelines

B

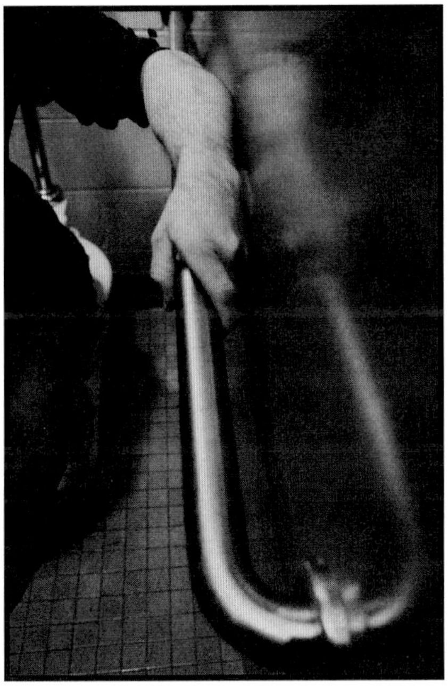

federal register

Wednesday
March 6, 1991

Part VI

Department of Housing and Urban Development

Office of the Assistant Secretary for Fair Housing and Equal Opportunity

24 CFR Chapter I

Final Fair Housing Accessibility Guidelines

DEPARTMENT OF HOUSING AND URBAN DEVELOPMENT

Office of the Assistant Secretary for Fair Housing and Equal Opportunity

24 CFR Ch. I

[Docket No. N-91-2011; FR 2665-N-06]

Final Fair Housing Accessibility Guidelines

AGENCY: Office of the Assistant Secretary for Fair Housing and Equal Opportunity, HUD.

ACTION: Notice of Final Fair Housing Accessibility Guidelines.

SUMMARY: This document presents guidelines adopted by the Department of Housing and Urban Development to provide builders and developers with technical guidance on how to comply with the specific accessibility requirements of the Fair Housing Amendments Act of 1988. Issuance of this document follows consideration of public comment received on proposed accessibility guidelines published in the **Federal Register** on June 15, 1990. The guidelines presented in this document are intended to provide technical guidance only, and are not mandatory. The guidelines will be codified in the 1991 edition of the Code of Federal Regulations as Appendix II to the Fair Housing regulations (24 CFR Ch. I, Subch. A, App. II). The preamble to the guidelines will be codified in the 1991 edition of the Code of Federal Regulations as Appendix III to the Fair Housing regulations (24 CFR Ch. I, Subch. A, App. III).

EFFECTIVE DATE: March 6, 1991.

FOR FURTHER INFORMATION CONTACT: Merle Morrow, Office of HUD Program Compliance, room 5204, Department of Housing and Urban Development, 451 Seventh Street, SW., Washington, DC. 20410-0500, telephone (202) 708-2618 (voice) or (202) 708-0015 (TDD). (These are not toll-free numbers.)

SUPPLEMENTARY INFORMATION:

I. Adoption of Final Guidelines

The Department of Housing and Urban Development (Department) is adopting as its Fair Housing Accessibility Guidelines, the design and construction guidelines set forth in this notice (Guidelines). Issuance of this document follows consideration of public comments received in response to an advance notice of intention to develop and publish Fair Housing Accessibility Guidelines, published in the **Federal Register** on August 2, 1989 (54 FR 31856), and in response to proposed accessibility guidelines published in the **Federal Register** on June 15, 1990 (55 FR 24730).

The Department is adopting as final Guidelines, the guidelines designated as Option One in the proposed guidelines published on June 15, 1990, with modifications to certain of the Option One design specifications. In developing the final Guidelines, the Department was cognizant of the need to provide technical guidance that appropriately implements the specific accessibility requirements of the Fair Housing Amendments Act of 1988, while avoiding design specifications that would impose an unreasonable burden on builders, and significantly increase the cost of new multifamily construction. The Department believes that the final Guidelines adopted by this notice (1) are consistent with the level of accessibility envisioned by Congress; (2) simplify compliance with the Fair Housing Amendments Act by providing guidance concerning what constitutes acceptable compliance with the Act; and (3) maintain the affordability of new multifamily construction by specifying reasonable design and construction methods.

The Option One design specifications substantially revised in the final Guidelines include the following:

(1) Site impracticality. The final Guidelines provide that covered multifamily dwellings with elevators shall be designed and constructed to provide at least one accessible entrance on an accessible route regardless of terrain or unusual characteristics of the site. Every dwelling unit on a floor served by an elevator must be on an accessible route, and must be made accessible in accordance with the Act's requirements for covered dwelling units.

For covered multifamily dwellings without elevators, the final Guidelines provide two alternative tests for determining site impracticality due to terrain. The first test is an individual building test which involves a two-step process: measurement of the slope of the undisturbed site between the planned entrance and all vehicular or pedestrian arrival points; and measurement of the slope of the planned finished grade between the entrance and all vehicular or pedestrian arrival points. The second test is a site analysis test which involves an analysis of the existing natural terrain (before grading) by topographic survey with 2 foot contour intervals, with slope determination made between each successive contour interval.

A site with a single building (without an elevator), having a common entrance for all units, may be analyzed only under the first test—the individual building test. All other sites, including a site with a single building having multiple entrances serving either individual dwelling units or clusters of dwelling units, may be analyzed either under the first test or the second test. For sites for which either test is applicable (that is, all sites other than a site with a single nonelevator building having a common entrance for all units), the final Guidelines provide that regardless of which test is utilized by a builder or developer, at least 20% of the total ground floor units in nonelevator buildings, on any site, must comply with the Act's accessibility requirements.

(2) An accessible route into and through covered dwelling units. The final Guidelines distinguish between (i) single-story dwelling units, and (ii) multistory dwelling units in elevator buildings, and provide guidance on designing an accessible entrance into and through each of these two types of dwelling units.

(a) Single-story dwelling units. For single-story dwelling units, the final Guidelines specify the same design specification as presented in the proposed Option One guidelines, except that design features within the single-story dwelling units, such as a loft or a sunken living room, are exempt from the access specifications, subject to certain requirements. Lofts are exempt provided that all other space within the units is on an accessible route. Sunken or raised functional areas, such as a sunken living room, are also exempt from access specifications, provided that such areas do not interrupt the accessible route through the remainder of the unit. However, split-level entries or areas will need ramps or other means of providing an accessible route.

(b) Multistory dwelling units in buildings with elevators. For multistory dwelling units in buildings with elevators, the final Guidelines specify that only the story served by the building elevator must comply with the accessible features for dwelling units required by the Fair Housing Act. The other stories of the multistory dwelling units are exempt from access specifications, provided that the story of the unit that is served by the building elevator (1) is the primary entry to the unit; (2) complies with Requirements 2 through 7 with respect to the rooms located on the entry/accessible level; and (3) contains a bathroom or powder room which complies with Requirement 7.

(c) Thresholds at patio, deck or balcony doors. The final Guidelines provide that exterior deck, patio, or balcony surfaces should be not more than ½ inch below the floor level of the interior of the dwelling unit, unless they are constructed of impervious materials such as concrete, brick or flagstone, in which case the surface should be no more than 4 inches below the floor level of the interior dwelling units, unless the local building code requires a lower drop. This provision and the following provision were included in order to minimize the possibility of interior water damage when exterior surfaces are constructed of impervious materials.

(d) Outside surface at entry door. The final Guidelines also provide that at the primary entry door to dwelling units with direct exterior access, outside landing surfaces constructed of impervious materials such as concrete, brick, or flagstone should be no more than ½ inch below the interior of the dwelling unit. The Guidelines further provide that the finished surface of this area, located immediately outside the entry door, may be sloped for drainage, but the sloping may be no more than ⅛ inch per foot.

(3) Usable bathrooms. The final Guidelines provide two alternative sets of specifications for making bathrooms accessible in accordance with the Act's requirements. The Act requires that an accessible or "usable" bathroom is one which provides sufficient space for an individual in a wheelchair to maneuver about. The two sets of specifications provide different approaches as to how compliance with this maneuvering space requirement may be achieved. The final Guidelines for usable bathrooms also provide that the usable bathroom specifications (either set of specifications) are applicable to powder rooms (i.e., a room with only a toilet and a sink) when the powder room is the only toilet facility on the accessible level of a covered multistory dwelling unit.

The details about, and the reasons for these modifications, and additional minor technical modifications made to certain design specifications of the Option One guidelines, are discussed more fully in the section-by-section analysis which appear later in this preamble.

Principal features of the Option One guidelines that were not changed in the final Guidelines include the following:

(1) Accessible entrance and an accessible route. The Option One guidelines for these two requirements remain unchanged in the final Guidelines.

(2) Accessible and usable public and common use areas. The Option One guidelines for public and common use areas remain unchanged in the final Guidelines.

(3) Door within individual dwelling units. The final Guidelines recommend that doors intended for user passage within individual dwelling units have a clear opening of at least 32 inches nominal width when the door is open 90 degrees.

(4) Doors to public and common use areas. The final Guidelines continued to provide that on accessible routes in public and common use areas, and for primary entry doors to covered units doors that comply with ANSI 4.13 meet the Act's requirement for "usable" doors.

(4) Thresholds at exterior doors. Subject to the exceptions for thresholds and changes in level at exterior areas constructed of impervious materials, the final Guidelines continue to specify that thresholds at exterior doors, including sliding door tracks, be no higher than ¾ inch.

(5) Reinforced walls for grab bars. The final Guidelines for bathroom wall reinforcement remains essentially unchanged from the Option One guidelines. The only change made to these guidelines has been to subject powder rooms to the reinforced wall requirement when the powder room is the only toilet facility on the accessible floor of a covered multistory dwelling unit.

The text of the final Guidelines follows the Preamble, which includes a discussion of the public comments received on the proposed guidelines, and the section-by-section analysis referenced above.

The design specification presented in the Fair Housing Accessibility Guidelines provide technical guidance to builders and developers in complying with the specific accessibility requirements of the Fair Housing Amendments Act of 1988. The Guidelines are intended to provide a safe harbor for compliance with the accessibility requirements of the Fair Housing Amendments Act, as implemented by 24 CFR 100.205 of the Department's Fair Housing regulations. The Guidelines are not mandatory. Additionally, the Guidelines do not prescribe specific requirements which must be met, and which, if not met, would constitute unlawful discrimination under the Fair Housing Amendments Act. Builders and developers may choose to depart from the Guidelines, and seek alternate ways to demonstrate that they have met the requirements of the Fair Housing Act.

II. Statutory and Regulatory Background

Title VIII of the Civil Rights Act of 1968 makes it unlawful to discriminate in any aspect relating to the sale, rental or financing of dwellings, or in the provision of brokerage services or facilities in connection with the sale or rental of a dwelling, because of race, color, religion, sex or national origin. The Fair Housing Amendments Act of 1988 (Pub. L. 100–430, approved September 13, 1988) (Fair Housing Act or the Act) expanded coverage of title VIII (42 U.S.C. 3601–3620) to prohibit discriminatory housing practices based on handicap and familial status. As amended, section 804(f)(3)(C) of the Act provides that unlawful discrimination includes a failure to design and construct covered multifamily dwellings for first occupancy after March 13, 1991 (30 months after the date of enactment in accordance with certain accessibility requirements. The Act defines "covered multifamily dwellings" as "(a) buildings consisting of 4 or more units if such buildings have one or more elevators; and (b) ground floor units in other buildings consisting of 4 or more units" (42 U.S.C. 3604).

The Act makes it unlawful to fail to design and construct covered multifamily dwellings so that:

(1) Public use and common use portions of the dwellings are readily accessible to and usable by persons with handicaps;

(2) All doors within such dwellings which are designed to allow passage into and within the premises are sufficiently wide to allow passage by persons in wheelchairs; and

(3) All premises within such dwellings contain the following features of adaptive design:

(a) An accessible route into and through the dwelling;

(b) Light switches, electrical outlets, thermostats, and other environmental controls in accessible locations.

(c) Reinforcements in bathroom walls to allow later installation of grab bars; and

(d) Usable kitchens and bathrooms such that an individual in a wheelchair can maneuver about the space.

The Act provides that compliance with (1) the appropriate requirements of the American National Standard for Buildings and Facilities—Providing Accessibility and Usability for Physically Handicapped People (commonly cited as "ANSI A117.1"), or (2) with the laws of a State or unit of general local government, that has incorporated into such laws the accessibility requirements of the Act, shall be deemed to satisfy the accessibility requirements of the Act. (See section 804(f)(4) and (5)(A).) The Act also provides that the Secretary of the Department of Housing and Urban

Development shall provide technical assistance to States and units of local government and other persons to implement the accessibility requirements of the Act. (See section 804(f)(5)(C).)

Congress believed that the accessibility provisions of the Act would (1) facilitate the ability of persons with handicaps to enjoy full use of their homes without imposing unreasonable requirements on homebuilders, landlords and non-handicapped tenants; (2) be essential for equal access and to avoid future *de facto* exclusion of persons with handicaps; and (3) be easy to incorporate in housing design and construction. Congress predicted that compliance with these minimal accessibility design and construction standards would eliminate many of the barriers which discriminate against persons with disabilities in their attempts to obtain equal housing opportunities. (See H.R. Rep. No. 711, 100th Cong. 2d Sess. 27–28 (1988) ("House Report").)

The Fair Housing Act became effective on March 12, 1989. The Department implemented the Act by a final rule published January 23, 1989 (54 FR 3232), and which became effective on March 12, 1989. Section 100.205 of that rule incorporates the Act's design and construction requirements, including the requirement that multifamily dwellings for first occupancy after March 13, 1991 be designed and constructed in accordance with the Act's accessibility requirements. The final rule clarified which multifamily dwellings are subject to the Act's requirements. Section 100.205 provides, in paragraph (a), that covered multifamily dwellings shall be deemed to be designed and constructed for first occupancy on or before March 13, 1991, if they are occupied by that date, or if the last building permit or renewal thereof for the covered multifamily dwellings is issued by a State, County or local government on or before January 13, 1990. The Department selected the date of January 13, 1990 because it is fourteen months before March 13, 1991. Based on data contained in the Marshall Valuation Service, the Department found that fourteen months represented a reasonable median construction time for multifamily housing projects of all sizes. The Department chose the issuance of a building permit as the appropriate point in the building process because such permits are issued in writing by governmental authorities. The issuance of a building permit has the advantage of being a clear and objective standard. In addition, any project that actually achieves first occupancy before March 13, 1991 will be judged to have met this standard even if the last building permit or renewal thereof was issued after January 13, 1990 (55 FR 3251).

Section 110.205 of the final rule also incorporates the Act's provisions that compliance with the appropriate requirements of ANSI A117.1, or with State or local laws that have incorporated the Act's accessibility requirements, suffices to satisfy the accessibility requirements of the Act as codified in § 100.205. In the preamble to the final rule, the Department stated that it would provide more specific guidance on the Act's accessibility requirements in a notice of proposed guidelines that would provide a reasonable period for public comment on the guidelines.

III. Proposed Accessibility Guidelines

On August 2, 1989, the Department published in the **Federal Register** an advance notice of intention to develop and publish Fair Housing Accessibility Guidelines (54 FR 31856). The purpose of this document was to solicit early comment from the public concerning the content of the Accessibility Guidelines, and to outline the Department's procedures for their development. To the extent practicable, the Department considered all public comments submitted in response to the August 2, 1989 advance notice in its preparation of the proposed accessibility guidelines.

On June 15, 1990, the Department published proposed Fair Housing Accessibility guidelines (55 FR 24370). The proposed guidelines presented, and requested public comment on, three options for accessible design:

(1) Option one (Option One) provided guidelines developed by the Department with the assistance of the Southern Building Code Congress International (SBCCI), and incorporated suggestions received in response to the August 2, 1989 advance notice;

(2) Option two (Option Two) offered guidelines developed by the National Association of Home Builders (NAHB) and the National Coordinating Council on Spinal Cord Injuries (NCCSCI); and

(3) Option three (Option Three) offered "adaptable accommodations" guidelines, an approach that provides for identification of certain features in dwelling units that could be made accessible to people with handicaps on a case-by-case basis.

In the June 15, 1990 notice of proposed guidelines, the Department recognized that projects then being designed, in advance of publication of the final Guidelines may not become available for occupancy until after March 13, 1991. The Department advised that efforts to comply with the proposed guidelines, Option One, in the design of projects which would be completed before issuance of the final Guidelines, would be considered as evidence of compliance with the Act in connection with the Department's investigation of any complaints. Following publication of the June 15, 1990 notice, the Department received a number of inquiries concerning whether certain design and construction activities in connection with projects likely to be completed before issuance of final Guidelines would be considered by the Department to be in compliance with the Act.

In order to resolve these questions, the Department, on August 1, 1990, published in the **Federal Register** a supplementary notice to the proposed guidelines (55 FR 31191). In the supplementary notice, the Department advised that it only would consider efforts to comply with the proposed guidelines, Option One, as evidence of compliance with the Act. The Department stated that evidence of compliance with the Option One guidelines, under the circumstances described in the supplementary notice, would be a basis for determination that there is no reasonable cause to believe that a discriminatory housing practice under section 804(f)(3) has occurred, or is about to occur in connection with the investigation of complaints filed with the Department relating to covered multifamily dwellings. The circumstances described in the August 1, 1990 supplementary notice that the Department found would be in compliance with the Act, were limited to:

(1) Any covered multifamily dwellings which are designed in accordance with the Option One guidelines, and for which construction is completed before publication of the final Fair Housing Accessibility Guidelines; and

(2) Any covered multifamily dwellings which have been designed in accordance with the Option One guidelines, but for which construction is not completed by the date of publication of the final Guidelines provided:

(a) Construction begins before the final Guidelines are published; or

(b) A building permit is issued less than 60 days after the final Guidelines are published.

On September 7, 1990, the Department published for public comment a Preliminary Regulatory Impact Analysis on the Department's assessment of the economic impact of the Guidelines, as implemented by each of the three design options then under consideration (55 FR 37072–37129).

IV. Public Comments and Commenters

The proposed guidelines provided a 90-day period for the submission of comments by the public, ending September 13, 1990. The Department received 562 timely comments. In addition, a substantial number of comments were received by the Department after the September 13, 1990 deadline. Although those comments were not timely filed, they were reviewed to assure that any major issues raised had been adequately addressed in comments that were received by the deadline. Each of the timely comments was read, and a list of all significant issues raised by those comments was compiled. All these issues were considered in the development of the final Guidelines.

Of the 562 comments received, approximately 200 were from disability advocacy organizations, or units of State or local government concerned with disability issues. Sixty-eight (68) additional commenters identified themselves as members of the disability community; 61 commenters identified themselves as individuals who work with members of the disability community (e.g., vocational or physical therapists or counselors), or who have family members with disabilities; and 96 commenters were members of the building industry, including architects, developers, designers, design consultants, manufacturers of home building products, and rental managers. Approximately 292 commenters supported Option One without any recommendation for change An additional 155 commenters supported Option One, but recommended changes to certain Option One design standards. Twenty-six (26) commenters supported Option Two, and 10 commenters supported Option Three. The remaining commenters submitted questions, comments and recommendations for changes on certain design features of one or more of the three options, but expressed no preference for any particular option, or, alternatively, recommended final guidelines that combine features from two or all three of the options.

The Commenters

The commenters included several national, State and local organizations and agencies, private firms, and individuals that have been involved in the development of State and local accessibility codes. These commenters offered valuable information, including copies of State and local accessibility codes, on accesibility design standards. These commenters included: the Southern Building Code Congress International (SBCCI); the U.S. Architectural and Transportation Barriers Compliances Board (ATBCB); the Building Officials & Code Administrators International, Inc. (BOCA); the State of Washington Building Code Council; the Seattle Department of Construction and Land Use; the Barrier-free Subcode Committee of the New Jersey Uniform Construction Code Advisory Board; the Department of Community Planning, Housing and Department of Arlington County, Virginia; the City of Atlanta Department of Community Development, Bureau of Buildings; and members of the Department of Architecture, the State of University of New York at Buffalo. In addition to the foregoing organizations, a number of the commenters from the building industry submitted detailed comments on the proposed guidelines.

The commenters also included a number of disability organizations, several of which prepared detailed comments on the proposed guidelines. The comments of two disability organizations also were submitted as concurring comments by many individuals and other disability advocacy organizations. These two organizations are the Disability Rights Education & Defense Fund, and the Consortium for Citizens with Disabilities (CCD). The CCD represents the following organizations: the Association for Education and Rehabilitation of the Blind and Visually Impaired, Association for Retarded Citizens of the United States, International Association of Psychological Rehabilitation Facilities, National Alliance for the Mentally Ill, National Association of Protection and Advocacy Systems, National Association of Developmental Disabilities Councils, National Association of State Mental Health Program Directors, National Council of Community Mental Health Centers, National Head Injury Foundation, National Mental Health Association, United Cerebral Palsy Associations, Inc. Both the Disability Rights Education and Defense Fund and the CCD were strongly supportive of Option One.

A coalition of 20 organizations (Coalition), representing both the building industry and the disability community, also submitted detailed comments on the proposed guidelines. The members of the Coalition include: American Institute of Architects, American Paralysis Association, American Resort and Residential Development Association, American Society of Landscape Architects, Apartment and Office Building Association, Association of Home Appliance Manufacturers, Bridge Housing Corporation, Marriott Corporation, Mortgage Bankers Association, National Apartment Association, National Assisted Housing Management Association, National Association of Home Builders (NAHB), National Association of Realtors, National Association of Senior Living Industries, National Conference of States on Building Codes and Standards, National Coordinating Council on Spinal Cord Injury (NCCSCI), National Leased Housing Association, National Multi Housing Council, National Organization on Disability, and the Paralyzed Veterans of America.

The commenters also included U.S. Representatives Don Edwards, Barney Frank and Hamilton Fish, Jr., who advised that they were the primary sponsors of the Fair Housing Act, and who expressed their support of Option One.

Comments on the Three Options

In addition to specific issues and questions raised about the design standards recommended by the proposed guidelines, a number of commenters simply submitted comments on their overall opinion of one or more of the options. Following is a summary of the opinions typically expressed on each of the options.

Option One. The Option One guidelines drew a strong reaction from commenters. Supporters stated that the Option One guidelines provided a faithful and clearly stated interpretation of the Act's intent. Opponents of Option One stated that its design standards would increase housing costs significantly—for everyone. Several commenters who supported some features of Option One were concerned that adoption of Option One in its entirety would escalate housing costs. Another frequent criticism was that Option One's design guidelines were to complex and cumbersome.

Option Two. Supporters of Option Two state that this option presented a reasonable compromise between Option One and Option Three. Supporters stated that the Option Two guidelines provided more design flexibility than the Option One guidelines, and that this flexibility would allow builders to deliver the required accessibility features at a lower cost. Opponents of Option Two stated that this option allowed builders to circumvent the Act's intent with respect to several essential accessibility features.

Option Three. Supporters of Option Three stated that Option Three presented the best method of achieving the accessibility objectives of the Act, at the lowest possible cost. Supporters stated that Option Three would contain housing costs, because design adaptation only would be made to those units which actually would be occupied by a disabled resident, and the adaptation would be tailored to the specific accessibility needs of the individual tenant. Opponents of Option Three stated that this option, with its "add-on" approach to accessibilty, was contrary to the Act's intent, which, the commenter claimed, mandates accessible features at the time of construction.

Comments on the Costs of Implementation

In addition to the comments on the specific features of the three design options, one of the issues most widely commented upon was the cost of compliance with the Act's accessibility requirements, as implemented by the Guidelines. Several commenters disputed the Department's estimate of the cost of compliance, as presented in the Initial Regulatory Flexibility Analysis, published with the proposed guidelines on June 15, 1990 (55 FR 24384–24385), and in the Preliminary Regulatory Impact Analysis published on September 7, 1990 (55 FR 37072–37129). The Department's response to these comments is discussed in the Final Regulatory Impact Analysis, which is available for public inspection during regular business hours in the Office of the Rules Docket Clerk, room 10276, Department of Housing and Urban Development, 451 Seventh Street, SW., Washington, DC 20410–0500.

V. Discussion of Principal Public Comment Issues, and Section-by-Section Analysis of the Final Guidelines.

The following presents a discussion of the principal issues raised by the commenters, and the Department's response to each issue. This discussion includes a section-by-section analysis of the final Guidelines that addresses many of the specific concerns raised by the commenter, and highlights the differences between the proposed Option One guidelines and the final Guidelines. Comments related to issues outside the purview of the Guidelines, but related to the Act (e.g., enforcement procedures, statutory effective date), are discussed in the final section of the preamble under the preamble heading "Discussion of Comments on Related Fair Housing Issues".

1. Discussion of General Comments on the Guidelines

ANSI Standard

Comment. Many commenters expressed their support for the ANSI Standard as the basis for the Act's Guidelines, because ANSI is a familiar and accepted accessibility standard.

Response. In developing the proposed and final Guidelines, the Department was cognizant of the need for uniformity, and of the widespread application of the ANSI Standard. The original ANSI A117.1, adopted in 1961, formed the technical basis for the first accessibility standards adopted by the Federal Government, and most State governments. The 1980 edition of that standard was based on research funded by the Department, and became the basis for the Uniform Federal Accessibility Standards (UFAS), published in the Federal Register on August 4, 1984 (47 FR 33862). The 1980 edition also was generally accepted by the private sector, and was recommended for use in State and local building codes by the Council of American Building Officials. Additionally, Congress, in the Fair Housing Act, specifically referenced the ANSI Standard, thereby encouraging utilization of the ANSI Standard as guidance for compliance with the Act's accessibility requirements. Accordingly, in using the ANSI Standard as a reference point for the Fair Housing Act Accessibility Guidelines, the Department is issuing Guidelines based on existing and familiar design standards, and is promoting uniformity between Federal accessibility standards, and those commonly used in the private sector. However, the ANSI Standard and the final Guidelines have differing purposes and goals, and they are by no means identical. The purpose of the Guidelines is to describe minimum standards of compliance with the specific accessibility requirements of the Act.

Comment. Two commenters suggested that the Department adopt the ANSI Standard as the guidelines for the Fair Housing Act's accessibility requirements, and not issue new guidelines.

Response. The Department has incorporated in the Guidelines those technical provisions of the ANSI Standard that are consistent with the Act's accessibility requirements. However, with respect to certain of the Act's requirements, the applicable ANSI provisions impose more stringent design standards than required by the Act. (In the preamble to the proposed rule (55 FR 3251), and again in the preamble to the proposed guidelines (55 FR 24370), the Department advised that a dwelling unit that complies fully with the ANSI Standard goes beyond what is required by the Fair Housing Act.) The Department has developed Guidelines for those requirements of the Act where departures from ANSI were appropriate.

Comment. A few commenters questioned whether the Department would revise the Guidelines to correspond to ANSI's periodic update of its standard.

Response. The ANSI Standard is reviewed at five-year intervals. As the ANSI Standard is revised in the future, the Department intends to review each version, and, if appropriate to make revisions to the Guidelines in accordance with any revisions made to the ANSI Standard. Modifications of the Guidelines, whether or not reflective of changes to the ANSI Standard, will be subject to notice and prior public comment.

Comment. A few commenters requested that the Department republish the ANSI Standard in its entirety in the final Guidelines.

Response. The American National Standards Institute (ANSI) is a private, national organization, and is not connected with the Federal Government. The Department received permission from ANSI to print the ANSI Standard in its entirety, as the time of publication of the proposed guidelines (55 FR 24404–24487), specifically for the purpose of assisting readers of the proposed guidelines in developing timely comments. In the preamble to the proposed guidelines, the Department stated that since it was printing the entire ANSI Standard, as an appendix to the proposed guidelines, the final notice of the Accessibility Guidelines would not include the complete text of the ANSI Standard (55 FR 24371). Copies of the ANSI Standard may be purchased from the American National Standards Institute, 1430 Broadway, New York, NY 10018.

Comment. Another commenter requested that the Department confirm that any ANSI provision not cited in the final Guidelines is not necessary for compliance with the Act.

Response. In the proposed guidelines, the Department stated that: "Where the guidelines rely on sections of the ANSI Standard, the ANSI sections are cited. * * * For those guidelines that differ from the ANSI Standard, recommended specifications are provided" (55 FR 24385). The final Guidelines include this statement, and further state that the ANSI sections not cited in the Guidelines have been determined by the

Department not to be necessary for compliance with the Act's requirements.

Bias Toward Wheelchair Users

Comment. Two commenters stated that the proposed guidelines were biased toward wheelchair users, and that the Department has erroneously assumed that the elderly and the physically disabled have similar needs. The commenters stated that the physical problems suffered by the elderly often involve arthritic and back problems, which make bending and stooping difficult.

Response. The proposed guidelines, and the final Guidelines, reflect the accessibility requirements contained in the Fair Housing Act. These requirements largely are directed toward individuals with mobility impairments, particularly those who require mobility aids, such as wheelchairs, walkers, or crutches. In two of the Act's accessibility requirements, specific reference is made to wheelchair users. The emphasis of the law and the Guidelines on design and construction standards that are compatible with the needs of wheelchair users is realistic because the requirements for wheelchair access (e.g., wider doorways) are met more easily at the construction stage. (See House Report at 27.) Individuals with nonmobility impairments more easily can be accommodated by later nonstructural adaptations to dwelling units. The Fair Housing Act and the Fair Housing regulations assure the right of these individuals to make such later adaptations. (See section 804(f)(3)(A) of the Act and 24 CFR 100.203 of the regulations. See also discussion of adaptations made to units in this preamble under the heading "Costs of Adaptation" in the section entitled "Discussion of Comments on Related Fair Housing Issues".)

Compliance Problems Due to Lack of Accessibility Guidelines

Comment. A number of commenters from the building industry attributed difficulty in meeting the Act's March 13, 1991 compliance deadline, in part, to the lack of accessibility guidelines. The commenters complained about the time that it has taken the Department to publish proposed guidelines, and the additional time it has taken to publish final Guidelines.

Response. The Department acknowledges that the development and issuance of final Fair Housing Accessibility Guidelines has been a time-consuming process. However, the building industry has not been without guidance on compliance with the Act's accessibility requirements. The Fair Housing Act identifies the ANSI Standard as providing design standards that would achieve compliance with the Act's accessibility requirements. Additionally, in the preamble to both the proposed and final Fair Housing rule, and in the text of § 100.205, the Department provided examples of how certain of the Act's accessibility requirements may be met. (See 53 FR 45004–45005, 54 FR 3249–3252 (24 CFR Ch. I, Subch. A, App. I, at 583–586 (1990)), 24 CFR 100.205.)

The delay in publication of the final Guidelines has resulted, in part, because of the Department's pledge, at the time of publication of the final Fair Housing regulations, that the public would be provided an opportunity to comment on the Guidelines (54 FR 3251, 24 CFR Ch. I, Subch. A, at 585–586 (1990)). The delay in publication of the final Guidelines also is attributable in part to the Department's effort to develop Guidelines that would (1) ensure that persons with disabilities are afforded the degree of accessibility provided for in the Fair Housing Act, and (2) avoid the imposition of unreasonable requirements on builders.

Comment. Two commenters requested that interim accessibility guidelines should be adopted for projects "caught in the middle", i.e. those projects started before publication of the final Guidelines.

Response. The preamble to the June 15, 1990 proposed guidelines and the August 1, 1990 supplementary notice directly addressed this issue. In both documents, the Department recognized that projects being designed in advance of publication of the Guidelines may not become available for occupancy until after March 13, 1991. The Department advised that efforts to comply with the Option One guidelines, in the design of projects that would be completed before issuance of the final Guidelines, would be considered as evidence of compliance with the Act in connection with the Department's investigation of any complaints. The August 1, 1990 supplementary notice restated the Department's position on compliance with the Act's requirements prior to publication of the final Guidelines, and addressed what "evidence of compliance" will mean in a complaint situation.

Conflict with Historic Preservation Design Codes

Comment. Two commenters expressed concern about a possible conflict between the Act's accessibility requirements and local historic preservation codes (including compatible design requirements). The commenters stated that their particular concerns are: (1) The conversion of warehouse and commercial space to dwelling units; and (2) new housing construction on vacant lots in historically designated neighborhoods.

Response. Existing facilities that are converted to dwelling units are not subject to the Act's accessibility requirements. Additionally, alteration, rehabilitation or repair of covered multifamily dwellings are not subject to the Act's accessibility requirements. The Act's accessibility requirements only apply to new construction. With respect to new construction in neighborhoods subject to historic codes, the Department believes that the Act's accessibility requirements should not conflict with, or preclude building designs compatible with historic preservation codes.

Conflict with Local Accessibility Codes

Comment. Several commenters inquired about the appropriate course of action to follow when confronted with a conflict between the Act's accessibility requirements and local accessibility requirements.

Response. Section 100.205(i) of the Fair Housing regulations implements section 804(f)(8) of the Act, which provides that the Act's accessibility requirements do not supplant or replace State or local laws that impose higher accessibility standards (53 FR 45005). For accessibility standards, as for other code requirements, the governing principle to follow when Federal and State (or local) codes differ is that the more stringent requirement applies.

This principle is equally applicable when multifamily dwellings are subject to more than one Federal law requiring accessibility for persons with physical disabilities. For example, a multifamily dwelling may be subject both to the Fair Housing Amendments Act and to section 504 of the Rehabilitation Act of 1973. Section 504 requires that 5% of units in a covered multifamily dwelling be fully accessible—thus imposing a stricter accessibility standard for those units than would be imposed by the Fair Housing Act. However, compliance only with the section 504 requirements would not satisfy the requirements of the Fair Housing Act. The remaining units in the covered multifamily dwelling would be required to meet the specific accessibility requirements of the Fair Housing Act.

Comment. One commenter, the Seattle Department of Construction and Land Use, presented an example of how a local accessibility code that is more stringent with respect to some accessibility provisions may interact with the Act's accessibility requirements, where they are more stringent with respect to other provisions. The commenter pointed out that the State of Washington is very hilly, and that the State of Washington's accessibility code requires accessible buildings on sites that would be deemed impractical under the Option One guidelines. The commenter stated that the State of Washington's accessibility code may require installation of a ramp, and that the ramp may then create an accessible entrance for the ground floor, making it subject to the Act's accessibility requirements. The commenter asked that, since the project was not initially subject to the Act's requirements, whether the creation of an accessible ground floor in accordance with the State code provisions would require all units on the ground floor to be made accessible in accordance with the Fair Housing Act. (The State of Washington's accessibility code would require only a percentage of the units to be accessible.)

Response. The answer to the commenter's question is that a nonelevator building with an accessible entrance on an accessible route is required to have the ground floor units designed and constructed in compliance with the Act's accessibility requirements. This response is consistent with the principle that the stricter accessibility requirement applies.

Design Guidelines for Environmental Illness

Comment. Twenty-three (23) commenters advised the Department that many individuals are disabled because of severe allergic reactions to cerrtain chemicals used in construction, and in construction materials. These commenters requested that the Department develop guidelines for constructing or renovating housing that are sensitive to the problems of individuals who suffer from these allergic reactions (commonly referred to as environmental illnesses). These commenters further advised that, as of February 1988, the Social Security Administration lists as a disability "Environmental Illness" (P.O.M.S. Manual No. 24515.065).

Response. The Guidelines developed by the Department are limited to providing guidance relating to the specific accessibility requirements of the Fair Housing Act. As discussed above, under the preamble heading "Bias Toward Wheelchair Users," the Act's requirements primarily are directed to providing housing that is accessible to individuals with mobility impairments. There is no statutory authority for the Department to create the type of design and construction standards suggested by the commenters.

Design Guidelines for the Hearing and Visually-Impaired

Comment. Several commenters stated that the proposed guidelines failed to provide design features for people with hearing and visual impairments. These commenters stated that visual and auditory design features must be included in the final Guidelines.

Response. As noted in the response to the preceding comment, the Department is limited to providing Guidlines for the specific accessibility requirements of the Act. The Act does not require fully accessible individual dwelling units. For individual dwelling units, the Act requires the following: Doors sufficiently wide to allow passage by handicapped persons in wheelchairs; accessible route into and through the dwelling unit; light switches; electrical outlets, thermostats, and other environmental controls in accessible locations; reinforcements in bathroom walls to allow later installation of grab bars; and usable kitchens and bathrooms such that an individual in a wheelchair can maneuver about the space. To specify visual and auditory design features for individual dwelling units would be to recommend standards beyond those necessary for compliance with the Act. Such features were among those identified in Congressional statements discussing modifications that would be made by occupants.

The Act, however, requires public and common use portions of covered multifamily dwellings to be "readily accessible to and usable by handicapped persons." The more comprehensive accessibility requirement for public and common use areas of dwellings necessitates a more comprehensive accessibility standard for these areas. Accordingly, for public and common use areas, the final Guidelines recommend compliance with the appropriate provisions of the ANSI Standard. The ANSI Standard for public and common use areas specifies certain design features to accommodate people with hearing and visual impairments.

Guidelines as Minimum Requirements

Comment. A number of commenters requested that the Department categorize the final Guidelines as minimum requirements, and not as performance standards, because "recommended" guidelines are less effective in achieving the objectives of the Act. Another commenter noted that a safe harbor provision becomes a *de facto* minimum requirement, and that it should therefore be referred to as a minimum requirement.

Response. The Department has not categorized the final Guidelines as either performance standards or minimum requirements. The minimum accessibility requirements are contained in the Act. The Guidelines adopted by the Department provide one way in which a builder or developer may achieve compliance with the Act's accessibility requirements. There are other ways to achieve compliance with the Act's accessibility requirements, as for example, full compliance with ANSI A117.1. Given this fact, it would be inappropriate on the part of the Department to constrain designers by presenting the Fair Housing Accessibility Guidelines as minimum requirements. Builders and developers should be free to use any reasonable design that obtains a result consistent with the Act's requirements. Accordingly, the design specifications presented in the final Guidelines are appropriately referred to as "recommended guidelines".

It is true, however, that compliance with the Fair Housing Accessibility Guidelines will provide builders with a safe harbor. Evidence of compliance with the Fair Housing Accessibility Guidelines adopted by this notice shall be a basis for a determination that there is no reasonable cause to believe that a discriminatory housing practice under section 804(f)(3) has occurred or is about to occur in connection with the investigation of complaints filed with the Department relating to covered multifamily dwellings.

National Accessibility Code

Comment. Several commenters stated that there are too many accessibility codes—ANSI, UFAS, and State and local accessibility codes. These commenters requested that the Department work with the individual States to arrive at one national uniform set of accessibility guidelines.

Response. There is no statutory authority to establish one nationally uniform set of accessibility standards. The Department is in agreement with the commenters' basic theme that increased uniformity in accessibility standards is desirable. In furtherance of this objective, the Department has relied upon the ANSI Standard as the design basis for the Fair Housing Accessibility Guidelines. The Department notes that the ANSI Standard also serves as the design basis for the Uniform Federal

Accessibility Standards (UFAS), the Minimum Guidelines and Requirements for Accessible Design (MGRAD) issued by the U.S. Architectural and Transportation Barriers Compliance Board, and many State and local government accessibility codes.

One Set of Design Standards

Comment. A number of commenters objected to the fact that the proposed guidelines included more than one set of design standards. The commenters stated that the final Guidelines should present only one set of design standards so as not to weaken the Act's accessibility requirements.

Response. The inclusion of options for accessibility design in the proposed guidelines was both to encourage a maximum range of public comment, and to illustrate that there may be several ways to achieve compliance with the Act's accessibility requirements. Congress made clear that compliance with the Act's accessibility standards did not require adherence to a single set of design specifications. In section 804(f)(4) of the Act, the Congress stated that compliance with the appropriate requirements of the ANSI Standard suffices to satisfy the accessibility requirements of the Act. In House Report No. 711, the Congress further stated as follows:

> However this section (section 804(f)(4)) is not intended to require that designers follow this standard exclusively, for there may be other local or State standards with which compliance is required or there may be other creative methods of meeting these standards. (House Report at 27)

Similarly, the Department's Guidelines are not the exclusive standard for compliance with the Act's accessibility requirements. Since the Department's Guidelines are a safe harbor, and not minimum requirements, builders and developers may follow alternative standards that achieve compliance with the Act's accessibility requirements. This policy is consistent with the intent of Congress, which was to encourage creativity and flexibility in meeting the requirements of the Act.

Reliance on Preamble to Guidelines

Comment. One commenter asked whether the explanatory information in the background section of the final Guidelines may be relied upon, and deemed to have the same force and effect as the Guidelines themselves.

Response. The Fair Housing Accessibility Guidelines are—as the name indicates—only guidelines, not regulations or minimum requirements. The Guidelines consist of recommended design specifications for compliance with the specific accessibility requirements of the Fair Housing Act. The final Guidelines provide builders with a safe harbor that, short of specifying all of the provisions of the ANSI Standard, illustrate acceptable methods of compliance with the Act. To the extent that the preamble to the Guidelines provide clarification on certain provisions of the Guidelines, or illustrates additional acceptable methods of compliance with the Act's requirements, the preamble may be relied upon as additional guidance. As noted in the "Summary" portion of this document, the preamble to the Guidelines will be codified in the 1991 edition of the Code of Federal Regulations as Appendix III to the Fair Housing regulations (24 CFR Ch. I, Subch. A, App. III.).

"User Friendly" Guidelines

Comment. A number of commenters criticized the proposed guidelines for being too complicated, too ambiguous, and for requiring reference to a number of different sources. These commenters requested that the final Guidelines be clear, concise and "user friendly". One commenter requested that the final Guidelines use terms that conform to terms used by each of the three major building code organizations: the Building Officials and Code Administrators International, Inc. (BOCA); the International Conference of Building Officials (ICBO), and the Southern Building Code Congress International (SBCCI).

Response. The Department recognizes that the Accessibility Guidelines include several highly technical provisions. In drafting the final Guidelines, the Department has made every effort to explain these provisions as clearly as possible, to use technical and building terms consistent with the terms used by the major building code organizations, to define terms clearly, and to provide additional explanatory information on certain of the provisions of the Guidelines.

2. Section-by-Section Analysis of Final Guidelines

The following presents a section-by-section analysis of the final Guidelines. The text of the final Guidelines is organized into five sections. The first four sections of the Guidelines provide background and explanatory information on the Guidelines. Section 1, the Introduction, describes the purpose, scope and organization of the Guidelines. Section 2 defines relevant terms used. Section 3 reprints the text of 24 CFR 100.205, which implements the Fair Housing Act's accessibility requirements, and Section 4 describes the application of the Guidelines. Section 5, the final section, presents the design specifications recommended by the Department for meeting the Act's accessibility requirements, as codified in 24 CFR 100.205. Section 5 is subdivided into seven areas, to address each of the seven areas of accessible design required by the Act.

The following section-by-section analysis discusses the comments received on each of the sections of the proposed Option One Guidelines, and the Department's response to these comments. Where no discussion of comments is provided under a section heading, no comments were received on this section.

Section 1. Introduction

Section 1, the Introduction, describes the purpose, scope and organization of the Fair Housing Accessibility Guidelines. This section also clarifies that the accessibility guidelines apply only to the design and construction requirements of 24 CFR 100.205, and do not relieve persons participating in a federal or federally-assisted program or activity from other requirements, such as those required by section 504 of the Rehabilitation Act of 1973 (29 U.S.C. 794), or the Architectural Barriers Act of 1968 (42 U.S.C. 4151–4157). (The design provisions for those laws are found at 24 CFR Part 8 and 24 CFR Part 40, respectively.) Additionally, section 1 explains that only those sections of the ANSI Standard cited in the Guidelines are required for compliance with the accessibility requirements of the Fair Housing Act. Revisions to section 1 reflect the Department's response to the request of several commenters for further clarification on the purpose and scope of the Guidelines.

Section 2. Definitions

This section incorporates appropriate definitions from § 100.201 of the Department's Fair Housing regulations, and provides additional definitions for terms used in the Guidelines. A number of comments were received on the definitions. Clarifications were made to certain definitions, and additional terms were defined. New terms defined in the final Guidelines include: *adaptable, assistive device, ground floor, loft, multistory dwelling unit, single-story dwelling unit,* and *story.* The inclusion of new definitions reflects the comments received, and also reflects new terms introduced by changes to certain of the Option One design specifications. In several instances, the clarifications of existing definitions, or the new terms defined, were derived from definitions of certain terms used by one or more of the major building code organizations. Comments on specific definitions are discussed either below or in that portion of the preamble under the particular section heading of the Guidelines in which these terms appear.

Accessible

Comment. A number of commenters stated that the Department used the terms "accessible" and "adaptable" interchangeably, and requested clarification of the meaning of each. The commenters noted that, under several State building codes, these terms denote different standards for compliance. The commenters requested that if the Department intends these two terms to have the same meaning, this should be clearly stated in the final Guidelines, and, if the terms have different meanings, "adaptable" should also be defined.

Response. The Department's use of the terms "adaptable" and "accessible" in the preamble to the proposed guidelines generally reflected Congress' use of the terms in the text of the Act, and in the House and Senate conference reports. However, to respond to commenters' concerns about the distinctions between these terms, the Department has included a definition of "adaptable dwelling units" to clarify the meaning of this term, within the context of the Fair Housing Act. In the final Guidelines, "adaptable dwelling units", when used with respect to covered multifamily dwellings, means dwelling units that include features of adaptable design specified in 24 CFR 100.205(c)(2)–(3).

The Fair Housing Act refers to design features that include both the minimal "accessibility" features required to be built into the unit, and the "adaptable" feature of reinforcement for bathroom walls for the future installation of grab bars. Accordingly, under the Fair Housing Act, an "adaptable dwelling unit" is one that meets the minimal accessibility requirements specified in the Act (i.e., usable doors, an accessible route, accessible environmental controls, and usable kitchens and bathrooms) and the "adaptable" structural feature of reinforced bathroom walls for later installation of grab bars.

Assistive Device

Comment. Several commenters requested that we define the phrase "assistive device."

Response. "Assistive device" means an aid, tool, or instrument used by a person with disabilities to assist in activities of daily living. Examples of assistive devices include tongs, knob turners, and oven rack pusher/pullers. A definition for "assistive device" has been included in the final Guidelines.

Bathroom

In response to the concern of several commenters, the Department has revised the definition of "bathroom" in the final Guidelines to clarify that a bathroom includes a "compartmented" bathroom. A compartmented bathroom is one in which the bathroom fixtures are distributed among interconnected rooms. The fact that bathroom facilities may be located in interconnecting rooms does not exempt this type of bathroom from the Act's accessibility requirements. This clarification, and minor editorial changes, were the only revisions made to the definition of "bathroom". Other comments on this term were as follows:

Comment. Several commenters requested that the Department reconsider its definition of "bathroom", to include powder rooms, i.e., rooms with only a toilet and sink. These commenters stated that persons with disabilities should have access to all bathrooms in their homes, not only full bathrooms. One commenter believed that, unless bathroom was redefined to include single- or two-fixture facilities, some developers will remove a bathtub or shower from a proposed second full bathroom to avoid having to make the second bathroom accessible. The commenter suggested that bathroom be redefined to include any room containing at least two of the possible bathroom fixtures (toilet, sink, bathtub or shower).

Response. In defining "bathroom" to include a water closet (toilet), lavatory (sink), and bathtub or shower, the Department has followed standard dictionary usage, as well as Congressional intent. Congressional statements emphasized that the Act's accessibility requirements were expected to have a minimal effect on the size and design of dwelling units. In a full-size bathroom, this can be achieved. To specify space for wheelchair maneuvering in a powder room would, in most cases, require enlarging the room significantly. However, a powder room would be subject to the Act's accessibility requirements if the powder room is the only toilet facility on the accessible level of a covered multistory dwelling unit. Additionally, it should be noted that doors to powder rooms (regardless of the location of the powder room), like all doors within dwelling units, are required by the Act to be wide enough for wheelchair passage. Some powder rooms may, in fact, be usable by persons in wheelchairs.

Comment. One commenter requested that the final Guidelines provide that a three-quarters bathroom (water closet, lavatory and shower) would not be subject to the accessibility requirements—specifically, the requirement for grab bar reinforcement.

Response. The Fair Housing Act requires reinforcements in bathroom walls to allow for later installation of grab bars at toilet, bathtub or shower, if provided. Accordingly, the Fair Housing regulations specifically require reinforcement in bathroom walls to allow later installation of grab bars around the shower, where showers are provided. (See 24 CFR 100.205(c)(3)(iii).)

Building

Comment. One commenter suggested that the Department use the term "structure" in lieu of "building". The commenter stated that, in the building industry, "building" is defined by exterior walls and fire walls, and that an apartment structure of four units could be subdivided into two separate buildings of two units each by inexpensive construction of a firewall. The commenter suggested that the final definition of "building" include the following language: "For the purpose of the Act, firewall separation does not define buildings."

Response. The term "building" is the term used in the Fair Housing Act. The Department uses this term in the Guidelines to be consistent with the Act. With respect to the comment on firewall separation, the Department believes that, within the context of the Fair Housing Act, the more appropriate place for the language on firewall separation is in the definition of "covered multifamily dwellings". Since many building codes in fact define "building" by exterior walls and firewalls, a definition of "building" in the Fair Housing Accessibility Guidelines that explicitly excludes firewalls as a means of identifying a building would place the Guidelines in conflict with local building codes. Accordingly, to avoid this conflict, the Department has clarified the definition of "covered multifamily dwelling" (which is discussed below) to address the issue of firewall separation.

Covered Multifamily Dwellings

The Department has revised the definition of "covered multifamily dwellings" to clarify that dwelling units within a single structure separated by firewalls do not, for purposes of these Guidelines, constitute separate buildings.

A number of questions and comments were received on what should, or should not, be considered a covered multifamily dwelling. Several of these comments requested clarification concerning "ground floor dwelling units". These comments generally concluded with a request that the Department define "ground floor" and "ground floor unit". The Department has included a definition of "ground floor" in the final Guidelines. The Department believes that this definition is sufficiently clear to identify ground floor units, and that therefore a separate definition for "ground floor unit" is unnecessary. Specific questions concerning ground floor units are discussed below under the heading "Ground Floor". Comments on other covered multifamily dwellings are as follows:

Comment. (Garden apartments) One commenter requested that the Department clarify whether single family attached dwelling units with all living space on one level (i.e. garden units) fall within the definition of covered multifamily dwellings.

Response. The Fair Housing Act and its regulations clearly define "covered multifamily dwellings" as buildings consisting of four or more dwelling units, if such buildings have one or more elevators, and ground floor dwelling units in other buildings consisting of four or more dwelling units. Garden apartments located in an elevator building of four or more units are subject to the Act's requirements. If the garden apartment is on the ground floor of a nonelevator building consisting of four or more apartments, and if all living space is on one level, then the apartment is subject to the Act's requirements (unless the building is exempt on the basis of site impracticality).

Comment. (Townhouses) Several commenters requested clarification concerning whether townhouses are covered multifamily dwellings.

Response. In the preamble to the Fair Housing regulations, the Department addressed this issue. Using an example of a single structure consisting of five two-story townhouses, the Department stated that such a structure is *not* a covered multifamily dwelling if the building does not have an elevator, because the entire dwelling unit is not on the ground floor. Thus, the first floor of a two-story townhouse in the example is not a ground floor unit, because the entire unit is not on the ground floor. In contrast, a structure consisting of five single-story townhouses would be a covered multifamily dwelling. (See 54 FR 3244; 24 CFR Ch. I, Subch. A, App. I at 575–576 (1990).)

Comment. (Units with basements) One commenter asked whether a unit that contains a basement, which provides additional living space, would be viewed as a townhouse, and therefore exempt from the Act's accessibility requirements. The commenter stated that basements are generally designed with the top of the basement, including the basement entrance, above finished grade, and that basement space cannot be made accessible without installation of an elevator or a lengthy ramp.

Response. If the basement is part of the finished living space of a dwelling unit, then the dwelling unit will be treated as a multistory unit, and application of the Act's accessibility requirements will be determined as provided in the Guidelines for Requirement 4. If the basement space is unfinished, then it would not be considered part of the living space of the unit, and the basement would not be subject to the Act's requirements. Attic space would be treated in the same manner.

Dwelling Unit

"Dwelling unit" is defined as a single unit of residence for a household of one or more persons. The definition provides a list of examples of dwelling units in order to clarify the types of units that may be covered by the Fair Housing Act. The examples include condominiums and apartment units in apartment buildings. Several commenters submitted questions on condominiums, and one commenter requested clarification on whether vacation time-sharing units are subject to the Act's requirements. Their specific comments are as follows:

Comment. (Condominiums) A few commenters requested that condominiums be excluded from covered dwelling units because condominiums are comparable to single family homes. The commenter stated that condominiums do not compete in the rental market, but compete in the sale market with single family homes, which are exempt from the Act's requirements.

Response. The Fair Housing Act requires all covered multifamily dwellings for first occupancy after March 13, 1991 to be designed and constructed in accordance with the Act's accessibility requirements. The Act does not distinguish between dwelling units in covered multifamily dwellings that are for sale, and dwelling units that are for rent. Condominium units in covered multifamily dwellings must comply with the Act's accessibility requirements.

Comment. (Custom-designed condominium units) Two commenters stated that purchasers of condominium units often request their units to be custom designed. The commenters questioned whether custom-designed units must comply with the Act's accessibility requirements. Another commenter stated that the Department should exempt from compliance those condominium units which are pre-sold, but not yet constructed, and for which owners have expressly requested designs that are incompatible with the Act's accessibility requirements.

Response. The fact that a condominium unit is sold before the completion of construction does not exempt a developer from compliance with the Act's accessibility requirements. The Act imposes affirmative duties on builders and developers to design and construct covered multifamily dwellings for first occupancy after March 13, 1991 in accordance with the Act's accessibility requirements. These requirements are mandatory for covered multifamily dwellings for first occupancy after March 13, 1991, regardless of the ownership status of covered individual dwelling units. Thus, to the extent that the pre-sale *or* post-sale construction included features that are covered by the Act (such as framing for doors in pre-sale "shell" construction), they should be built accordingly.

Comment. (Vacation timeshare units) One commenter questioned whether vacation timeshare units were subject to the Act's requirements. The commenter stated that a timeshare unit may be owned by 2 to 51 individuals, each of whom owns, or has the right to use, the unit for a proportionate period of time equal to his or her ownership.

Response. Vacation timeshare units are subject to the Act's accessibility requirements, when the units are otherwise subject to the accessibility requirements. "Dwelling" is defined in 24 CFR 100.20 as "any building, structure, or portion thereof which is occupied as, or designed or intended for occupancy as, a residence by one or more families, and any vacant land which is offered for sale or lease for the construction or location thereon of any such building, structure or portion thereof". The preamble to the final Fair Housing rule states that the definition of "dwelling" is "broad enough to cover each of the types of dwellings enumerated in the proposed rule: mobile home parks, trailer courts, condominiums, cooperatives, *and time-*

sharing properties." (Emphasis added.) (See 54 FR 3238, 24 CFR Ch. I, Subch. A, App. I, at 567 (1990).) Accordingly, the fact of vacation timeshare ownership of units in a building does not affect whether the structure is subject to the Act's accessibility requirements.

Entrance

Comment. One commenter requested clarification on whether "entrance" refers to an entry door to a dwelling unit, or an entry door to the building.

Response. As used in the Guidelines, "entrance" refers to an exerior entry door. The definition of "entrance" has been revised in the final Guidelines to clarify this point, and the term "entry" is used instead of "entrance" when referring to the entry into a unit when it is interior to the building.

Ground Floor

As noted above, under the discussion of covered multifamily dwellings, several commenters requested clarification concerning "ground floor" and "ground floor dwelling unit". In response to these comments, the Department has included a definition for "ground floor" in the final Guidelines. The Department has incorporated the definition of "ground floor" found in the Fair Housing regulations (24 CFR 100.201), and has expanded this definition to address specific concerns related to implementation of the Guidelines. In the final Guidelines, "ground floor" is defined as follows:

"Ground floor" means a floor of a building with a building entrance on an accessible route. A building may have one or more ground floors. Where the first floor containing dwelling units in a building is above grade, all units on that floor must be served by a building entrance on an accessible route. This floor will be considered to be a ground floor.

Specific comments concerning ground floor units are as follows:

Comment. (Nonresidential ground floor units) Two commenters advised that, in many urban areas, buildings are constructed without an elevator and with no dwelling units on the ground floor. The ground floor contains either parking, retail shops, restaurants or offices. To bring these buildings into compliance with the Act, one of the commenters recommended that the Department adopt a proposal under consideration by the International Conference of Building Officials (ICBO). The commenter stated that the proposal provides that, in buildings with ground floors occupied by parking and other nonresidential uses, the lowest story containing residential units is considered the ground floor. Another commenter recommended that a building should be exempt from compliance with the Act's requirements if the ground floor is occupied by a non-residential use (including parking). The commenter stated that if an elevator is to be provided to serve the upper residential floors, then the elevator should also serve the ground floor, and access be provided to all the dwelling units.

Response. The Department believes that the definition of "ground floor unit" incorporated in the final Guidelines addresses the concerns of the commenters.

Comment. (More than one ground floor) One commenter requested guidance on treatment of nonelevator garden apartments (i.e., apartment buildings that generally are built on slopes and contain two stories in the front of the building and three stories in the back). The commenter stated that these buildings arguably may be said to have two ground floors. The commenter requested that the Department clarify that, if a building has more than one ground floor, the developer must make one ground floor accessible—but not both—and the developer may choose which floor to make accessible. Another commenter suggested that, in a garden-type apartment building, the floor served by the primary entrance, and which is located at the parking lot level, is the floor which must be made accessible.

Response. In the preamble to the final Fair Housing rule, the Department addressed the issue of buildings with more than one ground floor. (See 54 3244, 24 CFR Ch. I, Subch. A, App. I at 576 (1990).) The Department stated that if a covered building has more than one floor with a building entrance on an accessible route, then the units on each floor with an accessible building entrance must satisfy the Act's accessibility requirements. (See the discussion of townhouses in nonelevator buildings above.)

Handicap

Comment. Several commenters requested that the Department avoid use of the terms "handicap" and "handicapped persons", and replace them with the terms "disability" and "persons with disabilities".

Response. "Handicap" and "handicapped persons" are the terms used by the Fair Housing Act. These terms are used in Guidelines and regulations to be consistent with the statute.

Principle of Reasonableness and Cost

Comment. Four commenters noted that, in the preamble to the proposed guidelines, the Department indicated that the Fair Housing Accessibility Guidelines were limited by a "principle of reasonableness and cost". The commenters requested that the Department define this phrase.

Response. In the preamble to the proposed guidelines, the Department stated in relevant part as follows: "These guidelines are intended to provide a safe harbor for compliance with respect to those issues they cover. * * * Where the ANSI Standard is not applicable, the language of the statute itself is the safest guide. The degree of scoping, accessibility, and the like are of course limited by a principle of reasonableness and cost." (55 FR 24371)

In House Report No. 711, the accessibility requirements of the Fair Housing Act were referred to by the Congress as "modest" (House Report at 25), "minimal" and "basic features of adaptability" (House Report at 25). In developing the Fair Housing Accessibility Guidelines, the Department was attentive to the fact that Congress viewed the Act's accessibility requirements as reasonable, and that the Guidelines for these requirements should conform to this "reasonableness" principle—that is, that the Guidelines should provide the level of reasonable accessibility envisioned by Congress, while maintaining the affordability of new multifamily construction. The Department believes that the final Guidelines conform to this principle of reasonableness and cost.

Slope

Comment. One commenter, the Building Officials & Code Administrators International, Inc. (BOCA), requested clarification of the term, "slope". The commenter stated the definition indicates that slope is calculated based on the distance and elevation between two points. The commenter stated that this is adequate when there is a uniform and reasonably consistent change in elevation between point (i.e., one point is at the top of a hill and the other is at the bottom), but the definition does not adequately address land where a valley, gorge, or swale occurs between two points. The commenter stated that the definition also does not adequately address conditions where there is an abrupt change in the rate of slope between the points (i.e. a sharp drop off within a short distance, with the remaining distance being flat or sloped much more gradually).

Response. Slope is measured from ground level at the entrance to all arrival points within 50 feet, and is considered impractical only when it exceeds 10 percent between the entrance and all these points. Since multifamily dwellings typically have an arrival point fairly close to the building, a significant change such as a sharp drop would likely result in an impractical slope. Minor variations, such as a swale, if more than 5 percent, would be easily graded or ramped; a gorge would be bridged or filled, in any event, if it was on an entrance route.

Usable Door

Comment. One commenter stated that a clear definition of "usable door" is required.

Response. The Guidelines for Requirement 3 (usable doors) fully describe what is meant by "usable door" within the meaning of the Act.

Section 3. Fair Housing Act Design and Construction Requirements

This section reprints § 100.205 (Design and Construction Requirements) from the Department's final rule implementing the Fair Housing Act. A reprint of § 100.205 was included to provide easy reference to (1) the Act's accessibility requirements, as codified by § 100.205; and (2) the additional examples of methods of compliance with the Act's requirements that are presented in this regulation.

Section 4. Application of the Guidelines

This section states that the design specifications that comprise the final Guidelines apply to all "covered multifamily dwellings" as defined in Section 2 of the Guidelines. Section 4 also clarifies that the Guidelines, are "recommended" for designing dwellings that comply with the requirements of the Fair Housing Amendments Act of 1988.

Under the discussion of Section 4 in the proposed guidelines, the Department requested comment on the Act's application to dwelling units with design features such as a loft or sunken living room (55 FR 24377). A number of comments were received on this issue. Since the Act's application to units with such features is relevant within the context of an accessible route into and through a dwelling unit, the comments and the Department's response to these comments are discussed in section 5, under the subheading, "Guidelines for Requirement 4".

Section 5. Guidelines

The Guidelines contained in this Section 5 are organized to follow the sequence of requirements as they are presented in the Fair Housing Act and in the regulation implementing these requirements, 24 CFR 100.205. There are Guidelines for seven requirements: (1) An accessible entrance on an accessible route; (2) accessible and usable public common use areas; (3) doors usable by a person in a wheelchair; (4) accessible route into and through the covered dwelling unit; (5) light switches, electrical outlets and environmental controls in accessible locations; (6) bathroom walls reinforced for grab bars; and (7) usable kitchens and bathrooms.

For each of these seven requirements, the Department adopted the corresponding Option One guidelines, but changes were made to certain of the Option One design specifications. The following discussion describes the Guidelines for each of the seven requirements, and highlights the changes that have been made.

Guidelines for Requirement 1

The Guidelines for Requirement 1 present guidance on designing an accessible entrance on an accessible route, as required by § 100.205(a), and on determining when an accessible entrance is impractical because of terrain or unusual characteristics of the site.

The Department has adopted the Option One guidelines for Requirement 1, with substantial changes to the specifications for determining site impracticality. These changes, and the guidelines that remain unchanged for Requirement 1 are discussed below.

Site Impracticality Determinations. The Guidelines for Requirement 1 begin by presenting criteria for determining when terrain or unusual site characteristics would make an accessible entrance impractical. Section 100.205(a) recognizes that certain sites may have characteristics that make it impractical to provide an accessible route to a multifamily dwelling. This section states that all covered multifamily dwellings shall be designed and constructed to have at least one building entrance on an accessible route unless it is impractical to do so because of the terrain or unusual characteristics of the site.

Comments. The Department received many comments on the site impracticality specifications presented in the proposed guidelines (55 FR 24377–24378). The majority of the members of the disability community who commented on this issue supported the Option One guidelines, and recommended no change. However, other commenters, including a few disability organizations, members of the building industry, State and local government agencies involved in the development and enforcement of accessibility codes, and some of the major building code organizations, criticized one or more aspects of the Option One and Option Two guidelines for Requirement 1. Specific comments are noted below.

A few commenters suggested that the 10% slope criterion was too low, and easily will be met by a project site having a hilly terrain which could (and typically would) be made more level. These commenters recommended a higher slope criterion ranging anywhere from 12% to 30%. Other commenters stated that the slope criterion for the planned finished grade should not exceed 8.33%. The Congressional sponsors of the Act (U.S. Representatives Edwards, Fish, and Frank) stated that a limited exemption for slopes greater than 10% "was not contemplated by the Act"; but that they believed the Department has the discretion to develop such an exemption if it is "carefully crafted and narrowly tailored".

Several commenters stated that any evaluation of the undisturbed site should be done only on the percentage of land that is buildable. Several commenters stated that the final Guidelines should not require an evaluation of the undisturbed site between the planned entrance and the arrival points—that the only evaluation of the undisturbed site should be the initial threshold slope analysis.

There were a number of questions on arrival points, and requests that these points be more clearly defined. Several commenters presented specific examples of possible problems with the use of arrival points, as specified in the Option One guidelines. A few commenters stated that the individual building analysis should involve a measurement between the entrance and only one designated vehicular or pedestrian arrival point.

Other commenters stated that single buildings on a site should be subject to the same analysis as multiple buildings on a site.

A number of commenters criticized the Option One site impracticality analysis as being too cumbersome and confusing. A number of commenters objected to Option Two's requirement that covered multifamily dwellings with elevators must comply with the Act's accessibility requirements, regardless of site conditions or terrain.

Response. Following careful consideration of these comments, the Department has revised significantly the procedure for determining site impracticality, and its application to covered multifamily dwellings.

For covered multifamily dwellings with elevators, the final Guidelines would not exempt these dwellings from the Act's accessibility requirements. The final Guidelines provide that covered multifamily dwellings with elevators shall be designed and constructed to provide at least one accessible entrance on an accessible route regardless of terrain or unusual characteristics of the site. Every dwelling unit on a floor served by an elevator must be on an accessible route, and must be made accessible in accordance with the Act's requirements for covered dwelling units. The Department has excluded elevator buildings from any exemption from the Act's accessibility requirements because the Department believes that the type of site work that is performed in connection with the construction of a high rise elevator building generally results in a finished grade that would make the building accessible. The Department also notes that the majority of elevator buildings are designed with a primary building entrance and a passenger drop-off area which are easily made accessible to individuals with handicaps. Additionally, many elevator buildings have large, relatively level areas adjacent to the building entrances, which are normally provided for moving vans. These factors lead the Department to conclude that site impracticality considerations should not apply to multifamily elevator buildings.

For covered multifamily dwellings without elevators, the final Guidelines provide two alternative tests for determining site impracticality due to terrain. The first test is an individual building test which involves a two-step process: measurement of the slope of the undisturbed site between the planned entrance and all vehicular or pedestrian arrival points; and measurement of the slope of the planned finished grade between the entrance and all vehicular or pedestrian arrival points. The second test is a site analysis test which involves an analysis of the topography of the existing natural terrain.

A site with a single building, having a common entrance for all units, may be analyzed only under the first test—the individual building test.

All other sites, including a site with a single building having multiple entrances serving either individual dwelling units or clusters of dwelling units, may be analyzed either under the first test or the second test. For these sites for which either test is applicable, the final Guidelines provide that regardless of which test is utilized by a builder or developer, at least 20% of the total ground floor units in nonelevator buildings, on any site, must comply with the Act's accessibility requirements.

The distinctive features of the two tests for determining site impracticality due to terrain, for nonelevator multifamily dwellings, are as follows:

1. *The individual building test.*

a. This test is applicable to all sites.

b. This test eliminates the slope analysis of the entire undisturbed site that was applicable only to multiple building sites, and, concomitantly, the table that specifies the minimum percentage of adaptable units required for every multiple building site. The only analysis for site impracticality will be the individual building analysis. This analysis will be applied to each building regardless of the number of buildings on the site.

c. The individual building analysis has been modified to provide for measurement of the slopes between the planned entrance and all vehicular or pedestrian arrival points within 50 feet of the planned entrance. The analysis further provides that if there are no vehicular or pedestrian arrival points within 50 feet of the planned entrance, then measurement will be made of the slope between the planned entrance and the closest vehicular or pedestrian arrival point. Additionally, the final Guidelines clarify how to measure the slope between the planned entrance and an arrival point.

d. The individual building analysis retains the evaluation of both the undisturbed site and the planned finished grade. Buildings would be exempt only if the slopes of both the original undisturbed site and the planned finished grade exceed 10 percent (1) as measured between the planned entrance and all vehicular or pedestrian arrival points within 50 feet of the planned entrance; or (2) if there are no vehicular or pedestrian arrival points within that 50 foot area, as measured between the planned entrance and the closest vehicular or pedestrian arrival point.

2. *The site analysis test.*

a. This test is only applicable to sites with multiple buildings, or to sites with a single building with multiple entrances.

b. This test involves an analysis of the existing natural terrain (before grading) of the buildable area of the site by topographic survey with 2 foot contour intervals, with slope determination made between each successive contour interval. The accuracy of the slope analysis is to be certified by a professional licensed engineer, landscape architect, architect or surveyor.

c. This test provides that the minimum number of ground floor units to be made accessible on a site must equal the percentage of the total buildable area (excluding floodplains, wetlands, or other restricted use areas) of the undisturbed site that has an existing natural grade of less than 10% slope.

The Department believes that both tests for determining site impracticality due to terrain present enforceable criteria for determining when terrain makes accessibility, as required by the Act, impractical. The Department also believes that by offering a choice of tests, the Department is providing builders and developers with greater flexibility in selecting the approach that is most appropriate, or least burdensome, for their development project, while assuring that accessible units are provided on every site. As noted earlier in this preamble, this policy is consistent with the intent of Congress which was to encourage creativity and flexibility in meeting the Act's requirements, and thus minimize the impact of these requirements on housing affordability.

With respect to determining site impracticality due to unusual characteristics of the site, the test in the final Guidelines is essentially the same as that provided in the Option One guidelines. This test has been modified to limit measurement of the finished grade elevation to that between the entrance and all vehicular or pedestrian arrival points within 50 feet of the planned entrance.

Finally, the final Guidelines for Requirement 1 contemplate that the site tests recommended by the Guidelines will be performed, generally, on "normal" soil. The Department solicits additional public comment only on the issue of the feasibility of the site tests on areas that have difficult soil, such as areas where expansive clay or hard granite is prevalent.

Additional specific comments on the site impracticality determination are as follows:

Comment. One commenter stated that the site impracticality determination seems to suggest that only the most direct path from the pedestrian or vehicular arrival points will be used to evaluate the ability to create an accessible route of travel to the building. The commenter stated that it may be possible to use natural or finished contours of the site to provide an accessible route other than a straight-line route.

Response. To be enforceable, the Guidelines must specify where the line is drawn; otherwise it is not possible to specify what is "practical". Generally, developers provide relatively direct access from the entrance to the pedestrian and vehicular arrival points. If, in fact, the route as built was accessible, then the building would be expected to have an accessible entrance and otherwise comply with the Act.

Comment. Another commenter stated that the site impracticality determination does not take into account the many building types and unit arrangements. The commenter stated that some buildings have a common entrance with unit entrances off a common corridor, while others have individual, exterior entrances to the units. The commenter stated that if the Department is going to permit exemptions from the Act's requirements caused by terrain, the commenter did not understand why every entrance in a building containing individually-accessed apartments must comply with the Act's requirements, simply because they are in one building.

Response. The final Guidelines recognize (as did the proposed guidelines) the difference in building types. If there is a single entry point serving the entire building (or portions thereof), that entry point is considered the "entrance". If each unit has a separate exterior entrance, then each entrance is to be evaluated for the conditions at that entrance. Thus, a building with four entrances, each serving one of four units, might have only one accessible entrance, depending upon site conditions, or it might have any combination up to four.

Comment. Another commenter stated that the evaluation for unusual characteristics of the site only takes into account floodplains or high hazard coastal areas, and excludes other possible unique and unusual site characteristics.

Response. The provision for unusual characteristics of the site clearly provides that floodplains or high hazard coastal areas are only two examples of unusual site characteristics. The provision states that "unusual site characteristics" includes "sites subject to similar requirements of law or code."

Comment. A number of commenters expressed concern that the site impracticality determination of the Guidelines may conflict with local health, safety, environmental or zoning codes. A principal concern of one of the commenters was that the final Guidelines may require "massive grading" of a site in order to achieve compliance with the Act. The commenter was concerned that such grading may conflict with local laws directed at minimizing environmental damage, or with zoning codes that severely limit substantial fill activities at a site.

Response. The Department believes that the site impracticality determination adopted in these final Guidelines will not conflict with local safety, health, environmental or zoning codes. The final Guidelines provide, as did the proposed guidelines, that the site planning involves consideration of all State and local requirements to which a site is subject, such as "density constraints, tree-save or wetlands ordinances and other factors impacting development choices" (55 FR 24378), and explicitly accept the site plan that results from balancing these and other factors affecting the development. The Guidelines would not require, for example, that a site be graded in violation of a tree-save ordinance. If, however, access is required based on the final site plan, then installation of a ramp for access, rather than grading, could be necessary in some cases so as not to disturb the trees. Where access is required, the method of providing access, whether grading or a ramp, will be decided by the developer, based on local ordinances and codes, and on business or aesthetic factors. It should be noted that these nonmandatory Guidelines do not purport to preempt conflicting State or local laws. However, where a State or local law contradicts a specification in the Guidelines, a builder must seek other reasonable cost-effective means, consistent with local law, to assure the accessibility of his or her units. The accessibility requirements of the Fair Housing Act remain applicable, and State and local laws must be in accord with those requirements.

Additional Design Specifications for Requirement 1. In addition to the site impracticality determinations, the final Guidelines for Requirement 1 specify that an accessible entrance on an accessible route is practical when (1) there is an elevator connecting the parking area with any floor on which dwelling units are located, and (2) an elevated walkway is planned between a building entrance and a vehicular or pedestrian arrival point, and the planned walkway has a slope no greater than 10 percent. The Guidelines also provide that (i) an accessible entrance that complies with ANSI 4.14, and (2) an accessible route that complies with ANSI 4.3, meets with the accessibility requirements of § 100.205(a). Finally, the Guidelines provide that if the slope of the finished grade between covered multifamily dwellings and a public or common use facility exceeds 8.33%, or where other physical barriers, or legal restrictions, outside the control of the owner, prevent the installation of an accessible pedestrian route, an acceptable alternative is to provide access via a vehicular route. (These design specifications are unchanged from the proposed Option One guidelines for Requirement 1.)

Comment. Several comments were received on the additional design specifications for Requirement 1. The majority of commenters supported 8.33% as the slope criterion for the finished grade between covered multifamily dwellings and a public or common use facility. A few commenters stated that vehicular access was not an acceptable alternative to pedestrian access. Other commenters stated that the 10% slope criterion for the planned walkway was inconsistent with accessibility requirements that prohibit ramps from having a slope in excess of 8.33%.

Response. With respect to access via a vehicular route, the Department's expectation is that public and common use facilities generally will be on an accessible pedestrian route. The Department, however, recognizes that there may be situations in which an accessible pedestrian route simply is not practical, because of factors beyond the control of the owner. In those situations, vehicular access may be provided. With respect to the 10% slope criterion for planned elevated walkways, this is the criterion for determining whether it is practical to provide an accessible entrance. If the site is determined to be practical, then the slope of the walkway must be reduced to 8.33%.

Guidelines for Requirement 2

The Guidelines for Requirement 2 present design standards that will make public and common use areas readily accessible to and usable by handicapped persons, as required by § 100.205(c)(1).

The Department has adopted the Option One guidelines for Requirement 2, without change. The Guidelines for Requirement 2 identify components of public and common use areas that should be made accessible, reference the section or sections of the ANSI Standard which apply in each case, and describe the appropriate application of the design specifications. In some cases, the Guidelines for Requirement 2 describe variations from the basic ANSI provision that is referenced.

The basic components of public and common use areas covered by the Guidelines include, for example: accessible route(s); protruding objects; ground and floor surface treatments; parking and passenger loading zones;

curb ramps; ramps; stairs; elevator; platform lifts; drinking fountains and water coolers; toilet rooms and bathing facilities, including water closets, toilet rooms and stalls, urinals, lavatories and mirrors, bathtubs, shower stalls, and sinks; seating, tables or work surfaces; places of assembly; common-use spaces and facilities, including swimming pools, playgrounds, entrances, rental offices, lobbies, elevators, mailbox areas, lounges, halls and corridors and the like; and laundry rooms.

Specific comments on the Guidelines for Requirement 2 are as follows:

Comment. A number of comments were received on the various components listed in the Guidelines for Requirement 2, and the accessibility specifications for these components provided by both options One and Two. A few commenters, including the Granite State Independent Living Foundation, submitted detailed comments on the design standards for the listed components of public and common use areas, and, in many cases, recommended specifications different than those provided by either Option One or Option Two.

Response. Following careful consideration of the comments submitted on the design specifications of Requirement 2, the Department has decided not to adopt any of the commenters' proposals for change. The Department believes that application of the appropriate ANSI provisions to each of the basic components of public and common use areas, in the manner specified on the Option One chart, and with the limitations and modifications noted, remains the best approach to meeting the requirements of § 100.205(c)(1) for accessible and usable public and common use areas, both because Congress clearly intended that the ANSI Standard be used where appropriate, and because it is consistent with the Department's support for uniform standards to the greatest degree possible.

Comment. Other commenters requested that the ANSI provisions applicable to certain components in public and common use areas also should be applied to these components when they are part of individual dwelling units (for example, floor surface treatments, carpeting, and work surfaces).

Response. To require such application in individual dwelling units would exceed the requirements imposed by the Fair Housing Act. The Fair Housing Act does not require individual dwelling units to be fully accessible and usable by individuals with handicaps. For individual dwelling units, the Act limits its requirements to specific features of accessible design.

Comment. A number of commenters indicated confusion concerning when the ANSI standard was applicable to stairs.

Response. Stairs are subject to the ANSI Standard only when they are located along an accessible route not served by an elevator. (Accessibility between the levels served by the stairs or steps would, under such circumstances, be provided by some other means such as a ramp or lift located with the stairs or steps.) For example, a ground floor entry might have three steps up to an elevator lobby, with a ramp located besides the steps. The steps in this case should meet the ANSI specification since they will be used by people with particular disabilities for whom steps are more usable than ramps.

In nonelevator buildings, stairs serving levels above or below the ground floor are not required to meet the ANSI standard, unless they are a part of an accessible route providing access to public or common use areas located on these levels. For example, mailboxes serving a covered multifamily dwelling in a nonelevator building might be located down three steps from the ground floor level, with a ramp located beside the steps. The steps in this case would be required to meet the ANSI specifications.

Comment. Other commenters indicated confusion concerning when handrails are required. A few commenters stated that the installation of handrails limits access to lawn areas.

Response. Handrails are required only on ramps that are on routes required to be accessible. Handrails are not required on any on-grade walks with slopes no greater than 5%. Only on those walks that exceed 5% slope, and that are parts of the required accessible route, would handrails be required. Accordingly, walks from one building containing dwelling units to another, would not be affected even if slopes exceeded 5%, because the Guidelines do not require such walks as part of the accessible route. The Department believes that the benefits provided to persons with mobility-impairments by the installation of handrails on required assessible routes outweigh any limitations on access to lawn areas.

Comment. A number of proposals for revisions were submitted on the final Guidelines for parking and passenger loading zones.

Response. The Department has not adopted any of these proposals. The Department has retained the applicable provisions of the ANSI Standard for parking space. As noted previously in the preamble, the ANSI Standard is a familiar and widely accepted standard. The Department is reluctant to introduce a new or unfamiliar standard, or to specify parking specifications that exceed the minimal accessibility standards of the Act. However, if a local parking code requires greater accessibility features (e.g. wider aisles) with respect to parking and passenger loading zones, the appropriate provisions of the local code would prevail.

Comment. A number of commenters requested that the final Guidelines for parking specify minimum vertical clearance for garage parking. other commenters suggested that the Department adopt ANSI's vertical height requirement at passenger loading zones as the minimal vertical clearance for garage parking.

Response. No national accessibility standards, including UFAS, require particular vertical clearances in parking garages. The Department did not consider it appropriate to exceed commonly accepted standards by including a minimum vertical clearance in the Fair Housing Accessibility Guidelines, in view of the minimal accessibility requirements of the Fair Housing Act.

Comment. Two commenters stated that parking spaces for condominiums is problematic because the parking spaces are typically deeded in ownership to the unit owner at the time of purchase, and it becomes extremely difficult to arrange for the subsequent provision of accessible parking. one of the commenters recommended that the Guidelines specify that a condominium development have two percent accessible visitor parking, and that these visitor accessible spaces be reassigned to residents with disabilities as needed.

Response. Condominiums subject to the requirements of the Act must provide accessible spaces for two percent of covered units. One approach to the particular situation presented by the commenters would be for condominium documents to include a provision that accessible spaces may be reassigned to residents with disabilities, in exchange for nonaccessible spaces that were initially assigned to units that were later purchased by persons with disabilities.

Comment. Several commenters stated that Option One's requirement of "sufficient accessible facilities" of each type of recreational facility is too vague. The commenters preferred option Two's guidelines on recreational facilities, which provides that a minimum of 25% (or at least one of each type) of recreational facilities must be accessible.

Response. The Department decided to retain its more flexible approach to recreational facilities. The final Guidelines specify that where multiple recreational facilities are provided, accessibility is met under § 100.205(c)(1) if sufficient accessible facilities of each type are provided.

Comment. Several commenters suggested that all recreational facilities should be made accessible.

Response. To specify that all recreational facilities should be accessible would exceed the requirements of the Act. Congress stated that the Act did not require every feature and aspect of covered multifamily housing to be made accessible to individuals with handicaps. (See House Report at 26.)

Comment. Several commenters submitted detailed specifications on how various recreational facilities could be made accessible. These comments were submitted in response to the Department's request, in the proposed guidelines, for more specific guidance on making recreational facilities accessible to persons with handicaps (55 FR 24376). The Department specifically requested information about ways to provide access into pools.

Response. The Department appreciates all suggestions on recommended specifications for recreational facilities, and, in particular, for swimming pools. For the present, the Department has decided not to change the specifications for recreational facilities, including swimming pools, as provided by the Option One guidelines, since there are no generally accepted standards covering such facilities. Thus, access to the pool area of a swimming facility is expected, but not specialized features for access into the pool (e.g., hoists, or ramps into the water).

Comment. Several commenters criticized the chart in the Option One guidelines, stating that it was confusing and difficult to follow.

Response. The chart is adapted from ANSI's Table 2 pertaining to basic components for accessible sites, facilities and buildings. The ANSI chart is familiar to persons in the building industry. Accordingly, the Option One chart (and now part of the final Guidelines), which is a more limited version of ANSI's Table 2, is not a novel approach.

Guidelines for Requirement 3

The Guidelines for Requirement 3 present design standards for providing doors that will be sufficiently wide to allow passage into and within all premises by handicapped persons in wheelchairs (usable doors) as required by § 100.20(c)(2).

The Department has adopted the Option One guidelines for Requirement 3 with minor editorial changes. No changes were made to the design specifications for "usable doors".

The Guidelines provide separate guidance for (1) doors that are part of an accessible route in the public and common use areas of multifamily dwellings, including entry doors to individual dwelling units; and (2) doors within individual dwelling units.

(1) For public and common use areas and entry doors to dwelling units, doors that comply with ANSI 4.13 would meet the requirements of § 100.205(c)(2).

(2) For doors within individual dwelling units, the Department has retained, in the final Guidelines, the design specification that a door with a clear opening of at least 32 inches nominal width when the door is open 90 degrees, as measured between the face of the door and the stop, would meet the requirements of § 100.205(c)(2).

Specific comments on the design specifications presented in the Guidelines for Requirement 3 are as follows:

Minimum Clear Opening

Comment. The issue of minimum clear opening for doors was one of the most widely commented-upon design features of the guidelines. The majority of commenters representing the disability community supported the Option One specification of a minimum clear opening of 32 inches. A few commenters advocated a wider clear opening. U.S. Representatives Edwards, Frank, and Fish expressed their support for the Option One specification on minimum clearance which is consistent with the ANSI Standard.

Commenters from the building industry were almost unanimous in their opposition to a minimum clear opening of 32 inches. Several builders noted that a 32-inch clear opening requires use of 36-inch doors. These commenters stated that a standard 2′10″ door (34″) provides only a 31¾ inch clear opening. The commenters therefore recommended amending the Guidelines to permit a "nominal" 32 inch clear space, allowing the use of a 2′10″ door, which provides a 31¾ inch clear opening. Other commenters stated that, generally, door width should provide a 32-inch clear opening, but that this width can be reduced if sufficient maneuvering space is provided at the door. These commenters supported Option Two's approach, which provided for clear width to be determined by the clear floor space available for maneuvering on both sides of the door, with the minimum width set at 29¼ inches. (See Option 2 chart and accompanying text at 55 FR 24382.)

Response. The Department considered the recommendations for both wider clear openings, and more narrow clear openings, and decided to maintain the design specification proposed in the Option One guidelines (a clear opening of at least 32 inches nominal width). The clear opening of at least 32 inches nominal width has been the accepted standard for accessibility since the issuance of the original ANSI Standard in 1961. While the Department recognizes that it may be possible to maneuver most wheelchairs through a doorway with a slightly more narrow opening, such doors do not permit ready access on the constant-use basis that is the reality of daily living within a home environment. The Department also recognizes that wider doorways may ensure easier passage for wheelchair users. However, by assuring that the minimum 36-inch hallway and 32-inch clear openings are provided, the Department believes that its recommended opening for doors should accommodate most people with disabilities. In the preamble to the proposed guidelines, the Department stated that the clear width provided by a standard 34-inch door would be acceptable under the Guidelines.

Maneuvering Space at Doors

Comment. Several commenters requested that the final Guidelines incorporate minimum maneuvering clearances at doors, as provided by the ANSI Standard. These commenters stated that maneuvering space on the latch side of the door is as important a feature as mininum door width. Other commenters stated that the maneuvering space was necessary to ensure safe egress in cases of emergency.

Response. The Department has carefully considered these comments, and has declined to adopt this approach. The Department believes that, by adhering to the standard 32-inch clear opening, it is possible to forego other accessibility requirements related to doors (e.g. door closing forces, maneuvering clearances, and hardware) without compromising the Congressional directive requiring doors to be "sufficiently wide to allow passage by handicapped persons in wheelchairs." However, as the Department noted in the preamble to the proposed guidelines, approaches to, and maneuvering spaces at, the exterior side of the entrance door to an individual dwelling unit would be considered part of the public spaces, and therefore would be subject to the appropriate ANSI provisions. (See 55 FR 24380.)

Doors in a Series

Comment. A few commenters expressed concern that the Guidelines did not provide design specification for an entrance that consists of a series of more than one door. The commenters were concerned that, without adequate guidance, a disabled resident or tenant could be trapped between doors.

Response. Doors in a series are not typically part of an individual dwelling unit. Doors in a series generally are used in the entries to buildings, and are therefore part of public spaces. Section 4.13 of the ANSI Standard, which is applicable to doors in public and common use areas, provides design specifications for doors in a series. However, where doors in a series *are* provided as part of a dwelling unit, the Department notes that the requirements of an accessible route into and through the dwelling unit would apply.

Door Hardware

Comment. A few commenters requested that lever hardware be required on doors throughout dwelling units, not only at the entry door to the dwelling unit.

Response. For doors within individual dwelling units, the Fair Housing Act only requires that the doors be sufficiently wide to allow passage by handicapped persons in wheelchairs. Lever hardware is required for entry doors to the building and to individual dwelling units because these doors are part of the public and common use areas, and are, therefore, subject to the ANSI provisions for public and common use areas, which specify lever hardware. Installing lever hardware on doors is the type of adaptation that individual residents can make easily. The ANSI standard also recognizes this point. Under the ANSI Standard, only the entry door into an accessible dwelling unit is required to comply with the requirements for door hardware. (See ANSI section 4.13.9.)

Multiple Usable Entrances

Comment. Several commenters noted that the Guidelines do not provide more than one accessible entrance/exit, and that without a second means of egress, wheelchair users may find themselves in danger in an emergency situation.

Response. As stated previously, the Department is limited to providing Guidelines that are consistent with the accessibility requirements of the Act. The Act requires "an accessible entrance", rather than requiring all entrances to be accessible. However, the requirements for usable doors and an accessible route to exterior spaces such as balconies and decks does respond to this concern.

Guidelines for Requirement 4

The Guidelines for Requirement 4 present design specifications for providing an accessible route into and through the covered dwelling unit, as required by § 100.205(c)(3)(i).

The Department has adopted the Option One guidelines for Requirement 4 with the following changes:

First, the Department has eliminated the specification for maneuvering space if a person in a wheelchair must make a T-turn.

Second, the Department has eliminated the specification for a minimum clear headroom of 80 inches.

Third, and most significantly, the Department has revised the design specifications for "changes in level" within a dwelling unit to include separate design specifications for: (a) single-story dwelling units, including single-story dwelling units with design features such as a loft or a sunken living room; and (b) multistory dwelling units in buildings with elevators.

Fourth, the Department has revised the specifications for changes in level at exterior patios, decks or balconies in certain circumstances, to minimize water damage. For the same reason, the final Guidelines also include separate specifications for changes in level at the primary entry doors of dwelling units in certain circumstances.

Specific comments on the Guidelines for Requirement 4, and the rationale for the changes made, are discussed below.

Minimum Clear Corridor Width

A few commenters from the disability community advocated a minimum clear corridor width of 48 inches. However, the majority of commenters on this issue had no objection to the minimum clear corridor width of 36 inches. The 36-inch minimum clear corridor width, which has been retained, is consistent with the ANSI Standard.

T-turn Maneuvering Space

Comment. Several commenters stated that this design specification was unclear in two respects. First, they stated that it was unclear when it is necessary for a designer to provide space for a T-turn. The commenters stated that it was difficult to envision circumstances where a wheelchair could be pulled into a position traveling forward and then not be capable of backing out. Second, the commenters stated that the two descriptions of the T-turn provided by the Department were contradictory. The commenters stated that the preamble to the proposed guidelines provided one description of the T-turn (55 FR 24380), while Figure 2 of the guideline 4 (55 FR 24392), presented a different description of the T-turn.

Response. The Department has decided to delete the reference to the T-turn dimensions in the Guidelines for Requirement 4. The Guidelines adequately address the accessible route into and through the dwelling unit by the minimum corridor width and door width specifications, given typical apartment layouts. Should a designer find that a unique layout in a particular unit made a T-turn necessary for a wheelchair user, the specifications provided in the ANSI Standard sections referenced for public and common use areas could be used.

Minimum Clear Headroom

Comment. Several commenters from the building industry objected to the specification for a minimum clear headroom of 80 inches. The commenters stated that standard doors provide a height range from 75 to 79 inches, and that an 80-inch specification would considerably increase the cost of each door installed.

Response. The specification for minimum clear headroom of 80 inches was included in the proposed guidelines because it is a specification included in the major accessibility codes. This design specification was not expected to conflict with typical door heights. However, since the principal purpose of the requirement is to restrict obstructions such as overhanging signs in public walkways, the Department has determined that this specification is not needed for accessible routes within individual dwellings units, and has therefore deleted this standard from the final Guidelines for such routes. (The requirement, however, still applies in public and common use spaces.)

Changes in Level within a Dwelling Unit

In the preamble to the proposed guidelines, the Department advised that the Act appears to require that dwelling units with design features such as lofts or with more than one floor in elevator buildings be equipped with internal elevators, chair lifts, or other means of access to the upper levels (55 FR 24377). The Department stated that, although it is not clear that Congress intended this result, the Department's preliminary assessment was that the statute appears to offer little flexibility in this regard. The Department noted that several commenters, including the NAHB and the NCCSCI, suggested that units with more than one floor in elevator buildings should be required to comply with the Act's accessibility requirements only on the floor that is served by the building elevator. (This was the position taken by Option Two.) The Department solicited comments on this issue, and received a number of responses opposing the Department's interpretation.

Comment. The commenters opposing the Department's interpretation stated that the Department's interpretation would place an undue burden on developers and needlessly increase housing costs for everyone; defeat the purpose of having multilevel units, which is to provide additional space at a lower cost; eliminate multilevel designs which may be desirable to disabled residents (e.g., to provide living accommodations for live-in attendants); and "create a backlash" against the Accessibility Guidelines.

Response. Following careful consideration of these comments, and a reexamination of the Act and its legislative history, the Department has determined that its previous interpretation ot the Act's application to units with changes in level (whether lofts, or additional stories in elevator buildings), which would have required installation of chair lifts or internal elevators in such units, runs contrary to the purpose and intent of the Fair Housing Act, which is to place "modest accessibility requirements on covered multifamily dwellings." (See House Report at 25.)

In House Report No. 711, the Congress repeatedly emphasized that the accessibility requirements of the Fair Housing Act were minimal basic requirements of accessibility.

> These modest requirements will be incorporated into the design of new buildings, resulting in features which do not look unusual and will not add significant additional costs. The bill does not require the installation of elevators or 'hospital-like' features, or the renovation of existing units." (House Report at 18)

> Accessibility requirements can vary across a wide range. A standard of total accessibility would require that every entrance, doorway, bathroom, parking space, and portion of buildings and grounds be accessible. Many designers and builders have interpreted the term 'accessible' to mean this type of standard. The committee does not intend to impose such a standard. Rather, the committee intends to use a standard of adaptable' design, a standard developed in recent years by the building industry and by advocates for handicapped individuals to provide usable housing for handicapped persons without necessarily being significantly different from conventional housing." (House Report at 26)

The Department has determined that a requirement that units with lofts or multiple stories in elevator buildings be equipped with internal elevators, chair lifts, or other means of access to lofts or upper stories would make accessible housing under the Fair Housing Act significantly different from conventional housing, and would be inconsistent with the Act's "modest accessibility requirements". (See House Report at 25.)

The Department also has determined that a requirement that dwelling units with design features, such as sunken living rooms, must provide some means of access, such as ramps or lifts, as submitted in the proposed guidelines (55 FR 24380) is inconsistent with the Act's modest accessibility requirements. Sunken living rooms are not an uncommon design feature. To require a ramp or other means of access to such an area, at the time of construction, would reduce, perhaps significantly, the space provided by the area. The reduced space might interfere with the use and enjoyment of this area by a resident who is not disabled, or whose disability does not require access by means of a ramp or lift. The Department believes that had it maintained in the final Guidelines the access specifications for design features, such as sunken living rooms, as set forth in the proposed guidelines, the final Guidelines would have interfered unduly with a developer's choice of design, or would have eliminated a popular design choice. Accordingly, the final Guidelines provide that access is not required to design features, such as a sunken living room, provided that the area does not have the effect of interrupting the accessible route through the remainder of the unit.

The Department believes that the installation of a ramp or deck in order to make a sunken room accessible is the type of later adaptation that easily can be made by a tenant. The Department, however, does require that design features, such as a split-level entry, which is critical to providing an accessible route into and through the unit, must provide a ramp or other means of access to the accessible route.

In order to comply with the Act's requirement of an accessible route into and through covered dwelling units, the Department has revised the Guidelines for Requirement 4 to provide separate technical guidance for two types of dwelling units: (1) Single-story dwelling units, including single-story dwelling units with design features such as a loft or a sunken living room; and (2) multistory dwelling units in elevator buildings. (Definitions for "single-story dwelling unit," "loft," "multistory dwelling unit" and "story" have been included in section 2 of the final Guidelines.)

"Single-story dwelling unit" is defined as a dwelling unit with all finished living space located on one floor.

"Loft" is defined as an intermediate level between the floor and ceiling of any story, located within a room or rooms of a dwelling.

"Multistory dwelling unit" is defined as a dwelling unit with finished living space located on one floor and the floor or floors immediately above or below it.

"Story" is defined as that portion of a dwelling unit between the upper surface of any floor and the upper surface of the floor next above, or the roof of the unit. Within the context of dwelling units, the terms "story" and "floor" are synonymous.

For single-story dwelling units and multistory dwelling units, the Guidelines for Requirement 4 are as follows:

(1) For single-story dwelling units, the design specifications for changes in level, are the same as proposed in the Option One guidelines. Changes in level within the dwelling unit with heights between ¼ inch and ½ inch are beveled with a slope no greater than 1:2. Changes in level greater than ½ inch (excluding changes in level resulting from design features such as a loft or a sunken living room) must be ramped or must provide other means of access. For example, split-level entries must be ramped or use other means of providing and accessible route into and through the dwelling unit.

For single-story dwelling units with design features such as a loft or a raised or sunken functional area, such as a sunken living room, the Guidelines specify that: (a) access to lofts is not required, provided that all spaces other than the loft are on an accessible route; and (b) design features such as a sunken living room are also exempt from the access specifications, provided that the sunken area does not interrupt the accessible route through the remainder of the unit.

(2) In multistory dwelling units in buildings with elevators, access to the additional story, or stories, is not required, provided that the story of the unit that is served by the building elevator (a) is the primary entry to the unit; (b) complies with Requirements 2 through 7 with respect to the rooms located on the entry/accessible level; and (3) contains a bathroom or powder room which complies with Requirement

7. (As previously noted, multistory units in buildings without elevators are not considered ground floor units, and therefore are exempt.)

The Department believes that the foregoing revisions to the Guidelines for Requirement 4 will provide individuals with handicaps the degree of accessibility intended by the Fair Housing Act, without increasing significantly the cost of multifamily housing.

Comment. Two commenters suggested that the same adaptability requirement that is applied to bathrooms should be applied to dwelling units with more than one story, or with lofts, i.e. that stairs, and the wall along the stairs, contain the appropriate reinforcement to provide for later installation of a wheelchair lift by a disabled resident, if so desired.

Response. The only blocking or wall reinforcement required by the Fair Housing Act is the reinforcement in bathroom walls for later installation of grab bars. As noted earlier in this preamble, the Fair Housing Act does not actually require that features in covered units be "adaptable", except for bathrooms. The adaptable feature is the reinforcement in bathroom walls which allows later installation of grab bars. Accordingly, the Department believes that a specification for reinforcement of the walls along stairs would exceed the Act's requirements, because the necessary reinforcement could vary by type of lift chosen, and more appropriately would be specified and installed as part of the installation of the lift.

Thresholds at Exterior Doors/ Thresholds to Balconies or Decks

Comment. A number of commenters from the building industry objected to the provision of the Option One guidelines that specified that an exterior deck, balcony, patio, or similar surface may be no more than ¾ inch below the adjacent threshold. Several commenters stated that, in many situations, this height is unworkable for balconies and decks because of waterproofing and safety concerns. This was a particular concern among commenters from the South Florida building industry, who stated that the ¾" height is ineffective for upper floors of high rise buildings in a coastal environment and invites water control problems. Others noted that the suggestion of a wooden decking insert, or the specification of a ¾ inch maximum change in level, in general, might conflict with fire codes.

Response. In response to these concerns, and mindful that Congress did not intend the accessibility requirements of the Act to override the need to protect the physical integrity of multifamily housing, the Department has included two additional provisions for changes in level at thresholds leading to certain exterior surfaces, as a protective measure against possible water damage. The final Guidelines provide that exterior deck, patio or balcony surfaces should be no more than ½ inch below the floor level of the interior of the dwelling unit, unless they are constructed of impervious material such as concrete, brick or flagstone. In such case, the surface should be no more than 4 inches below the floor level of the interior dwelling unit, unless the local code requires a lower drop. Additionally, the final Guidelines provide that at the primary entry doors to dwelling units with direct exterior access, outside landing surfaces constructed of impervious materials such as concrete, brick, or flagstone should be no more than ½ inch below the floor level of the interior of the dwelling unit. The Guidelines further provide that the finished surface of this area, located immediately outside the entry door, may be sloped for drainage, but the sloping may be no more than ⅛ inch per foot.

In response to commenters' concern that the Guidelines for an accessible route to balconies and decks may conflict with certain building codes that require higher thresholds, or balconies or decks lower than the ¾ inch specified by the Guidelines, the Department notes that the Guidelines are "recommended" design specifications, not building code "requirements". Accordingly, the Guidelines cannot preempt State or local law. However, the builder confronted with local requirements that thwart the particular means of providing accessibility suggested by the Guidelines is under a duty to take reasonable steps to provide for accessibility by other means consistent with local law constraints and considerations of cost-effectiveness, in order to provide dwelling units that meet the specific accessibility requirements of the Fair Housing Act.

Guidelines for Requirement 5

The Guidelines for Requirement 5 present design specifications for providing dwelling units that contain light switches, electrical outlets, thermostats, and other environmental controls in accessible locations, as required by § 100.205(c)(2)(ii).

The Department has adopted the Option One guidelines for Requirement 5 with minor technical changes. The final Guidelines clarify that to be in an accessible location within the meaning of the Act, the maximum height for an environmental control, for which reach is over an obstruction, is 44 inches for forward approach (as was proposed in the Option One guidelines), or 46 inches for side approach, provided that the obstruction is no more than 24 inches in depth. The inclusion of this additional specification for side approach is consistent with the comparable provisions in the ANSI standard.

Specific comments on the Guidelines for Requirement 5 are as follows:

Comments. Three comments stated that lowered thermostats could pose a safety hazard for children. However, the majority of comments requested clarification as to what is meant by "other environmental controls". Several commenters from the disability community requested that circuit breakers be categorized as environmental controls. Other commenters asked whether light and fan switches on range hoods fall within the category of light switches and environmental controls.

Response. With regard to concerns about lowered thermostats, the Act specifically identifies "thermostats" as one of the controls that must be in accessible locations, and the mounting heights specified in the Guidelines are necessary for an accessible location. The only other environmental controls covered by the Guidelines for Requirement 5 would be heating, air conditioning or ventilation controls (e.g., ceiling fan controls). The Department interprets the Act's requirement of placing environmental controls in accessible locations as referring to those environmental controls that are used by residents or tenants on a daily or regular basis. Circuit breakers do not fall into this category, and therefore are not subject to accessible location specifications. Light and fan switches on range hoods are appliance controls and therefore are not covered by the Act.

Comment. Other commenters asked whether light switches and electrical outlets in the inside corners of kitchen counter areas, and floor outlets are permissible.

Response. Light switches and electrical outlets in the inside corners of kitchen counters, and floor outlets, are permissible, if they are not the only light switches and electrical outlets provided for the area.

Comment. Another commenter pointed out that some electrical outlets that are installed specifically to serve individual appliances, such as refrigerators or microwave ovens, cannot realistically be mounted in an accessible location.

Response. Electrical outlets installed to serve individual appliances, such as refrigerators or built-in microwave ovens, may be mounted in non-accessible locations. These are not the type of electrical outlets which a disabled resident or tenant would need access to on a regular or frequent basis.

Comment. One commenter stated that Figure 3 in the proposed guidelines (Figure 2 in the final Guidelines) specifies a reach requirement more stringent than the ANSI Standard.

Response. The ANSI Standard presents reach ranges for both forward and side approaches for two situations: (1) unobstructed; and (2) over an obstruction. The proposed guidelines specified only the heights for forward reach, because those heights also are usable in side approach. The diagram in Figure 2 (formerly Figure 3) showing forward reach is identical to that of Figure 5 in the ANSI Standard. The ANSI Standard also includes a figure (Figure 6) for side reach that permits higher placement. The reach range for forward approach was the only one referenced in the proposed guidelines for use in the dwelling unit, because it was considered simpler and easier to use a single specification that would work in all situations. The reach range for forward approach has been retained in the final Guidelines for situations where there is no built-in obstruction in order to assure usability when the unit was furnished. However, the final Guidelines have added the specification for side reach over a built-in obstruction that is consistent with the ANSI requirement, and that permits placement two inches higher than forward reach.

Guidelines for Requirement 6

The Guidelines for Requirement 6 present design standards for installation of reinforcement in bathroom walls to allow for later installation of grab bars around the toilet, tub, shower stall and shower seat where such facilities are provided, as required by § 100.205(c)(3)(iii).

The Department adopted the Option One guidelines for Requirement 6 with two modifications. First, the final Guidelines provide that a powder room is subject to the requirement for reinforced walls for grab bars when the powder room is the only toilet facility located on the accessible level of a covered multistory dwelling unit. Second, the final Guidelines further clarify that reinforced bathroom walls will meet the accessibility requirement of § 100.205(c)(3)(iii), if reinforced areas are provided at least at those points where grab bars will be mounted.

Specific comments on this guideline were as follows:

Comment. A number of commenters requested that the Department specify the dimensions for grab bar reinforcement, and suggested that grab bar reinforcing material run horizontally throughout the entire length of the space given for grab bars, as provided by the ANSI Standard. These commenters stated that if this type of reinforcement was required, residents could locate more easily the studs for future grab bar installation, and have flexibility in the placement of grab bars for optimal use, and safety in bathrooms. One commenter noted that many grab bars are of such a length that they require an intermediate fastener, but the proposed standard does not permit intermediate fastening. Two commenters recommended that the final Guidelines follow ANSI and UFAS Standards for requirements for mounting grab bars. One commenter recommended the installation of panels of plywood behind bathroom walls because this would provide greater flexibility in the installation of grab bars.

Response. The illustrations of grab bar wall reinforcement accompanying the Guidelines for Requirement 6 are intended only to show where reinforcement for grab bars is needed. The illustrations are not intended to prescribe how the reinforcing should be provided, or that the bathtub or shower is required to be surrounded by three walls of reinforcement. The additional language added to the Guidelines is to clarify that the Act's accessibility requirement for grab bar reinforcement is met if reinforced areas are provided, at a minimum, at those points where grab bars will be mounted. The Department recognizes that reinforcing for grab bars may be accomplished in a variety of ways, such as by providing plywood panels in the areas illustrated, or by installing vertical reinforcement (in the form of double studs, for example) at the points noted on the figures accompanying the Guidelines.

Comment. Several commenters stated that the final Guidelines should incorporate Option Two's specification of reinforcement for shower seats when shower stalls are provided.

Response. The Fair Housing Act only requires reinforcement for later installation of grab bars. The Act does not cover reinforcement for shower seats; rather, it mentions shower seats (if provided) as an area where grab bar reinforcement would be needed. However, as will be discussed more fully in the following section concerning the Guidelines for Requirement 7 (Usable Bathrooms), reinforcement for shower seats would provide adaptability to increase usability of shower stalls, and is a design option available to builders and developers in designing "usable" bathrooms.

Comment. One commenter recommended that the final Guidelines incorporate Option Two's specification that prefabricated tub/shower enclosures would have to be fabricated with reinforcement for grab bar enclosures.

Response. The Department did not incorporate this specification in the final Guidelines. The Department believes that it is inappropriate to specify product design. A builder should have the flexibility to choose how reinforcement for grab bars will be provided.

Comment. Two commenters stated that half-baths should also contain grab-bar reinforcements.

Response. Half-baths are not considered "bathrooms", as this term is commonly used, and, therefore are not subject to the bathroom wall reinforcement requirement, unless a half-bath facility is the only restroom facility on the accessible level of a covered multistory dwelling unit.

Comment. One commenter requested that the final Guidelines incorporate language clearly to specify that the builder's responsibility is limited solely to wall reinforcement, and later installation is the responsibility of the resident or tenant.

Response. It is unnecessary to incorporate the suggested language in the final Guidelines. The Guidelines for Requirement 6 are solely directed to reinforcement. No guidelines are provided for the actual installation of grab bars. Accordingly, there should be no confusion on this issue.

Guidelines for Requirement 7

The Guidelines for Requirement 7 present design specifications for providing usable kitchens and bathrooms such that an individual in a wheelchair can maneuver about the space, as required by § 100.205(c)(3)(iv).

For usable kitchens, the Department adopted the Option One guidelines with one change. The Department has eliminated the specification that controls for ranges and cooktops be placed so that reaching across burners is not required.

For usable bathrooms, the final Guidelines provide two alternative sets of design specifications. The Fair Housing Act requires that an accessible or "usable" bathroom is one which provides sufficient space for an individual in a wheelchair to maneuver about. The two sets of specifications provide different approaches as to how compliance with this maneuvering space requirement may be accomplished. The first set of specifications also includes size dimensions for shower stalls, but only when a shower stall is the only bathing facility provided in a dwelling unit. Additionally, either set of specifications is applicable to powder rooms, when a powder room is the only restroom facility on the accessible level of a covered multistory dwelling unit.

With the exception of the inclusion of shower stall dimensions, the first set of "usable bathroom" specifications remain the same as the Option One guidelines for usable bathrooms. The second set of "usable bathroom" specifications provide somewhat greater accessibility than the first set, but would be applicable only to one bathroom in a dwelling unit that has two or more bathrooms. The second set of specifications include clear space specifications for bathrooms with in-swinging doors and for bathrooms with outswinging doors. This second set of specifications also provides that toilets must be located in a manner that permits a grab bar to be installed on one side of the fixture, and provides specifications on the installation of vanities and lavatories.

To meet the Act's requirements for usable bathrooms, the final Guidelines provide that (1) in a dwelling unit with a single bathroom, either set of specifications may be used; and (2) in a dwelling unit with more than one bathroom, all bathrooms in the unit must comply with the first set of specifications, or, alternatively, at least one bathroom must comply with the second set of specifications, and all other bathrooms must be on an accessible route, and must have a usable entry door in accordance with the guidelines for Requirements 3 and 4. However, in multistory dwelling units, only those bathrooms on the accessible level are subject to the Act's requirements for usable bathrooms. Where a powder room is the only restroom facility provided on the accessible level of a multistory dwelling unit, the powder room must meet either the first set of specifications or the second set of specifications. All bathrooms and powder rooms that are subject to Requirement 7, must have reinforcements for grab bars as provided in the Guideline for Requirement 6.

In developing the final Guidelines for the usable bathroom requirement, the Department recognized that the Option One guidelines for usable bathrooms presented the minimum specifications necessary to meet the Act's requirements. Accordingly, the Department believes that it is appropriate to provide a second set of specifications which provide somewhat different accessibility accommodations than the Option One guidelines. The Department believes that by offering two sets of specifications for usable bathrooms, the Department is providing builders and developers with more development choices in designing dwelling units that contain more than one bathroom; and it is providing individuals and families with more housing options. Builders and developers may design all bathrooms to meet the minimal specifications of the first set of specifications, or they may design only one bathroom to meet the somewhat greater accessibility specifications of the second set. Regardless of which set of usable bathroom specifications is selected by a builder or developer, all doors to bathrooms and powder rooms must meet the minimum door width specifications of Requirement 3.

The following presents a discussion of the specific comments received on usable kitchens and usable bathrooms.

Controls for Ranges and Cooktops

Comment. A few commenters stated that the Department lacks authority under the Fair Housing Act to impose design standards on appliances. The commenter stated that standards that specify certain design features for appliances in individual dwelling units exceed the scope of the Department's statutory authority. Other commenters objected to front range controls as a safety hazard for children. Commenters from the disability community were strongly supportive of this design specification.

Response. With respect to usable kitchens, the Act solely requires that kitchens have sufficient space such that an individual in a wheelchair can maneuver about. Accordingly, a specification that controls for ranges and cooktops be placed so that they can be used without reaching across burners is not consistent with the Act's requirement for usable kitchens.

In the proposed guidelines, the Option One guidelines for usable kitchens specified that controls should be located so as to be usable without reaching across burners. As the preamble to the proposed guidelines noted, many standard styles of ranges and cooktops meeting this specification (other than those with front controls) are available on the market. However, in reviewing the entire rulemaking history on the design and constructions requirements, the Department has concluded that the requirements of the Fair Housing Act did not cover any appliance controls. Accordingly, this specification was not included in the final Guidelines.

Maneuvering Space, Adjustable Cabinetry, Fixtures and Plumbing

Comment. A number of commenters from the disability community stated that it was important that the Guidelines for both kitchens and bathrooms specify a five-foot turning radius; adjustable cabinetry, fixtures and plumbing; and fixture controls that comply with the appropriate provisions of the ANSI Standard.

Response. The legislative history of the Fair Housing Act clearly indicates that Congress did not envision usable kitchens and bathrooms to be designed in accordance with the specifications suggested by the commenters. In House Report No. 711, the Congress stated as follows:

> The fourth feature is that kitchens and bathrooms be usable such that an individual in a wheelchair can maneuver about the space. This provision is carefully worded to provide a living environment usable by all. Design of standard sized kitchens and bathrooms can be done in such a way as to assure usability by persons with disabilities without necessarily increasing the size of space. The Committee intends that such space be usable by handicapped persons, but this does not necessarily require that a turning radius be provided in every situation. This provision also does not require that fixtures, cabinetry or plumbing be of such design as to be adjustable. (House Report at 27)

Accordingly, the Department is unable to adopt any of the proposals suggested by the commenters. The Act's requirement for usable kitchens and bathrooms only specifies maneuverability for wheelchair users, and this maneuverability does not require the specification advocated by the commenters. (See previous discussion of this issue in the preamble to the proposed Fair Housing regulations at 53 FR 45005.)

Comment. Two commenters requested clarification concerning what is meant by "sufficient maneuvering space". One of the commenters recommended that this term be defined to include "such space as shall permit a person in a wheelchair to use the features and appliances of a room without having to leave the room to obtain an approach to an appliance, work surface, or cabinet".

Response. The Guidelines for Requirement 7 (usable kitchens and bathrooms) describe what constitutes sufficient maneuvering space in the kitchen and the bathroom. Additionally, the preamble to the proposed guidelines explicitly states that sufficient maneuvering space for kitchens does not require a wheelchair turning radius (55 FR 24381). As noted in response to the preceding comment, a wheelchair turning radius also is not required for either usable kitchens or usable bathrooms. The Guidelines for usable bathroom state that sufficient maneuvering space is provided within the bathroom for a person using a wheelchair or other assistive device to enter and close the door, use the fixtures, reopen the door and exit. This specification was not changed in the final Guidelines.

Kitchen Work Surfaces

Comment. One commenter stated that "Element 12" in the chart accompanying the Guidelines for Requirement 2 (public and common use areas) seems to require a portion of the kitchen counters to be accessible since they are work surfaces. This commenter stated that if this interpretation is correct then it should be made clear in the Guidelines.

Response. The commenter's interpretation is not correct. The chart accompanying the Guidelines for Requirement 2 is only applicable to the public and common use areas, not to individual dwelling units.

Showers

Comments. Several commenters requested that the final Guidelines provide dimensions on the appropriate width and height of showers and shower doors. Another commenter asked whether showers were required to comply with dimensions specified by the ANSI Standard.

Response. The final Guidelines for usable bathrooms (the first set of specifications) specify size dimensions for shower stalls in only one situation—when the shower stall is the only bathing facility provided in a covered dwelling unit. The Department believes that, where a shower stall is the only bathing facility provided, size specification for the shower stall is consistent with the Act's requirement for usable bathrooms. However, if a shower stall is not the only bathing facility provided in the dwelling unit, then the only specification for showers, appropriate under the Act, concerns reinforced walls in showers. (The titles under the illustrations (figures) related to showers in the final Guidelines for Requirement 6 have been revised to make it clear that the figures are specifying only the different areas required to be reinforced in showers of different sizes, not the required sizes of the shower stalls.)

In-swinging Bathroom Doors

Comment. One commenter stated that in-swinging bathroom doors generally are problematic, unless the bathroom is unusually large. The commenter noted that an in-swinging door makes it extremely difficult to enter and exit. The commenter recommended that in-swinging doors be prohibited unless there is sufficient internal bathroom space, exclusive of the swing of the door, which allows either a five foot turning radius or two mutually exclusive 30" x 48" wheelchair spaces. Another commenter stated that in-swinging bathroom doors create a serious obstacle for the wheelchair user.

Response. The Department declines to prohibit in-swinging bathroom doors. Adjusting an in-swinging door to swing out is the type of later adaptation that can be made fairly easily by a resident or tenant. Once a minimum door width is provided, a tenant who finds a bathroom not readily usable can have the door rehung as an outswinging door. Note, however, that the second set of guidelines for usable bathrooms specifies clear space for bathrooms with in-swinging doors.

Bathroom Design Illustrations

Comment. A number of commenters from the disability community stated that two of the six bathroom drawings in the preamble to the proposed guidelines (numbers 4 and 6 at 55 FR 24374–24375) did not allow for a parallel approach to the tub. These commenters requested that these drawings be removed from the final Guidelines. Other commenters stated that the Department's bathroom design illustrations at 55 FR 24374–24375 are not consistent with the Figure 8 bathroom design illustrations at 55 FR 24401.

Response. While a parallel approach to the tub would provide somewhat greater accessibility, the Department believes that to indicate, through the Guidelines, that a parallel approach to the tub is necessary to meet the Act's requirements, exceeds the Fair Housing Act's minimal design expectations for bathrooms. Accordingly, the first set of specifications for usable bathrooms does not specify a parallel approach to the tub. However, the second set of specifications provides for a clear access aisle adjacent to the tub that would permit a parallel approach to the tub. Either method would meet the Act's requirements. With respect to the comments on the bathroom design illustrations, these illustrations have been revised to make the clear floor space requirements more readily understood. The illustrations are adapted from ANSI A117.1.

Number of Accessible Bathrooms

Comment. A number of comments were received on how many bathrooms in a dwelling unit should be subject to the Act's "usable" bathroom requirement. Many commenters recommended that all full bathrooms be made accessible. Other commenters recommended that only one full bathroom be required to be made accessible. A few commenters recommended that half-baths/powder rooms also be subject to the Act's requirement.

Response. In House Report No. 711, the Congress distinguished between "total accessibility" and the level of accessibility required by the Fair Housing Act. The report referred to standards requiring every aspect or portion of buildings to be totally accessible, and pointed out that this was not the level of accessibility required by the Act. The final Guidelines for bathrooms are consistent with the Act's usable bathroom requirement, and provide the level of accessibility intended by Congress. As discussed previously in this preamble, the final Guidelines for usable bathrooms provide two sets of specifications. The second set of specifications provides somewhat greater accessibility than the first set of specifications. In view of this fact, the final Guidelines provide that in a dwelling unit with a single bathroom, the bathroom may be designed in accordance with either set of specifications—the first set or the second set. However, in a dwelling unit with more than one bathroom, all bathrooms in the unit must comply with the first set of specifications, or a minimum of one bathroom must comply with the second set of specifications, and all other bathrooms must be on an accessible route, and must have a usable entry door in accordance with the guidelines for Requirements 3 and 4. Additionally, the final Guidelines provide that a powder room must comply with the Act's usable bathroom requirements when the powder room is the only restroom facility provided on the accessible level of a multistory dwelling unit.

3. Discussion of Comments on Related Fair Housing Issues Compliance Deadline

Section 100.205 of the Fair Housing regulations incorporates the Act's design and construction requirements, including the requirement that multifamily dwellings for first occupancy after March 13, 1991 be designed and constructed in accordance with the Act's accessibility requirements. Section 100.205(a) provides that covered multifamily dwellings shall be deemed to be designed and constructed for first occupancy on or before March 13, 1991 (and, therefore, exempt from Act's accessibility requirements), if they are occupied by that date, or if the last building permit or renewal thereof for the covered multifamily dwellings is issued by a State, County, or local government on or before January 13, 1990.

Comment. The Department received a number of comments on the March 13, 1991 compliance deadline, and on methods of achieving compliance. Many commenters objected to the March 13, 1991 compliance deadline on the basis that this deadline was unreasonable. Several commenters from the building industry stated that, in many cases, design plans for buildings now under construction were submitted over two years ago, and it would be very expensive to make changes to buildings near completion. Other commenters stated that it is unreasonable to impose additional requirements on a substantially completed project that unexpectedly has been delayed for occupancy beyond the March 13, 1991 effective date.

Response. Section 804(f)(3)(C) of the Fair Housing Act states that the design and construction standards will be applied to covered multifamily dwelling units for first occupancy after the date that is 30 months after the date of enactment of the Fair Housing Amendments Act. The Fair Housing Act was enacted on September 13, 1988. The date that is 30 months from that date is March 13, 1991. Accordingly, the inclusion of a March 13, 1991 compliance date in § 100.205 is a codification of the Act's compliance deadline. The Department has no authority to change that date. Only Congress may extend the March 13, 1991 deadline.

The Department, however, has been attentive to the concerns of the building industry, and has addressed these concerns, to the extent that it could, in prior published documents. In the preamble to the final Fair Housing rule, the Department addressed the objections of the building industry to the Department's reliance on "actual occupancy" as the sole basis for determining "first occupancy". (See 54 FR 3251; 24 CFR Ch. I, Subch. A, App. I at 585 (1990).) Commenters to the proposed Fair Housing rule, like the commenters to the proposed guidelines, argued that coverage of the design and construction requirements must be determinable at the beginning of planning and development, and that projects delayed by unplanned and uncontrollable events (labor strikes, Acts of God, etc.) should not be subject to the Act.

In order to accommodate the "legitimate concerns on the part of the building industry" the Department expanded § 100.205 of the final rule to provide that covered multifamily dwellings would be deemed to be for first occupancy if the last building permit or renewal thereof was issued on or before January 13, 1990. A date of fourteen months before the March 13, 1991 deadline was selected because the median construction time for multifamily housing projects of all sizes was determined to be fourteen months, based on data provided by the Marshall Valuation Service.

More recently, the Department addressed similar concerns of the building industry in the preamble to the proposed accessibility guidelines. In the June 15, 1990 publication, the Department recognized that projects designed in advance of the publication of the final Guidelines, may not become available for first occupancy until after March 13, 1991. To provide some guidance, the Department stated in the June 15, 1990 notice that compliance with the Option One guidelines would be considered as evidence of compliance with the Act, in projects designed before the issuance of the final Guidelines. The Department restated its position on this issue in a supplementary notice published in the Federal Register on August 1, 1990 (55 FR 31131). The specific circumstances under which the Department would consider compliance with the Option One guidelines as compliance with the accessibility requirements of the Act were more fully addressed in the August 1, 1990 notice.

Comment. A number of commenters requested extending the date of issuance of the last building permit from January 13, 1990 to some other date, such as June 15, 1990, the date of publication of the proposed guidelines; August 1, 1990, the date of publication of the supplementary notice; or today's date, the date publication of the final Guidelines.

Response. The date of January 13, 1990 was not randomly selected by the Department. This date was selected because it was fourteen months before the compliance deadline of March 13, 1991. As previously noted in this preamble, fourteen months was found to represent a reasonable median construction time for multifamily housing projects of all sizes, based on data contained in the Marshall Valuation Service. Builders have been on notice since January 23, 1989—the publication date of the final Fair Housing rule, that undertaking construction after January 13, 1990 without adequate attention to accessibility considerations would be at the builder's risk.

Comment. One commenter requested that the applicable building permit be the "primary" building permit for a particular building. Other commenters inquired about the status of building permits that are issued in stages, or about small modifications to building plans during construction which necessitate a reissued building permit.

Response. Following publication of the proposed Fair Housing regulation, and the many comments received at that time from the building industry expressing concern that "actual occupancy" was the only standard for determining "first occupancy", the Department gave careful consideration to the steps and stages involved in the building process. On the basis of this study, the Department determined that an appropriate standard to determine "first occupancy", other than actual occupancy, would be issuance of the last building permit on or before January 13, 1990. This additional standard was added to the final Fair Housing Act regulation. The Department believes that, aside from actual occupancy, issuance of the last building permit remains the appropriate standard.

Compliance Determinations bv State and Local Jurisdictions

Comment. A few commenters questioned the role of States and units of local government in determining compliance with the Act's accessibility requirements. The commenters noted that (1) § 100.205(g) encourages States and units of general local government to include, in their existing procedures for the review and approval of newly constructed covered multifamily dwellings, determinations as to whether the design and construction of such dwellings are consistent with the Act's accessibility requirements; but (2) § 100.205(h) provides that determinations of compliance or noncompliance by a State or a unit of general local government are not conclusive in enforcement proceedings under the Fair Housing Act. These commenters stated that, unless determinations of compliance or noncompliance by a State or unit of general local government are deemed to be conclusive, local jurisdictions will be discouraged from performing compliance reviews because they will not be able to provide a building permit applicant with a sense of finality that proposed design plans are in compliance with the Act.

Response. Sections 100.205 (g) and (h) of the Fair Housing regulations implement sections 804(f)(5) (B) and (C), and section 804(f)(6)(b) of the Fair Housing Act. The language of §§ 100.205 (g) and (h) is taken directly from these statutory provisions. The Congress, not the Department, made the decision that determinations of compliance or noncompliance with the Act by a State or unit of general local government shall not be conclusive in enforcement proceedings. The Department, however, agrees with the position taken in the statute. The Department believes that it would be inappropriate to accord particular "weight" to determinations made by a wide variety of State and local government agencies involving a new civil rights law, without first having the benefit of some experience reviewing the accuracy of the determinations made by State and local authorities under the Fair Housing Act.

Comment. Two commenters stated that local building departments, especially those in smaller urban areas and in rural areas, do not have the manpower or expert knowledge to assure a proper determination of compliance, particularly in "close call" situations. The commenters recommended that liability for any infractions exclude local building departments unless the Department is willing to provide qualified personnel from its local field office to attend staff reviews of every building permit request.

Response. The Department is reluctant to assume that State and local jurisdictions, by performing compliance reviews, will subject themselves to liability under the Fair Housing Act, particularly in light of section 804(f)(5)(C) of the Act, which encourages States and localities to make reviews for compliance with the statute; and the implicit recognition, under Section 804(f)(6)(B), that these reviews may not be correct.

Comment. With reference to a violation of the Act's requirements, several commenters questioned how violations of the Act would be determined, and what the penalty would be for a violation. The commenters asked whether a builder would be cited, and fined, for each violation per building, or for each violation per unit.

Response. If it is determined that a violation of the Act has occurred, a Federal District Court or an administrative law judge (ALJ) has the authority to award actual damages, including damages for humiliation and emotional distress; punitive damages (in court) or civil penalties (in ALJ proceedings); injunctive relief; attorneys fees (except to the United States); and any other equitable relief that may be considered appropriate. Whether a violation will be found for each violation per building, for each violation per unit, or on any other basis, is properly left to the courts and the ALJs.

Enforcement Mechanisms

In the proposed guidelines, the Department solicited public comment on effective enforcement mechanisms (55 FR 24383–24384). Specifically, the Department requested comment on the effectiveness of: annual surveys to assess the number of projects developed with accessible buildings; recordkeeping requirements; and a "second opinion" by an independent, licensed architect or engineer on the site impracticality issue. The Department stated that comments on these proposals would be considered in connection with forthcoming amendments to the Fair Housing regulation.

The Department appreciates all comments submitted on the proposed enforcement mechanisms, and the suggestions offered on other possible enforcement mechanisms, such as a preconstruction review process, certification by a licensed architect, engineer or other building professional that a project is in compliance with the Act, and certification of local accessibility codes by the Department. All these comments will be considered in connection with future amendments to the Fair Housing Act regulation.

First Occupancy

Comment. A number of commenters requested clarification of the determination of "first occupancy" after March 13, 1991. A few commenters referred to the Act's first occupancy requirement as that of "ready for occupancy" by March 13, 1991.

Response. The phrase "ready for occupancy" does not correctly describe the standard contained in the Fair Housing Act. The Act states that covered multifamily dwellings subject to the Act's accessibility requirements are those that are "for first occupancy" after March 13, 1991. The standard, "first occupancy," is based on actual occupancy of the covered multifamily dwelling, or on issuance of the last building permit, or building permit renewal, on or before January 13, 1990. Where an individual is relying on a claim that a building was actually occupied on March 13, 1991, the Department, in making a determination of reasonable cause, will consider each situation on a case-by-case basis. As long as one dwelling unit in a covered multifamily dwelling is occupied, the one occupied dwelling unit is sufficient to meet the requirements for actual occupancy. However, the question of whether the occupancy was in compliance with State and local law (e.g., pursuant to a local occupancy permit, where one is required) will be a crucial factor in determining whether first occupancy has been achieved.

Comment. Several commenters requested clarification of "first occupancy", with respect to projects involving several buildings, or projects with extended build-out terms, such as planned communities with completion dates 5 to 10 years into the future.

Response. "First occupancy" is determined on a building-by-building basis, *not* on a project-by-project basis. For a project that involves several buildings, one building in the project could be built without reference to the accessibility requirements, while a building constructed next door might have to comply with the Act's requirements. The fact that one or more buildings in a multiple building project were occupied on March 13, 1991 will not be sufficient to afford an exemption from the Act's requirements for other buildings in the same project that are developed at a later time.

Costs of Adaptation

Comment. A few commenters requested clarification on who incurs the cost of making a unit adaptable for a disabled tenant.

Response. All costs associated with incorporating the new design and construction requirements of the Fair Housing Act are borne by the builder. There are, of course, situations where a tenant may need to make modifications to the dwelling unit which are necessary to make the unit accessible for that person's particular type of disability. The tenant would incur the cost of this type of modification—whether or not the dwelling unit is part of a multifamily dwelling exempt from the Act's accessibility requirements. For dwellings subject to the statute's accessibility requirements, the tenant's costs would be limited to those modifications that were not covered by the Act's design and construction requirements. (For example, the tenant would pay for the cost of purchasing and installing grab bars.) For dwellings not subject to the accessibility requirements, the tenant would pay the cost of all modifications necessary to meet his or her needs. (Using the grab bar example, the tenant would pay both the cost of buying and installing the grab bars and the costs associated with adding bathroom wall reinforcement.)

Section 100.203 of the Fair Housing regulations provides that discrimination includes a refusal to permit, at the expense of a handicapped person, reasonable modifications of existing premises occupied or to be occupied by that person, if modifications are necessary to afford the person full enjoyment of the premises. In the case of a rental, the landlord may reasonably condition permission for a modification on the renter's agreeing to restore the interior of the unit to the condition that existed before its modification—reasonable wear and tear excepted. This regulatory section provides examples of reasonable modifications that a tenant may make to existing premises. The examples include bathroom wall reinforcement. In House Report No. 711, the Congress provided additional examples of reasonable modifications that could be made to existing premises by persons with disabilities:

> For example, persons who have a hearing disability could install a flashing light in order to 'see' that someone is ringing the doorbell. Elderly individuals with severe arthritis may need to replace the doorknobs with lever handles. A person in a wheelchair may need to install fold-back hinges in order to be able to go through a door or may need to build a ramp to enter the unit. Any modifications protected under this section [section 804(f)(3)(A)] must be reasonable and must be made at the expense of the individual with handicaps. (House Report at 25)

Reasonable Modification

Comment. One commenter requested clarification concerning what is meant by "reasonable modification".

Response. What constitutes "reasonable modification" is discussed to some extent in the preceding section, "Costs of Adaptation", and also was discussed extensively in the preambles to both the proposed and final Fair Housing rules. (See 53 FR 45002–45003, 54 FR 3247–3248; 24 CFR Ch. I, Subch. A, App. I at 580–583 (1990).) Additionally, examples of reasonable modifications are provided in 24 CFR 100.203(c).

Scope of Coverage

Comment. A number of comments were received on the issue of which types of dwelling units should be subject to the Act's accessibility requirements, and the number or percentage of dwelling units that must comply with the Act's requirements.

Response. The Department lacks the authority to adopt any of the proposals recommended by the commenters. The type of multifamily dwelling subject to the Fair Housing Act's accessibility requirements, and the number of individual dwelling units that must be made accessible were established by the Congress, not the Department. The Fair Housing Act defines "covered multifamily dwelling" to mean buildings consisting of four or more units if such buildings have one or more elevators; and ground floor units in other buildings consisting of four or more units." (See Section 804(f)(7) of the Act.) The Fair Housing Act requires that covered multifamily dwellings for first occupancy after March 13, 1991 be designed and constructed in accordance with the Act's accessibility requirements. The Act does not permit only a percentage of units in covered multifamily dwellings to be designed in accordance with the Act's requirements, nor does the Department have the authority so to provide by regulation.

VI. Other Matters

Codification of Guidelines. In order to assure the availability of the Guidelines, and the preamble to the Guidelines, to interested persons in the future, the Department has decided to codify both documents. The Guidelines will be codified in the 1991 edition of the Code of Federal Regulations as appendix II to the Fair Housing regulations (i.e., 24 CFR Ch. I, Subch. A, App. II), and the preamble to the Guidelines will be codified as appendix III (i.e., 24 CFR Ch. I, Subch. A, App. III).

Regulatory Impact Analysis. A Preliminary Impact Analysis was published in the **Federal Register** on September 7, 1990 (55 FR 37072–37129). A Final Regulatory Impact Analysis is available for public inspection during regular business hours in the Office of the Rules Docket Clerk, room 10276, Department of Housing and Urban Development, 451 Seventh Street, SW., Washington, DC 20410–0500.

Environmental Impact. A Finding of No Significant Impact with respect to the environment has been made in accordance with HUD regulations at 24 CFR part 50, which implement section 102(2)(C) of the National Environmental Policy Act of 1969. The Finding of No Significant Impact is available for public inspection during regular business hours in the Office of the Rules Docket Clerk, Office of the General Counsel, Department of Housing and Urban Development, room 10276, 451 Seventh Street, SW., Washington, DC 20410–0500.

Executive Order 12606, The Family. The General Counsel, as the Designated Official under Executive Order No. 12606, The Family, has determined that this notice will likely have a significant beneficial impact on family formation, maintenance or well-being. Housing designed in accordance with the Guidelines will offer more housing choices for families with members who have disabilities. Housing designed in accordance with the Guidelines also may be beneficial to families that do not have members with disabilities. For example, accessible building entrances, as required by the Act and implemented by the Guidelines, may benefit parents with children in strollers, and also allow residents and visitors the convenience of using luggage or shopping carts easily. Additionally, with the aging of the population, and the increase in incidence of disability that accompanies aging, significant numbers of people will be able to remain in units designed in accordance with the Guidelines as the aging process advances. Compliance with these Guidelines may also increase the costs of developing a multifamily building, and, thus, may increase the cost of renting or purchasing homes. Such costs could negatively affect families' ability to obtain housing. However, the Department believes that the benefits provided to families by housing that is in compliance with the Fair Housing Amendments Act outweigh the possible increased costs of housing.

Executive Order 12611, Federalism. The General Counsel, as the Designated Official under section 6(a) of Executive Order No. 12611, Federalism, has determined that this notice does not involve the preemption of State law by Federal statute or regulation and does not have federalism implications. The Guidelines only are recommended design specifications, not legal requirements. Accordingly, the Guidelines do not preempt State or local laws that address the same issues covered by the Guidelines.

Dated: February 27, 1991.

Gordon H. Mansfield,

Assistant Secretary for Fair Housing and Equal Opportunity.

Accordingly, the Department adds the Fair Housing Accessibility Guidelines as Appendix II and the text of the preamble to these final guidelines beginning at the heading "Adoption of Final Guidelines" and ending before "VI. Other Matters" as appendix III to 24 CFR, ch. I, subchapter A to read as follows:

Appendix II to Ch. I, subchapter A—Fair Housing Accessibility Guidelines

BILLING CODE 4210-28-M

U.S. Department of Housing and Urban Development
Office of Fair Housing and Urban Development

Fair Housing Accessibility Guidelines

Design Guidelines for Accessible/Adaptable Dwellings

Issued by the Department of Housing and Urban Development

NOTE: This is a reprint of the final Fair Housing Accessibility Guidelines published in the Federal Register on March 6, 1991, Vol. 56, No. 44, pages 9472-9515. This reprint incorporates corrections to the final Guidelines which were published in the Federal Register on June 24, 1991.

Contents

Fair Housing Accessibility Guidelines

Section 1. Introduction

Authority

Section 804(f)(5)(C) of the Fair Housing Amendments Act of 1988 directs the Secretary of the Department of Housing and Urban Development to provide technical assistance to States, local governments, and other persons in implementing the accessibility requirements of the Fair Housing Act. These guidelines are issued under this statutory authority.

Purpose

The purpose of these guidelines is to provide technical guidance on designing dwelling units as required by the Fair Housing Amendments Act of 1988 (Fair Housing Act). These guidelines are not mandatory, nor do they prescribe specific requirements which must be met, and which, if not met, would constitute unlawful discrimination under the Fair Housing Act. Builders and developers may choose to depart from these guidelines and seek alternate ways to demonstrate that they have met the requirements of the Fair Housing Act. These guidelines are intended to provide a safe harbor for compliance with the accessibility requirements of the Fair Housing Act.

Scope

These guidelines apply only to the design and construction requirements of 24 CFR 100.205. Compliance with these guidelines do not relieve persons participating in a Federal or Federally-assisted program or activity from other requirements, such as those required by section 504 of the Rehabilitation Act of 1973 (29 U.S.C. 794) and the Architectural Barriers Act of 1968 (42 U.S.C. 4151-4157). Accessible design requirements for Section 504 are found at 24 CFR Part 8. Accessible design requirements for the Architectural Barriers Act are found at 24 CFR Part 40.

Organization of Guidelines

The design guidelines are incorporated in Section 5 of this document. Each guideline cites the appropriate paragraph of HUD's regulation at 24 CFR 100.205; quotes from the regulation to identify the required design features, and states recommended specifications for each design feature.

Generally, these guidelines rely on the American National Standards Institute (ANSI) A117.1-1986, American National Standard for Buildings and Facilities--Providing Accessibility and Usability for Physically Handicapped People (ANSI Standard). Where the guidelines rely on sections of the ANSI Standard, the ANSI sections are cited. Only those sections of the ANSI Standard cited in the guidelines are recommended for compliance with 24 CFR 100.205. For those guidelines that differ from the ANSI Standard, recommended specifications are provided. The texts of cited ANSI sections are not reproduced in the guidelines. The complete text of the 1986 version of the ANSI A117.1 Standard may be purchased from the American National Standards Institute, 1430 Broadway, New York, NY 10018.

Section 2. Definitions

As used in these Guidelines:

"Accessible", when used with respect to the public and common use areas of a building containing covered multifamily dwellings, means that the public or common use areas of the building can be approached, entered, and used by individuals with physical handicaps. The phrase "readily accessible to and usable by" is synonymous with accessible. A public or common use area that complies with the appropriate requirements of ANSI A117.1-1986, a comparable standard or these guidelines is "accessible" within the meaning of this paragraph.

"Accessible route" means a continuous unobstructed path connecting accessible elements and spaces in a building or within a site that can be negotiated by a person with a severe disability using a wheelchair, and that is also safe for and usable by people with other disabilities. Interior accessible routes may include corridors, floors, ramps, elevators and lifts. Exterior accessible routes may include parking access aisles, curb ramps, walks, ramps and lifts. A route that complies with the appropriate requirements of ANSI A117.1-1986, a comparable standard, or Section 5, Requirement 1 of these guidelines is an "accessible route". In the circumstances described in Section 5, Requirements 1 and 2, "accessible route" may include access via a vehicular route.

"Adaptable dwelling units", when used with respect to covered multifamily dwellings, means dwelling units that include the features of adaptable design specified in 24 CFR 100.205(c)(2)-(3).

"ANSI A117.1-1986" means the 1986 edition of the American National Standard for buildings and facilities providing accessibility and usability for physically handicapped people.

"Assistive device" means an aid, tool, or instrument used by a person with disabilities to assist in activities of daily living. Examples of assistive devices include tongs, knob-turners, and oven-rack pusher/pullers.

"Bathroom" means a bathroom which includes a water closet (toilet), lavatory (sink), and bathtub or shower. It does not include single-fixture facilities or those with only a water closet and lavatory. It does include a compartmented bathroom. A compartmented bathroom is one in which the fixtures are distributed among interconnected rooms. A compartmented bathroom is considered a single unit and is subject to the Act's requirements for bathrooms.

"Building" means a structure, facility or portion thereof that contains or serves one or more dwelling units.

"Building entrance on an accessible route" means an accessible entrance to a building that is connected by an accessible route to public transportation stops, to parking or passenger loading zones, or to public streets or sidewalks, if available. A building entrance that complies with ANSI A117.1-1986 (see Section 5, Requirement 1 of these guidelines) or a comparable standard complies with the requirements of this paragraph.

"Clear" means unobstructed.

"Common use areas" means rooms, spaces or elements inside or outside of a building that are made available for the use of residents of a building or the guests thereof. These areas include hallways, lounges, lobbies, laundry rooms, refuse rooms, mail rooms, recreational areas and passageways among and between buildings. See Section 5, Requirement 2 of these guidelines.

"Controlled substance" means any drug or other substance, or immediate precursor included in the definition in Section 102 of the Controlled Substances Act (21 U.S.C. 802).

"Covered multifamily dwellings" or "covered multifamily dwellings subject to the Fair Housing Amendments" means buildings consisting of four or more dwelling units if such buildings have one or more elevators; and ground floor dwelling units in other buildings consisting of four or more dwelling units. Dwelling units within a single structure separated by firewalls do not constitute separate buildings.

"Dwelling unit" means a single unit of residence for a household of one or more persons. Examples of dwelling units covered by these guidelines include: condominiums; an apartment unit within an apartment building; and other types of dwellings in which sleeping accommodations are provided but toileting or cooking facilities are shared by occupants of more than one room or portion of the dwelling. Examples of the latter include dormitory rooms and sleeping accommodations in shelters intended for occupancy as a residence for homeless persons.

"Entrance" means any exterior access point to a building or portion of a building used by residents for the purpose of entering. For purposes of these guidelines, an "entrance" does not include a door to a loading dock or a door used primarily as a service entrance, even if nonhandicapped residents occasionally use that door to enter.

"Finished grade" means the ground surface of the site after all construction, levelling, grading, and development has been completed.

"Ground floor" means a floor of a building with a building entrance on an accessible route. A building may have one or more ground floors. Where the first floor containing dwelling units in a building is above grade, all units on that floor must be served by a building entrance on an accessible route. This floor will be considered to be a ground floor.

"Handicap" means, with respect to a person, a physical or mental impairment which substantially limits one or more major life activities; a record of such an impairment; or being regarded as having such an impairment. This term does not include current, illegal use of or addiction to a controlled substance. For purposes of these guidelines, an individual shall not be considered to have a handicap solely because that individual is a transvestite.

As used in this definition:

(a) "Physical or mental impairment" includes:
   (1) Any physiological disorder or condition, cosmetic disfigurement, or anatomical loss affecting one or more of the following body systems: Neurological; musculoskeletal; special sense organs; respiratory, including speech organs; cardiovascular; reproductive; digestive; genito-urinary; hemic and lymphatic; skin; and endocrine; or
   (2) Any mental or psychological disorder, such as mental retardation, organic brain syndrome, emotional or mental illness, and specific learning disabilities. The term "physical or mental impairment" includes, but is not limited to, such diseases and conditions as orthopedic, visual, speech and hearing impairments, cerebral palsy, autism, epilepsy, muscular dystrophy, multiple sclerosis, cancer, heart disease, diabetes, Human Immunodeficiency Virus infection, mental retardation, emotional illness, drug addiction (other than addiction caused by current, illegal use of a controlled substance) and alcoholism. These guidelines are designed to make units accessible or adaptable for people with physical handicaps.

(b) "Major life activities" means functions such as caring for one's self, performing manual tasks, walking, seeing, hearing, speaking, breathing, learning and working.

(c) "Has a record of such an impairment" means has a history of, or has been misclassified as having, a mental or physical impairment that substantially limits one or more major life activities.

(d) "Is regarded as having an impairment" means:
   (1) Has a physical or mental impairment that does not substantially limit one or more major life activities but that is treated by another person as constituting such a limitation;
   (2) Has a physical or mental impairment that substantially limits one or more major life activities only as a result of the attitudes of others toward such impairment; or
   (3) Has none of the impairments defined in paragraph (a) of this definition but is treated by another person as having such an impairment.

"Loft" means an intermediate level between the floor and ceiling of any story, located within a room or rooms of a dwelling.

"Multistory dwelling unit" means a dwelling unit with finished living space located on one floor and the floor or floors immediately above or below it.

"Public use areas" means interior or exterior rooms or spaces of a building that are made available to the general public. Public use may be provided at a building that is privately or publicly owned.

"Single-story dwelling unit" means a dwelling unit with all finished living space located on one floor.

"Site" means a parcel of land bounded by a property line or a designated portion of a public right of way.

"Slope" means the relative steepness of the land between two points and is calculated as follows: The distance and elevation between the two points (e.g., an entrance and a passenger loading zone) are determined from a topographical map. The difference in elevation is divided by the distance and that fraction is multiplied by 100 to obtain a percentage slope figure. For example, if a principal entrance is ten feet from a passenger loading zone, and the principal entrance is raised one foot higher than the passenger loading zone, then the slope is $1/10 \times 100 = 10\%$.

"Story" means that portion of a dwelling unit between the upper surface of any floor and the upper surface of the floor next above, or the roof of the unit. Within the context of dwelling units, the terms "story" and "floor" are synonymous.

"Undisturbed site" means the site before any construction, levelling, grading, or development associated with the current project.

"Vehicular or pedestrian arrival points" means public or resident parking areas, public transportation stops, passenger loading zones, and public streets or sidewalks.

"Vehicular route" means a route intended for vehicular traffic, such as a street, driveway or parking lot.

Section 3. Fair Housing Act Design and Construction Requirements

The regulations issued by the Department at 24 CFR 100.205 state:

§ 100.205 Design and construction requirements.

(a) Covered multifamily dwellings for first occupancy after March 13, 1991 shall be designed and constructed to have at least one building entrance on an accessible route unless it is impractical to do so because of the terrain or unusual characteristics of the site. For purposes of this section, a covered multifamily dwelling shall be deemed to be designed and constructed for first occupancy on or before March 13, 1991 if they are occupied by that date or if the last building permit or renewal thereof for the covered multifamily dwellings is issued by a State, County or local government on or before January 13, 1990. The burden of establishing impracticality because of terrain or unusual site characteristics is on the person or persons who designed or constructed the housing facility.

(b) The application of paragraph (a) of this section may be illustrated by the following examples:

Example (1): A real estate developer plans to construct six covered multifamily dwelling units on a site with a hilly terrain. Because of the terrain, it will be necessary to climb a long and steep stairway in order to enter the dwellings. Since there is no practical way to provide an accessible route to any of the dwellings, one need not be provided.

Example (2): A real estate developer plans to construct a building consisting of 10 units of multifamily housing on a waterfront site that floods frequently. Because of this unusual characteristic of the site, the builder plans to construct the building on stilts. It is customary for housing in the geographic area where the site is located to be built on stilts. The housing may lawfully be constructed on the proposed site on stilts even though this means that there will be no practical way to provide an accessible route to the building entrance.

Example (3): A real estate developer plans to construct a multifamily housing facility on a particular site. The developer would like the facility to be built on the site to contain as many units as possible. Because of the configuration and terrain of the site, it is possible to construct a building with 105 units on the site provided the site does not have an accessible route leading to the building entrance. It is also possible to construct a building on the site with an accessible route leading to the building entrance. However, such a building would have no more than 100 dwelling units. The building to be constructed on the site must have a building entrance on an accessible route because it is not impractical to provide such an entrance because of the terrain or unusual characteristics of the site.

(c) All covered multifamily dwellings for first occupancy after March 13, 1991 with a building entrance on an accessible route shall be designed and constructed in such a manner that—

(1) The public and common use areas are readily accessible to and usable by handicapped persons;

(2) All the doors designed to allow passage into and within all premises are sufficiently wide to allow passage by handicapped persons in wheelchairs; and

(3) All premises within covered multifamily dwelling units contain the following features of adaptable design:

(i) An accessible route into and through the covered dwelling unit;

(ii) Light switches, electrical outlets, thermostats, and other environmental controls in accessible locations;

(iii) Reinforcements in bathroom walls to allow later installation of grab bars around the toilet, tub, shower, stall and shower seat, where such facilities are provided; and

(iv) Usable kitchens and bathrooms such that an individual in a wheelchair can maneuver about the space.

(d) The application of paragraph (c) of this section may be illustrated by the following examples:

Example (1): A developer plans to construct a 100 unit condominium apartment building with one elevator. In accordance with paragraph (a), the building has at least one accessible route leading to an accessible entrance. All 100 units are covered multifamily dwelling units and they all must be designed and constructed so that they comply with the accessibility requirements of paragraph (c) of this section.

Example (2): A developer plans to construct 30 garden apartments in a three story building. The building will not have an elevator. The building will have one accessible entrance which will be on the first floor. Since the building does not have an elevator, only the "ground floor" units are covered multifamily units. The "ground floor" is the first floor because that is the floor that has an accessible entrance. All of the dwelling units on the first floor must meet the accessibility requirements of paragraph (c) of this section and must have access to at least one of each type of public or common use area available for residents in the building.

(e) Compliance with the appropriate requirements of ANSI A117.1-1986 suffices to satisfy the requirements of paragraph (c)(3) of this section.

(f) Compliance with a duly enacted law of a State or unit of general local government that includes the requirements of paragraphs (a) and (c) of this section satisfies the requirements of paragraphs (a) and (c) of this section.

(g)(1) It is the policy of HUD to encourage States and units of general local government to include, in their existing procedures for the review and approval of newly constructed covered multifamily dwellings, determinations as to whether the design and construction of such dwellings are consistent with paragraphs (a) and (c) of this section.

(2) A State or unit of general local government may review and approve newly constructed multifamily dwellings for the purpose of making determinations as to whether the requirements of paragraphs (a) and (c) of this section are met.

(h) Determinations of compliance or noncompliance by a State or a unit of general local government under paragraph (f) or (g) of this section are not conclusive in enforcement proceedings under the Fair Housing Amendments Act.

(i) This subpart does not invalidate or limit any law of a State or political subdivision of a State that requires dwellings to be designed and constructed in a manner that affords handicapped persons greater access than is required by this subpart.

Section 4. Application of the Guidelines

The design specifications (guidelines) presented in Section 5 apply to new construction of "covered multifamily dwellings", as defined in Section 2. These guidelines are recommended for designing dwellings that comply with the requirements of the Fair Housing Amendments Act of 1988.

Section 5. Guidelines

Requirement 1. Accessible building entrance on an accessible route.

Under section 100.205(a), covered multifamily dwellings shall be designed and constructed to have at least one building entrance on an accessible route, unless it is impractical to do so because of terrain or unusual characteristics of the site.

Guideline

(1) Building entrance. Each building on a site shall have at least one building entrance on an accessible route unless prohibited by the terrain, as provided in paragraphs (2)(a)(i) or (2)(a)(ii), or unusual characteristics of the site, as provided in paragraph (2)(b). This guideline applies both to a single building on a site and to multiple buildings on a site.

(a) Separate ground floor unit entrances. When a ground floor unit of a building has a separate entrance, each such ground floor unit shall be served by an accessible route, except for any unit where the terrain or unusual characteristics of the site prohibit the provision of an accessible route to the entrance of that unit.

(b) Multiple entrances. Only one entrance is required to be accessible to any one ground floor of a building, except in cases where an individual dwelling unit has a separate exterior entrance, or where the building contains clusters of dwelling units, with each cluster sharing a different exterior entrance. In these cases, more than one entrance may be required to be accessible, as determined by analysis of the site. In every case, the accessible entrance should be on an accessible route to the covered dwelling units it serves.

(2) Site impracticality. Covered multifamily dwellings with elevators shall be designed and constructed to provide at least one accessible entrance on an accessible route, regardless of terrain or unusual characteristics of the site. Covered multifamily dwellings without elevators shall be designed and constructed to provide at least one accessible entrance on an accessible route unless terrain or unusual characteristics of the site are such that the following conditions are found to exist:

(a) Site impracticality due to terrain. There are two alternative tests for determining site impracticality due to terrain: the individual building test provided in paragraph (i), or the site analysis test provided in paragraph (ii). These tests may be used as follows.

A site with a single building having a common entrance for all units may be analyzed only as described in paragraph (i).

All other sites, including a site with a single building having multiple entrances serving either individual dwelling units or clusters of dwelling units, may be analyzed using the methodology in either paragraph (i) or paragraph (ii). For these sites for which either test is applicable, regardless of which test is selected, at least 20% of the total ground floor units in nonelevator buildings, on any site, must comply with the guidelines.

(i) Individual building test. It is impractical to provide an accessible entrance served by an accessible route when the terrain of the site is such that:

(A) the slopes of the undisturbed site measured between the planned entrance and all vehicular or pedestrian arrival points within 50 feet of the planned entrance exceed 10 percent; and

(B) the slopes of the planned finished grade measured between the entrance and all vehicular or pedestrian arrival points within 50 feet of the planned entrance also exceed 10 percent.

If there are no vehicular or pedestrian arrival points within 50 feet of the planned entrance, the slope for the purposes of this paragraph (i) will be measured to the closest vehicular or pedestrian arrival point.

For purposes of these guidelines, vehicular or pedestrian arrival points include public or resident parking areas; public transportation stops; passenger loading zones; and public streets or sidewalks. To determine site impracticality, the slope would be measured at ground level from the point of the planned entrance on a straight line to (i) each vehicular or pedestrian arrival point that is within 50 feet of the planned entrance, or (ii) if there are no vehicular or pedestrian arrival points within that specified area, the vehicular or pedestrian arrival point closest to the planned entrance. In the case of sidewalks, the closest point to the entrance will be where a public sidewalk entering the site intersects with the sidewalk to the entrance. In the case of resident parking areas, the closest point to the planned entrance will be measured from the entry point to the parking area that is located closest to the planned entrance.

(ii) Site analysis test. Alternatively, for a site having multiple buildings, or a site with a single building with multiple entrances, impracticality of providing an accessible entrance served by an accessible route can be established by the following steps:

(A) The percentage of the total buildable area of the undisturbed site with a natural grade less than 10% slope shall be calculated. The analysis of the existing slope (before grading) shall be done on a topographic survey with two foot (2') contour intervals with slope determination made between each successive interval. The accuracy of the slope analysis shall be certified by a professional licensed engineer, landscape architect, architect or surveyor.

(B) To determine the practicality of providing accessibility to planned multifamily dwellings based on the topography of the existing natural terrain, the minimum percentage of ground floor units to be made accessible should equal the percentage of the total buildable area (not including floodplains, wetlands, or other restricted use areas) of the undisturbed site that has an existing natural grade of less than 10% slope.

(C) In addition to the percentage established in paragraph (B), all ground floor units in a building, or ground floor units served by a particular entrance, shall be made accessible if the entrance to the units is on an accessible route, defined as a walkway with a slope between the planned entrance and a pedestrian or vehicular arrival point that is no greater than 8.33%

(b) Site impracticality due to unusual characteristics. Unusual characteristics include sites located in a federally-designated floodplain or coastal high-hazard area and sites subject to other similar requirements of law or code that the lowest floor or the lowest structural member of the lowest floor must be raised to a specified level at or above the base flood elevation. An accessible route to a building entrance is impractical due to unusual characteristics of the site when:

(i) the unusual site characteristics result in a difference in finished grade elevation exceeding 30 inches and 10 percent measured between an entrance and all vehicular or pedestrian arrival points within 50 feet of the planned entrance; or

(ii) if there are no vehicular or pedestrian arrival points within 50 feet of the planned entrance, the unusual characteristics result in a difference in finished grade elevation exceeding 30 inches and 10 percent measured between an entrance and the closest vehicular or pedestrian arrival point.

(3) Exceptions to site impracticality . Regardless of site considerations described in paragraphs (1) and (2), an accessible entrance on an accessible route is practical when:

(a) There is an elevator connecting the parking area with the dwelling units on a ground floor. (In this case, those dwelling units on the ground floor served by an elevator, and at least one of each type of public and common use areas, would be subject to these guidelines.) However:

(i) Where a building elevator is provided only as a means of creating an accessible route to dwelling units on a ground floor, the building is not considered an elevator building for purposes of these guidelines; hence, only the ground floor dwelling units would be covered.

(ii) If the building elevator is provided as a means of access to dwelling units other than dwelling units on a ground floor, then the building is an elevator building which is a covered multifamily dwelling, and the elevator in that building must provide accessibility to all dwelling units in the building, regardless of the slope of the natural terrain; or

(b) An elevated walkway is planned between a building entrance and a vehicular or pedestrian arrival point and the planned walkway has a slope no greater than 10 percent.

(4) Accessible entrance. An entrance that complies with ANSI 4.14 meets section 100.205(a).

(5) Accessible route. An accessible route that complies with ANSI 4.3 would meet section 100.205(a). If the slope of the finished grade between covered multifamily dwellings and a public or common use facility (including parking) exceeds 8.33%, or where other physical barriers (natural or manmade) or legal restrictions, all of which are outside the control of the owner, prevent the installation of an accessible pedestrian route, an acceptable alternative is to provide access via a vehicular route, so long as necessary site provisions such as parking spaces and curb ramps are provided at the public or common use facility.

Requirement 2. Accessible and usable public and common use areas.

Section 100.205(c)(1) provides that covered multifamily dwellings with a building entrance on an accessible route shall be designed in such a manner that the public and common use areas are readily accessible to and usable by handicapped persons.

Guideline

The following chart identifies the public and common use areas that should be made accessible, cites the appropriate section of the ANSI Standard, and describes the appropriate application of the specifications, including modifications to the referenced Standard.

BASIC COMPONENTS FOR ACCESSIBLE AND USABLE PUBLIC AND COMMON USE AREAS OR FACILITIES

Accessible element or space	ANSI A117.1 section	Application
1. Accessible route(s)	4.3	Within the boundary of the site: (a) From public transportation stops, accessible parking spaces, accessible passenger loading zones, and public streets or sidewalks to accessible building entrances (subject to site considerations described in section 5). (b) Connecting accessible buildings, facilities, elements and spaces that are on the same site. On-grade walks or paths between separate buildings with covered multifamily dwellings, while not required, should be accessible unless the slope of finish grade exceeds 8.33% at any point along the route. Handrails are not required on these accessible walks. (c) Connecting accessible building or facility entrances with accessible spaces and elements within the building or facility, including adaptable dwelling units. (d) Where site or legal constraints prevent a route accessible to wheelchair users between covered multifamily dwellings and public or common-use facilities elsewhere on the site, an acceptable alternative is the provision of access via a vehicular route so long as there is accessible parking on an accessible route to at least 2% of covered dwelling units, and necessary site provisions such as parking and curb cuts are available at the public or common use facility.
2. Protruding objects	4.4	Accessible routes or maneuvering space including, but not limited to halls, corridors, passageways, or aisles.
3. Ground and floor surface treatments	4.5	Accessible routes, rooms, and spaces, including floors, walks, ramps, stairs, and curb ramps.
4. Parking and passenger-loading zones	4.6	If provided at the site, designated accessible parking at the dwelling unit on request of residents with handicaps, on the same terms and with the full range of choices (e.g., surface parking or garage) that are provided for other residents of the project, with accessible parking on a route accessible to wheelchairs for at least 2% of the covered dwelling units; accessible visitor parking sufficient to provide access to grade-level entrances of covered multifamily dwellings; and accessible parking at facilities (e.g., swimming pools) that serve accessible buildings.
5. Curb ramps	4.7	Accessible routes crossing curbs.
6. Ramps	4.8	Accessible routes with slopes greater than 1:20.
7. Stairs	4.9	Stairs on accessible routes connecting levels not connected by an elevator.
8. Elevator	4.10	If provided.
9. Platform lift	4.11	May be used in lieu of an elevator or ramp under certain conditions.
10. Drinking fountains and water coolers	4.15	Fifty percent of fountains and coolers on each floor, or at least one, if provided in the facility or at the site.
11. Toilet rooms and bathing facilities (including water closets, toilet rooms and stalls, urinals, lavatories and mirrors, bathtubs, shower stalls, and sinks.)	4.22	Where provided in public-use and common-use facilities, at least one of each fixture provided per room.
12. Seating, tables, or work surfaces	4.30	If provided in accessible spaces, at least one of each type provided.
13. Places of assembly	4.31	If provided in the facility or at the site.
14. Common-use spaces and facilities (including swimming pools, playgrounds, entrances, rental offices, lobbies, elevators, mailbox areas, lounges, halls and corridors, and the like.)	4.1 through 4.30	If provided in the facility or at the site: (a) Where multiple recreational facilities (e.g., tennis courts) are provided sufficient accessible facilities of each type to assure equitable opportunity for use by persons with handicaps. (b) Where practical, access to all or a portion of nature trails and jogging paths.
15. Laundry rooms	4.32.6	If provided in the facility or at the site, at least one of each type of appliance provided in each laundry area, except that laundry rooms serving covered multifamily dwellings would not be required to have front-loading washers in order to meet the requirements of § 100.205(c)(1). (Where front loading washers are not provided, management will be expected to provide assistive devices on request if necessary to permit a resident to use a top loading washer.)

Requirement 3. Usable doors.

Section 100.205(c)(2) provides that covered multifamily dwellings with a building entrance on an accessible route shall be designed in such a manner that all the doors designed to allow passage into and within all premises are sufficiently wide to allow passage by handicapped persons in wheelchairs.

Guideline

Section 100.205(c)(2) would apply to doors that are a part of an accessible route in the public and common use areas of multifamily dwellings and to doors into and within individual dwelling units.

(1) On accessible routes in public and common use areas, and for primary entry doors to covered units, doors that comply with ANSI 4.13 would meet this requirement.

(2) Within individual dwelling units, doors intended for user passage through the unit which have a clear opening of at least 32 inches nominal width when the door is open 90 degrees, measured between the face of the door and the stop, would meet this requirement. (See Fig. 1 (a), (b), and (c).) Openings more than 24 inches in depth are not considered doorways. (See Fig. 1 (d).)

Note:
A 34-inch door, hung in the standard manner, provides an acceptable nominal 32-inch clear opening. This door can be adapted to provide a wider opening by using offset hinges, by removing lower portions of the door stop, or both. Pocket or sliding doors are acceptable doors in covered dwelling units and have the added advantage of not impinging on clear floor space in small rooms. The nominal 32-inch clear opening provided by a standard six-foot sliding patio door assembly is acceptable.

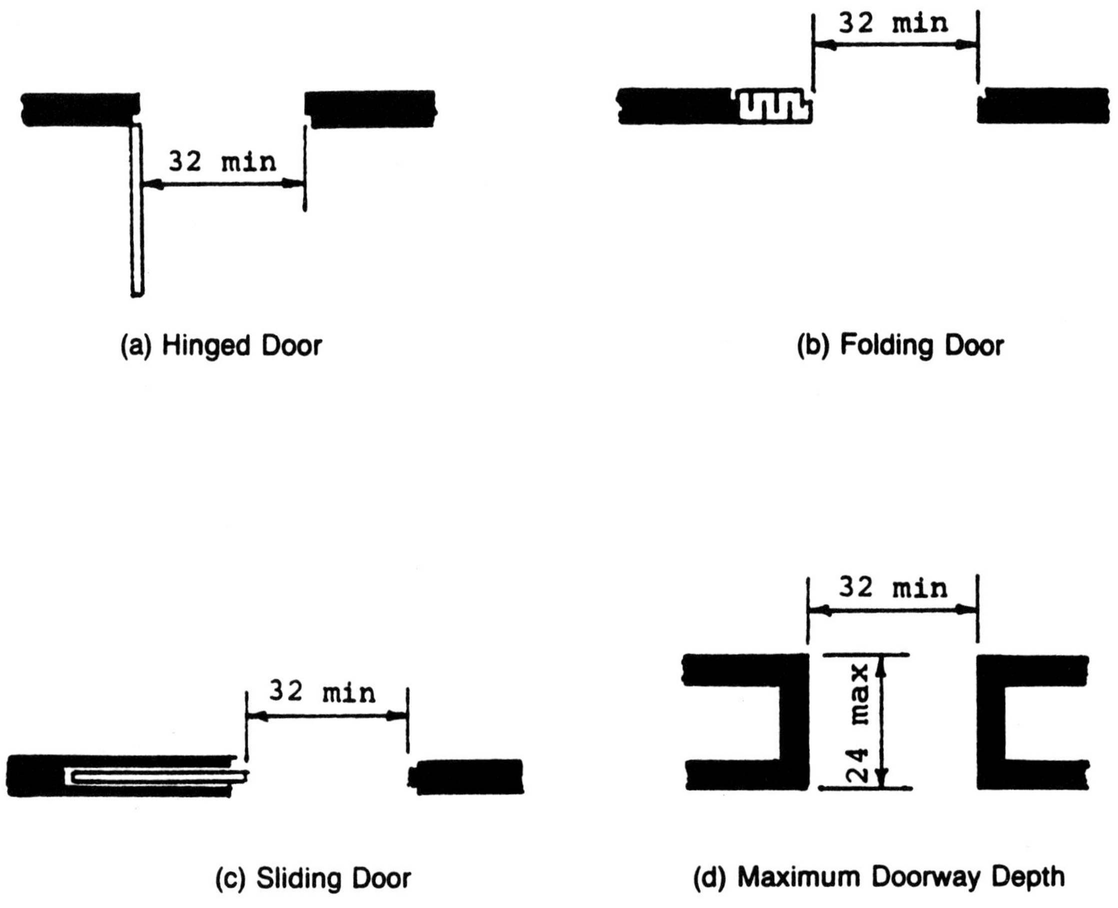

Fig. 1 Clear Doorway Width and Depth

Requirement 4. Accessible route into and through the covered dwelling unit.

Section 100.205(c)(3)(i) provides that all covered multifamily dwellings with a building entrance on an accessible route shall be designed and constructed in such a manner that all premises within covered multifamily dwelling units contain an accessible route into and through the covered dwelling unit.

Guideline

Accessible routes into and through dwelling units would meet section 100.205(c)(3)(i) if:

(1) A minimum clear width of 36 inches is provided.

(2) In single-story dwelling units, changes in level within the dwelling unit with heights between 1/4 inch and 1/2 inch are beveled with a slope no greater than 1:2. Except for design features, such as a loft or an area on a different level within a room (e.g., a sunken living room), changes in level greater than 1/2 inch are ramped or have other means of access. Where a single story dwelling unit has special design features, all portions of the single-story unit, except the loft or the sunken or raised area, are on an accessible route; and

(a) In single-story dwelling units with lofts, all spaces other than the loft are on an accessible route.

(b) Design features such as sunken or raised functional areas do not interrupt the accessible route through the remainder of the dwelling unit.

(3) In multistory dwelling units in buildings with elevators, the story of the unit that is served by the building elevator (a) is the primary entry to the unit, (b) complies with Requirements 2 through 7 with respect to the rooms located on the entry/accessible floor; and (c) contains a bathroom or powder room which complies with Requirement 7. (Note: multistory dwelling units in non-elevator buildings are not covered dwelling units because, in such cases, there is no ground floor unit.)

(4) Except as provided in paragraphs (5) and (6) below, thresholds at exterior doors, including sliding door tracks, are no higher than 3/4 inch. Thresholds and changes in level at these locations are beveled with a slope no greater than 1:2.

(5) Exterior deck, patio, or balcony surfaces are no more than 1/2 inch below the floor level of the interior of the dwelling unit, unless they are constructed of impervious material such as concrete, brick or flagstone. In such case, the surface is no more than 4 inches below the floor level of the interior of the dwelling unit, or lower if required by local building code.

(6) At the primary entry door to dwelling units with direct exterior access, outside landing surfaces constructed of impervious materials such as concrete, brick or flagstone, are no more than 1/2 inch below the floor level of the interior of the dwelling unit. The finished surface of this area that is located immediately outside the entry may be sloped, up to 1/8 inch per foot (12 inches), for drainage.

Requirement 5. Light switches, electrical outlets, thermostats and other environmental controls in accessible locations.

Section 100.205(c)(3)(ii) requires that all covered multifamily dwellings with a building entrance on an accessible route shall be designed and constructed in such a manner that all premises within covered multifamily dwelling units contain light switches, electrical outlets, thermostats, and other environmental controls in accessible locations.

Guideline

Light switches, electrical outlets, thermostats and other environmental controls would meet section 100.205(c)(3)(ii) if operable parts of the controls are located no higher than 48 inches, and no lower than 15 inches, above the floor. If the reach is over an obstruction (for example, an overhanging shelf) between 20 and 25 inches in depth, the maximum height is reduced to 44 inches for forward approach; or 46 inches for side approach, provided the obstruction (for example, a kitchen base cabinet) is no more than 24 inches in depth. Obstructions should not extend more than 25 inches from the wall beneath a control. (See Fig.2.)

Note

Controls or outlets that do not satisfy these specifications are acceptable provided that comparable controls or outlets (i.e., that perform the same functions) are provided within the same area and are accessible, in accordance with this guideline for Requirement 5.

(a) Forward Reach Limit

NOTE: Clear knee space should be as deep as the reach distance.

(b) Maximum Forward Reach
Over an Obstruction

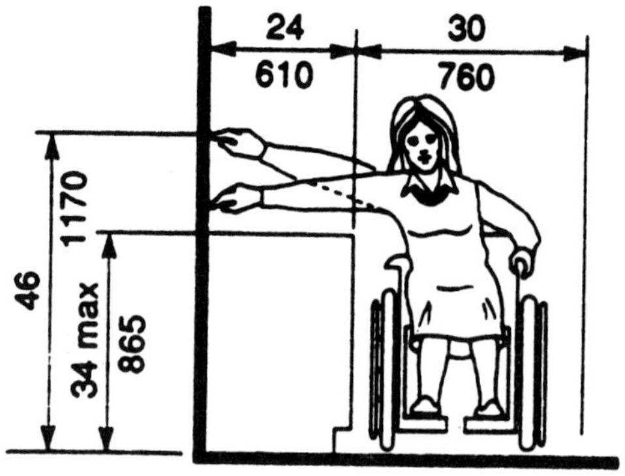

(c) Maximum Side Reach Over Obstruction

Fig. 2 Reach Ranges

Requirement 6. Reinforced walls for grab bars.

Section 100.205(c)(3)(iii) requires that covered multifamily dwellings with a building entrance on an accessible route shall be designed and constructed in such a manner that all premises within covered multifamily dwelling units contain reinforcements in bathroom walls to allow later installation of grab bars around toilet, tub, shower stall and shower seat, where such facilities are provided.

Guideline

Reinforced bathroom walls to allow later installation of grab bars around the toilet, tub, shower stall and shower seat, where such facilities are provided, would meet section 100.205(c)(3)(iii) if reinforced areas are provided at least at those points where grab bars will be mounted. (For example, see Figs. 3, 4 and 5.) Where the toilet is not placed adjacent to a side wall, the bathroom would comply if provision was made for installation of floor mounted, foldaway or similar alternative grab bars. Where the powder room (a room with a toilet and sink) is the only toilet facility located on an accessible level of a multistory dwelling unit, it must comply with this requirement for reinforced walls for grab bars.

Note:
Installation of bathtubs is not limited by the illustrative figures; a tub may have shelves or benches at either end; or a tub may be installed without surrounding walls, if there is provision for alternative mounting of grab bars. For example, a sunken tub placed away from walls could have reinforced areas for installation of floor-mounted grab bars. The same principle applies to shower stalls -- e.g., glass-walled stalls could be planned to allow floor-mounted grab bars to be installed later.

Reinforcement for grab bars may be provided in a variety of ways (for example, by plywood or wood blocking) so long as the necessary reinforcement is placed so as to permit later installation of appropriate grab bars.

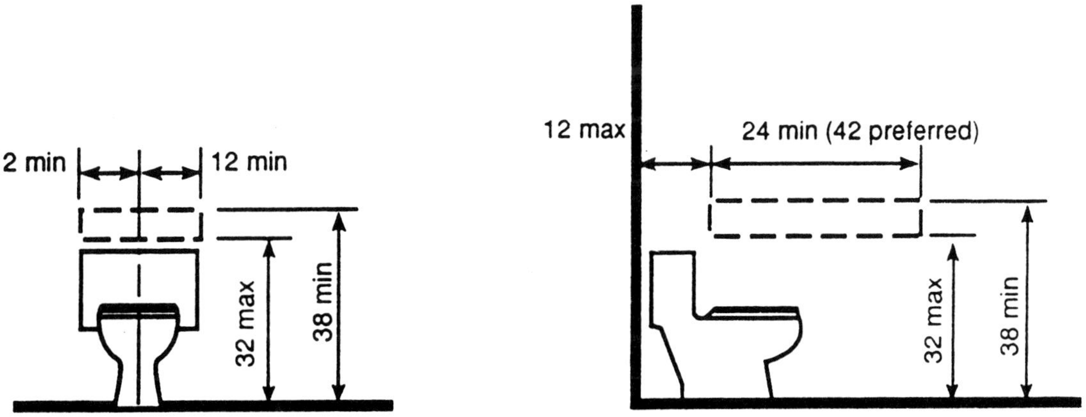

Reinforced Areas for Installation
of Grab Bars

Fig. 3 Water Closets in Adaptable Bathrooms

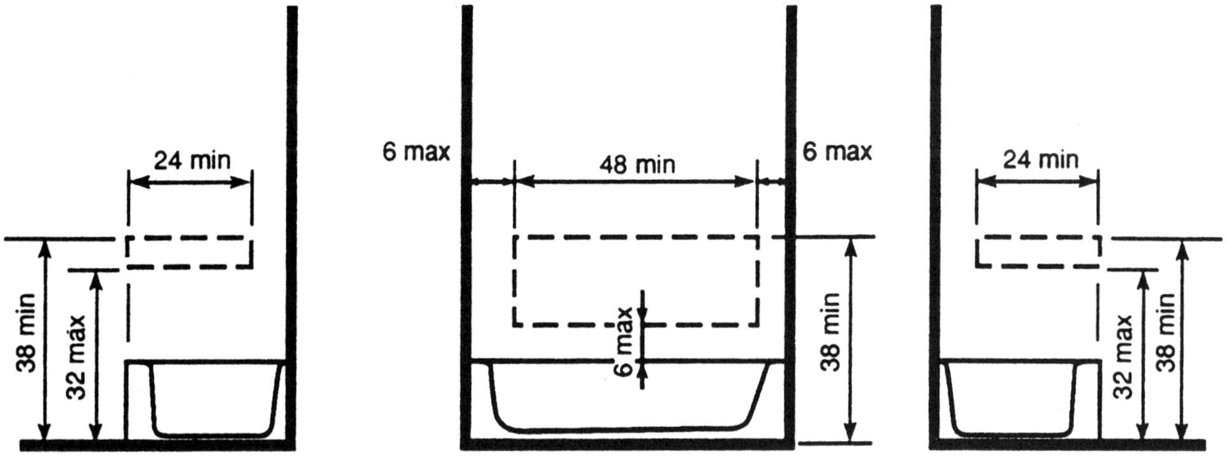

Fig. 4 Location of Grab Bar Reinforcements for Adaptable Bathtubs

NOTE: The areas outlined in dashed lines represent locations for future installation of grab bars for typical fixture configurations.

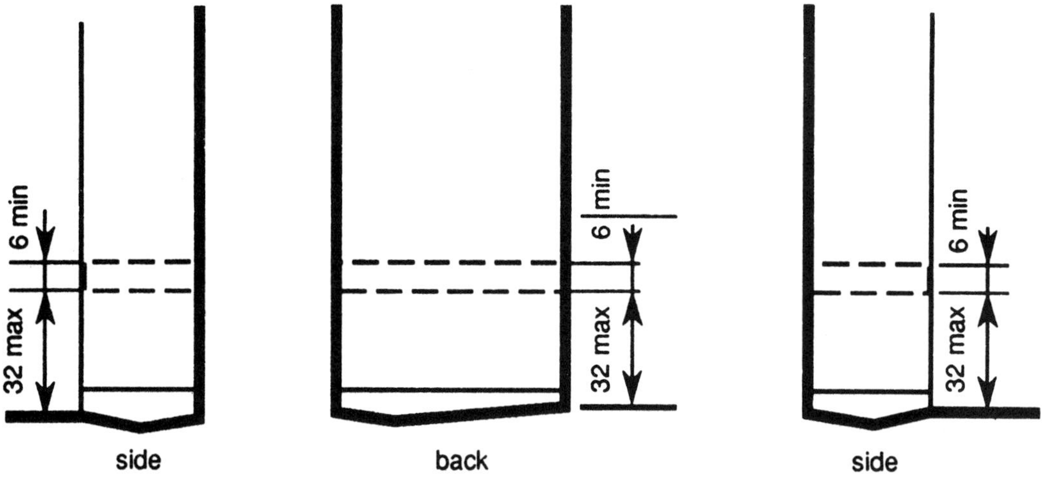

Fig. 5 Location of Grab Bar Reinforcements for Adaptable Showers

NOTE: The areas outlined in dashed lines represent locations for future installation of grab bars.

Requirement 7. Usable kitchens and bathrooms.

Section 100.205(c)(3)(iv) requires that covered multifamily dwellings with a building entrance on an accessible route shall be designed and constructed in such a manner that all premises within covered multifamily dwelling units contain usable kitchens and bathrooms such that an individual in a wheelchair can maneuver about the space.

Guideline

(1) Usable kitchens. Usable kitchens would meet section 100.205(c)(3)(iv) if:

(a) A clear floor space at least 30 inches by 48 inches that allows a parallel approach by a person in a wheelchair is provided at the range or cooktop and sink, and either a parallel or forward approach is provided at oven, dish washer, refrigerator/freezer or trash compactor. (See Fig. 6)

(b) Clearance between counters and all opposing base cabinets, countertops, appliances or walls is at least 40 inches.

(c) In U-shaped kitchens with sink or range or cooktop at the base of the "U", a 60-inch turning radius is provided to allow parallel approach, or base cabinets are removable at that location to allow knee space for a forward approach.

(2) Usable bathrooms. To meet the requirements of section 100.205(c)(3)(iv) either:

All bathrooms in the dwelling unit comply with the provisions of paragraph (a); or

At least one bathroom in the dwelling unit complies with the provisions of paragraph (b), and all other bathrooms and powder rooms within the dwelling unit must be on an accessible route with usable entry doors in accordance with the guidelines for Requirements 3 and 4.

However, in multistory dwelling units, only those bathrooms on the accessible level are subject to the requirements of section 100.205(c)(3)(iv). Where a powder room is the only facility provided on the accessible level of a multistory dwelling unit, the powder room must comply with provisions of paragraph (a) or paragraph (b). Powder rooms that are subject to the requirements of section 100.205(c)(3)(iv) must have reinforcements for grab bars as provided in the guideline for Requirement 6.

(a) Bathrooms that have reinforced walls for grab bars (see Requirement 6) would meet section 100.205(c)(3)(iv) if:

(i) Sufficient maneuvering space is provided within the bathroom for a person using a wheelchair or other mobility aid to enter and close the door, use the fixtures, reopen the door and exit. Doors may swing into the clear floor space provided at any fixture if the maneuvering space is provided. Maneuvering spaces may include any kneespace or toespace available below bathroom fixtures.

(ii) Clear floor space is provided at fixtures as shown in Fig. 7 (a), (b), (c) and (d). Clear floor space at fixtures may overlap.

(iii) If the shower stall is the only bathing facility provided in the covered dwelling unit, the shower stall measures at least 36 inches x 36 inches.

Note:
Cabinets under lavatories are acceptable provided the bathroom has space to allow a parallel approach by a person in a wheelchair; if parallel approach is not possible within the space, any cabinets provided would have to be removable to afford the necessary knee clearance for forward approach.

(b) Bathrooms that have reinforced walls for grab bars (see Requirement 6) would meet section 100.205(c)(3)(iv) if:

(i) Where the door swings into the bathroom, there is a clear space (approximately, 2' 6" by 4'0") within the room to position a wheelchair or other mobility aid clear of the path of the door as it is closed and to permit use of fixtures. This clear space can include any kneespace and toespace available below bathroom fixtures.

(ii) Where the door swings out, a clear space is provided within the bathroom for a person using a wheelchair or other mobility aid to position the wheelchair such that the person is allowed use of fixtures. There also shall be clear space to allow persons using wheelchairs to reopen the door to exit.

(iii) When both tub and shower fixtures are provided in the bathroom, at least one is made accessible. When two or more lavatories in a bathroom are provided, at least one is made accessible.

(iv) Toilets are located within bathrooms in a manner that permit a grab bar to be installed on one side of the fixture. In locations where toilets are adjacent to walls or bathtubs, the center line of the fixture is a minimum of 1'6" from the obstacle. The other (non-grab bar) side of the toilet fixture is a minimum of 1'3" from the finished surface of adjoining walls, vanities or from the edge of a lavatory. (See Figure 7(a).)

(v) Vanities and lavatories are installed with the centerline of the fixture a minimum of 1'3" horizontally from an adjoining wall or fixture. The top of the fixture rim is a maximum height of 2'10" above the finished floor. If kneespace is provided below the vanity, the bottom of the apron is at least 2'3" above the floor. If provided, full kneespace (for front approach) is at least 1'5" deep. (See Figure 7(c).)

(vi) Bathtubs and tub/showers located in the bathroom provide a clear access aisle adjacent to the lavatory that is at least 2'6" wide and extends for a length of 4'0" (measured from the foot of the bathtub). (See Figure 8.)

(vii) Stall showers in the bathroom may be of any size or configuration. A minimum clear floor space 2'6" wide by 4'0" should be available outside the stall. (See Figure 7(d).) If the shower stall is the only bathing facility provided in the covered dwelling unit, or on the accessible level of a covered multistory unit, and measures a nominal 36 x 36, the shower stall must have reinforcing to allow for installation of an optional wall hung bench seat.

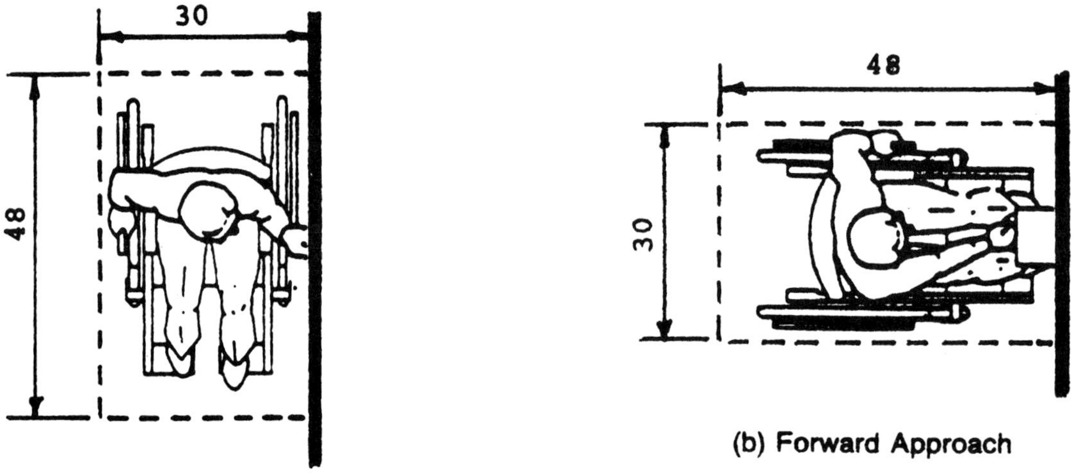

(a) Parallel Approach

(b) Forward Approach

Fig. 6 Minimum Clear Floor Space for Wheelchairs

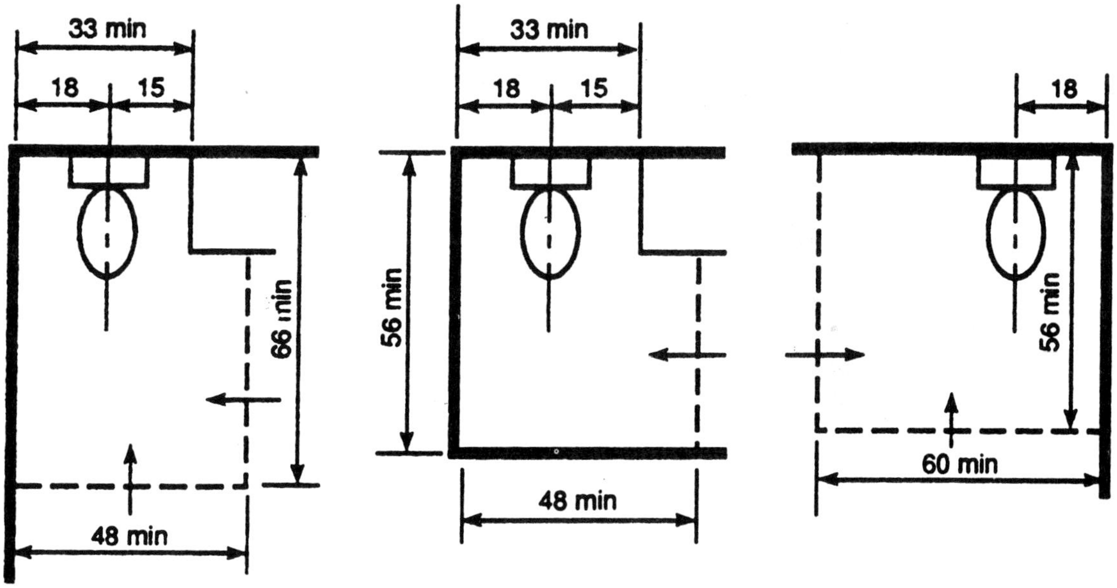

(a) Clear Floor Space for Water Closets

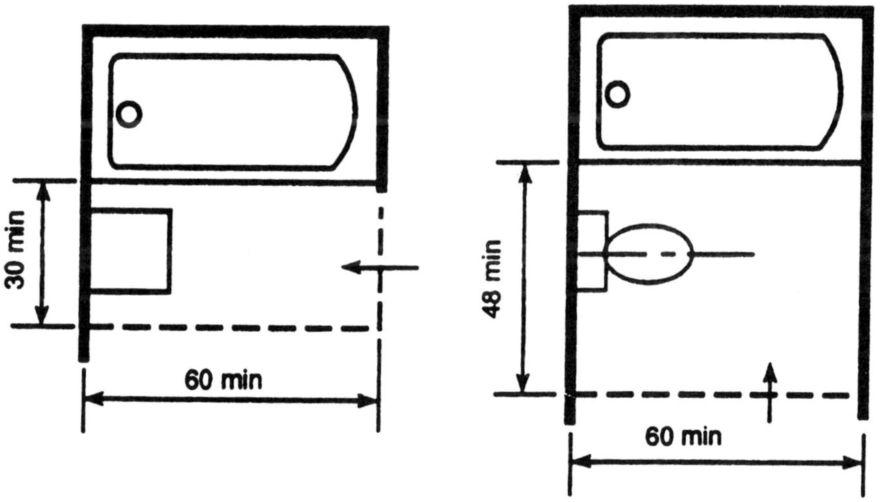

(b) Clear Floor Space at Bathtubs

Fig. 7 Clear Floor Space for Adaptable Bathrooms

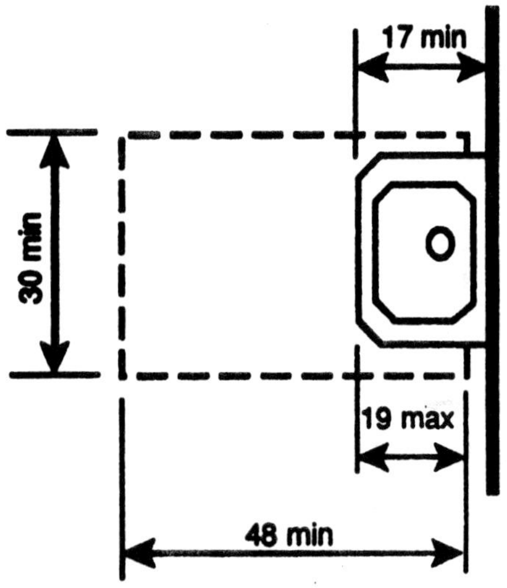

Lavatory With Knee Space

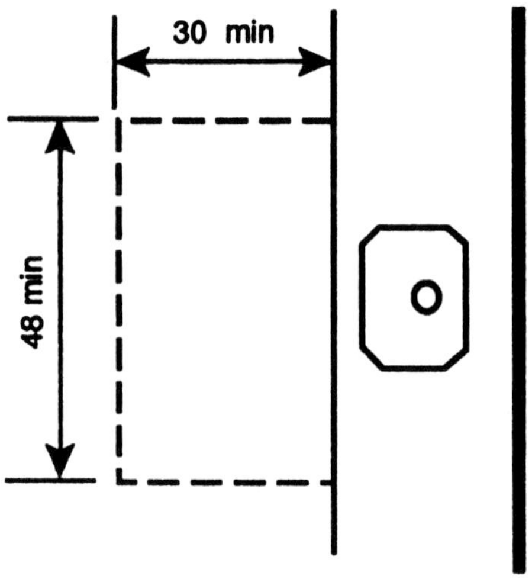

Lavatory Without Knee Space

(c) Clear Floor Space at Lavatories

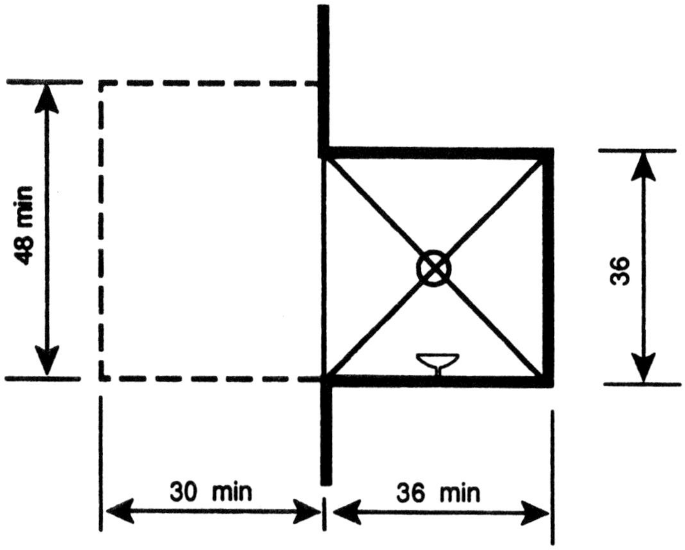

(d) Clear Floor Space at Shower

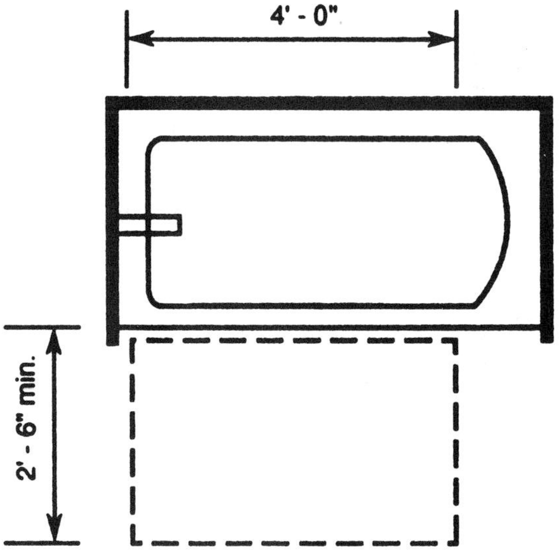

Fig. 8 Alternative Specification – Clear Floor Space at Bathtub

NOTE: Clear floor space beside tub may overlap with clear floor space beneath adjacent fixtures.

Appendix III to Ch. I, Subchapter A—Preamble to Final Housing Accessibility Guidelines (Published March 6, 1991).

[FR Doc. 91-5228 Filed 3-5-91; 8:45 am]

BILLING CODE 4210-28-M

BILLING CODE 4210-28-C

☆U.S. Government Printing Office : 1992 - 312-228/41080

Appendix C

Supplemental Notice
Fair Housing Accessibility Guidelines:
Questions and Answers
about the Guidelines

federal register

Tuesday
June 28, 1994

Part III

Department of Housing and Urban Development

Office of the Assistant Secretary for Fair Housing and Equal Opportunity

24 CFR Ch. I

Fair Housing: Accessibility Guidelines; Questions and Answers; Supplement to Notice

DEPARTMENT OF HOUSING AND URBAN DEVELOPMENT

Office of the Assistant Secretary for Fair Housing and Equal Opportunity

24 CFR Chapter I

[Docket No. N-94-2011; FR-2665-N-09]

Supplement to Notice of Fair Housing Accessibility Guidelines: Questions and Answers About the Guidelines

AGENCY: Office of the Assistant Secretary for Fair Housing and Equal Opportunity, HUD.

ACTION: Supplement to notice of fair housing accessibility guidelines.

SUMMARY: On March 6, 1991, the Department published final Fair Housing Accessibility Guidelines (Guidelines) to provide builders and developers with technical guidance on how to comply with the accessibility requirements of the Fair Housing Amendments Act of 1988 (Fair Housing Act) that are applicable to certain multifamily dwellings designed and constructed for first occupancy after March 13, 1991. Since publication of the Guidelines, the Department has received many questions regarding the applicability of the technical specifications set forth in the Guidelines to certain types of new multifamily dwellings and certain types of units within covered multifamily dwellings. The Department also has received several questions concerning the types of new multifamily dwellings that are subject to the design and construction requirements of the Fair Housing Act.

This document reproduces the questions that have been most frequently asked by members of the public, and the Department's answers to these questions. The Department believes that the issues addressed by these questions and answers may be of interest and assistance to other members of the public who must comply with the design and construction requirements of the Fair Housing Act.

EFFECTIVE DATE: June 28, 1994.

FOR FURTHER INFORMATION CONTACT: Judith Keeler, Director, Office of Program Compliance and Disability Rights. For technical questions regarding this notice, contact Office of Fair Housing and Equal Opportunity, room 5112, Department of Housing and Urban Development, 451 Seventh Street, Washington, DC 20410, telephone 202-708-2618 (voice), 202-708-1734 TTY; for copies of this notice contact the Fair Housing Information Clearinghouse at 1-800-795-7915 (this is a toll-free number), or 1-800-483-2209 (this is a toll-free TTY number).

SUPPLEMENTARY INFORMATION:

Background

The Fair Housing Amendments Act of 1988 (Pub.L. 100-430, approved September 13, 1988) (the Fair Housing Amendments Act) amended title VIII of the Civil Rights Act of 1968 (Fair Housing Act or Act) to add prohibitions against discrimination in housing on the basis of disability and familial status. The Fair Housing Amendments Act also made it unlawful to design and construct certain multifamily dwellings for first occupancy after March 13, 1991, in a manner that makes them inaccessible to persons with disabilities, and established design and construction requirements to make these dwellings readily accessible to and usable by persons with disabilities.[1] Section 100.205 of the Department's regulations at 24 CFR part 100 implements the Fair Housing Act's design and construction requirements (also referred to as accessibility requirements).

On March 6, 1991 (56 FR 9472), the Department published final Fair Housing Accessibility Guidelines (Guidelines) to provide builders and developers with technical guidance on how to comply with the accessibility requirements of the Fair Housing Act. (The Guidelines are codified at 24 CFR Ch.I, Subch.A., App. II. The preamble to the Guidelines is codified at 24 CFR Ch.I, Subch.A., App.III.) The Guidelines are organized to follow the sequence of requirements as they are presented in the Fair Housing Act and in 24 CFR 100.205. The Guidelines provide technical guidance on the following seven requirements:

Requirement 1. Accessible building entrance on an accessible route.
Requirement 2. Accessible common and public use areas.
Requirement 3. Usable doors (usable by a person in a wheelchair).
Requirement 4. Accessible route into and through the dwelling unit.
Requirement 5. Light switches, electrical outlets, thermostats and other environmental controls in accessible locations.
Requirement 6. Reinforced walls for grab bars.
Requirement 7. Usable kitchens and bathrooms.

The design specifications presented in the Guidelines are recommended guidelines only. Builders and developers may choose to depart from these guidelines and seek alternate ways to demonstrate that they have met the requirements of the Fair Housing Act. The Fair Housing Act and the Department's implementing regulation provides, for example, for use of the appropriate requirements of the ANSI A117.1 standard. However, adherence to the Guidelines does constitute a safe harbor in the Department's administrative enforcement process for compliance with the Fair Housing Act's design and construction requirements.

Since publication of the Guidelines, the Department has received many questions regarding applicability of the design specifications set forth in the Guidelines to certain types of new multifamily dwellings and to certain types of interior housing designs. The Department also has received several questions concerning the types of new multifamily dwellings that are subject to compliance with the design and construction requirements of the Fair Housing Act. Given the wide variety in the types of multifamily dwellings and the types of dwelling units, and the continual introduction into the housing market of new building and interior designs, it was not possible for the Department to prepare accessibility guidelines that would address every housing type or housing design. Although the Guidelines cannot address every housing design, it is the Department's intention to assist the public in complying with the design and construction requirements of the Fair Housing Act through workshops and seminars, telephone assistance, written replies to written inquiries, and through the publication of documents such as this one. The Department has contracted for the preparation of a design manual that will further explain and illustrate the Fair Housing Act Accessibility Guidelines.

The questions and answers set forth in this notice address the issues most frequently raised by the public with respect to types of multifamily dwellings subject to the design and construction requirements of the Fair Housing Act, and the technical specifications contained in the Guidelines.

The question and answer format is divided into two sections. Section 1, entitled "Dwellings Subject to the New Construction Requirements of the Fair Housing Act" addresses the issues raised in connection with the types of multifamily dwellings (including portions of such dwellings) constructed for first occupancy after March 13, 1991 that must comply with the Act's design and construction requirements. Section

[1] Although this notice uses the terms "disability" and "disabilities," the terms used in the Fair Housing Amendments Act are "handicap" and "handicaps."

2, entitled "Accessibility Guidelines," addresses the issues raised in connection with the design and construction specifications set forth in the Guidelines.

Dated: March 23, 1994.

Roberta Achtenberg,

Assistant Secretary for Fair Housing and Equal Opportunity.

Accordingly, the Department adds the "Questions and Answers about the Fair Housing Accessibility Guidelines" as Appendix IV to 24 CFR Chapter I, Subchapter A to read as follows:

U.S. Department of Housing and Urban Development
Office of the Assistant Secretary for
Fair Housing and Equal Opportunity

Supplement to Notice of Fair Housing Accessibility Guidelines: Questions and Answers about the Guidelines

24 CFR Ch.I

Appendix IV to Subchapter A—

Note:* *This is a reprint of the Supplement to Notice of Fair Housing Accessibility Guidelines: Questions and Answers About the Guidelines published in the Federal Register on June 28, 1994, Vol. 59, No. 123, pages 33362-33368.

Questions and Answers about the Fair Housing Accessibility Guidelines

Introduction

On March 6, 1991 (56 FR 9472), the Department published final Fair Housing Accessibility Guidelines (Guidelines). (The Guidelines are codified at 24 CFR Ch. I, Subch. A, App. II.) The Guidelines provide builders and developers with technical guidance on how to comply with the accessibility requirements of the Fair Housing Amendments Act of 1988 (Fair Housing Act) that are applicable to certain multifamily dwellings designed and constructed for first occupancy after March 13, 1991. Since publication of the Guidelines, the Department has received many questions regarding the applicability of the technical specifications set forth in the Guidelines to certain types of new multifamily dwellings and certain types of units within covered multifamily dwellings. The Department also has received several questions concerning the types of new multifamily dwellings that are subject to the design and construction requirements of the Fair Housing Act.

The questions and answers contained in this document address some of the issues most frequently raised by the public with respect to the types of multifamily dwellings subject to the design and construction requirements of the Fair Housing Act, and the technical specifications contained in the Guidelines.

The issues addressed in this document are addressed only with respect to the application of the Fair Housing Act and the Guidelines to dwellings which are "covered multifamily dwellings" under the Fair Housing Act. Certain of these dwellings, as well as certain public and common use areas of such dwellings, may also be covered by various other laws, such as section 504 of the Rehabilitation Act of 1973 (29 U.S.C. 794); the Architectural Barriers Act of 1968 (42 U.S.C. 4151-4157); and the Americans with Disabilities Act of 1990 (42 U.S.C. 12101-12213).

Section 504 applies to programs and activities receiving federal financial assistance. The Department's regulations for section 504 are found at 24 CFR part 8.

The Architectural Barriers Act applies to certain buildings financed in whole or in part with federal funds. The Department's regulations for the Architectural Barriers Act are found at 24 CFR parts 40 and 41.

The Americans with Disabilities Act (ADA) is a broad civil rights law guaranteeing equal opportunity for individuals with disabilities in employment, public accommodations, transportation, State and local government services, and telecommunications. The Department of Justice is the lead federal agency for implementation of the ADA and should be contacted for copies of relevant ADA regulations.

The Department has received a number of questions regarding applicability of the ADA to residential housing, particularly with respect to title III of the ADA, which addresses accessibility requirements for public accommodations. The Department has been asked, in particular, if public and common use areas of residential housing are covered by title III of the ADA. Strictly residential facilities are not considered places of public accommodation and therefore would not be subject to title III of the ADA, nor would amenities provided for the exclusive use of residents and their guests. However, common areas that function as one of the ADA's twelve categories of places of public accommodation within residential facilities are considered places of public accommodation if they are open to persons other than residents and their guests. Rental offices and sales office for residential housing, for example, are by their nature open to the public, and are places of public accommodation and must comply with the ADA requirements in addition to all applicable requirements of the Fair Housing Act. As stated above, the remainder of this notice addresses issues most frequently raised by the public with respect to the types of multifamily dwellings subject to the design and construction requirements of the Fair Housing Act, and the technical specifications contained in the Guidelines.

Section 1: Dwellings Subject to the New Construction Requirements of the Fair Housing Act.

The issues addressed in this section concern the types of multifamily dwellings (or portions of such dwellings) designed and constructed for first occupancy after March 13, 1991 that must comply with the design and construction requirements of the Fair Housing Act.

1. Townhouses

(a) **Q.** Are townhouses in non-elevator buildings which have individual exterior entrances required to be accessible?
A. Yes, if they are single-story townhouses. If they are multistory townhouses, accessibility is not required. (See the discussion of townhouses in the preamble to the Guidelines under "Section 2--Definitions [Covered Multifamily Dwellings]" at 56 FR 9481, March 6, 1991, or 24 CFR Ch. I, Subch. A, App. III.)

(b) **Q.** Does the Fair Housing Act cover four one-story dwelling units that share common walls and have individual entrances?
A. Yes. The Fair Housing Act applies to all units in buildings consisting of four or more dwelling units if such buildings have one or more elevators; and ground floor dwelling units in other buildings consisting of four or more dwelling units. This would include one-story homes, sometimes called "single-story townhouses," "villas," or "patio apartments," regardless of ownership, even though such homes may not be considered multifamily dwellings under various building codes.

(c) **Q.** What if the single-story dwelling units are separated by firewalls?
A. The Fair Housing Act would still apply. The Guidelines define covered multifamily dwellings to include buildings having four or more units within a single structure separated by firewalls.

2. Commercial Space

Q. If a building includes three residential dwelling units and one or more commercial spaces, is the building a "covered multifamily dwelling" under the Fair Housing Act?
A. No. Covered multifamily dwellings are buildings consisting of four or more dwelling units, if such buildings have one or more elevators; and ground floor dwelling units in other buildings consisting of four or more dwelling units. Commercial space does not meet the definition of "dwelling unit." Note, however, that title III of the ADA applies to public accommodations and commercial facilities, therefore an independent determination should be made regarding applicability of the ADA to the commercial space in such a building (see the introduction to these questions and answers, which provides some background on the ADA).

3. Condominiums

(a) **Q.** Are condominiums covered by the Fair Housing Act?
A. Yes. Condominiums in covered multifamily dwellings are covered by the Fair Housing Act. The Fair Housing Act makes no distinctions based on ownership.

(b) **Q.** If a condominium is pre-sold as a shell and the interior is designed and constructed by the buyer, are the Guidelines applicable?
A. Yes. The Fair Housing Act applies to design and construction of covered multifamily dwellings, regardless of whether the person doing the design and construction is an architect, builder, or private individual. (See discussion of condominiums in the preamble to Guidelines under "Section 2--Definitions [Dwelling Units]" at 56 FR 9481, March 6, 1991, or 24 CFR Ch. I, Subch. A, App. III.)

4. Additions

(a) **Q.** If an owner adds four or more dwelling units to an existing building, are those units covered by the Fair Housing Act?
A. Yes, provided that the units constitute a new addition to the building and not substantial rehabilitation of existing units.

(b) **Q.** What if new public and common use spaces are also being added?
A. If new public and common use areas or buildings are also added, they are required to be accessible.

(c) **Q.** If the only new construction is an addition consisting of four or more dwelling units, would the existing public and common use spaces have to be made accessible?
A. No, existing public and common use areas would not have to be made accessible. The Fair Housing Act applies to new construction of covered multifamily dwellings. (See section 804(f)(3)(C)(i) of the Act.) Existing public and common use facilities are not newly constructed portions of covered multifamily dwellings. However, reasonable modifications to the existing public and common use areas to provide access would have to be allowed, and the Americans with Disabilities Act (ADA) may apply to certain public and common use areas. An independent determination should be made regarding applicability of the ADA. (See the introduction to these questions and answers, which provides some background on the ADA.)

5. Units Over Parking

(a) **Q.** Plans for a three-story building consist of a common parking area with assigned stalls on grade as the first story, and two stories of single-story dwelling units stacked over the parking. All of the stories above the parking level are to be accessed by stairways. There are no elevators planned to be in the building. Would the first story of single-story dwelling units over the parking level be required to be accessible?
A. Yes. The Guidelines adopt and amplify the definition of "ground floor" found in HUD's regulation implementing the Fair Housing Act (see 24 CFR 100.201) to indicate that ". . .where the first floor containing dwelling units is above grade, all units on that floor must be served by a building entrance on an accessible route. This floor will be considered to be a ground floor." (See definition of "ground floor" in the Guidelines at 24 CFR Ch. I, Subch. A, App. II, Section 2.) Where no dwelling units in a covered multifamily dwelling are located on grade, the first floor with dwelling units will be considered to be a ground floor, and must be served by a building entrance on an accessible route. However, the definition of "ground floor" does not require that there be more than one ground floor.

(b) **Q.** If a building design contains a mix of single-story flats on grade and single-story flats located above grade over a public parking area, do the flats over the parking area have to be accessible?
A. No. In the example in the above question, because some single-story flats are situated on grade, these flats would be the ground floor dwelling units and would be required to be accessible. The definition of ground floor in the Guidelines states, in part, that "ground floor means a floor of a building with a building entrance on an accessible route. A building may have one or more ground floors. . ." Thus, the definition includes situations where the design plan is such that more than one floor of a building may be accessed by means of an accessible route (for an example, see Question 6, which follows). There is no requirement in the Department's regulations implementing the Fair Housing Act that there be more than one ground floor.

6. More Than One Ground Floor

Q. If a two or three story building is to be constructed on a slope, such that the lowest story can be accessed on grade on one side of the building and the second story can be accessed on grade on the other side of the building, do the dwelling units on both the first and second stories have to be made accessible?

A. Yes. By defining "ground floor" to be any floor of a building with an accessible entrance on an accessible route, the Fair Housing Act regulations recognize that certain buildings, based on the site and the design plan, have more than one story which can be accessed at or near grade. In such cases, if more than one story can be designed to have an accessible entrance on an accessible route, then all such stories should be so designed. Each story becomes a ground floor and the dwelling units on that story must meet the accessibility requirements of the Act. (See the discussion on this issue in Question 12 of this document.)

7. Continuing Care Facilities

Q. Do the new construction requirements of the Fair Housing Act apply to continuing care facilities which incorporate housing, health care and other types of services?

A. The new construction requirements of the Fair Housing Act would apply to continuing care facilities if the facility includes at least one building with four or more dwelling units. Whether a facility is a "dwelling" under the Act depends on whether the facility is to be used as a residence for more than a brief period of time. As a result, the operation of each continuing care facility must be examined on a case-by-case basis to determine whether it contains dwellings. Factors that the Department will consider in making such an examination include, but are not limited to: (1) the length of time persons stay in the project; (2) whether policies are in effect at the project that are designed and intended to encourage or discourage occupants from forming an expectation and intent to continue to occupy space at the project; and (3) the nature of the services provided by or at the project.

8. Evidence of First Occupancy

Q. The Fair Housing Act applies to covered multifamily dwellings built for first occupancy after March 13, 1991. What is acceptable evidence of "first occupancy"?

A. The determination of first occupancy is made on a building by building basis. The Fair Housing Act regulations provide that "covered multifamily dwellings shall be deemed to be designed and constructed for first occupancy on or before March 13, 1991 (and therefore exempt from the Act's accessibility requirements) if they are occupied by that date or if the last building permit or renewal thereof for the covered multifamily dwellings is issued by a State, county or local government on or before June 15, 1990."

For buildings that did not obtain the final building permit on or before June 15, 1990, proof of the date of first occupancy consists of (1) a certificate of occupancy, and (2) a showing that at least one dwelling unit in the building actually was occupied by March 13, 1991. For example, a tenant has signed a lease and has taken possession of a unit. The tenant need not have moved into the unit, but the tenant must have taken possession so that, if desired, he or she could have moved into the building by March 13, 1991. For dwelling units that were for sale, this means that the new owner had completed settlement and taken possession of the dwelling unit by March 13, 1991. Once again, the new owner need not have moved in, but the owner must have been in possession of the unit and able to move in, if desired, on or before March 13, 1991. A certificate of occupancy alone would not be an acceptable means of establishing first occupancy, and units offered for sale, but not sold, would not meet the test for first occupancy.

9. Converted Buildings

Q. If a building was used previously for a nonresidential purpose, such as a ware-

house, office building, or school, and is being converted to a multifamily dwelling, must the building meet the requirements of the Fair Housing Act?
A. No, the Fair Housing Act applies to "covered multifamily dwellings for first occupancy after" March 13, 1991, and the Fair Housing Act regulation defines "first occupancy" as "a building that has never before been used for any purpose." (See 24 CFR 100.201, for the definition of "first occupancy," and also 24 CFR Ch. I, Subch. A, App. I.)

Section 2: Accessibility Guidelines.

The issues addressed in this section concern the technical specifications set forth in the Fair Housing Accessibility Guidelines.

Requirement 1 -- Accessible Entrance on an Accessible Route

10. Accessible Routes to Garages

(a) **Q.** Is it necessary to have an accessible path of travel from a subterranean garage to single-story covered multifamily dwellings built on top of the garage?
A. Yes. The Fair Housing Act requires that there be an accessible building entrance on an accessible route. To satisfy Requirement 1 of the Guidelines, there would have to be an accessible route leading to grade level entrances serving the single-story dwelling units from a public street or sidewalk or other pedestrian arrival point. The below grade parking garage is a public and common use facility. Therefore, there must also be an accessible route from this parking area to the covered dwelling units. This may be provided either by a properly sloped ramp leading from the below grade parking to grade level, or by means of an elevator from the parking garage to the dwelling units.

(b) **Q.** Does the route leading from inside a private attached garage to the dwelling unit have to be accessible?
A. No. Under Requirement 1 of the Guidelines, there must be an accessible entrance to the dwelling unit on an accessible route. However, this route and entrance need not originate inside the garage. Most units with attached garages have a separate main entry, and this would be the entrance required to be accessible. Thus, if there were one or two steps inside the garage leading into the unit, there would be no requirement to put a ramp in place of the steps. However, the door connecting the garage and dwelling unit would have to meet the requirements for usable doors.

11. Site Impracticality Tests

(a) **Q.** Under the individual building test, how is the second step of the test performed, which involves measuring the slope of the finished grade between the entrance and applicable arrival points?
A. The slope is measured at ground level from the entrance to the top of the pavement of all vehicular and pedestrian arrival points within 50 feet of the planned entrance, or, if there are none within 50 feet, the vehicular or pedestrian arrival point closest to the planned entrance.

(b) **Q.** Under the individual building test, at what point of the planned entrance is the measurement taken?
A. On a horizontal plane, the center of each individual doorway should be the point of measurement when measuring to an arrival point, whether the doorway is an entrance door to the building or an entrance door to a unit.

(c) **Q.** The site analysis test calls for a calculation of the percentage of the buildable areas having slopes of less than 10 percent. What is the definition of "buildable areas"?
A. The "buildable area" is any area of the lot or site where a building can be located in compliance with applicable codes and zoning regulations.

12. Second Ground Floors

(a) **Q.** The Department's regulation for the Fair Housing Act provides that there can be more than one ground floor in a covered multifamily dwelling (such as a three-story building built on a slope with three stories at and above grade in front and two stories at grade in back). How is the individual building test performed for additional stories, to determine if those stories must also be treated as "ground floors"?
A. For purposes of determining whether a non-elevator building has more than one ground floor, the point of measurement for additional ground floors, after the first ground floor has been established, is at the center of the entrance (building entrance for buildings with one or more common entrance and each dwelling unit entrance for buildings with separate ground floor unit entrances) at floor level for that story.

(b) **Q.** What happens if a builder deliberately manipulates the grade so that a second story, which also might have been treated as a ground floor, requires steps?
A. Deliberate manipulation of the height of the finished floor level to avoid the requirements of the Fair Housing Act would serve as a basis for the Department to determine that there is reasonable cause to believe that a discriminatory housing practice has occurred.

Requirement 2 -- Public and Common Use Areas

13. No Covered Dwellings

Q. Are the public and common use areas of a newly constructed development that consists entirely of buildings having four or more multistory townhouses, with no elevators, required to be accessible?
A. No. The Fair Housing Act applies only to new construction of covered multifamily dwellings. Multistory townhouses, provided that they meet the definition of "multistory" in the Guidelines, are not covered multifamily dwellings if the building does not have an elevator. (See discussion of townhouses in the preamble to the Guidelines under "Section 2--Definitions [Covered Multifamily Dwellings]" at 56 FR 9481, March 6, 1991, or 24 CFR Ch. I, Subch. A, App. III.) If there are no covered multifamily dwellings on a site, then the public and common use areas of the site are not required to be accessible. However, the Americans with Disabilities Act (ADA) may apply to certain public and common use areas. Again, an independent determination should be made regarding applicability of the ADA. (See the introduction to these questions and answers, which provides some background on the ADA.)

14. Parking Spaces and Garages

(a) **Q.** How many resident parking spaces must be made accessible at the time of construction?
A. The Guidelines provide that a minimum of two percent of the parking spaces serving covered dwelling units be made accessible and located on an accessible route to wheelchair users. Also, if a resident requests an accessible space, additional accessible parking spaces would be necessary if the two percent are already reserved.

(b) **Q.** If both open and covered parking spaces are provided, how many of each type must be accessible?
A. The Guidelines require that accessible parking be provided for residents with disabilities on the same terms and with the full range of choices, e.g., surface parking or garage, that are provided for other residents of the project. Thus, if a project provides different types of parking such as surface parking, garage, or covered spaces, some of each must be made accessible. While the total parking spaces required to be accessible is only two percent, at least one space for each type of parking should be made accessible even if this number exceeds two percent.

(c) **Q.** If a project having covered multifamily dwellings provides parking garages where there are several individual garages grouped together either in a separate area of the building (such as at one end of the building, or in a detached building), for assignment or rental to residents, are there any requirements for the inside dimensions of these individual parking garages?
A. Yes. These garages would be public and common use space, even though the individual garages may be assigned to a particular dwelling unit. Therefore, at least two percent of the garages should be at least 14' 2" wide and the vehicular door should be at least 10'-0" wide.

(d) **Q.** If a covered multifamily dwelling has a below grade common use parking garage, is there a requirement for a vertical clearance to allow vans to park?
A. This issue was addressed in the preamble to the Guidelines, but continues to be a frequently asked question. (See the preamble to the Guidelines under the discussion of "Section 5--Guidelines for Requirement 2" at 56 FR 9486, March 6, 1991, or 24 CFR Ch. I, Subch. A, App. III.) In response to comments from the public that the Guidelines for parking specify minimum vertical clearance for garage parking, the Department responded: No national accessibility standards, including UFAS, require particular vertical clearances in parking garages. The Department did not consider it appropriate to exceed commonly accepted standards by including a minimum vertical clearance in the Fair Housing Accessibility Guidelines, in view of the minimal accessibility requirements of the Fair Housing Act.

Since the Guidelines refer to ANSI A117.1 1986 for the standards to follow for public and common use areas, and since the ANSI does not include a vertical clearance for garage parking, the Guidelines likewise do not. (Note: UFAS is the Uniform Federal Accessibility Standard.)

15. Public Telephones

Q. If a covered multifamily dwelling has public telephones in the lobby, what are the requirements for accessibility for these telephones?
A. The requirements governing public telephones are found in Item #14, "Common use spaces and facilities," in the chart under Requirement 2 of the Guidelines. While the chart does not address the quantity of accessible public telephones, at a minimum, at least one accessible telephone per bank of telephones would be required. The specifications at ANSI 4.29 would apply.

Requirement 3 -- Usable Doors

16. Required Width

Q. Will a standard hung 32-inch door provide sufficient clear width to meet the requirements of the Fair Housing Act?
A. No, a 32-inch door would not provide a sufficient clear opening to meet the requirement for usable doors. A notation in the Guidelines for Requirement 3 indicates that a 34-inch door, hung in the standard manner, provides an acceptable nominal 32-inch clear opening.

17. Maneuvering Clearances and Hardware

Q. Is it correct that only the exterior side of the main entry door of covered multifamily dwellings must meet the ANSI requirements?
A. Yes. The exterior side of the main entry door is part of the public and common use areas and therefore must meet ANSI A117.1 1986 specifications for doors. These specifications include necessary maneuvering clearances and accessible door hardware. The interior of the main entry door is part of the dwelling unit and only needs to meet the requirements for usable doors within the dwelling intended for user passage, i.e., at least 32 inches

nominal clear width, with no requirements for maneuvering clearances and hardware. (See 56 FR 9487-9488, March 6, 1991, or 24 CFR Ch. I, Subch. A, App. III.)

18. Doors to Inaccessible Areas

Q. Is it necessary to provide usable doors when the door leads to an area of the dwelling that is not accessible, such as the door leading down to an unfinished basement, or the door connecting a single-story dwelling with an attached garage? (In the latter case, there is a separate entrance door to the unit which is accessible.)
A. Yes. Within the dwelling unit, doors intended for user passage through the unit must meet the requirements for usable doors. Such doors would have to provide at least 32 inches nominal clear width when the door is open 90 degrees, measured between the face of the door and the stop. This will ensure that, if a wheelchair user occupying the dwelling unit chooses to modify the unit to provide accessibility to these areas, such as installing a ramp from the dwelling unit into the garage, the door will be sufficiently wide to allow passage. It also will allow passage for people using walkers or crutches.

Requirement 4 -- Accessible Route Into and Through the Unit

19. Sliding Door

Q. If a sliding door track has a threshold of 3/4", does this trigger requirements for ramps?
A. No. The Guidelines at Requirement 4 provide that thresholds at doors, including sliding door tracks, may be no higher than 3/4" and must be beveled with a slope no greater than 1:2.

20. Private Attached Garages

(a) **Q.** If a covered multifamily dwelling has an individual, private garage which is attached to and serves only that dwelling, does the garage have to be accessible in terms of width and length?
A. Garages attached to and which serve only one covered multifamily dwelling are part of that dwelling unit, and are not covered by Requirement 2 of the Guidelines, which addresses accessible and usable public and common use space. Because such individual garages attached to and serving only one covered multifamily dwelling typically are not finished living space, the garage is not required to be accessible in terms of width or length. The answer to this question should be distinguished from the answer to Question 14(c). Question 14(c) addresses parking garages where there are several garages or stalls located together, either in a separate, detached building, or in a central area of the building, such as at one end. These types of garages are not attached to, and do not serve, only one unit and are therefore considered public and common use garages.

21. Split-Level Entry

Q. Is a dwelling unit that has a split entry foyer, with the foyer and living room on an accessible route and the remainder of the unit down two steps, required to be accessible if it is a ground floor unit in a covered multifamily dwelling?
A. Yes. Under Requirement 4, there must be an accessible route into and through the dwelling unit. This would preclude a split level foyer, unless a properly sloped ramp can be provided.

Requirement 5 -- Environmental Controls

22. Range Hood Fans

Q. Must the switches on range hood kitchen ventilation fans be in accessible locations?
A. No. Kitchen ventilation fans located on a range hood are considered to be part of the appliance. The Fair Housing Act has no requirements for appliances in the interiors of dwelling units, or the switches

that operate them. (See "Guidelines for Requirement 5" and "Controls for Ranges and Cooktops" at 56 FR 9490 and 9492, March 6, 1991, or 24 CFR Ch. I, Subch. A, App. III.)

Requirement 6 -- Reinforced Walls for Grab Bars

23. Type of Reinforcement

Q. What type of reinforcement should be used to reinforce bathroom walls for the later installation of grab bars?
A. The Guidelines do not prescribe the type of material to use or method of providing reinforcement for bathroom walls. The Guidelines recognize that grab bar reinforcing may be accomplished in a variety of ways, such as by providing plywood panels in the areas illustrated in the Guidelines under Requirement 6, or by installing vertical reinforcement in the form of double studs at the points noted on the figures in the Guidelines. The builder/owners should maintain records that reflect the placement of the reinforcing material, for later reference by a resident who wishes to install a grab bar.

24. Type of Grab Bar

Q. What types of grab bars should the reinforcement be designed to accommodate and what types may be used if the builder elects to install grab bars in some units at the time of construction?
A. The Guidelines do not prescribe the type of product for grab bars, or the structural strength for grab bars. The Guidelines only state that the necessary reinforcement must be placed "so as to permit later installation of appropriate grab bars." (Emphasis added.) In determining what is an appropriate grab bar, builders are encouraged to look to the 1986 ANSI A117.1 standard, the standard cited in the Fair Housing Act. Builders also may follow State or local standards in planning for or selecting appropriate grab bars.

Requirement 7 -- Usable Kitchens and Bathrooms

25. Counters and Vanities

Q. It appears from Figure 2(c) of the Guidelines (under Requirement 5) that there is a 34 inch height requirement for kitchen counters and vanities. Is this true?
A. No. Requirement 7 addresses the requirement for usable kitchens and bathrooms so that a person in a wheelchair can maneuver about the space. The legislative history of the Fair Housing Act makes it clear that the Congress intended that the Act affect ability to maneuver within the space of the kitchen and bathroom, but not to require fixtures, cabinetry or plumbing of adjustable design. Figure 2(c) of the Guidelines is illustrating the maximum side reach range over an obstruction. Because the picture was taken directly from the ANSI A117.1 1986 standard, the diagram also shows the height of the obstruction, which, in this picture, is a countertop. This 34 inch height, however, should not be regarded as a requirement.

26. Showers

Q. Is a parallel approach required at the shower, as shown in Figure 7(d) of the Guidelines?
A. Yes. For a 36" x 36" shower, as shown in Figure 7(d), a person in a wheelchair would typically add a wall hung seat. Thus the parallel approach as shown in Figure 7(d) is essential in order to be able to transfer from the wheelchair to the shower seat.

27. Tub Controls

Q. Do the Guidelines set any requirements for the type or location of bathtub controls?
A. No, except where the specifications in Requirement 7(2)(b) are used. In that case, while the type of control is not

specified, the control must be located as shown in Figure 8 of the Guidelines.

28. Paragraph (b) Bathrooms

Q. If an architect or builder chooses to follow the bathroom specifications in Requirement 7, Guideline 2, paragraph (b), where at least one bathroom is designed to comply with the provisions of paragraph (b), are the other bathrooms in the dwelling unit required to have reinforced walls for grab bars?
A. Yes. Requirement 6 of the Guidelines requires reinforced walls in bathrooms for later installation of grab bars. Even though Requirement 6 was not repeated under Requirement 7--Guideline 2, it is a separate requirement which must be met in all bathrooms. The same would be true for other Requirements in the Guidelines, such as Requirement 5, which applies to usable light switches, electrical outlets, thermostats and other environmental controls; Requirement 4 for accessible route; and Requirement 3 for usable doors.

29. Bathroom Clear Floor Space

Q. Is it acceptable to design a bathroom with an in-swinging 2'10" door which can be retrofitted to swing out in order to provide the necessary clear floor space in the bathroom?
A. No. The requirements in the Guidelines must be included at the time of construction. Thus, for a bathroom, there must be sufficient maneuvering space and clear floor space so that a person using a wheelchair or other mobility aid can enter and close the door, use the fixtures and exit.

30. Lavatories

Q. Would it be acceptable to use removable base cabinets beneath a wall-hung lavatory where a parallel approach is not possible?
A. Yes. The space under and around the cabinet should be finished prior to installation. For example, the tile or other floor finish must extend under the removable base cabinet.

31. Wing Walls

Q. Can a water closet (toilet) be located in an alcove with a wing wall?
A. Yes, as long as the necessary clear floor space shown in Figure 7(a) is provided. This would mean that the wing wall could not extend beyond the front edge of a lavatory located on the other side of the wall from the water closet.

32. Penalties

Q. What types of penalties or monetary damages will be assessed if covered multifamily dwellings are found not to be in compliance with the Fair Housing Act?
A. Under the Fair Housing Act, if an administrative law judge finds that a respondent has engaged in or is about to engage in a discriminatory housing practice, the administrative law judge will order appropriate relief. Such relief may include actual and compensatory damages, injunctive or other equitable relief, attorney's fees and costs, and may also include civil penalties ranging from $10,000 for the first offense to $50,000 for repeated offenses. In addition, in the case of buildings which have been completed, structural changes could be ordered, and an escrow fund might be required to finance future changes.

Further, a Federal district court judge can order similar relief plus punitive damages as well as civil penalties for up to $100,000 in an action brought by a private individual or by the U.S. Department of Justice.

U. S. Department of Housing and Urban Development
Washington, D.C. 20410-0500

December 16, 1991

OFFICE OF GENERAL COUNSEL

MEMORANDUM FOR: Gordon Mansfield, Assistant Secretary for Fair Housing and Equal Opportunity, E

FROM: Frank Keating, General Counsel, G

SUBJECT: Carriage House Units

You have inquired about the application of the accessibility requirements under the Fair Housing Amendments Act ("Act") to carriage house unit designs.

In the examples which you provided, stacked housing units are designed to incorporate parking for each unit into the dwelling unit design in non-elevator buildings. Specifically, you have indicated that the garage footprint is used as the footprint for the remaining floor or floors of the units.

Since these carriage houses are located in buildings without elevators, the remaining question is whether they are ground floor units. See Section 804(f)(7) of the Act.

The Preamble to the regulations implementing the Act discusses the applicability of the Act to townhouses. Because the accessiblity provisions of the Act "extend only to ground floor units in buildings without elevators," and a townhouse of more than one story is not a ground floor unit, multistory townhouses were not required to be made accessible in buildings where there was no elevator. 24 CFR Ch. 1, Subch. A., App. 1, P. 702 (1991).

Because this carriage house design does not include the entire dwelling unit on the ground floor, it is not a covered multifamily dwelling within the meaning of the Act.

Revised April 1998
HUD - 1733-FHEO

EQUAL HOUSING OPPORTUNITY

04758

U.S. DEPARTMENT OF JUSTICE
CIVIL RIGHTS DIVISION

Multi-Family Housing Access Forum
Tuesday, November 14, 2006
8:30 - 11:00 a.m.

Embassy Suites Phoenix-Scottsdale
4415 East Paradise Village Parkway South
Phoenix, Arizona
(602) 765-5800

AGENDA

Registration and Breakfast

Welcome and Introductions
STEVEN H. ROSENBAUM
Chief, Housing and Civil Enforcement Section
Civil Rights Division, U.S. Department of Justice

Opening Remarks
GRACE CHUNG BECKER
Deputy Assistant Attorney General
Civil Rights Division, U.S. Department of Justice

Presentations
MICHAEL PYATOK, FAIA
Pyatok Architects, Inc.
Director, Stardust Center for Affordable Homes and the Family
Arizona State University

CURTIS CATON, AIA
Pyatok Architects, Inc.
Oakland, California

DOUGLAS T. WHITNEYBELL, AIA
Whitneybell Architects, Inc.
Phoenix, Arizona

Comments from Participants

Concluding Remarks
STEVEN H. ROSENBAUM

4 ACCESSIBLE ROUTES INTO AND THROUGH DWELLING UNIT

- Thresholds of unit's exterior doors may not exceed 3/4" (also applies to sliding tracks).
- In single-story units, changes of height of 1/4" to 1/2" must be beveled. Those greater than 1/2" must be ramped or have other means of access.
- Minimum **clear** width for accessible route inside the unit is 36".
- Hallways, passages, and corridors must be wide enough to allow room to maneuver a wheelchair throughout the unit.

5 ACCESSIBLE LIGHT SWITCHES, ELECTRICAL OUTLETS, AND ENVIRONMENTAL CONTROLS

- Operable parts of controls must be no lower than 15" and no higher than 48".
- Switches, outlets, thermostats and controls must be accessible to people in wheelchairs.

6 REINFORCED WALLS IN BATHROOM

- Walls in bathrooms must be reinforced so that grab bars near the toilet, tub, shower, and shower seat, if provided, can be added later.

Refer to diagrams in HUD Guidelines for locations and acceptable dimensions of wall reinforcements.

7 USABLE KITCHENS AND BATHROOMS

- A minimum of 40" of **clear** floor space is required in kitchens to allow a person in a wheelchair to maneuver between opposing base cabinets, countertops, appliances, or walls.
- A U-shaped design requires a minimum of 5' in diameter **clear** space, or removable cabinets at the base of the "U."
- Appliances must be located so a person in a wheelchair can use them. A 30" x 48" **clear** floor space is required for a parallel or forward approach.
- Adequate maneuvering space is required in bathrooms so that a person in a wheelchair can easily enter, close the door, use the facilities and fixtures, and exit.

HUD Guidelines provides two sets of specifications for usable bathrooms: Option A and Option B.

- With Option A, **all** bathrooms must include providing a basic degree of maneuverability to meet Option A requirements.
- With Option B, only one bathroom must meet Option B requirements, which provide for a stricter degree of maneuverability. Other bathrooms require usable doors, reinforced walls, switch/outlets in accessible locations, and must be an accessible route.

REQUIREMENTS

1. Accessible Entrance on an Accessible Route
2. Accessible Public and Common-Use Areas
3. Usable Doors
4. Accessible Routes Into and Through the Dwelling Unit
5. Accessible Light Switches, Electrical Outlets, and Environmental Controls
6. Reinforced Walls in Bathrooms
7. Usable Kitchens and Bathrooms

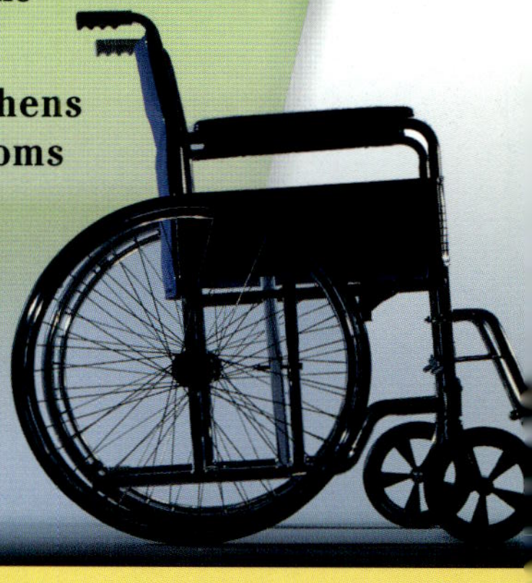

Based on the Fair Housing Act, as amended, there are seven technical requirements in the *Accessibility Guidelines* for covered buildings.

ACCESSIBILITY GUIDELINES

1 ON AN ACCESSIBLE ROUTE

- If separate entrances for ground-floor units, each entrance must be accessible.
- If common entrances to a multi-unit building, at least one entrance — typically used by residents for entering the building — must be accessible.
- An accessible entrance must be located on a route that a person in a wheelchair can easily travel, leading to and from meaningful locations, e.g., parking, public transportation, other buildings in the complex, amenities such as laundry room, recreational facilities.

Refer to ANSI, Section 4.3.

2 ACCESSIBLE PUBLIC AND COMMON-USE AREAS

- Parking areas, curb ramps, passenger loading areas, building lobbies, lounges, halls and corridors, elevators, public use restrooms, and rental or sales offices must be accessible to people with disabilities.
- Included are drinking fountains/ water coolers, mailboxes, laundry rooms, community and exercise rooms, swimming pools, playgrounds, recreation facilities, nature trails.

3 USABLE DOORS

- Doors must be wide enough to enable a person in a wheelchair to maneuver through them easily.
- Included are public and common-use doors, doors leading into an individual dwelling unit, and **all** doors within the dwelling unit itself.

Doors in public or common-use areas can comply by using ANSI standards.

- For wheelchairs, doors must have a minimum **clear** opening width of 32" (measure from face of door to the stop, with the door open 90 degrees).
- All types of doors are covered:
  - hinged doors
  - sliding doors
  - folding doors
- Doors leading to any outdoor amenities the dwelling may have… balcony, patio, deck… are covered. If a deck or patio has doorways leading into two or more separate rooms, **all** these doors must be usable.

AS AMENDED

- Prohibits housing discrimination on the basis of race, color, religion, sex, national origin, familial status, or disability.
- Sets certain requirements for accessible design in new construction.
- Covers residential multi-family dwellings for first occupancy after March 13, 1991 (covered multi-family dwellings are **all** types of buildings with four or more units).
- Includes condos, single-story townhouses, garden apartments, vacation timeshares, dormitories, and homeless shelters.
- Requires covered buildings with an elevator to make **all** units in buildings accessible.
- Requires covered buildings without an elevator to make **all** ground-floor units (including ground-floors at different levels in the same building) accessible.

4703

U.S. Department of Housing and Urban Development
Equal Housing Opportunity

For further information
about the Fair Housing Accessibility Guidelines,
www.hud.gov/fairhousing
HUD Distribution Center: **1-800-767-7468**
TTY: **1-800-877-8339**

The Fair Housing Amendments Act of 1988 amends Title VIII of the Civil Rights Act of 1968, which prohibits discrimination on the basis of race, color, religion, sex, or national origin in the sale, rental, and financing of dwellings, to prohibit discriminatory housing practices based on disability and familial status. The 1988 Amendments also establish certain design and construction requirements for new multifamily housing built for first occupancy after March 13, 1991.

WHAT ARE THE NEW CONSTRUCTION REQUIREMENTS?

The Fair Housing Amendments Act of 1988 requires that covered multifamily dwellings built for first occupancy after March 13, 1991 include certain features of accessible design. Therefore, architects, builders, and other persons involved in the design and construction of housing must be aware of the Fair Housing Amendments Act design and construction requirements.

WHAT ARE COVERED MULTIFAMILY DWELLINGS?

Covered multifamily dwellings are buildings consisting of four or more dwelling units, if such buildings have one or more elevators, and ground floor dwelling units in other buildings consisting of four or more dwelling units. This includes apartments, condominiums, single-story townhouses, vacation time-sharing properties, homeless shelters and other, similar residential buildings.

- Architects;
- Builders;
- Building Contractors;
- Site Engineers; and
- Any other person(s) involved in the design and construction of residential housing.

WHAT ARE FAIR HOUSING ACCESSIBILITY GUIDELINES?

The purpose of the Fair Housing Accessibility Guidelines (Guidelines) is to provide technical guidance on designing dwelling units as required by the Fair Housing Amendments Act of 1988. These Guidelines are not mandatory, but are intended to provide a safe harbor for compliance with the accessibility requirements of the Fair Housing Amendments Act.

WHAT ARE THE PENALTIES FOR NON-COMPLIANCE?

Responsibility for complying with the law rests with any and all persons involved in the design and construction of covered multifamily dwellings. When the law has been violated, an administrative law judge or a Federal District Court will order relief. Such relief may include actual and compensatory damages, attorneys' fees and costs, and may also include civil penalties ranging from $11,000 to $60,000. In the case of buildings which have already been completed, structural changes could be ordered.

The Guidelines provide technical guidance on the specific requirements stated in the Fair Housing Amendments Act, which are:

- An accessible building entrance on an accessible route;
- accessible and usable public and common use areas;
- doors designed to be usable by persons in wheelchairs;
- an accessible route into and through the covered dwelling unit;
- light switches, electrical outlets, thermostats and other environmental controls in accessible locations;
- reinforcements in bathroom walls for later installation of grab bars; and
- kitchen and bathroom space organized so an individual in a wheelchair can maneuver about the space.

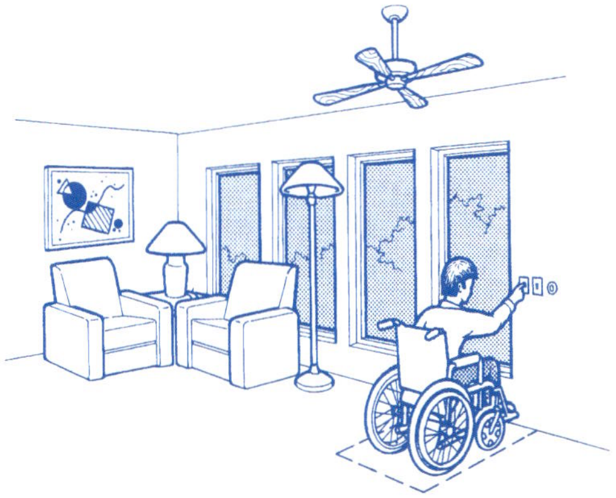

The Fair Housing Amendments Act does not invalidate any law of a state or local government that requires dwellings to be designed and constructed in a manner that affords persons with disabilities greater accessibility than the requirements of the Fair Housing Amendments Act. Likewise, other Federal laws which require greater accessibility in certain housing, such as Section 504 of the Rehabilitation Act of 1973 or the Architectural Barriers Act of 1968, are not invalidated or replaced by the Fair Housing Amendments Act requirements.

WHERE TO GET MORE INFORMATION?

For more information concerning the Fair Housing Amendments Act design and construction requirements contact your local HUD field office.

For copies of this publication, contact the HUD Distribution Center at
1-800-767-7468 (voice);
1-800-927-9275 (TTY)

Please visit our website:
www.hud.gov/fairhousing

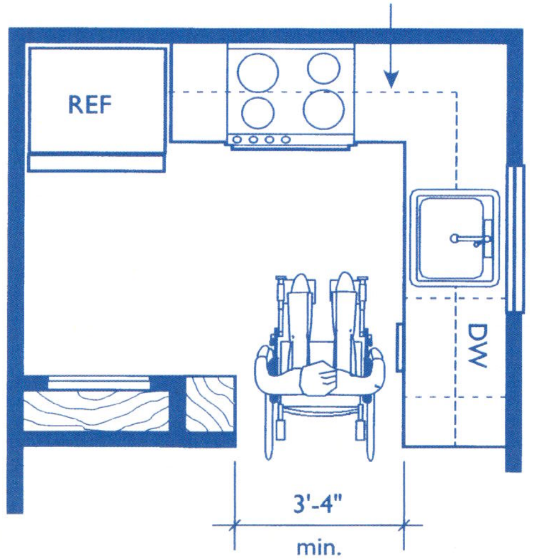

U.S. Department of Housing and Urban Development
451 Seventh Street, S.W.
Washington, D.C. 20410

Official Business
Penalty for Private Use, $300

EQUAL HOUSING OPPORTUNITY

"Good Access is Good Business...."
www.usdoj.gov/crt/housing/fairhousing

AND BUILDERS

Are you in compliance with the Fair Housing Act?

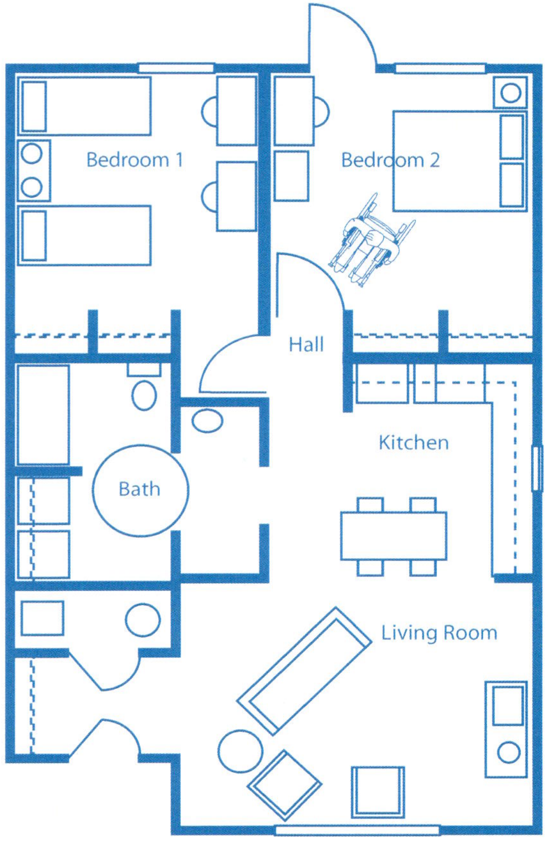

U.S. Department of Housing and Urban Development

What's the solution?

1

Provide lever hardware.

3

Provide a 30" X 48" clear floor space centered on the lavatory.

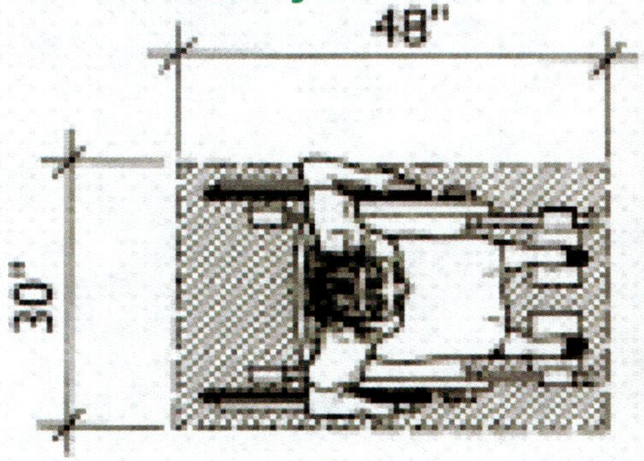

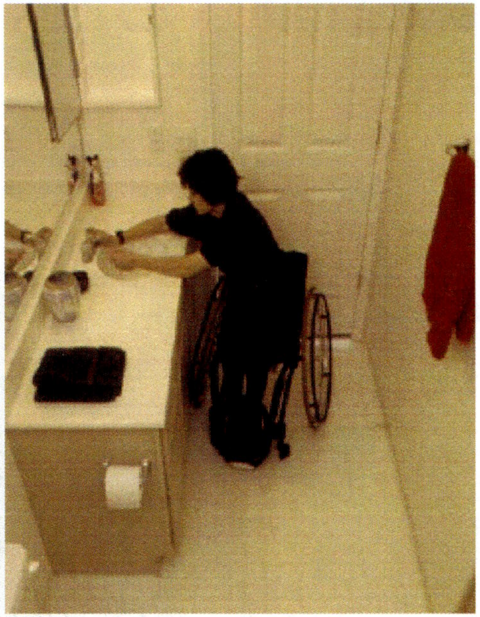

2

Provide wheel stops.

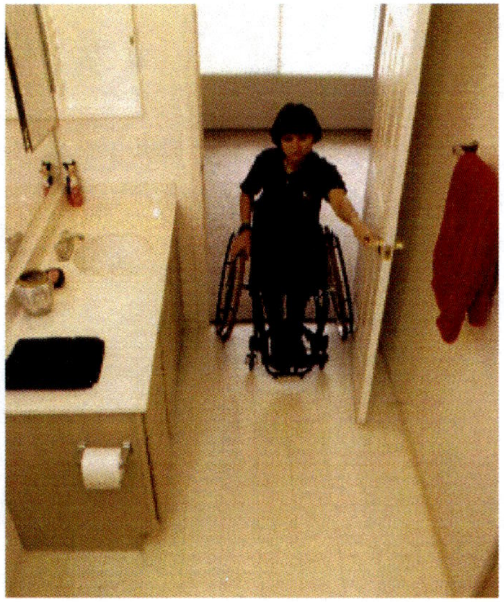

4

Provide 32" minimum clear opening for accessible doors; 32" nominal clear opening for usable doors. (Primary entry is accessible door; bathroom door is usable door.)

What's wrong with the picture?

1

Dwelling unit

2

3

4

26" nominal
clear opening
at door

WHITNEYBELL PERRY INC
ARCHITECTURE & PLANNING

PHOENIX ■ CHANDLER
p:602.265.1891 f: 602.230.8458

D.O.J. Access Forum

14 November 2006

Phoenix, Arizona

WPI Standard – EXCEED minimum requirements whenever possible (exception when exact dimensions are required – i.e. 18" to CL of toilet).

3 Standard Guidelines:

- Fair Housing Act Design Manual 1996, 1999
- ANSI A117.1 1992, 1998, 2003 (note: HUD projects or other federally funded projects – UFAS will need to be referenced as well)
- ADA Guidelines (latest edition 2004)
-

Fair Housing Act Design Manual

- Applies "to all new multifamily housing consisting of four or more dwelling units."
- Applies to all units in a project if all floors are accessible (upper floors or floors below grade) via elevator (even applies to two-story t.h. units if elevator used) OR applies to all ground floor units.
- Only exception: if it can be proven that there are site impracticality issues that must limit the number of "covered" units; however, the guidelines mandate that at least 20% of the units must meet the requirements regardless of site impracticality issues (p. 1.41). Reference FHA manual starting at page 1.38 for detailed description of site impracticality tests.

ANSI:

- Applicable year is typically determined by UBC/IBC year currently in use by jurisdiction or by jurisdiction's amendments to the building code. (Trend is to refer to most current ANSI). However, funding agencies may also dictate required year.
- Applies to public spaces and residential units as required by UBC/IBC (typically 2% of the total number of units; however, federally funded projects typically require 5% of the total number of units plus hearing/visual impaired units – reference UFAS).

ADA:

- Applies to public areas – office/recreation buildings, site, commercial/retail uses, etc.

1102 EAST MISSOURI AVENUE PHOENIX, ARIZONA 85014-2784
575 WEST CHANDLER BOULEVARD, SUITE 123 CHANDLER, ARIZONA 85225-7532

TIPS

- 30" x 48" clear floor dimension – either forward approach or side approach **centered** on appliance or fixture (FHA) (type of fixture will determine).
- 60" clear in U-shaped kitchens (FHA).
- Washer/dryer accessibility requires 30" x 48" centered side approach (2003 ANSI section 1003.10).
- Required door clearances – 32" clear with door open 90º.
- Site impracticality test (FHA): Must have **certified** slope analysis by civil engineer.
- Parking: must provide equal amenities, i.e. if project has covered, garage and open parking then there must also be accessible parking of each type. This means that space itself must meet accessibility guidelines and an accessible route must lead to the space from the residential units or amenities (WPI usually provides for van parking).
- Use "accessible" in lieu of "handicap".
- Full ANSI units: provide at least one of each bedroom type – i.e. one-bedroom, two-bedroom, three-bedroom, etc.
- All trash enclosures must be accessible – must have an accessible route leading to them and must be usable by persons with disabilities.
- Grab bar blocking in bathrooms required in all FHA/ANSI units.
- Verify that jurisdiction hasn't amended the code to require more strict accessibility compliance (i.e. parking stall sizes, number, etc.).
- Jurisdiction and/or client cannot dictate that we use less strict guidelines regarding <u>federal</u> accessibility requirements.

WHITNEYBELL PERRY INC
ARCHITECTURE & PLANNING

QUIZ

1. What is the maximum slope? ANSI/ADA

   Typical sidewalk (non-ramp) ____ *1:20 = 5%*
   Ramp ____ *1:12 = 8.33%*
   Cross slope on sidewalk ____ *1:48 = 2%*
   Curb ramp ____ *1:12 = 8.33%*

   (These slopes requirements should be noted in civil engineer's general notes as well as on the accessibility site plan.)

   BONUS: What is the maximum rise dimension allowed before handrails are required on ramps? ____ *6"*

2. Which residential unit(s) does FHA cover? *All ground floor units and units served by elevators.*

3. How many van accessible parking spaces are required if there are 8 total accessible parking spaces required for a multifamily project? *ADA requires 1.*

4. How many van accessible parking spaces are required if there are 9 total accessible parking spaces required for a multifamily project? *ADA requires 2.*

5. What is the minimum door width allowed for interior, swinging passage doors in FHA/ANSI units? *ANSI governs with 36" or 34" with special hinges.*

6. Site has 100 first floor units and 100 second floor units not elevator served (4 accessible) plus clubhouse, 2 pools, exercise building, detached mail kiosk, and tot lot. There are 300 total parking spaces and a train is heading west from Chicago at 70 mph on the same track as a train heading east from L.A. at 84 mph. How many accessible parking spaces are required? *FHA requires 2% of the spaces required of the covered units by the municipality plus one per amenity including clubhouse.*

WHITNEYBELL PERRY INC

ARCHITECTURE & PLANNING

PHOENIX ■ CHANDLER

Douglas T. Whitneybell Architects

WHITNEYBELL PERRY INC
HIGH DESERT VILLAGE

AFFORDABLE HOUSING

Central Phoenix

FRIDAY
May 24, 2002

Downtown • East Phoenix • North-Central Phoenix • South Phoenix

Casa Nueva's American dream

Low-income families get affordable housing

By Yvonne Wingett
The Arizona Republic

Joining hands over a dinner of hot dogs and macaroni, the Sanders-Davis family prayed together for the first time ever.

They thanked the Lord for their new home. They thanked the Lord for the first home-made meal in two years. And they thanked the Lord for the strength to kick a drug habit that two years ago sucked away every dollar and landed them in a homeless shelter.

"We're not sleeping on top of each other any more," said Stephen Sanders, 49, a computer-technician student at Maricopa Skill Center.

"And I have my privacy now," added 13-year-old Johna Davis, who can't wait to have her first slumber party.

The Sanders-Davis family isn't the only lucky one.

At a time when Arizona is suffering from a shortage of affordable housing, other low-income families have a chance to move into brand-spanking new digs for less than market rate. Apartments range from $279 to $680, with the tax credit.

Casa Nueva, a $5.2 million development near 18th and Van Buren streets, has 26 tax-credit-funded units available to formerly homeless, low-income families that earn up to 60 percent of state median income, or about $52,000 for a family of four. And 38 apartments are available with no income restrictions, which range from $510 to $705.

"You don't see a lot of the tax-credit affordable, multi-family housing in the downtown core, and they're a necessity," said Brian Champeau, director of Phoenix Local Initiatives Support Corp. "The need is here and the city is really coming to the table and understanding they need to be here to provide quality housing to everyone — not just folks who can afford $1,000 a month."

For single mom Linda Johnson and her four children, shelling out $399 a month for a three-bedroom apartment still bruises the pocketbook. But she's pinching pennies on groceries and "extras" because she's determined to keep her kids out of the drug-infested hotels and shelters they've known for half their lives.

"I cried the first night we were here," said Johnson, a janitor. "We feel like we're in a mansion. A dishwasher, my own bathroom, a walk-in closet — I was totally awesomed about it."

The new home is what the Johnson and Sanders-Davis families needed to jump-start their "new lives."

"It's like heaven, a new start," said Shirley Davis, 43.

And developers hope that the complex will help revitalize the primarily Hispanic neighborhood that is packed with dilapidated single and multifamily housing.

SENIOR HUSING - GUADALUPE
WHITNEYBELL ARCHITECTS INC
NUESTO PUEBLITO - I'TOM PUEBLO

Mesa Senior Meadows

WHITNEYBELL PERRY INC
DESERT PARKS VISTA

WHITNEYBELL PERRY INC
DESERT PARKS VISTA

DESERT PARKS VISTA

DESERT PARKS VISTA

WHITNEYBELL PERRY INC
DOWNTOWN OCOTILLO

WHITNEYBELL PERRY INC
THE CARLYLE

WHITNEYBELL PERRY INC
Casa Blanca

WHITNEYBELL PERRY INC
Casa Blanca

WHITNEYBELL PERRY INC
VILLA PALLAVICINI

WHITNEYBELL PERRY INC
VILLA PALLAVICINI

WHITNEYBELL ARCHITECTS INC
LEGACY PARK

WHITNEYBELL ARCHITECTS INC
LEGACY PARK

GROUNDBREAKING
CITY OF PHOENIX
INFILL APARTMENTS
WHITNEYBELL ARCHITECTS INC
THE MET

WHITNEYBELL PERRY INC
The Met

WHITNEYBELL PERRY INC
The Met

WHITNEYBELL PERRY INC
The Met

WHITNEYBELL PERRY INC
THE METROPOLITAN

METRO LOFTS

TURKEY TROT "22" INVITATIONAL
WHITNEYBELL ARCHITECTS INC
YOU ARE INVITED, PLEASE JOIN US !
N
MARYLAND
FINISH
BETHANY HOME
SQUAW PEAK FWY
CAMELBACK
INDIAN SCHOOL
START

$30,784 DONATED THIS LAST THANKSGIVING BRINGS THE TOTAL TO $214,784 ENTIRELY DONATED TO ARIZONA DIABETIC CHILDREN
THE REWARDING FINISH
22ND TURKEY TROT INVITATIONAL 2001
WHITNEYBELL ARCHITECTS INC
20 YEARS OF TURKEY TROT SHIRTS
GENEROUS FRIENDS

Arizona Business Magazine | May | June 2000
Whitneybell Architects Inc
Architecture Planning

ARCHITECT RANGERS

N

CAL ASSOCIATION

ARIZONA MEDICAL ASSOCIATION
810

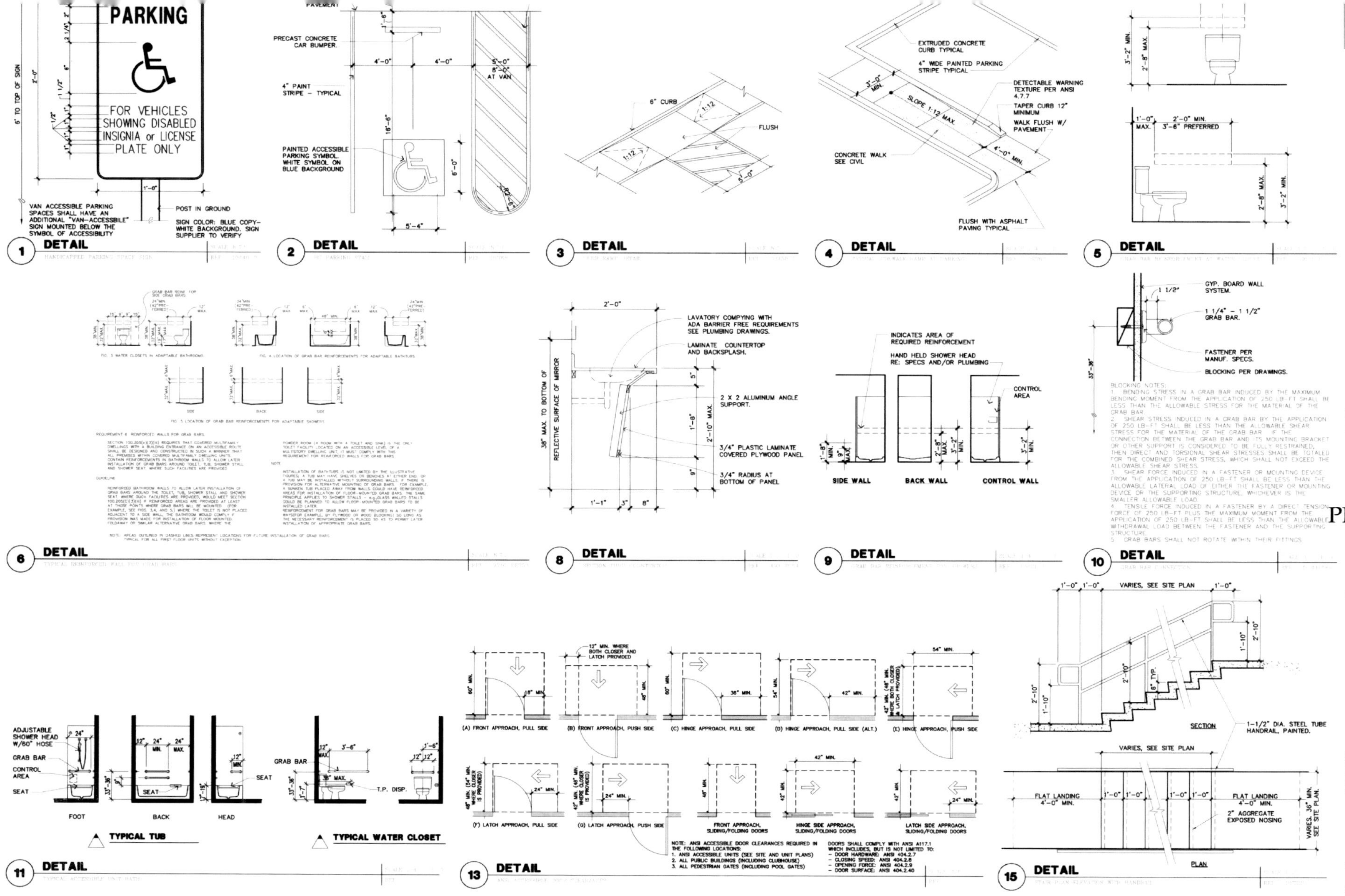

NOTE: REFER TO STRUCTURAL DETAILS AND PLANS FOR STRUCTURAL RELATED INFORMATION TYPICAL. THESE DETAILS ARE ARCHITECTURAL ONLY.

LAS MANANITAS

ALBUQUERQUE, NEW MEXICO

PRELIMINARY

WHITNEYBELL ARCHITECTS INC
1102 East Missouri Avenue
Phoenix, Arizona 85014-2784
(602)265-1891

ARCHITECTURE AND PLANNING

7.00

0122

ACCESSIBILITY DETAILS

ACCESSIBILITY DETAILS

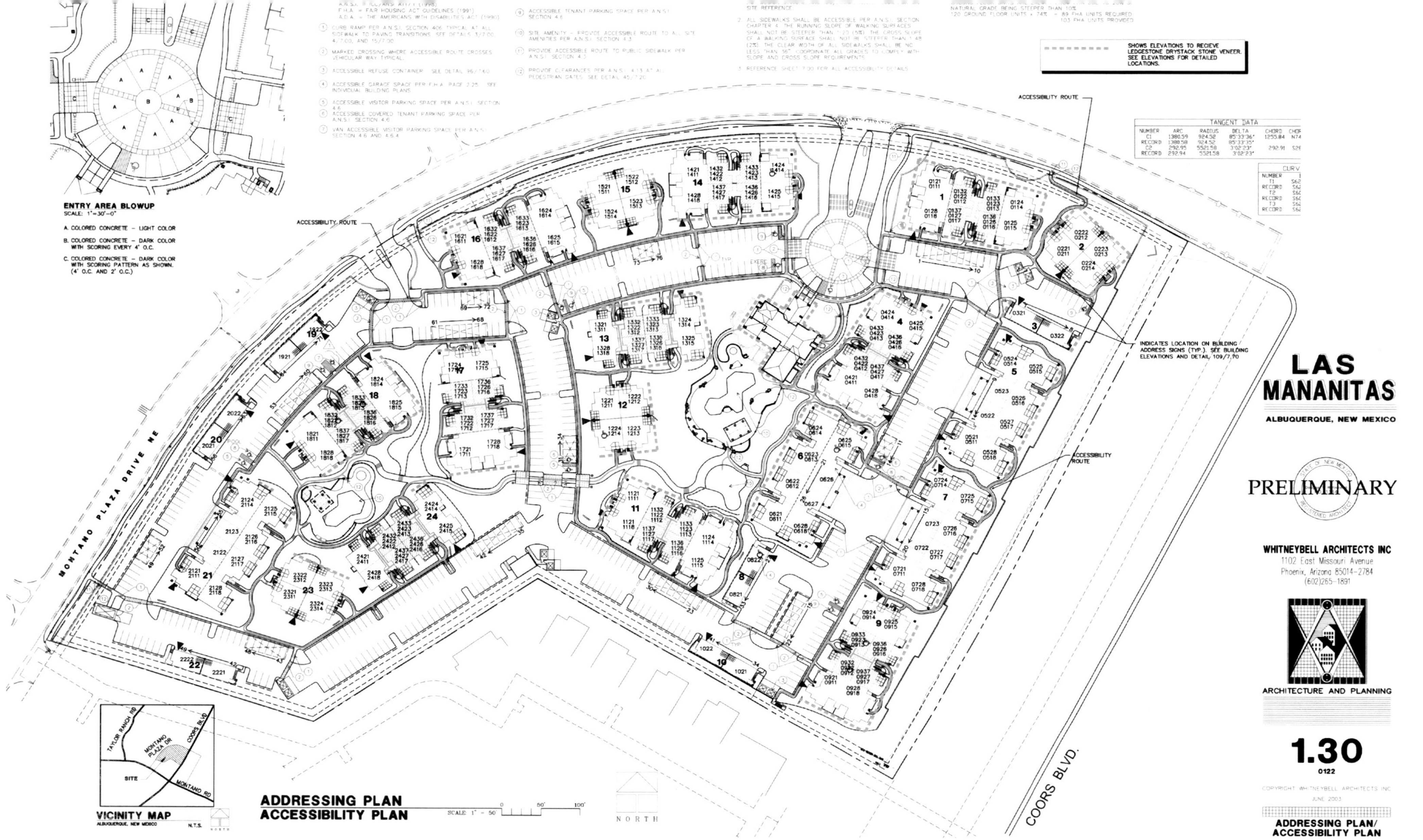

ACCESSIBILITY PLAN

ADA Compliance
INTERNATIONAL BUILDING CODE
2006
UNIVERSAL DESIGN HANDBOOK
ANSI
UFAS UNIFORM FEDERAL ACCESSIBILITY STANDARDS
FACILITIES COMPLIANCE WORKBOOK
EVAN TERRY ASSOCIATES, P.C.
ADA Compliance
THOMPSON
ADA

Fair Housing Act
Design Manual
A Manual to Assist
Designers and Builders
in Meeting the
Accessibility Requirements
of the Fair Housing Act
U. S. Department
of Housing and Urban Development
Office of Fair Housing and Equal Opportunity
Office of Housing

Revised Edition
POCKET GUIDE
TO THE
ADA
Americans with
Disabilities Act
Accessibility Guidelines
for Buildings and Facilities
Provides quick reference to primary
requirements of ADAAG
Edited from the Federal Register's
ADA Accessibility Guidelines
for Buildings and Facilities
Edited by
EVAN TERRY
ASSOCIATES, P.C.

HANDBOOKS
McGraw-Hill
UNIVERSAL
DESIGN
HANDBOOK
CD-ROM INCLUDED
Foreword by Robert Ivy, FAIA, Editor in Chief, Architectural Record
WOLFGANG F.E. PREISER, Editor in Chief
ELAINE OSTROFF, Senior Editor

PORTÉ VINE
Optical
FLUR DE LIE
Piazza Cafe